ELIZABETH THE QUEEN

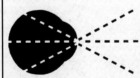

Elizabeth the Queen

THE LIFE OF A MODERN MONARCH

Sally Bedell Smith

THORNDIKE PRESS
A part of Gale, Cengage Learning

Detroit • New York • San Francisco • New Haven, Conn • Waterville, Maine • London

Copyright © 2012 by Sally Bedell Smith.

Thorndike Press, a part of Gale, Cengage Learning.

ALL RIGHTS RESERVED

Thorndike Press® Large Print Biography.

The text of this Large Print edition is unabridged.

Other aspects of the book may vary from the original edition.

Set in 16 pt. Plantin.

LIBRARY OF CONGRESS CATALOGING-IN-PUBLICATION DATA

Smith, Sally Bedell, 1948–
    Elizabeth the Queen : the life of a modern monarch / by Sally Bedell Smith.
      p. cm. — (Thorndike Press large print biography)
    Originally published: New York : Random House, 2011.
    Includes bibliographical references.
    ISBN-13: 978-1-4104-4527-8 (hardcover)
    ISBN-10: 1-4104-4527-5 (hardcover)
    1. Elizabeth II, Queen of Great Britain, 1926– 2. Great Britain
— History — Elizabeth II, 1952– 3. Queens — Great Britain —
Biography. I. Title.
DA590.S55 2012
941.085092—dc23
[B]
                                          2011048545

Published in 2012 by arrangement with Random House, Inc.

Printed in Mexico
2 3 4 5 6 7 15 14 13 12

For Stephen

They love her for her wisdom and her pride,
Her friendship and her quiet majesty;
And soon the streets of Britain will be thronged
With crowds rejoicing in her Jubilee

But as the cool unfaltering voice reads on,
A different picture forms upon the air —
A small quick figure, walking all alone
Across a glen studded with standing deer . . .

She notes a crumbling wall, an open gate,
With countrywoman's eyes she views the scene;
Yet, walking free upon her own estate
Still, in her solitude, she is the Queen

From "The Opening of Parliament,"
MARY WILSON,
wife of Harold Wilson,
Prime Minister, 1964–70 and 1974–76

"She sort of expands when she laughs. She laughs with her whole face."

Queen Elizabeth II and Prince Philip, the Duke of Edinburgh, in New Brunswick, Canada, during her Golden Jubilee celebrations, October 2002. NORM BETTS/REX USA

PREFACE

At the end of the wedding of Prince William and Catherine Middleton on April 29, 2011, the radiant couple turned before walking down the aisle at Westminster Abbey and stood before his grandparents, Queen Elizabeth II and Prince Philip. The newlyweds were celebrated for their romantic love match, and for the young prince's determination to marry his soul mate despite her being a "commoner" — having neither royal nor aristocratic origins. The bride and groom gave a low curtsy and neck bow to the Queen, who looked sturdy and stoic at age eighty-five. She signaled her approval with an almost imperceptible nod.

Seventy-two years earlier the Queen had made a similarly independent decision about love. When she was only thirteen, on the first afternoon she spent with eighteen-year-old Prince Philip of Greece, a strikingly handsome but impecunious British naval officer in training, Elizabeth fell in love. Eight years later they married under the same Gothic arches of Westminster Abbey. While everything else in the life of Lilibet, as she was called, was laid out for her, she made the most important decision on her own, against the wishes of her mother, who preferred a titled English aristocrat.

"She never looked at anyone else," said Elizabeth's cousin Margaret Rhodes.

It was a sign of remarkable certitude on the part of then-Princess Elizabeth, not to mention strength and confidence in a girl so young. But that unwavering decision is just one of many surprising aspects I discovered about the woman who has reigned for sixty years as Queen of the United Kingdom of England, Wales, Scotland, and Northern Ireland, along with fifteen other realms and fourteen territories around the world. Her role and how she manages to perform it seemed to me to defy rational explanation: a hereditary position consecrated by God, embodying a multicultural and multifaith nation far different from the homogenous land ruled by her predecessors over the thousand-year history of the British monarchy. I understood that much of her life is ceremonial, an unvarying routine of yearly set pieces that date from the time of Queen Victoria. A singular and internationally famous figure, Elizabeth II is the world's longest-serving leader — seemingly as familiar, predictable, and unchanging as she is dutiful.

In her epic life, the Queen has played her part like a great actress — the only person about whom it can truly be said that all the world is a stage. Billions have watched her evolve from a beautiful ingenue to a businesslike working mother to a wise grandmother. When she was twenty-eight years old and had been on the throne for three years, her first private secretary, Sir Alan Lascelles, said, "People will not realize for years how intelligent she is. . . . Eventually it will become an accepted national fact." Yet while her public persona conveys gravitas, she has concealed much of that intelligence, much of her personality and humor. Behind her enigmatic and dignified facade resides a largely unknown woman.

"Her private side took me totally by surprise," said Howard Morgan, an artist who painted the Queen's portrait in the 1980s. "She talks like an Italian. She waves her hands about. She is enormously expressive." Friends and family have often witnessed the joie de vivre seldom seen in public — blowing bubbles during a birthday party at the London Aquarium, belting out songs while perched atop a wooden box on an island in the Outer Hebrides, jumping up to serve the American artist George "Frolic" Weymouth from the buffet in a dining room at Windsor Castle. "She stacked the plates!" Weymouth recalled, "which is what we were taught *never* to do when we were growing up."

During informal conversation her eyes sparkle, her voice is merry and warm. "You can hear her laughter sometimes throughout the house," said Tony Parnell, the former foreman at Sandringham, the monarch's estate in Norfolk. "It is a joyous laugh."

At five foot four, the Queen's small stature is another surprise to people seeing her for the first time. Yet like her great-great-grandmother Queen Victoria, who barely reached five feet, she has the kind of bearing that makes her size beside the point. She emphasizes her authority by walking at what her longtime dress designer Norman Hartnell called her "intentionally measured and deliberate pace."

Equally paradoxical is the Queen's becoming humility, a trait inculcated in her early years. "She can uphold the identity of herself as Queen and still be humble," said Margaret Rhodes. "Her inner modesty stops her getting spoiled." When the Queen goes to the theater she tries to arrive unannounced after the house lights have gone down. One of her former private secretaries described how odd it was "to watch her sidle into a room. . . . She doesn't ever try to make an entrance." If someone else is being celebrated, she effortlessly slips into the background. When her cousin Lady Mary Clayton had her ninetieth birthday party in December 2007, a caricaturist memorialized the occasion with a cartoon. Mary's figure is the largest, in the center, while the bespectacled Queen is tucked in among the others in the last row.

While known for her caution, Elizabeth II refuses to wear a hard hat when riding on horseback — for a practical reason, it turns out — prompting the staff at Windsor Castle to joke that "the only thing that comes between the Queen and her heir is an Hermès scarf." Nor does she use a seat belt in her cars, and she drives on the private roads of her estates "like a bat out of hell," said Margaret Rhodes.

Even her eyebrows remain defiantly untamed. A quarter century ago biographer Elizabeth Longford first recognized the Queen's no-nonsense integrity in those natural brows, which added "interest and character to the face" and made it "a living record rather than a meaningless statement."

Elizabeth II has chosen to age gracefully without

the enhancements of cosmetic surgery, keeping her hairstyle essentially the same. "To be that consistent for that long is amazingly comforting," said Dame Helen Mirren, who won an Oscar for her portrayal of the Queen in the 2006 film *The Queen.* "It shows such reliability. She has never lurched in one direction or another. It is self-discipline, which I think comes from within rather than imposed from without."

She has kept a daily diary, but the contents won't be available for historians until after her death. "It's just like scrubbing your teeth," she once said. "It's not really a diary like Queen Victoria's, you know . . . or as detailed as that. It's quite small." Friends who have heard her savvy opinions and sharp character sketches speculate that she may have committed those kinds of observations to paper, without betraying confidences.

To maintain her status, Elizabeth II must be extraordinary. The expectations of her subjects dictate that she must be human as well — if not exactly ordinary. Throughout her time as monarch she has worked to find a balance between the two dispositions. If she is too mysterious and distant, she loses her connection with the people; if she seems too much like everyone else, she loses her special mystique.

At a Buckingham Palace garden party in 2007, the Queen asked guests such standard questions as "Have you come far?" After one introduction, a woman said to the Queen, "What do you do?" Recounting the exchange to a group of friends several days later, Elizabeth II recalled, "I had no idea what to say." In all her years of meeting people, it was the first time anyone had asked her that question.

In Britain, the power and the glory are kept separate. Elizabeth II reigns rather than rules, with a commitment to serve until death. Winston Churchill, who was the Queen's first prime minister, put it this way in 1953: "A great battle is lost: parliament turns out the government. A great battle is won: crowds cheer the Queen." Those holding the power — the prime ministers who lead the government when their party achieves a parliamentary majority — come and go with the vagaries of elections, while the Queen endures as head of state. She lacks the power to govern, but she has a sort of negative power. Because she is there, no prime minister can be number one. "She makes a dictatorship more difficult, she makes military coups more difficult, rule by decree more difficult," said Robert Gascoyne-Cecil, the 7th Marquess of Salisbury, a Conservative politician and former leader of the House of Lords. "It is more difficult because she occupies space, and due process must be followed."

She also has the positive power of influence: "the right to be consulted, the right to encourage, and the right to warn." In public she influences through her example, by setting a high standard for service and citizenship, by rewarding achievement, and by diligently carrying out her duties. Tony Blair, the tenth of her twelve prime ministers, called her "a symbol of unity in a world of insecurity . . . simply the best of British."

There is never a moment in her life when Elizabeth II is not the Queen, which puts her in a solitary position and affects the behavior of everyone around her, even her family. She holds neither a passport nor a driver's license, she can't vote or appear as a witness in court, and she can't change her faith from Anglican to Roman Catholic. Because she stands for national unity and must avoid alienating her subjects, she needs to remain scrupulously neutral — not just about politics but even seemingly innocuous matters such as favorite colors or songs or television shows. But she does have strong preferences and opinions that occasionally emerge.

A straightforward streak is one of Elizabeth II's appealing qualities. "When she says something she means it. And the public picks that up and admires it," said Gay Charteris, the widow of Martin Charteris (Lord Charteris of Amisfield), a senior adviser to the Queen for three decades — one of the many people I spoke to who are close to the royal family.

I was fascinated to think that from the mid-nineteenth century through the first decades of the twenty-first century — for 123 of the past 174 years — the monarchy has been dominated by two formidable women, Queen Victoria and Queen Elizabeth II. Between them they have symbolized Britain far longer than the four men who occupied the throne between their reigns. Matriarchs face special demands, which in the case of Elizabeth II have meant carrying out duties expected of a man and a woman.

As a career woman, Elizabeth II has been an anomaly both in her generation and in the British upper class. She had no model for balancing

15

the roles of monarch, wife, and mother. All too often the requirements of her job, combined with her ingrained sense of duty, pulled her away from motherhood. Her laissez-faire attitude toward child rearing had unfortunate consequences, and her children have given her more than her share of heartache. She has occasionally revealed some of her anguish, but more often has kept it to herself, letting off steam on long walks with her dogs. "There is a weed in Scotland nicknamed the Stinking Willie that is deeply rooted," said Lady Elizabeth Anson, a cousin of the Queen. "I have seen her go into a field and pull up lots of that."

Prince Philip has said that "supporting the Queen" defined his life as the longest-serving consort in British history. As they move through public events, they resemble a royal Fred and Ginger with their expert choreography of turns and cues that transmit lively interest and look effortless. He also provides the spritz of vinegar to her Windsor cream, with his pointed and often irreverent comments. "Prince Philip is the only man in the world who treats the Queen simply as another human being," said Martin Charteris. "And, of course, it's not unknown for the Queen to tell Prince Philip to shut up. Because she's Queen, that's not something she can easily say to anybody else."

The routine of the Queen's life — outlined a year ahead, mapped in detail six months in advance — has been practical and reassuring. One of her friends, John Julius Cooper, the 2nd Viscount Norwich, jokingly said the secret of her equanimity might be "never having to look for a parking place." In the view of one of her private secretaries, "She has two great assets. First of all she sleeps very well, and secondly she's got very good legs, and she can stand for a long time. . . . The Queen is as tough as a yak." She finds refuge for four months at intervals throughout the year at her country estates. On each return to Sandringham, her staff "present[s] the house to her as she left it," said Tony Parnell, who worked there for fifty years. "If bits and knickknacks were left on chairs, they are kept on chairs."

The story of Elizabeth II turns on what she has made of the life that was given her. I wanted to know what elements of her character and personality and upbringing have helped her carry out her unique role. Who is she, what are her days like? How did she learn on the job to deal with politicians and heads of state as well as coal miners and professors? How has she experienced the world while living in a virtual cocoon? What is her approach to leadership, has it changed, and if so how? How has she dealt with mistakes and setbacks? Her family? How has she maintained her equilibrium and kept her basic values? How has she lived the most public of lives but preserved her privacy? Would she ever abdicate in favor of her eldest son, Prince Charles, or even her grandson Prince William? How, in the winter season of her life, has she managed to bring stability and vigor to the monarchy?

I first met Queen Elizabeth II in Washington, D.C., in May 2007. The occasion was a garden party at the British ambassador's residence, and it was a warm and cloudless day. Some seven hundred Washingtonians turned out — the men in their best suits, many of the women wearing hats.

Highly efficient military men organized us into lanes about thirty feet apart. As the appointed hour approached, the sovereign's flag was raised to indicate that Her Majesty was on the premises. The Queen, then eighty-one, and her husband, Prince Philip, came out onto the terrace and passed between two Grenadier Guards in scarlet tunics and bearskin hats. After the regimental band of the Coldstream Guards struck up "God Save the Queen," the royal couple walked down a short flight of steps.

My husband, Stephen, and I happened to be in the lane where Philip was making his way on his own, while Elizabeth II was on the other side.

The Queen disappeared into the distance of the gardens, but we stayed in place, and eventually she doubled back along our lane toward the residence. The British ambassador, Sir David Manning, was making introductions to every twelfth person or so. He signaled that he would be stopping in front of us as he whispered into her ear. He presented me, and Elizabeth II extended her white-gloved hand, while I said, according to protocol, "How do you do, Your Majesty?" Next came my husband, and the Queen said she understood that he edited a Washington newspaper. Like her husband, she is not enamored of the press — she has not granted an interview during her sixty-year reign — but she didn't let on.

Her politeness was badly rewarded when Stephen decided to commit two protocol infractions simultaneously: asking the Queen a question and mentioning the possibility that she gambled at the racetrack. "Did you put a wager on Street Sense at Churchill Downs?" he inquired, referring to the winner of the Kentucky Derby, which she had attended for the first time the previous Saturday. With masterful diplomatic deflection, she ignored the question, but lingered. Something about the phrasing must have piqued her interest. Stephen and I had watched the race on television; as a fan of the turf for many years, he knew how to "read a race," seeing maneuvers on the track that utterly eluded me. He made a quick observation about the race, and Elizabeth II replied that it was startling to see the winning horse covered with so much mud afterward — the result of running on dirt rather than the grass tracks she was accustomed to seeing in England.

Evidently relieved to be discussing horses, one of her favorite topics, she went back and forth with my husband, replaying the race and its thrilling finish, in which Street Sense went from nineteenth place to first. "You could see the yellow cap!" she said excitedly. Stephen told her that the handicapper at his newspaper, *The Washington Examiner,* had picked the top three horses in their order of finish. "That's really quite extraordinary," the Queen said. And then she was gone.

I had not anticipated the animated gestures, the expressive blue eyes, the flashing smile. For a minute or so, I had glimpsed the gaiety so often obscured by the dignity of the Queen's role. While I didn't realize it at the time, I had also witnessed her control and skill. By ignoring my husband's inappropriate question about making a bet, she didn't make him feel ill at ease. She simply let it slide away, and moved the conversation back to

19

comfortable terms.

Throughout her reign, Elizabeth II has managed to float above politics and, for the most part, controversy. If not exactly a Hollywood star, she is a major celebrity. She has long been the most popular member of the royal family on Google, generating considerably more searches, although her grandsons, Prince William and Prince Harry (along with Catherine Middleton after she and William became engaged), have followed her closely and periodically surpassed her in the Google Trends data since 2004. She has even been portrayed on *The Simpsons* by comedian Eddie Izzard.

With her good health and her determination to keep fit, the Queen could continue to carry out her duties effectively for a decade or more, leaving the prospect of a short reign for Prince Charles, the next in line, who will turn sixty-four in 2012 during his mother's Diamond Jubilee celebrating her sixty years on the throne.

It was probably fitting that the second time I chatted with the Queen was with a group dedicated to Anglo-American fellowship, the Pilgrims, at a reception for some six hundred members and guests that she hosted at St. James's Palace in London in June 2009. I had been working on this biography for more than a year. My admittance card also contained a slip of paper assigning me to the crimson and gilt Throne Room, specifically to "Group Five," led by General Sir Richard Dannatt, then chief of the General Staff of the British Army.

Frequently in large receptions, people are selected in advance and clustered in small groups to be presented to Elizabeth II. For the Pilgrims, she would greet about a hundred or so, and General Dannatt would make the introductions for my group. This time, she offered a black-gloved hand, while her ubiquitous Launer handbag dangled from her other arm. I knew she had been briefed several months earlier about this book, and her press secretary, who stood nearby, had been told I would be attending the gathering. But many people had passed before the Queen's gaze.

I told her that it was good to see her again in an Anglo-American setting, having previously met her in Washington. "Is that what brought you over here?" she asked. "No, my daughter is getting married here in London," I replied. "When is the wedding?" asked the Queen. "The Fourth of July," I replied. Yet again I saw those twinkling eyes. "Oh," she said, "that's a little dangerous!" "I hope all is forgiven," I replied. Another smile, and once more, she moved on.

CONTENTS

23

CHAPTER ONE
A ROYAL EDUCATION

It was a footman who brought the news to ten-year-old Elizabeth Alexandra Mary Windsor on December 10, 1936. Her father had become an accidental king just four days before his forty-first birthday when his older brother, King Edward VIII, abdicated to marry Wallis Warfield Simpson, a twice-divorced American. Edward VIII had been sovereign only nine months after taking the throne following the death of his father, King George V, making him, according to one mordant joke, "the only monarch in history to abandon the ship of state to sign on as third mate on a Baltimore tramp."

"Does that mean that you will have to be the next queen?" asked Elizabeth's younger sister, Margaret Rose (as she was called in her childhood). "Yes, someday," Elizabeth replied. "Poor you," said Margaret Rose.

Although the two princesses had been the focus of fascination by the press and the public, they had led a carefree and insulated life surrounded by governesses, nannies, maids, dogs, and ponies. They spent idyllic months in the English and Scottish countryside playing games like "catching the days" — running around plucking autumn leaves

25

His "steadfastness" had been her model.

Princess Elizabeth watching her father reading documents from his government boxes, April 1942. Lisa Sheridan/Getty Images

from the air as they were falling. Their spirited Scottish nanny, Marion "Crawfie" Crawford, had managed to give them a taste of ordinary life by occasionally taking them around London by tube and bus, but mostly they remained inside the royal bubble.

Before the arrival of Margaret, Elizabeth spent four years as an only — and somewhat precocious — child, born on the rainy night of April 21, 1926. Winston Churchill, on first meeting the two-year-old princess, extravagantly detected "an air of authority and reflectiveness astonishing in an infant." Crawfie noted that she was "neat and methodical . . . like her father," obliging, eager to do her best, and happiest when she was busy. She also showed an early ability to compartmentalize — a trait that would later help her cope with the demands of her position. Recalled Lady Mary Clayton, a cousin eight years her senior: "She liked to imagine herself as a pony or a horse. When she was doing that and someone called her and she didn't answer right away, she would then say, 'I couldn't answer you as a pony.' "

The abdication crisis threw the family into turmoil, not only because it was a scandal but because it was antithetical to all the rules of succession. While Elizabeth's father had been known as "Bertie" (for Albert), he chose to be called George VI to send a message of stability and continuity with his father. (His wife, who was crowned by his side, would be known as Queen Elizabeth.) But Bertie had not been groomed for the role. He was in tears when he talked to his mother about his new responsibilities. "I never wanted this to happen," he told his cousin Lord Louis "Dickie" Mountbatten. "I've never even seen a State Paper. I'm only a Naval Officer, it's the only thing I know about." The new King was reserved by nature, somewhat frail physically, and plagued by anxiety. He suffered from a severe stammer that led to frequent frustration, culminating in explosions of temper known as "gnashes."

Yet he was profoundly dutiful, and he doggedly set about his kingly tasks while ensuring that his little Lilibet — her name within the family — would be ready to succeed him in ways he had not been. On his accession she became "heiress presumptive," rather than "heiress apparent," on the off chance that her parents could produce a son. But Elizabeth and Margaret Rose had been born by cesarean section, and in those days a third operation would have been considered too risky for their mother. According to custom, Lilibet would publicly refer to her mother and father as "the King and Queen," but privately they were still Mummy and Papa.

When Helen Mirren was studying for her role in 2006's *The Queen,* she watched a twenty-second piece of film repeatedly because she found it so revealing. "It was when the Queen was eleven or twelve," Mirren recalled, "and she got out of one of those huge black cars. There were big men waiting for her, and she extended her hand with a look of gravity and duty. She was doing what she thought she had to do, and she was doing it beautifully."

"I have a feeling that in the end probably that training is the answer to a great many things," the Queen said on the eve of her fortieth year as

28

monarch. "You can do a lot if you are properly trained, and I hope I have been." Her formal education was spotty by today's standards. Women of her class and generation were typically schooled at home, with greater emphasis on the practical than the academic. "It was unheard of for girls to go to university unless they were very intellectual," said Lilibet's cousin Patricia Mountbatten. While Crawfie capably taught history, geography, grammar, literature, poetry, and composition, she was "hopeless at math," said Mary Clayton, who had also been taught by Crawfie. Additional governesses were brought in for instruction in music, dancing, and French.

Elizabeth was not expected to excel, much less to be intellectual. She had no classmates against whom to measure her progress, nor batteries of challenging examinations. Her father's only injunction to Crawfie when she joined the household in 1932 had been to teach his daughters, then six and two, "to write a decent hand." Elizabeth developed flowing and clear handwriting similar to that of her mother and sister, although with a bolder flourish. But Crawfie felt a larger need to fill her charge with knowledge "as fast as I can pour it in." She introduced Lilibet to the *Children's Newspaper,* a current events chronicle that laid the groundwork for following political news in *The Times* and on BBC radio, prompting one Palace adviser to observe that at seventeen the princess had "a first-rate knowledge of state and current affairs."

Throughout her girlhood, Elizabeth had time blocked out each day for "silent reading" of books by Stevenson, Austen, Kipling, the Brontës, Tennyson, Scott, Dickens, Trollope, and others in the standard canon. Her preference, then and as an adult, was for historical fiction, particularly about "the corners of the Commonwealth and the people who live there," said Mark Collins, director of the Commonwealth Foundation. Decades later, when she conferred an honor on J. K. Rowling for her Harry Potter series, the Queen told the author that her extensive reading in childhood "stood me in good stead because I read quite quickly now. I have to read a lot."

Once she became first in line to the throne, Elizabeth's curriculum intensified and broadened. Her most significant tutor was Sir Henry Marten, the vice provost of Eton College, the venerable boys' boarding school down the hill from Windsor Castle whose graduates were known as Old Etonians. Marten had coauthored *The Groundwork of British History,* a standard school textbook, but he was hardly a dry academic. A sixty-six-year-old bachelor with a moon face and gleaming pate, he habitually chewed a corner of his handkerchief and kept a pet raven in a study so heaped with books that Crawfie likened them to stalagmites. Sir Alec Douglas-Home, who would serve as Queen Elizabeth II's fourth prime minister, remembered Marten as "a dramatic, racy, enthusiastic teacher" who humanized figures of history.

Beginning in 1939, when Elizabeth was thirteen, she and Crawfie went by carriage to Marten's study twice a week so she could be instructed in history and the intricacies of the British constitution. The princess was exceedingly shy at first,

30

often glancing imploringly at Crawfie for reassurance. Marten could scarcely look Elizabeth in the eye, and he lapsed into calling her "Gentlemen," thinking he was with his Eton boys. But before long she felt "entirely at home with him," recalled Crawfie, and they developed "a rather charming friendship."

Marten imposed a rigorous curriculum built around the daunting three-volume *The Law and Custom of the Constitution* by Sir William Anson. Also on her reading list were *English Social History* by G. M. Trevelyan, *Imperial Commonwealth* by Lord Elton, and *The English Constitution* by Walter Bagehot, the gold standard for constitutional interpretation that both her father and grandfather had studied. Marten even included a course on American history. "Hide nothing," Sir Alan "Tommy" Lascelles, private secretary to King George VI, had told Marten when asked about instructing the princess on the crown's role in the constitution.

Unlike the written American Constitution, which spells everything out, the British version is an accumulation of laws and unwritten traditions and precedents. It is inherently malleable and dependent on people making judgments, and even revising the rules, as events occur. Anson called it a "somewhat rambling structure . . . like a house which many successive owners have altered." The constitutional monarch's duties and prerogatives are vague. Authority rests more in what the king doesn't do than what he does. The sovereign is compelled by the constitution to sign all laws passed by Parliament; the concept of a veto is unthinkable, but the possibility remains.

Elizabeth studied Anson for six years, painstakingly underlining and annotating the dense text in pencil. According to biographer Robert Lacey, who examined the faded volumes in the Eton library, she took note of Anson's assertion that a more complex constitution offers greater guarantees of liberty. In the description of Anglo-Saxon monarchy as "a consultative and tentative absolutism" she underlined "consultative" and "tentative." Marten schooled her in the process of legislation, and the sweeping nature of Parliament's power. Elizabeth's immersion in the "procedural minutiae" was such that, in Lacey's view, "it was as if she were studying to be Speaker [of the House of Commons], not queen." Prime ministers would later be impressed by the mastery of constitutional fine points in her unexpectedly probing questions.

When Elizabeth turned sixteen, her parents hired Marie-Antoinette de Bellaigue, a sophisticated Belgian vicomtesse educated in Paris, to teach French literature and history. Called "Toni" by the two princesses, she set a high standard and compelled them to speak French with her during meals. Elizabeth developed a fluency that impressed even Parisians, who praised her for speaking with "cool clear precision" on her visit to their city in 1948, at age twenty-two.

De Bellaigue worked in tandem with Marten, who suggested essay topics for Elizabeth to write in French. The governess later recounted that Marten had taught the future Queen "to appraise both sides of a question, thus using [her] judgment." In de Bellaigue's view, Lilibet "had from the beginning a positive good judgment. She had an instinct for the right thing. She was her simple self, 'très naturelle.' And there was always a strong sense of duty mixed with joie de vivre in the pattern of her character."

Elizabeth's mother had an enormous influence on the development of her character and personality. Born Elizabeth Bowes Lyon to the Earl and Countess of Strathmore, she had grown up in an aristocratic Scottish-English family of nine children. In 1929, Time magazine had pronounced her a "fresh, buxom altogether 'jolly' little duchess." She read widely and avidly, with a particular fondness for P. G. Wodehouse. Somewhat improbably, she was also a fan of Damon Runyon's stories about New York gangsters and molls, once writing to a friend in the author's vernacular: "The way that Dame Pearl gets a ripple on, there was a baby for you — Oh boy."

Queen Elizabeth taught her daughter to read at age five and devoted considerable time to reading aloud the children's classics. As soon as Lilibet could write, her mother encouraged her to begin the lifelong habit of recording her impressions in a diary each night. During her father's coronation in 1937, the eleven-year-old princess kept a lively journal, "From Lilibet by Herself." "The arches and beams at the top [of Westminster Abbey] were covered with a sort of haze of wonder as Papa was crowned," she wrote. When her mother was crowned and the white-gloved peeresses put on their coronets simultaneously, "it looked wonderful to see arms and coronets hovering in the air and then the arms disappear as if by magic."

■ ■ ■ ■

At an early age, Elizabeth's parents began arranging for her to sit for portraits. She would repeat this ritual more than 140 times throughout her life, making her the most painted monarch in history. For the royal family, portraits have long been an essential part of image making, helping to shape the way the public sees its regal icons. When asked if she kept her portraits, the Queen replied, "No, none. They're all painted for other people."

Hungarian Alexius de László, a widely admired society portrait artist, was hired to capture Lilibet in oils for the first time. She was just seven. László found her to be "intelligent and full of character," although he conceded she was "very sleepy and restless." Aristocratic matrons enjoyed the company of the smooth-talking sixty-four-year-old artist, but Elizabeth thought he was "horrid," as she recalled years later with a grimace. "He was one of those people who wanted you to sit permanently looking at you." The resulting ethereal image — a favorite of her mother's — shows the young princess in ruffled silk, with blond curls and wide blue eyes, holding a basket of flowers. Yet her unsmiling expression betrays a whiff of exasperation.

The second artist to capture Elizabeth's image was another Hungarian, sculptor Zsigmond Strobl, who had eighteen sessions with her from 1936 to 1938. She was older, by then the heiress presumptive, and eager to chat with the Hungarian journalist who joined the sittings to help her pass the time in conversation. Being painted or sculpted from life reinforced the virtue of patience. As Queen she would also find her sittings to be an oasis of uncluttered time when she could unwind, connect with a stranger in a private and unthreatening way, speak expansively — sometimes quite personally — and even crack jokes. "It's quite nice," she said during a sitting before her eightieth birthday as she flashed an impish smile. "Usually one just sits, and people can't get at you because one's busy doing nothing."

A favorite topic during the Strobl sculpting sessions was the world of horses, which had become Elizabeth's full-blown passion as well as another opportunity for learning. Her father bred and raced thoroughbreds, continuing a royal tradition, and he introduced her to all aspects of the equine world, starting with her first riding lesson at age three. By 1938 she began learning how to ride sidesaddle, a necessary skill for the yearly Trooping the Colour ceremony celebrating the sovereign's birthday when she would be required to ride in a red military tunic, long navy blue riding skirt, and black tricorn cap at the head of a parade of more than 1,400 soldiers.

Her twice weekly riding lessons helped her develop athleticism and strength and taught her how to keep a cool head in moments of danger. She experienced the uninhibited joy of vaulting fences and cantering across fields and through woodlands — sensations that would temporarily liberate her from the restrictions of her official life. Although she tried fox hunting while in her teens — first with the Garth Foxhounds in Berkshire, then with the Beaufort Hunt in Gloucestershire — she was already captivated by breeding and racing.

During girlhood visits with her father to his stables at Hampton Court and Sandringham, she took in the rudiments of a breeding operation, and she began to master the genealogical permutations of temperament and physical conformation vital to producing successful horses. She saw the formidable stallions as well as mares and their foals, and she watched young horses training on the Wiltshire "gallops," great swaths of springy turf on the crests of rolling hills that mimic the straightaways and curves of a racetrack. She came to know the grooms and stable boys, the trainers and jockeys — an unaffected community that views life differently because of the primacy of their animals. As she told artist Frolic Weymouth years later, "horses are the greatest levelers in the world."

She also had a natural rapport with dogs. In 1933 her father became fascinated with Welsh corgis — a breed with pointed snout, outsize ears, and stumpy legs — and gave her Dookie, the first in a long line of corgis that became her trademark. She has had as many as a dozen at a time, and they often precede her like a "moving carpet," as Diana, Princess of Wales, put it. The dogs served as icebreakers, although they could sometimes intimidate guests or employees with their snappish personalities. "They're heelers," Elizabeth II once explained. "They're cattle dogs so they bite," adding with a sly smile, "They chase people."

Even before the family moved to Buckingham Palace in 1937 when Lilibet's father took the throne, making friends was complicated for the young princess. When she became heiress presumptive, the little girls who visited had to curtsy and call her "Ma'am." "It was a very inhibiting experience," recalled Lady Elizabeth Cavendish, who was invited to play and take tea at Buckingham Palace. During one visit by the royal family to the 12th Earl and Countess of Airlie's Cortachy Castle in Scotland, the Airlies' son, Jamie Ogilvy, took Princess Elizabeth and tossed her onto a sofa. Moments later, his father came up, punched him in the stomach, and said, "Never do that to royalty." "The Princess didn't mind," recalled Ogilvy, "but that was the structure in which she was brought up."

As Crawfie observed, life in the Palace brought down "a glass curtain between you and the outer world." Buckingham Palace is an overwhelming place, with 775 rooms, more the head office of the monarchy than a home. Lilibet spent many hours gazing out the windows watching the world pass below her, wondering about the lives of the "real people."

To expand her horizons beyond the family, and to diminish the sense of isolation, Crawfie organized a troop of Girl Guides (the equivalent of American Girl Scouts) at the Palace. The original group of twenty included relatives such as Patricia Mountbatten, the "quite fierce" (in Lilibet's view) leader of the Kingfisher patrol to whom the heiress presumptive actually had to defer, and aristocratic friends such as Lady Camilla "Micky" Wallop (daughter of the 9th Earl of Portsmouth), as well as daughters of chauffeurs and other Palace employees.

Using either a designated room in the Palace or the summerhouse in the forty-acre garden as the headquarters, the girls built campfires, watched birds, and played team games. The future Queen was rough-and-ready. She "was brought up knowing she mustn't cry in public, which becomes a way of life," Patricia Mountbatten recalled. "As a child she was told, 'If you fall down, you don't make a face.'"

Dignitaries who visited the King and Queen were introduced to the princesses, who were expected to make intelligent conversation with them during dinner. Elizabeth was as interested in people as her mother, but she lacked Queen Elizabeth's spontaneous enjoyment of others. Queen Elizabeth helped Lilibet overcome her diffidence by role-playing exercises in which she would pretend to be the Archbishop of Canterbury or another distinguished guest. The Queen drilled in her own mother's maxim that "if you find something or somebody a bore, the fault lies in you." She also taught her daughters how to withstand the stares of three thousand people during garden parties at Buckingham Palace, and how to walk at a measured pace. As Lilibet lectured her sister, "You must *not* be in too much of a hurry to get through the crowds to the tea table. That's not polite."

Through her chatty and descriptive letters while she and the King were on tour overseas, Queen Elizabeth introduced her daughter to the wider world and the exacting demands of royal service. When their parents traveled to Canada and the United States in June 1939, Lilibet and Margaret Rose kept track of their progress on maps displayed in their schoolroom. Their mother wrote

38

that Americans were "particularly easy and pleasant . . . and delighted to find that we were ordinary & fairly polite people with a big job of work." She revealed that "sometimes I have tears in my eyes when one sees the emotion in their faces" but also confessed to the strain of being "almost continually 'on show' . . . there comes a moment when one's resistance nearly goes."

With her mother's guidance, Lilibet also developed a deeply held Christian faith. Queen Elizabeth read Bible stories and instructed her daughter in the collects and psalms from the Book of Common Prayer. "The Queen knows the prayer book backwards," said George Carey, the 103rd Archbishop of Canterbury and later Lord Carey of Clifton. Queen Elizabeth showed her devotion by kneeling to pray each night, a practice her daughter was said to continue. "She comes from a generation in which kneeling by the side of the bed is quite natural," said Carey. "Attitude helps you to pray, and if you are on your knees it creates a mood of submission before the Almighty."

Queen Elizabeth also instructed her daughter in practical matters. Clarissa Eden, the widow of Sir Anthony Eden (the 1st Earl of Avon), Elizabeth II's second prime minister, marveled that the Queen would "sit up at a slight distance from the chair back. She can sit like that for hours." This habit she learned early from her mother, who firmly believed "a lady's back should never touch the back of her chair."

As a little girl, Lilibet had a hot temper — a family trait shared not only by her father, but George V and Edward VII — that her mother's soothing personality tamed through example and exhortation. Queen Elizabeth's mother, the Countess of Strathmore, "brought up her children and they brought up their children to be in control of their temper and moods, and to never allow their moods to dominate," said Mary Clayton. Queen Elizabeth's enlightened tenets for parenting were grounded in encouragement and understanding: avoid ridicule, discourage showing off, speak quietly, and "never shout or frighten" or "you lose their delightful trust in you." As she wrote in one letter to Lilibet, "remember to keep your temper & your word & be loving."

With her 150 dolls and lineup of thirty foot-high toy horses saddled and bridled for play, her every creature comfort cared for, and her meals served by footmen in scarlet livery, how did Elizabeth avoid being spoiled and arrogant? "She was brought up by strict nannies," explained a friend from the age of five. "I remember once when Princess Elizabeth and Princess Margaret came to tea, and Princess Elizabeth put her elbows on the table. Mrs. Knight said, 'Take them off.' I didn't expect a princess would have to be told, but she was brought up properly, as a nanny would bring you up, and the Queen has never broken the rules."

Clara "Allah" Knight was the family's Hertfordshire-born nursery nanny, who along with Lilibet's Scottish nursemaid, Margaret "Bobo" MacDonald, regulated the quotidian details of life outside the classroom, and spent far more time with the two princesses than did their parents. Bobo — described by valet John Dean as "small, very smart, and rather peremptory" — would remain in the Queen's service until her death in 1993. "The Queen just enjoyed talking to a sensible Scottish countrywoman," said Mary Clayton.

To encourage tidiness and frugality, Allah and Bobo taught Lilibet to keep her belongings in neat rows, to save wrapping paper and ribbon in fastidiously folded parcels and carefully wound rolls, and to turn off unneeded lights. The princess received a weekly allowance of 5 shillings, a useful if artificial discipline, since her annual income was £6,000 a year. When she undressed, she obediently folded her clothes and placed them under a lace and net "clothes tidy," never leaving anything on the floor or thrown over a chair. Allah and Bobo also helped stop her nail biting, although they didn't entirely extinguish what Helen Mirren called Elizabeth's "internal fast beat" behind her tranquil demeanor: a tendency in adulthood to fidget with her engagement and wedding rings.

The other crucial enforcer in Elizabeth's life was her paternal grandmother, Queen Mary, the consort of King George V. She was a stiff and formal figure who wore a tiara every night at dinner, even when she and the King were dining alone. She was unable to "look anyone straight in the face," noted photographer Cecil Beaton. "Queen Mary wore tiaras like she wore her toques," observed Deborah Mitford, the Duchess of Devonshire, "as if they were part of her being." Her manner was thoroughly proper, her dedication to duty absolute. Not long before she died at age eighty-five, Queen Mary touchingly said she wished that just once she had climbed over a fence.

A stickler for protocol, Queen Mary insisted Lilibet and Margaret Rose curtsy to her whenever they met. She rigorously suppressed her emotions — exhibiting, at most, a slight shift of her lips to indicate amusement — and impressed on Lilibet that it was inappropriate for a monarch to smile in public. When Lilibet spoke of "all the people who'll be waiting to see us outside" a concert, her grandmother punished her self-important remark by taking her home immediately. Lilibet absorbed even the difficult lessons readily, in part because she and her grandmother were similarly self-contained, focused, and industrious. In the years to come she would frequently quote her stern grandmother.

Churchill observed that despite Queen Mary's rigidity and apparent intolerance of change, "new ideas held no terrors for her." Her paradoxical open-mindedness injected rigor into Lilibet's education when Queen Elizabeth was inclined to relax her daughters' routine, on the theory that they should have "a happy childhood which they can always look back on." Through a back channel to Crawfie, Queen Mary suggested revisions to the curriculum and schedules, raised the caliber of the literature selections, and encouraged learning poetry by heart as "wonderful memory training." She took Lilibet and Margaret on cultural excursions to museums and galleries, the British Mint, the Bank of England, Greenwich Palace, and the Tower of London.

Queen Mary's passion was history — specifically the genealogical heritage of the royal family — and for Lilibet she was a living link to the past. Her grandfather, Prince Adolphus, the Duke of

Cambridge, was one of the sons of King George III; Queen Victoria had been her godmother; and she knew two of Britain's most noteworthy prime ministers, William Gladstone and Benjamin Disraeli. She could tell tales of the magnificent Delhi Durbar of 1911, when she and King George V were celebrated as Emperor and Empress of India, and she could describe the origins and particulars of the royal jewelry that she unabashedly flaunted, sometimes wearing the spectacular Cullinan I and II diamonds (530.2 and 317.4 carats respectively) as a brooch between her ample bosom.

In Lilibet's pantheon of mentors and tutors, her father had a singular place. George VI alone could tell her what it was like to be monarch, what the challenges were, and how best to meet them. She was brighter than her father, who labored to commit facts and figures to memory, and more even-tempered, but she shared his shyness and his sense of dedication. She watched with admiration his struggle to overcome his stammer for his annual Christmas broadcast, and she noted his diligence in jotting down ideas on a pad he kept nearby during meals. His "steadfastness," she later said, had been her model.

She learned timeless lessons about perseverance, courage, and duty from her father's conduct during World War II. Lilibet was only thirteen when Britain declared war on Germany on September 3, 1939, after Hitler's invasion of Poland. Six weeks later, she was in Scotland with Margaret Rose and Crawfie, reading "At a Solemn Musick" by Milton as word came over the radio that the Nazis had sunk the battleship *Royal Oak,* one of the first major blows to Britain's morale. The King opened a spacious house on his Balmoral estate in the Scottish Highlands to children and their mothers who had been evacuated from the port city of Glasgow ahead of Nazi bombing. Crawfie directed the princesses to serve them tea, and to talk to the women about their sons and husbands serving in the armed forces.

On May 10, 1940, German troops surged into Holland, Belgium, Luxembourg, and France, and Neville Chamberlain resigned as Britain's prime minister, to be succeeded by Winston Churchill. Lilibet wept while listening to Chamberlain's resignation speech on the radio; it was clear that after nearly nine months of tense anticipation, the real war was beginning. Two days later, the princesses were sent to the safety of the medieval fortress of Windsor Castle twenty-one miles from the center of London, where they would live within its thirteen acres surrounded by thick walls until the defeat of Germany in May 1945. For security reasons, their location was kept secret, although they were able to venture beyond the castle.

Throughout the war the King and Queen spent their days either at Buckingham Palace or traveling around the country on the ten-car Royal Train, visiting troops, factories, hospitals, and bombed-out neighborhoods. Many nights they would join their daughters at Windsor and sleep in a cavernous shelter built under the castle's Brunswick Tower or in a fortified ground-floor apartment in the Victoria Tower. Their resolve to continue working in London exposed them to considerable danger and endeared them to the British populace. After Germany launched its Luftwaffe bombing campaign against British cities and military targets in the summer of 1940, Buckingham Palace was hit nine times. The second bomb, which fell in mid-September, destroyed the Palace chapel and nearly killed both the King and Queen.

Like the rest of her generation, Elizabeth was thrown by the war into an extraordinary situation that deeply affected her adolescence. But contrary to what some observers have said, she wasn't consigned to "purdah" or kept in a state of suspended animation. If anything, her life in the castle gave her an early introduction to the male world she would inhabit as Queen, since she mixed frequently with the young officers in the Grenadier Guards assigned to protect the royal family. (The Grenadiers, founded in 1656, are one of the seven prestigious regiments of the Household Division under the aegis of the monarch. The four other regiments of foot guards are the Coldstream, Scots, Irish, and Welsh, along with two Household Cavalry regiments, the Life Guards and what became known as the Blues and Royals after the merger of the Royal Horse Guards and the Royal Dragoons.) "I was brought up amongst men," her sister, Margaret, would later say.

At age sixteen, Elizabeth was named an honorary colonel of the Grenadiers and applied her gimlet eye to the first of many regimental inspections. Her rigorous critique prompted one of the majors to advise Crawfie to tactfully remind the princess that "the first requisite of a really good officer is to be able to temper justice with mercy."

45

The officers came to tea as well as more formal luncheons where Elizabeth arranged the seating and developed her skills as a hostess. The group included Lord Rupert Nevill and Hugh Euston (later the Duke of Grafton), who would become lifelong friends. Other guests included officers who were convalescing or on leave, among them airmen from New Zealand, Australia, Canada, and the United States. From having been "a rather shy little girl," Elizabeth "became a very charming young person able to cope with any situation without awkwardness," Crawfie observed. "She was an excellent conversationalist."

Elizabeth and her sister "never forgot there was a war on," said Antoinette de Bellaigue, "but there was no feeling of doom and gloom." Windsor's windows were blacked out, the castle was reinforced with barbed wire and protected by batteries of antiaircraft guns, the vast rooms were illuminated by bare low-wattage bulbs, and hot water was so limited that lines were drawn at five inches in all bathtubs — although the family ate well, with supplies of meat and game from various royal estates. The princesses became accustomed to what their mother described as "the whistle & scream of bombs," yet she fretted that they were "looking different" because "the noise of guns is so heavy" and so much ordnance landed in the vicinity — nearly three hundred high-explosive bombs by the war's end. "Though they are so good & composed," she wrote to Queen Mary, "there is always the listening, & occasionally a leap behind the door, and it does become a strain."

Several times the family escaped for brief holidays at Balmoral, where Queen Elizabeth was delighted to see her daughters revive with "pink cheeks and good appetites" after walks in the crisp air on the heather-covered hills rising above Royal Deeside, the valley along the River Dee that had been the sentimental heart of the family since the time of Queen Victoria and Prince Albert. The heiress presumptive's great-great-grandparents had bought the Balmoral estate in 1852 after falling in love with the Scottish Highlands. "All seemed to breathe freedom and peace," Victoria wrote in her journal, "and to make one forget the world and its sad turmoils."

Victoria and Albert tore down the existing residence and built a larger Balmoral castle of gleaming off-white granite that would weather into a gray hue, with a hundred-foot-high tower, turrets and gables, all according to Albert's own exacting adaptation of the baronial style. They decked out the interior with a riot of different-colored tartan plaid rugs, curtains, carpets, and linoleum, thistle-patterned wallpaper, landscape paintings by Sir Edwin Landseer, and stags' heads lining the hallways. Large windows captured vistas of lawns, gardens, pine forests, and hills up the valley of the Dee — the outdoor paradise that shaped their family expeditions.

In the four decades since Victoria's death in 1901, remarkably little had changed at Balmoral, and her descendants felt the magic of the place intensely. It was the sanctuary where the family had spent two months each autumn, a sacrosanct interlude they would resume at war's end. During their quick wartime Highland respites Lilibet shot her first

47

stag and caught her first salmon — a modest eight pounds. The King, his wife, daughters, and courtiers amused themselves after dinner with games of charades lasting until midnight, highlighted by Tommy Lascelles imitating a St. Bernard so noisily that he lost his voice.

In the early part of the war, the King and Queen kept up their social life with periodic balls at Buckingham Palace and Windsor Castle. One dance in December 1943 for "young men and maidens" at Windsor lasted until 4 A.M. The King was famous for being "the best waltzer in the world," and he let loose on the dance floor, even leading a conga line through the glittering state rooms. Later in the war, Elizabeth slipped into London from time to time — for the occasional dinner party, and to attend her first opera, *La Bohème,* performed by the Sadler's Wells Company at the New Theatre.

Crawfie worked to keep the atmosphere light at the castle by organizing games of hide and seek and sardines as well as treasure hunts with the officers, and she set up a Madrigal Society so the girls could sing with guardsmen and boys from Eton. At Christmas the princesses appeared with local schoolchildren in the annual pantomime, a full-scale production staged in the Waterloo Chamber. Elizabeth was called on to sing and tap-dance before audiences of more than five hundred, including townspeople and soldiers. Crawfie remarked on her poise, and her riding instructor, Horace Smith, was struck by her "confidence and vigour," as well as her droll delivery of comic lines.

Periodically word came that officers she knew had died in battle — including, in 1942, her uncle

Prince George, the Duke of Kent, in a plane crash while serving in the Royal Air Force, leaving three children, the youngest only seven weeks old. "What a beastly time it is for people growing up," Queen Elizabeth wrote to her brother David in 1943. "Lilibet meets young Grenadiers at Windsor and then they get killed, & it is horrid for someone so young." While later in life friends would remark that the Queen found it nearly impossible to write condolence notes about the deaths of those close to her, during the war she readily would take up her pen to write to an officer's mother, "and give her a little picture of how much she had appreciated him at Windsor and what they had talked about," Crawfie recalled.

Antoinette de Bellaigue, Marion Crawford, and Henry Marten continued their instruction during the war years. Marten traveled up the hill to the castle in a dog cart, his Gladstone bag bulging with the princess's textbooks. Sir Owen Morshead, the royal librarian, augmented the curriculum with regular tours of Windsor's collections, including artifacts such as the shirt worn by King Charles I when he was beheaded, and the lead shot that killed Lord Nelson at the Battle of Trafalgar. (The priceless paintings had been removed from their frames and sent away for safekeeping.) The future Queen would later say that she considered Windsor to be her home because it represented "all the happiest memories of childhood."

The Girl Guides kept up their activities as well, giving Elizabeth an unexpectedly democratic experience when refugees from London's bomb-ravaged East End were taken in by families on the Windsor estate and joined the troop. The girls earned their cooking badges, with instruction from a castle housekeeper, by baking cakes and scones (a talent Elizabeth would later display for a U.S. president) and making stew and soup. With their Cockney accents and rough ways, the refugees gave the future Queen no deference, calling her Lilibet, the nickname even daughters of aristocrats were forbidden to use, and compelling her to wash dishes in an oily tub of water and clean up the charred remains of campfires.

The most unusual — and memorable — training received by Elizabeth was a three-week stint she did in 1945 when she was eighteen, at the Mechanical Transport Training Centre run by the Auxiliary Territorial Service. The skills she acquired there figure in a pivotal scene in *The Queen* when Helen Mirren confidently drives a Land Rover across the hills of Balmoral, only to run aground on a rock while fording the River Dee. In a phone call to Thomas, her head ghillie, she says briskly, "I think I've broken the prop-shaft." "Are you sure, Ma'am?" he replies. "Yes perfectly," says the Queen. "The front one, not the rear. I've lost the four-wheel drive. You forget, I used to be a mechanic during the war."

Although the scene was invented, her automobile expertise was a genuine source of pride for Elizabeth II. She told Labour politician Barbara Castle more than two decades after the war that her ATS training was the only time she had ever been able to measure herself against her contemporaries. The other eleven young women at the training center were actually several years older, but Second Subaltern Elizabeth Alexandra Mary Windsor wore the same drab uniform and was given the same instruction: learning to drive a three-ton truck in heavy London traffic, changing wheels and spark plugs, understanding the workings of ignition systems, bleeding brakes, and stripping down engines. Her face and hands got grimy from the grease, and she had to salute her senior officers. But the experience gave her confidence and expert driving skills. "I've never worked so hard in my life," she told a friend. "Everything I learnt was brand new to me — all the oddities of the insides of a car."

With the exception of her first tightly scripted radio broadcast in 1940 to children displaced by the war — a sentimental speech delivered in a little-girl voice after numerous rehearsals to master her breathing and phrasing — Elizabeth carried out few official duties until the last years of the war. In 1944 she traveled to Wales with the King and Queen to visit miners, gave her first public speeches in London at the Queen Elizabeth Hospital for Children and the National Society for the Prevention of Cruelty to Children, launched her first battleship, and attended her first official dinner at Buckingham Palace in honor of the prime ministers of the British Dominions.

When England celebrated Victory in Europe Day on May 8, 1945, Elizabeth joined her family and Prime Minister Winston Churchill on the balcony at Buckingham Palace to greet the cheering throngs. That night, she and Margaret Rose escaped the confines of the Palace with Crawfie, Toni de Bellaigue, and the King's equerry as their chaperones. Among the group of sixteen were their cousin Margaret Rhodes and several guards officers, including Henry Porchester, who would become her lifelong friend and closest adviser on horse breeding and racing. Proudly wearing her ATS uniform, the future Queen linked arms with her friends and surged through the crowds, tearing along St. James's Street, and joyfully dancing the conga, the Lambeth Walk, and the hokey-cokey. When they returned to the Palace railings, the princesses joined the crowds shouting, "We want the King; we want the Queen," and cheered when their parents appeared on the balcony. Elizabeth and Margaret Rose slipped back into the Palace through a garden gate, and Queen Elizabeth "provided us with sandwiches she made herself," recalled Toni de Bellaigue.

The following night, the revels continued. "Out in crowd again," Elizabeth recorded in her diary. "Embankment, Piccadilly, Pall Mall, walked simply miles. Saw parents on balcony at 12:30 am — ate, partied, bed 3am!" "It was a unique burst of personal freedom," wrote Margaret Rhodes, "a Cinderella moment in reverse, in which they could pretend that they were ordinary and unknown."

Three months later, the group ventured out again to mark the victory over Japan. Once more they "walked miles," Elizabeth wrote. "Ran through Ritz . . . drank in Dorchester, saw parents twice, miles away, so many people." This time Elizabeth was recognized and cheered, although police cautioned the revelers that "the princesses wished to be treated as private individuals, and they were allowed to go on their way."

Elizabeth was barely nineteen years old at the war's end. Despite her years behind the walls of Windsor, she had experienced life in ways she certainly would not have if she had passed through adolescence in the conventional style of a young member of the royal family. She had seen her parents in a heroic new light as the embodiments of duty and brave service, she had felt the losses of wartime deaths, and she had been exposed to people outside the royal orbit. She had taken on new responsibilities and had caught a glimpse of what the next stage of her life would likely be, not only her role as heiress presumptive, but even more profoundly her personal life — a secret she held tight with the discretion that would characterize her conduct in the decades ahead. She had entered the war as a little girl, and now she was a young woman.

CHAPTER TWO
LOVE MATCH

"There was a whole battalion of lively young men," recalled Lady Anne Glenconner, whose parents, the Earl and Countess of Leicester, were friends and neighbors of King George VI and Queen Elizabeth at Sandringham in Norfolk. But Lilibet "realized her destiny and luckily set her heart on Prince Philip at an early age. He was ideal — good looking and a foreign prince."

Her choice was in some respects traditional, because the princess and Philip were relatives, but not too close to raise eyebrows. They were third cousins, sharing the same great-great-grandparents, Queen Victoria and Prince Albert. Philip was in fact more royal than Elizabeth, whose mother was mere British nobility (with distant links to English and Scottish kings), while his parents were Princess Alice of Battenberg (a great-grandchild of Queen Victoria) and Prince Andrew of Greece, the descendant of a Danish prince recruited for the Greek throne in the mid-nineteenth century. Lilibet and Philip were both connected to most of Europe's reigning families, where consanguinity had been common for centuries. Queen Victoria and her husband had been even closer: first cousins who shared the same grandmother, the Dowa-

"People thought 'Aha!' at that point."

Princess Elizabeth and Philip exchange a telltale glance at the wedding of their cousin Lady Patricia Mountbatten, October 1946.
© TopFoto/The Image Works

ger Duchess of Coburg. Victoria's mother (also Victoria) and Albert's father, Ernest, were sister and brother.

In other ways, Philip was an outlier with a decidedly unconventional background. Queen Elizabeth had made no secret of her preference for one of her daughter's aristocratic English friends from a family similar to the Strathmores — the future Dukes of Grafton, Rutland, and Buccleuch, or Henry Porchester, the future Earl of Carnarvon. Philip could boast none of their extensive landholdings, and in fact had very little money.

Although he was born on June 10, 1921, on the isle of Corfu, Philip spent scarcely a year in Greece before the entire royal family was expelled in a coup. His parents took him, along with his four older sisters, to Paris where they lived rent-free in a house owned by wealthy relatives. A proud professional soldier with an extroverted personality and quick wit, Prince Andrew found himself at loose ends, while Alice (properly known as Princess Andrew of Greece after her wedding) had difficulty managing a large family, not least because she was congenitally deaf. Still, during these early years Philip flourished in an overwhelmingly female household that showered attention on him. He attended the American school in St. Cloud, learned to speak fluent French, and developed an assertive personality.

But his childhood took a dysfunctional turn after his parents sent him at the age of eight to Cheam, a boarding school in England. A year later his mother had a nervous breakdown and was committed to a sanatorium for several years, which precipitated his parents' permanent separation. She eventually moved to Athens and established a Greek Orthodox order of nuns, dedicating herself with religious fervor to carrying out good works.

Prince Andrew was mostly absent from his son's life as well, living as a "boulevardier" in Monte Carlo with a mistress, and subsisting on a small annuity, while beneficent relatives and friends paid Philip's school fees. Philip's four sisters married prosperous German princes — several with connections to the Nazi Party — and welcomed their little brother on school holidays until Hitler's intensifying belligerence made the visits impossible. Philip was also touched twice by tragedy while in his teens when his sister Cecile and her family were killed in a plane crash, and a year later his favorite uncle and guardian, George Mountbatten, the 2nd Marquess of Milford Haven, died of cancer.

Philip was consigned to an itinerant life as an exile, with neither home nor parents to sustain him. Asked years later about the rootlessness of his upbringing, he said, "The family broke up. . . . I just had to get on with it. You do. One does." He left Cheam in 1933 to spend one year at Salem, a boarding school in Germany run by a progressive Jewish educator named Kurt Hahn. After the Nazis briefly detained Hahn, he fled in 1934 to the North Sea coast of Scotland and founded Gordonstoun School, where Philip soon enrolled.

Gordonstoun's educational philosophy was rooted in leadership and service, and meeting tests of physical endurance (harsh drills, cold showers) in addition to academic work. Philip embraced the challenges and became the school's head boy (known as the "Guardian"). "He was one of those boys who very early rendered disinterested service and who never asked for any privilege on account of his birth," Hahn recalled. In his final report, Hahn wrote that Philip was a "born leader" who would "need the exacting demands of a great service to do justice to himself." The headmaster saw "intelligence and spirit" as well as "recklessness," and noted that Philip's leadership qualities were "marred at times by impatience and intolerance."

Once in the United Kingdom, Philip came under the wing of his relatives there, chiefly his Battenberg grandmother, the Dowager Marchioness of Milford Haven, who lived in a grace-and-favor apartment in Kensington Palace, and his mother's younger brother, Louis "Dickie" Mountbatten, later the 1st Earl Mountbatten of Burma, who assiduously cultivated his royal relatives.

Six feet tall, with intense blue eyes, chiseled features, and blond hair, Philip was an Adonis as well as athletic and engaging, exuding confidence and a touch of impudence. He was a resourceful and energetic self-starter, yet he was also something of a loner, with a scratchy defensiveness that sprang from emotional deprivation. "Prince Philip is a more sensitive person than you would appreciate," said his first cousin Patricia Mountbatten, Dickie's older daughter. "He had a tough childhood, and his life constrained him into a hard exterior in order to survive."

As cousins, Philip and young Elizabeth had crossed paths twice, first at a family wedding in 1934 and then at the coronation of King George VI in 1937. But it wasn't until July 22, 1939, when the King and Queen took their daughters to the Royal Naval College at Dartmouth, that the thirteen-year-old princess spent any time with Philip, who was a cadet in training at the school.

At the behest of Dickie Mountbatten, an officer in the British navy, Philip was invited to have lunch and tea with the royal family. Crawfie observed the sparks, later writing that Lilibet "never took her eyes off him," although he "did not pay her any special attention" — no surprise since he was already a man of the world, and she only on the cusp of adolescence. More revealing was the depth and durability of Elizabeth's attraction, and her single-minded determination to marry him.

During the war years, Philip came to visit his cousins occasionally at Windsor Castle, and he and the princess corresponded when he was at sea. He served with the British Royal Navy in the Mediterranean and the Pacific, and was cited for gallantry after the Battle of Matapan against Italian forces in 1942. Friends and relatives detected a flutter of romance between Philip and Elizabeth by December 1943, when he was on leave at Windsor for Christmas and watched Elizabeth, then seventeen, perform in the "Aladdin" pantomime. Queen Mary wrote to her friend Mabell, the Countess of Airlie, shortly afterward that the cousins had "been in love for the past eighteen months. In fact longer, I think." The King was quite taken by Philip, telling his mother the young man was "intelligent, has a good sense of humour and thinks about things in the right way." But both the King and Queen thought that Lilibet was too young to consider a serious suitor.

Philip visited Balmoral in the summer of 1944, and he wrote Queen Elizabeth about how he had savored "the simple enjoyment of family pleasures and amusements and the feeling that I am welcome to share them." That December, while Philip was away on active duty, his father died of cardiac arrest at age sixty-two in the room where he lived at the Hotel Metropole in Monte Carlo. All he left his twenty-three-year-old son were some trunks containing clothing, an ivory shaving brush, cuff links, and a signet ring that Philip would wear for the rest of his life.

While Philip was completing his deployment in the Far East, Lilibet enjoyed the freedom of the postwar period. In August 1945 she reveled in the country life at Balmoral, stalking stags and picnicking on the moors, singing "descants and ditties" with her parents. Her one unanticipated sadness came in December 1945 when her nanny, Allah, died after a brief illness during the family's first Christmas at Sandringham, which had just been reopened after being shuttered for six years.

Back in London that autumn, Lilibet had her own suite in Buckingham Palace with a view of Big Ben and a decor of "pink and fawn" floral fabric, as well as her own small household: two ladies-in-waiting, a footman (also known as a page), a housemaid, and Bobo, now serving as her dresser (the royal term for a lady's maid who attends to personal matters). She invited Mrs. Vicary Gibbs, who was one of her ladies-in-waiting, her cousin Lady Mary Cambridge, and several guardsmen to a house party at Sandringham, turned up the radio, entertained them at dinner, and joined in games.

At a party given by the Grenfell family at their Belgravia home in February 1946 to celebrate the peace, the princess impressed Laura Grenfell as "absolutely natural. . . . She opens with a very easy and cosy joke or remark. . . . She had everyone in fits talking about a sentry who lost his hat while presenting arms." Elizabeth "danced every dance." She was "thoroughly enjoying herself" as the "Guardsmen in uniform queued up."

Philip finally returned to London in March 1946. He took up residence at the Mountbatten home on Chester Street, where he relied on his uncle's butler to keep his threadbare wardrobe in good order. He was a frequent visitor to Buckingham Palace, roaring into the side entrance in a black MG sports car to join Lilibet in her sitting room for dinner, with Crawfie acting as duenna. Margaret was invariably on hand as well, and Philip included her in their high jinks, playing ball and tearing around the long corridors. Crawfie was taken with Philip's breezy charm and shirtsleeve informality — a stark contrast to the fusty courtiers surrounding the monarch.

During a month-long stay at Balmoral in the summer of 1946, Philip proposed to Elizabeth, and she accepted on the spot, without even consulting her parents. Her father consented on the condition that they keep their engagement a secret until it could be announced after her twenty-first birthday the following April. Like the princess, Philip didn't believe in public displays of affection, which made it easy to mask his feelings. But he revealed them

61

privately in a touching letter to Queen Elizabeth in which he wondered if he deserved "all the good things which have happened to me," especially "to have fallen in love completely and unreservedly."

Palace courtiers and aristocratic friends and relatives of the royal family viewed Philip suspiciously as a penniless interloper. They were irked that he seemed to lack proper deference toward his elders. But mostly, they viewed him as a foreigner, specifically a "German," or in their less gracious moments, a "Hun," a term of deep disparagement after the bloody conflict so recently ended. Even though his mother had been born in Windsor Castle, and he had been educated in England and served admirably in the British navy, Philip had a distinctly continental flavor, and he lacked the clubby proclivities of the Old Etonians. What's more, the Danish royal family that had ruled in Greece *was* in fact predominantly German, as was his maternal grandfather, Prince Louis of Battenberg, and his sisters' German husbands continued to be a touchy subject.

Glossed over was the fact that German bloodlines had been tightly woven into the British royal family since the eighteenth century. After the Glorious Revolution of 1688 when Catholic King James II fled England, the crown passed to his Protestant daughter Mary II and her husband William III, who ruled together. Following their deaths, Mary's sister Queen Anne took the throne until she died in 1714. But Anne left no successor, which triggered the provisions of the Act of Settlement of 1701, a constitutional law passed by Parliament to ensure a Protestant would occupy the throne. It stipulated that the crown could only pass to the descendants of Sophia, the Electress of Hanover, the granddaughter of James I. At the time of Queen Anne's death, the successor was Sophia's son, George Louis, who became King George I of Great Britain, the first sovereign in the House of Hanover. Neither he nor his German-born son, King George II, spoke English. King George III, who took the throne in 1760, was the first in the Hanover line born in Britain.

In the nineteenth century, the German strain in the British line of succession was further strengthened when Edward the Duke of Kent, the fourth son of George III, married the Princess of Saxe-Coburg-Saalfield and produced Princess Victoria, who took the throne on the death of her uncle, King William IV. Queen Victoria raised the German stakes yet again by choosing Prince Albert of Saxe-Coburg-Gotha as her husband, taking on his name and dropping the House of Hanover. Their grandson, George V, in turn married Queen Mary, who had a German father, Prince Francis, the Duke of Teck. Although born in Kensington Palace, Princess Victoria Mary of Teck always spoke with a slight German accent.

During World War I, amid strong anti-German feeling in Britain, King George V made a strategic decision to dispel the long Teutonic shadow from the royal family's image. By royal proclamation in 1917, he transformed the House of Saxe-Coburg-Gotha into the House of Windsor, after the ancient castle. At the same time, he anglicized the names of collateral members of the family: Battenberg became Mountbatten, and Teck became Cambridge and Athlone.

None of the criticisms of Philip's German blood or cheeky attitude was of any concern to Princess Elizabeth. A man of ideas and appealing complexity, he was a breath of fresh air to the heiress presumptive. It was clear he would not be easy, nor would he be boring, as might have been the case with one of her mother's chosen suitors. He shared her commitment to duty and service, but he also had an irreverence that could help lighten her official burdens at the end of a tiring day. His life had been as unfettered as hers had been structured, and he was unencumbered by the properties and competing responsibilities of a landed British aristocrat. According to their mutual cousin, Patricia Mountbatten, the princess also saw that behind his protective shell, "Philip had a capacity for love which was waiting to be unlocked, and Elizabeth unlocked it."

The princess "would not have been a difficult person to love," said Patricia Mountbatten. "She was beautiful, amusing and gay. She was fun to take dancing or go to theater." In the seven years since their first meeting, Lilibet (which is what Philip now called her, along with "darling") had indeed become a beauty, her appeal enhanced by being petite. She did not have classical features but rather what *Time* magazine described as "pin-up" charm: big bosom (taking after her mother), narrow shoulders, a small waist, and shapely legs. Her curly brown hair framed her porcelain complexion, with cheeks that Cecil Beaton described as "sugar pink," vivid blue eyes, an ample mouth that widened into a dazzling smile, and an infectious laugh. "She sort of expands when she laughs," said her cousin Margaret Rhodes. "She laughs with her whole face."

There was nothing daring or even particularly stylish about Elizabeth's appearance. Until she was well into her teens, she and her sister had dressed alike in childish outfits, primarily to assuage Margaret, who "was always trying to catch up," explained Anne Glenconner, a good friend of Margaret. Only when Lilibet turned nineteen did she begin choosing clothing for herself, and even then she tended toward the conservative styles and pastel colors favored by her mother, avoiding any hint of décolletage. Crawfie had to badger her into choosing a bold red dinner dress with a pleated skirt and figure-hugging jacket piped in white silk — "one of the most becoming frocks she ever had," the governess concluded. The princess was intrigued by the process of selecting bespoke clothing from the royal couturier, Norman Hartnell — the sketches, the models, and the fittings. But she had little patience for gazing at herself in mirrors. Vain preening was alien to her nature.

The press caught wind of the cousins' romance as early as October 1946 at the wedding of Patricia Mountbatten to Lord Brabourne at Romsey Abbey. Philip was an usher, and when the royal family arrived, he escorted them from their car. The princess turned as she removed her fur coat, and the cameras caught them gazing at each other lovingly. "I think people thought 'Aha!' at that point," recalled Patricia Brabourne. But no official confirmation followed, and the couple kept up an active social life. Elizabeth's guardsmen friends served as her escorts to restaurants and fashionable clubs like The 400, and Philip would take Elizabeth and Margaret out to a party or the theater. But he was only one among many young men to dance with the heiress presumptive.

Lilibet had a growing number of official duties in what her father wryly called the "Royal Firm" (later shortened to the "Firm"). In July 1945, her parents took her to Northern Ireland — her first flight on an airplane. Eight months later she returned for her first solo visit to the six predominantly Protestant counties that were created when Ireland was divided by the British government in 1922. Ireland had been a British colony since England's King Henry II invaded in the twelfth century. After more than eight centuries of oppressive British rule, Irish nationalists rebelled in 1916, resulting in the violent six-year war for independence that led to partition. While the north (also to be known as Ulster) remained within the United Kingdom, the predominantly Catholic twenty-six counties in the south became the self-governing Irish Free State, a British dominion (similar to Canada and Australia) that grudgingly recognized the British monarch as its head of state.

George VI continued to be his daughter's most important tutor. During long walks at Sandringham, Balmoral, and Windsor Home Park, he gave her advice and shared his views on government and politics.

The King's popularity was at its peak, but the postwar years proved difficult for him. In the July 1945 election, the Labour Party won control of Parliament. After heroically leading Britain through the war, Winston Churchill, the King's confidant and valued partner, was replaced at 10 Downing Street by Clement Attlee, the leader of the Labour party. Not only was Attlee taciturn and reserved, his socialist policies — an ambitious Labour platform to create a far-reaching welfare state, nationalize industry, and redistribute wealth — were anathema to both the King and Queen (although Queen Elizabeth shrewdly sized him up as "a practical little man . . . quite cagey . . . difficult to get along with, but he soon melted"). The King didn't hesitate to express his outrage in private, but publicly he remained rigorously neutral. His elder daughter could also see how the strain of his job was wearing her father down. He had begun to suffer from arteriosclerosis, which affected the circulation in his legs and gave him considerable pain. But instead of pacing himself, he kept late hours, chain-smoking as he worked.

On February 1, 1947, King George VI, Queen Elizabeth, Princess Elizabeth, and Princess Margaret embarked on their first official overseas trip together — three months in the British colonies of South Africa and Rhodesia, plus a month for the round-trip ocean voyage on the forty-thousand-ton battleship HMS *Vanguard,* where the admiral's quarters had been transformed into a suite of day and sleeping cabins decorated with prints of London scenes, sofas and chairs in cheerful patterns of ivory, blue, and beige, and satinwood furniture. With a household entourage of ten, they left England from Portsmouth on a gray day at a time when Britain was suffering through a winter of record-breaking cold along with food rationing and fuel shortages.

The journey marked Lilibet's emergence as a major presence in the royal family and introduced her to the distant reaches of British power. The idea of the British Commonwealth began taking shape in the early twentieth century to describe colonies in the empire making the transition to independence but keeping their connection to the crown. What would become the modern Commonwealth in 1949 was still inchoate, but George VI wanted to transmit to the heiress presumptive his devotion to the countries of the formerly robust British Empire. On a personal level, her time away from Philip would be a final test of her commitment and some time for "we four," the affectionate name King George VI had given to his family, to spend their last stretch of time together.

The first several days shipboard left the entire royal party seasick and confined to their cabins in heavy swells and gales so fierce that the Royal Standard — the sovereign's red, gold, and blue flag bearing lions passant and rampant as well as a gold harp — was torn to shreds. When the sun came out as they cruised into the tropics, the princesses leaned hatless against the rails in their flowered dresses, lay on the deck of the rifle range to compete in shooting contests, and dashed around playing tag with the boisterous naval officers. The King, in shirtsleeves and shorts displaying spindly legs, played deck tennis with midshipmen while the women watched. When the ship passed the equator, the crew staged a "Crossing the Line" ceremony featuring sailors dressed in wigs, falsies, and skirts, presided over by Father Neptune with his trident. The "novices" crossing for the first time were dunked and otherwise tormented, although the two princesses only had their faces dabbed with outsized powder puffs.

Elizabeth carried a photograph of her fiancé and kept a steady correspondence with him throughout the trip, recounting their adventures. The princesses were enchanted by the beauty of southern Africa's dramatic vistas, and amazed by the abundance of food and profusion of goods in shop windows compared to the deprivation in London. Sitting in an aerodrome in the Zulu territory, Lilibet and Margaret stared wide-eyed as five thousand half-naked warriors wearing loincloths, animal skins, beads, and feathers brandished their spears and shields, chanting and stomping in a great tribal dance. The princesses gaped at Victoria Falls, marveled at wildlife in the Kruger National Park, hiked the trails in the Drakensberg mountains of the Natal National Park, and clipped the feathers off ostriches. Yet Elizabeth couldn't help feeling "guilty that we had got away to the sun while everyone else was freezing," she wrote to Queen Mary. "We hear such terrible stories of the weather and fuel situation at home. . . . I do hope you have not suffered too much."

The royal party followed a relentless schedule, including thirty-five days on the "White Train" of fourteen air-conditioned railway carriages painted ivory and gold. Elizabeth watched her parents make their rounds, displaying lively interest as they endured endless receiving lines and tributes, taking in all manner of performances and celebrations.

The strain of being on constant display — of feeling "quite sucked dry sometimes," as her mother described it to a niece midway through the tour — she now saw firsthand. She witnessed her father's short fuse when he was exhausted or tense, and her mother's ability to still his "gnashes" with a deft touch on his arm. Either from some unknown underlying illness or the toll of his exertions, the King was visibly losing weight.

There were serious tensions in South Africa, a predominantly black country controlled by a white minority that was itself divided between the Afrikaners of mainly Dutch descent and the English-speaking population — the angry legacy of the nineteenth-century Boer wars in which the British brutally suppressed the Dutch settlers' rebellions and created British colonies. In part, the royal family's trip was an effort by the King to promote reconciliation and to support the prime minister, Field Marshal Jan Smuts, an Afrikaner educated in England.

As Smuts faced a general election in 1948, many Afrikaners felt he was too close to Britain and too sympathetic to blacks. While he opposed giving blacks political power, Smuts favored paternalistic policies to help improve their lives. The opposition Afrikaner National Party, however, advocated apartheid policies of racial separation and subjugation. The pro-apartheid extremists eventually prevailed over Smuts and his party, setting South Africa on an isolationist course for nearly half a century. Lilibet saw how onlookers at events were segregated by race, and she understood the political divisions among the whites. Her insights into

70

the repressive policies in South Africa and neighboring Rhodesia later proved invaluable when she dealt with racial questions that threatened to tear apart the Commonwealth.

The high point of the journey for Elizabeth was her twenty-first birthday on April 21. South Africa celebrated her coming of age as a national holiday with military reviews, a ball in her honor, fireworks, and a necklace of twenty-one diamonds presented by Smuts. She marked the milestone with an eloquent speech dedicated to the young people who had shared her experience of the "terrible and glorious years of the second world war." The address was written by Dermot Morrah, a historian sympathetic to the monarchy and an editorial writer for *The Times,* and polished by Tommy Lascelles, who thought it had "the trumpet-ring of the other Elizabeth's Tilbury speech, combined with the immortal simplicity of Victoria's 'I will be good.' "

Reading the text for the first time brought Elizabeth to tears. While she hadn't crafted the words she spoke, her emotional reaction explains why her delivery was so authentic, and why her sentiments still strike a powerful chord and define her to this day. Lascelles told her that if "200 million other people cry when they hear you deliver it . . . that is what we want."

Her remarks, which were broadcast from Cape Town "to all the peoples of the British Commonwealth and Empire," lasted six minutes. In a piping voice, she spoke of the Commonwealth countries as her "home," and challenged her contemporaries to lift the "burden" from their elders who had "fought and worked and suffered to protect our childhood" and to take on the challenges of the postwar world. "If we all go forward together with an unwavering faith, a high courage, and a quiet heart," she said, "we shall be able to make of this ancient Commonwealth . . . an even grander thing — more free, more prosperous, more happy, and a more powerful influence for good in the world." This turned out to be her credo for the Commonwealth, and it took root during her three months in Africa, just as her father intended.

But it was her personal vow — "my solemn act of dedication" — at the end of her speech that became her north star. "I should like to make that dedication now," she said with palpable feeling. "It is very simple. I declare before you all that my whole life whether it be long or short shall be devoted to your service and the service of our great imperial family to which we all belong." Only the word "imperial" would fail to stand the test of time. With the imminent independence of India and restiveness in other British colonies, it was clear that the empire was coming to an end.

Lilibet did indeed coax "a lump into millions of throats," including Queen Mary's. "Of course I wept," she wrote to Queen Elizabeth. The heiress presumptive had become the royal family's fresh face for the future, "solid and endearing," in the judgment of Tommy Lascelles, with "a healthy sense of fun" and an ability to "take on the old bores with much of her mother's skill." He observed that she showed "an astonishing solicitude for other people's comfort; such unselfishness is not a normal characteristic of that family."

By the standard measures, the Africa journey was a big success for the royal family, setting the seal on their image as a force for continuity, unity, and stability during uncertain times. They had made a great effort to see every corner of the region, stopping the White Train at remote villages, the princesses sometimes in their dressing gowns bedecked with jewelry to put on a good show. The crowds in cities and bush alike had been huge and enthusiastic, the press coverage overwhelmingly positive. After boarding the *Vanguard* at the end of April for the trip home, "we four" stood above the forward gun turret and waved as they listened to the crowds below singing what a newsreel announcer described as "songs of hope." Lilibet would not return to South Africa until 1995, after the end of apartheid and the election of Nelson Mandela as president.

Back in London, Philip had been working as an instructor at the Naval Staff College in Greenwich, and with the help of Dickie Mountbatten had secured his British citizenship in February 1947, giving up his title as H.R.H. Prince Philip of Greece. Since he had no surname, Philip decided on Mountbatten, the English version of his mother's Battenberg. As it turned out, his naturalization was unnecessary, since all the descendants of Sophia Electress of Hanover, who included Philip, were automatically considered citizens of Britain.

The long-postponed engagement announcement came on July 9, 1947, followed by the happy couple's introduction at a Buckingham Palace garden party the next day. Philip's mother retrieved a tiara from a bank vault, and he used some of the diamonds to design an engagement ring created by Philip Antrobus, Ltd., a London jeweler. Several months later Philip was confirmed in the Church of England by the Archbishop of Canterbury.

In July 1947, Princess Elizabeth was assigned her first private secretary, a bright and energetic civil servant named John "Jock" Colville, who had served as an assistant private secretary to both Neville Chamberlain and Winston Churchill during World War II. Colville had ambitious plans for broadening Elizabeth's horizons. In another example of Queen Mary's farsightedness, she advised Colville shortly after his appointment that he should arrange for the heiress presumptive to travel, to mix with people beyond her social circle, and even to get to know Labour politicians. Colville found Elizabeth to be less engaged politically than he had hoped for, but he judged her worth to be "real." He arranged for her to see telegrams from the Foreign Office, to watch a debate on foreign policy in the House of Commons, to spend a day observing juvenile court, and to attend a dinner in the prime minister's residence at 10 Downing Street with up-and-coming Labour leaders.

Philip now had his own valet and bodyguard, and spent much of his time before the November 20 wedding with the royal family, including the late summer sojourn at Balmoral. "There was luxury, sunshine and gaiety," wrote Jock Colville, with "picnics on the moors every day; pleasant siestas in a garden ablaze with roses, stocks and antirrhinums; songs and games."

Elsewhere in Britain, the situation was unrelentingly bleak — an *"annus horrendus,"* as described by Hugh Dalton, the chancellor of the exchequer — characterized by high unemployment, idle factories, and food shortages. A government financial crisis led to tax increases and further austerity measures. Under these difficult circumstances, the Palace negotiated with the Labour government an increase in the annual income for Elizabeth from the £15,000 she had been granted on reaching the age of twenty-one to £40,000 plus £10,000 for Philip. These sums were allocated under the provisions of what was known as the Civil List through arrangements between the sovereign and Parliament dating from the eighteenth century.

William the Conqueror had seized vast amounts of English property following his successful invasion in 1066, and subsequent monarchs added holdings in Scotland, Wales, and Ireland even as they rewarded loyal subjects by giving them large tracts of land. What remained in the monarch's possession was called the Crown Estate, which encompassed vast urban and rural holdings. When George III became king in 1760, these properties weren't generating much revenue, so he struck an agreement with Parliament to turn over the income from the crown lands to the Exchequer (the government treasury) in exchange for a fixed annual payment called the Civil List. At the same time, he and his successors kept the income from a separate portfolio of property known as the Duchy of Lancaster.

These two sources of funds financed the royal household as well as members of the sovereign's family. In 1947 the Crown Estate provided the

75

government with nearly £1 million in "surplus revenue" from commercial and residential properties, mines, farms, forests, and fisheries. That year Parliament authorized the Treasury to return £410,000 to King George VI as a Civil List stipend, plus £161,000 for family members, leaving the government with nearly £400,000 to use for general expenses.

Just before his daughter's wedding, the King gave his future son-in-law a collection of grand titles — the Duke of Edinburgh, Earl of Merioneth, and Baron Greenwich — and decreed that he should be addressed as "His Royal Highness." He would be called the Duke of Edinburgh, although he would continue to be known popularly as Prince Philip and would use his Christian name for his signature. (His official designation as a Prince of the United Kingdom would not come for another decade.) The King also invested Philip with the Order of the Garter, which dates from 1348 and is the highest personal honor that a monarch can confer; Elizabeth had received the Garter a week earlier as a mark of her seniority to her husband.

On November 18, the King and Queen had a celebratory ball at Buckingham Palace that dramatist Noel Coward called a "sensational evening. . . . Everyone looked shiny and happy." Elizabeth and Philip were "radiant. . . . The whole thing was pictorially, dramatically and spiritually enchanting." As was his habit, the King led a conga line through the state rooms of the palace, and the festivities ended after midnight. Philip was in charge of distributing gifts to his fiancée's attendants: silver compacts in Art Deco style with a gold crown above the bride's and groom's entwined initials and a row of five small cabochon sapphires. With typical insouciance, "he dealt them out like playing cards," recalled Lady Elizabeth Longman, one of the two non–family members among the eight bridesmaids.

The morning of the wedding two days later, Philip gave up smoking, a habit that had kept his valet, John Dean, "busy refilling the cigarette boxes." But Philip knew how anguished Elizabeth was by her father's addiction to cigarettes, so he stopped, according to Dean, "suddenly and apparently without difficulty." Patricia Brabourne, who was also with her cousin that morning, said that Philip wondered if he was being "very brave or very foolish" by getting married, although not because he doubted his love for Lilibet. Rather, he worried that he would be relinquishing other aspects of his life that were meaningful. "Nothing was going to change for her," his cousin recalled. "Everything was going to change for him." Before he left Kensington Palace, where he had spent the night in his grandmother's apartment, Philip indulged in a favorite royal ritual by downing a gin and tonic.

Outside Westminster Abbey, tens of thousands of spectators gathered in freezing temperatures to welcome the princess and her father in the Irish State Coach. Two thousand guests enjoyed the splendor of the 11:30 A.M. ceremony in the Abbey, an event that Winston Churchill called "a flash of colour on the hard road we have to travel." Elizabeth's dress by Norman Hartnell was of pearl-and-crystal-encrusted ivory silk satin, with a fifteen-foot train held by the two five-year-old pages, Prince William of Gloucester and Prince Michael of Kent, who wore Royal Stewart tartan kilts and silk shirts. Her tulle veil was embroidered with lace and secured by Queen Mary's diamond tiara, and Philip's naval uniform glinted with the new Garter insignia pinned to his jacket. The men in the congregation wore morning dress or uniforms, while the women were resplendent in long dresses, elbow-length white gloves, splendid jewels, and either tiaras or hats, many bedecked with feathered plumes. The Archbishop of York, Cyril Garbett, presided, telling the young couple that they should have "patience, a ready sympathy, and forbearance."

After the hour-long service, the bride and groom led a procession down the nave that included five kings, five queens, and eight princes and princesses, among them the crowned heads of Norway, Denmark, Romania, Greece, and Holland. Philip's mother was present, but his three sisters and their German husbands were pointedly not invited. Also noticeably absent was the king's brother, former King Edward VIII, now the Duke of Windsor, and his wife the Duchess, for whom he had abdicated the throne. The estranged Windsors were living in Paris, unwelcome in London except for periodic visits. Although their exile may have seemed harsh, George VI, Queen Elizabeth, and their advisers had seen no alternative. A king and former king living in the same country would have resulted in two rival courts.

While the bells of the Abbey pealed, Elizabeth

and Philip were driven to Buckingham Palace in the Glass Coach, preceded and followed by the two regiments of the Household Cavalry on horseback, wearing full ceremonial dress: the Royal Horse Guards in their blue tunics, the Life Guards in red, all with white leather breeches, black thigh-high boots, shiny steel cuirasses, and gleaming helmets with either red or white plumes. It was the most elaborate public display since the war, and the crowds responded with cheers and thunderous applause. More than 100,000 people broke through police lines to surge toward the Palace railings, shouting, "We want Elizabeth! We want Philip!" When the royal family stepped out on the balcony to smile and wave, they received a "tumultuous expression of good will."

As a concession to Britain's hard times, only 150 guests attended the "wedding breakfast," which was actually luncheon in the Ball Supper Room. The "austerity" menu featured *Filet de Sole Mountbatten, Perdreau en Casserole,* and *Bombe Glacée Princess Elizabeth,* served on plates of silver gilt (solid silver covered with gold) by footmen in scarlet livery. The tables were decorated with pink and white carnations, as well as small keepsake bouquets of myrtle and white Balmoral heather at each place setting. The bride and groom cut the wedding cake — four tiers standing nine feet high — with Philip's Mountbatten sword.

The King didn't subject himself to the strain of making a speech, celebrating the moment instead with a raised glass of champagne to "the bride." After being showered with rose petals in the Palace forecourt, the newlyweds were transported in an open carriage drawn by four horses — "the bride snugly ensconced in a nest of hot-water bottles" — to Waterloo Station, crossing the Thames on Westminster Bridge, illuminated by streetlights in the gloaming. As they alighted on the red carpet at the station, Elizabeth's beloved corgi, Susan, hopped out as her owner handed the leash to Cyril Dickman, the footman, who would accompany the couple on their honeymoon, along with John Dean, Bobo, and a detective.

They spent the first week at Broadlands, the Mountbatten estate in Hampshire, and more than two more weeks in snowbound seclusion at Birkhall, an early-eighteenth-century white stone lodge on the Balmoral estate, set in the woods on the banks of the River Muick. With its Victorian decor — pine furniture, tartan carpets, walls covered with Landseer paintings and Spy caricatures — and memories of childhood summers before her parents became King and Queen, Elizabeth could relax in a place she considered home. Dressed in army boots and a sleeveless leather jacket lined with wool, Elizabeth went deer stalking with her husband, feeling "like a female Russian commando leader followed by her faithful cut-throats, all armed to the teeth with rifles," she wrote to her cousin Margaret Rhodes.

She also sent her parents tender letters thanking them for all they had given her, and the example they had set. "I only hope that I can bring up my children in the happy atmosphere of love and fairness which Margaret and I have grown up in," she wrote, adding that she and her new husband "behave as though we had belonged to each other for years! Philip is an angel — he is so kind and thoughtful." Philip revealed his carefully cloaked emotions when he wrote to his mother-in-law, "Cherish Lilibet? I wonder if that word is enough to express what is in me." He declared that his new wife was "the only 'thing' in this world which is absolutely real to me, and my ambition is to weld the two of us into a new combined existence that will not only be able to withstand the shocks directed at us but will also have a positive existence for the good."

CHAPTER THREE
DESTINY CALLS

The honeymooners were back in London in time for the fifty-second birthday of King George VI on December 14, ready to begin their new life. Elizabeth and Philip chose to live in Clarence House, the nineteenth-century residence adjacent to St. James's Palace, just down the Mall from her parents. But the house needed extensive renovations, so they moved temporarily into an apartment in Buckingham Palace. For weekend getaways, they rented Windlesham Moor in Surrey, not far from Windsor. Philip had a paper-pushing job at the Admiralty on the other end of the Mall, where he would walk on the weekdays. Elizabeth was kept busy by Jock Colville, whose tutorial seemed to be yielding results. Eleanor Roosevelt, who had first spotted Elizabeth's ability to ask "serious questions" during a visit to England in 1942, was delighted six years later when she came to Windsor Castle and found that the princess showed a keen interest in "social problems and how they were being handled."

Colville's biggest project was organizing Elizabeth and Philip's first official visit to Paris in May 1948. During their four days in the city, the glamorous young couple proved effective at generating

"The Queen in her own way is immensely kind, but she had too little time to fulfill her family care."

Princess Elizabeth with her first child and heir apparent, Prince Charles, November 1948. PHOTOGRAPH BY CECIL BEATON, CAMERA PRESS LONDON

goodwill for Britain among the wary French. The crowds along the Champs-Élysées were so passionate in their cheering that Elizabeth's eyes were "brimming with tears." The British ambassador, Sir Oliver Harvey, noted that even the usually contemptuous communist newspapers "published good photographs and sympathetic accounts of the visit."

Unknown to either the French or the British, Elizabeth was four months pregnant, and behind closed doors was suffering from nausea. Even so, she and Philip kept up an active social life. They went to the races at Epsom and Ascot and joined friends at restaurants, nightclubs, and dances. For a costume party at Coppins, the home of the Duchess of Kent, Elizabeth dressed "in black lace, with a large comb and mantilla, as an Infanta," wrote diarist Chips Channon, and "danced every dance until nearly 5 a.m." Philip "was wildly gay," Channon observed, in a "policeman's hat and hand-cuffs. He leapt about and jumped into the air as he greeted everybody. . . . He and Princess Elizabeth seemed supremely happy and often danced together." When they were with friends such as Rupert Nevill and his wife, Micky, the former Camilla Wallop (who had been in Elizabeth's Girl Guides troop), and John and Patricia Brabourne, the royal couple showed an easy affection toward each other. During a visit to the Brabournes in Kent, John said to Philip, "I never realized what lovely skin she has." "Yes," Philip replied, "she's like that all over."

In the early evening of November 14, 1948, word went out that Princess Elizabeth had gone into labor in her second-floor bedroom at Buckingham Palace, where a hospital suite had been prepared for the baby's arrival. In attendance were four physicians led by gynecologist Sir William Gilliatt, and a midwife, Sister Helen Rowe. Philip passed the time playing squash with three courtiers, beating each of them in turn. Around 9 P.M. senior members of the household gathered in the Equerry's Room, a ground-floor drawing room that was equipped with a well-stocked bar, and shortly afterward were told that Elizabeth had given birth to a seven-pound, six-ounce son at 9:14. They set to work writing "Prince" on telegrams and calling the Home Office, Prime Minister Attlee, and Winston Churchill, the leader of the opposition. "I knew she'd do it!" exclaimed Commander Richard Colville, press secretary to the King, exultant over the arrival of a male heir. "She'd never let us down."

Ainslie, the Palace steward, phoned for "any spare pages to put their flippin' skates on" as family members converged on the Equerry's Room. Eighty-one-year-old Queen Mary brought her brother, the Earl of Athlone, and his wife, Princess Alice, Countess of Athlone. "Glad it's all over," mumbled the earl. "All for the best, I suppose — horrid business." After the elderly trio had been taken to see the newborn, they returned with the King and Queen as well as the doctors for a round of champagne. Sir John Weir, one of the official physicians to the royal family, confided to Queen Elizabeth's private secretary, Major Thomas Harvey, that he'd "never been so pleased to see a male organ in all his life." Queen Elizabeth was "beaming with happiness," and George VI was "simply delighted by the success of everything." Queen Mary, sitting in "the straightest-backed chair we could find," was busy grilling Sir William Gilliatt "from A to Z." Philip, still dressed in sneakers and sports clothes, joined his wife as her anesthesia wore off, presented her with a bouquet of roses and carnations, and gave her a kiss.

Shortly before midnight, the baby was brought to the ballroom for viewing by the courtiers. Thomas Harvey described him as "just a plasticene head emerging from a cocoon, with Nurse Rowe proudly standing guard: a simple little cot, with white blankets. . . . Poor little chap, two-and-a-half hours after being born, he was being looked at by outsiders — but with great affection and good-will." Well-wishers who had been given the news of the heir's birth by a policeman were still cheering along the Buckingham Palace railing. Finally Richard Colville and Lieutenant Michael Parker, Prince Philip's equerry, persuaded them to go home.

Elizabeth and Philip named their son Charles Philip Arthur George. "I had no idea that one could be kept so busy in bed — there seems to be something happening all the time!" Elizabeth wrote to her cousin Lady Mary Cambridge two weeks after giving birth. "I still find it hard to believe that I really have a baby of my own!" The new mother was particularly taken with her son's "fine, long fingers — quite unlike mine and certainly unlike his father's," as she described them in a letter to her former music teacher, Mabel Lander. For nearly two months, the princess breast-fed her son until she fell ill with measles — one of several childhood diseases she had missed by not attending a school — and Charles had to be sent away temporarily so he wouldn't catch the illness at such a young age.

In addition to parenthood, Elizabeth and Philip were collaborating on the refurbishment of Clarence House. He took the lead on matters of design, orchestrating the placement of pictures on the walls, as he would do throughout their marriage, and indulging in his passion for technology by having a speaker system installed in their bedroom. She made practical suggestions, according to biographer Sarah Bradford, who recounted that "when someone complained about the smell of paint in the room, she said, 'Put a bucket of hay in there and that'll take it away.'" Elizabeth was sensitive about her husband's need to assert himself in his domain. "Philip is terribly independent," she had written to her mother during her honeymoon, adding that she wanted him to be "boss in his own home."

They moved early in the summer of 1949, delighted at last to be in their own home together. They had adjacent bedrooms, connected by a door, his with masculine paneling, hers a feminine pink and blue, with canopy hangings "suspended from a crown" over the double bed. "In England the upper class always have had separate bedrooms," explained their cousin Lady Pamela Mountbatten (later Hicks). "You don't want to be bothered with snoring, or someone flinging a leg around. Then when you are feeling cozy you share your room sometimes. It is lovely to be able to choose."

The couple had a full complement of household staff to serve them — Elizabeth's private secretary Jock Colville; her ladies-in-waiting, including Lady Margaret Egerton (who would later marry Colville); equerry Michael Parker, a cheeky Australian who was a friend of Philip's from the navy; General Sir Frederick "Boy" Browning, comptroller (treasurer) for the household; Philip's valet John Dean; the dresser Bobo MacDonald; and several butlers, footmen, housemaids, chauffeurs, detectives, a chef, and culinary helpers. Continuing the family tradition, Prince Charles had two Scottish nurses, Helen Lightbody, who was the enforcer, and Mabel Anderson, the nurturer, as well as his own nursery footman, John Gibson, who served all meals and maintained the pram, much as a chauffeur would keep a car in good working order.

It was understood that those employed by the royal family would regard their work as confidential, so Elizabeth and her parents were dismayed when they learned early in 1949 that Crawfie planned to publish a memoir of her years in royal service. However affectionate the portrayal — and it was as loving as it was acute in its recollections — she had betrayed their trust. They cut her off completely, forever branding any similar act of perceived disloyalty — of which there would be plenty more in the coming years — as "Doing a Crawfie."

Philip was determined to pursue a career in the navy, so for more than a year he had been taking courses at the Naval Staff College at Greenwich, where he had to spend many weeknights. As a new mother, Elizabeth kept a light schedule of royal duties, which included the occasional speech. One at a Mothers' Union meeting in the autumn of 1949 drew unusual criticism from advocates for modernizing the marriage laws when she condemned divorce for creating "some of the darkest evils in our society today." As usual, the words had been written by courtiers, but the sentiments reflected the prevailing view in the royal family about the need to keep families intact under any circumstance. Still, it was a rare moment of controversy for a young woman who otherwise kept her opinions private.

In October 1949 Philip resumed active service when he was appointed second-in-command of the destroyer HMS *Chequers,* based on the small island nation of Malta in the Mediterranean, which had been part of the British Empire since 1814 and served as an important shipping center and outpost for the Mediterranean Fleet. For the wife of a naval officer, such a posting was expected. According to John Dean, the royal couple "were advised that conditions [in Malta] were not suitable for the infant prince." Elizabeth could have stayed in London with her son, but she decided instead to spend as much time as possible with her husband. She had been accustomed to long parental absences while she was growing up, so her decision to leave Charles wouldn't have raised eyebrows. She had expert nannies in charge, not to mention her own parents, who were eager to keep their grandson company. Elizabeth would visit Malta for long stretches of time, returning at intervals to Clarence House.

She left six days after Charles's first birthday, in

time to join Philip for their second wedding anniversary. At the outset she fulfilled her role as heiress presumptive, visiting historic sites, touring an industrial exhibition and a hospital, inspecting ships, and dedicating a plaque to mark the heroism of the Maltese during World War II when they withstood a siege by Axis forces.

Beyond minimal royal obligations, Elizabeth was given unaccustomed freedom and anonymity. "I think her happiest time was when she was a sailor's wife in Malta," said Margaret Rhodes. "It was as nearly an ordinary a life as she got." She socialized with other officers' wives, went to the hair salon, chatted over tea, carried and spent her own cash — although shopkeepers "noticed that she was slow in handling money." The royal couple lived a significant cut above the ordinary, however, in the Earl Mountbatten's Villa Guardamangia, a spacious sandstone house built into a hill at the top of a narrow road, with romantic terraces, orange trees, and gardens. Dickie Mountbatten was commanding the First Cruiser Squadron, and his wife, Edwina, accompanied Elizabeth on her first flight to Malta.

Philip and Elizabeth spent the Christmas of 1949 on the island, while their son stayed with his grandparents at Sandringham. After *Chequers* sailed out for duty in the Red Sea at the end of December, the princess flew back to England. She stopped first for several days in London, with a detour to Hurst Park to see her steeplechaser Monaveen win a race before she was reunited with Charles in Norfolk after five weeks apart.

When Philip returned from naval maneuvers,

Elizabeth rejoined him in Malta at the end of March 1950 for an idyllic six weeks. Elizabeth dispensed with the chauffeur to drive her Daimler Saloon, a gift from her father on her eighteenth birthday. If the royal couple wanted to be less conspicuous, they zoomed around in Philip's Hillman Minx.

Much to Uncle Dickie's delight, the two couples spent a lot of time together, exploring the island's coves by boat, sunbathing and picnicking. They cheered the Mountbattens' younger daughter, Pamela, when she won the ladies' race at the riding club, and in the evenings they went to the Phoenicia Hotel for dinner and dancing.

During these weeks, Elizabeth grew closer to the uncle who had taken such a prominent role in her husband's life. He gave her a polo pony and went riding with her, encouraging her to perfect her skills at sidesaddle, which she "loathed," recalled his daughter Pamela, "because she felt out of touch with the horse. She felt marooned up there and much preferred to ride astride." But in part because of Uncle Dickie's persistence, "she was a very good sidesaddle rider."

Also at Dickie's urging, Philip took up polo — "a very fast, very dangerous, very exciting game" that he figured his nephew would enjoy. But it was Elizabeth who shrewdly advised how to persuade her husband: "Don't say anything. Don't push it. Don't nag. Just leave it alone." Once Philip made the transition from watching matches to participating, his wife caught the action on her new movie camera, the beginning of her lifelong photographic hobby.

On May 9 she flew back to London, six months pregnant and ready to resume some of her royal duties. Jock Colville had left the household the previous autumn to return to the diplomatic corps, and his replacement was thirty-six-year-old Martin Charteris, who was enraptured by the princess on their first meeting.

An Old Etonian who trained at Sandhurst and rose to the rank of lieutenant colonel in the army, Charteris was the younger brother of the 12th Earl of Wemyss, one of Scotland's most prominent titles. He had a refreshing unconventional streak, sculpting in his spare time and indulging in the retro habit of taking snuff, which he would offer to flagging ladies on arduous royal tours. Married to the daughter of Viscount Margesson, the former Conservative chief whip and war minister under Churchill, Charteris was intelligent, worldly, decent, and free of pomposity. For more than a quarter century he was a wise and steadying influence in Elizabeth's life. When he was well into his eighties, his eyes still lit up when he spoke of her.

Colville had never taken to Philip, writing that the duke could be "vulgar" in his comments and "off-hand" in his treatment of the princess. With his gentle wit and easy manner, Martin Charteris was a more emollient presence in the household. He also worked to expand Elizabeth's knowledge of public affairs, arranging in June 1950 for her to receive memoranda and minutes of cabinet meetings, as well as daily reports on the proceedings in Parliament in addition to Foreign Office papers.

Elizabeth gave birth at Clarence House on August 15, 1950, at 11:50 A.M. to her second child, Anne Elizabeth Alice Louise. Philip had returned to London more than two weeks earlier, which gave him time to get reacquainted with his twenty-one-month-old son after almost a year away. But his first command of the frigate HMS *Magpie* — and a promotion to lieutenant commander — sent him back to Malta in early September. As she had with Charles, Elizabeth breast-fed her daughter for several months. She celebrated Charles's second birthday, and left shortly thereafter for Malta. Yet again the family was split at Christmas, with mother and father celebrating on their own while the children were at Sandringham with their grandparents, who unabashedly doted on them. Queen Elizabeth sent regular letters to her daughter, reporting Charles "giving himself an ecstatic hug" and Anne "so pretty & neat & *very* feminine. . . . Everybody loves them so, and they cheer us up more than I can say."

The following spring, Elizabeth made her first trips to Italy and Greece, where Philip showed her the Parthenon and other sights in his homeland. Always vigilant about his own weight, he helped his wife return to trim form by encouraging her to give up potatoes, wine, and sweets. But their time in the Mediterranean was coming to an end. King George VI had been in declining health since 1948, increasingly plagued by pain and numbness resulting from his arteriosclerosis. In March 1949 he had undergone surgery to improve circulation in his legs. He continued to carry out his duties but his appearance was gaunt, and by May 1951 he was seriously ill, this time with a fever and chronic cough that did not respond to treatment.

Elizabeth came home to stand in for her father at a variety of events, most prominently the Trooping the Colour parade in June, when for the first time she took the salute on behalf of the King. The lone woman leading masses of straight-backed men, she rode sidesaddle on a chestnut police horse called Winston. She wore the scarlet and gold tunic of the Grenadier Guards — the regiment presenting its flag in an intricate hour-long ceremony — and a tricorn cap with white osprey plume, an exact replica of the hat worn by a Grenadier colonel in 1745. At age twenty-five, she projected an image of composure, her crop and reins held lightly in her left hand, her right hand in confident salute. Watching from a window above Horse Guards Parade was a large family contingent including Queen Elizabeth; Queen Mary; Prince Charles; his godfather, King Haakon of Norway; and Earl Mountbatten, who hoisted the little prince to a windowsill and taught him a proper salute. Prince Philip was back in Malta, and George VI was too weak to attend.

Philip returned to London in July when it became clear that the royal couple would be needed full-time to represent the sovereign. He took an open-ended leave from the navy, but in effect the thirty-year-old duke was ending his military career after only eleven months of enjoying the satisfaction of his own command — "the happiest of my sailor life." Much later Philip would say philo-

94

sophically, "I thought I was going to have a career in the Navy but it became obvious there was no hope. . . . There was no choice. It just happened. You have to make compromises. That's life. I accepted it. I tried to make the best of it."

In September George VI had a biopsy that revealed a malignancy, and surgeons removed his left lung in a three-hour operation. The cancer diagnosis was not openly discussed and certainly not given out to the press, but the family understood the severity of the King's condition. As a precaution, the Queen and the two princesses were named Counsellors of State to act on the King's behalf, even as bulletins from the Palace indicated he was making good progress.

Elizabeth and Philip had been scheduled to leave for a state visit to Canada and the United States, which they postponed by two weeks until they were reassured that her father was in no imminent danger. Instead of traveling on the ocean liner *Empress of Britain,* they decided to take a BOAC Stratocruiser on their first transatlantic flight. The double-decker plane was upholstered in royal blue in their honor, and they could sleep in pull-down berths made up in white linen. They left at midnight on October 8, 1951, after saying goodbye at the airport to Queen Elizabeth and Princess Margaret and arrived sixteen hours later in Montreal — the beginning of a thirty-five-day trek of more than ten thousand miles from the east coast to the Pacific and back. They traveled in a ten-coach royal train with a paneled sitting room and sleeping cars outfitted with floral fabrics for Elizabeth and tailored upholstery for Philip.

Everywhere they went, from French-speaking Quebec (where she reviewed "one of the largest military parades in Quebec's history") to Vancouver Island (which they reached after an eighty-mile boat trip), they were greeted by enthusiastic crowds. In Toronto 38,000 schoolchildren serenaded them in a stadium, and 100,000 people filled the city's Riverside Park. They tried to be as visible as possible, often riding in a convertible in cold and snowy weather with a traveler's rug — a routine source of "comfort, softness, and discretion," even in the tropics — tucked around them. In frigid Winnipeg, however, a transparent plastic bubble was fitted over the car. Their personal greetings were primarily limited to VIPs (including the famous seventeen-year-old Dionne quintuplets, five sisters who dressed in identical suits and matching hats), but they managed to talk to some ordinary people, mainly children, and also to former servicemen who had been wounded during the war.

The essential public routine that the royal couple would use over the decades took shape in those long days: Elizabeth was the restrained presence, her smiles tentative and infrequent, which prompted criticism in some press accounts. "My face is aching with smiling," she complained to Martin Charteris when she heard the reports on her dour demeanor. Philip, always at a discreet distance behind, was already providing comic relief, grinning and teasing onlookers. When the royal couple watched bronco bucking and chuck wagon races at a rodeo in Calgary, they sat under electric blankets, both looking uncomfortably cold. But Philip was in good spirits, sporting his new ten-gallon hat, which he waved during the races. Once he went over the line, committing the first of his legendary "gaffes" when he jokingly observed that Canada was "a good investment" — a remark that stuck in the Canadians' craw for its neo-imperial implication.

The scope and pace of the trip were punishing. They made more than seventy stops, and on a single day in Ontario they visited eight towns. Through it all, Elizabeth worried about the health of her father 3,400 miles away. Prepared for the worst, Martin Charteris carried the documents required for Elizabeth's accession, and she had black mourning clothes as part of her traveling wardrobe. The princess was buoyed periodically by encouraging phone calls from her mother that made her feel "much refreshed and strengthened."

In private on the train Philip tried to keep the atmosphere light, but he clearly found the journey stressful. "He was impatient. He was restless," recalled Martin Charteris. "He hadn't yet defined his role. . . . He was certainly very impatient with the old style courtiers and sometimes, I think, felt that the Princess paid more attention to them than to him. He didn't like that. If he called her a 'bloody fool' now and again, it was just his way. I think others would have found it more shocking than she did."

For much of the trip, Philip wore his naval uniform, and Elizabeth favored discreetly tailored suits and close-fitting hats, sometimes trimmed with veils, as well as fur coats and capes. During their visit to Niagara Falls, everyone donned oilskin suits on the spray-lashed observation deck. Pulling her hood tight, Elizabeth exclaimed, "This will ruin my hair!"

While most of their time was devoted to sightseeing (which she filmed on her movie camera), they also visited steel and paper mills, and Elizabeth got a first glimpse of the United States from Windsor, Ontario, when she saw the skyline of the Motor City across the Detroit River. Several weeks later, the royal couple boarded a plane for Washington and set foot on American soil for the first time on October 31 — the beginning of an important connection with the United States that would grow deeper in the years to come.

President Harry S. Truman, his wife, Bess, and daughter, Margaret, greeted them at the airport with a twenty-one-gun salute. Truman expressed relief that the King had "recovered so promptly" and observed that Margaret, who had met the princess during a visit to England, "tells me when everyone becomes acquainted with you, they immediately fall in love with you." The sixty-seven-year-old president counted himself among them, calling Elizabeth a "fairy princess." Elizabeth enunciated every word of her reply, her high voice a model of cut-glass precision, proclaiming that "free men everywhere look towards the United States with affection and with hope." She later told Martin Charteris that she was taken by Truman's natural manner.

They drove into the capital in a procession of convertibles as 600,000 people shouted and cheered along the route. Philip and Elizabeth stayed with the Trumans at Blair House, the official guest quarters, and the president took the princess across Pennsylvania Avenue for a tour of the White House, which was undergoing a top-to-bottom renovation.

The royal couple's whirlwind itinerary started with a reception at the Statler Hotel (later the Capital Hilton) on 16th Street for nine hundred representatives of "press, radio, television and newsreels." Elizabeth made some brief remarks, the royal couple met a small number of journalists, and Philip diverted himself by sneaking a look at the notebooks of two women reporters, a gambit he would enjoy repeating in future encounters with the news media.

The following day they visited the Capitol, inspected the Declaration of Independence and Constitution at the Library of Congress, paid tribute at the grave of George Washington in Mount Vernon and the Tomb of the Unknown Soldier in Arlington National Cemetery, and spent two hours shaking hands with 1,500 guests at a British embassy party. At a Rose Garden ceremony, they presented the Trumans with an overmantel mirror adorned with a painting of flowers, to be hung in the refurbished Blue Room as a "welcome ornament . . . a mark of our friendship." (It was eventually moved to the pink bedroom suite in the private quarters.) Their visit ended with a white-tie dinner in honor of the Trumans at the Canadian embassy.

They had a rough return trip across the North Atlantic aboard the *Empress of Scotland.* Only Elizabeth managed to avoid seasickness and show up regularly at mealtimes, and veteran sailor Philip was furious about his own weakness. On arrival at the Liverpool Dockyards three days after Prince Charles's third birthday, they boarded the Royal Train for London's Euston Station. Waiting on the platform were Queen Elizabeth, Princess Margaret, and Prince Charles, who had not seen his parents in over a month. He was in a mischievous mood, asking a guardsman, "Where is your sword?" but he obediently walked along a line of dignitaries shaking hands.

When the princess and duke stepped off the train, Elizabeth rushed to hug her mother and kiss her on both cheeks. For tiny Charles, she simply leaned down and gave him a peck on the top of his head before turning to kiss Margaret. "Britain's heiress presumptive puts her duty first," explained a newsreel announcer. "Motherly love must await the privacy of Clarence House." Prince Philip was even less demonstrative, touching his son on the shoulder to indicate they should move along to the waiting limousines. As they passed through the station, Prince Charles was again with his grandmother, while his parents walked ahead.

In the royal couple's absence, a general election had taken place. On October 25, 1951, the Conservatives had narrowly won a parliamentary majority, sending Attlee off and returning seventy-six-year-old Winston Churchill to 10 Downing Street six years after his crushing loss. When the City of London welcomed Elizabeth and Philip back with a luncheon in their honor at the Guildhall, Churchill raised a glass to toast their health.

The King and Queen celebrated Christmas at

Sandringham with their daughters, son-in-law, two grandchildren, Queen Mary, and an assortment of relatives — the first time the entire clan had enjoyed the holiday together. Like their autumnal escape to Balmoral, the royal family's six-week sojourn in Norfolk each winter was an ingrained tradition dating back to King Edward VII and his mother, Queen Victoria, who bought the Sandringham estate for him when he was Prince of Wales.

In 1870 the future Edward VII built a new and considerably larger house at Sandringham, in Jacobean Revival style with more than three hundred rooms. The red-brick facade is trimmed with stone, ornamented with balconies and bay windows, and extravagantly topped with gables, chimneys, and onion domes. The spacious rooms are decorated with paneling, intricate plasterwork, arches, columns, and coffered ceilings. The centerpiece of the house — only steps from the front entrance — is the grand two-story Saloon, a Jacobean-style great hall overlooked by a minstrel's gallery and dominated by two massive stone fireplaces. The bedroom suites are huge as well, with furniture described by the writer David Cecil as "sturdily philistine." Deborah, the Duchess of Devonshire, was astounded to discover three marble sinks in her bathroom, the first engraved "HEAD & FACE ONLY," the second "HANDS," and "good heavens the last was blank, so what can it have been for?" she wrote in a letter to a friend.

Christmas in 1951 followed the pattern set by Queen Victoria, with the family opening gifts on Christmas Eve in the German style. They gathered in the ballroom, where trestle tables covered with cloths were arranged with gifts in piles marked for each family member. After tearing off the wrappings and ribbons, the adults changed into black tie and long dresses for a dinner complete with champagne toasts and popping open Christmas crackers, gaily wrapped party favors containing paper hats and trinkets. The next morning they all walked to St. Mary Magdalene, the nearby parish church, then returned for Christmas luncheon. After a big breakfast on Boxing Day — the extra holiday observed in Britain on December 26 when in earlier times landowners would give their employees gifts or reward their service — the men went out for the traditional pheasant shoot. The King felt well enough to join them, carrying a light gun.

But failing health prevented him from keeping his commitment to travel with the Queen on a long-planned state visit to the Commonwealth nations of Australia, New Zealand, and Ceylon in the new year, so he deputed Elizabeth and Philip to take the nearly six-month journey instead. They decided to add several days in the beginning of the trip to visit the British colony of Kenya, which had given them a retreat at the foot of Mount Kenya called Sagana Lodge as a wedding gift.

The King and Queen accompanied the royal party to the airport on January 31, 1952, to say farewell. Standing on the tarmac, George VI looked haggard as he stoically waved to his daughter and son-in-law when they took off on their BOAC Argonaut. Five days later, after settling into the secluded Sagana Lodge, Elizabeth and Philip spent a night at Treetops Hotel, a three-bedroom cabin built among the branches of a large fig tree above an illuminated salt lick in a game preserve. Dressed in khaki trousers and a bush scarf, Elizabeth excitedly filmed the elephants, rhinos, monkeys, and other animals with her movie camera. At sunset, she and Philip spotted a herd of thirty elephants. "Look, Philip, they're pink!" she said, not realizing that the gray pachyderms had been rolling in pink dust. After staying up much of the night, Elizabeth stood at dawn with Michael Parker, now her husband's private secretary, to watch a white eagle swoop above their heads.

Back at Sagana, Parker took a phone call in the mid-afternoon from Martin Charteris at the nearby Outspan Hotel. The private secretary bore the grim news that the fifty-six-year-old King was dead, and Princess Elizabeth Alexandra Mary was now Queen at age twenty-five. After a pleasant day shooting hares on the Sandringham Estate, George VI had dined with his wife and Princess Margaret before retiring to his ground-floor bedroom at 10:30 P.M. Early in the morning of February 6, he had died in his sleep from a blood clot in his heart. Parker immediately informed Prince Philip, who muttered that it would be "the most appalling shock" for his wife, then walked into her bedroom where she had been resting and broke the news to her. She shed no tears, but looked "pale and worried." Philip led her down a path through the garden to the Sagana River, where they took a long walk along the bank.

When Elizabeth's cousin Pamela Mountbatten, who was serving as her lady-in-waiting, expressed her condolences, the new Queen could only say, "Oh, thank you. But I am so sorry that it means we've got to go back to England and it's upsetting everybody's plans."

There has been much speculation, not least because of historical parallels, about when precisely Elizabeth became Queen. It undoubtedly happened when she was atop the African fig tree, which draws a romantic line to the moment in 1558 when Elizabeth I, seated next to an oak tree at Hatfield House, heard that the death of her sister, Queen Mary, meant she was the monarch, also at age twenty-five.

With preternatural composure, her mid-twentieth-century successor set about her business, writing letters, telegrams, and memoranda — vivid proof, as Charteris recalled, that she had "seized her destiny with both hands."

CHAPTER FOUR
"READY, GIRLS?"

"What are you going to call yourself?" asked Martin Charteris, as Elizabeth came to grips with the loss of her father. "My own name, of course. What else?" she replied. But some clarification was necessary, since her mother had been called Queen Elizabeth. The new monarch would be Queen Elizabeth II (following her sixteenth-century predecessor, Elizabeth I) but she would be known as the Queen. Her mother would become Queen Elizabeth the Queen Mother, rather than the more fusty Dowager Queen. Elizabeth II would be Queen Regnant, and her royal cypher E II R.

"It was all very sudden," she recalled four decades later. Her task, she said, was "kind of taking it on, and making the best job you can. It's a question of maturing into something that one's got used to doing, and accepting the fact that here you are, and it's your fate, because I think continuity is important."

Elizabeth II returned to England on the Argonaut that had flown her to Kenya only a week earlier. When the erstwhile princess walked by his seat several times, Philip's valet John Dean noted that "she looked as if she might have been crying." Mike Parker said Philip "was like the Rock of Gi-

"It was the most poignant moment. She looked so young, with nothing on her head, wearing only the white shift over her dress."

Queen Elizabeth II, age twenty-seven, before the anointing at her coronation in Westminster Abbey, June 1953. GETTY IMAGES

braltar, comforting her as best he could."

Dressed in a simple black coat and hat, she held her composure as she arrived at London Airport near dusk on February 7, 1952, after a nineteen-hour flight. Waiting on the tarmac was a small delegation of men in dark overcoats, top hats, and homburgs led by her uncle the Duke of Gloucester and Prime Minister Winston Churchill. Foreign Minister Anthony Eden and his fellow government ministers stood bareheaded as she slowly shook hands with each of them, and they gave her deep bows. A Daimler bearing the sovereign's coat of arms on its roof drove her to Clarence House, where eighty-four-year-old Queen Mary honored her by reversing roles, curtsying and kissing her hand, although she couldn't help adding, "Lilibet, your skirts are much too short for mourning."

The next day, the new Queen went to St. James's Palace, the sovereign's official residence. Built by Henry VIII in the sixteenth century, the turreted red-brick complex in the heart of London was the home of the monarch until Queen Victoria moved to much larger Buckingham Palace. At St. James's, Elizabeth II appeared for twenty minutes before several hundred members of the Accession Council, a ceremonial body including the Privy Council — the principal advisory group to the monarch drawn from senior ranks of politicians, the clergy, and the judiciary — along with other prominent officials from Britain and the Commonwealth. Under the terms of the Act of Settlement of 1701, she had been monarch since the moment of her father's death, but the council was convened to hear her proclamation and religious oath. She would not be crowned until her coronation in sixteen months, but she was fully empowered to carry out her duties as sovereign.

The men of the council bowed simultaneously to the fortieth monarch since William the Conqueror took the English throne after the Battle of Hastings in 1066. Elizabeth II declared in a clear voice that "by the sudden death of my dear father, I am called to assume the duties and responsibilities of sovereignty. My heart is too full for me to say more to you today than I shall always work, as my father did throughout his reign, to advance the happiness and prosperity of my peoples, spread as they are the world over. . . . I pray that God will help me to discharge worthily this heavy task that has been lain upon me so early in my life."

As her husband escorted her out, by several accounts she was in tears. They drove to Sandringham to join the Queen Mother and Princess Margaret in paying respects privately at the late King's coffin before it was transported by train to London for the official lying in state at Westminster Hall, followed by the funeral and burial in St. George's Chapel at Windsor on February 15. The most enduring image was of the three queens — Mary the grandmother, the Queen Mother, and Elizabeth II — standing by the catafalque with Princess Margaret, shrouded in opaque black veils to their waists.

In an unprecedented message to her countrymen, the Queen Mother asked that "protection and love" be given to her daughter "in the great and lonely station to which she has been called." Privately, she wrote to Queen Mary, "I cannot bear to think of Lilibet, so young to bear such a burden."

Churchill, who had first met Elizabeth II as a toddler, grieved over George VI and seemed non-plussed by the new sovereign. Jock Colville, who by then had returned to Churchill as private secretary, recalled that "I tried to cheer him up by saying how well he would get on with the new queen, but all he could say was that he did not know her and that she was only a child."

According to Churchill's youngest daughter, Mary Soames, "my father realized very quickly she was much more than that." As Martin Charteris observed, "He was impressed by her. She was conscientious, she was well-informed, she was serious-minded. Within days of her Accession she was receiving prime ministers and presidents, ambassadors and High Commissioners . . . and doing so faultlessly." The Queen recognized the change in herself, confiding to a friend, "Extraordinary thing, I no longer feel anxious or worried. I don't know what it is — but I have lost all my timidity."

With his gift for eloquence and keen sense of occasion, Churchill set the stage for what the press would optimistically herald as "a new Elizabethan age." Britain was still gripped by shortages, with rationing of foodstuffs such as tea, sugar, and butter, while rubble from World War II bombing blighted the London landscape. The imperial decline was inexorable, and the fears of communist expansion around the world had ushered in the Cold War.

In a speech to the House of Commons five days after Elizabeth took the throne, Churchill described her as "a fair and youthful figure . . . the heir to all our traditions and glories," assuming her position "at a time when a tormented mankind stands uncertainly poised between world catastrophe and a golden age." He expressed hope that the new Queen would be "a signal for . . . a brightening salvation of the human scene." A promising young Conservative politician named Margaret Thatcher had her own sanguine view, writing in a newspaper column that "if, as many earnestly pray, the accession of Elizabeth II can help to remove the last shreds of prejudice against women aspiring to the highest places, then a new era for women will indeed be at hand."

On February 27 at 11 A.M., Elizabeth II presided over her first investiture in the vast ballroom at Buckingham Palace, honoring private citizens and members of the military with awards for exemplary service to their country. While the Queen hands out these honors known as the orders of chivalry, the government chooses the 2,500 individuals to be recognized each year. With Britain's world role vastly diminished, investitures have helped sustain national pride, and the Queen has presided over these ceremonies with care and precision. By her sixtieth year on the throne, she had conferred more than 404,500 honors and awards, bestowing them in person over 610 times. "People need pats on the back sometimes," she once said. "It's a very dingy world otherwise."

At each investiture she greets more than a hundred recipients individually and presents their medals or brooches (and in the case of knights, taps the kneeling men on the shoulders with a sword), offering personal comments to all. The impressive hour-long ceremonies are attended by Yeomen of the Guard in red and gold uniforms and her Gurkha Orderly Officers.

The very first honor she bestowed on February 27 was the Victoria Cross, the highest military decoration for valor in battle, to Private William Speakman of the King's Own Scottish Borderers. He had shown "gallantry and utter contempt of personal danger" during "fierce hand-to-hand fighting" in Korea the previous November, when he led more than ten charges, sustaining serious wounds while inflicting "enormous losses to the enemy." Speakman was one of only fifteen British subjects who received the award in the six decades after World War II.

Conferring that honor had special meaning for the new Queen, who had also become the head of the armed forces. Members of the military pledge their loyalty to the sovereign, not to the government, keeping their allegiance above politicians who come and go. In the years to come, Elizabeth II would personally approve the appointments to the highest ranks, sign all officers' commissions, and serve as honorary colonel-in-chief of all seven regiments in the Household Division, the guardsmen designated as her personal troops.

By April, the royal family completed its move to Buckingham Palace, and the new Queen adapted to an office schedule that has scarcely varied throughout her reign. She awoke at 7:30 A.M. when a housemaid pulled open the curtains in her first-floor bedroom, and Bobo (the only member of the household to call her "Lilibet," along with "my little lady") carried in a "calling tray" with Earl Grey tea and Marie biscuits. Right behind Bobo, surging through the doorway, came the Queen's pack of corgis, which had spent the night down the corridor in their room adjacent to the Page's Pantry, each of them assigned a wicker dog basket. A footman had already given them their first walk of the day in the garden.

After bathing (in water kept at around seventy degrees), dressing, and having her hair styled and sprayed, Elizabeth II walked through her sitting room, often listening to the BBC on her portable radio along the way, for breakfast in her private dining room amid eighteenth-century paintings. The morning papers were arranged on a sideboard. *Sporting Life* was her first read (supplanted in later years by *The Racing Post*), with a focus on news of the turf, followed by the *Daily Telegraph* (including its two crossword puzzles that became a daily task, but never with a thesaurus) and *The Times,* plus a look at the *Express, Mail,* and *Mirror* tabloids. In the early days she tended to eat a boiled egg and toast with a pat of butter from the Windsor dairy stamped with her cypher, tossing scraps of bread to her eager dogs. She later replaced her cooked breakfast with tea and toast thinly spread with marmalade.

At nine o'clock sharp each morning, a Scottish bagpiper would play for fifteen minutes while marching under her window, skirling familiar Highland reels and strathspeys — a tradition at each of her palaces begun by Queen Victoria. By 10 A.M. Elizabeth II was at the desk by a tall window in her sitting room looking out over the Palace gardens. She sat on a mahogany Chippendale chair with a seat embroidered by her father (one of his hobbies had been needlework), surrounded by papers and books, family photos in silver frames, and oil paintings, including a portrait of Susan, her favorite corgi. There was a Hepplewhite mahogany bookcase, a satinwood chest of drawers, comfortable sofas, and vases of roses, narcissi, or other fresh-cut flowers. "I like my rooms to look really lived in," she said.

On her desk were two telephones as well as an intercom, with buttons to summon her private secretaries — Tommy Lascelles and his deputies Michael Adeane, Martin Charteris, and Edward Ford — who came one by one, giving a brisk neck bow on arrival, bearing baskets of papers to be signed and discussed. Standing throughout the meeting, each man covered a different area of expertise, and their agendas ranged across schedules for domestic and foreign travel, ecclesiastical and military appointments, legislation before Parliament, and other issues of the day. Edward Ford called her "a bureaucrat's dream. She was wonderful to work for, always so accessible. . . . You talked with her as you might talk to a friend who was staying for the weekend. . . . 'The prime minister is delayed, shall we put it off till tomorrow?' . . . The whole conduct of affairs was very informal and relaxed, far more so than it had been with the King."

She was also conscientious about dealing with correspondence from the public. She leafed through a stack of envelopes in a basket, reading quickly, and jotting notes for replies to be written either by her ladies-in-waiting or private secretaries. She once explained that she had always regarded letters as "rather personal to oneself, that people write them thinking that I'm going to open them and read them." She said that the letters "give one an idea of what is worrying people."

She was required to meet monthly for ten minutes with four government ministers from her Privy Council. In these meetings — always conducted with everyone standing up to keep the proceedings short — she would say "approved" to various government actions read out to her, mostly concerning regulations and government appointments.

Every day except Christmas and Easter — whether at home in London or Windsor, on vacation at Sandringham or Balmoral, weekends visiting friends, travels around the United Kingdom, or visits overseas — she attended to the red leather dispatch boxes of official government papers that could be unlocked only by her key plus three others kept by her private secretaries. Each box brimmed with Foreign Office cables, budget documents, cabinet minutes, orders requiring her signature, and classified intelligence reports.

A smaller evening box, delivered before dinner, contained a summary by the chief whip of the day's activities in Parliament. Her stated preference: "a piece of 300 to 900 words . . . a 'light' approach is welcomed." The parliamentary scribes complied with references to "low wattage" debates and descriptions of "shouts and jeers" as well as accolades for speeches of "wit, passion and stinging phrases." If she were entertaining any politicians for dinner, according to one observer, she could be "as well informed as any of her guests that evening."

The Queen customarily received a copy of the daily Court Circular, the official list of royal activities prepared by a Palace information officer that she would scrutinize for mistakes before its publication the next day in *The Times* and the *Daily Telegraph.* She made similar corrections and comments on government documents, all of which she signed and delivered to her private secretary's office by 8 A.M. the next day. Michael Adeane estimated that she spent three hours daily doing her paperwork, and it was not unusual for her to be at her desk late into the evening.

For the weekends she received a larger box with enough material to keep her deskbound in the mornings, reading rapidly but thoroughly. Once while staying with some good friends, the Queen said, "I must go do my boxes." "Oh must you ma'am?" said the friend. "If I missed one once, I would never get it straight again," the Queen replied.

An essential part of her schedule was her series of private audiences in a sitting room on the ground floor of the Palace — "my way of meeting people, without anybody else listening," she once explained. These sessions would give her "a very broad picture of what is actually going on, either in government or in the civil service. . . . The fact that there's nobody else there gives them a feeling that they can say what they like." She said that the confidentiality and resulting outspokenness helped form the "basis of where I get my information from."

For ninety minutes or so on most mornings she would receive the credentials of newly appointed ambassadors in morning dress or native costume, and bid other envoys goodbye, meet with clergy, government officials, military officers, and distinguished citizens, sometimes using the time to confer honors privately rather than at the larger investiture ceremonies. All these encounters were guided by time-honored rules: waiting in the spacious and gilded Bow Room, the Queen pressing a buzzer, the doors thrown open, the announcement of the guest, one pace into the room followed by a bow or curtsy, three more paces and another bow or curtsy, the handshake and a conversation while standing or an invitation to sit and chat. All visitors were instructed in the protocol by ladies-in-waiting, equerries, and private secretaries, and the Queen read briefing papers about everyone she would meet. As if governed by a well-calibrated internal clock, she invariably knew the precise moment to end the conversation, which she would signal by extending her hand. She would then press a buzzer, summoning one of her senior staff to escort her guest from the room.

Even if she were dining either alone or with Prince Philip, the table in the dining room in her private apartment was set impeccably by footmen responsible for three separate pantries: glass, silver, and china. Yet another footman rolled the ancient wooden trolley with platters of food down long corridors from the basement kitchen on the other side of the Palace. To unwind before luncheon, Elizabeth II would have a gin and Dubonnet (half portions of each, with ice and lemon) and before dinner a strong gin martini, prepared neat, unlike Philip's, which was an expertly mixed concoction in its own pitcher. The page, a senior footman, served the meal, which tended to be simple — grilled meat, chicken, or fish (always boned), vegetables from the Windsor farm, and cheese. Strong spices were forbidden, along with garlic, pasta with sauce, and raw shellfish such as oysters and mussels. She tended to avoid rich desserts as well, although when served strawberries and cream, she reverted to her nursery ways and crushed them into a puree.

"She is not particular about food," said a former royal household official. "To her, food is fuel. If she were being served steak, we would make sure the Queen got the smallest piece and that it was well done." One staple was a constant supply of Malvern water, which was also used for her ice, particularly on trips overseas when tap water might cause illness.

The Queen's midday meal seldom ran more than an hour, and her afternoons were more variable than her mornings. She might have an outside engagement, more work at her desk, another audience, a long walk with her corgis around the Palace gardens, a wash and set by her hairdresser, or wardrobe fittings in her dressing room furnished with mirrors and a skirted dressing table adorned with gold hairbrushes and framed photographs.

Teatime was sacrosanct, served by her page each day at five from a lace-draped cart with plates of sandwiches made of thin bread cut into rounds and filled with cucumber, egg, and watercress, along with freshly baked scones, gingerbread, and muffins. The Queen would brew the Earl Grey or Darjeeling in a silver teapot, allocating one spoonful for each cup. She preferred her tea lukewarm and usually limited herself to the sandwiches, feeding bits of scones to the corgis.

Charles was only three when his mother took the throne, and Anne was eighteen months old, so their life was spent mainly in the six-room nursery complex on the second floor of Buckingham Palace or out in the extensive gardens, overseen by their two nannies. In her first gesture of modernity, Elizabeth II dropped the tradition of requiring formal bows and curtsies from her children when they were very young. On weekdays Charles and Anne came downstairs after breakfast at 9:30 for some brief playtime with their parents. They didn't see the Queen and duke until tea, when the nannies brought them down for "a final romp" that sometimes included a splash in the swimming pool for Charles with his father.

Preparations for their bedtime began at 6 P.M., which caused the Queen to make one adjustment in the official routine. Her father had held his audience with the prime minister at 5:30 P.M. on Tuesdays, but when she initially kept to the same schedule, Charles and Anne complained, "Why isn't Mummy going to play with us tonight?" So she moved the audience to 6:30, which allowed her to go to the nursery to join in their nightly bath and tuck them into bed before discussing matters of state with Winston Churchill.

■ ■ ■ ■

Adjusting to his new position as the Queen's consort proved troublesome for Philip. "For a real action man, that was very hard to begin with," said Patricia Brabourne. While everything was mapped out for Elizabeth II, he had to invent his job under the scrutiny of her courtiers, and he had no role model to follow.

Prince Albert had "wielded over the Sovereign an undefined and unbounded influence," wrote Lytton Strachey in his biography of Queen Victoria, "the natural head of her family, superintendent of her household, manager of her private affairs, sole CONFIDENTIAL adviser in politics, and only assistant in her communications with the officers of the Government . . . tutor of the royal children, the private secretary of the Sovereign, and her permanent minister." In 1857, Victoria officially rewarded her husband by naming him Prince Consort, recognizing his unique status during the seventeen years since she married him as a new Queen.

Not only was Philip excluded from the substance of his wife's official life, with no access to the state papers in her daily boxes, neither he nor his wife considered an official designation of Prince Consort desirable or appropriate in the twentieth century. "The monarchy changed," Philip later explained to biographer Gyles Brandreth. "It became an institution. I had to fit into the institution. . . . There were plenty of people telling me what *not* to do. 'You mustn't interfere with this.' 'Keep out.' I had to try to support the Queen as best I could without getting in the way. The difficulty was to find things that might be useful."

Like Prince Albert, Prince Philip was considered an outsider by senior officials of the court. "Refugee husband," he mockingly referred to himself. He was wounded by the slights he experienced. "Philip was constantly being squashed, snubbed, ticked off, rapped over the knuckles," said John Brabourne. Much of the wariness stemmed from Philip's closeness to Dickie Mountbatten. "My father was considered pink — very progressive," Patricia Brabourne recalled. "The worry was that Prince Philip would bring into court modern ideas and make people uncomfortable."

The most hurtful rebuff had occurred in the days following the King's death, after Queen Mary heard that Dickie Mountbatten had triumphantly announced that "the House of Mountbatten now reigned." She and her daughter-in-law, the Queen Mother, were angered by his presumption, and the Queen shared their view that she should honor the allegiance of her grandfather and her father to the House of Windsor by keeping the Windsor name rather than taking that of her husband. Churchill and his cabinet agreed. Philip responded with a memo to Churchill vigorously objecting to the prime minister's advice and pressing instead for the House of Mountbatten, which was ironic. It was his mother's family name since his father had given him no surname.

The most immediate precedent was actually on Philip's side, when Queen Victoria dropped her own House of Hanover and adopted her husband's family name. Her son Edward VII ruled

120

as the first King of Saxe-Coburg-Gotha, which George V then changed to Windsor for political reasons. Elizabeth II had every right to make her own change. Her reluctance to do so reflected not only her unwillingness to stand up to Churchill, but also to her mother and her grandmother. The Queen failed to foresee that her actions would have a profound impact on Philip, leading to strains in their marriage. "She was very young," said Patricia Brabourne. "Churchill was elderly and experienced, and she accepted his constitutional advice. I felt that if it had been later she would have been able to say, 'I don't agree.' "

"I am the only man in the country not allowed to give his name to his children," Philip fumed to friends. "I'm nothing but a bloody amoeba." Dickie Mountbatten was even more outspoken, blaming "that old drunk Churchill" who "forced" the Queen's position. The prime minister mistrusted and resented Earl Mountbatten, largely because as India's last viceroy, appointed by Prime Minister Clement Attlee, he had presided over that country's move to independence. "Churchill never forgave my father for 'giving away India,' " said Patricia Brabourne.

Behind the scenes, Dickie continued a campaign to reverse the decision, with his nephew's acquiescence. Meanwhile, Philip resolved to support his wife while finding his own niche, which would lead in the following decades to the active patronage of more than eight hundred different charities embracing sports, youth, wildlife conservation, education, and environmental causes. Within the family Philip also took over management of all the royal estates, to "save her a lot of time," he said. But even more significantly, as Prince Charles's official biographer, Jonathan Dimbleby, wrote in 1994, the Queen "would submit entirely to the father's will" in decisions concerning their children.

She made Philip the ultimate domestic arbiter, Dimbleby wrote, because "she was not indifferent so much as detached." Newspaper editor and Conservative politician William Deedes, himself a remote father, saw in Elizabeth II's detachment "her struggle to be a worthy head of state, which was a heavy burden for her. The Queen in her own quiet way is immensely kind, but she had too little time to fulfill her family care. I find it totally understandable, but it led to problems."

Particularly at the outset, Elizabeth II's focus was on showing gravitas as monarch. "In the first five years she was more formal," recalled one of her longtime ladies-in-waiting. The freedom she enjoyed as a young princess — she once attended a ball at the American ambassador's residence dressed as an Edwardian parlor maid, with Philip costumed as a waiter — had to be subdued, at least in public. Keeping her dignity was paramount, and in doing so she frequently obeyed Queen Mary's injunction against smiling, even as her youth and beauty gave her an automatic advantage. "How *much* nicer to have a young queen than that very dull man," wrote the novelist Nancy Mitford. Elizabeth II was also fortunate in having said little of consequence in public, which let her maintain an enigmatic aura.

She had to walk her most delicate line with her

mother, a widow at age fifty-one. Elizabeth II was well aware, as she wrote at the time, that her own life was more full than ever, while the future of both her mother and her sister, Margaret, "must seem very blank." The Queen Mother was too well trained to show her emotions in public, but she shared her grief with friends, telling Edith Sitwell she was "engulfed by great black clouds of unhappiness and misery." Along with losing her husband, she no longer had her homes or her position at center stage. She agreed to move to Clarence House, but she would stay in Buckingham Palace for more than a year before making the shift.

In the interim, during a visit to friends in Caithness on the bleak northern coast of Scotland, she impulsively bought a small run-down castle tucked behind a grove of trees stunted and twisted from the persistent winds, with a panoramic view of the Orkney Islands. "How sad it looks," she said. "Just like me." She called it the Castle of Mey, and planned to "escape there occasionally when life became hideous." Although the purchase price was a token £100, the Queen funded an extensive renovation, including the installation of bathrooms and electricity, a project that would take three years.

It wouldn't do for the Queen Mother to retreat in mourning as Queen Victoria had done after the death of Prince Albert, so Churchill met with her in the autumn of 1952 to urge her to continue the public service that had earned worldwide admiration and to help her daughter carry out her duties. She agreed, in effect, to assume the role of national grandmother, always smiling and twinkling, a patron of charities and goodwill ambassador for her country and the monarchy, carrying out her essential credo: "The point of human life and living [is] to give and to create new goodness all the time."

Cecil Beaton called her "the great mother figure and nannie to us all. . . . The warmth of her sympathy bathes us and wraps us in a counterpane by the fireside." She combined an ability to connect instantly with virtually anyone and a flair for high drama, "like a great musical comedy actress in the 1930s descending the stairs," said Sir Roy Strong, the former director of the National Portrait Gallery and the Victoria and Albert Museum. No one looked askance when she wore pearls while fishing in Scottish rivers or arrived late for engagements in what Beaton once described as a "pink cushiony cloud."

Her destiny was to remain single, and to deny herself the love of another man, although few could have predicted that she would be a widow for fully half of her life. She needed to find compensations beyond her public duties, so the Queen permitted — in fact indulged with generous financial support — her mother to live a carefree and extravagant private life marked by nonstop entertaining and the stimulation of a lively group of friends.

Mother and daughter spoke nearly every day on the telephone. When the Queen placed the call, the Palace operator said to her mother, "Good morning, Your Majesty, Her Majesty is on the line for Your Majesty," which became a standing joke among friends and courtiers. They usually exchanged news about horses and racing, as well as gossip and family matters. "They were great confidantes," recalled the Queen Mother's long-serving lady-in-waiting, Dame Frances Campbell-Preston. "The Queen could talk to her about her troubles. Queen Elizabeth was aware of the tremendous responsibility the Queen had. She and the King had had it, so she knew the pressures."

The Queen Mother was in many ways "an Edwardian lady with rigid views," recalled Campbell-Preston. "A lot of the importance the Queen attached to tradition and doing things the right way came from her mother," said a former household official. As a consequence, the Queen Mother was a brake on changes to the status quo proposed by Prince Philip and senior advisers. "The Queen Mother was always in the equation," said another former member of the household. "The Queen would ask, 'Does Queen Elizabeth know about this?' "

There were inevitable comparisons — not always flattering — between the staid young Queen, trapped within the restraints of neutrality and propriety, and the spirited dowager who had the freedom to display her enjoyment and the gaiety to light up a room. The two women deferred to each other in private, although only the Queen Mother was required to curtsy. Still, by June 1952, Richard Molyneux, a former equerry to Queen Mary, reported that during a visit to Windsor Castle, the Queen was "very much the Sovereign. She enters the room at least ten yards ahead of her husband or mother."

Much of the Queen's first year on the throne was devoted to preparing for her coronation on Tuesday, June 2, 1953. The biggest question was whether to let the ceremony be televised, and her initial decision, supported by Churchill, was to keep the lights and cameras away, fearing an intrusion on the sanctity of the rituals. But after the ban on televising was announced in October, the Palace faced an outcry from broadcasters as well as the public over being excluded from such a significant ceremony.

The Queen yielded after recognizing that her subjects wanted to see her crowned, so she agreed to a compromise permitting live coverage of everything except the most sacred moments, including her anointing and taking Communion, and excluding any close-ups as well. In her first Christmas radio broadcast she declared with evident satisfaction that during the coronation "millions outside Westminster Abbey will hear the promises and prayers being offered up within its walls, and see much of the ancient ceremony. . . . I want to ask you all, whatever your religion may be, to pray for me on that day — to pray that God may give me wisdom and strength to carry out the solemn promises I shall be making, and that I may faithfully serve Him and you, all the days of my life."

That autumn, Elizabeth II also made a conciliatory gesture toward her husband by announcing that during the State Opening of Parliament he should "henceforth have, hold and enjoy the Place, Pre-eminence and Precedence next to Her Majesty." When she opened Parliament for the first time in November, the Duke of Edinburgh sat in the Chair of State to the left and several inches below her throne in the House of Lords, just as Prince Albert had done. Unlike her father's hesitant delivery, Elizabeth II made a flawless seven-minute address, which was written by Churchill. Ever observant, Cecil Beaton noted that her eyes were "not those of a busy, harassed person."

The honor given Prince Philip in Parliament would not be repeated in Westminster Abbey the following June. At the Queen's suggestion he was made chairman of the committee to oversee the coronation ceremony, but he would not walk by her side. "We took it for granted that she would be alone," recalled Gay Charteris. "That must have been hard for him. It was how it was done. She is the monarch. Yet if she had been a man, the wife would have been there." Such was the case in 1937 when Queen Elizabeth was first anointed on her uncovered head, and then crowned with her husband. But by tradition, the Queen's consort is neither crowned nor anointed.

Two months before the big celebration, on March 24, 1953, Queen Mary died in her sleep at age eighty-five. She received all the suitable honors at Westminster Hall followed by a funeral at St. George's Chapel in Windsor. Her son the Duke of Windsor attended, but the Queen did not include him in a dinner that evening, nor did she invite him to the coronation. She agreed with Churchill's advice that it would be "quite inappropriate for a King who had abdicated." The embittered duke wrote to his wife, "What a smug stinking lot my relations are."

The buildup to the coronation pulled the British together in a burst of patriotism and great expectations, as the country began to emerge from postwar rationing and economic stagnation. Princess Margaret said it was "like a phoenix-time. Everything was being raised from the ashes. There was this gorgeous-looking lovely young lady, and nothing to stop anything getting better and better." Churchill's notion of a new Elizabethan Age may have been an illusion, but for a time it caught the imagination of the British public and emphasized the importance of the monarch, in the words of Rebecca West, as "the emblem of the state, the symbol of our national life, the guardian of our self-respect."

For weeks, the Queen applied herself to learning every nuance of the three-hour service. She met several times with Geoffrey Fisher, the ninety-ninth Archbishop of Canterbury, who instructed her in the spiritual significance of the various rites and gave her prayers to say. She practiced her lines and her steps every day in the ballroom at Buckingham Palace. Tied to her shoulders were sheets stitched together and augmented with weights to simulate her heavy robe and train. She sat at her desk wearing the five-pound St. Edward's Crown dating from the coronation of Charles II, and listening to recordings of her father's coronation.

The 16th Duke of Norfolk, a small, ruddy, and highly efficient peer who carried the additional title of Earl Marshal, was responsible for choreographing the ceremony (an ironic coincidence, since he was a Roman Catholic supervising a deeply Protestant service). His wife, Lavinia, the Duchess of Norfolk, stood in for the Queen at numerous rehearsals in Westminster Abbey, several of which were watched intently by Elizabeth II. The

Queen's six maids of honor, unmarried daughters of the highest-ranking hereditary peers (dukes, earls, and marquesses) who were responsible for carrying the train, also rehearsed frequently in the Abbey and had one trial run at the Palace. When asked whether she would like to take a break midway through the service the Queen replied, "I'll be all right. I'm as strong as a horse."

An estimated one million people streamed into London to witness the pageantry, including forty thousand Americans. The official delegation from the United States was led by General George Marshall and included Earl Warren, governor of California, and General Omar Bradley. Also in the crowd was twenty-three-year-old Jacqueline Bouvier — the future wife of President John F. Kennedy — then a reporter for the *Washington Times Herald,* who filed whimsical reports on the London scene. "All the deposed monarchs are staying at Claridge's," she wrote, and ladies had to have their hair done at 3:30 A.M. on Coronation Day so they could be in their seats at 6:30 A.M. wearing their tiaras, "and that takes a bit of arranging."

The night before the coronation, hundreds of thousands of spectators endured unseasonably cold temperatures, lashing wind, and downpours to stake out positions along the route of the procession, which began at 9 A.M. The parade included twenty-nine bands and twenty-seven carriages, as well as thirteen thousand soldiers representing some fifty countries, among them Indians, Pakistanis, Malayans, Fijians, Australians, and Canadians. Queen Salote of Tonga, a British territory in the South Pacific, was the runaway crowd pleaser, oblivious to the weather in her open landau, "a great big, warm personality" who was "swathed in purple silk and with a magnificent plume waving in the wind from the crown."

Elizabeth II traveled to Westminster Abbey in the twenty-four-foot-long Gold State Coach, with gilded sculptures and door panels featuring classical scenes painted in the eighteenth century. Eight gray horses, one of which was named Eisenhower, pulled the fairytale carriage. The Queen wore her great-great-grandmother's diadem and a coronation gown of white satin with short sleeves and a heart neckline, its bodice and bell-shaped skirt adorned with the symbols of Great Britain and its Commonwealth realms (among them a rose, thistle, shamrock, maple leaf, and fern), all extravagantly embroidered in pale colored silk, gold and silver threads, semiprecious stones, seed pearls, and shimmering crystals. She could be seen smiling at the thunderous cheering as she waved her white-gloved arm up and down. Prince Philip wore the full dress uniform of an Admiral of the Fleet, which he covered during the ceremony with his peer's robes of scarlet topped by an ermine cape.

Awaiting the Queen's arrival at the Abbey door promptly at 11 A.M. were the maids of honor, dressed identically in white satin with pearl embroidery. "She was relaxed, and she looked so beautiful," recalled Anne Glenconner (then Lady Anne Coke, daughter of the Earl of Leicester). "She had a wonderful little figure, with a tiny waist and wonderful complexion with great big eyes. Prince Philip looked after her, saying to us, 'Do this and do that.' " One of the Queen's attendants said, "You must be feeling nervous, Ma'am." "Of course I am," replied Elizabeth II, "but I really do think Aureole will win," a reference to her horse running in the Derby four days later.

The maids of honor, assisted by the Mistress of the Robes, the Dowager Duchess of Devonshire, arranged the monarch's crimson velvet Robe of State edged with ermine and gold lace. As the maids grabbed the satin handles on the eighteen-foot train, the Queen looked over her shoulder and said, "Ready, girls?" They lifted the heavy velvet, and proceeded down the long aisle toward the gold-carpeted coronation "theater" in the center of the Abbey before the high altar gleaming with regalia of scepters, swords, and crowns and draped with gold, crimson, and blue tapestry, all illuminated by bright arc lights for television.

The procession included heads of state, diplomats, an African chieftain in leopard skin and feather headdress, a Muslim in plain black robe, crown princes, and members of the royal family, including Philip's mother wearing a dove gray nun's habit and wimple, and the Queen Mother and Princess Margaret trailing twelve-foot trains. All the women wore ball gowns, and those men not in flowing robes or traditional costumes ("plucked indiscriminately out of the dead pages of British history," wrote Russell Baker in the *Baltimore Sun*) wore white tie and tails, although Labour politician Aneurin Bevan defiantly appeared in a black business suit.

When the Queen approached the high altar, her

heavy skirt swinging "backwards and forwards in a beautiful rhythmic effect," the Boys Choir of Westminster School sang out, *"Vivat Regina Elizabetha! Vivat! Vivat! Vivat!,"* the sole remnant of Latin in the entire service. During the ceremony, most of which dates from the first Abbey coronation of William the Conqueror on Christmas Day in 1066, she was seated in three different places. The Chair of Estate faced the center of the theater, in front of the royal gallery, which was behind a long table filled with silver gilt and solid gold pieces including giant platters, chalices, and salt cellars. The carved oak King Edward's Chair, used for every coronation since 1308, faced the high altar. Behind it on an elevated platform, also facing the altar, was the Queen's throne where she would sit after being anointed and crowned.

Elizabeth II stood by King Edward's Chair as the archbishop began the "recognition," presenting her in turn to the 7,500 distinguished guests seated in the four sides of the Abbey. As the occupants of each quadrant cried "God Save Queen Elizabeth!" followed by a trumpet fanfare, she gave a slight neck bow and slow half curtsy, the only time she would ever make that dual gesture as Queen.

After swearing the coronation oath in which she pledged to honor the laws of Great Britain, its realms, territories, and possessions, and "maintain the Laws of God," the most spiritual part of the ceremony took place. She stood in front of the Chair of Estate as her maids of honor removed her crimson robe, her gloves, her jewelry and diadem. The Dowager Duchess of Devonshire and the Lord Great Chamberlain, the Marquess of Cholmondeley, then helped Elizabeth II put on her Colobium Sindonis, a simple scoop neck white linen dress with a full pleated skirt that fitted over her gown. "Lord Cholmondeley had to do up the shift in the back," recalled Anne Glenconner. "He couldn't do hooks and eyes, so they put on press fasteners so he just had to push them shut."

Four Knights of the Garter held silver poles supporting a canopy of woven silk and gold over King Edward's Chair, where the Queen sat awaiting her anointing out of television camera range. "It was the most poignant moment," Anne Glenconner continued. "She looked so young, with nothing on her head, wearing only the white shift over her dress." The Archbishop of Canterbury poured holy oil from a 22-karat gold ampulla in the form of an eagle into a twelfth-century silver-gilt anointing spoon. He anointed Elizabeth II with oil, making a sign of the cross on the palms of each of her hands, her forehead, and exposed upper chest. "Some small interest was generated," according to one account, "by the fact that Elizabeth unlike Victoria did not refuse to let the archbishop anoint her breast."

She was then invested with coronation robes weighing thirty-six pounds. They were made of stiff woven golden cloth — the long-sleeved Supertunica held by a wide belt, the embroidered Stole draped around her neck, and the Imperial Mantle, a large gleaming cloak fastened with a gold eagle clasp. Her garments, from the simple linen dress to the splendid vestments, along with the symbolism of her anointment, were designed to signify her priestlike status. British sovereigns long ago gave up the notion of a divine right, responsible to God alone, which allowed them to rule without necessarily listening to the advice of their merely mortal ministers or Parliament. But as a devout Christian, the Queen believed that the coronation sanctified her before God to serve her people, much as the Pope is blessed in his ordination.

"The real significance of the coronation for her was the anointing, not the crowning," said Canon John Andrew, a friend of the royal family and senior chaplain to the 100th Archbishop of Canterbury. "She was consecrated, and that makes her Queen. It is the most solemn thing that has ever happened in her life. She cannot abdicate. She is there until death."

In a further series of rituals, she was presented with her regalia, each "ornament" a symbol of royalty, starting with two armills, thick 22-karat gold bracelets that signified sincerity and wisdom. She received gold spurs, a thick white glove to encourage "gentleness in levying taxes," and the Jewelled Sword of Offering to help her protect good and punish evil, which she carried to the altar, reverently balancing it between her hands. A ruby and sapphire coronation ring was placed on the fourth finger of her right hand to show her fidelity to her subjects, jeweled scepters represented queenly power, mercy, and leadership, and the orb topped by a cross of precious jewels displayed Christ's power over mankind.

Still seated in King Edward's Chair, nearly engulfed by her ponderous golden robes and holding a jeweled scepter upright in each hand, she looked with "intense expectancy" as the archbishop blessed the enormous St. Edward's Crown of solid gold, set with 444 semiprecious stones. He held it aloft, then placed it firmly on her head, which momentarily dropped before rising again. Simultaneously, the scarlet and ermine robed peers in one section of the Abbey, and the bejeweled peeresses in another, also identically dressed in red velvet and fur-trimmed robes, crowned themselves with their gold, velvet, and ermine coronets. The congregation shouted "God Save the Queen," and cannons boomed in Hyde Park and at the Tower of London. As the archbishop intoned, "God crown you with a crown of glory and righteousness," Elizabeth II could literally feel the weight of duty — between her vestments, crown, and scepters, more than forty-five pounds' worth — on her petite frame.

Accompanied by the archbishop and Earl Marshal, the Queen held the scepters while ascending the platform to sit on her throne and receive the homage of her "princes and peers." The first was the archbishop, followed by the Duke of Edinburgh, who approached the throne bareheaded in his long red robe, mounted the five steps, and knelt before his wife, placing his hands between hers and saying, "I, Philip, do become your liege man of life and limb, and of earthly worship; and faith and truth I will bear unto you, to live and die, against all manner of folks. So help me God." When he stood up, he touched her crown and kissed her left cheek, prompting her to quickly adjust the crown as he walked backward and gave his wife a neck bow.

In the royal gallery, tiny Prince Charles, wearing a white satin shirt and dark shorts, arrived through a rear entrance and sat between the Queen Mother and Princess Margaret to witness his mother's anointing, investiture with regalia, crowning, and homage paid by his father. "Look, it's Mummy!" he said to his grandmother, and the Queen flashed a faint smile. The four-and-a-half-year-old heir to the throne watched wide-eyed, variously excited and puzzled, while the Queen Mother leaned down to whisper explanations.

The woman who only sixteen years earlier was at the center of the same ceremony smiled throughout, but Beaton also caught in the Queen Mother's expression "sadness combined with pride." "She used to say it was like a priesthood, being a monarch," said Frances Campbell-Preston. "I imagine seeing your daughter go into the anointing must be unusual." Princess Margaret had a slightly glazed look, and by one account, during the Queen's investiture "never once did she lower her gaze from her sister's calm face." But at the end of the service, she wept. "Oh ma'am you look so sad," Anne Glenconner said to the princess with the red-rimmed eyes. "I've lost my father, and I've lost my sister," Margaret replied. "She will be so busy. Our lives will change."

The lengthy ceremony ended after a parade of noblemen paid homage, and the congregation celebrated Holy Communion, as the Queen knelt to take the wine and bread "as a simple communicant." Elizabeth II and her maids of honor took a short break by retiring into the Chapel of St. Edward the Confessor, where she shed her golden vestments, put on her jewelry, and was fitted with a new robe of ermine-bordered purple velvet, lined in white silk and embroidered with a gold crown and E.R. She also exchanged the St. Edward's Crown, which is worn only once for the coronation, for the somewhat lighter — at three pounds — Imperial State Crown that she would use for the State Opening of Parliament and other major state occasions. This celebrated crown contains some of the most extraordinary gems in the world — the Black Prince's Ruby, which Henry V wore at the Battle of Agincourt in 1415, the Stuart Sapphire, and the Cullinan II diamond weighing over 317 carats. Before leaving the chapel, the archbishop produced a flask of brandy from beneath his gold and green cope. He passed it around to the Queen and her maids so they could each have a sip as a pick-me-up before the processional.

Carrying the two-and-a-half-pound orb and two-pound scepter, with her maids holding the eighteen-foot train of her robe, the newly crowned Queen walked through the nave of the Abbey to the annex, where she and her attendants had a luncheon of Coronation Chicken — cold chicken pieces in curried mayonnaise with chunks of apricot. Afterward Elizabeth II and Philip settled into the Gold State Coach for two hours in a seven-mile progress through London, this time in the pouring rain.

Back at the Palace, the Queen had a chilled nose and hands from the drafty carriage. But she was ebullient as she relaxed with her maids in the Green Drawing Room. "We were all running down the corridor, and we all sat on a sofa together," recalled

Anne Glenconner. "The Queen said, 'Oh that was marvelous. Nothing went wrong!' We were all laughing." Elizabeth II took off her crown, which Prince Charles put on his head before toppling over, while Princess Anne scampered around giggling underneath her mother's train. The Queen Mother managed to subdue their wild excitement. She "anchored them in her arms," Beaton wrote, "put her head down to kiss Prince Charles's hair."

It was a day of jubilation not only over the coronation's success, but because that morning had brought the news that Edmund Hillary of New Zealand and his Tibetan Sherpa, Tenzing Norgay, members of a British mountain climbing team, had been the first to reach the summit of Mount Everest. The "Elizabethan explorers" toasted the Queen with brandy and flew her standard atop the highest mountain in the world, five and a half miles above sea level.

As Earl Warren reported to President Dwight Eisenhower, "the Coronation has unified the nation to a remarkable degree." An astonishing number of people saw the ceremony on television. In Britain an estimated 27 million out of a population of 36 million watched the live broadcast, and the number of people owning television sets doubled. Future prime minister John Major, then ten years old, fondly recalled seeing the ceremony on his first television, as did Paul McCartney. "It was a thrilling time," McCartney said. "I grew up with the Queen, thinking she was a babe. She was beautiful and glamorous." About one third of Americans — some 55 million out of a total population of 160 million — also tuned in, either on the day when they saw only photographs accompanied by a radio feed, or the next day for the full broadcast.

One notably alert viewer in Paris was former King Edward VIII, who had abdicated before he was crowned (an important distinction: as one of the Queen's friends put it, "he was never anointed, so he never really became king") and had last attended a coronation in 1911 when he was the sixteen-year-old Prince of Wales and his father was crowned King George V. Now dressed in a stylish double-breasted gray pinstripe suit, the Duke of Windsor watched at the home of Margaret Biddle, a wealthy American who had a "television lunch" for one hundred friends. She positioned three television sets in one room filled with rows of gilt chairs, and the duke sat in the middle of the front row, where he observed the entire telecast "without a sign of envy or chagrin." At the conclusion of the coronation, he stretched his arms in the air, lit a cigarette, and said coolly, "It was a very impressive ceremony. It's a very moving ceremony and perhaps more moving because she is a woman."

CHAPTER FIVE
AFFAIRS OF STATE

Aureole, the spirited three-year-old chestnut colt that had been the Queen's preoccupation in the hours before her crowning, was one of the favorites in the Coronation Derby Day on Saturday, June 6, 1953, the 174th running of the Derby Stakes at Epsom Downs. His sire was Hyperion and his dam Angelola, but his name derived from his grand-sire, the stallion Donatello, named for the Italian Renaissance artist who carved bold halos around the heads of his angelic sculptures.

The Queen relishes choosing names for her foals. With her aptitude at crossword puzzles and parlor games such as charades, she is imaginative and quick to make combinations — the filly Angelola, for example, by Donatello out of the mare Feola, and Lost Marbles out of Amnesia by Lord Elgin. "She would pull on all sorts of knowledge, including old Scottish names," recalled Jean, the Countess of Carnarvon, whose husband, Henry Porchester — later the Earl of Carnarvon, but known to the Queen as "Porchey" — was Elizabeth II's racing manager for more than three decades.

The Queen was driven down the Epsom Downs track with her husband in the open rear seat of

"She would especially miss the weekly audiences which she has found so instructive and, if one can say so of state matters, so entertaining."

Winston Churchill saying goodbye to Elizabeth II after his farewell dinner on stepping down as prime minister, April 1955. ASSOCIATED PRESS

a Daimler to the cheers of a half million spectators, a record for the course. From the royal box
she peered through binoculars as her racing colors (purple body with gold braid, scarlet sleeves,
and gold-fringed black velvet cap) flashed along
the mile-and-a-half course with twenty-six other
galloping thoroughbreds. Aureole held second
place, but couldn't catch Pinza, the winner by
four lengths. In her sunglasses and cloche hat, the
Queen smiled and waved despite her disappointment. The victorious jockey, forty-nine-year-old
Sir Gordon Richards, had received his knighthood (the first ever for a jockey) from the Queen
only days earlier. After being invited to meet the
Queen, he said she was a "marvelous sport" and
"seemed to be just as delighted as I was with the
result of the race."

Also in the royal box was Winston Churchill,
the Queen's most ardent booster throughout the
coronation festivities. In the sixteen months — to
the day — since she took the throne, she had developed a close and unique bond with Britain's
most formidable statesman. His fondness for both
of her parents, along with the shaping experience of World War II, gave them a reservoir of
memories and a common perspective, despite their
five-decade age difference. She appreciated his
wisdom, experience, and eloquence, and looked
to him for guidance on how she should conduct
herself as monarch.

Churchill was also great company, not least because he shared his monarch's love of breeding and
racing, a passion that came to him late in life. For
his Tuesday evening meetings with the Queen, he

always arrived at the Bow Room in a frock coat and top hat. The rules of the prime minister's audience called for complete discretion, so few details of the discussions emerged. Years later when Elizabeth II was asked whose audiences she most enjoyed, she replied, "Winston of course, because it was always such fun." Churchill's reply to a query about their most frequent topic of discussion was "Oh, racing," and his daughter Mary Soames concurred that "they spent a lot of the audience talking about horses."

Palace courtiers escorted the prime minister to the audiences, waited in the room next door, and afterward enjoyed whisky and soda with him while chatting for a half hour or so. "I could not hear what they talked about," Tommy Lascelles recorded in his diary, "but it was, more often than not, punctuated by peals of laughter, and Winston generally came out wiping his eyes. 'She's *en grande beauté ce soir,*' he said one evening in his schoolboy French."

The relationship between the Queen and Churchill prompted comparisons with Queen Victoria, who took the throne at age eighteen, and fifty-eight-year-old William Lamb, Viscount Melbourne, her first prime minister. Melbourne's manner, wrote Lytton Strachey, "mingled, with perfect facility, the watchfulness and the respect of a statesman and a courtier with the tender solicitude of a parent. He was at once reverential and affectionate, at once the servant and the guide." Yet when asked directly by former courtier Richard Molyneux early in her reign whether Churchill treated her as Melbourne treated Victoria, Elizabeth II said, "Not a bit of it. I find him very obstinate."

Nor was she shy about catching out her prime minister when he hadn't adequately prepared, as happened when Churchill failed to read an important cable from the British ambassador in Iraq. "What did you think about that most interesting telegram from Baghdad?" the Queen asked him that Tuesday. He sheepishly admitted he hadn't seen it, and returned to 10 Downing Street "in a frightful fury." When he read the cable, he realized that it was indeed significant.

"If it was a case of teaching her, it was not done in a didactic way," said Mary Soames. "She was very well versed in her constitutional position. My father knew very well what the position of constitutional monarch is vis à vis prime minister, cabinet and parliament. So it was a great advantage for her first prime minister to be somebody who really did know that. Most of them don't, and his massive experience in government would surely have been a help. They talked about the present. They must have talked about people. Young though she was, she had experience. She traveled. She probably knew some of the people better than he, so she would have told him about them. What struck my father was her attentiveness. She has always paid attention to what she was doing. He never said she was lacking confidence."

One small glimpse of Elizabeth II's growing self-assurance came when Churchill was finishing his memoirs of World War II and asked her permission to publish two letters he had written to her father. She granted his request but observed that his language was "rather rough on the Poles" and asked that "in the interests of international amity" his words "be toned down a bit." Churchill readily changed the original version of the letter he had written a decade earlier.

In the weeks before the coronation, the seventy-eight-year-old prime minister had assumed a greater workload than usual when Anthony Eden had a botched gall bladder operation, causing him to fly to Boston for extensive repair surgery and a long recovery in the United States. Although Eden was foreign secretary, he functioned as Churchill's deputy. In the view of Clementine Churchill, "the strain" of the additional burdens "took its toll" on her husband. While Eden was overseas, Churchill suffered a stroke after a dinner in honor of the Italian prime minister on June 23. Amazingly, since his mind remained sharp, Churchill and his aides were able to conceal his paralytic symptoms as "fatigue," keeping the truth about his illness under wraps.

The Queen kept informed about Churchill's condition, writing a lighthearted letter to buoy his spirits, and inviting him in September to join her at the Doncaster races to watch the St. Leger, followed by a weekend at Balmoral. He made a surprisingly rapid recovery, although his condition was still frail. When the prime minister lingered in the rear of the royal box at the racetrack, the Queen said to him, "They want you." He appeared at the front, he later told his doctor, and "got as much cheering as she did."

After a period of rest in the south of France, Churchill was back at work by October, making speeches and presiding over cabinet meetings. But he tired easily, and his memory had slipped. It was obviously time for his retirement, but the Queen declined to use their weekly audience to apply any pressure. Churchill made a series of pledges to Eden that he would step down on a certain date, only to find one excuse after another to extend his time in office. In the view of Eden's wife, Clarissa, the prime minister "prevaricated continuously for nearly two years."

Besides dealing with Churchill's illness and recovery, the young Queen became embroiled that summer in a highly sensitive family matter with constitutional implications. Princess Margaret had fallen in love and was determined to marry one of the royal household's most trusted employees, thirty-eight-year-old Group Captain Peter Townsend, who had been working for the family since 1944. Not only was he sixteen years her senior, he was the divorced father of two sons.

Handsome and mild-mannered, Townsend had been a highly decorated Royal Air Force pilot in World War II, a dashing hero who had brought down eleven German planes in the Battle of Britain. He had originally been assigned to Buckingham Palace for three months as an equerry, who is an aide-de-camp who assists the monarch at events, organizes logistics, and helps look after guests. Lascelles noted that Townsend was "a devilish bad equerry: one could not depend on him to order the motor-car at the right time of day, but we always made allowances for his having been three times shot down into the drink in our defence."

Yet Townsend's calm and empathetic temperament endeared him to George VI, who made him a permanent member of the staff, first as equerry and then as Deputy Master of the Household, overseeing all private social engagements.

Although Margaret was just thirteen when Townsend arrived, her sparkling personality made her the center of attention in the royal family. "Lilibet is my pride, Margaret my joy," their father used to say. Margaret had always been the impish counterpoint to her sister, the witty entertainer who knew how to brighten her father's moods, with a quicksilver mind that ran in unpredictable directions and didn't yield easily to discipline. She was willful and competitive, and she would always remain resentful that her older sister received a better education. She had asked to join Lilibet's tutorials with Henry Marten, but was told by the tutor, "It is not necessary for you." Perhaps to compensate, her father indulged and spoiled his younger daughter, which only encouraged her mercurial tendencies. "She would not listen ever," recalled her cousin Mary Clayton. "She would go on doing something terribly naughty just the same. She was so funny she didn't get scolded, which would have been good for her."

Her younger sister was often vexing, but Elizabeth invariably stood up for her. "Margaret was an awful tease," said Mary Clayton, "which helped her sister in her own way to control difficult situations." She also kept Elizabeth humble. "The Queen never shows off, unlike Princess Margaret, who was always pirouetting," said historian Kenneth Rose. Despite their different natures, the two sisters could laugh at the same jokes, although Elizabeth's wit is gentler and more dry. Both excelled at mimicry and enjoyed singing popular songs together at the piano, which Margaret played with great flair.

As Margaret matured, Townsend was drawn to her "unusual, intense beauty." At five foot one, she had a voluptuous figure and what Townsend described as "large purple-blue eyes, generous sensitive lips, and a complexion as smooth as a peach." He was struck by her "astonishing power of expression" that "could change in an instant from saintly, almost melancholic, composure, to hilarious uncontrollable joy." And he saw that "behind the dazzling façade, the apparent self-assurance, you could find, if you looked for it, a rare softness and sincerity."

By the time Margaret turned twenty in August 1950, Townsend's marriage had come apart after his wife, Rosemary, strayed into several affairs. The princess and the equerry with blue eyes and chiseled features found themselves in long conversations, and by August 1951 on the Balmoral moors the King spotted his daughter gazing lovingly at Townsend dozing in the heather. Yet both he and his wife averted their eyes, engaging in the royal penchant for "ostriching," an almost congenital ability to ignore unpleasant situations.

Margaret turned to Townsend for consolation in the months following her father's death when she was "in a black hole." That June he initiated divorce proceedings against Rosemary, citing her adultery with John de László, son of the portrait artist who had painted Lilibet as a child. After his divorce from Rosemary was granted in November 1952, Townsend told Tommy Lascelles that he and the princess were "deeply in love" and wanted to get married — a plan the couple had shared only with the Queen and Duke of Edinburgh.

The following day Lascelles had the first in a series of conversations with the Queen describing the "formidable obstacles" posed by the Royal Marriages Act of 1772, which was designed to prevent unsuitable matches from damaging the royal family. The act specifies that no member of the family in the line of succession can marry without the consent of the sovereign, but if the family member is over the age of twenty-five, he or she could marry one year after giving notice to the Privy Council, unless both houses of Parliament specifically disapproved of the proposed marriage. The problem for Margaret was that marriage to a divorced man would not be recognized by the Church of England, of which her sister was the Supreme Governor — a circumstance that would cause the Queen to forbid the union. Princess Margaret was third in line to the throne after the Queen's two children, but because Charles and Anne were both so young, she could plausibly serve as Regent. The issue remained unresolved, and was swept temporarily out of mind by the all-consuming coronation preparations.

Other than telling the Queen Mother in February, Margaret and Townsend kept their intentions secret until Coronation Day, when a tabloid reporter caught Margaret flicking a piece of "fluff" from the lapel of Townsend's uniform with a proprietary and flirtatious glance. Several days later,

149

the Palace learned that *The People,* a Sunday tabloid, would run a story on the affair, prompting Lascelles to notify Churchill on June 13. "This is most important!" Churchill exclaimed. "One motor accident, and this young lady might be our queen." Not only was the prime minister troubled about the censure of the Anglican Church, he worried that parliaments in the Commonwealth would disapprove of Margaret marrying Townsend on the grounds that their child would be an unsuitable king or queen. Churchill "made it perfectly clear that if Princess Margaret should decide to marry Townsend, she must renounce her rights to the throne."

Churchill, Lascelles, and Michael Adeane all agreed that the only remedy was to offer Townsend "employment abroad as soon as possible," Lascelles recalled. "And with this the Queen agreed." Until the publication in 2006 of a memorandum written by Lascelles in 1955 detailing the sequence of events, the common assumption was that the Queen had "stood on the sidelines" while others banished Townsend, and that Princess Margaret was misled by Lascelles into thinking she could freely marry on reaching the age of twenty-five. In fact, by Lascelles's account, "the Queen, after consulting Princess Margaret — and presumably Townsend himself — told me a few days later that she considered Brussels to be the most suitable post." Elizabeth II also asked for a statement clarifying the "implications" if she were to forbid the marriage. The government's attorney general produced a memo, and Lascelles wrote a letter outlining the possibility of a split within the Commonwealth if "several parliaments . . . might take a diametrically opposite view of that held by others." He was scheduled to retire at the end of the year, but before his departure, the private secretary sent this information to the Queen as well as Margaret, who thanked him for it in February 1954.

Once Townsend left for his Belgian exile in July 1953, the Queen and her advisers hoped the separation would cool the couple's ardor. But the princess and her lover continued to correspond daily, and Margaret deluded herself into thinking that after her twenty-fifth birthday she could prevail, even if her sister was compelled to withhold her approval. By postponing a decision, everyone involved only prolonged the agony and kept the Queen's younger sister in limbo for two years.

In retrospect, it's clear why Elizabeth II did not want to force the issue. Divorced people were excluded from royal garden parties and other gatherings in the sovereign's palaces and on the royal yacht. Her grandfather had first admitted "innocent parties" in divorce to the Royal Enclosure at Ascot, and the Queen had relented to include "guilty parties" as well. Still, she had an almost visceral reaction to divorce, which she had inveighed against in her only major speech as a princess. "She strongly believed that divorce was catching," said Lady Elizabeth Anson, a cousin of the Queen through the Queen Mother's Bowes Lyon family. "If one got divorced, it made it easier for another unhappy couple to get divorced."

With the resolution of Margaret's dilemma delayed, the Queen turned her full attention to the culmination of the continuing coronation celebration: an ambitious five-and-a-half-month tour of Commonwealth countries, covering 43,000 miles from Bermuda to the Cocos Islands, by plane and ship. It was her first extended trip as sovereign, and the first time a British monarch had circled the globe. By one accounting, she heard 276 speeches and 508 renditions of "God Save the Queen," made 102 speeches, shook 13,213 hands, and witnessed 6,770 curtsies.

Elizabeth II's role as the symbolic head of the Commonwealth of Nations not only enhanced her place in the world and extended her reach, it became a source of pride and pleasure and an essential part of her identity. "She sees herself fused into that instrument that was originally an empire," said former Canadian prime minister Brian Mulroney after she had been leader of the organization for nearly sixty years. Sir Philip Moore, her private secretary from 1977 to 1986, once estimated that she devoted half of her time to the Commonwealth. Over the course of her reign she would visit most member nations multiple times.

In 1949 the London Declaration created the modern Commonwealth with the removal of "British" from its name, while recognizing King George VI as "Head of the Commonwealth." That year, newly independent India pledged to keep its membership when it became a republic, setting the stage for British colonies to join as they sought independence. The Irish Free State had become a republic the previous year, ending the British monarch's role as head of state. In a further demonstration of antipathy for Britain rooted in centuries of domination as well as bitterness over the island's partition, the new Republic of Ireland left the Commonwealth. Other newly independent nations eagerly joined in the years to come, however. "The transformation of the Crown from an emblem of dominion into a symbol of free and voluntary association . . . has no precedent," Elizabeth II observed after twenty-five years on the throne.

What began as a cozy group of eight members — Britain, Canada, Australia, New Zealand, South Africa, Pakistan, Ceylon, and India — would grow to fifty-four by the early twenty-first century, representing almost one third of the world's population. Most of the member nations became republics, but some (Brunei and Tonga among them) had monarchs of their own, and all twenty-nine realms and territories where Elizabeth II reigned as Queen belonged as well.

Embracing First and Third World countries, large and small, from all regions except the Middle East, the Commonwealth dedicated itself to giving its members equal voice and a sense of kinship. With English as the shared language, it served as a forum for the promotion of good government, education, economic development, and human rights — although its main weakness was a tendency to dither over the egregious abuses of tyrants.

In preparation for her first Commonwealth tour, the Queen supervised the creation of one hundred new outfits by her couturier Norman Hartnell. Her priorities were comfort for her daytime clothes, which were usually sewn with weights in the hems as a safeguard against windy conditions, bright colors so she could be easily visible at outdoor events, and sumptuous fabrics for her evening gowns, which often incorporated motifs to pay homage to her host countries. Her coronation dress was part of her wardrobe as well, to be worn opening parliaments in a number of countries.

Watching the televised departure ceremony on the evening of November 23, 1953, Noel Coward thought the Queen "looked so young and vulnerable and valiant," and the royal couple had "star quality *in excelsis*." They traveled on a BOAC Stratocruiser for nearly ten hours to a refueling stop in Gander, Newfoundland, followed by another five and a half hours to Bermuda, tracked along the way by naval vessels from Britain and Canada that stayed in continuous radio contact.

After a day of official rounds on Britain's oldest colony, the royal party visited Jamaica, where they boarded the SS *Gothic* for their three-week voyage through the Panama Canal to the South Pacific archipelago of Fiji. On the way the Queen worked in her sitting room and wrote letters (posted from each port of call, where airplanes transported them in diplomatic bags). One message to Churchill commended his efforts for "the good of the world" at his summit in Bermuda with President Eisenhower and French premier Joseph Laniel to plan a strategy for dealing with the threat of a nuclear confrontation in the Cold War standoff with the Soviet Union. Otherwise, Elizabeth II watched members of the royal household play shuffleboard, quoits, and deck tennis, and she filmed the customary "Crossing the Line" initiation. Lady-in-waiting Pamela Mountbatten was tipped into a tank of water by Prince Philip, dressed as the Demon Barber of King Neptune's Court, who was then unceremoniously pushed into the pool as well.

Their visit to Fiji challenged the Queen's ability to cope smoothly with exotic customs. A group of native chieftains came aboard the *Gothic* and welcomed her with a lengthy dance featuring clapping and sequences of grunts while sitting cross-legged, followed by a solemn presentation of whale's teeth. On shore, the chiefs painstakingly prepared quantities of kava, a strong sedating beverage made by pulverizing roots of the kava plant, liberally lubricated with spit. The Queen, who had been warned of the potency of the drink, watched the long preparation, and when she was somberly offered a draft in a seashell, warily took just half a mouthful. Back on the *Gothic* that night after their black-tie dinner, Elizabeth II marveled at the experience. "Didn't you LOVE this?" she exclaimed, and then sat cross-legged in her evening gown on the floor of the dining room. "As she was in the middle of the grunts and claps, the steward came in and was transfixed," said Pamela Mountbatten.

The next stop was the island kingdom of Tonga, and a joyful reunion with the exuberant Queen Salote, who drove her British counterpart around in the London taxicab she had acquired during the coronation and laid on a feast for seven hundred people, all seated on the ground, eating with their fingers. "The Queen suffered through that," recalled Pamela Mountbatten. "She has a very small appetite, but she knows if she stops, everyone stops. So out of consideration she had to play with her food and extend the time eating."

The royal party arrived in New Zealand before Christmas. They celebrated the holiday at the Auckland home of Governor General Sir Willoughby Norrie, where the Queen broadcast her Christmas speech, declaring her intention to show the people of the Commonwealth that "the Crown is not merely an abstract symbol of our unity but a personal and living bond between you and me." She also touched on the expectation of a new Elizabethan Age and admitted, "frankly I do not myself feel at all like my great Tudor forebear, who was blessed with neither husband nor children, who ruled as a despot and was never able to leave her native shores." She emphasized that the Commonwealth "bears no resemblance to the Empires of the past," but rather was built on "friendship, loyalty and the desire for freedom and peace." And she echoed her twenty-first birthday pledge by declaring her intention to give her "heart and soul every day of my life" to this "equal partnership of nations and races."

Two keen listeners to the broadcast were five-year-old Prince Charles and three-year-old Princess Anne, who were spending Christmas at Sandringham with their grandmother. They spoke to the Queen and Prince Philip by radio telephone, but otherwise news of their progress came in regular letters from the Queen Mother, who had them for weekends at Royal Lodge, her pale pink house tucked among the trees in Windsor Great Park. Just as Elizabeth and Margaret had followed their parents' travels on maps, Prince Charles traced his parents' route on a globe in his nursery. "He is intensely affectionate & loves you & Philip most tenderly," reassured the Queen Mother in a letter to her daughter.

The crowds everywhere were enormous and enthusiastic. Masses of welcoming boats jammed Sydney's harbor, and by one count, three quarters of Australia's population came out to see the Queen. At age twenty-seven she was hailed as the "world's sweetheart." But the royal couple refused to let their celebrity go to their heads. "The level of adulation, you wouldn't believe it," Prince Philip recalled. "It could have been corroding. It would have been very easy to play to the gallery, but I took a conscious decision not to do that. Safer not to be too popular. You can't fall too far." The Queen Mother reinforced this instinct to separate their public and private personae. "How moving & humble making," she wrote her daughter in early March 1954, "that one can be the vehicle through which this love for country can be expressed. Don't you feel that?"

The Duke of Edinburgh also helped his wife stay on an even keel when she became frustrated after endless hours of making polite conversation. "I remember her complaining in Australia, 'All these mayors are so boring. Why are they so boring?'" recalled Pamela Mountbatten. "Prince Philip explained to her, 'You don't have to sit next to them every day in England. We are two months in Australia so you have to sit next to them a lot more.' This was easy for Prince Philip, who charges in and makes things happen. The Queen early on was not a natural conversationalist or mixer. So for her it was much harder work. Also, they were intimidated by her. The protocol was they shouldn't speak first, which made for stilted conversation."

The Queen's style was sparing — "never . . . a superfluous gesture," the photographer Cecil Beaton once observed — smiling only when delighted or amused, rather than incessantly as a politician would do. Meeting and greeting thousands of people at receptions and garden parties actually gave her a temporary facial tic. But when she was watching a performance or a parade, and her face was in repose, she looked grumpy, even formidable. The portrait painter Michael Noakes observed that "she has no intermediate expression," just a "great smile or dour." As the Queen herself once ruefully acknowledged, "The trouble is that unlike my mother, I don't have a naturally smiley face." From time to time, Philip would jolly his wife. "Don't look so sad, sausage," he said during an event in Sydney. Or he might provoke a grin by reciting scripture at odd moments, once inquiring sotto voce, "What meaneth then this bleating of the sheep?"

During the long and repetitive days, the Queen developed coping techniques, including her preternatural ability to stand for hours without tiring. Years later she described her technique to Susan Crosland, the wife of Foreign Secretary Anthony Crosland: "One plants one's feet apart like this," said the Queen as she lifted her evening gown above her ankles. "Always keep them parallel. Make sure your weight is evenly distributed. That's all there is to it." Her handshaking was similarly designed with self-preservation in mind: she extends her hand, allowing her to grasp the fingers and do the squeezing, usually protected by a size seven white glove, which guards against picking up illness and being cut by women's diamond rings.

Elizabeth II has always carried a handbag on her left arm. Its ubiquity has prompted fascination about its significance and speculation about its contents. Phil Brown, the manager of the Hull City football team, got a good look inside when he sat next to the Queen at a luncheon in 2009. "It was almost like a lady's prop with essential items," he said. "It had things that you would expect — makeup, [coin] purse, sweeteners she put in her coffee, the normal stuff. You expect that a lady-in-waiting would carry her handbag, but for the Queen, it was almost like a comfort blanket."

Her ladies-in-waiting are responsible for necessities such as extra pairs of gloves as well as needles, thread, and safety pins to make emergency repairs. Her private secretary keeps the texts of her speeches, which he hands to her at the appointed time. But the Queen "is a very practical down-to-earth lady," said one of her long-serving ladies-in-waiting. "She needs a comb or lipstick or Kleenex, and if she hasn't got it, what does she do?" For the same reason, her handbag usually contains reading glasses, mint lozenges, and a fountain pen, although rarely cash, except for a precisely folded £5 or £10 note on Sundays for the church collection plate.

Elizabeth II has also been known to carry a bag hook, an ingenious item designed for practicality. "I watched the Queen open her handbag and remove a white suction cup and discreetly spit into it," recalled a dinner guest at the Berkshire home of the Queen's cousin Jean Wills. "The Queen then attached the cup to the underside of the table. The cup had a hook on it, and she attached her handbag to it."

Elizabeth II taught herself to keep engaged in the moment by sharpening her powers of observation. Once when she spotted a Franciscan monk in a crowd, she said to an official nearby, "I'm always fascinated by their toes, aren't you?" She would store up these moments for later and recount them, often with expert dialect, for her husband and advisers. She used her mimicry in part as "a way of relieving the boredom and shattering the formality," said a former courtier.

On many evenings during the Commonwealth tour the royal party shared reminiscences over private black-tie dinners aboard the *Gothic.* They relaxed by going to stud farms and the races at Rondwich and Flemington in Australia. During weekend visits to the beach, the Queen's advisers became accustomed to hearing Philip speak with spousal directness. When she balked at wearing a swimsuit on a trip to the Great Barrier Reef, he said, "Do come in, you have nothing to do, at least have a nice swim." "I need to keep out of the sun," the Queen replied. "You are a premature grandmother!" he exclaimed in exasperation.

Philip's principal diversion at public events continued to be wisecracks and lighthearted banter. In motorcades he took to finding the most unlikely people and waving at them. But when he was off on his own, he gave speeches reflecting his growing portfolio of interests. To a gathering of scientists in Wellington, New Zealand, he spoke at length about the applications of science to agriculture, medicine, and the military. While the Queen spoke briefly and carefully hewed to written texts, Philip began to enjoy the luxury of discursive and off-the-cuff remarks.

The last leg of the tour brought the royal couple back to exotic locales, with stops in Ceylon (now Sri Lanka), the Cocos Islands in the Indian Ocean, Uganda, and Libya. The Queen wore her coronation dress to open the Ceylonese parliament in an outdoor pavilion. As she sat in the sun on the throne for an hour, her bejeweled dress heated up and she nearly roasted, but she showed no sign of discomfort. Her attendants noticed that even in the hottest temperatures the Queen scarcely perspired — a phenomenon still evident into her eighties. On a visit to Ground Zero in New York City in July 2010, she spent nearly a half hour in record-shattering 103-degree heat greeting families of those who had lost their lives on 9/11. "We were all pouring sweat," said Debbie Palmer, the widow of a firefighter. "She didn't have a bead of sweat on her. I thought that is what it must be like to be royal." But Pamela Mountbatten, who witnessed the Queen's uncanny cool nearly six decades earlier, said, "There are certain people whose skin runs water, but she doesn't. That means she can't get relief, so she suffers twice as much from the heat. She says no perspiration makes it much worse. It is very convenient because it looks wonderful, but at a cost."

At Tobruk in Libya, the Queen and Prince Philip transferred to *Britannia,* the new 412-foot royal yacht with a gleaming deep blue hull, which they had designed together with architect Sir

Hugh Casson. The duke supervised technical features as well as overall decor, and the Queen selected the understated chintz fabrics, and even doorknobs and lamp shades. With its grand staircase, spacious drawing rooms, and state dining room, *Britannia* was suitable for entertaining world leaders and hosting large receptions of dignitaries. A less formal sun lounge furnished with bamboo and wicker chairs was used for afternoon tea, and the Queen and Prince Philip each had cozy bedrooms fitted with single beds and connected by a door, as well as his and hers sitting rooms with built-in desks. *Britannia* was not only the monarch's floating embassy — a unique bubble of British distinctiveness — to be deployed in future tours around the world, but a secluded "country house at sea" where the Queen said she could "truly relax."

For its maiden voyage, *Britannia* brought Prince Charles and Princess Anne to be reunited with their parents in early May 1954 for the first time in nearly half a year. The Queen was pleased that she would be seeing her children earlier than she had anticipated, but she worried that they wouldn't know their parents. The Queen Mother wrote to allay her daughter's concerns, saying, "You may find Charles much older in a very endearing way."

Still, when the moment came and the Queen was piped aboard, her strict control and conformity to protocol prevailed as it had when she met her son after her Canada trip. "No, not you dear," she said as she greeted dignitaries first, then shook the five-year-old's extended hand. The private reunion was warm and affectionate, as Prince Charles showed his mother all around the yacht where he had been living for more than a week. The Queen told her mother how happy she was to be with her "enchanting" children again. They had both "gravely offered us their hands," she wrote, "partly I suppose because they were somewhat overcome by the fact that we were really there and partly because they have met so many new people recently! However the ice broke very quickly and we have been subjected to a very energetic routine and innumerable questions which have left us gasping!" But the repercussions of that chilly first encounter were evident four decades later in a biography of Prince Charles by Anthony Holden, who titled a chapter about the prince's childhood "No, Not You Dear."

The Queen and her family arrived at the Isle of Wight, where Churchill joined them on board *Britannia* for a sail into London up the Thames. "One saw this dirty commercial river as one came up," the Queen recalled. Yet Churchill "was describing it as the silver thread which runs through the history of Britain." Her prime minister, she observed, saw things "in a very romantic and glittering way; perhaps one was looking at it in a rather too mundane way." Stilted though she sounded, her oft-mocked use of "one" was her unassuming way to avoid the more self-referential word "I."

Churchill had set his retirement date for her return from the tour, but once again he wavered. The Queen remained hopeful he would keep his commitment, telling Anthony Eden during an audience after a Buckingham Palace garden party in July that Churchill "seemed less truculent about going now." The prime minister would cling to power for eight more months, and during this time, according to Jock Colville, his half-hour audiences with the Queen "dragged out longer and longer . . . and very often took an hour and a half, at which I may say racing was not the only topic discussed."

Finally the eighty-year-old leader agreed to yield his premiership on April 5, 1955. Even at the eleventh hour, he nearly backed off when he thought he might act as a peacemaker by convening a four-power summit with the Soviet Union. The Queen remained patient during their audience on March 29, telling him she didn't mind a delay. Two days later, he gave formal notification that he would go as planned. Private secretary Michael Adeane replied that the Queen "felt the greatest personal regrets" and had said "she would especially miss the weekly audiences which she has found so instructive and, if one can say so of state matters, so entertaining."

Churchill gave a farewell dinner on April 4 in which he toasted the Queen as a "young, gleaming champion" of "the sacred causes and wise and kindly way of life." He had advised his cabinet that afternoon to "never be separated from the Americans." At his last audience on April 5, Elizabeth II offered him a dukedom to honor his special place in British history, even though that title was now reserved only for "royal personages." Jock Colville had assured her that Churchill would decline the offer because he "wished to die in the House of Commons." But when the prime minister set out for Buckingham Palace in his frock coat and top hat, Colville became apprehensive that in a burst of sentimentality Churchill might change his mind. "I very nearly accepted," he tearfully told his private secretary back at Number 10. "I was so moved by her beauty and her charm and the kindness with which she made this offer, that for a moment I thought of accepting. But finally I remembered that I must die as I have always been — Winston Churchill. And so I asked her to forgive my not accepting it. And do you know, it's an odd thing, but she seemed almost relieved."

Writing to Churchill afterward, Elizabeth II told him none of his successors "will ever, for me, be able to hold the place of my first Prime Minister." She thanked him for his "wise guidance" and for his leadership during the Cold War, "with its threats and dangers which are more awe-inspiring than any which you have had to contend with before, in war or peace." Churchill replied that he had tried "to keep Your Majesty squarely confronted with the grave and complex problems of our time." He revealed that at the beginning of her reign he had recognized her grasp of "the august duties of a modern Sovereign and the store of knowledge which had already been gathered by an upbringing both wise and lively," including her "Royal resolve to serve as well as rule, and indeed to rule by serving."

It was the Queen's constitutional prerogative to choose, after consulting with members of the Conservative Party, the next leader of the party capable of commanding the necessary majority in the House of Commons. After Churchill resigned, she asked him during their final audience if he would

165

recommend a successor. Since he was no longer prime minister, he could not technically offer such advice, so he demurred, saying he would leave it to her. She told him, according to Colville, "the case was not a difficult one and that she would summon Anthony Eden."

She had presumably taken soundings with Tory officials, but she didn't disclose the nature or extent of those consultations. Her emphasis then, as it would be throughout her reign, was strict adherence to constitutionally correct procedures and an unwillingness to impose her personal preference.

In her first audience with Eden, the Queen was almost offhand in discharging her duties. After they had chatted for a while, he finally said, "Well, Ma'am?" to which the Queen replied, "I suppose I ought to be asking you to form a government."

An Old Etonian son of a baronet, the fifty-seven-year-old prime minister was "the best looking politician of his time," a cultivated man with an Oxford First in Oriental Languages, including Persian and Arabic. He brought extensive experience to his role, having served in Parliament since 1923, with leadership positions in prewar, wartime, and postwar governments. He had considerable charm, but he could be tense and sometimes unpredictable, with an "odd and violent temper," observed Cynthia Gladwyn, the wife of diplomat Sir Gladwyn Jebb, along with a need for praise and flattery. A shy streak made him seem remote, which put more of a burden on the Queen to establish rapport.

Her success in doing so was evident that summer when Eden and his wife, Clarissa, a niece of Winston Churchill, were attending a military event in Winchester with the Queen. Afterward the prime minister had his weekly audience, which Clarissa overheard when she was resting in a room next door. "Anthony was telling her the menu he had had at Ike's — there was a lot of merriment," she wrote in her diary. Recalling the moment years later, she said, "They were chatting away and laughing like anything. It was very noisy, and it surprised me. I would have thought it would be more structured questions and answers."

Eden had married Clarissa after his first wife, Beatrice, bolted with another man, making him the first divorced prime minister. That circumstance put him in a delicate position when Princess Margaret turned twenty-five on August 21, 1955, and her romance with Peter Townsend — like Eden, the innocent party in a divorce — again moved to center stage. Six days before her birthday, Margaret wrote Eden a letter explaining that she would remain at Balmoral until October when Townsend was expected in London for his annual leave. "It is only by seeing him in this way that I feel I can properly decide whether I can marry him or not," she wrote. "I hope to be in a position to tell you and the other Commonwealth Prime Ministers what I intend to do."

While the press whipped up popular sentiment for a royal love match ("COME ON MARGARET! PLEASE MAKE UP YOUR MIND!" pleaded the *Daily Mirror*), the Queen, the prime minister, and Michael Adeane debated how to proceed once she was compelled to deny permission as head of the Church of England, requiring Margaret to ask for approval from the parliaments in the United Kingdom and Commonwealth realms. In early October the Edens visited Balmoral for the annual prime minister's weekend, which featured long consultations, some of them including Prince Philip. The Queen wanted her sister to be happy, but was equally committed to the royal family's role as a model for her subjects. She took pains to remain neutral and let Margaret make up her own mind.

Back in London, after determining that Parliament would not approve a union opposed by the Church, Eden informed Margaret that if she wished to wed Townsend in a civil ceremony, she needed to renounce her right to the throne. This would mean giving up her Civil List income and the rights of any of her heirs in the line of succession.

On October 20, 1955, the cabinet prepared the points to be covered by a Bill of Renunciation in Parliament, and four days later an editorial in *The Times* laid out in moralistic terms the princess's stark choice: either she could keep her "high place" in the estimation of the Commonwealth and give up Townsend, or she could contract a civil marriage and relinquish her royal status.

On October 31 Princess Margaret announced that she and Townsend were parting company. Although her sorrowful statement, written in collaboration with Townsend, emphasized her religious beliefs and sense of obligation to the Commonwealth, the true deciding factor was that she had been raised in luxury as a princess, and she couldn't face the prospect of living, as Kenneth

Rose put it, "in a cottage on a group captain's salary" — outside the royal family that was the very essence of her identity.

The controversy over Margaret's dashed marital plans prompted some mild criticism, but mainly she drew praise for her willingness to sacrifice her happiness on the altar of royal duty. Margaret continued to live in Clarence House with her mother, making public appearances and cutting a glamorous figure, although some could see, as Tommy Lascelles described it, that she had become "selfish and hard and wild." Like her father before her, the Queen coddled her sister rather than confronting her when she misbehaved.

The image of the Queen in the public imagination in the mid-1950s was set by two of her most celebrated portraits, each romanticized in a particular way. To commemorate her Commonwealth tour, the bespectacled Australian artist William Dargie captured her in seven sessions at the end of 1954 in the Yellow Drawing Room on the first floor of Buckingham Palace. Dargie found her to be chatty and marveled that her "straight back . . . never slumped once," but noted that "she had a difficult mouth to paint." His image combines dignity with accessibility: "a nice friendly portrait," in the Queen's words. It was commissioned to hang in Australia's Parliament House in Canberra, but she liked it so much that she asked Dargie to make a copy for her private apartment at the Palace. The only other portrait of herself that she has kept in her personal collection is the official state portrait in her coronation dress by Sir James Gunn, hanging at Windsor Castle.

From October 1954 through February 1955, the Queen also sat sixteen times for Pietro Annigoni. The forty-four-year-old Florentine artist was barely five feet tall, with a burly physique, intense brown eyes, and big peasant hands. He spoke broken English, so they conversed entirely in French. He found her to be "kind, natural and never aloof," and was taken by the unaffected way she talked, referring to "my husband," "my mother," and "my sister." Her memories of childhood, "watching the people and the cars down there in the Mall," inspired him to show her "alone and far off" despite being "dear to the hearts of millions of people whom she loved."

The result is an arresting three-quarter view of the Queen bareheaded, in her capacious dark blue robes of the Order of the Garter against a bleak imaginary landscape. Her demeanor is regal, her expression contemplative, with a hint of determination. The Queen was happy with the portrait, and Margaret praised the artist's success with her sister's elusive mouth. The following year Margaret sat thirty-three times for her own Annigoni portrait, which she considered so beautiful it moved her to tears. When American artist Frolic Weymouth asked Margaret her opinion of her sister's portrait, she sniffed, "Mine was better than hers."

As Elizabeth II approached her thirtieth birthday in 1956, she was still benefiting from a honeymoon glow, although her prime minister was grappling with an array of domestic crises. Only a month after taking office, he had called an election in May 1955, which the Tories had won easily. But the country was plagued with labor unrest; the Queen's birthday parade that June even had to be canceled when Eden declared a state of emergency during a railway strike. Churchill had done nothing to slow the growth of the welfare state created by the postwar Labour government, and the costs were hobbling the economy.

The Queen took several noteworthy steps to shrink the traditional distance from her subjects. During a trip to Nigeria in February, she visited the Oji River Leper Settlement at a time when victims of leprosy were considered outcasts. Her "qualities of grace and compassion," wrote British journalist Barbara Ward, "shine through the spectacle of a young queen shaking hands with cured Nigerian lepers to reassure timid villagers who do not believe in the cure." The gesture was every bit as groundbreaking as Princess Diana's handshake in 1987 with an AIDS patient at a time of public fear about catching the disease through touch.

On May 11, 1956, the Queen began hosting informal luncheons at Buckingham Palace for "meritocrats" from fields such as medicine, sports, literature, the arts, religion, education, and business. She holds them to this day. The inspiration came from Prince Philip, who thought gatherings of a half dozen luminaries every month or so could keep the Queen better connected to the outside world. One peculiarity of the get-togethers is that the guests have little or nothing in common with each other, which some participants liken to being shipwrecked. Elizabeth II, invariably preceded by her pack of corgis and her special cross-breed of corgis and dachshunds called "dorgis," typically mixes with everyone over cocktails and then makes more extensive conversation with her two luncheon partners at the oval table in the 1844 Drawing Room or the Chinese Dining Room.

As with her public events, the Queen enjoys mild mishaps. Once one of her corgis had an accident on the rug, prompting the Queen to signal her Master of the Household, Vice Admiral Sir Peter Ashmore, who retrieved an old-fashioned blotter from a nearby desk and dropped to his hands and knees to remove the stain — while everyone else pretended not to notice.

That spring, Elizabeth II deployed her diplomatic skills on Premier Nikita Khrushchev and Prime Minister Nikolai Bulganin, the newly installed leaders of the Soviet Union. The two tough-minded Cold War foes did not come to Britain on a state visit as the Queen's guests. But they were eager to spend time with her, so she invited them to Windsor Castle. After meetings with Eden, they left London "looking very smart in new black suits and clean shirts and different ties."

The Russian leaders were enchanted by the monarch's casual appearance. "She was dressed in a plain, white dress," Khrushchev wrote in his memoirs. "She looked like the sort of young woman you'd be likely to meet walking along Gorky Street on a balmy summer afternoon."

The Queen gave them a guided tour and served each leader a glass of tea, Russian style. Philip quizzed them about Leningrad, while Elizabeth II inquired about their airplane, the TU-104, which she had seen flying over the castle on its descent into London Airport. Khrushchev was impressed that she "had such a gentle, calm voice. She was completely unpretentious, completely without the haughtiness that you'd expect of royalty. . . . In our eyes she was first and foremost the wife of her husband and the mother of her children." In the car back to Claridge's in London, the two Russians excitedly tried to top each other: "The Queen said to me . . ." "No, she said that to me!"

The tranquillity of the spring and early summer was shattered by the Suez Crisis that escalated from mid-July until the end of the year. It began when Gamal Abdel Nasser, the president of Egypt, nationalized the Suez Canal, which had been controlled by Britain and France through the Suez Canal Company. The 120-mile waterway linking the Mediterranean and Red Sea had long been a strategic conduit for the British navy, but was increasingly important for the transport of oil to Europe. Nasser sought to rid the region of British influence, chiefly its close alliance with the kingdoms of Iraq and Jordan, and to set himself up as the Arab world's dominant leader. Eden viewed Nasser, who had overthrown Egypt's King Farouk four years earlier, as a dangerous dictator who should be stopped.

In the following months, Britain publicly pursued various diplomatic options for international supervision of the canal while secretly plotting military action against Egypt with France and Israel. The plan called for Israel to invade Egypt through the Sinai Peninsula on October 29, 1956, which would then prompt several thousand British and French troops to intervene in a so-called effort to save the canal from the battling Israeli and Egyptian forces. The entire misbegotten operation was a ruse to ensure that Britain and France could recapture the canal by force.

The invasion succeeded after a week of hostilities. But Eden made a terrible miscalculation by keeping the United States in the dark, infuriating Dwight Eisenhower, who had been working with the British government in the spirit of the "special relationship." Not only did the newly reelected American president oppose the Suez military adventure for destabilizing the Middle East, he worried that the Soviet Union's offer to assist Egypt could trigger a wider war. The United States joined other countries, including many of Britain's Commonwealth allies, in the United Nations to condemn the Suez action and demand a cease-fire. The crisis caused a run on the pound — the sale of millions from sterling accounts, especially in the United States — which enabled Eisenhower to exert further leverage by refusing to back an international loan to Britain unless the invading forces were withdrawn. The U.N. cease-fire took effect at midnight on November 6, and by the end of December the French and British troops had completed a humiliating retreat.

Through her daily boxes, the Queen had access to the Foreign Office documents about the Suez strategy. "Nothing was kept from her. She knew about the secret deals beforehand," said one Palace adviser. In Eden's view, "she understood what we were doing very well." During the weeks before the invasion, she had two audiences with the prime minister, whose nerves were frayed from the tension. He began taking Benzedrine, which aggravated his insomnia and volatile moods. Martin Charteris later described him as "edgy" and "jumpy," and unable to sit still when he came to Buckingham Palace. "I think the Queen believed Eden was mad," recalled Charteris.

Despite misgivings by some members, Eden's cabinet backed the Suez operation with near unanimity. Michael Adeane supported the prime minister, but the Queen's assistant private secretaries Martin Charteris and Edward Ford were adamantly opposed. Elizabeth II might have raised her signature question: "Are you sure you are being wise?" The most Eden would reveal two decades later to biographer Robert Lacey was that the Queen did not express her disapproval, "nor would I claim that she was pro-Suez." She maintained scrupulous neutrality in keeping with her constitutional role. "I don't think she was really for it," recalled Gay Charteris. "That is the impression Martin got, and he was frightfully against it."

Mentally and physically shattered — by one account "in such a bad way that he didn't make sense" — Eden flew to Jamaica in mid-November for a rest cure at Goldeneye, the home of writer Ian Fleming, leaving R. A. "Rab" Butler in charge during the interim. Churchill, who criticized Eden's failure to consult Eisenhower, dispatched a letter to his old friend, emphasizing that the two countries needed to stop second-guessing Eden's decisions and concentrate on having a united front against the Soviet Union. Replying on November 23, Eisenhower agreed that the Soviets were "the real enemy" and that the United States and Britain should focus on "achieving our legitimate objectives in the Middle East."

Churchill sent Eisenhower's letter to the Queen, who observed that "it is most interesting to learn his appreciation of the situation, and I hope it means that the present feeling that this country and America are not seeing eye-to-eye will soon be speedily replaced by even stronger ties between us." Britain would in fact work more harmoniously with America on the international stage in the following decades, even as its prestige as a world power faded and its colonies pushed for independence.

Although the Queen bore no blame personally, the setback of Suez inevitably cast a shadow on her reign. The most immediate casualty was Eden himself. His health still fragile, he decided to resign on January 9, 1957, at age fifty-nine, after only twenty months in office. The Queen praised his "highly valued" leadership "in tempestuous times," and Eden expressed gratitude for her "wise and impartial reaction to events." But his reputation as a statesman was in tatters, never to be fully rehabilitated.

Once again it fell to Elizabeth II to select the party leader, but this time she was caught up in political machinations that for the first time reflected badly on her reputation for impartiality. While the Labour Party elected its leaders by democratic vote, the more elitist Conservatives preferred an obscure process of private soundings they called "emergence." The two leading candidates were sixty-two-year-old Harold Macmillan, the chancellor of the exchequer, and fifty-four-year-old Rab Butler, the leader of the House of Commons, who had been the prime minister's deputy and expected to get the top job.

It seemed reasonable to reward Butler for his decades of service in leadership roles. He had also objected to Suez, while Macmillan had been one of its architects, even as he managed to distance himself from the fiasco. Eden had no formal say in the selection of a successor, although he did tell the Queen he preferred Butler.

At the retiring prime minister's suggestion, her point men for the decision were the party's top mandarins, sixty-three-year-old Lord Salisbury, and fifty-six-year-old David Maxwell Fyfe, Viscount Kilmuir, who served as Lord Chancellor, one of the senior officers of Parliament. Together they polled the cabinet, along with several former ministers and the leader of the backbenchers. Salisbury reported to the Queen that Macmillan came out ahead by a wide margin. Churchill also weighed in, advising the Queen to "choose the older man."

But when she summoned Macmillan to the Palace on January 10 and asked him to form a government, her choice surprised the Tory rank and file, many of whom supported Butler. Rather than making a well-considered decision, Elizabeth II seemed to have ceded her judgment to a pair of hidebound aristocrats whose soundings were too narrow. In fairness to the Queen, she was only following the improvisational rules of the Conservative Party. If she had made an independent choice — a highly unlikely outcome, given her cautious temperament — she would have been accused of overreaching her role. Even so, the lingering impression was of a young woman out of touch, and too beholden to the wishes of an Establishment coterie. The new Elizabethan Age, so buoyant five years before, was losing altitude in the cool air of criticism.

CHAPTER SIX
MADE FOR TELEVISION

The one missing voice in the tense days of Suez conflict and leadership change was Prince Philip's. It was a time when the Queen could have used his moral support. But on October 15 the thirty-five-year-old duke had set out, with his wife's encouragement, on a four-month solo tour of Commonwealth countries on *Britannia* covering nearly forty thousand miles.

His primary destination was Melbourne, where he was to open the 1956 Olympic Games and, as Philip later explained, "it would have been much simpler to have flown out and back." But he and the Queen decided to expand the scope of the trip to include more stops in Australia and visits to New Zealand, Kenya, and Gambia, as well as a number of "remote communities who are loyal members of the Commonwealth" such as Papua New Guinea, Seychelles, Ceylon, and Malaya. He also went to the Falklands in the South Atlantic, and British bases in the Antarctic.

By his own description, Philip is "by profession a sailor" who owes his "allegiance to another of the world's few really great fraternities, the fraternity of the sea." So in the autumn of 1956 he relished reliving the camaraderie of the Officers' Ward-

"Wheeeee!" the Queen exclaimed as she caught her first glimpse of the lower Manhattan skyline. It reminded her of *"a row of great jewels."*

The royal couple approaching New York City on a ferryboat, October 1957. Associated Press

room, but in considerably more luxurious circumstances than his navy days, with formal dinners at a table for twenty set with silver and crystal, accompanied by the best vintages from the royal yacht's wine cellar.

The trip also allowed him to free himself from the strictures of Palace life and the suspicious gaze of courtiers. Unlike other men of his generation and class, he was dependent on and subordinate to his wife. Only when on his own could he claim the control that his contemporaries took for granted. He pursued his fascination with exploring by bringing along the famous veteran of Antarctic expeditions, Sir Raymond Priestley; grew a trim mustache and beard known in the Royal Navy as a "full set"; and practiced painting with a private tutor, Norfolk artist Edward Seago, who had been instructing him since the beginning of the year. In a nostalgic touch, Philip signed his paintings with the Greek "Phi" — a circle bisected by a vertical line.

Back home, critics began calling his protracted journey "Philip's Folly," noting his conspicuous absence during the aborted Middle East invasion, not to mention his ninth wedding anniversary (although he did send the Queen white roses and a photo of two iguanas embracing), and Christmas, when he broadcast a brief radio address from halfway between New Zealand and Cape Horn, referring to men and women in the Commonwealth "willing to serve others rather than themselves."

By the fifth year of his wife's reign, Philip had firmly established a range of causes and passions that he would expand in the years to come. "He has one of those minds where you may be sure the door that is closed is the one he wants to look behind," said one Buckingham Palace adviser. "He wants to know what is going on. That is the nature of the man."

From his years as a naval officer, he had been absorbed by science and technology, and he spoke frequently on improving education in those fields. But he equally emphasized the development of the "whole man" by building character along with intellect. He was passionate about the links between mental, moral, and physical health, and the need to give young people opportunities for physical fitness to prevent the spread of what he called "sub-health." He was an early promoter of Outward Bound, the wilderness schools launched by Gordonstoun founder Kurt Hahn to develop leadership skills and self-confidence by meeting rigorous physical challenges. In 1956 Philip began the Duke of Edinburgh's Award, a worldwide program to recognize teenagers and young adults for completing courses of community service and physical endurance.

Toward the end of Philip's trip, his longtime friend and loyal private secretary, Mike Parker, suddenly left for London when his wife, Eileen, filed for divorce, accusing her husband of adultery. The news splashed across the British tabloids, and Fleet Street conflated Parker's prominent position in the royal household with Philip's months overseas to raise questions about the stability of the royal marriage. The press focused on the duke's attendance for several years at a stag luncheon group in Soho called the Thursday Club that included Parker as well as actors David Niven and Peter Ustinov. While nothing untoward was said to have occurred at these gatherings except drinking, smoking, and telling racy tales, one of the participants, celebrity photographer Stirling Henry Nahum, popularly known as "Baron," was alleged to have provided his apartment for assignations between the duke and an unnamed "party girl," causing a "rift" in his marriage.

Given Philip's matinee idol looks and eye for feminine beauty, he had been linked in the rumor mill for some time to various actresses and society beauties such as Pat Kirkwood, Helene Cordet, and Katie Boyle — all of whom denied anything more than friendship or a glancing acquaintance. The story of the "party girl" had no basis in fact, and Philip was "very hurt, terribly hurt, very angry" about the allegation. The Queen took the unusual step of authorizing her usually tight-lipped press secretary, Commander Richard Colville, to issue an explicit denial, saying, "It is quite untrue that there is any rift between the Queen and the Duke." There the matter rested, although rumors of Philip's supposed dalliances would continue to surface whenever he was spotted on the dance floor or in lively conversation with a pretty woman.

Parker resigned his position to quell the publicity while his case wound through the courts. Elizabeth II and Philip were reunited on February 16, 1957, in Portugal, a moment she used in her own sly fashion to dispel questions about the state of her marriage. When her tanned and freshly shaven consort boarded the Queen's plane, he found her and the members of her household all wearing false

183

beards. The royal couple spent two days alone before they resumed their public roles on a three-day state visit in Portugal. Reporting on his tour at a luncheon in London on the 26th, the duke took pains to note that in his younger days being away for four months would have meant "nothing at all," while now for the "obvious reasons" of his wife and family, the prolonged absence "meant much more to me." But he went on to say that "making some personal sacrifice" was worthwhile to advance the well-being of the Commonwealth "even a small degree."

Just four days earlier, the Queen had rewarded that sacrifice and Philip's work generally as her consort by officially making him a Prince of the United Kingdom — a more elevated title than the royal duke designation he had held since their marriage. The idea had come from Harold Macmillan, the new prime minister, who shrewdly saw it as a way to further reinforce Philip's standing with his wife, as well as in the eyes of Britain and the Commonwealth.

Despite a naturally gloomy cast of mind, Macmillan took charge with a burst of optimism, moving smartly away from the Suez shame and reaffirming Britain's status as a great country filled with industrious citizens. "Most of our people have never had it so good," he famously said on July 20, 1957. Under his watch, Britain did indeed grow more prosperous. Shortly after moving into 10 Downing Street, Macmillan also worked deftly to mend the special relationship frayed by Suez, quietly orchestrating an invitation from Eisenhower to the Queen for a state visit to the United

States in the fall of 1957.

Macmillan had an easier relationship with Elizabeth II than his jittery predecessor, not as cozy as Churchill's but sympathetic, notably on her part, although she sometimes became irritated by his antique affectations and tendency to pontificate. Like Churchill, Macmillan had an American mother (invariably described as pushy or dominating) and what his biographer Alistair Horne characterized as an "instinctive reverence towards the monarchy." The prime minister was astute, witty, and urbane, capable of the sort of penetrating character assessments that intrigued the Queen, who savored political gossip.

Macmillan was a complicated character, a combination of cunning and vulnerability, deeply religious as well as ruthless. The grandson of an impoverished Scottish farmer who built a fortune as a book publisher, Harold had received all the advantages of an education at Eton and Oxford. In World War I, he was wounded five times, an experience that gave him unusual affinity with the working-class men who had served with him in the trenches, along with a measure of survivor's guilt.

He vaulted into the aristocracy when he married the third daughter of the 9th Duke of Devonshire, Lady Dorothy Cavendish, who tormented him by conducting a decades-long affair with Robert Boothby, a flamboyant and amusing bisexual politician. The relationship was an open secret ("We all knew about it," the Queen Mother years later told her friend Woodrow Wyatt, a conservative columnist for *The Times* and *News of the World*) that made Macmillan's humiliation even more agonizing. At the beginning, he suffered a nervous breakdown, and over time he coped by developing "a mask of impenetrable calm." Yet behind what U.S. ambassador David Bruce called a "Victorian languor," Macmillan was capable of "force" and "determination," as well as "swift action."

More at ease in the like-minded company around the bar at White's, the men's club on St. James's Street, he nevertheless quickly warmed to the Queen, a different sort of woman from his social acquaintances, with an intelligence and detailed mastery of domestic and foreign policy issues that astonished him from the outset. He readily took advantage of her total discretion and maternal kindness, describing her as "a great support, because she is the one person you can talk to."

Butler, the veteran lieutenant who made the Tuesday evening trip to Buckingham Palace when Macmillan was traveling abroad, held a similar view of her gifts as an interlocutor. "She never reacted excessively," he later said. "She never used a phrase carelessly. She would never give away an opinion early on in the conversation." Rather, she would solicit an opinion and "listen to it right through."

In his nearly seven years in office, Macmillan and Elizabeth II had a genuine working partnership. He frequently sent her long letters filled with appraisals of world leaders and confessions about his setbacks, as well as droll vignettes and grim prognostications.The Queen dispatched handwritten replies that were unfailingly encouraging and appreciative. Macmillan was taken with her informality and her sense of fun. Like many others, he wished she could "be made to smile more" in public. On learning of his reaction, she remarked that she "had always assumed people wanted her to look solemn most of the time."

After a hiatus of six years, the thirty-one-year-old sovereign was now keen to have more children, as was her husband. Dickie Mountbatten blamed the delay on Philip's anger over the Queen's rejection of his family name after the accession. But by her own account, she had postponed her dream of having a large family primarily because she wanted to concentrate on establishing herself as an effective monarch.

During a visit to Buckingham Palace in May 1957, Eleanor Roosevelt met with Elizabeth II for nearly an hour the day after Prince Charles had undergone a tonsillectomy. The former first lady found her to be "just as calm and composed as if she did not have a very unhappy little boy on her mind." The Queen reported that Charles had already been fed ice cream to soothe his painful throat, yet it was 6:30 in the evening, and she was compelled to entertain the widow of a former U.S. president rather than sit at the bedside of her eight-year-old son.

While the Queen certainly loved her children, she had fallen into professional habits that kept her apart from them much of the time. They benefited from nurturing nannies — for Charles in particular, Mabel Anderson was a "haven of security" — and a doting grandmother. But because of her dogged devotion to duty, amplified by her natural inhibitions and aversion to confrontation,

Elizabeth II had missed out on many maternal challenges as well as satisfactions. "She let things go," said Gay Charteris. "She did have work every day. It was easier to go back to that than children having tantrums. She always had the excuse of the red boxes." An iconic 1957 photograph taken by Princess Margaret's future husband, Antony Armstrong-Jones, inadvertently crystallized the distance between the royal parents and their children. It shows Elizabeth II and Philip leaning on a stone bridge in the gardens of Buckingham Palace, gazing with admiration at Anne and Charles sitting on a rock below, reading a book.

The downside of the Queen's approach to motherhood had been clear to Clarissa Eden during a stay at Windsor Castle in April 1955 when she and her husband joined the royal family for a picnic. Six-year-old Charles flopped onto Anthony Eden's chair, prompting the Queen to tell the boy to move. When he refused, she asked him again, "because it is the prime minister's cushion and he is tired." But the young prince wouldn't budge. Then when Charles wouldn't eat his food because he hadn't washed his hands, the Queen Mother indulged him by saying, "Oh I do understand the feeling. Put some water in a saucer for him." Clarissa Eden was mildly amused by the prince's spoiled behavior, but surprised that the Queen "didn't say, 'Come on Charles, get up,' but I suppose she doesn't like scenes at all cost."

On that particular spring afternoon Philip, the resident disciplinarian, was enjoying himself on the nearby lake in a flat-bottomed punt. If the Queen erred toward leniency, her husband was often too tough. In his role as head of the family — "the natural state of things," in the view of Elizabeth II — he enforced the rules, insisting, for example, that Charles make his bed each morning and arrive punctually for breakfast. Philip called all the shots for the heir apparent, who was in many ways markedly different from his father: diffident, insecure, introspective, and athletically awkward. From an early age he was, in the words of the Queen Mother, "a very gentle boy, with a very kind heart." Although two years her brother's junior, Princess Anne was a much sturdier character: self-confident, rigorous, and assertive like Philip.

The most important decision for Charles concerned his education. (As was traditional among the upper classes, Anne would continue to be taught by a governess until she was ready for boarding school at age thirteen.) In an effort to create a semblance of normal life, the duke and Queen decided to send their son to a private primary school — the first ever for an heir apparent. Philip selected Hill House School in London, a five-year-old academy founded on Plutarch's credo that a child's mind was "not a vessel to be filled but a fire to be kindled." After Charles's years in the nursery, being in a classroom with other boys was a novelty, and he was exposed to such leveling experiences as sweeping the floors and riding a bus to the athletic fields. But Charles had only one year in which the embers barely began to glow before his parents packed him off in the autumn of 1957, two months before his ninth birthday — the year when upper-class boys customarily went to boarding school — to his father's alma mater, Cheam School in Hampshire.

Philip chose a school that conformed to his vision of educating the "whole" child. But he also saw his mission to toughen up his son's apparent softness. Describing his rationale years later, the duke wrote, "Children may be indulged at home, but school is expected to be a Spartan and disciplined experience in the process of developing into self-controlled, considerate and independent adults."

From the moment he entered his dormitory, Charles was miserable. Although over the following five years he would adjust to the strict regimen and coexist with more than eighty boys in the classroom and on the playing fields, he always remained slightly apart, pining for the distant solace of home. Explaining his inability to make many friends, he later said, "I always preferred my own company, or just a one to one."

He became even more self-conscious about his singular position when at the end of his first year his mother gave him the title Prince of Wales — the most vivid symbol of his place in the royal succession. He had no idea what was coming as he and several other boys met in the headmaster's study during the summer of 1958 to watch the telecast of the Queen's message closing the Commonwealth Games in Cardiff — the quadrennial sporting competition sponsored by member nations. When she made the momentous announcement, Charles cringed with embarrassment as the crowds on the small screen cheered, "God Bless the Prince of Wales."

His parents were well aware of his unhappiness at school; the Queen even wrote of her son's "dread" on returning to Cheam after a holiday. But they believed in the need for a stiff upper lip, and the Queen deflected her son's complaints to her husband. With his brusque manner and tendency to criticize rather than encourage, Philip was notably unsympathetic, which drove an ever-widening wedge between father and son.

As a practical matter, boarding school made sense for Charles given the busy schedules of the Queen and Prince Philip. It also kept him away from the prying eyes of the press. Until then, coverage of the monarch in newspapers and magazines — and in the hushed and impeccable voices of the British Broadcasting Corporation — had been reliably deferential to the Queen, according her praise verging on adoration while directing episodes of sensationalism at others such as her husband and her sister. The press was now for the first time publishing articles critical of Elizabeth II and her closest advisers.

In the usually slow month of August 1957, when the Queen and her court had decamped for their annual holiday in the Scottish Highlands, an obscure publication called *National and English Review* ran a piece called "The Monarch Today" by the magazine's editor, thirty-three-year-old John Grigg, the 2nd Baron Altrincham. He was a contrarian Tory who had already attracted attention for campaigning against his fellow hereditary peers who sat in Parliament's House of Lords, many of whom he said were "not necessarily fitted to serve." He had also advocated the ordination of women in the Anglican Church, and fiercely criticized Anthony Eden's Suez invasion.

Now he was taking aim at those who served — or rather in his view failed to serve — the monarchy, which he said he supported. His title gave him instant credibility, as did his education at Eton and Oxford and his service as an officer in the Grenadier Guards — all spawning grounds for the Buckingham Palace courtier class. Altrincham denounced those advisers as a "tight little enclave" of "tweedy" aristocrats who filled the Queen's official speeches with platitudes. "The personality conveyed by the utterances which are put into her mouth," he wrote, "is that of a priggish schoolgirl," preventing her from coming into her own "as an independent and distinctive character." Altrincham urged the royal family to surround itself with a more racially and socially diverse group, creating a "truly classless and Commonwealth court" that could more imaginatively help the Queen achieve the "seemingly impossible task of being at once ordinary and extraordinary."

This line of criticism echoed a little-noticed essay by journalist and broadcaster Malcolm Muggeridge in the *New Statesman* two years earlier. Prompted by the media circus created by Princess Margaret's drama with Peter Townsend, Muggeridge had warned in October 1955 of the dangers of overexposure in the press. He presciently advised the royal family to install an "efficient public relations set-up" to replace "rather ludicrous courtiers" in an effort to control the press and "check some of the worst abuses." Better advisers, he wrote, would help the royal family "prevent themselves and their lives from becoming a sort of royal soap opera." Muggeridge, a clever polemicist, offered this sound advice in a restrained and respectful way. His most provocative observation was that the monarchy had "become a kind of *ersatz* religion," and he suggested that the British royal family might consider the Scandinavian approach of living "simply and unaffectedly among their subjects."

Altrincham's like-minded analysis might have attracted little more than raised eyebrows among the 4,500 readers of his journal had he not had the temerity to attack the Queen personally for her "debutante stamp" and her "woefully inadequate training" for the job of sovereign. " 'Crawfie,' Sir Henry Marten, the London season, the race-course, the grouse-moor, canasta and the occasional royal tour," he wrote, "would not have been good enough for Elizabeth I!"

What's more, he singled out Elizabeth II's "style of speaking, which is frankly 'a pain in the neck.' Like her mother, she appears to be unable to string even a few sentences together without a written text. . . . Even if the Queen feels compelled to read all her speeches, great and small, she must at least improve her method of reading them. With practice, even a prepared speech can be given an air of spontaneity." In the spirit of what he described as "loyal and constructive criticism," Altrincham observed that once she had "lost the bloom of youth," her reputation would depend primarily on her personality. "She will have to say things which people can remember," he wrote, "and do things which will make people sit up and take notice."

His words drew a torrent of indignant criticism in the press and within the Establishment. The tabloids ran banner headlines about the "attack" on the Queen. *The Sunday Times* called Altrincham a cad and a coward, and Henry Fairlie wrote in the *Mail* that the Queen's critic dared "to pit his infinitely tiny and temporary mind against the accumulated experience of centuries." Geoffrey Fisher, the Archbishop of Canterbury, dismissed Altrincham as "a very silly man." B. K. Burbidge of the League of Empire Loyalists slapped Altrincham in the face during an encounter on a London street. The magistrate who fined Burbidge one pound for the assault couldn't help sympathizing with the man's anger, saying that "95 per cent of the population of this country are disgusted and offended by what was written."

Inside the Palace, the essay was taken as constructive criticism. Martin Charteris privately described it as a "real watershed for the post-war monarchy" and said the author had performed a "terrific service." By some accounts, Prince Philip — no fan of crusty courtiers — felt the same way. With help from her husband and various professionals such as the BBC's David Attenborough and Antony Craxton, a friend of Philip's from Gordonstoun days, the Queen improved her delivery of speeches, mainly by lowering her voice and smoothing out her clipped accent. But she continued to read her prepared scripts rather than risk violating her neutral position as monarch with a misspoken word. Contrary to Altrincham's prediction, even after she had lost her youthful bloom, the public respected her stolid style, along with her self-effacing refusal to "make people sit up and take notice."

Charteris's gratitude for Altrincham's wake-up call reflected other ways the Queen adapted to the times, democratizing some of her activities and eventually diversifying her staff. The following year marked the last of the elitist "presentation parties" for debutantes at Buckingham Palace, an antiquated upper-class ritual dating back to the court of George III, to be replaced by additional royal garden parties open to a wider spectrum of people.

While these changes were beginning to take shape behind the scenes, Malcolm Muggeridge added to the imbroglio in October 1957 by writing an essay titled "Does England Really Need a Queen?" in the American weekly magazine *The Saturday Evening Post*. He not only expanded his earlier themes of "royal soap opera," he raised the ante with his sarcastic tone and blunt criticism of the Queen and those who revered her.

He reported that "those who mix socially with the royal family" are the most "contemptuously facetious" about the Queen. "It is the duchesses, not shop assistants," he wrote, "who find the Queen dowdy, frumpish and banal." He said the Queen fulfilled her duties with "a certain sleep-walking quality about the gestures, movements and ceremonial." Worse still, she was "a generator of snobbishness and a focus of sycophancy."

Muggeridge got an even more vehement pummeling in the press than Altrincham. He was harassed on the street, his house was vandalized, and he received vitriolic hate mail, some of which contained excrement and razor blades. The BBC even temporarily banned him from its airwaves. When he returned, he became one of the network's preeminent broadcasters.

One reason for the intensity of the reaction was the article's intentional timing to coincide with the Queen's much anticipated visit to North America. Arriving in Canada on October 12 for a five-day visit, she made her first live television broadcast, speaking alternately in English and French to an audience of fourteen million out of Canada's 16.5 million population. She used a TelePrompTer for the first time, which enabled her to look straight into the camera. She came across as "shy, a bit bashful and sometimes awkward," but endearing because her performance "was so human," according to *The New York Times*.

Perhaps the criticisms of Altrincham and Muggeridge had already sunk in, because she uncharacteristically began her seven-minute speech by telling her viewers, "I want to talk to you more personally." She went on to say, in almost confidential fashion, "There are long periods when life seems a small dull round, a petty business with no point, and then suddenly we are caught up in some great event which gives us a glimpse of the solid and durable foundations of our existence."

The following day she was the first sovereign to open the Canadian parliament. So Canadians could feel they were "taking part in a piece of Canada's history," she also agreed to television coverage of her speech from the throne in Ottawa's

Senate chamber.

The Queen was especially looking forward to her second trip to America. Writing to Anthony Eden, she said, "there does seem to be a much closer feeling between the U.S. and ourselves, especially since the Russian satellite [Sputnik] has come to shake everyone about their views on Russian scientific progress!" Unlike her lightning visit in 1951, this would be a full-dress affair: six days in Washington, New York, and Jamestown, Virginia, where she would celebrate the 350th anniversary of the founding of the first British colony in America.

She had an affectionate relationship with the sixty-seven-year-old American president that dated back to World War II when Eisenhower was in London as Supreme Allied Commander. He had enjoyed a "devoted friendship" with her parents, and he liked to recount how they had once arranged for him to have a special tour of the private areas of Windsor Castle. To ensure the general's privacy, they had decided to remain in their apartments. But on the appointed day George VI had forgotten, and he and his family were on a terrace above the rose garden having tea with Margaret Rhodes at a table covered to the ground with a white tablecloth. As Eisenhower and his group approached, the King knew that their presence would stop the tour. "We all dived under the table and hid," the Queen said years later. "If [Eisenhower] and his party had looked up . . . they would have seen a table shaking from the effect of the concerted and uncontrollable giggles of those sheltering beneath it," recalled Margaret Rhodes. When George VI later recounted the story to Eisenhower, the general "was so staggered by the King of England hiding," said Elizabeth II.

A crowd of ten thousand greeted the Queen and duke on their arrival in Virginia on October 16 for a day-long celebration in Jamestown and Williamsburg. They were accompanied by an entourage of sixty-six, including the British foreign secretary, Selwyn Lloyd. In Williamsburg the Queen gave a brief speech from a balcony at the College of William and Mary, praising the "enlightened and skilled statesmen" who founded the American republic. "Lord what's-his-name was way off base," wrote *The Washington Post.* "She is no orator, but those who heard her today thought that there was a nice lilt to her voice."

The following morning they flew to Washington on Eisenhower's aircraft, the *Columbine III,* a swift and sleek propeller plane with four powerful engines on its long wings. As they waited to take off, Philip immersed himself in the sports section of the newspaper while Elizabeth II unlocked her monogrammed leather writing case with a small gold key and began writing postcards to her children. "Philip?" she suddenly said. Her husband kept reading. "Philip!" she repeated. He glanced up, startled. "Which engines do they start first on a big plane like this?" Her husband looked momentarily perplexed. "Come on now," she said with a laugh. "Don't wait until they actually *start* them, Philip!" He offered a guess, which turned out to be correct. (They went in sequence, first on one wing from the inner engine to the outer, then the inner followed by the outer on the other wing.) "He was flustered," recalled Ruth Buchanan, wife of Wiley T. Buchanan, Jr., Eisenhower's chief of protocol, who sat nearby. "It was so like what an ordinary wife would do when her husband wasn't paying attention."

Riding into the capital with the president and his wife, Mamie, in a bubble-top limousine accompanied by sixteen bands, they were cheered along the route by more than a million people who were undaunted by intermittent rain showers. The royal couple spent their four nights in the most elegant guest quarters in the recently renovated White House — the Rose Suite furnished in Federal style for the Queen (later the Queens' Bedroom and Sitting Room, named in honor of all its royal guests) and the Lincoln Bedroom, with its eight-foot-long carved rosewood bed, for the Duke of Edinburgh.

Much of the visit was given over to the usual receptions, formal dinners at the White House and British embassy (complete with gold plates flown over from Buckingham Palace), and tours of local sights, several of which offered unguarded glimpses of the Queen, described in news accounts as "the little British sovereign" or "the little monarch."

It was evident to Ruth Buchanan that the Queen was "very certain, and very comfortable in her role. But she didn't let the barrier down. She would maintain a stance, and she was very much in control of what she did, although she did laugh at my husband's jokes." Once when Buchanan was waiting for her husband to escort the royal couple to their limousine, "I could hear her guffawing. You didn't realize she had that hearty laugh. But the minute she rounded the corner and saw us, she just straightened up."

British ambassador Harold Caccia threw a garden party for two thousand under five tents lined with fiberglass that shimmered like silk, preceded by a more exclusive meeting with eighty diplomats and their wives. During a tour of the National Gallery, the Queen confessed to its director, John Walker, that she had recently longed to buy a Monet at a London auction, but couldn't afford the "staggering amount."

Vice President Richard Nixon treated the royal couple to a luncheon with ninety-six guests in the orchid-bedecked old Supreme Court chamber in the Capitol. It was their first encounter with the incisive but socially awkward vice president. Perhaps taking note of the recent criticism of the Queen, Nixon talked to her about speaking techniques. The next day he even sent her a book with some "rather startling ideas" that he thought could be helpful: *The Art of Readable Writing,* by noted language expert Dr. Rudolf Flesch, an advocate of "plain talk."

On the third day the Queen indulged in some unusual departures from the normal run of activities. She had specifically asked to see an American football "match," as she put it, so the White House arranged for her to sit in a "royal box" at the fifty yard line at the University of Maryland's Byrd Stadium for a game against the University of North Carolina. On the way she spotted a Giant supermarket and asked if a visit might be arranged so she "could see how American housewives shop for food."

To the cheers of 43,000 spectators, the Queen

walked onto the field to chat with two opposing players, both strapping lads in crew cuts. Dressed in a $15,000 mink coat given to her by Mutation Mink Breeders Association, a group of American fur farmers, she watched the game intently but seemed "perturbed" whenever the players threw blocks. It was a quintessential American display: cheerleaders doing cartwheels, high-stepping drum majorettes, marching bands, and North Carolina girls costumed in large cigarette packs covering their heads and torsos, dancing as an announcer boasted about their state's "parade of industries."

While the royal pair was being entertained at halftime, security men raced back to the supermarket to arrange for a visit on the fly. After Maryland's 21–7 victory, the motorcade arrived at the Queenstown Shopping Center at 5 P.M., to the amazement of hundreds of shoppers. Elizabeth II and Philip had never before seen a supermarket, a phenomenon then unknown in Britain, and their visit was noteworthy for its spontaneity and novelty.

With the curiosity of anthropologists and an informality they had not displayed publicly in Britain, they spent fifteen minutes shaking hands, quizzing customers, and inspecting the contents of shopping carts. "How nice that you can bring your children along," said Elizabeth II, nodding toward the little seat in one housewife's cart. Queen and consort were amazed not only at the quantities of food but the range of products — clothing, stationery, toiletries, even Halloween costumes. She took a particular interest in frozen chicken pot pies, while he nibbled on sample crackers with cheese and joked, "Good for mice!" They both heard about refrigeration techniques and were particularly intrigued by the checkout counters, which cashier David Ferris explained as the monarch walked through the lane. "Thank you for the tour," the Queen said to supermarket manager Donald D'Avanzo. "I enjoyed it very much." D'Avanzo announced afterward that he had been "amazed and scared. . . . It was the greatest thing that ever happened to me."

On their final day in Washington, the Queen and Philip made their only private visit of the entire tour, a sunny drive out to Virginia so she could inspect eighteen yearlings at the Middleburg Training Track. She spent nearly an hour looking at the horses and talking to the owners and their trainers. Elizabeth II's host was the sportsman and philanthropist Paul Mellon, a friend and fellow thoroughbred breeder, who entertained her at tea that afternoon at his four-thousand-acre estate in nearby Upperville.

A far more exuberant welcome awaited Elizabeth II and Philip in New York City the next morning. The Queen had asked specifically to see Manhattan "as it should be approached" from the water, a vista she had been dreaming about since childhood. "Wheeeee!" she exclaimed as she caught her first glimpse of the glistening lower Manhattan skyline from the deck of a U.S. Army ferryboat. The sight reminded her, she said, of "a row of great jewels."

A crowd of 1.25 million lined the streets from Battery Park to City Hall and northward to the Waldorf-Astoria, waving British and American flags and cheering her motorcade with shouts of "Hi Liz" and "Hooray for Prince Phil," along with spontaneous bursts of "God Save the Queen." Driving along Wall Street in Eisenhower's bubble-top limousine, she and Philip passed through a blizzard of ticker tape, confetti, and torn-up phone books. As she looked up at the canyon of skyscrapers, she exclaimed, "I never realized they were so close together!"

She had only fifteen hours in the city — "a teaser," she admitted — to fulfill her wish list and shake some three thousand hands. Wearing a dark blue satin cocktail dress and close-fitting pink velvet hat, she addressed the representatives of eighty-two countries in the United Nations General Assembly. At the conclusion of her six-minute speech praising the organization's laudable ideals and urging all its member nations to persevere in the pursuit of peace, the audience of two thousand responded with "a thunderous standing ovation." Afterward, she had an hour-long tour of the five-year-old U.N. headquarters, asking at one point how the thirty-nine-story glass Secretariat building "kept standing up." During a reception with delegates, Philip talked to Soviet ambassador Andrei Gromyko about the recently launched Sputnik satellite that his wife had mentioned in her letter to Anthony Eden.

The royal couple used a Louis XV–style suite on the twenty-eighth floor of the Waldorf Towers as their temporary headquarters, and they were feted at two meals in the legendary hotel: a luncheon for 1,700 hosted by Mayor Robert Wagner, and a dinner for 4,500 given by the English-Speaking

Union and the Pilgrims of the United States, both groups committed to Anglo-American amity. In between, the Queen took in the "tremendous" view from the 102nd floor of the Empire State Building at twilight — another specific request — when "the evening sky was purple and the offices were still blazing, and the whole midtown skyline is composed of vast hanging sheets of exquisite lace," in the words of British writer Alistair Cooke.

As the white-tie banquet began in the grand ballroom, the punishing schedule was beginning to take its toll, even on an energetic thirty-one-year-old Queen. A closed-circuit television set up for the six adjoining banquet rooms gave guests an unusual view of Elizabeth II in her three-inch-high diamond tiara and evening gown glittering with pastel paillettes. She was never supposed to be filmed in the act of eating, but there she was, on the TV screens, fork in left hand, eating striped bass with champagne sauce, filet of beef with truffle sauce, beignet potatoes, string beans almandine, and Waldorf savarin au rhum. Guests could watch her follow strict mealtime protocol, talking for the first two courses to her partner on the left, former U.S. ambassador to Britain Lewis Douglas, then turning to the right at the main course to converse with Pilgrims president Hugh Bullock.

The New York Times noted that her speech was the "one time during the program . . . when the fatigue showed through. . . . She made no effort to force a smile . . . and although she stumbled over her text only once, her voice plainly showed it." Despite her somber demeanor, she warmly praised the dinner's two sponsors for their emphasis on the "common language and the heritage of history" between Britain and America, as well as their "conscious effort" to ensure that the two nations did not "take each other for granted."

She had one more stop that night, a Royal Commonwealth ball for another 4,500 guests at the Seventh Regiment Armory on Park Avenue. Protocol chief Wiley Buchanan marveled that despite her fatigue, she sat on the dais "straight as a ruler, not even touching the back of her chair." As the Queen and Philip made their way to a waiting limousine well after midnight, she stopped frequently to speak to war veterans. One aviator blinded in World War I tried to get up from his wheelchair to greet her. "She put a gentle hand on his shoulder and told him that he should not rise," recalled Buchanan. "She spoke to him for several moments, then moved on."

Buchanan had arranged for a light to be placed on the floor of the royal couple's car that was switched on for their drive to Idlewild Airport, illuminating the Queen's dress and tiara for the throngs of spectators lining the streets of Manhattan and Queens. Many of the women wore bathrobes and had curlers in their hair. "Philip," said Elizabeth II, "look at all those people in their nightclothes. *I* certainly wouldn't come out in *my* nightclothes to see anyone drive by, no matter who it was!"

By 2 A.M. the Queen and Philip were on board the *Seven Seas,* a BOAC DC-7, for their nearly fourteen-hour flight home. "You both have captivated the people of our country by your charm and graciousness," Eisenhower wrote in his farewell letter to the royal couple.

American and British papers pronounced the visit "extraordinarily successful" and a "tremendous American triumph." No one was more pleased than Prime Minister Harold Macmillan, who was due to follow his sovereign to Washington the next week for a round of meetings with Eisenhower. The Queen, Macmillan wrote in his diary, "has buried George III for good and all." But the British people felt left out as they read about her impromptu forays, not to mention the extensive television coverage she had permitted. "Why did she have to cross the Atlantic to become real?" wondered the London *Daily Herald*.

The Queen's new reliance on television was no accident, and her husband had much to do with the change. Given Philip's fascination with technology, it was only natural that he would see the potential of broadcasting for the monarchy. As early as November 1952 he had predicted that radio and television had "gone beyond the stage of being amusing and entertaining novelties." He was the first member of the royal family to host his own television program, a documentary about his Commonwealth tour featuring film he had shot.

From the time of the coronation, Elizabeth II had been wary of the intrusiveness of TV cameras. In her letter to Eden before her North American trip, she confessed her trepidation, saying, "Television is the worst of all, but I suppose when one gets used to it, it is not so terrible as at first sight." She had decided the previous summer to shift from radio and to televise her annual Christmas broadcast for the first time, on the twenty-fifth anniversary of the inaugural radio broadcast by her grandfather, King George V. Days before her departure to Canada, she had even practiced with a TelePrompTer in a makeshift studio in Buckingham Palace. Philip, who had urged her to use the device, acted as her "producer" as she read an old speech. When she sounded flat, he spent a few moments with her, and on the second run-through she was reported to be "more vivacious," nodding and smiling at appropriate moments.

The Canadian broadcast had been the Queen's dry run for her live telecast at 3 P.M. on December 25, but she was no less apprehensive. It was her sixth Christmas message, which from the beginning had been prepared without benefit of "advice" from the government — the one predictable occasion during the year when she can talk directly to the people. She always takes great trouble over this personal homily, which reaffirms her religious beliefs and sense of duty as she seeks to inspire others to adhere to high standards and do good works. The message typically incorporates ideas from her private secretaries, but it is mainly written in close collaboration with Philip over a period of months, often building on a specific theme that can be linked to events in the preceding year.

Philip took a particularly active role in the 1957 telecast, bringing in his friend at the BBC, Antony Craxton. They chose the Long Library at Sandringham for its excellent acoustics and set up a small desk in front of a cabinet filled with Christmas cards and family pictures. An arrangement of holly on the desk concealed a microphone, and two cameras were set up, each with a TelePrompTer.

dition to getting the knack of reading large
scrolling on a machine, the Queen studied an
instructional film made by BBC announcer Sylvia
Peters. Even after three rehearsals, Elizabeth II
told a guest at the staff holiday party at Windsor
Castle, "My husband seems to have found the secret of how to relax on television. I am still worried
because I have not found the secret yet." A few
days before the broadcast, Craxton spent forty-five
minutes with her, going over the script sentence by
sentence.

The Queen spoke for seven minutes, interrupt-
ing her eye contact with the audience by occasionally looking at her sheaf of papers and turning over
the pages periodically for effect. She smiled tentatively from time to time, and clasped her hands
for emphasis. Television could help her be less of
a "remote figure," she said, and make her annual
message to Britain and the Commonwealth "more
personal and direct." Yet she warned of the new
medium's dangers in the "speed at which things
are changing all around us," causing people to
"feel lost and unable to decide what to hold on to
and what to discard, how to take advantage of the
new life without losing the best of the old."

The "inventions" themselves weren't the problem, she added. Rather, "the trouble is caused
by unthinking people who carelessly throw away
ageless ideals as if they were old and outworn ma-
chinery." To uphold endangered "fundamental
principles," she called for a "special kind of courage . . . which makes us stand up for everything
we know is right, everything that is true and honest. We need the kind of courage that can with-

stand the subtle corruption of the cynics so that we can show the world that we are not afraid of the future."

"I cannot lead you into battle," Elizabeth II said. "But I can do something else. I can give you my heart, and my devotion to these old islands and to all the peoples of our brotherhood of nations." As she signed off with her Christmas wishes, she glanced quickly toward her husband standing behind one of the cameras and flashed a luminous smile at her viewers.

An estimated thirty million people tuned in, and the press, especially in the United States, hailed her performance as an effective reply to her critics, a "post-Altrincham royal speech." Her manner, said *The New York Times,* was "unstrained and natural." "All her charm, grace and simplicity were there," wrote a London *Daily Express* commentator. "I was moved . . . to the point of tears." Harry Truman called her reference to the "unthinking people" a "lovely statement. We haven't lost the ideals, but we've certainly been neglecting them."

No Christmas message in the five decades since has had such an impact, or conveyed such surprisingly dark undertones. "The final draft was, in fact, Prince Philip's," Craxton wrote afterward. But it was also a product of ideas exchanged between the Queen and her husband. She has always taken care to avoid saying anything she does not believe, declining even to use the word "very" unless she means "very." Her pledge of fealty to her people and plea to "stand up for what we believe to be right" were undeniably authentic, as were the deep spiritual threads running through the message.

209

■ ■ ■ ■

A year later the government permitted the State Opening of Parliament to be televised for the first time. (It had declined to do so in 1957 when the Queen announced a genuine reform originated by Macmillan and his ministers to create life peers, thereby admitting women to the House of Lords for the first time in their own right.) One of the great British spectacles, the opening of Parliament is as much a made-for-television phenomenon as any event in the royal calendar. It also serves as a reminder of the Queen's place as the "Crown in Parliament" by gathering the House of Commons, the House of Lords, and the sovereign in one place, as the Queen reads out the government's legislative program.

The ceremony itself draws on centuries of tradition and ageless rituals. The setting is always the House of Lords chamber, with its richly ornamented high ceilings, stained glass windows, and elaborately carved wood.

The day before the ceremony, the Imperial State Crown and seventeenth-century Sword of State are brought from the Tower of London to Buckingham Palace, where the Queen has a chance to get reaccustomed to having nearly three pounds sitting on her head. In the evening she often works at her desk wearing the purple velvet crown glittering with three thousand diamonds; one year her butler noted that she was wearing pink mule slippers as well.

On the morning of the opening, a horse-drawn carriage carries the crown and Sword of State, along with the Cap of Maintenance, a crimson velvet hat trimmed with white ermine, down the Mall to the Houses of Parliament. A second coach transports the gold maces. The Queen calls these symbols of royal power "the working pieces of kit," and she makes certain that the front of the crown, with its huge Black Prince's Ruby and Cullinan II diamond, faces forward in the carriage. "There is one thing to remember," she said with a twinkle to Crown Jeweler David Thomas before he made his first trip to the Palace of Westminster with the priceless cargo. "The horses are always in the front of the carriage."

Wearing a long white gown, jeweled Garter collar, elbow-length gloves, and diamond tiara, she and Prince Philip, as always in the uniform of Admiral of the Fleet, travel in the horse-drawn Irish State Coach to the Palace of Westminster with her Household Cavalry escort. In the Robing Room, adorned with frescoes depicting the Arthurian legend, she puts on her eighteen-foot-long scarlet velvet robe of state and her crown.

The House of Lords chamber is invariably packed, a tableau vivant of peers in their red robes with white fur collars (including, for the first time in 1958, fifteen recently appointed life peers, four of them women), bewigged justices draped in black and clustered on the large red hassock called the Woolsack, military officers, ecclesiastics, and ambassadors in white tie.

The processional is led by men with quaint medieval titles such as Maltravers Herald Extraordinary, Clarenceaux King of Arms, and Rouge Dragon Pursuivant, all decked out in gold-encrusted scarlet tabards, knee breeches, and silk stockings. Lining the route are the Queen's bodyguards, the Gentlemen at Arms in helmets waving swan plumes, and the Yeomen of the Guard (also known as Beefeaters), wearing crimson and gold knee-length tunics, crimson knee breeches, white neck ruffs, and black Tudor bonnets.

Elizabeth II, attended by four page boys and two of her ladies-in-waiting, with Prince Philip clasping her raised left hand, makes a stately progress along the Royal Gallery into the chamber. She is preceded by two dignitaries holding the sword and the cap, which dangles from a long stick, as well as two Great Officers of State, the Earl Marshal and Lord Great Chamberlain, walking backward. On the dot of 11:30 A.M., she arranges herself on her ornately gilded throne beneath a golden canopy, with Philip seated to her left, several inches lower.

Black Rod, an official representing the Queen, strides to the House of Commons, where the door is vigorously slammed in his face to show the independence of the lower house. (No monarch has been permitted in the House of Commons since 1642, when King Charles I barged in and tried to arrest five members.) After three loud knocks with his ebony staff, Black Rod is admitted to the chamber, where he commands the members to "attend Her Majesty immediately in the House of Peers." Led by the prime minister, his cabinet, and the leader of the opposition, the members of Parliament crowd behind the Bar of the House of Lords, a wooden barrier near the entrance, where they are required to stand. Squeezed into a space roughly eighteen by twelve feet, the politicians bring an earthy and slightly raffish touch to the proceedings, "looking like culprits in a law court," wrote American ambassador David Bruce.

The Lord Chancellor climbs the dais, reaches into a red silk bag, and hands the Queen the speech that has been prepared by the prime minister and his cabinet. Seldom taking more than fifteen minutes, she dutifully recites the government's legislative program for the coming year. "I think I have made the dullest and most boring speech of my life," she confided to Pietro Annigoni while sitting for him after the ceremony in 1969. "But it dealt with such dry material. One tries at least to put a little expression into one's voice, but it's not humanly possible to produce something even remotely lively." Wearing the heavy crown is as tiring as it looks. Hours afterward, "my neck is still feeling the effects," she once confessed.

At two minutes and ten seconds, her speech on October 28, 1958, was one of the shortest on record, with sentences she could actually read with conviction, mostly generalities about advancing the Commonwealth and supporting the United Nations and the Atlantic Alliance. She spoke of the historic significance of broadcasting the ceremony to enable "many millions of my subjects . . . to witness this renewal of the life of parliament." She mentioned as well her planned visit "with my dear husband" to Canada the following summer and later in the year to Ghana, which had declared its independence from Britain in 1957.

But before they were to leave for Ghana, Philip set off again on another goodwill tour aboard *Bri-*

tannia, spending four months visiting India, Pakistan, Singapore, Brunei, Borneo, Hong Kong, the Solomon, Gilbert, and Ellice Islands in the Pacific, Panama, the Bahamas, and Bermuda. He returned at the end of April 1959, and soon afterward Elizabeth II got pregnant at last. Some years later the rumor arose that Prince Andrew, the child from this pregnancy, was fathered during her husband's long absence by Henry Porchester, her good friend and fellow thoroughbred enthusiast. But given the timing of the baby's arrival in mid-February 1960, the conception had to have occurred during the preceding May when the Queen and Philip "were scarcely separated," according to subsequent research by gossip columnist Nigel Dempster, the repentant promoter of the original tale.

As soon as the Queen confirmed her condition, she sent Martin Charteris on a confidential mission. "I am going to have a baby, which I have been trying to do for some time," she told her assistant private secretary, "and that means I won't be able to go to Ghana as arranged. I want you to go and explain the situation to [President Kwame] Nkrumah and tell him to keep his mouth shut."

She and Philip went ahead with their six-week trip across fifteen thousand miles of Canada, which included stops in every province and territory. As part of the opening of the St. Lawrence Seaway with the United States, they invited the Eisenhowers to join them for luncheon aboard *Britannia* on June 26. Ten days later the royal couple touched down in Chicago for fourteen hours, and once again the president provided them with a limousine, this time a convertible. Mayor Richard Daley rolled the red carpet across Lake Shore Drive, introduced Elizabeth II to his seven children, and proclaimed, "Chicago is yours!" Eisenhower wrote the Queen that his chauffeur reported that "he had never witnessed greater enthusiasm among the crowds lining the streets."

She was suffering from morning sickness that she managed to conceal, although during her journey through the Yukon Territory she took to her bed for several days. Her press office said she had a minor stomach ailment, and once she had rested, she resumed her travels. A week after her return to London on August 1, the Palace announced that she was expecting, and she headed to Balmoral for her annual holiday.

Harold Macmillan, who had delayed calling an election until the Queen's return, used her as a lure to pressure Eisenhower to visit Britain as part of his planned world tour. The prime minister knew that a visit from the American president could help bolster his party's prospects in the coming campaign. When Eisenhower wavered, Macmillan sent word that if he bypassed the United Kingdom, "this will be an insult to the Queen." She had no intention of returning to London, so Eisenhower took up her invitation to spend two days at Balmoral.

Prince Philip met Ike, Mamie, and their son John at Aberdeen airport on August 28 and accompanied them to Balmoral. The presidential party quickly fell into the rhythms of the Highlands, socializing with the Queen's family as well as friends including the Earl of Westmorland, Lord and Lady Porchester, and Dominic Elliot, son of the 5th Earl of Minto and a friend of Princess Margaret.

"The Queen and Eisenhower got on famously," Elliot recalled. "The President was quite a character, a marvelous chap, and he fitted in very well." While Ike didn't join the men shooting out on the grouse moors, the Queen did treat him to a picnic luncheon near Loch Muick, including drop scones that she prepared on a griddle, drawing on the lessons she had learned from the cook at Windsor Castle during the war. He was so impressed that he asked for the recipe, and several months later she obliged, writing everything out in longhand and apologizing that the quantity was for sixteen people. "When there are fewer I generally put in less flour and milk," she wrote helpfully, adding that "the mixture needs a great deal of beating."

The Queen Mother gave the Eisenhowers a jolly cocktail party at Birkhall before they departed. The president declared the trip "perfect in every respect," and thanked the Queen in particular for her parting gift of grouse from the day's shoot. He and the prime minister had the birds for dinner the following evening at Chequers.

Macmillan and the Tories won a decisive victory six weeks later in the general election. The prime minister wrote the Queen, who was by then nearly five months pregnant, that there was no reason for her to return to London prematurely. Because of her condition, she missed the State Opening of Parliament, and the Lord Chancellor read the speech instead.

While her own trip to Ghana was necessarily postponed, Philip went as her representative in late November, in part to assuage Nkrumah, who was deeply disappointed by the loss of the sovereign's visit. Philip gave eight speeches in six days, ranging across promoting academic freedom in universities, encouraging scientific research, and inspiring young people to become doctors and nurses. His praise for the country's "great national awakening" went down well, and he promised to return with his wife in 1961.

Once the Queen hit the six-month mark in her pregnancy, she withdrew from her official duties. But one bit of unfinished business needed to be resolved. When Macmillan visited her at Sandringham in early January 1960, she told him that she needed to revisit the issue of her family name that had been irritating her husband since she decided in 1952 to use Windsor rather than her husband's Mountbatten. "The Queen only wishes (properly enough) to do something to please her husband — with whom she is desperately in love," the prime minister wrote in his diary. "What upsets me . . . is the Prince's almost brutal attitude to the Queen over all this." Somewhat cryptically he added, "I shall never forget what she said to me that Sunday night at Sandringham."

Macmillan left shortly afterward for a trip to Africa, leaving the resolution of the Queen's tricky family problem to Rab Butler, his deputy prime minister, and Lord Kilmuir, who served as the government's legal arbiter as the Lord Chancellor. Butler sent a telegram to Macmillan in Johannesburg on January 27 saying that the Queen had "absolutely set her heart" on making a change for Philip's sake. By one account, Butler confided to a friend that Elizabeth II had been "in tears."

Following discussions among her private secretaries and government ministers, a formula emerged in which the royal family would continue to be called "The House and Family of Windsor," but the Queen's "de-royalised" descendants — starting with any grandchildren who lacked the designation of "royal highness" — would adopt the surname "Mountbatten-Windsor." Those in the immediate line of succession, including all of the Queen's children, would continue to be called "Windsor." It seemed clear-cut, but thirteen years later Princess Anne, at the urging of Dickie and Prince Charles, would contravene the policy on her wedding day by signing the marriage register as "Mountbatten-Windsor."

Elizabeth II told Macmillan that the compromise was "a great load off her mind." She announced it in a statement on February 8 saying, "The Queen has had this in mind for a long time and it is close to her heart." On February 19, 1960, she gave birth to her second son at Buckingham Palace, with the usual crowds along the railings to cheer the news. In a gesture of wifely devotion, Elizabeth II named the boy after the father Philip had lost fifteen years earlier.

CHAPTER SEVEN
NEW BEGINNINGS

Elizabeth II was two months from her thirty-fourth birthday when she gave birth for the third time. Unlike the arrivals of Charles and Anne in the early years of her marriage, she now had the sovereign's obligations competing for her postpartum time. "Nothing, but *nothing* deflected her from duty," recalled assistant private secretary Sir Edward Ford. "She'd go into labor and have a baby, so we knew we weren't going to see her for a while. But within a very short time, twenty-four or forty-eight hours at most, she'd be asking whether there were any papers and would we care to send them up?"

Andrew Albert Christian Edward, second in the line of succession, was barely a week old when twenty-nine-year-old Princess Margaret seized the limelight by announcing her engagement to the prominent photographer Antony Armstrong-Jones, also twenty-nine. Since the bitter disappointment of her dashed romance with Peter Townsend more than four years earlier, the Queen's sister had cut a showy figure among London's smart set. Her hairstyles changed with her moods, and she displayed her curvy figure in flamboyant outfits featuring vivid colors and leg-revealing skirts. (Dismayed by her unaristocratic open-toed shoes, Nancy Mitford

Macmillan was enchanted by "those brightly shining eyes which are her chief beauty."

Elizabeth II with Harold Macmillan, her third prime minister, at Oxford University, November 1960. © Popperfoto/Getty Images

called her "Pigmy-Peep-a-toes.") A heavy smoker, Margaret was known for her ten-inch cigarette holders, and for drinking Famous Grouse whisky, often to excess.

While the Queen would engage people in conversation, Princess Margaret would *address* them in what museum director Roy Strong described as a "slightly explosive drawl." She was more insistent on formalities than the sovereign, rebuking friends when they unwittingly violated protocol with a word or a gesture. "If you missed the 'royal' in 'Your Royal Highness,' she would rip you to shreds," said one of her friends. "She would say, 'There are members of Arab states who are highnesses. I am a royal one.'" One slyly believable moment in the film *The Queen* had Helen Mirren's Elizabeth II remarking, "I don't measure the depth of a curtsy. . . . I leave that to my sister."

Since 1953 Princess Margaret had been enjoying a prolonged adolescence while living with her mother at Clarence House, where she often slept late after long evenings at parties — frequently exhausting the other guests, who knew it was impolite to leave before a member of the royal family. To the embarrassment of their friends, Margaret could be cavalier with her mother, walking into the room where she was watching television, for example, and changing the channel, or criticizing her food at a luncheon party. "You mustn't worry," the Queen Mother said to her friend Prudence Penn, who expressed concern about Margaret's rude treatment. "I'm quite used to it."

The Queen adopted a similarly phlegmatic approach, even when Margaret was an hour and a half late to her tenth anniversary party at Buckingham Palace. "I felt the Queen was not served well by her sister, who was not a good advertisement for the monarchy," said Patricia Brabourne. "The Queen dealt with it by acting in private as the sister giving support she needed and probably giving the hard advice that probably wasn't followed."

Margaret could also be affectionate and warmhearted — the "rare softness" that Peter Townsend had observed — as well as caring and kind, notably to those who were ill. She had a keen interest in theater and the performing arts, principally ballet. She enchanted her loyal friends with her quick wit and vivacity, enhanced by a sharp intelligence.

When Margaret fell in love with Tony Armstrong-Jones, it came as a relief to the Queen, who wanted above all for her sister to be happy. He was not an aristocrat but his background was privileged. His father, Ronald Armstrong-Jones, was a barrister with deep roots in Wales, and his beautiful mother, Anne Messel, came from a family of wealthy bankers who had made their original fortune in Germany before converting from Judaism to Christianity in London, a genealogical fact that the royal family chose to disregard. The Armstrong-Joneses had divorced when Tony was just five, and his mother had acquired aristocratic cachet when she married the Earl of Rosse. An education at Eton and Cambridge gave Tony entrée into upper-class circles where he found clients for his growing photography business.

He was several inches taller than tiny Margaret, and good-looking, with a dazzling smile and a hint of vulnerability from a slight limp caused by polio that he contracted at sixteen. Sophisticated and charming, he moved easily from the raffish world of artists and writers to the rarefied atmosphere of the Queen's court. Equally important, he could match wits with Margaret, and he shared her taste for the high life. He also captivated both the Queen Mother and the Queen, who offered him an earldom before the wedding. He initially declined the title, only to accept it the following year when he became the Earl of Snowdon (after the highest mountain in Wales) before Margaret gave birth to their first child, David, ensuring that the Queen's nephew would receive his own title — Viscount Linley — rather than being known as Mr. Armstrong-Jones.

Elizabeth II provided generously for the couple. Two days before their marriage, she and Prince Philip hosted a sumptuous court ball at Buckingham Palace, where the "whole atmosphere," wrote Noel Coward, conveyed "supreme grandeur without pomposity."

The wedding day on Friday, May 6, 1960, sparkled with sunshine. White banners bearing the initials A and M woven in gold fluttered over the Mall, where an estimated 100,000 people crowded the route to Westminster Abbey, resembling "endless, vivid herbaceous borders," wrote Coward. "The police were smiling, the Guards beaming, and the air tingled with excitement and the magic of spring."

Margaret was the image of a fairytale princess, dressed in an artfully simple gown of white silk organza, nominally a Norman Hartnell creation but in fact designed by Tony. The three-inch-high

Poltimore diamond tiara encircled her chignon and anchored her long silk tulle veil. Prince Philip walked his sister-in-law to the altar, where Tony waited, looking "pale" and "a bit tremulous." Eight bridesmaids aged six to twelve, led by nine-year-old Princess Anne, followed in floor-length white silk dresses.

Noel Coward watched the Queen, elegant in a pale blue gown and matching long-sleeved bolero jacket, "scowl a good deal," and wondered whether this "concealed sadness or bad temper." Close observers of Elizabeth II understood her expression meant she was straining to contain powerful emotions. "When she is deeply moved and tries to control it she looks like an angry thunder-cloud," wrote Labour politician Richard Crossman.

As with other royal spectaculars, the Duke of Norfolk organized the day's pageantry, and the BBC presented the first televised royal wedding ceremony. The Glass Coach — the traditional conveyance for royal brides for the previous five decades — transported the smiling couple back to Buckingham Palace, where they had a wedding breakfast for just 120 of the two thousand Abbey guests. The Queen gave her sister and brother-in-law *Britannia* for their six-week honeymoon. The £26,000 cost of the wedding was paid by the Queen Mother, who was in turn heavily subsidized by the Queen, although the Macmillan government picked up the £60,000 tab for the honeymoon. On their return to London, Margaret and Tony moved into a twenty-room apartment on four floors of Kensington Palace provided by the Queen and refurbished at a cost of £85,000,

£50,000 of which was allocated by the government's Ministry of Public Works to repair structural damage caused by bombs during the war.

Elizabeth II curtailed her foreign travel during her third child's first year in 1960 but otherwise remained fully engaged in affairs of state as Macmillan sent her a stream of letters and memos, mainly on foreign policy. For their weekly audiences, Macmillan provided clear agendas that gave her "an opportunity to consider the issues involved, and frame her own views (by custom, generally put in the form of questions) on them," wrote his biographer Alistair Horne. Macmillan's respect for the Queen deepened with time as he observed the consistent "assiduity with which she absorbed the vast mass of documents passed to her, and — even after so few years on the throne — her remarkable accumulation of political experience."

On his trip through Africa early in 1960, Macmillan had told the white South African parliament that "the wind of change is blowing through this continent, and whether we like it or not, this growth of national consciousness is a political fact." Scarcely a month later, South African police killed sixty-seven protesters in Sharpeville, and the biennial Commonwealth Prime Ministers' Conference in London threatened to fracture over apartheid.

After ten days of wrangling, Macmillan engineered a communiqué that mollified both black and white African leaders. "The official text is weak," he confided to the Queen, "but has the advantage of being agreed. . . . It does at least keep the Commonwealth for the time being from being broken up." But South Africa continued on its separatist path, and in October 1960 the white population voted overwhelmingly to abolish the monarchy in South Africa and establish a white-dominated republic.

One of the cornerstones of Macmillan's foreign policy was his campaign to secure Britain's admission to the Common Market, the European free trade zone consisting of France, West Germany, Italy, Belgium, Luxembourg, and the Netherlands, which he believed was essential for Britain's economic progress. The main power broker was French president Charles de Gaulle, who needed to be persuaded that the United Kingdom intended to be a full-fledged partner, since he suspected that the British had stronger affinities with the Commonwealth and the United States. To help with the sales pitch, Macmillan enlisted the Queen, who presided over a lavish three-day state visit for de Gaulle and his wife.

Twice a year since the beginning of her reign, Elizabeth II had been entertaining heads of state at Buckingham Palace according to strict protocol and unchanging rituals. (Later in the 1960s she would add Windsor Castle as an alternative setting.) These state visits were an essential part of her portfolio of duties, and she extended her legendary hospitality with the same care and attention to leaders of nations large and small. The British government would choose the head of state to be honored, but only the Queen could extend the invitation.

The visits typically lasted three days, and the head of state would stay in the most opulent accommodations in Buckingham Palace — the six-room Belgian Suite on the ground floor, overlooking the gardens. The set routine began with a ceremonial welcome (usually on a Tuesday) with a military guard of honor and marching bands followed by a carriage procession to the Palace for a luncheon with the royal family. After an exchange of gifts, the Queen presented an exhibit in the Picture Gallery featuring royal memorabilia of interest to the visiting head of state. In the evening she would host a white-tie state banquet for around 160 in the Palace ballroom. Over the next two days, the visiting leader would meet with officials in government and business, and on the second evening would host a "return" dinner in honor of Elizabeth II and Prince Philip.

For the French president, the British government added an extra layer of magnificence to the usual pomp and pageantry "to appeal to de Gaulle's sense of grandeur — and vanity." In addition to his impressive arrival on April 5 in an open carriage with the Queen and the state banquet including her effusive toast, he was heralded by trumpeters from the Household Cavalry before his address to the House of Lords and House of Commons in Westminster Hall, and he was treated to a gala at Covent Garden as well as a nighttime fireworks spectacular outside the Palace. De Gaulle, who could be a difficult dinner partner prone to speaking elliptically, later wrote that Elizabeth II was "well informed about everything, that her judgments on people and events were as clear-cut as they were thoughtful, that no one was more preoccupied by the cares and problems of our storm-tossed age."

As for Britain and the Common Market, he remained coyly noncommittal.

Shortly after the turn of 1961, the Queen resumed her travels, embarking with Philip on a five-week tour of India, Pakistan, Nepal, Iran, Cyprus, and Italy, missing the first birthday of Prince Andrew. Not long after her return in early March, Macmillan gave her his insights into America's new first couple, John Fitzgerald Kennedy and his glamorous young wife, Jacqueline. Jack Kennedy had been a familiar presence in England in the years before World War II when his father, Joseph P. Kennedy, had served as U.S. ambassador to the Court of St. James's (the official title of the American envoy to Britain). No modern American president before or since had such close connections to Britain as Jack Kennedy.

Nearly a decade older than Elizabeth II, Jack had been a college student in the late 1930s while she was still a child, so they hadn't known each other. But she had seen Joe Kennedy and his wife, Rose, on their visits to Windsor Castle and Buckingham Palace. The Queen revealed to Canadian prime minister Brian Mulroney the affection she had for JFK's mother, mentioning a time when a relative had died and she and Margaret had been confined to a small room while their parents received dignitaries. "Only Rose Kennedy came into the room and chatted with them," Mulroney recalled. "They were ignored by the other guests — and she remembered it some forty years later!"

Joe Kennedy had failed as ambassador, serving only two years before Franklin D. Roosevelt recalled him in November 1940. Kennedy had urged appeasing the Nazis and drew the scorn of the British for his cowardice when he retreated to an estate in the country during the Blitz. The humiliating performance of his father had "eaten into [JFK's] soul," in the view of the president's friend, the philosopher Isaiah Berlin. But rather than creating resentment, Kennedy's experiences in England as a young man deepened his affection for the country and its leaders, above all Winston Churchill, whom he regarded as "the greatest man he ever met."

Macmillan actively disliked Joe Kennedy and was initially dubious about his son, worrying that he was a "young cocky Irishman" and a "strange character" who could be "obstinate, sensitive, ruthless and highly sexed." Yet Dorothy Macmillan's nephew, Billy, the Marquess of Hartington, had been married to Jack Kennedy's sister Kathleen (both died in plane crashes in the 1940s), and this sharpened Macmillan's curiosity.

Following his first two encounters with Kennedy in March and April 1961, the sixty-six-year-old prime minister forged an instant bond with the forty-three-year-old president. "We seemed to be able (when alone) to talk freely and frankly to each other," Macmillan later wrote, "and to *laugh* (a vital thing) at our advisers and ourselves." He reported to the Queen that Kennedy had "surrounded himself with a large retinue of highly intelligent men."

At Kennedy's suggestion, Macmillan appointed as British ambassador to the United States forty-two-year-old Sir William David Ormsby Gore, a friend of Jack's since prewar days, and first cousin to Billy Hartington. Gore's sister Katharine was also married to Macmillan's son Maurice, further sealing what became known as the "special relationship within a special relationship." Kennedy named as his ambassador to the Court of St. James's sixty-three-year-old David K. E. Bruce, a highly regarded veteran of the diplomatic corps who had previously headed the embassies in France and West Germany. Bruce's first wife, Ailsa, was the sister of Paul Mellon, the Queen's closest American friend in horse racing circles. At ease in plus fours on the shooting field and in jodhpurs riding to hounds, Bruce melded perfectly with the Queen's social set. Known among his peers as a "professional statesman," he won the confidence of senior members of the royal household as well as top politicians, and would serve for eight years, the longest tenure of an American ambassador in London.

In June 1961 the first couple visited London after they had dazzled the French on a swing through Paris, and JFK had faced a truculent and intransigent Nikita Khrushchev during a sobering two-day meeting in Vienna that put Cold War tensions between the United States and the Soviet Union in sharp relief. Billed as a private stopover to attend the christening of the daughter of Jackie's sister, Lee Radziwill, and her husband, Stas, the real purpose was for Jack to unburden himself to Macmillan about his discussions with Khrushchev. The prime minister would later report to the Queen that Kennedy had been "completely overwhelmed by the ruthlessness and barbarity of the Russian premier."

The evening after the christening, the Queen

and Prince Philip gave a dinner for the Kennedys at Buckingham Palace — the first time an American president had dined there since 1918 when Woodrow Wilson was entertained by King George V. The royal couple "put on a good show in the beautiful reception rooms," David Bruce wrote afterward. Yet the thirty-one-year-old first lady, who eight years earlier had written with confident insouciance about the coronation, now felt uneasy with the thirty-five-year-old Queen, whom she dismissed as "pretty heavy going." "I think [she] resented me," Jackie told author Gore Vidal. "Philip was nice, but nervous. One felt absolutely no relationship between them."

The first lady was equally indiscreet with photographer Cecil Beaton. While conceding that "they were all tremendously kind and nice," Jackie said that she "was not impressed by the flowers or the furnishings of the apartments at Buckingham Palace, or by the Queen's dark-blue tulle dress and shoulder straps, or her flat hairstyle." The first lady recounted to Vidal that "the Queen was human only once." Jackie had complained about the pressures of being on tour in Canada, causing the Queen to throw her a conspiratorial glance and reply cryptically, "One gets crafty after a while and learns how to save oneself."

Later in the year during her rescheduled state visit to Ghana, Elizabeth II proved her worth to the American president in an unanticipated way. Following the African country's independence from Britain in 1957, newly elected president Kwame Nkrumah had appeared to be an enlightened leader, hospitable to Western political and business interests and committed to multiracialism. He had an Egyptian wife who was a Coptic Christian, and several of his top aides were English, including an army captain as his secretary and a woman who served as his aide and amanuensis.

But in the two years since the Queen's visit was postponed, Nkrumah had hardened into a dictator presiding over what Winston Churchill character- ized as a "corrupt and tyrannical regime," im- prisoning hundreds of members of the opposition without trial, expelling British officers and advis- ers, and railing against Britain in speeches. Just as ominously, after a visit to Moscow in September 1961, Nkrumah had edged toward an alliance with the Soviet Union and a possible departure from the Commonwealth.

Despite the specter of violence triggered by dem- onstrations, labor unrest, and death threats against Nkrumah, Macmillan advised the Queen to pro- ceed with her travel plans for mid-November. At the same time, he urged Kennedy to help thwart Soviet designs on Ghana by offering the country millions of dollars for the Volta Dam project, a request the American president held in abeyance. Members of Parliament and some elements in the press pushed for the Queen to cancel the trip. Churchill wrote to Macmillan of the "widespread uneasiness both over the physical safety of the Queen and perhaps more, because the visit would seem to endorse a regime . . . which is thoroughly authoritarian." Macmillan replied that day, say- ing that "her wish is to go. This is natural with so courageous a personality."

The Queen was profoundly irritated by the pressure from the "fainthearts in Parliament and the press. . . . How silly I should look if I was scared to visit Ghana and then Khrushchev went and had a good reception." Even after bombs exploded in Accra five days before her trip was to begin, she refused to waver.

She melted Nkrumah, with whom she was photographed dancing at a state ball, and she charmed the Ghanaian press, who called her "the greatest Socialist monarch in the world." The people of Ghana "fell for her — went out of their minds for her," said the BBC's Audrey Russell. "In that open car . . . she didn't bat an eyelid — Nkrumah next to her. You just saw the Queen very calm, very poised — not smiling too much — just right." Afterward Elizabeth II sized up Nkrumah with uncanny precision in a letter to her friend Henry Porchester, expressing surprise at "how muddled his views on the world seemed to be, and how naïve and vainglorious were his ambitions for himself and his country," along with her dismay at his "short term perspective" and inability to "look beyond his own lifetime."

On her return to London in late November, Macmillan called Kennedy and said, "I have risked my Queen. You must risk your money!" JFK responded that he would meet Elizabeth II's "brave contribution" with his own, and less than two weeks later he announced the U.S. financing of the Volta Dam. With that, the fear of Ghana's departure from the Commonwealth abated.

The Queen did not see Jack Kennedy again, although Jackie and Lee came through London in March 1962 on the way home from India and Pak-

233

istan. This time Elizabeth II gave the American sisters a Buckingham Palace luncheon with the Macmillans, Andrew Devonshire (the 11th Duke), Michael Adeane, Master of the Household Patrick Plunket, and other guests. Unlike the previous visit, the first lady and the Queen seemed to click. "It was a great pleasure to meet Mrs. Kennedy again," Elizabeth II wrote to JFK. "I hope her Pakistan horse [a bay gelding named Sardar given her by President Mohammad Ayub Khan] will be a success — please tell her that mine became very excited by jumping with the children's ponies in the holidays, so I hope hers will be calmer!"

That spring it was time for Prince Charles to take the next step in his education after his final year at Cheam. In April he was dispatched at age thirteen to Gordonstoun. If anything, Philip had become even more convinced that the rigors of his alma mater were vital to strengthening his timid and introspective son and making him more resilient. He felt it was important that a boy should be shown "the stuff he is made of, to find himself, or become even dimly aware of his own possibilities." After a young man had overcome physical challenges, Philip could see "a light in his eye, and a look about him that distinguishes him from his fellows." The reason such young men looked different, he said, was their discovery that "they can take it," that "they were only frightened of themselves to begin with and now they know they have no cause to be frightened of themselves or of anything else either."

Yet as with Cheam, Philip transmuted his own

successful experience at Gordonstoun into wishful thinking about his son, and neither Elizabeth II nor her mother could dissuade him. The Queen Mother had advocated Eton as an easier fit, a place where Charles could find familiar companionship with the sons of aristocrats. But Philip argued against its proximity to Windsor Castle and London, where tabloid journalists were lurking. The modernist in Philip also saw advantages in exposing his son to a more egalitarian and diverse environment than Eton, with its deeply rooted upper-class traditions.

Charles suffered what he later called his "prison sentence" of five years in northeastern Scotland under conditions even worse than at Cheam. More than the short pants in frigid weather, the early morning runs, the cold showers, and open windows in all seasons, Charles found the constant bullying intolerable. He wrote to his parents of the "hell . . . especially at night," when his dorm mates would throw slippers and pillows at him or "rush across the room and hit me as hard as they can." He pleaded to come home, but his father responded that Charles should find strength in the adversity.

The only respite for Charles came from visits to Balmoral, and particularly Birkhall, where he could be pampered by his grandmother and share her interest in art and music. But even then, "an awful cloud came down three or four days before he had to return," recalled David Ogilvy, the 13th Earl of Airlie, a family friend. "He hated returning to Gordonstoun."

Following the royal family's annual Balmoral

holiday that year, the world stood still for thirteen days in October when the United States confronted the Soviet Union over the installation of nuclear missiles in Cuba and narrowly averted a nuclear war. The Queen was kept informed throughout the crisis by Macmillan, who was in frequent contact with Kennedy. The missile crisis further solidified British-American ties. Kennedy had relied on David Ormsby Gore's counsel for some crucial tactical decisions, most importantly the size of the blockade perimeter, and Macmillan had served as a useful sounding board.

By the Queen's seventh and final year with Macmillan as her prime minister, they had settled into an amiable relationship of mutual understanding and respect. He had his own sense of grandeur, yet he treated her with a courtly deference in the spirit of Churchill. "She loves her duty and means to be Queen and not a puppet," he wrote. He had particularly earned her admiration with his conscientious efforts to stabilize the Commonwealth. She in turn knew how to offer him levity, strength, compassion, or admiration as his mood required, and in 1963 she would deploy her entire range of reactions.

In January she commiserated over his disappointment when de Gaulle condescendingly vetoed British membership in the Common Market. Shortly afterward she and Philip left on *Britannia* for another major tour of Commonwealth nations in the Pacific, including Australia and New Zealand. On her return to Britain that March, she learned of a disturbing sex scandal that threatened to topple Macmillan's government. His secretary of state for war, John Profumo, had been having an affair with a "fashionable London call girl" named Christine Keeler, who in turn was the mistress of a Soviet military attaché, leading to suspicions of espionage by Keeler and an impression of "political squalor" in a "frivolous and decadent" government, in the words of Kennedy adviser Arthur Schlesinger.

Profumo initially denied his sexual intimacy with Keeler both to Macmillan and to the House of Commons, but in June he was forced to resign in disgrace after admitting he had lied. Macmillan was compelled to tell Parliament that he had been "grossly deceived" — which David Bruce called "pitiable and extremely damaging." Bruce feared that confidence in Macmillan had been "greatly undermined."

To the Queen, the prime minister wrote a letter expressing his "deep regret at the development of recent affairs" and offering his apology for "the undoubted injury done by the terrible behavior of one of Your Majesty's Secretaries of State," adding that he had "of course no idea of the strange underworld" of Profumo and his coterie. Elizabeth II replied with what Alistair Horne described as a "charmingly consoling letter . . . sympathizing with her prime minister over the horrible time he had been experiencing."

Profumo withdrew from the public stage and devoted the rest of his life to working quietly on behalf of the poor and homeless. Years later he was discreetly befriended by Prime Minister Margaret Thatcher, who so admired his dignified and responsible service that for her seventieth birthday party at Claridge's in 1995 she seated him next to Elizabeth II. The Palace approved his place of honor, reflecting the Queen's tolerance and capacity for forgiveness. She shared Thatcher's respect for Profumo's dedication to good works, and that evening she was seen "in animated conversation with him," recalled Charles Powell, Baron Powell of Bayswater, one of Thatcher's senior advisers.

As David Bruce feared, Profumo's conduct had seriously damaged Macmillan, who told the Queen in September 1963 that he planned to relinquish his party's leadership before the next general election the following year. Less than a month later he was stricken with severe pain from an inflamed and enlarged prostate and was rushed into surgery on October 10 to remove what was thought to be a malignant tumor. The operation was successful and the tumor benign. Yet in a panic not unlike Eden's, Macmillan nevertheless decided to resign immediately, and the Queen interrupted her annual summer holiday in Balmoral to return to London.

The drama that unfolded over the following week cast Elizabeth II in an unnecessarily bad light as Macmillan schemed to prevent his deputy, Rab Butler, from succeeding him. Through an extraordinary series of maneuvers, Macmillan set himself up as the ultimate arbiter by interviewing all four candidates from his sickbed at King Edward VII Hospital. He chose his sixty-year-old foreign secretary, the 14th Earl of Home, as the leader who would attract the most Conservative Party support. Macmillan buttressed his case with a poll of the cabinet showing ten ministers in

Home's favor, three for Butler, and three each for the other two candidates. However, the backing of the party rank and file was not as clear-cut.

Because of his post-operative confinement, Macmillan sent his letter of resignation to the Palace and arranged with private secretary Michael Adeane for the Queen to visit him in the hospital for their final audience. On the morning of October 18, 1963, the Palace announced that Macmillan had resigned. Shortly afterward the Queen, dressed in a peacock green coat and hat, set out for the hospital. Macmillan awaited her in his bed, which had been wheeled into the boardroom. He wore an old brown sweater over a white silk shirt, and he was tethered to a tube draining bile into a pail under the bed, with a bottle nearby in case he had an accident of incontinence.

As Elizabeth II entered the room, Macmillan was enchanted by her "firm step, and those brightly shining eyes which are her chief beauty." The prime minister's physician, Sir John Richardson, recorded that "there were in fact tears in her eyes." Seated in a tall chair at his bedside, the Queen "seemed moved," Macmillan later wrote, and said "how sorry she had been to get my letter of resignation." From that moment, he was a former prime minister, and she had no constitutional necessity to heed his advice. In fact, in the two previous situations in which she had used her prerogative to select a leader for the Tory party, Churchill and Eden had specifically withheld any official guidance following their resignations.

Yet according to Macmillan, "the Queen asked for my advice as to what she should do," and he obliged by reading aloud his memorandum arguing the case for Lord Home, adding that she should send for him "immediately." Macmillan also urged her to refrain from appointing Home directly as prime minister. Instead, she should instruct him to "take his soundings" and report whether he had sufficient support from his party to form a government.

The Queen followed her former prime minister's counsel to the letter. Home received the backing of the cabinet, including Butler, for whom refusing to serve as one of Home's ministers would have been an act of disloyalty. The next morning, Home renounced his peerage and traveled to Buckingham Palace to kiss hands — the act of being officially received as the head of government, which requires picking up the Queen's hand and brushing it lightly with the lips — as Sir Alec Douglas-Home, her fourth prime minister.

The selection process was criticized in the press and among politicians in both parties. Despite his oft-professed concern for constitutional propriety, Macmillan had boxed in the Queen, critics agreed, by virtually compelling her to take his advice after he had resigned. And for all his insistence on guarding her prerogatives, his actions effectively ended her role in naming the leader of the Tories. Not long afterward, the party adopted new Labour-style rules for choosing its leader through an election.

Critics blamed Macmillan and the familiar "magic circle" of aristocratic men for shaping a decision that should have been based on wider soundings. But Elizabeth II could be faulted as well for failing to organize her own independent canvassing beyond the cabinet — especially after being accused of consulting too narrowly for her selections in 1955 and 1957 — and for yielding to Macmillan's anti-Butler agenda. It was her most controversial decision to date, a curious abandonment of the astute political judgment she had developed in the twelve years of her reign.

Palace aides pointed out that Douglas-Home happened to be her personal preference as well. She reportedly regarded Butler as "too remote" and "too complex," while Douglas-Home was another Old Etonian — also taught by the eccentric Sir Henry Marten — and a longtime family friend with whom she enjoyed country pursuits on their Scottish estates. Thin to the point of frailty, her new prime minister was a consummate gentleman with a fondness for flower arranging. David Bruce considered him "excruciatingly amusing."

He was a familiar presence in the Queen's official life as well, not only as a member of Macmillan's cabinet, but also the highly dignified peer who carried the Cap of Maintenance on a stick at the Opening of Parliament. He took a progressive stance when he introduced the Life Peerages bill in the House of Lords in 1957, adding mischievously that "taking women into a parliamentary embrace seemed to be only a modest extension of the normal functions of a peer." Further to his credit, he was an experienced hand in foreign policy with knowledge that included a year spent reading Marxist works including *Das Kapital* during his youth when he was afflicted with tuberculosis of the spine. He regarded the Queen as a "friendly headmaster receiving the head prefect in his study," always listening intently, quizzing him astutely, and expressing concern about his problems.

Macmillan was sixty-nine when he retired, and he would lead an active life for twenty-three more years. The Queen wrote him a long and heartfelt letter while he was still recuperating, thanking him for being her "guide and supporter through the mazes of international affairs and my instructor in many vital matters relating to our constitution and to the political and social life of my people." She offered him an earldom so he might "continue to take part in public life from the benches of the Upper House," as well as the Order of the Garter, both of which he rather imperiously declined. More than two decades later, on his ninetieth birthday, he would finally relent, accepting the title of Earl of Stockton, conferred personally by the Queen as one of the rare hereditary peerages in the late twentieth century.

When the transfer of Conservative power took place in October 1963, Elizabeth II was four months pregnant. Her nest was already two thirds empty, with Charles at Gordonstoun, and Anne off to boarding school at Benenden that September. By November the Queen had essentially retired from public appearances, although in mid-month she came to a black-tie dinner party given by Ambassador David Bruce and his second wife, Evangeline, at Winfield House, their residence in Regent's Park. Because of her condition, the Queen asked that it be a small party, with just sixteen guests, all of whom she approved after discussions between

Bruce and Michael Adeane.

"It is almost incredible how much detailed planning is involved in a dinner for the Queen," Bruce wrote in his diary. The Polish butler, Russian chef, four footmen, and countless maids prepared "as if for a mammoth carnival," including chasing down unfounded rumors that the Queen disliked soup and would only drink tomato juice while pregnant. The one admonition to the chef from the Palace was not to garnish his pastry with Amorini, the small Italian chocolate heart-shaped candies coated in bright colors or edible silver. When asked, the Queen said she was indifferent whether women wore long or short dresses.

It was a high-powered but lively British-American group: Mollie and Robert Cranborne (the future 6th Marquess and Marchioness of Salisbury); Conservative politician Ian Gilmour and his wife, Caroline (a daughter of the 8th Duke of Buccleuch); American journalist Walter Lippmann and his wife, Helen; Lee and Stas Radziwill; the Dowager Duchess of Devonshire; Michael Adeane; Tory cabinet minister and future prime minister Edward Heath; and Katharine Macmillan (the wife of the former prime minister's son, Maurice). The Queen knew everyone except the Lippmanns, and she was pleased to greet the Bruces' spaniels as well.

"All went with a swing," Bruce recalled. "The Queen appeared to like all the dishes and wines, she was ready and gay in conversation, as was her husband. . . . She blends openness with dignity, has a dazzling complexion, and cordial, sympathetic, unaffected manners." After dinner she talked first to Walter Lippmann, then moved on to each of the men, while Philip conversed with the women. It was nearly midnight when the royal couple left.

Just ten days later, on the 22nd of November, President John F. Kennedy was assassinated. "The unprecedented intensity of that wave of grief mixed with something akin to disaster swept over our people," Elizabeth II recalled. Prince Philip and Alec Douglas-Home flew to Washington for the funeral, but because of her pregnancy, the Queen's doctors advised her against attending the memorial service at St. Paul's Cathedral. She insisted on having her own service at St. George's Chapel, Windsor, to which she invited nearly four hundred American servicemen stationed in England.

Some eighteen months later, on May 14, 1965, she would preside over the dedication of a unique memorial to the fallen president: an acre of land at Runnymede, the site where King John sealed the Magna Carta in 1215, given by the British people to the United States in perpetuity. Marking the ground was a plinth with Kennedy's birth and death dates along with an inscription from his inaugural address: "Let every Nation know, whether it wishes us well or ill, that we shall pay any price, bear any burden, meet any hardship, support any friend or oppose any foe, in order to assure the survival and success of liberty." A committee chaired by David Ormsby Gore oversaw the fund-raising, design, and construction of the memorial, all of which the Queen followed with marked interest.

At the dedication, Elizabeth II and the Duke of Edinburgh accompanied Jackie Kennedy and her children up a woodland path to the memorial site. Four-year-old John Kennedy, Jr., gave the Queen a small bow, and his seven-year-old sister, Caroline, dropped a quick curtsy. As they climbed the hill, Prince Philip tenderly held John's hand.

During the ceremony, Macmillan spoke sentimentally of his late friend and ally, and Elizabeth II's graceful remarks showed "generosity, sympathy and understanding," recalled David Bruce. She touched on JFK's many ties to Britain — his life in England during the "doom laden period" before World War II, the death of his elder brother, Joe, "on a hazardous mission" during the war, and his "dearly loved sister" Kathleen, who lay "buried in an English churchyard." The Queen talked of Kennedy's "wit and style," adding that "with all our hearts, my people shared his triumphs, grieved at his reverses, and wept at his death." Jackie did not speak, but issued a statement of thanks to the British people, saying "you share with me thoughts that lie too deep for tears."

On March 10, 1964, the thirty-seven-year-old Queen gave birth to her fourth child, Edward Antony Richard Louis, in the Belgian Suite at Buckingham Palace. She remained out of the public eye until May, but she kept up with her office work. When her baby was barely a month old, her government boxes revealed a disquieting secret she would be compelled to keep until its unmasking fifteen years later. Sir Anthony Blunt, since 1945 the Surveyor of the Queen's Pictures, the man responsible for the art collections in her palaces, was a spy for the Soviet Union. In exchange for "immensely valuable" information about Soviet collaborators, the British intelligence service gave Blunt immunity. "The Queen knew for years that this man was a spy," said Peter Rawlinson, Baron Rawlinson of Ewell, the government's solicitor-general, who arranged the immunity deal. "It was essential to keep him in his position at Buckingham Palace looking after the Queen's pictures. Otherwise Russia would have realized that his cover had been blown."

If she was unnerved by the revelation of Blunt's treachery, she gave no sign. "I find that I can often put things out of my mind which are disagreeable," she told one courtier. Partly from training, but also her instinctive discretion, Elizabeth II had accustomed herself to absorbing information from so many different sources — intelligence reports, cabinet papers on proposed government reforms, a conversation with a judge on problems in the courts — that she learned how to seal off sensitive information. "She has a compartmentalized brain, with lots of boxes," said Margaret Rhodes. "She can appear frightfully jolly while a constitutional question is going on in another part of her mind."

Less than a week after Blunt made his shocking confession, Elizabeth II was hosting one of her springtime series of "dine-and-sleep" gatherings at Windsor Castle. "She talked of all sorts of things," David Bruce recalled, "including such political questions as Laos, Cyprus, and Zanzibar, revealing extensive briefing and reading. On lighter topics she was humorous and communicative."

These periodic entertainments, which Queen Victoria began in the nineteenth century when the court was officially in residence at Windsor each April, bring together eight to ten prominent guests drawn from the arts, diplomacy, the clergy, business, the military, academia, the judiciary, and politics for a leisurely evening of dinner and conversation. Although formal in structure, the Windsor dinners are more relaxed than the Buckingham Palace luncheons organized for a similar purpose. "She regards Windsor as her home," said Alec Douglas-Home, "just like anyone else's home. It's hard for us to realize." In addition to the Easter season, Elizabeth spends every possible weekend at Windsor and takes pride in being its chatelaine. She inspects the guest rooms before the visitors' arrivals and selects reading material for their enjoyment.

The pattern of the dine-and-sleeps has varied little from the days of King George VI and Queen Elizabeth, who revived them after World War II. Each couple arrives between six and seven o'clock, to be greeted by an equerry and lady-in-waiting and escorted to their suite in the Lancaster, York, or King Edward III tower. The customary accommodation includes two large bedrooms and bathrooms, a ladies' dressing room and commodious sitting room furnished with desks equipped with writing paper and pens, tables laden with mineral water, decanters of whisky, sherry, and gin, cornucopias of fruit, bowls of peppermint candies, jars of biscuits, and vases of fresh flowers.

She assigns a footman and housemaid to serve as each guest's valet or ladies' maid. Their job is to unpack the suitcases, fold underwear in gauzy organza bags, line up cosmetics and perfume bottles in perfect order, whisk away clothing for washing and ironing ("better than any dry cleaner in London," said the wife of a Commonwealth diplomat), draw the bath at the guest's requested temperature, drape a large bath towel over a nearby chair, lay out clothes, and before departure time repack everything with tissue paper. The size of the staff and level of pampering are unequaled, although museum director Roy Strong found it "unnerving to be descended upon by so many."

The houseguests meet in one of the castle's vast drawing rooms, where the Queen and Prince Philip, accompanied by the inevitable scuffling corgis, join them, along with a half dozen courtiers, for a round of drinks. The Queen tells stories about previous visitors, slipping into personalities and accents, and laughs about her misbehaving corgis. "It is always amusing to see when dogs fail to obey a royal command," recalled one former courtier. Everybody is then escorted back to their rooms off the 550-foot, red-carpeted Grand Corridor curving along the east and south sides of the castle quadrangle.

Racing the clock, the guests have less than a half hour to change for dinner in the State Dining Room, which begins with drinks at 8:15 before the prompt arrival of the Queen and Prince Philip fifteen minutes later. Elizabeth II wears a long gown and glitters with large diamonds at her neck, ears, and wrists. Philip appears in a dinner jacket of his own design, a black-tie version of the "Windsor Uniform" originally created by George III for gentlemen at court: dark blue velvet, with brass buttons, scarlet collar, and cuffs.

The Queen doesn't believe in general or even three-way conversation at meals, so everyone follows her lead. When she turns first to the left everyone follows suit, and all heads swivel suddenly when she turns to the right for the second half of the meal. She expects her dinner partners to know the protocol, although she sometimes offers practical tips. "I need to explain about the napkins," she once told a guest. "Look over there. They're doing it all wrong. They've got the starched side down. The napkin will slip off their knees. You do it like this, the unstarched side on your lap and then you tuck it under your bottom."

Her conversation is congenial, but she never engages deeply, preferring to move from one topic to another. At the end of the meal, she has the somewhat outré habit of opening her evening bag, pulling out a compact, and reapplying her lipstick. When First Lady Laura Bush made a similar cosmetic fix during a Washington ladies' luncheon, she cheerily commented, "The Queen told me it was all right to do it."

Hewing to an upper-class ritual long after the advent of feminism in the 1970s, Elizabeth II and the women withdraw from the dining room after dinner, leaving the men to enjoy port and cigars at the table. "She never batted an eye," recalled Jean Carnarvon, the widow of her longtime racing manager. "It was just expected." Conversation in these vestigial female groupings might touch on harmless personal matters while yielding little about the Queen's views.

The next stop is always the castle library, where the Queen has arranged to have objects of particular interest to each guest on display. "The selections are to entertain rather than inform," said Oliver Everett, the Royal Librarian for nearly two decades. In the days preceding the dinner, the librarian sends her a note describing the proposed items and their importance. For an American official there could be correspondence from George Washington, or Mrs. Lincoln's reply to Queen Victoria's condolence note after her husband was assassinated, while the director of the Victoria and Albert Museum could be shown the original letter from the 8th Duke of Devonshire to Queen Victoria suggesting the museum's name. "It gives people something to talk about," said Jean Seaton, the widow of writer Ben Pimlott. "It is a good mechanism for the Queen, who is a fundamentally shy person."

The culmination of the evening is the world's most exclusive guided tour led by the Queen and duke through the priceless collections of the castle's state rooms. "I suppose landscape is quite nice," she said when asked her favorite style of painting. The equestrian scenes by George Stubbs give her the most pleasure, and it distresses her, she once said, that "he experimented terribly with his canvases, and we've got one which is flaking off and you can't stop it." She is also known to dislike most modern art. When she opened the Tate Modern gallery, "she was steered away from the unmade bed and the bits of animals preserved in tanks of brine and allowed to look at a few bright abstracts," Diana Mitford, Lady Mosley wrote to her sister Deborah, the Duchess of Devonshire.

Yet the Queen's commentary on the Windsor

Castle masterpieces by the likes of van Dyck, Holbein, and Rubens often surprises guests as she reels off the date painted, the subject, and a brief story about each artwork. "Her assessment of a picture is invariably honest and often shrewd," said a former Surveyor of the Queen's Pictures. "She has a good visual memory. She will never pretend to appreciate something she doesn't like or understand." Unlike Queen Victoria, Elizabeth II is not a passionate collector who scours the sale catalogues for new finds. "She is neither an art historian nor a connoisseur," said Oliver Everett. "But she knows what she has and the significance of it." Her preference is for "beauty in nature," as one of her former advisers put it. But she takes seriously her role as custodian of the royal collection, which includes some seven thousand paintings.

After coffee in one of the drawing rooms, the Queen and Prince Philip say their goodbyes, and are not seen again. Breakfast is served early in the individual suites, where printed cards ask guests to "refrain from offering presents of money to the Servants of Her Majesty's establishment," although tips are permitted for the acting valets and ladies' maids. Some people take time to wander once more through the state rooms before being escorted out by a senior member of the household, who reminds them to sign the visitor's book with its pages of heavy white cards. "What surprised me was not how many, but how few people ever stayed here," observed Roy Strong.

By the summer of 1964 the Queen had resumed her full public program. Once again she led her annual birthday parade in June riding sidesaddle, and she hosted a succession of garden parties in July at Buckingham Palace and the Palace of Holyroodhouse in Scotland. Queen Victoria began the parties in the 1860s for her aristocratic court, and Queen Elizabeth II democratized them in the 1960s after she abolished debutante presentations. With a guest list of around eight thousand for each, the garden parties are intended to reward people across the socioeconomic spectrum for their contributions to British life.

Personalized invitations of white pasteboard embossed in gold with the Queen's crown and cypher announce that "the Lord Chamberlain is commanded by Her Majesty" to invite the individual on the designated day. (The Lord Chamberlain, distinct from the ceremonial Lord Great Chamberlain, is the senior official at Buckingham Palace who supervises more than eight hundred staff.) When the Palace doors open at 3 P.M., the men in morning suits and the women in hats and afternoon dresses, along with members of the military in uniform and clergy in their vestments, wander through the gardens and rolling lawns. They patiently line up at the four-hundred-foot buffet in the enormous green and white striped tea tent for a cup of the Queen's blend of Darjeeling and Assam and a selection of sandwiches, cakes, and pastries — all of which have been inspected earlier by the Queen. Two military bands play sprightly tunes, while the crowd is organized into lanes by the Yeomen of the Guard wearing scarlet and gold tunics, white ruffs, and red, white, and blue beribboned black velvet hats.

At the stroke of 4 P.M., the Queen, Prince Philip, and assorted other members of the royal family arrive on the terrace for the national anthem and fan out to the various lanes. The Gentlemen Ushers, retired military officers in morning dress and top hats, select around a hundred guests to be introduced to the Queen by the Lord Chamberlain, seeking as wide a cross section as possible. She spends an hour moving along the line, an expert in the art of fleeting but unhurried concentration on each of her interlocutors, and ends up at the Royal Tent emblazoned with a large gleaming crown.

A footman serves her a cup of tea from a tray as she takes a break for ten minutes before moving to the adjacent Diplomatic Tent to greet dignitaries and then returning to the Palace at 6 P.M. One year a diplomat's wife was riveted as the Queen "drank her tea, kicked off her shoes and stood in her stockings with one hand on her hip. She was drinking and laughing and chatting with her butler." Elizabeth II shows no sign of weariness at the familiar routine and understands the sense of occasion for the thousands of guests. As Cecil Beaton once watched her "standing talking quietly to a very moth-eaten couple," he mused that "these people were all so admirable, the salt of the earth. They had done good deeds, worked for their country. They were the country's backbone, and I feel the Queen knew this well."

In the autumn of 1964, the Queen and Prince Philip traveled to Canada for a nine-day state visit. They returned to London two days before a general election on October 15. Throughout Alec

Douglas-Home's year as prime minister, the media, primarily two new satirical outcroppings of 1960s popular culture, the magazine *Private Eye* and the television revue *That Was the Week That Was,* had mercilessly mocked him as an out-of-touch toff. Labour leader Harold Wilson had piled on, repeatedly referring to him by his hereditary title, the 14th Earl of Home. "I suppose," Douglas-Home responded, "that Mr. Wilson, when you come to think of it, is the 14th Mr. Wilson" — a nickname that stuck.

In fact, Douglas-Home had acquitted himself well, and he was popular with the electorate. But an impulse for change pushed the Labour Party ahead by a small margin — 44.1 percent of the vote and 317 seats to 43.4 percent and 303 seats for the Tories. Harold Wilson became the first Labour prime minister since Attlee took office in 1945. It was also the first time the Queen had not been involved in choosing the premier, since the party had already elected Wilson as their leader.

While Attlee, who counted three Old Etonians in his cabinet, had been a predictable sort of Labour politician, Wilson was an unfamiliar breed to the Queen: a lower-middle-class product of the academically selective English grammar schools who rose to attain top honors at Oxford, where he taught economics for nearly a decade. He was proudly provincial, with a pronounced Yorkshire accent, although he was passionately fond of Gilbert and Sullivan, and cultivated the donnish habit of pipe smoking. Still, his simple tastes, reflexive geniality, and quick wit made him good company.

When he arrived at Buckingham Palace on October 16 to kiss hands, he not only brought his wife, Mary, but his two sons, his father, and his political secretary and confidante, Marcia Williams. Rather than full morning dress, the pudgy new leader made a democratic statement by pairing his striped trousers incongruously with an ordinary suit jacket. The courtiers took it in stride, offering the family sherry in the Equerry's Room while Wilson met with the Queen.

One of her obligations is to disregard her first minister's political leanings, and Wilson's certainly diverged from the Tory line of the previous dozen years. After Wilson accommodated labor unions with a "Social Contract," Sir Michael Oswald, the manager of the Queen's stud at Sandringham, suggested she give that name to one of her foals. "I got a bleak look from the monarch," Oswald recalled.

Elizabeth II taught her fifth prime minister at once to take her seriously; when he came to his first audience expecting a general chat, she drilled him with specific questions about his views on shoring up the pound and addressing the balance of payments deficit. Like Churchill at a similar moment, Wilson was embarrassed to be "caught out," and years later advised his successor to "read all his telegrams and cabinet committee papers in time" lest he "feel like an unprepared schoolboy."

"We have to work very hard on him," the Queen said to one of her ladies-in-waiting with a giggle after the first audience. "Within three months he would have died for her," recalled the lady-in-waiting. "She is savvy in knowing what you have to work on." The unabashedly Tory Queen Mother found Wilson "a bit touchy . . . uncomfortable to talk to," so she was pleased that her daughter had "tamed him." He was, in fact, more than amenable. "Harold was never a republican," said Marcia Williams, later Baroness Falkender. "His family were very pro the Queen." He admired the "real ceremonies of the monarchy," he once said. "I have a great respect for tradition."

It also helped that at age forty-eight, Wilson was only a decade older than Elizabeth II. "She started with Winston Churchill, who treated her in a fatherly way, but with Harold it was sort of an equal thing," said his wife, Mary. Wilson found he could relax with the Queen in a way he hadn't anticipated. "He was surprised that she used to sit this way," said Marcia Falkender, leaning forward and grasping her wrists attentively. "She would sit down with him not like a lady does it, not sitting in a prim way. Her very stance gave him to believe she was interested." Before long, added his loyal political secretary, "nobody came between Harold and the Queen. He had his audience once a week at 6:30 in the evening on Tuesdays. We would meet him in the hall and we would know where he was going. He would suck on his pipe, make a quip, and off he would go. And when he returned, you'd know he'd had a good time."

CHAPTER EIGHT
REFUGE IN ROUTINES

If Harold Wilson's premiership marked the turning of a page, an epochal event three months later closed an important chapter in the life of the Queen. On January 24, 1965, Winston Churchill died at age ninety. Instantly the wheels began turning for a full state funeral, the first with such panoply for a nonroyal since the death of the Duke of Wellington in 1852.

The preparations, code-named "Operation Hope Not," had begun in 1958 when the former prime minister nearly died from a sudden attack of pneumonia and the Queen decided that he should be given the supreme honor, overseen by her ceremonial expert, the 16th Duke of Norfolk. "It was entirely owing to the Queen that it was a state funeral," recalled Churchill's daughter Mary Soames. "She indicated that to him several years before he died, and he was gratified."

President Lyndon Johnson was supposed to represent the United States, but he was bedridden at Bethesda Naval Hospital with acute bronchitis, and his doctors resisted. The president was eager to attend, not least because Churchill was confidently Anglo-American and regarded the bond between the countries as a "living entity to be

"She has an ability to get horses psychologically attuned to what she wants and then to persuade them to enjoy it."

The Queen, as always without a hard hat, tearing up the course at Ascot in a race with family members, June 1961. POPPERFOTO/GETTY IMAGES

fostered and prized." Johnson desperately pressed for three days to obtain special accommodations including bringing his own chair to the funeral, arranging shelter from inclement weather, and gaining permission to sit while others were standing. He also secured an agreement from the Queen to receive him privately in Buckingham Palace after the funeral.

In the end, his physicians prevailed. Johnson not only lost his chance to participate in a grand occasion, but he would never again have a chance to meet the Queen. The president's designated replacement, Secretary of State Dean Rusk, fell ill with influenza and had to bow out as well, reducing the official American delegation to only Chief Justice Earl Warren and David Bruce. Dwight Eisenhower attended as a private citizen and issued his own tribute hailing Churchill as "a great maker of history" who was the "embodiment of British defiance to threat, her courage in adversity, her calmness in danger, her moderation in success . . . the leader to whom the entire body of free men owes so much."

By Elizabeth II's decree, Churchill lay in state in Westminster Hall for three days, followed by a funeral at St. Paul's Cathedral on Saturday, January 30, to "acknowledge our debt of gratitude . . . for the life and example of a national hero." It was one of the most magnificent spectacles of the twentieth century, with 120 slow-marching naval ratings (noncommissioned officers) pulling the coffin on the gun carriage used at the funerals of Queen Victoria and Kings George V and VI, detachments from all branches of the armed services, nine military bands, and guns fired ninety times, once a minute for each year of his life. The male members of the Churchill family walked behind the coffin, followed by Churchill's widow and daughters in a carriage provided by the Queen, who equipped it with rugs and hot-water bottles to help them ward off the cold. Hundreds of thousands of mourners lined the roads to watch the procession from Westminster to St. Paul's, which took a full hour.

At the cathedral, the Queen arrived before the procession to join the congregation of three thousand (including leaders of 110 nations) and sit with her husband and mother in three red upholstered gilt chairs in front of the catafalque under the 365-foot dome. "Waiving all custom and precedence," noted Mary Soames, the Queen "waited the arrival of her greatest subject." Elizabeth II also told the Churchill family "we were not to curtsy or bow as we passed her, because it would have held everything up."

The service lasted a half hour, with neither sermon nor eulogies, only prayers, scriptures, and three of Churchill's favorite hymns. The second, Julia Ward Howe's stirring "The Battle Hymn of the Republic," paid homage to his American roots (his mother was a New Yorker, Jennie Jerome), previously sung at St. Paul's just over a year earlier at the memorial service for John F. Kennedy. At Churchill's service, it was the hymn "most enthusiastically rendered," wrote David Bruce.

Once a trumpeter had sounded the "Last Post" and a bugler had played "Reveille," the Queen again broke precedent and left after the Churchill family had followed the coffin, borne by eight Grenadier guardsmen. The royal family stood silently on the cathedral steps with the other world leaders, "the clouds of cold coming from the Queen's mouth" as the funeral cortege departed amid muffled drums for Tower pier. From there, the coffin, escorted by the family, was transported by launch up the Thames, and by train for burial in a churchyard near Churchill's birthplace at Blenheim Palace.

In another unprecedented gesture, the Queen hosted a buffet luncheon at Buckingham Palace for all the chief mourners and foreign dignitaries. "It hit between wind and water," David Bruce recorded, "restrained but informal." Rather than greet her guests in a receiving line, the Queen circulated among them, her introductions managed by members of the household. Prince Charles, Princess Anne, and Prince Andrew "wandered casually about," ten-month-old Prince Edward "was brought in for a speedy tour," and the Queen left just before two o'clock.

Of all the striking scenes of the day, one of the most memorable was of Churchill's coffin draped in the Union Jack, its only adornment a black pillow holding the insignia of the Most Noble Order of the Garter: the elaborate chain known as the Collar of the Order, with the enameled emblem of St. George and the dragon attached, and the badge with the cross of St. George and the Garter motto, "Honi soit qui mal y pense" (Shame on him who thinks evil of this). The Nobel laureate and recipient of countless other awards considered the Garter in a class by itself because, Churchill said, "only the Queen decides." With a maximum twenty-four recipients — "Companions" they are called — at any given time, plus members of the royal family and foreign sovereigns, the Garter knights are probably the most exclusive club in the world. The Order was founded in 1348 by King Edward III, and the members serve until their death.

In June 1965, the Queen assembled her knights for their annual gathering, which included the installation of two new Companions, Basil Brooke, the former prime minister of Northern Ireland, and Edward Bridges, the former head of the Civil Service. Elizabeth II gives no specific reason for conferring her unique "mark of Royal favour," but she has included eight of her prime ministers and other distinguished figures from politics, the law, business, the military, diplomacy, and the judiciary as well as hereditary peers, a number of whom she has chosen for serving her personally. With the exception of the royal members, women weren't allowed in the Order until 1987, when the Queen decided to create full-fledged "Lady Companions," the first of whom was Lavinia Fitzalan-Howard, the Duchess of Norfolk, who had been the Queen's stand-in during rehearsals for the coronation, and who had regularly hosted Elizabeth II and Philip at her ancestral home, Arundel Castle, during the summertime Goodwood races. Intriguingly, Elizabeth II never honored her sister, Princess Margaret, although she appointed Princess Anne in 1994 and her cousin Princess Alexandra in 2003, both widely admired for their dedicated royal service.

Forty years after her father's death, Mary

Soames was appointed to the Order. When she came to Buckingham Palace, the Queen had laid out the insignia on a grand piano. "Well, here it is," said Elizabeth II. As she pointed toward the collar, she said, "That is your father's chain!" "Oh, Ma'am," replied Mary, "that can't be." Feeling slightly abashed at contradicting the monarch, she explained that the collar was in a display case at Chartwell, the Churchill home in Kent. "I caused it to be retrieved," said the Queen with a twinkle, explaining that she had arranged for a replica to go on display.

Garter Day, which is held on the Monday after Trooping the Colour in June, is a particularly enjoyable fixed point on the Queen's yearly calendar. The Garter knights meet at Windsor Castle to witness the installation of new members in the Garter Throne Room. Conjuring a medieval tableau, they wear their gleaming chains and badges over heavy dark blue velvet robes embellished with white satin bows on the shoulders. "Whoever invented these robes wasn't very practical," the Queen once remarked, "even in the days when somebody wore clothes like these." As she administers the oath and exhorts the knights in their faith, "she is highly practical, quick & neat," noted Deborah Devonshire when her husband, Andrew, the 11th Duke of Devonshire, was invested. "The language is thrilling, ancient & rather frightening, nothing but battling with things & people."

The Queen treats the knights to luncheon in the Waterloo Chamber, a long gallery with an intricately carved ceiling and clerestory windows resembling a man-o'-war ship from the nineteenth century. The table is splendidly set with silver gilt and flowers. Like other royal banquets, there is "no hanging about for a slow eater," Deborah Devonshire recalled.

Following the luncheon, the knights ready themselves for a colorful procession, fastening their robes and adjusting their badges, collars, and flat black velvet hats with waving ostrich plumes. They walk from the main part of the castle down a cobbled street to St. George's Chapel, preceded by regimental bands in gold tunics, the Military Knights of Windsor in scarlet uniforms, and Officers of Arms in scarlet and gold tabards and black knee breeches, passing by dismounted members of the Household Cavalry lining the route. Many of the Garter knights are elderly, and some shuffle unsteadily under the weight and volume of their robes. "The Queen is always very concerned for their well-being," said Lieutenant Colonel Sir Malcolm Ross, former Comptroller for the Queen. "She will say, 'Pay attention to this one. Make sure he is not puffed,' so I would take him by a short-cut."

Garter Day is one of the monarchy's popular tourist attractions, with eight thousand spectators each year, and a thousand more filling St. George's Chapel for the service of thanksgiving, where the Garter knights are tucked away in the choir stalls. Afterward, the Queen, the Duke of Edinburgh, and knights ride in carriages and cars back to the castle. "It's always very lucky to plod downhill and not uphill," the Queen observed. Once the royal family members take their leave, the Companions meet in the Waterloo Chamber for tea, a happy atmosphere of "hats off, hair down, and general relaxation," recalled Deborah Devonshire.

It would be more than a decade before Harold Wilson, the Queen's first socialist prime minister, would participate in the rarefied rituals of the Garter — pageantry he embraced with enthusiasm. In the meantime, he pursued an agenda of wide-ranging social reforms and increased government spending on housing, pensions, health, and welfare subsidies. Once a government captures a working majority in Parliament, however slender, the ruling party has virtually untrammeled power, with no prospect of compromise with the opposition. The postwar Conservative governments had done little to reduce the welfare state constructed by the Attlee government, and Wilson significantly broadened the reach of those programs.

Starting in 1965, his Labour majority pushed through laws abolishing capital punishment, ending government censorship, liberalizing abortion, lowering the voting age to eighteen, reforming divorce, and decriminalizing homosexuality. Wilson's government nearly doubled the number of universities, significantly expanding free higher education (a practice that would end thirty-three years later with the introduction of means-tested tuition fees). At the same time, he eroded the quality of secondary education by eliminating the publicly funded selective grammar schools that had educated not only Wilson but other prominent British leaders such as Margaret Thatcher and Edward Heath. Those academically rigorous schools were replaced by egalitarian comprehensive schools with lower scholastic standards. To pay for the expanded government programs, the Labour Party binged on borrowing and raised taxes.

The prime minister shared his plans in the Tuesday evening audiences at Buckingham Palace. Wilson felt the Queen "had very good views on everything," Marcia Falkender recalled. "She didn't tender it in a way of saying, 'This is my advice and you should take it.' She knew she was not there to give advice, but she was there, if possible, to discuss it in a decent way." Wilson's press secretary Joe Haines said that the Queen's Socratic approach forced the prime minister to "justify any proposals to her, which was good discipline. It meant he had to have his arguments very clear in his own mind." In the larger sense, however, she doesn't appear to have slowed the march of socialist policies, although Harold Macmillan, for one, believed she had a "restraining influence."

Like Macmillan, Wilson catered to the Queen's fascination with political gossip. Among other things, he told her about French president Valéry Giscard d'Estaing's alleged penchant for trolling the streets of Paris for women. "The fact that she was Queen, she could take it all in, and nothing would shock her," said Marcia Falkender. "She has a very good understanding of people and reading them. . . . She is a highly intelligent raconteur of the political scene." Wilson also relied on the Queen's confidentiality. When he was worried about fellow cabinet members undercutting him, she gave him a shoulder to weep on.

While her relationship with Wilson was warm from the outset, Elizabeth II knew that most of his class-conscious colleagues took a dim view of the monarchy and the Queen. Yet she managed over time to win over some of the hardest cases, among them Barbara Castle, the flame-haired firebrand known as Labour's Red Queen, and Richard Crossman, described by historian A. N. Wilson as a "large, shambolic bisexual." When Harold Wilson's cabinet first met with Elizabeth II to be sworn in as members of the Privy Council, they grudgingly went along with what Wedgwood Benn, an outspoken socialist, called a "terribly degrading" ritual of kneeling, swearing on the Bible, taking the Queen's hand, and walking backward. He petulantly offered "the most miniature bow ever seen."

Crossman, like so many others, appreciated how the Queen put him at ease, noting that she had a "lovely laugh" and was "a really very spontaneous person." The Queen felt relaxed enough with Crossman to unburden herself on a variety of topics in their audiences, and he came to pride himself on being an astute observer of her nuances. When Crossman mentioned Dame Evelyn Sharp, an intimidating civil servant in charge of urban renewal, the Queen snapped, "Oh that woman. I can tell you I don't like her." As for her Privy Council ritual, she said, "Philip always said it was a waste of time." Unbeknownst to Elizabeth II, her interlocutor was busily recording her comments in his copious diaries. When after his death in 1974 his literary executors planned to publish his observations, Martin Charteris dissuaded them from including the "most objectionable passages" involving the Queen's comments.

Barbara Castle, who had a spiky sense of humor and a vivacious personality, was taken with the Queen's wit and "natural charm" and established an easy camaraderie with the Queen. After a state banquet in 1965, Castle was standing with Elizabeth II and Princess Margaret as they chatted about Prince Charles's anxiety over taking his university admission examination. "You and I would never have got into university," the Queen suddenly said to her sister, as the Labour politician hastened to reassure the monarch that it "wasn't as formidable as it seemed." Castle was impressed that Elizabeth II could shift quickly between politicians of opposing viewpoints by remembering as many biographical details as possible, "which kept the conversation going in a perfectly safe, politically neutral way."

Benn, however, remained unrepentantly opposed to the Queen and all she stood for — an attitude unsoftened by his marriage to a wealthy American with a large house in fashionable Holland Park. As postmaster general in the Wilson cabinet, he even launched a quixotic campaign to remove the image of Elizabeth II from postage stamps. She patiently listened to his proposal and examined sketches of his suggested alternatives. He left his forty-minute audience convinced she had agreed to the scheme. "She took him for a mug," said historian Kenneth Rose. "He thought he had wrapped her round his finger." Privately, she let Wilson know her displeasure, and the prime minister squelched the matter. When Benn later came to the Palace to be sworn in after Wilson had switched him to minister of technology, the Queen couldn't resist saying, "I'm sure you'll miss your stamps." He thanked her for her "kindness and encouragement in helping me to tackle them," before obediently bowing and walking backward from the audience room.

One of her other detractors was Labour Party foreign secretary Michael Stewart. During a dine-and-sleep visit to Windsor Castle in 1968, he announced to Lydia Katzenbach, wife of the U.S. attorney general, that "except in knowledge of horse flesh," the Queen was "a stupid woman." When Katzenbach recounted the criticism afterward, David Bruce expressed his surprise, "in view of the common understanding that the Prime Minister finds the Queen remarkably well informed on international problems. That she prefers, if given a choice — which she is not — horses to affairs of state, may well be the case, but no one can accuse her of neglecting her interminable and I should imagine often boring duties of an official character."

As Elizabeth II entered middle age, horses were indeed both her passion and her refuge. Over the years she has seldom purchased horses, preferring them to be "home-bred," a tradition stretching back to Queen Elizabeth I. By the 1960s, she had been supervising the royal equine enterprise for more than a decade, with breeding operations located at Sandringham and nearby Wolferton as well as Hampton Court, along with Polhampton Lodge Stud in Berkshire, which she began leasing in 1962. Ten years later she bought Polhampton to use as a bucolic camp for recently weaned yearlings and runners needing a rest — what her veteran stud manager Michael Oswald calls the "walking wounded."

In her private as well as public life, the Queen is a woman of predictable routines, which, in the case of her racehorses, are timed to their rhythms of mating, birth, weaning, training, and racing. She typically visits the mares and stallions at the Sandringham stud farm twice in the first six weeks of each year when the breeding season begins, and again in April and July to see the foals resulting from the previous season's mating. With her trusty old-fashioned camera, she methodically photographs the mares and their offspring.

In the early spring as well as the fall she inspects her yearlings at Polhampton, and whenever possible in the spring and summer she observes more than a score of her young thoroughbreds in training at stables in Wiltshire, Hampshire, and Berkshire. She follows their progress at races throughout the year, only a small number of which she sees in person because of the demands of her job. The Derby in early June and Royal Ascot later that month are indelible dates in her calendar, and she attends other major race meetings when she can.

The Royal Stud at Sandringham is a picturesque late-nineteenth-century complex of red-brick and native brown carrstone stables topped by chimneys and cupolas. The mares inhabit roomy boxes that can easily accommodate newborn foals, but each stallion lives like a king in his considerably larger box with tiled walls, ten inches of wood chips on the floor, high windows, a pitched roof of wood and Norfolk reed, and infrared lights for drying off. There are four paddocks of two acres apiece for the stallions, enclosed by brick walls and hedges, with nearby gardens and fountains.

The main business of the stud takes place in the covering shed, a cavernous structure with a sandy floor. The Queen's breeding and racing advisers make suggestions about mating, but unlike her role as sovereign, where she follows the guidance of others, she often takes the initiative, based on her observations as well as her extensive knowledge of bloodlines. She knows which horses are good for stamina, which for speed, and which possess the ineffable trait of courage. She is an astute judge of conformation — whether, as Henry Porchester observed, "a horse had a good shoulder, short cannon bones, good feet, flat feet, bent or straight hocks, good quarters, a nice eye or quality head." She famously discovered that a stable had mixed up two of her yearlings, Doutelle and Agreement, that she had only previously seen once as foals. "She reads a lot, and she knows a lot," said Michael Oswald. "If you want to discuss a sales catalogue you should do your homework, because she'll know who a horse's great-great-grandmother was." The final decision "rests always with the Queen," wrote Arthur FitzGerald in his official history of the Royal studs.

Oswald jocularly refers to the Sandringham Stud as the "Maternity Help and Marriage Guidance Center for Horses." But the act of live cover — breeding a multimillion-dollar prize-winning stallion with one of the Queen's valuable mares — is not for the faint of heart. Rather, it is a serious exercise in controlled lust between two powerful and highly strung creatures, each weighing nearly a ton. As a measure of her earthy nature as a countrywoman, the Queen has witnessed the raw reality of thoroughbred matchmaking any number of times. The otherwise prim and proper Queen would stand in a corner of the covering shed with her stud manager and grooms, wearing a hard hat for protection before the health and safety authorities required her to build an elevated viewing stand. "She is very matter-of-fact," said Michael Oswald. "She knows how it works."

The fast, furious, and potentially dangerous mating act begins when a mare in heat is brought into the covering shed. Her rear legs are encased in heavy leather boots to prevent her from kicking the stallion, and a thick leather "false mane" is strapped across her neck and withers so she is not bitten during the frenzy of coitus.

The mare is first brought to one side of the shed, a padded wall with a large opening where she and a "teaser" stallion engage in equine foreplay, and if she is sufficiently aroused — an unmistakable reaction known as clitoral "winking" — the veterinarian will examine her by palpation and ultrasound to determine whether she is about to ovulate. If so, she returns to the covering shed, where she stands in a slight hollow in the middle. One groom holds her bridle and another has a "twitch," a pole with a loop of rope that sedates the mare when twisted around the end of her nose. The highly excited stallion of choice is held by four men as he strains, snorts, whinnies, and rears before mounting the mare, his violent exertions guided by a stud groom standing near her tail.

Once conception has been confirmed by ultrasound, the Queen tracks the eleven-month gestation, and occasionally she watches the mare foaling, which usually occurs at night. Typically she is sent a photograph of the foal, which she sometimes will name even before birth, and she follows its development until it is weaned and shipped out as a yearling to Polhampton.

During one of the Queen's visits to Polhampton, she accompanied Henry Porchester, her stud groom Sean Norris, her trainer Ian Balding and his wife, Emma, into a field to have a better look at six colts about to be broken in. Suddenly the colts started galloping around in a circle and "dive bombing," rearing up and kicking out. Only Balding and the Queen stayed in place, while their three companions bolted for the gate. Elizabeth II and her trainer knew that if they remained motionless, the young horses would not attack them and would eventually settle down.

"Oh, that was scary," the Queen said afterward. "She was completely unruffled," Balding recalled, having witnessed an unflinching physical courage that is one of her defining traits. "She has the ability to get calmer in the face of problems rather than allowing herself to get her adrenaline up and to panic," said Monty Roberts, the California horse trainer known as the "horse whisperer," who was to become her close friend.

Preparing her yearlings for the racetrack occupies nearly as much of the Queen's attention as breeding. Her expertise is such that, as Henry Porchester said, "talking to her is almost like talking to a trainer." "If she had been a normal person, she probably would have become a trainer," observed Ian Balding. "She loves it so much." She has always divided her horses among several trainers, mainly because she wants to see their different approaches. "Some trainers suit a particular horse better than others," said Oswald. "It's rather like deciding on schools for your children." She can stand for hours in the early morning mist on the gallops, wearing a head scarf, tweed coat, and Wellington boots, binoculars fixed on the horses streaking across the rolling downs. "She would watch how her horses moved, how they would stretch out," said Ian Balding. "She could see how they run."

She revisits her horses in their boxes during "evening stables," when she takes the time to inspect them one by one, offering each a carrot or a bunch of clover with an affectionate pat, and chatting with its groom. She knows all the stable hands and grooms, and she respects their expertise. Their world is one of the very few places where the barriers of protocol disappear, where she can talk to people on the same level. She knows about their problems and concerns just as much as those of their four-legged charges.

While touring Balding's stables at Kingsclere, she inquired about the ventilation system, knowing that since horses can breathe only through their noses, they are susceptible to respiratory infections. Back at the house for a drink, she blew her nose and startled her trainer by handing him her handkerchief so he could see the dark mucus. "I had a feeling that it was incredibly dusty in there, and there was no air," she said. It was her dramatic and no-nonsense way of showing that his horses were suffering. Balding knocked some holes in the rear of the stalls, covered them with screens, and added a vent in the roof to increase the air circulation.

While staying at one of her country residences, the Queen finds time to ride nearly every day, even in the rain, both as an escape and a physical fitness regimen. Since childhood she has ridden well, with a fine seat, light rein, and confident control. Although she is always accompanied by a groom and detective, when she hacks out across the countryside she is as alone as she can possibly be — a rarity for a queen.

She was never interested in jumping, and she knew how to avoid danger. But her prudence has always excluded wearing a hard hat while riding, even in her younger days when tearing down the racecourse with her sister and her daughter, her head scarf flying in the wind during the family's private morning race each year on Gold Cup Day during Royal Ascot. Jean Carnarvon recalled that her husband "used to be bananas about it. He would talk to her about it. She wasn't going to do it." Once when Ian Balding was hacking with her in Windsor Home Park, he took her to task. "I really think it is ridiculous that you above all others do not wear a crash helmet," he said. Replied the Queen, "I never have, and you don't have to have your hair done like I do" — an expression less of vanity than the practical need to be ready for her appointments.

Unlike his wife, Philip was not brought up on horseback. He took up polo in 1950 while living on Malta because he enjoyed the sport's vigorous physical challenge. From the start he rode aggressively, "keen to win at all costs," said Major Ronald Ferguson, who played frequently with Philip. Ferguson believed that Philip "needed to play polo to get rid of all his pent-up frustrations. He would arrive . . . with steam coming out of his ears and after a few games he would be a different man — the frustration gone."

To the duke, a polo pony is like a dirt bike. "He drives it, and he wants a machine out in front of him so when he steps on the throttle it goes, when he brakes, it stops, and it goes fast left or right," said Monty Roberts. "He is not interested in the why, but how to get it done." Horses are incomprehensible to Philip, who cares little how one differs from another.

Elizabeth II takes a more intuitive and inquisitive view, and appreciates how horses react. "She has an ability to get horses psychologically attuned to what she wants and then to persuade them to enjoy it," observed Sir John Miller, for many years the Crown Equerry and Horsemaster to the Queen. "She gets into it and investigates the innate tendencies," said Roberts.

Although no fan of the turf, Prince Philip dutifully accompanies his wife to Royal Ascot, the centerpiece of her racing life and one of the royal family's popular rituals going back to Queen Anne, who began it in 1711. For four days in June, starting the Tuesday after Garter Day (called by some "the Ascot Vigil," in which the knights "kneel in prayer for a winner later in the week"), the Queen entertains friends, mainly from the racing world, at Windsor Castle with a combination of graciousness and military precision. Everyone dresses to the teeth, the men in morning coats and top hats, the women in "formal day wear" and their best hats — required attire for the Royal Enclosure at the racecourse.

Elizabeth II hosts a sumptuous luncheon, and at the appointed hour she rises, usually followed by her platoon of corgis and dorgis who have been resting under the table. The royal party is driven in cars through Windsor Great Park to the Ascot Gate, where they climb into landaus, each drawn by a team of four horses ridden by two scarlet-coated postillions, with footmen in red livery and black top hats seated at the back. After a drive along two miles of country lanes, the Royal Procession, which had its origins in the 1820s during the reign of King George IV, enters the racecourse's Golden Gates at 2 P.M. for the traditional ride up the grassy straight mile.

Once in the royal box, the Queen's guests are free to entertain themselves while she focuses on the afternoon races, finding welcome relief even with the tension of having a runner. "The great thing about racing is she can get deeply immersed for two or three hours at a stretch, and it is completely different from her everyday work, a switch out from what is going on in the world that is worrying or unhappy," said Michael Oswald. "One of her private secretaries told me it has a very good therapeutic effect."

When she has a winner, she jumps up and down like a little girl, whooping and grinning, throwing off the inhibitions that usually restrain her in public. She does not, however, place bets. She is acknowledged to be unusually observant at reading a race, as she leans forward in her chair, her eyes transfixed. "Look, it's on the wrong leg," she would say. "No wonder it can't go round the corner. . . . I don't think that horse stayed. . . . Did you see it swerve? I didn't like the way its ears went back. I like the way it accelerated. . . . I think it will be better on a left-handed than a right-handed course."

With a television in the back and a line of big chairs behind a curving glass window at the front, her generously appointed box was designed to provide the best view of the course. After the fourth race, the Queen invites her guests, including various dignitaries summoned from the Royal Enclosure, for tea in her private room at the back of the box as footmen circulate and serve sandwiches, scones, strawberries and cream, and pastries. She sits for a while, making conversation, but leaps up at the start of the next race, lest she miss a moment. "As a human being one always has hope," the Queen once said when asked about her fascination with the turf, "and one always has perhaps the gambling instinct, that one's horse is going to be better than the next man's horse, and that's why one goes on doing it."

The Queen pays for her breeding and racing out of her private funds, offsetting some of the expenditure with prize money, stud fees for her stallions, and sales of selected winners to other breeders, with a net cost, by one estimate, of a half million pounds a year. The 1950s brought her a string of winners led by Aureole, her sentimental favorite who after losing the Derby won other top races including the prestigious King George VI and Queen Elizabeth Stakes at Ascot. In 1954 and 1957 the Queen was the top money winner in Britain.

More than anyone, Elizabeth II shared the ups and downs of breeding and racing with her mother. They first owned a horse together in 1949, a steeplechaser named Monaveen. But after he broke a leg on a jump during a race at Hurst Park and had to be put down, the Queen decided to concentrate on flat racing, while her mother devoted herself to jumpers. Because she had so much more free time, the Queen Mother attended many more races than the Queen and could more frequently feel the thrill of watching her own horses run.

The Queen Mother took a keen interest in her daughter's thoroughbred enterprise, and Elizabeth II transferred horses to her mother if they seemed better suited for going over jumps than running on a flat track. The two women found much in common based on their extensive knowledge of horseflesh. During daily phone calls, their chat about the turf ran the gamut from gossip about jockeys, trainers, winners, and losers to the latest news on injuries, breeding, foaling, and naming. When either was traveling they exchanged long letters sharing their experiences and offering advice. "Racing is incredible out here," the Queen wrote from New Zealand. "They all bet like mad and like their marathons of eight races at a dose."

Elizabeth II happily subsidized her mother's passion for racing, which she knew gave her great pleasure. One year when the jumpers had done badly, the Queen proposed paying the trainer's bill. "The Queen Mother accepted gratefully," wrote her biographer William Shawcross, "signed the bill and wrote underneath the total, 'Oh dear.' "

In her sixties and very much a blithe spirit, the "Queen Mum," an affectionate term coined by the tabloid press, was easy to indulge. She had become pleasingly plump, and was regarded as a "great gastronome," although her family teased her about her large appetite for food and drink. She had one serious health scare, a diagnosis of colon cancer in December 1966 that the family kept secret. Surgeons removed the tumor, no further treatment was needed, and the Queen Mother never had a recurrence of the malignancy. After a quiet recuperation at Sandringham, all her vitality returned.

She continued her rounds of official duties — one hundred or more events in most years — effectively and enthusiastically. Her enjoyment was infectious, notably when she threw up her hands in a theatrical outburst of delight. Deborah Devonshire nicknamed her "Cake" after observing her at a wedding reception. On hearing that the bride and groom were about to cut the cake, the Queen Mother exclaimed "Oh, the Cake!" as if seeing the ritual for the first time. "She really is superb at her own type of superbery," the Duchess wrote to her sister Diana in 1965. At a dinner party given by John Profumo at his home in Regent's Park a year before his fall from grace, the Queen Mother even joined Ted Heath, David Bruce, and several aristocrats in practicing the twist, the latest dance craze, late into the night.

She loved to entertain her friends with extravagant black-tie dinners at her various homes, and al fresco luncheons served by a half dozen liveried footmen on tables set with white cloths and fine silver under a canopy of trees in the garden of Clarence House. The crowd was more eclectic than at the monarch's table, since she could invite anybody she pleased, including dancers, artists, writers, and actors who amused her and could make bright conversation. The food was beautifully presented, and the claret flowed freely, along with her piquant opinions — outspoken criticisms of politicians, most of them Labour, her hatred of "the Japs," and suspicious view of the Germans and the French ("so nice & so nasty. . . . How can one trust them?"). Recalling an encounter with Dinka tribesmen in the Sudan, she declared, "They were naked, but they were so black it didn't matter!"

The Edwardian world of the Queen Mother had a certain air of unreality. When her longtime friend Tortor Gilmour moved to a smaller house in her village, the Queen Mother came to tea and lamented the mundane view from the front windows. "Darling," she said, "you must have them close the petrol station and move that school." Surveying the scene during one of her elegant luncheons at Clarence House, the Queen Mother and former Queen said, "Look at us. We are just ordinary people — look at us around this table — having an ordinary lunch."

The lives of the real ordinary people were changing rapidly in the 1960s. In tandem with the far-reaching social reforms of the Labour Party,

British culture underwent seismic shifts. Rock 'n' roll music loosened inhibitions, the birth control pill gave women new sexual freedom, and depictions of sexuality in film and the theater became more explicit. In 1967 even seventeen-year-old Princess Anne attended a performance of the musical *Hair,* with its full-frontal nudity.

At the apex of popular culture were the Beatles. Harold Wilson sought to signal his modernity by recommending that the Queen award each of the "Fab Four" with the MBE — Member of the Most Honourable Order of the British Empire — in October 1965. Only four years earlier the group had been playing in a Liverpool cellar, but their infectious tunes and mop-haired style had exploded into Beatlemania, with legions of screaming fans, and sales of their records in the millions. There was an outcry from the Establishment that the government had debased the award by giving it to pop stars, and some war heroes protested by returning their medals. Noel Coward called it a "major blunder on the part of the Prime Minister . . . I don't think the Queen should have agreed."

The Beatles had first met her when they played at the Royal Variety Show in 1963. After they had bowed respectfully during their introductions, she asked when they were next performing. "Tomorrow night, Ma'am," said Paul McCartney. "Oh, where is it?" she replied. "Slough, Ma'am," he replied. "Oh," she said brightly. "That's near us!" "She meant of course Windsor Castle," McCartney recalled. "It was funny and so unassuming."

Two years later she presented them with their honors at Buckingham Palace while police restrained crowds of shrieking girls trying to storm the gates. During their investiture in the opulent white and gold ballroom, the Queen was "lovely," said McCartney. "She was like a mum to us." But John Lennon's delight with the honor soon soured, and he returned it in 1969 as a protest against the Vietnam War.

He was not alone. The Wilson government supported the escalating U.S. involvement in Southeast Asia, but the prime minister refused Lyndon Johnson's request for troops — not even, the president complained, a "platoon of bagpipers." An embittered Johnson dismissed Wilson as a "little creep" even as the war provoked large-scale protests and riots on university campuses and in the streets of both Britain and the United States.

A different sort of violence exploded when "The Troubles" began in Northern Ireland where the Catholic minority — which suffered widespread discrimination — pressed for an independent union with the Republic of Ireland to the south. In the late 1960s the militant Irish Republican Army took the lead in the Catholic cause. As Protestants committed to the status quo clashed with Catholics, British troops were deployed to keep the peace. The IRA escalated the conflict with terrorist bombings and general mayhem, the beginning of three decades of bloodshed.

The convulsions of the 1960s unleashed a wave of antiestablishment feeling in Britain, and the monarchy became a prime target. By the middle of the decade, *Private Eye,* the satirical magazine that helped take down Alec Douglas-Home, began aiming its barbs at the royal family for being out of touch, pompous, and bound by outdated traditions. Prince Philip became known as "Phil the Greek." The magazine also lampooned the mainstream press for its sycophantic approach to the monarchy. Newspapers responded with more questioning and irreverent coverage of the Queen and her family, along with a steady drumbeat for greater access to information than the Palace had been accustomed to offering.

The Queen kept track of events by reading the newspapers, watching television newscasts, and studying the confidential documents in her boxes. David Bruce was struck, when he sat with her in the royal box at the Goodwood race meeting in 1968 — the year of widespread student rioting against university authorities as well as the Vietnam War, nuclear weapons, and other activist causes — that "the Queen talked at some length about violence, especially amongst young people throughout the world."

Elizabeth II held to her familiar routines as she carried out her own duties throughout the social changes of the turbulent 1960s, appearing mostly as a figure waving from a carriage or a maroon Rolls-Royce topped by her royal shield. In addition to her regular tours to Commonwealth countries in Asia, Africa, the Pacific, the Caribbean, and North America, she made a dozen state visits around the globe. Her ten days in the Federal Republic of Germany in May 1965 marked the first time a member of the British royal family had been there officially since 1913. The planning had begun two years earlier during the Macmillan government, but the new political subtext was Labour's expected reapplication for Common Market membership.

It was a delicate journey of reconciliation as well, marking the twentieth anniversary of the end of World War II. For the Queen it offered the prospect of exploring her German roots, and for Philip it marked a sentimental return to his family's homeland, to show his wife places where he had spent happy times with his sisters before World War II. After being excluded from the wedding of Elizabeth II and Philip because of bitter postwar feelings, his surviving three sisters — Theodora, Sophie (nicknamed "Aunt Tiny"), and Margarita, all princesses who married into German royalty — had been given prominent places in the royal box at Westminster Abbey during the coronation. They had also been quietly entertained by the Queen and Philip, particularly each spring at the Royal Windsor Horse Show, an extravaganza of equestrian competitions, military displays, and fireworks.

An emotional high point came in West Berlin, when cheering throngs packed John F. Kennedy Square and ecstatically chanted "Elizabeth!" Yet the Queen, who spoke of her German ancestry in her remarks, seemed discomfited by the passionate reaction. "I think she thought this was a bit too much of a good thing — too reminiscent of ritual Nazi shouting," recalled Foreign Secretary Michael Stewart. "That was the only time I saw her perhaps at all put out."

The moment Elizabeth II seemed to savor most occurred in Hanover, where she scrutinized the letter that launched her family's dynasty. Written in 1714 by British noblemen to George the Elector of Hanover — the future King George I — it said, "Queen Anne's dying. Come quick, certain persons want a Jacobite heir and not you."

In the autumn of 1965 the Queen's attention shifted to Africa, where she became embroiled in the British government's struggle with its colony of Southern Rhodesia. Rhodesian prime minister Ian Smith unilaterally declared independence from Britain and set up a white minority government mirroring the apartheid policies of neighboring South Africa. Since Britain's policy was to grant independence only to colonies that established majority rule, Harold Wilson responded by persuading the United Nations to impose economic sanctions. To attract support in Britain, Smith insisted that the Queen would remain as his country's head of state. Wilson countered by enlisting Elizabeth II to tell Smith directly that she would not preside as sovereign over a regime that failed to provide for black majority participation. She even sent a handwritten letter to the Rhodesian leader urging him to compromise.

Critics argued that such partisan involvement violated the Queen's neutrality. Smith continued to maintain the illusion that his country remained a monarchy despite the British government's contention that his country's government was illegitimate. He eventually dropped that pretense, and Rhodesia declared itself a republic, triggering a debilitating guerrilla war conducted by black militants.

A year later the Queen faced another round of criticism when her instincts lost touch with shifting public expectations. On October 21, 1966, an avalanche of water, mud, and debris cascaded down a mountain above the South Wales mining village of Aberfan, engulfing an elementary school and killing 116 children and 28 adults. Driven by an impulse to help his fellow Welshmen, Tony Snowdon left London without consulting the royal household and arrived at 2 A.M. to console grieving family members and visit survivors. He was followed by Prince Philip the next day, and the two men watched the rescue and recovery efforts. But despite urgings from her advisers, the Queen resisted visiting the scene. "People will be looking after me," she said. "Perhaps they'll miss some poor child that might have been found under the wreckage."

Her response reflected thoughtfulness as well as instinctive caution. Finally, after the last bodies had been recovered just over a week later, she and Philip went to Aberfan and spent more than two hours talking to relatives of the deceased, walking up the mound covering the school, and laying a wreath in the cemetery where eighty-one children had been buried in rows. A compelling circumstance had pulled her out of her bubble into direct and spontaneous contact with her subjects, who showed their appreciation. "As a mother, I'm trying to understand what your feelings must be," she said with tears in her eyes. "I'm sorry I can give you nothing at present except sympathy."

For someone who worked so hard to control her feelings in public, it was a difficult if heartfelt moment, a recognition that the villagers needed her soothing presence and that at such times a public display of emotion was now expected. But her tardy reaction to the crisis showed an unyielding side to her nature that would cause problems in the years to come.

When disaster struck at Aberfan, the Queen had recently returned from her two-month holiday at Balmoral, the most prolonged and restorative yearly retreat among her seasonal rituals. Her winter break at Sandringham from before Christmas until early February affords plenty of time for country pursuits, but genuine privacy is difficult because the twenty-thousand-acre Norfolk estate is crisscrossed with public roads and dotted with a half dozen villages. Only at Balmoral, where public roads border the estate, can the Queen truly get away from it all — except for her daily boxes. "It's nice to hibernate for a bit when one leads such a very moveable life," she once said.

The long drive from the gates to the castle through an enveloping forest of evergreen conifers casts an instant spell of privacy and tranquillity. In the style of a centuries-old summertime royal progress, trucks filled with clothing in trunks and wardrobes as well as moving vans containing household goods are driven up from London by soldiers a week before the Queen's arrival in early August. Horses are transported from Windsor and dogs from Sandringham. As soon as the Queen leaves Buckingham Palace, the furniture in the private quarters is covered in dust sheets, although the offices continue to run, albeit at a slower pace. Maids, cooks, housekeepers, footmen, security officers, and other household workers go northward in two contingents, each group of eighty spending a month in the staff quarters at Balmoral.

"There is a certain fascination in keeping the place as Queen Victoria had it," the Queen has remarked. The decor is remarkably unchanged, except for the welcome elimination of the potted palms. "The furniture has barely been moved," said her cousin Margaret Rhodes. "The pictures are the same too." Queen Victoria's favorite chair in the drawing room is so sacred that no one is allowed to sit in it. "Every new person goes for it, and everyone screams," said Jean Carnarvon.

Elizabeth II follows a timeless routine firmly rooted in the late nineteenth century, with some modern variations, and everyone falls into line. The atmosphere recalls summer camp, with boarding-school-style schedules. After the bagpiper does his 9 A.M. march, the Queen typically devotes several hours to her boxes, delivered on a trolley to her first floor study — the same room chosen by Queen Victoria for its view up the valley of the Dee. She also attends to developments on the fifty-thousand-acre estate. Although Balmoral is directly overseen by her husband, "Her Majesty is aware of everything," said Martin Leslie, for sixteen years the factor, or estate manager. She reads the factor's regular reports and checks on the status of the Highland Cattle she breeds, but she also questions the ghillies, gamekeepers, and stalkers she has known for decades. Her knowledge emerges in surprising ways. While driving a Scottish cleric on a tour of the estate, she suddenly shouted "Hooray!" as they passed one of her gamekeepers walking on the hills with a young woman.

The Queen explained that his wife had left him, and she was delighted that he was out with a new girlfriend.

Following her morning obligations, she tries to spend as much time outdoors as possible — often horseback riding or walking with her dogs through the great stands of fir trees, up the hills ablaze with purple heather and across the burns, tiny streams bubbling up from beneath the rocky soil. She can inhale the pine-scented air and gaze at the snow-capped North Cairngorns in the distance and what Byron called the "steep frowning glories" of Lochnagar, rising more than three thousand feet above nearby Loch Muick. "At Balmoral, she knows every inch," said Malcolm Ross, for many years a senior member of her household. "She can enjoy being a countrywoman."

From the age of sixteen, when she learned to expertly shoot a rifle, she developed a passion for stalking the indigenous Red Deer, and many days she would slip on her macintosh trousers and ride out on one of her home-bred Garron or Fell ponies, or drive one of the estate's dark green Range Rovers to a beat on a high ridge above the treeline. She and one of her stalkers would patiently track the stags from late morning until late afternoon, sometimes climbing as high as two thousand feet, and pausing only for a lunch of cold meat, fruit, and a slice of plum pudding retrieved from a canvas bag. Moving in for the kill, she would crawl through the undergrowth until the stag was within range. "It was always fun to see a new stalker out for the first time with the Queen," recalled Margaret Rhodes, who began stalking with her cousin when they were teenagers. "She would be crawling on her stomach with her nose up to the soles of the stalker's boots, which would be a surprise to the stalker." She shot her last stag in 1983, in a little glen near the Spittal of Glenmuick, a place subsequently called "the Queen's Corry."

When someone shoots a stag, it is gutted on the hillside, and its disemboweled carcass is strapped on the back of a rugged and sure-footed deer pony, which carries it down the boulder-strewn hills to the castle, where it is hung in the deer larder for skinning. (Even after she stopped stalking, the Queen continued to visit the larder at the end of the day.) Every part of the deer is used, from heads and antlers for trophies and meat for meals, to the hooves and the eyeballs, which are sold for export. The white Garron ponies are so streaked with blood that they need to be scrubbed each night.

Such carnage is second nature to the Queen, who is equally matter-of-fact about her other favorite country pursuit, picking up fallen grouse during shooting parties on the moors above the castle— a practice she was forced to stop at age eighty-five due to persistent pain in one of her knees. Shotguns never interested her, so while the men in her family — all attired smartly in tweed shooting suits and Barbours — joined the line of butts, their guns aimed at the unpredictable birds whizzing and swooping overhead, she would stand behind, dressed in a skirt, sturdy jacket, and head scarf, with two or three of her gun dogs, usually cocker spaniels (nicknamed "the hoovers") or Labradors. Using an impressive repertoire of whistles, hand signals, and calls, she would send out the dogs to retrieve the birds, sometimes at a distance of nearly a thousand yards, directing them from one point to another in search of the downed prey. If the bird wasn't dead, she would put it out of its misery by swiftly dispatching it with a stick. Once when a particularly versatile display of her "picker-up" skill prompted applause from the guns, ghillies, and beaters, she said, "If I'd known you were all watching, I'd never have tried it."

The shooting and stalking guests at Balmoral generally come on weekends, but most of the time the castle is filled with friends and relatives. The Queen issues all invitations to stay overnight, and she takes her hostess role seriously, often greeting guests at the side door where visitors enter the castle. "She shows you to your room," said one frequent guest. "She knows what books are there and she will make a reference to them. They change every year. It is a peculiar combination of relaxed formality or formal relaxation." To Malcolm Ross, being her guest in Scotland is "as if a switch has flipped. She is still the Queen, but she is a wonderful hostess in her own house. You are extremely privileged to see how relaxed she can be."

After a day on the hills, the guests change out of their shooting kit, and the Queen makes tea for everyone, measuring the leaves into a pot and pouring hot water from a silver urn. After another change of clothes, it's time for drinks in the drawing room, where Elizabeth II sits at a table playing patience, a vision from Victorian times. "She is conversing as she is playing," recalled a guest. "Everyone is sitting around. Some talk among themselves, others are at the table where she is playing. She is turning the cards and chatting, in her element, clearly very relaxed."

The prime minister visits for an obligatory weekend each September, and the Privy Counsellors come for a day, spending only a few minutes on formal business. Mostly there is a relentless round of socializing, which often includes picnic lunches and candlelit barbecues in lodges or cabins on the banks of lakes and rivers, deep in the Old Caledonian forest, or up in the hills. Frequently the guests don't learn until the last minute whether dinner will be black tie and gowns indoors or sweaters with trousers or skirts outdoors. By that time they will have already gone through three changes of clothing.

The Queen and Prince Philip organize the picnic ritual like a military drill. Chefs at the castle do the preliminary work, and all the food, plates, cutlery, and cooking equipment are loaded onto a trailer pulled by a Land Rover. Designed with a naval officer's efficiency by Philip, the trailer has compartments for every item. Household staff are conspicuously absent, allowing the Queen to almost gleefully undertake their chores. She always lays the table, and "she has to have it absolutely right," said Anne Glenconner, who was often invited by Princess Margaret. Philip does the grilling, wreathed in smoke. He is known as a creative cook, improvising recipes he has seen on television — from sausages to roast pig.

Once the Queen Mother and some friends staying at Birkhall ended up dining at the other end of the same bothy where the Queen was entertaining. "Our lunch was over before [the Queen Mother's] group had finished their drinks," said a guest. When the Queen puts on her yellow Marigold gloves to wash the dishes, everybody pitches in to clear the table, and the cleanup is rapid. Each item must be returned to the trailer exactly as it was packed. "Woe betide if you put the cutlery in the wrong place," said one veteran guest.

In the evenings, the family has a long tradition of playing vigorous games such as "Kick the Can" and "Stone," with guests as well as members of the household. Twice each autumn they gather in the castle ballroom for the Ghillies' Ball, where the men wear black tie and kilts, and the women dress in tiaras, long gowns, and tartan sashes fastened with diamond brooches. As military musicians play their tunes, the Queen and her family whirl through intricate reels and veletas with gamekeepers, ghillies, footmen, and maids — a montage of sights and sounds from an earlier century.

Balmoral echoes personal memories for Elizabeth II — of childhood, the war, Philip's proposal — and it represents a continuum back to Queen Victoria, even a connection to the Bavarian landscapes of her ancestors, which are conjured up by Prince Albert's adaptations of architectural styles from Germany. "At Balmoral, she never forgets she is Queen," said a Scottish cleric who visited there often. "*You* never forget she is Queen." All guests, including relatives who call her Lilibet and longtime friends, bow and curtsy when they greet her in the morning, and when she retires at night.

Yet her life in the Highlands offers her a taste of normality, and a sense of freedom. She goes into the nearby village of Ballater and stands in line at the local shops. She does household chores in remote cabins. She dresses unpretentiously in well-worn clothes — always the tartan skirts (never pants except for riding or field sports), but also plain black shoes with low socks, a buttoned-up cardigan with another sweater layered on top, and her ubiquitous strand of pearls. When she has downtime, she reads for pleasure, particularly historical novels — not, to anyone's knowledge, the seven volumes of Proust, "engrossed in the sufferings of Swann . . . while in the wet butts on the hills the guns cracked out their empty tattoo," as imagined by Alan Bennett in *The Uncommon Reader,* his droll novel about the Queen. For many years she would choose from a batch of volumes recommended by the Book Trust, a British charity founded in 1921 to promote books and reading. But the principal escape is through her primal communion with the countryside. "You can go out for miles and never see anybody," she has said. "There are endless possibilities." It is a world where she can live life "to the fullest."

CHAPTER NINE
DAYLIGHT ON THE MAGIC

In the 1960s, the Queen became a more relaxed and consistently engaged mother with her second set of children. "Goodness what fun it is to have a baby in the house again!" she said after Edward's birth in 1964. Mary Wilson recalled that on Tuesday evenings, as the prime minister's audience was drawing to a close, her husband "was very impressed by the fact that she always wanted to be there for the children's baths."

Elizabeth II felt comfortable spending more time in the nursery in part because she got along so well with Mabel Anderson. The principal nanny for Charles and Anne, Helen Lightbody, had been an autocrat nearly fifteen years older than the Queen, fierce in upholding her authority over the children. Lightbody had favored Charles over Anne, who bore the brunt of her reprimands. Displeased by her harsh treatment of his spirited daughter, Prince Philip had arranged for Lightbody's departure.

Mabel Anderson was a year younger than the Queen, and she had an affectionate and flexible nature as well as a firm sense of right and wrong. The Queen was not intimidated by Anderson as she had been by Lightbody, and the two women worked together with the younger children. When

"By far the most moving and meaningful moment came when I put my hands between Mummy's and swore to be her liege man of life and limb and to live and die against all manner of folks."

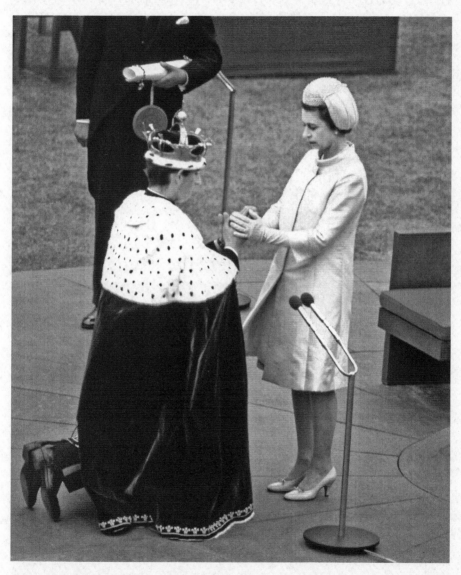

Prince Charles paying homage to his mother after his investiture as Prince of Wales, July 1969. REGINALD DAVIS MBE (LONDON)

Anderson took time off, the Queen felt relaxed enough to stay in the nursery with Andrew and Edward, putting on an apron for their baths and lulling them to sleep. Some critics have questioned whether she indulged Andrew and Edward too much, making up for not having spent more time with her older children.

Although still not inclined toward hugging and kissing, she showed more of her playful streak with Andrew and Edward. They knew Buckingham Palace was an office where the priorities were, in Andrew's words, "work and responsibilities and duties." Still, the passage outside the nursery echoed with the thuds of tennis balls and footballs barely missing the glass cabinets. When Sir Cecil Hogg, the family's ear, nose, and throat doctor for more than a dozen years, was paying a house call at the Palace, "he could hear the younger children rampaging in another room," recalled his daughter Min Hogg. "One of the children rushed into her bedroom and the Queen laughed and said to him, 'You and your monsters!' "

At Windsor Castle, which the boys considered their real home, they would race their bicycles and play "dodge-ems" with pedal cars along the gilded Grand Corridor, with its twenty-two Canalettos and forty-one busts on scagliola pedestals, or outside on the gravel paths. If the boys fell down, the Queen would "pick us up and say, 'Don't be so silly. There's nothing wrong with you. Go and wash off,' just like any parent," Andrew recalled. At teatime, they would sit with their parents to watch the BBC's *Grandstand* sports program on Saturdays and the Sunday Cricket League. "As a family we would always see more of the Queen at weekends than during the week," said Andrew.

Charles and Anne were away at school much of the time during the 1960s. Anne's experience at her prestigious boarding school in Kent, Benenden, was much happier than her older brother's. She had her father's thick skin and lacerating wit to protect her from mean girls — whom she called a "caustic lot." Her headmistress noted Anne's ability to "exert her authority in a natural manner without being aggressive." Like Prince Philip she was "extremely quick to grasp things" as well as impatient with those who could not. At five foot six, she was taller than her mother, with a trim and alluring figure. She had the Queen's porcelain complexion, but stronger features including a pendulous lower lip that gave her a sulky demeanor. As a teenager she wore her hair long, which softened her appearance.

Despite her sharp intelligence, Anne had scant interest in academics, and her examination results weren't strong enough for admission to a university. She enjoyed pushing the envelope physically, another trait inherited from her father, who taught her to sail in the rough waters off the Scottish coast and competed with her in the Cowes regatta. Anne wrote that sailing gave her "an utterly detached sensation that I have only otherwise experienced on a galloping horse . . . testing your skill against Nature, your ideals and the person you would like to be." Having ridden since the age of two when she first sat on a white pony named Fum, horses became Anne's passion. After graduating from Benenden in 1968 at age eighteen, she focused on competing in the arduous equestrian sport of three-day eventing.

When Charles was approaching his final year at Gordonstoun, his parents convened a meeting over dinner in December 1965 to map out the appropriate future for the heir to the throne, who was not included in the discussion. Three previous kings — Edward VII, Edward VIII, and George VI — had taken courses at Oxford and Cambridge but had never earned degrees. Since neither Philip nor Elizabeth II had university experience, they relied on the counsel of the Archbishop of Canterbury, Michael Ramsey; Prime Minister Harold Wilson; Dickie Mountbatten, then chief of the Defence Staff; Robin Woods, the dean of Windsor; and Sir Charles Wilson, principal and vice-chairman of Glasgow University and chairman of the Committee of Vice-Chancellors.

For several hours, they discussed various alternatives as the Queen listened. Harold Wilson advocated Oxford, but Dickie preferred Trinity College at Cambridge and the Royal Naval College at Dartmouth, followed by the Royal Navy, a plan the family eventually adopted a year later. Charles was pleased to be attending Cambridge, if only because it was so near the shooting at Sandringham, with its "crème de la crème of wild birds." When he enrolled in the autumn of 1967, he was the first royal student to live in rooms at the college. Former conservative politician Rab Butler, then the master of Trinity, was his mentor.

As a general principle, the Queen sought to expose Charles and Anne to challenging situations and preferred to talk to them "on level grown-up terms," one writer observed in 1968. "I remember the patience Prince Charles showed when he was around all those adults," said Mary Wilson. At one Buckingham Palace luncheon in honor of a delegation from Nigeria, Cynthia Gladwyn found him "charming . . . with his desire to please, his tentative interest in everybody, his wild-rose coloring . . . his sensitivity contrasting with his father's lack of it." Within the requirements of their royal existence, Elizabeth II encouraged her older children to work their way through difficulties, learning to think for themselves — an approach some intimates criticized as too lax.

"Right from the beginning, they were given a tremendously free rein," a lady-in-waiting told journalist Graham Turner, who wrote a damning account of the Queen's mothering skills. "Because of that early independence, it became more like a club than a family," the lady-in-waiting continued. "Charles and Anne, in particular, would also have thought, 'Don't let's bother Mummy, she's got enough on her plate already.' And she wouldn't have expected anything else. . . . The Queen and Prince Philip brought up the children very toughly."

Princess Anne countered that "it just beggars belief" to suggest that her mother was aloof and uncaring. "We as children may have not been too demanding, in the sense that we understood what the limitations were in time and the responsibilities placed on her as monarch in the things she had to do and the travels she had to make," said Anne, "but I don't believe that any of us, for a second, thought she didn't care for us in exactly the same way as any mother did. . . . We've all been allowed to find our own way and we were always encouraged to discuss problems, to talk them through. People have to make their own mistakes and I think she's always accepted that."

Of all the Queen's children, Anne was the most secure and self-sufficient. The mother-daughter relationship ran smoothly, largely because they shared such a strong bond through horses. And since Anne was cut from Prince Philip's cloth — feisty, confident, and straightforward — she could deal with his tough love.

Charles, however, struggled with his father's demands and expectations. He had shown his mettle in taking on physical challenges, notably during two terms in the Australian outback at the Timbertop school. On returning to Gordonstoun he achieved the same "Guardian" leadership position his father had held. He even mimicked some of his father's mannerisms — walking with one arm behind his back, making light jokes to put others at ease, tugging at his jacket sleeve, clasping his hands, or jabbing his right forefinger for emphasis.

But Philip continued to offer more criticism than praise to his son, deepening Charles's insecurity. Philip couldn't reconcile their "great difference," as he once put it. "He's a romantic, and I'm a pragmatist." Although Charles "was too proud to admit it," wrote Jonathan Dimbleby, "the Prince still craved the affection and appreciation that his father — and his mother — seemed unable or unwilling to proffer. . . . In self protection, he retreated more and more into formality with his parents." When it came to guidance about Charles's future, father and son minimized conflict by communicating through crisply composed letters.

It was at Sandringham and Balmoral that the children found common ground with their parents. To the Queen, Sandringham represents "an escape place, but it is also a commercially viable bit of England. I like farming . . . I like animals. I wouldn't be happy if I just had arable farming." The Queen and Prince Philip deeply imprinted their four children with knowledge of flora and fauna, and they all came to appreciate, as Anne wrote, the "pure luxury" of hours on horseback across the "miles of stubble fields around Sandringham," as well as "the autumn colours of the rowans and silver birches, the majesties of the old Scots pines" of Deeside. Charles was so inspired that at age twenty he wrote a book for his younger brothers about the mythical "Old Man of Lochnagar" who lived in a cave on the mountain above Balmoral, tried to travel to London but returned to the solitude of his "special" home.

Philip taught all four children to shoot, as well as to cast into the pools of the River Dee and catch salmon with a well-tied fly. Anne stalked with her mother, and was often the only other woman on the hills tracking deer. Parents and children were bound by an appreciation of country traditions and rituals, including being smeared with blood on their cheeks after killing their first stag.

The family frequently took the Royal Train to the Highlands, and occasionally began their holiday with a cruise on *Britannia* through the Western Isles of Scotland. Starting in the late 1960s, the sea voyage became a regular tradition. It was one of the few times when the Queen wore trousers other than on horseback or while participating in field sports, mainly so she could easily (and modestly) go up and down the ladders onto launches when they went ashore on deserted beaches for picnics. The culmination of the cruise was "*Britannia* Day," when they stopped in Caithness on the northern coast. They would disembark at the port of Scrabster and travel in a caravan of cars to the Castle of Mey, where the Queen Mother had been preparing for weeks, assisted by her lady-in-waiting Ruth Fermoy, giving instructions to her chef, and checking on the ripeness of the fruits and vegetables in her garden. One year the Queen Mother sent an urgent message to her daughter on *Britannia:* "There is a grave shortage of lemons. Could you please bring a couple with you? M." The Queen obligingly emerged from the royal yacht clutching a plastic bag filled with lemons.

The royal party strolled through the walled gardens before sitting down in the dining room at Mey for a luncheon of *oeufs Drumkilbo* (a mousse of eggs, prawns, and lobster, a favorite of the Queen Mother), salmon, chicken, lamb, and summer pudding. In the afternoon they visited the adjacent farm or walked toward the sea, and headed back to Scrabster after tea. By tradition, the Queen and her mother sent each other farewell poems through the Coast Guard ("A meal of such splendour, repast of such zest. It will take us to Sunday just to digest. To leafy Balmoral we are now on our way, but our hearts will remain at the Castle of Mey"). When *Britannia* steamed along the coast, flares were launched from both ship and shore as the

Queen Mother, her friends, and staff lined up behind the castle, waving tea towels and tablecloths. In the distance through binoculars, they could see the tiny figure of the Queen on deck, waving her own white cloth while *Britannia* blew its horn.

The royal family acquired an unusual addition in the spring of 1967 when Philip's mother came to live at Buckingham Palace at the Queen's invitation. Impoverished and frail, eighty-two-year-old Princess Alice had been living in Athens, where she had finally been forced to close her nursing sisterhood due to financial problems. Although she was not a real nun, she continued to wear her gray habit as a practical matter. "She did not have to worry about clothes or getting her hair done," Philip explained to Hugo Vickers, his mother's biographer.

Unlike the Queen Mother, who was an integral part of nearly every important gathering, Alice had always been a family satellite, orbiting in and out on visits to London, Windsor, Sandringham, and Balmoral. She disconcertingly referred to Philip by his nursery name, "Bubby-kins," and all the grandchildren called her "Yaya," the Greek name for grandmother. They were both fascinated and terrified by her eccentricities and her deep voice. A cigarette always in hand, she announced her rather spectral presence with a plume of smoke and hacking cough.

Alice had her son's direct manner, which her deafness made even more formidable. "Oh, I thought you were saying something interesting," she said to the Queen's assistant private secretary

Edward Ford after he had repeated an admittedly banal question about the circus several times during dinner. Anne acknowledged that Alice was not a "cuddly granny," and Charles admitted being intimidated at first. But they were soon enraptured by her childhood tales of Queen Victoria, and her intriguing theories, such as the need to "compartmentalize" the brain.

When she moved into her suite — two rooms on the first floor just to the right of the balcony in the front of Buckingham Palace — Andrew and Edward often came to play halma, a form of Chinese checkers. The Queen was also a frequent visitor, and communicated well with her mother-in-law, even joining the elderly princess to watch the Changing of the Guard outside her window. Philip, while devoted to his mother, had a prickly relationship with her — "not arguments, but let's say slight differences of agreement," Anne explained to Hugo Vickers. "My father would then go off down the corridor muttering, and she would be in her room muttering too."

Alice suffered from chronic bronchitis, and after her eighty-fourth birthday in February 1969 her health went into a steep decline. She died in her sleep on December 5, and she was buried at Windsor, where she had been born. Her worldly goods were even more meager than those of her late husband — just three dressing gowns that were immediately distributed to her nurses.

Alice had remained out of the public eye during her final years at the Palace, and she didn't make even a cameo appearance in the most consequential media project ever to involve the royal family, a unique documentary film offering a fly-on-the-wall view of them at work and at play. It was the collective brainchild of Prince Philip; John Brabourne, who was a successful filmmaker; Dickie Mountbatten; and the Queen's new press secretary, William Heseltine, who took over in 1968 after the retirement of Commander Sir Richard Colville, the man in charge of dealing with the press since King George VI appointed him in 1947. To recognize his long service, the Queen had knighted Colville in 1965.

For more than two decades, his mandate had been unabashedly protective. "We are not publicity agents for the royal family," he said in 1949. "We are here to tell the press how far they cannot go." His main job was to spoon-feed anodyne royal tidbits to the two court correspondents for the Press Association, the principal British news agency, who had their own office in Buckingham Palace, and to orchestrate silent newsreel footage of the Queen in her public appearances at home and abroad.

But by the 1960s, the perception had taken hold that the Queen was losing touch with her subjects, who were beginning to think she and her family were dull, to wonder what exactly she did for a living, and more ominously, to question whether she was giving good value for government money spent on her and her family. Philip was the only family member who had seen television as an effective communications tool. Since his 1957 documentary on his Commonwealth tour, he had hosted a second program about the Galápagos Islands a decade later, and he had also been the first to sit for a television interview in 1961.

Philip found a kindred spirit in William Heseltine, a forthright Australian — the very opposite of the buttoned-up aristocrats who traditionally served the monarch — with a modern point of view. "I was quite a different kind of person," Heseltine recalled. "I did think the strategy of keeping the private and public lives far apart had perhaps gone a little too far" and that the Queen and her family had become "rather one-dimensional figures." His idea, shared by Philip and the others, was to show the Queen hard at work in a variety of settings, to get across the "relentlessness" of her job, and to open the curtain on her private life as a wife and mother in places never before seen by the public. The film would be broadcast just before the investiture of Prince Charles as the Prince of Wales in July 1969, introducing him as the symbol of the monarchy's new generation as he reached his twenty-first year.

Above all, the architects of the film wanted to convey Elizabeth II's humanity behind the lofty position of sovereign, and to exploit the wholesome image of her model family. "I think it is quite wrong that there should be a sense of remoteness or majesty," said Philip. "If people see, whoever it happens to be, whatever head of state, as individuals, as people, I think it makes it much easier for them to accept the system or to feel part of the system."

The Queen was reluctant at first, discomfited by the intrusiveness of the cameras. But when her longtime friend John Brabourne presented the idea, she said, "You can do it, and then we'll see what it looks like." Brabourne brought in Richard Cawston of the BBC to direct, and Philip supervised an advisory committee drawn from both the BBC and rival ITV, coordinating everything with Heseltine and his team. Elizabeth II acquiesced, said Gay Charteris, because "the Queen goes with what she has to do." The film would be called, simply, *Royal Family.*

Shooting began on June 8, 1968, and continued for nearly a year. The Queen submitted to lights, cameras, and crews over seventy-five days in 172 locations around the world, resulting in forty-three hours of film that was eventually cut to 110 minutes. She was ill at ease initially, but Cawston managed to relax her, and she became less conscious of his presence, even when he was filming at close range. "She suddenly discovered it was something she could do," said John Brabourne. She teasingly called the director "Cawston," and invited him to meals so they could discuss camera angles and lighting. "Can't we avoid a shadow here?" she would say, slipping into the filmmaker's argot. "We can't have a backlit ambassador." When she asked to see the rushes, Cawston declined, saying she might feel self-conscious.

The novelty of the film was the juxtaposition of public and private, reinforcing a new image of the Queen as a working mother at a desk littered with papers in an office at once formal and cozy. For the first time, viewers could see the plain interior of the Royal Train, the country house comfort of *Britannia*'s drawing rooms, and the private apartments at Windsor Castle and Buckingham Palace.

The filmmakers covered the professional bases: the Queen dispensing honors; making her official rounds on state visits to Chile and Brazil; discussing her Brazil speech with private secretary Michael Adeane ("Not enough thanks . . . It seems a bit churlish not to thank them"); greeting Harold Wilson at his weekly audience; receiving ambassadors; making stilted conversation with President Richard Nixon before a Buckingham Palace luncheon; presiding over one of her garden parties; riding sidesaddle at her birthday parade; circulating through receptions at Buckingham Palace. Charles was shown in action on water skis and a bicycle, and joking about writing a paper for his history course. Philip was filmed while piloting an airplane and a helicopter, working on his charities in his office (more sleek and modern than his wife's), and painting a landscape. At crucial intervals the red boxes appeared — aboard the Royal Train, being lowered onto the deck of *Britannia* by helicopter, at Balmoral and Sandringham.

Aside from emphasizing the Queen's dedication, the film provided the first extended look at what she was like in her off-hours: in her riding habit feeding carrots to her horses and with Anne on the gallops in Berkshire; examining a necklace of enormous rubies with Bobo MacDonald; washing dishes; driving the children in a Land Rover to visit puppies at the Sandringham kennels; orchestrating a family barbecue at Loch Muick with Philip, Charles, Anne, Andrew, Edward, and the corgis; laughing with her children at an American sitcom on television and trading stories around the table at lunch; decorating a Christmas tree with her extended family, including the Queen Mother, who reminisced about "the King." Excluded were any scenes of stalking or shooting, for fear they would seem elitist or bloodthirsty.

A previously unseen tenderness emerged as the Queen sat on a sofa with her two young sons, pointing out photographs in a family album, and during an excursion with Edward to a shop near Balmoral. Fishing some coins out of a change purse she said to the woman at the counter, "This is all I've got." As Edward waited in the front seat of her car, she handed him some candy and said with a giggle, "Disgusting! This is going to be a gooey mess!"

In one of the most discussed sequences in the film, editing was used to distort reality and compound an unfortunate impression. U.S. ambassador to the Court of St. James's Walter Annenberg presented his credentials to the Queen on April 29, 1969, in one of the most formal and time-honored of her ceremonies. "Court Dress" is white tie, tailcoat, and top hat, and the ambassador is driven to the late-morning audience at Buckingham Palace in one of the Queen's gilded carriages with a coachman and footman in long red coats and silk hats. By that gesture, the Queen signals her personal responsibility for the diplomat, and she has been known to chastise Palace officials who don't send out the carriage in bad weather. "She never underplays the importance of ceremony," said a diplomat who assisted at many of the credentials presentations. "But part of the Queen's process and style is to put the other person at ease as soon as she can after the formal bit. She does combine

311

formality and informality in a remarkable way."

Walter Annenberg had rehearsed his lines repeatedly, and he and his wife, Lee, had practiced their bows and curtsys. On the appointed morning, after he had perfectly executed his steps, bows, and presentation of "the letter of recall of my predecessor and my own letters of credence," the Queen tried to lighten the mood in her usual manner by asking where he and his wife were living. "We're in the embassy residence," he replied, "subject, of course, to some of the discomfiture as a result of a need for, uh, elements of refurbishment and rehabilitation." Her expression momentarily puzzled, she swiftly moved to the next step of receiving embassy staff and Lee Annenberg.

As if to emphasize the ambassador's apparent buffoonery, the next scene in the film showed the Queen entering a Buckingham Palace party for diplomats. "He's not here," she murmured to her husband. "Who's not here?" Philip asked. "The American ambassador," she replied with an amused smile — implying she meant the hapless Annenberg, while in fact she was referring to his predecessor, David Bruce, and the reception had actually taken place the previous November.

Annenberg had reported to Richard Nixon that his credentials presentation had been "infinitely rewarding and impressive." But when *Royal Family* aired on the BBC on June 21, 1969, the American ambassador's "elements of refurbishment" remark produced howls of laughter and widespread ridicule in Britain. Newspapers challenged readers to produce even more egregious phrases; *The Sunday Times* called Annenberg the "flustered envoy";

and one magazine said he had the "verbal felic-ity of W. C. Fields." What the press did not know was that the sixty-one-year-old ambassador, like the Queen's own father, had suffered from a life-time of stuttering. Through speech therapy, he had learned the somewhat paradoxical strategy of framing complex sentences with ornate words to prevent verbal stumbling. Annenberg was so mor-tified by the outcry that he told Secretary of State William Rogers he would resign if Nixon thought he couldn't be effective in his job. Nixon reassured his ambassador that he should stay in place.

"When we reviewed the film before it was fin-ished, the great refurbishment thing was rather laughable and we debated whether to include it," Martin Charteris later admitted. "We allowed it to remain, but we should not have. As a result, I think the royal family felt a certain sense of guilt about Walter because they allowed a joke to be made about him. In fact, he was honorable and straightforward."

For all its appearance of spontaneity, the film was in fact a tightly controlled rebranding of the royal family as accessible and folksy, engaging in activi-ties ordinary people could relate to. Most critics applauded the film's humanizing effect. Cecil Bea-ton, who had observed the Queen closely for more than two decades, thought she "came through as a great character, quite severe, very self-assured, a bit bossy, serious, frowning a bit (and very lined). Her sentences are halting. She hesitates mid-way, you think she has dried up . . . but she goes on doggedly. She came out on top as the nice person she is."

There was some inevitable mockery of the family's old-fashioned traditions and stodgy costumes. One wag called the film "Corgi and Beth," and *Private Eye* came up with working-class nicknames: the Queen was Brenda, Prince Philip was Keith, Princess Margaret was Yvonne, and Prince Charles was Brian.

Some worried about the consequences of violating the precept set out in the nineteenth century by economist and constitutional expert Walter Bagehot that a sovereign should maintain a measure of mystery: "We must not let in daylight upon magic." Milton Shulman, the television critic for the *Evening Standard,* questioned the authenticity of the Queen and her family behaving "like a middle-class family in Surbiton or Croydon," and wondered about the precedent of using television "to act as an image-making apparatus for the monarchy," noting that "every institution that has so far attempted to use TV to popularize or aggrandize itself has been trivialized by it." Even the BBC's David Attenborough, one of the producers of *Royal Family,* declared that the film could kill the monarchy, an institution that "depends on mystique and the tribal chief in his hut. If any member of the tribe ever sees inside the hut, then the whole system of the tribal chiefdom is damaged and the tribe eventually disintegrates."

Neither the Queen nor the Palace hierarchy expressed second thoughts, although she never again permitted that kind of intimate entrée. Princess Anne later said that the film had been a "rotten idea" that she "never liked. . . . The attention that had been brought on one since one was a child, you just didn't want any more. The last thing you needed was great access." But the reaction of the public was overwhelmingly positive. *Royal Family* was repeated five times and was seen by forty million viewers in the United Kingdom and an estimated 400 million in 130 countries. Viewers were captivated by the informality of the Queen and her family and surprised to hear her conversational voice as well as her infectious laugh.

The glow of good feeling created by the film carried over to the investiture of Prince Charles on July 1, which was televised from the grassy courtyard of ancient Caernarvon Castle in Wales. Only one previous Prince of Wales, Charles's great-uncle, the Duke of Windsor, had been officially inducted in the role, in a ceremony at the castle in 1911. To help create a stronger bond with Wales, overcome historic resentments dating from the country's conquest by English kings in the thirteenth century, and restrain incipient nationalistic feelings, his mother had arranged for Charles to leave Cambridge the previous spring for eight weeks at University College, Aberystwyth. There he picked up some rudimentary Welsh, and was tutored in the history of the country's nationalism — valuable lessons, he said afterward, that helped him understand that the "language and culture" were "very unique and special to Wales" and "well worth preserving."

The actual investiture ceremony was a twentieth-century invention evoking medieval traditions, orchestrated by the Duke of Norfolk on a contemporary stage set created by Welshman

315

Lord Snowdon, who was a designer as well as a photographer. With TV cameras in mind, Snowdon designed a low round slate dais underneath a minimalist Plexiglas canopy supported by steel poles resembling pikestaffs. On the dais were three austere thrones of slate with scarlet cushions. Snowdon intended to project a "grand and simple" image of a modern monarchy. "I didn't want red carpets," Snowdon said. "I wanted him to walk across simple green grass."

The Queen was surprisingly on edge while she prepared for the procession into the courtyard. With noticeable agitation, she wondered aloud if the text of what she had to say would be on her seat. Philip snapped that he had no idea, "that it was her show not his." After exchanging more cross words, they moved off, their faces suitably arranged.

As she waited on the dais for the arrival of her son, Elizabeth II tucked her white handbag under one arm and held a furled umbrella in the other — an unnecessary precaution, since there was only a brief light drizzle. With four thousand invited guests looking on, Charles emerged from the Chamberlain Tower in his dark blue dress uniform of Colonel-in-Chief of the Royal Regiment of Wales, decorated with his gleaming Garter collar.

The climax of the ceremony came when he kneeled before his mother, who invested him with the insignia of his office in a solemn ritual punctuated with his periodic shy smiles. She first presented him with a sword inscribed with his motto "Ich Dien" (I serve), hanging it gently around his neck before adjusting the strap attached to its scabbard. She then crowned him with a coronet of 24-karat Welsh gold set sparingly with diamonds and emeralds over a purple velvet cap trimmed in ermine. Unlike other royal crowns, Charles's was strikingly stylized, with a single arch topped by an engraved orb, and crosses like stickpins interspersed with plainly wrought versions of the three-feathers emblem of the Prince of Wales.

As Elizabeth II put the coronet on his head, it settled just above his eyes, and he helped her by nudging it into place with his fingertips. She slipped onto his left hand a cabochon amethyst ring, symbolizing his unity with Wales, gave him his golden rod (for temporal rule), and draped a purple silk mantle with wide ermine collar on his shoulders, smoothing it into place in a practiced maternal gesture before fastening the gold clasp. After he had paid her homage, she raised him up and they exchanged the kiss of fealty on their left cheeks, signifying her pledge to protect the prince in his duties.

"By far the most moving and meaningful moment," he later wrote, "came when I put my hands between Mummy's and swore to be her liege man of life and limb and to live and die against all manner of folks." Those were the precise words his father had used during the Queen's coronation, and to Charles they were "magnificent, medieval, appropriate." The Queen looked suitably somber as well, although later that month, over lunch at Royal Lodge, Noel Coward told her that he had found the investiture moving. "She gaily shattered my sentimental illusions," Coward recorded, "by saying that they were both struggling not to giggle because at the dress rehearsal the crown was too big and extinguished him like a candle-snuffer!"

An estimated worldwide television audience of 500 million had watched the heir to the throne's official coming of age. For Charles, the investiture marked the start of his apprenticeship as king-in-waiting, the length of which he could never have imagined.

CHAPTER TEN
RING OF SILENCE

Pietro Annigoni returned to Buckingham Palace in the spring and fall of 1969 to paint the Queen's portrait for the second time. After an interval of fifteen years, Annigoni could detect changes that eluded those who saw the forty-three-year-old Queen every day. "Everything about her seemed smaller," he observed, "in some ways frailer and in some ways harder. As she posed her facial expression was mercurial — smiling, thoughtful, determined, uncertain, relaxed, taut, in rapid succession. . . . At every sitting the Queen chatted to me in the most natural way, and her disarming frankness never failed to surprise and fascinate me."

The diminutive artist forthrightly outlined to the Queen his vision for the portrait: "I see Your Majesty as being condemned to solitude because of your position," he said. "As a wife and mother you are entirely different, but I see you really alone as a monarch and I want to represent you that way. If I succeed, the woman, the Queen and, for that matter, the solitude will emerge." She nodded, examined the study he had painted during eight sittings and said, "One doesn't know one's self. After all, we have a biased view when we see ourselves in a mirror and, what's more, the image is always

319

He used to say to Elizabeth II, "Your job is to spread a carpet of happiness."

The Queen reviewing papers with her long-serving private secretary, Sir Martin Charteris, late at night aboard the royal yacht Britannia, *March 1972.* LICHFIELD/GETTY IMAGES

in reverse." She assented to his plan to portray her looking "thoughtful and severe, profoundly human," queenly yet unembellished. "I feel that the inspiration is there," she said.

They resumed their sittings at the end of October after she returned from Balmoral. In the interval, the world had been riveted by the landing of the first men on the moon. The Queen had become fascinated by these twentieth-century explorers after David Bruce brought *Apollo 8* astronaut Frank Borman — commander of the first crew to orbit the moon — his wife, and two young sons to Buckingham Palace the previous February.

When Neil Armstrong walked on the moon on July 20, he carried a microfilm message from the Queen to leave behind. She also sent her congratulations to the crew of *Apollo 11* "and to the American people on this historic occasion." She said the fortitude of astronauts Armstrong, Edwin "Buzz" Aldrin, and Michael Collins filled her with admiration, and that their exploits "add a new dimension to man's knowledge of the universe." The three American heroes came to London the following October as part of a world tour, and their first stop was Buckingham Palace, where they were greeted by Elizabeth II and her family. Somewhat sweetly, the men even bowed to little Andrew and Edward when they shook hands. The astronauts, all of whom were suffering from laryngitis and colds, remarked on how well informed the Queen was about their space voyage.

Elizabeth II now had a rooting interest in the *Apollo 12* crew when they blasted into space on November 14. She confessed to Annigoni that she had been waking up early to watch the television coverage of the second moon landing. During two of her sittings, she spent considerable time describing the mission's progress in detail, although she concurred with the artist that while "it filled us with wonder and admiration, it did not move us emotionally."

The second lunar launch coincided with Prince Charles's twenty-first birthday, which his mother marked with a grand ball at Windsor Castle for four hundred guests. It was a high-spirited celebration, and the Queen danced in her stocking feet past midnight. One party crasher, an Oxford undergraduate, scaled a garden wall and joined a group of guests. The Queen saw him and recalled that "he was so drunk that he couldn't say anything apart from a few incivilities." Yet after the police arrested the young man, who turned out to be an excellent student, she forgave his act of bravado. She said she hoped that he would not be expelled from college, and would only be "severely reprimanded and frightened."

The Windsor gala had been the handiwork of Patrick Plunket, 7th Baron Plunket, since 1954 the Queen's Deputy Master of the Household, who was one of her closest advisers as well as a friend since childhood. Three years older than the Queen, Plunket was a lifelong bachelor, always immaculately turned out, with military bearing and an impish grin. As the coordinator of the Queen's private social life, he had impeccable taste. He liked to fill Windsor Castle with imaginative floral arrangements incorporating zinnias, nicotiana, and alchemilla with peonies and tall white delphiniums, all dramatically spot-lit. "You must have emptied every greenhouse in Windsor Great Park," Elizabeth II once said to him. "Very nearly," he replied. "There's a little bit left."

Under Plunket's watch, Elizabeth II's guest lists expanded to include names from the artistic world — "people who never in the past would have been there," recalled a long-serving lady-in-waiting. He was a key adviser in creating a trendy mix for the Queen's informal luncheons at Buckingham Palace, and he even injected some variety into her weekend shooting parties. "He knew everybody and things like who Princess Margaret didn't like and who she shouldn't sit next to at dinner," said Margaret Rhodes.

But Plunket had a less obvious role as well, of equal importance to the Queen, that was grounded in their deep friendship. Plunket's parents, Teddy and Dorothé, who had been close to George VI and Elizabeth, had died in 1938 in an airplane crash. Plunket was just fifteen when he and his two younger brothers were orphaned, and the King and Queen took a strong interest in their upbringing. After Eton and Cambridge, Plunket served as an officer in the Irish Guards during World War II and was wounded in Belgium in 1944.

On his return to London, the King made him his equerry, and when Princess Elizabeth became Queen, she immediately asked Plunket to stay on and serve her as well. "She realized quickly that Patrick was someone she could depend on," recalled his brother Shaun Plunket. "He had a wonderful memory for names and faces, plus the knack of good judgment and an amazing instinct for the right and wrong thing to do, and she relied on that." In a household where many aides avoided delivering uncomfortable truths, Plunket spoke frankly to the woman he called "my boss" — "often with a smile, and she would smile back," said Shaun.

A connoisseur with several Rubenses in his collection of paintings, Plunket also advised the Queen on art purchases. Along with Prince Philip, he was a driving force behind transforming the bombed-out private chapel at Buckingham Palace into the Queen's Gallery, which exhibited royal artwork to the public for the first time in 1962. He shared his enthusiasm and knowledge with Elizabeth II, who came to appreciate her treasures with a zest evident in her after-dinner tours for guests at Windsor Castle and Buckingham Palace.

It was often said he was the brother she never had. He was certainly a trusted confidant. The Queen knew she could talk to him, even about personal matters, and depend on his total discretion. His cousin Lady Annabel Goldsmith called him "a great protector." If he thought the Queen looked tired, he would say, "Ma'am, do you feel I ought to close this down, or ask someone to close this down?" rather than, "I think you are looking tired." He always called her "Ma'am," and understood who she was and where she stood.

Yet he had an irreverent sense of humor perfectly pitched to hers. At ritualized events, Plunket would wink at his friends or nod at them in mock solemnity, sometimes over the Queen's shoulder. Afterward, he would regale her with stories, such as the time at a garden party when he found a sticky bun containing an entire set of dentures. He lightened the atmosphere and created a sense of fun, dancing with her when Philip was elsewhere, while never usurping her husband's role. The consort and the courtier enjoyed each other, and Philip was relieved that his wife had someone so capable to consult on matters beyond his own sphere.

With his wit and unstuffy demeanor, Plunket found a kindred spirit in Martin Charteris, who helped create a more open atmosphere around the Queen. The two men had been with Elizabeth II from the beginning, their admiration for her intensifying as their loyalty deepened. They both had country homes, but in London they each lived near the Queen, Plunket in a small bedroom, bathroom, and office in Buckingham Palace, and Charteris in an apartment on Friary Court in St. James's Palace.

Although he had served only as assistant private secretary for nearly twenty years, Charteris had his fingerprints on every important decision, and he was close to the Queen's children, particularly Charles, who felt "Martin was someone he could relate to," said Gay Charteris. But as the 1960s ended, the long-serving courtier figured his career would conclude where it began. Michael Adeane was just three years older, so when he reached retirement age, a promotion to private secretary "would have been too late for Martin," said his widow.

"One of the pleasant things about the Royal Household," David Bruce observed early in 1969, "is the admiration entertained by everyone in it for the Queen. I believe this is thoroughly deserved. . . . The atmosphere of cordiality in which she swims certainly impresses one as being completely genuine." She holds her employees to high standards, treats them with respect and fairness, only rarely showing anger.

In addition to her cadre of courtiers, the Queen from the outset has surrounded herself with an equally capable group of ladies-in-waiting, organized into a strict hierarchy, with medieval titles and clearly delineated tasks. They are almost exclusively drawn from the aristocracy, many of them are friends of the royal family, and all have shared interests, inbred caution, an intricate understanding of court etiquette, and sociable personalities.

The "head girl" beginning in 1967 was Fortune FitzRoy, the Duchess of Grafton, the Queen's Mistress of the Robes, although she had nothing to do with what the monarch wore. The position has historically been held by a duchess, and Fortune took over when the Dowager Duchess of Devonshire retired. Fortune Grafton was an experienced hand, having served in the second echelon as a Lady of the Bedchamber — again, bearing no relationship to the monarch's bedroom — since 1953. The third tier are called Women of the Bedchamber. Both the second and third levels have "Extra" ladies who are pulled in on special occasions, bringing the typical total to eleven.

As the senior lady-in-waiting, Fortune Grafton accompanies the Queen to the most prestigious events and tours, and the Ladies of the Bedchamber work in rotation at home and abroad, while the Women of the Bedchamber focus primarily on dealing with correspondence as well as attending the Queen on various occasions. All the ladies-in-waiting are adept at circulating through receptions, running interference for their boss by engaging overeager guests in conversation, or arranging for introductions.

The ladies understand — as do the equerries who perform the same duties — that even if Elizabeth II seems to be ignoring them, she always knows where they are. When she directly stares at them, she needs something done. They also know from her body language when she is ready to move along and one of them needs to step in to pick up the conversational thread. Sometimes she may shift her handbag or twirl her ring. The cues are subtle — the result of learning to read her over the years rather than any specific instructions she has given. "There are no set plays," said one former senior aide. "It is just intuition, like a wife knowing from long experience when her husband is ready to leave a drinks party."

The ladies-in-waiting have finely tuned antennae for what they call the "Awkward Squad," those who need to be calmed before meeting the monarch. On receiving lines, they stand ready to hold bouquets and unanticipated gifts pressed into the Queen's hands. "She will say, 'Can you cope? If you can't, get one of the policemen to help you,' " said one of her veteran attendants. "She will be given an enormous basket filled with flowers, and she will turn and say, 'What *are* we going to do with this?' "

Most of the time they do their drill perfectly,

but when they miss their mark, they can get what Elizabeth, the Countess of Leicester, for twenty years a Lady of the Bedchamber, called "a glare." Once when Lady Susan Hussey, a Woman of the Bedchamber, began arguing with historian Paul Johnson in a "fierce whisper," the Queen, who was standing nearby, gave them a "comprehensive monarchical glance" and "said sharply, 'stop bickering, you two!' "

Riding in the car with the Queen, her ladies-in-waiting generally let her take the conversational lead. "It would be ghastly for her to have a talkative lady-in-waiting," said Esme, the Dowager Countess of Cromer, who was appointed in 1967. "She would have to be thinking about what to do, whom to meet, giving speeches. It would drive her mad to have a wretched woman talking away, so I would keep my mouth shut."

The ladies-in-waiting often spend long hours on their feet, keeping up with their indefatigable boss, and since they have plenty of money, they can afford to work virtually as volunteers, with token compensation and small allowances for expenses. They can be rivalrous over choice assignments, but they tend to keep their competition among themselves. The point of their position is the honor of serving the monarch, and admission into an exclusive club where it is "easy to relax into luxury," wrote Frances Campbell-Preston, a lady-in-waiting to the Queen Mother.

While staying in one of the royal residences, they can choose from a pool of lady's maids to take care of their daily needs, and while on duty at Buckingham Palace, the Queen's attendants gather in their own sitting room on the second floor, opposite the nursery. Most days they have lunch in the household dining room with the private secretaries, equerries, and other senior officials. In the late afternoon they congregate for tea and drinks in the Equerry's Room. "We never talked about the Queen and Prince Philip," recalled Esme Cromer. "Never any complaining, or making observations. We were all very discreet, always. There was no telling stories, ever."

As with her top advisers, the Queen has always called her ladies-in-waiting and equerries by their Christian names. The staff (never servants, a word she dislikes) such as footmen, maids, and housekeepers go by their surnames, except for the Queen's closest personal aides, her dresser and her page. Two decades into the Queen's reign, dresser Bobo MacDonald was sui generis in the Palace hierarchy — a mother figure who had been caring for her boss's most private needs since she was a baby, generally acknowledged to be the sovereign's eyes and ears. In Buckingham Palace, the small, bespectacled Scotswoman lived in an apartment above the Queen's, where she had her meals served by liveried footmen instead of eating with the other staff in the dining room. She styled her wavy hair similarly to Elizabeth II and wore a triple strand of pearls as well as silk dresses tailored by royal couturier Norman Hartnell.

Nobody outside the family could match Bobo's knowledge of the Queen or the unbroken link to her childhood. They had shared a bedroom until Princess Elizabeth was a teenager, including the war years in Windsor Castle. Bobo had been there for the Queen's honeymoon, the King's death, the unfettered idyll in Malta, the months when Philip was traveling, the births of four children, the holidays, the foreign trips. "Bobo could say anything to the Queen, like 'You look awful in that dress,' or 'You can't wear green,' " said Margaret Rhodes. "She was a confidante, very much so."

Elizabeth II's principal clothing designers, Norman Hartnell and Hardy Amies, understood that Bobo not only organized the Tuesday afternoon fittings, but that her conservative taste weighed heavily in her employer's selections. To a certain extent, the Queen viewed her wardrobe as a military officer regards his various uniforms, clothes to be worn as the occasion required. But as Crawfie had observed when Elizabeth II was a princess, she took pleasure in crafting her look. "The sketches were put all over the floor and the rolls of fabric," recalled Valerie Rouse, a vendeuse for Hardy Amies. "She used to crawl around the floor saying, 'Well, I'll have this with that.' She absolutely knew she didn't want too many shoulder pads. She didn't want it too short. She did a lot of sitting down and waving."

Bobo inclined toward the practical and comfortable, especially in the winter when she fussed about her "little lady" being warm enough. She also considered accessories her bailiwick, particularly the Queen's boxy handbags that gave the couturiers fits. Bobo developed such a dislike for Amies that when the Queen knighted him she said, "Bobo will give me hell for this."

Monarch and faithful servant had a tight partnership, but few knew what passed between them, which made Bobo a powerful presence. "She knew everything about the Queen," said a long-serving footman. "They were stuck with each other. Miss MacDonald was not going to hand anything over to others." Nearly everybody — from the Lord Chamberlain to the housemaids — was intimidated by Bobo's strong personality, although she was "quite friendly when thawed," wrote valet John Dean, and had a good sense of humor. When the Queen visited a stud farm in Normandy owned by the Duc d'Audiffret-Pasquier in 1967 to see the stallions that had been covering her mares for several years, Bobo wandered away from the château for a walk in the woods and got lost, only to be arrested by the French secret service — a cause for much merriment among the royal party.

The Queen's small group of good friends has been known for the same rigorous discretion as her most faithful retainers. She has never particularly encouraged new friendships, but she has been open-minded enough to enlarge the circle from time to time. To be a friend of the Queen is an inherently lopsided experience. Those admitted to the inner sanctum understand the rules and have an instinctive sense of the invisible barriers. The women curtsy when they meet her, she kisses them on the cheek, and they feel free to return the affectionate gesture. They know how to make her relax and laugh, and she lets down her guard enough to share her piquant views of people and events, if not her innermost feelings.

They can seek her advice, which Patricia Brabourne described as "sound, very human, very wise." But they don't pick up the phone and unburden themselves. Above all, they are respectful. Even David Airlie (the 13th Earl), who first met her as a five-year-old, would never say "Oh, come off it." One ironclad principle is to avoid repeating her precise words — what has been called a "ring of silence." "Those who see the private side don't say anything specific for fear of violating her trust," said the son of one of her lifelong friends. Yet those who know her best have a knack for speaking perceptively about her character and personality without betraying confidences.

"She is not someone who is enormously intimate," said a friend of nearly six decades. "She is a wonderful friend, hugely amusing and incredible. She is straightforward and down-to-earth, and she is thoughtful. If one of one's children is terribly ill, she will know, and say 'How is so and so.' But you can't go too close. There is an aura. You wouldn't treat her like your best friend sitting on a sofa. It is not because she is doing it on purpose. It is just part of her. You cannot encroach on her personal life. You just don't go there."

Superficially, the Queen's circle might easily be dismissed as tweedy toffs, but in fact the men are capable and accomplished, the women bright and lively, all made of strong stuff and utterly reliable. "One of her greatest strengths is she is not associated with the old landed peerage," said Robert Gascoyne-Cecil, the 7th Marquess of Salisbury, very much of that group, which also includes the grand dukes of Marlborough, Devonshire, and Beaufort. "She doesn't have a clique. She has old friends, and the people she is related to. She is family minded."

For friendship she has relied on her extended network of cousins on the Bowes Lyon side, mainly Mary Colman, Jean Elphinstone Wills and her sister Margaret Rhodes, Mountbatten cousins Patricia Brabourne and Pamela Hicks, as well as Henry "Porchey" Carnarvon, Hugh Grafton, and Rupert Nevill, who all knew her from the wartime days in Windsor Castle, longtime family friends in the sporting set such as the Earls of Airlie and Westmorland, and Sir Eric and Prudence Penn, who were linked to the Queen in several different ways. Prudence had been a friend from teenage years, and her husband served more than twenty years at the Palace organizing ceremonial events. His uncle and de facto guardian, Arthur Penn, had been one of the Queen Mother's best friends and advisers, and had doted on the Queen as a child, calling her "the Colonel."

"There is absolutely no such thing as snobbism for the Queen," said Patricia Brabourne. "Dukes and butlers or maids are all treated with courtesy and friendship." Much the same could be said for her attitude toward Americans. Woven through her friendships are a remarkable number of strands from Britain's former colony. David Airlie's wife, Virginia, is the daughter of John Barry Ryan and his wife, Nin, who were prominent in New York and Newport society. Porchey himself had an American mother, Catherine Wendell from New York, and his wife, the former Jean Wallop, grew up in Wyoming. Her paternal grandfather, the 8th Earl of Portsmouth, had settled in the United States and married the daughter of a Kentucky judge. Jean's first cousin is the Queen's childhood friend Micky Nevill, the daughter of an American mother and the 9th Earl of Portsmouth.

When Jean Wallop arrived in England in 1955, she met the Queen over drinks at the London house of her cousin's friends, Gavin Astor, the 2nd Baron Astor of Hever, and his wife, Irene. "I nearly died of fright," she recalled. "The idea of the Queen was intimidating. She was a star, but she made me feel fine." Wallop was impressed immediately by Elizabeth II's "tremendous steadiness. She is difficult to know, but it is worth the wait. You sort of become friends. It takes a long time to know her."

Being entertained privately by her friends has long been an important escape valve for Elizabeth II, and she is equally comfortable in a grand country estate or a tiny mews house. The hostess sends her the guest list, but the Queen relies on her to organize the seating for luncheon or dinner. She arrives in a small car, accompanied only by a detective, who discreetly sits in another room. Over dinner at John and Patricia Brabourne's in 1966, Noel Coward found the Queen to be "easy and gay and ready to giggle." Two years later she was in high spirits at Raffles nightclub on the King's Road for the twenty-first birthday party for the Brabournes' son Norton Knatchbull. She even showed up that year at the wedding of lady-in-waiting Henriette Abel Smith's daughter, where the groom wore a flowered caftan and Mick Jagger was a guest.

More often than not, Philip has been by her side for these private moments. Approaching his fiftieth year as the 1960s drew to a close, his life as consort was a swirl of activity, with an average of 370 solo official engagements a year, many of them overseas. He was, if anything, becoming even more combative in his public persona. "You have mosquitoes. We have the press," he told the matron of a Caribbean hospital in 1966, provoking a protest from the royal reporters that he finally quelled by apologizing. Several years later he remained unrepentant, telling an audience at Edinburgh University, "I get kicked in the teeth for saying things." He insisted to a Scottish television interviewer that "the monarchy functions because occasionally you've got to stick your neck out. . . . The idea that you don't do anything on the off-chance you might be criticized, you'd end up living like a cabbage and it's pointless. You've got to stick up for something you believe in."

While touring North America in the autumn of 1969, Philip followed his own advice — and generated unfortunate headlines in the process. He first told a group in Ottawa, "The answer to this question of the monarchy is very simple. If the people don't want it, they should change it. But let us end it on amicable terms and not have a row. The monarchy exists not for its own benefit, but for that of the country. We don't come here for our health. We can think of better ways of enjoying ourselves." Having annoyed the Queen's subjects in Canada, he then made his way to the United States to stir up even more controversy.

It had been ten years since the Queen had been to America, but Philip had made several subsequent trips to promote trade with Britain and gather support for his favorite causes. During a ten-day swing in 1966, he even jumped into a swimming pool on a dare at a Miami Beach reception to secure a $100,000 donation for the Variety Club charities. Three years later, President Nixon organized a stag dinner for the duke on November 4, with 105 men from the administration, Congress, military, and judiciary as well as leaders from business, communications, and academia.

By sheer happenstance, Barbara Walters of NBC's *Today* show was at the White House filming an interview with Nixon's daughter Tricia. When Walters saw the president, she chided him for failing to include any women in his dinner that evening for Philip. He tried to make amends by offering to persuade the duke to appear on her show, a request that had already been turned down. "I had never thought of the President of the United States as a booking agent," Walters recalled.

But the next morning, Philip was on the air when Walters asked, "Might Queen Elizabeth ever abdicate and turn the throne over to Prince Charles?" "Who can tell?" Philip replied. "Anything might happen." His flippant remark made a big splash in the British press and prompted an outpouring of support for the Queen in the streets before the Palace issued an emphatic statement that she would remain on the throne. Walters wrote to apologize to Philip for causing such an uproar. He thanked her, saying he was happy to have been the "means of unlocking such a spectacular display of cheerfulness and goodwill . . . particularly in this day and age when most demonstrations seem to reflect nothing but anger and provocation." To Nixon, he declared that he had found Walters "particularly charming and intelligent."

Far more significant were comments Philip made the following Sunday on NBC's *Meet the Press,* which was billed by *Time* magazine as the forum in which the "Duke of Edinburgh jousts verbally with his friendly adversary, the Fourth Estate." Asked how the royal family was coping with inflation, he said, "We go into the red next year. Now, inevitably, if nothing happens we shall either have to — I don't know, we may have to move into smaller premises, who knows? . . . We had a small yacht which we had to sell, and I shall probably have to give up polo fairly soon." Philip's answer was too candid by half, and certainly damaging in its off-hand tone. But the topic was serious. Inflation had been eroding the British economy, and had taken its toll on royal finances as well. Consumer prices had risen by 74 percent since 1953, and salaries for royal employees, typically lower than in private industry, had increased by 167 percent.

The Civil List, the principal allowance from the government for the Queen's official expenditures, had been fixed since her accession at £475,000 annually, which was adequate for the early years when she had even been able to set aside the surplus for future contingencies. But as inflation picked up steam in 1962, expenses began outrunning income, and her surplus funds were used to cover growing deficits. By the time Prince Philip spoke out, the Queen faced the prospect of subsidizing the Civil List from other sources. The Queen had access to substantial income from the Duchy of Lancaster, a tax-free portfolio of properties and investments earmarked for both public and private purposes, as well as purely private income (also untaxed) of indeterminate amount, that supported Balmoral, Sandringham, her racing enterprise, and a range of personal expenses.

Other costs of the monarchy were supported by grants from government departments for the upkeep of the royal palaces, transportation, and security. But the Civil List expenditure was a political lightning rod for Labour Party critics who objected to underwriting the wealthy royal family — not only the Queen but her husband, mother, sister, daughter, and assorted other relatives who shared royal duties. (Charles, as the Duke of Cornwall as well as the Prince of Wales, had access to his own income through the extensive holdings of the Duchy of Cornwall, dating from the Middle Ages.) The critics ignored the fact that the source of the Civil List funds was the monarch's Crown Estate, and that the amount allocated to the royal family represented a sliver of the revenue that the Crown Estate had been handing over to the government Treasury for more than two hundred years.

Philip's remarks lit a fuse just as the Queen formally requested an increase in the Civil List payment. The issue exploded into heated debate in Parliament, with calls for a thorough examination of royal finances. Even Harold Wilson expressed his dismay over Philip's comments, and on November 11, 1969, he announced that a select committee would conduct an investigation and make recommendations to Parliament.

The Queen's image at the dawn of the new decade was captured in the Annigoni painting unveiled at the National Portrait Gallery on February 25, 1970. It was a striking depiction, shorn of the glamour and beauty of his first portrayal, at once wonderful and strange. This time she wore the red mantle of the Order of the British Empire, unadorned and again bareheaded, against a plain evening sky above a deep, long, and low horizon. She appeared at full length, and the emptiness of the background accentuated the solitary burdens of her office. Her expression was stern, yet her eyes looked slightly wistful. At a time of political and social ferment, Annigoni captured a reassuring certitude and dedication about the Queen, looking across her nation and her people.

CHAPTER ELEVEN
"NOT BLOODY LIKELY!"

In June 1970, Harold Wilson called a general election on the assumption that he could bolster Labour's majority in Parliament. But he misread the opinion polls as well as public dissatisfaction over rising prices and an increase in unemployment. The Conservatives won decisively in a surprising upset. Fifty-three-year-old Edward Heath came to Buckingham Palace on the 19th to kiss hands, the first Tory premier to be elected by his party rather than appointed by the Queen.

That night Elizabeth II gave a grand ball at Windsor Castle to celebrate the seventieth birthdays of the Queen Mother; the Queen's cousin Dickie Mountbatten; her uncle Harry, the Duke of Gloucester; and Henry Somerset, the 10th Duke of Beaufort, who had been her ceremonial Master of the Horse since the beginning of her reign.

The ball was a Patrick Plunket production, with the castle floodlit and fuchsias in pots lining the Gothic entrance hall. Many of the guests were celebrating the Tory victory. "We had been expecting to put up with Wilson and his loathsome mob for another five years," wrote Cecil Beaton, "and quite dramatically all was changed." When the new prime minister arrived like a conquering hero, the

Like the wedding of the Queen and Philip a quarter century earlier, the pageantry of their daughter's celebration struck a bright spark at a particularly bleak moment for Britain.

The royal family on the Buckingham Palace balcony after the wedding of Princess Anne and Captain Mark Phillips, November 1973.

guests cheered. "I was told that he blushed to his collar," Beaton recorded.

Yet Heath, who was Wilson's exact contemporary, proved to be heavy going for the Queen, who was ten years his junior. Like his Labour predecessor, his origins were modest. He had excelled in the grammar school system and earned his degree at Oxford. Heath's provincialism had a cultured gloss from his expertise in classical music and skill as a yachtsman, although neither was a fruitful source of small talk with Elizabeth II. A confirmed bachelor described as "celibate" by Philip Ziegler, his official biographer, Heath was at best indifferent to women and at worst contemptuous of them.

The Queen's sixth prime minister had a reputation for being brusque, even rude. Wilson described him as "cold and uncompassionate." He lacked Wilson's bonhomie and instinctive deference. Even worse, from the Queen's standpoint, he was humorless and remote. She could find traits to admire: certainly his political talent and accomplishments as well as his determination and his honesty. But given his personality, Heath's unfailing courtesy to his sovereign could be cloying at times.

Heath learned quickly to appreciate the Queen's value and found their audiences rewarding, especially since he had no spouse in whom to confide or share his frustrations. He described her as a patient listener when he unburdened himself "a good deal" beyond the agenda drawn up by their private secretaries that she kept on a card placed on a nearby table. "The fact that she has all these years of experience and is imperturbable is a source of encouragement in itself," he said. Heath also found that extensive correspondence with foreign leaders made her "very useful . . . particularly on overseas stuff."

He did not, however, share her passion for the Commonwealth, which led to tensions between them. From the moment of his election, Heath was determined to pick up Macmillan's quest for admission to the Common Market after French president Charles de Gaulle had twice rebuffed Britain's application. Heath applied a messianic zeal to the task of persuading French president Georges Pompidou, who continued to hold the veto power. To demonstrate to France that his country was truly European, Heath downplayed the importance of the Commonwealth. He also antagonized a number of its African members when he dropped the arms embargo against South Africa enacted by Wilson in 1967 and resumed weapons sales to the apartheid regime. Both Kenneth Kaunda of Zambia and Julius Nyerere of Tanzania threatened to leave the Commonwealth.

Fearing confrontations at the Commonwealth leaders' meeting in Singapore in January 1971, Heath banned the Queen from attending. As he expected, the Africans pummeled him, but nobody bolted. According to Heath biographer John Campbell, the Queen was "deeply unhappy with Heath's undisguised disrespect" for her beloved Commonwealth and "greatly upset by the rows which disfigured" the 1971 meeting. Martin Charteris said that if she had been allowed to attend, the acrimony would have been reduced if not eliminated. "It's like Nanny being there," he said. "She demands that they behave properly in her presence. . . . She knows them all and they like her." She resented being excluded and "she was determined it was not going to happen again."

The United States was also given short shrift by Heath in his pursuit of stronger European connections. Richard Nixon's national security adviser, Henry Kissinger, wrote that not only did the prime minister fail to cultivate the "special relationship," he "actively sought to downgrade it." Nixon did everything he could to establish good rapport with Heath, and to please the Queen as well. On the heels of his dinner for Philip, the president invited Charles and Anne to the White House in July 1970 — their first trip to America and the fourth such visit by a Prince of Wales since 1860.

Elizabeth II's two older children were being introduced to the round of royal duties, much as she had been instructed during her childhood. "I learnt the way a monkey learns — by watching its parents," Charles once said. During Anne's trip to New Zealand with her mother and father in March 1970, royal image maker William Heseltine modernized the Queen's regular routine by adding the "walkabout" — taking a casual stroll to chat and shake hands with ordinary people. Her daughter was expected to follow suit. "At nineteen years old suddenly being dropped in the middle of the street," Anne recalled. "Suddenly being told to pick someone and talk to them. Fun? No I don't think so. A challenge."

Nixon laid on an ambitious program for Charles and Anne's two days in Washington: lunch on the presidential yacht *Sequoia* and a cruise to Mount

Vernon, a steak cookout at the presidential retreat at Camp David, a dinner dance for seven hundred on the White House lawn, a Washington Senators baseball game, and visits to monuments and museums. Their socializing included the Nixons' twenty-four-year-old daughter, Tricia, who had attended Charles's investiture in Wales the previous year, as well as her younger sister, Julie, and Julie's husband, David Eisenhower, the grandson of the former president. More than three decades later, when Charles and his new wife, Camilla, visited George W. and Laura Bush at the White House, he joked that the Bushes had better not try to fix up their twin daughters with his sons William and Harry the way Nixon had worked to set him up with Tricia.

Nixon set aside a half hour to meet Charles in the Oval Office. In a briefing paper, Kissinger advised him to solicit the twenty-one-year-old prince's views on the Commonwealth, Wales, Scotland, and Northern Ireland, his impression of Canada, and of the "hopes and aspirations of his generation." They ended up talking for ninety minutes on a wide range of topics. When Nixon urged Charles to be a "presence" while not completely avoiding controversy, the prince "pointed out one must not become controversial too often otherwise people don't take you seriously." Charles added in his diary afterward, "to be just a presence would be fatal. . . . A presence alone can be swept away so easily."

The following October, Nixon was back in Britain for consultations with Heath. The Queen, who was on vacation at Balmoral, expressed concern that she would seem discourteous if she did not see the American president during his brief stay. Her advisers considered an invitation to Windsor or Buckingham Palace, but decided that neither place would be "suitable for entertaining a large party at short notice." Instead, she accepted Heath's invitation to fly down from Scotland and join Nixon for luncheon at Chequers — her first visit to the prime minister's country residence. It was an opportunity, said Heath's principal private secretary, Robert Armstong, for the Queen to meet Nixon "during his four-hour stay . . . without formality and without undue inroads into the time available for official discussions between the President and the Prime Minister." Nixon was grateful for the Queen's "signal kindness," and the visit was a success.

For all his impatience with the pomp and ceremony that Wilson had found thrilling, Heath had been brought up a royalist, and he was eager to do what was necessary to support an institution that worked well. The Civil List inquiry into royal finances promised by Wilson took shape under his successor as a select committee with a Tory majority that met a half dozen times in 1971. Michael Adeane gave detailed testimony about the Queen's official duties, the first comprehensive justification of her value to the government and the nation. He also revealed the concentration and care behind her seemingly uncomplicated daily rounds. "Taking a lively interest in everything, saying a kind word here and asking a question there," he said, "always smiling and acknowledging cheers when driving in her car, sometimes for hours, had to be experienced to be properly appreciated."

Labour critics questioned why the Queen was immune from taxation and demanded to know the size of her private fortune. William Hamilton, a strident republican member of the committee, called Princess Margaret — who had an admittedly light schedule of official engagements, including just thirty-one outside London in 1970 — an "expensive kept woman." The Palace pointed out that estimates of the Queen's net worth as high as 100 million pounds were overblown, since most of her assets — her art collection, the Crown Jewels, the contents of the three state-owned palaces — were held in trust for the monarchy, yielded no income, and could not be sold.

The committee issued its report on December 2, and Parliament passed the Civil List Act of 1972, which gave the Queen what she wanted: a rise in the Civil List payment to £980,000 a year for ten years, and increased disbursements for the other members of the royal family to cover their performance of public duties. (Princess Margaret's rose from £15,000 annually to £35,000.) Elizabeth II's Privy Purse, which covers personal as well as some public expenses such as staff pensions, would no longer receive a stipend from the Civil List and would be funded only by her Duchy of Lancaster income. For the first time, there would also be annual reviews. The press now had a way to raise such matters as taxation as well as support of peripheral members of the royal family in the years to come.

At the beginning of 1972, Michael Adeane decided to leave his post three years before his scheduled retirement, and Martin Charteris was named private secretary. "Martin was given his chance, and he blossomed," said Gay Charteris. "He said, 'The only thing I want to do is show the public what she is really like.' I think he helped do that." By way of reinforcement, Charteris used to say to Elizabeth II, "Your job is to spread a carpet of happiness." Once he took the number one spot, the Queen's speeches showed his deft touch, with dashes of humor that had previously been absent. He also got along well with William Heseltine, who became an assistant private secretary, and Ronald Allison, the new press secretary, who had worked on Fleet Street and understood the thinking of reporters.

The Queen at age forty-five was brimming with energy and blessed with a robust constitution. In November 1971 she somewhat improbably caught chicken pox — not even, she said, from one of her own children. She called it a "ridiculous disease" and submitted to confinement during her contagion. Once she was free of infection but still "covered in spots," she resumed her duties inside the Palace, including receiving the prime minister at the Tuesday audience. After Heath sent her a rather stiff note "to commiserate with you" about the illness, she replied in a lighthearted tone thanking him for his kindness, and expressing her frustration that she couldn't yet go out into crowds for fear she could be reinfected "from *them* — one can't win from a virus!"

It was a rare moment of ill health for the Queen. She was always a great believer in the virtues of fresh air and exercise, including her regular riding and daily walking. Wearing gloves on her public rounds and avoiding people with coughs and sniffles was also part of her routine. During her thirties and forties she nevertheless suffered from occasional colds, laryngitis, and bouts of sinusitis, which seldom prompted complaints or slowed her down. "She has a theory that you carry on working and your cold gets better," said a cousin of the Queen. One exception was after Charles's investiture, when a severe cold forced her to cancel engagements for four days.

Her ear, nose, and throat specialist for many years, Sir Cecil Hogg, used to make house calls at the various royal residences. After his first visit to Buckingham Palace, he reported "how unnerving it was to get under the bedclothes with the Queen in her nightie to test her chest and listen to bubbles inside," said Min Hogg, his daughter. "He said she was quite good at putting him at ease. When he was under the bedclothes she would say, 'I'm as nervous as you are.' "

While Elizabeth II has a full complement of doctors, including specialists, she also put great faith in homeopathic remedies long before such nostrums were commonplace in the culture. Her belief, shared with her mother, is that they "can do no harm and may well do you good," explained Lady Angela Oswald, a Norfolk neighbor and friend. Homeopathy — taking diluted substances that would induce symptoms of illness if used in larger doses — was embraced by Queen Victoria, and in 1923 Sir John Weir, a Scottish doctor, began administering such treatments to members of the royal family. On Weir's retirement in 1968, the Queen appointed her first female court physician, Dr. Margery Blackie, another homeopathic expert. Among Blackie's more exotic treatments was Malvern water with a trace of arsenic for sinus infections.

The homeopaths would come "for whatever was wrong with them," said Min Hogg. "The real physicians and surgeons would put their eyes to heaven." Still, Elizabeth II has always respected the professionalism of her medical specialists. When Sir Cecil turned seventy in 1971 and had to retire — a mandatory rule imposed by the Queen's medical advisers — she told him, "I am sorry, because you have such a steady hand."

In the third decade of the Queen's reign, she stepped up the pace of her foreign travels — fifteen Commonwealth trips, including six lengthy tours of Pacific countries, designed to reinforce their standing with Britain, along with state visits to seventeen non-Commonwealth countries. One of the most significant of these was a goodwill trip to France in May 1972 that set the stage for Parliament's ratification of a treaty allowing Britain to join the Common Market, which Heath had negotiated after intensively wooing a skeptical Georges Pompidou.

The principal apprehension before the trip was the precarious health of the Queen's uncle, the seventy-seven-year-old Duke of Windsor, who was suffering from terminal throat cancer. After excluding him from her wedding and her coronation, the Queen had extended an olive branch seven years earlier when the duke came to London for eye surgery. She cheered him considerably by visiting him twice during his convalescence, and, for the first time since the Windsors went into exile, she met with the duchess. Two years later the duke and duchess joined the rest of the family to unveil a plaque in honor of his mother, although the couple were not invited to the Queen's luncheon afterward, just as he had been excluded from the family dinner following Queen Mary's funeral. But in 1968 the Queen complied graciously when the duke asked for permission to be buried with the duchess in the royal family's cemetery at Frogmore in Windsor Home Park and pay a modest allowance for his wife if she were to survive him.

When doctors diagnosed his cancer in November 1971 and unsuccessfully treated him with radiation, the Queen alerted the Foreign Office that she wished to see him during her five-day state visit. In a confidential memo, British ambassador to France Sir Christopher Soames starkly laid out the high-stakes connection between the duke's health and Anglo-French relations. "If the Duke of Windsor were to die on 12, 13 or 14 May or on the morning of 15 May before the Queen leaves for Paris, the visit would have to be cancelled," Soames wrote. "I must emphasize that Pompidou clearly attaches the greatest importance to at least this part of the visit taking place, and I fear that a total cancellation though rationally understood would be taken amiss and would rankle him."

The duke survived, and after touring Provence and attending the races at Longchamp on the afternoon of May 18, the Queen, Philip, and Prince

Charles, along with Martin Charteris and Fortune Grafton, arrived at the Windsors' home in Neuilly-sur-Seine. The duchess nervously served them tea in the drawing room before taking Elizabeth II upstairs to her uncle David's sitting room. The old duke did his courtly best, rising from his wheelchair with great difficulty to bow to his niece and kiss her on both cheeks, despite being attached to an intravenous tube. He had shrunk to eighty-five pounds, yet, always the fashion plate, wore a smart blue blazer. They talked for about fifteen minutes, and as the Queen left, the duke's physician, Jean Thin, saw tears in her eyes.

Accompanied by an entourage of thirty-six, the Queen followed a full program in France, traveling in an open car with Pompidou, and in the evenings appearing at the banquets at Versailles and the British embassy in one dazzling tiara after another. "We may drive on different sides of the road, but we are going the same way," Elizabeth II declared at her banquet for the French president, with a nod toward an era of closer cooperation between Britain and Western Europe.

She left the country with a spectacular flourish, driving to Rouen at the mouth of the Seine to sail off on *Britannia.* It was a romantic setting, not least because Rouen is the capital of Normandy, home of William the Conqueror. "She went on board *Britannia* in the early evening," recalled Mary Soames, the wife of the British ambassador. "The rooftops were crowded with people. Almost to the mouth of the Seine people had driven their cars to the riverbank with their headlights on. The Queen stood for hours while people were waving her off."

The trip was a diplomatic success, and Pompidou was well pleased. Britain's *Observer* described "a conspicuous demonstration of political goodwill after a decade of coolness." The Queen "had seduced and conquered by her simplicity and charm," said *Le Figaro,* which proclaimed the visit "a consecration — of the beginning of a new era of Franco-British cooperation." "With the Queen's visit Britain seemed all but signed, sealed and delivered into the Common Market," declared *Time.*

On May 28, just ten days after the Queen's visit, the Duke of Windsor died. Back in England, Elizabeth II directed Patrick Plunket to arrange a dignified but muted funeral on Monday, June 5. Her one conundrum was how to handle Trooping the Colour two days earlier. Rather than cancel her annual birthday parade, she had bagpipers and drummers of the Scots Guards play a lament in memory of the former King, a compromise devised by Charteris. The duke's body lay in state for two days at St. George's Chapel, Windsor, where the half hour service took place, followed by his burial at Frogmore. Four senior clergymen — the Archbishop of Canterbury, the Archbishop of York, the Moderator of the Church of Scotland, and the Dean of Windsor — officiated, and all the adult members of the royal family attended except the duke's only surviving sibling, the Duke of Gloucester, who was ailing.

The seventy-five-year-old duchess stayed at Buckingham Palace, and during dinner the first night with the Queen and Prince Charles she oddly "prattled away," seemingly oblivious to her husband's death. The following evening she visited St. George's Chapel, where she repeated, "He gave up so much for so little," and pointed at herself "with a strange grin," Charles recalled. She was heavily sedated on the day of the funeral, and conspicuously disoriented as she sat in the choir with the Queen, who "showed a motherly and nanny-like tenderness and kept putting her hand on the Duchess's arm and glove," Clarissa Eden reported.

Elizabeth II's Christmas broadcast that year took note of the silver wedding anniversary she and Philip had celebrated the previous month, connecting the tolerance and understanding necessary for a successful marriage to the need for such values in achieving harmony among nations. Her main message was meant to reassure the countries of the Commonwealth on the eve of Britain's official entry into the European Economic Community, as the Common Market was now called, in January 1973. "The new links with Europe will not replace those with the Commonwealth," she said. "Old friends will not be lost; Britain will take her Commonwealth links into Europe with her." The goal, she added, was "to create a wider family of Nations."

The Christmas message now had an updated format that she had adopted following the success of the *Royal Family* documentary. In 1969 she had issued a written statement instead of her usual broadcast, while she and her advisers, as Philip put it, paused to "scratch our heads and see whether we can do something better." Instead of a static image of the Queen reading from a TelePrompTer, Richard Cawston injected a contemporary feel by juxtaposing her words with film footage from events of the previous year. There were images from royal tours overseas, of the Queen and her children, and scenes from the silver wedding anniversary festivities. As with the 1969 documentary, these revitalized year-end productions emphasized the wholesome happiness of the Queen and her family.

At the same time, the British tabloid press was beginning to take a more aggressive and sensational approach to the royal family. In the lead were *The Sun* and *News of the World,* which had been acquired in 1969 by Australian publisher Rupert Murdoch, an avowed republican who saw the monarchy as the apex of a "pyramid of snobbery." The Queen was his country's head of state; those who shared Murdoch's wish for a republic numbered around a quarter of the Australian population, including the Labour government that took power in December 1972, with Gough Whitlam as prime minister. In Britain, Murdoch saw an opportunity to scrutinize the behavior of the royal family and expose them if they misbehaved, a formula designed to drive up his newsstand sales while chipping away at the monarchy's standing.

Perhaps inevitably, the British media turned its attention in the 1970s to the younger generation of the royal family, Charles and Anne in particular. After his graduation from Cambridge in 1970, Charles had faithfully followed his family's plan and entered the Royal Naval College at Dartmouth a year later. In the eyes of the press he became an adventuresome figure called "Action Man." As he began his naval career, he met Camilla Shand, a pretty and sporty debutante one year his senior. She had a "slightly sexy, ginny voice," and above all she knew how to make the Prince of Wales relax and laugh. Their quiet romance lasted some six months before he left for a long tour at sea. While he was away, Camilla married Andrew Parker Bowles, a Household Cavalry officer, news that gave Charles a "feeling of emptiness."

Andrew Parker Bowles had also briefly dated Princess Anne, but as a Roman Catholic he was unsuitable for marriage to a member of the royal family. To her older brother's "shock and amazement," twenty-two-year-old Anne announced her engagement in May 1973 to twenty-four-year-old Mark Phillips, a handsome army captain and accomplished equestrian who had won a gold medal at the Mexico City Olympics in 1968. They had met at a party for the British team after the games, although they conceded it hadn't been love at first sight. "We had to be told that we'd met in 1968 before we remembered," Anne recalled. Charles initially dismissed Mark as dull and dim, but quickly sympathized with his future brother-in-law's abrupt introduction to the "interest, fascination (plus boorishness) shown by the press." The Queen and Philip considered Mark suitable enough. Like Tony Snowdon, he was a commoner. Although unprepossessing, Mark shared Anne's passion for horses and eventing.

They were married on Wednesday, November 14, Charles's twenty-fifth birthday, at Westminster Abbey before 1,500 guests in a ceremony presided over by the Archbishop of Canterbury. The Queen, in a bright blue coat and dress, smiled as Anne and her husband climbed into the famous Glass Coach for the trip back to Buckingham Palace for the wedding breakfast with family members. When they made the ritual appearance on the Palace balcony, a crowd of fifteen thousand cheered.

The day had been declared a national holiday, allowing tens of thousands of spectators to line the route of the procession. Hundreds of millions more in sixteen countries watched on television. As at the wedding of the Queen and Philip a quarter century earlier, the pageantry of their daughter's celebration — the coaches, the military bands, the sixteen trumpeters playing the fanfares, the guard of honor — struck a bright spark at a particularly bleak moment for Britain.

Since Heath took office, the economy had been ravaged by inflation and high unemployment. His attempt to restrain wage demands by the powerful miners' union had foundered after a crippling strike, and his efforts to freeze pay, prices, rents, and dividends late in 1972 proved ineffective as well. A perfect storm of crises in the autumn of 1973 nearly brought the country to a standstill. OPEC, the Organization of Petroleum Exporting Countries, had raised the price of oil by 12 percent early in 1973, and the Yom Kippur War in October after Egypt and Syria invaded Israel led to an outright oil embargo against the United States and Western Europe. Fuel supplies dwindled and costs quadrupled, even as the coal miners threatened yet another strike. On December 13, Heath announced he would impose a three-day workweek and mandatory power cuts to conserve energy.

The Queen felt it would be appropriate to inject a note of sympathy about her country's plight into her Christmas broadcast that year. Although her message was purely personal, and not written on advice from the government, she asked Martin Charteris to notify Heath that she wished to conclude her remarks with a "few sentences" about the crisis: "I cannot let Christmas pass without speaking to you directly of these difficulties because they are of deep concern to all of us as individuals and as a nation. Different people have different views, deeply and sincerely felt, about our problems and how they should be solved. Let us remember, however, that what we have in common is more important than what divides us."

The next day in their audience, Heath informed the Queen that she could not mention the crisis. Undaunted by his censorship — which was not revealed to the press — she tried again. Charteris wrote Heath to propose a shortened but no less anodyne single sentence, this time for the beginning of the broadcast: "I cannot let Christmas pass without speaking to you directly of the hardship and difficulties with which so many are faced because they are of deep concern to all of us as individuals and as a nation." But again Heath rebuffed the Queen's efforts, instructing his private secretary to tell her she had to omit any reference because of the country's "altogether exceptional circumstances." She had no choice but to comply.

In the new year, the miners went on strike, and the three-day week conjured up images of the dire postwar period of rationing and economic stagnation. Power was cut, candles illuminated offices, and workers bundled in overcoats at their desks. While Elizabeth II and Philip were on a Commonwealth tour of the Pacific, Heath suddenly called an election for February 28. The Queen flew back from Australia to receive Heath or kiss hands again with Harold Wilson.

Labour won 301 seats, the Conservatives 297, the Liberal Party 14, and a grab bag of minor parties held 23 seats. Neither of the major parties had enough votes in Parliament to allow them to easily put through legislation. Rather than tendering his resignation on Friday, March 1, Heath went to Buckingham Palace to tell the Queen he wanted to try to form a coalition with Liberal leader Jeremy Thorpe.

Elizabeth II was dealing with a hung Parliament for the first time in her reign, and she trod cautiously. "The Queen could only await events," wrote Robert Armstong. "She would not be called upon to take action unless and until Mr. Heath tendered his resignation." So she waited for four days while Heath negotiated, until he gave up on Monday, March 4, and submitted his resignation. Wilson arrived at Buckingham Palace to become prime minister for the second time at age fifty-eight, and, he recalled, "our relaxed intimacy was immediately restored."

With its tiny majority, Labour could have put Elizabeth II in a problematic position if Wilson had asked her to dissolve Parliament so he could call a quick second election in hopes of increasing his party's seats. She had the power to refuse such a request if she thought it would be bad for the nation at a time of economic instability, but she was loath to exercise that little used constitutional prerogative. Wilson never forced the issue, however. Martin Charteris said that when the prime minister had talked about an immediate election, "the Queen . . . let it be known she did not approve." Instead, Labour waited until October, when a second election gave them a decent working majority of three more seats.

Wilson yielded to the miners and disbanded the three-day week, but the malaise persisted — stagnating industrial production along with 15 percent inflation. By the mid-1970s, fully half of British adults were on government benefits. Yet Wilson charged ahead with increases in a host of social security programs. He also acquiesced when rapidly rising costs forced the Queen to request a further increase in the Civil List payment to £1.4 million annually.

While the Queen and Prince Philip were on a state visit to Indonesia on March 20, 1974, Princess Anne and her husband were the victims of a shocking kidnap attempt. An armed assailant named Ian Ball blocked their Rolls-Royce with his car on the Mall as the royal couple were returning to Buckingham Palace after a charity event. Ball opened fire and wounded Jim Beaton, Anne's lone bodyguard (who took three bullets in his efforts to protect her and was later rewarded with the George Cross, Britain's highest honor for bravery by civilians), as well as her chauffeur, a passer-by, and a policeman. But when Ball ordered Anne to leave the car she shouted, "Not bloody likely!" She continued to resist as Ball tried to drag her out while her husband held her other arm, until Ball was overpowered by police and arrested. Anne recounted the incident to Charles on the telephone "as if it were a perfectly normal occurrence. Her bravery and superb obstinacy were unbelievable." The Queen and Philip were immediately notified of the incident, but they kept to their schedule and returned to London on the 22nd.

By then Anne and Mark had already left for his home village of Great Somerford in Wiltshire to plant a commemorative tree as scheduled, both brushing off their violent encounter. "It wouldn't have been much good sitting and brooding about it," Anne said to the villagers. "We got back to life so quickly, we've practically forgotten it." The couple returned to Oak Grove, their five-bedroom house on the grounds of the Royal Military Academy at Sandhurst, where Mark worked as an instructor. Horses remained the center of their lives as they trained together and competed in cross-country jumping events, to all appearances a contented couple.

The Queen's own equine pursuits took a fortunate turn in 1974, although she mourned the death of her treasured stallion, Aureole, whose grave she marked with a copper beech in the paddock where he died. By then she had some fifty horses in training, and more than a score old enough to race. After middling success with her breeding and racing in the 1960s, she had applied a more systematic approach to the business in 1970 when she officially appointed Henry Porchester (later Carnarvon) as her first racing manager, and Sir Michael Oswald as her stud manager. "Henry was the Queen's closest personal friend, and a very influential adviser," said her longtime trainer Ian Balding. "One day he said to her, 'You don't have enough winners. Your horses are not well enough managed.' She said, 'You can be my manager. You can bloody well do it!' "

Her breeding operation at Sandringham became more complicated as she expanded it to include stallions owned by syndicates in which she had purchased shares. They would cover not only her own horses, but as many as one hundred visiting mares each year. Oswald, who lived nearby, became the on-site manager of the stallions and mares. At the same time, Porchester worked with her trainers, helped decide which races to run, advised her on buying and selling her thoroughbreds, consulted on mating, and represented her at the many races she was unable to attend because of her obligations as Queen.

Elizabeth II stayed in constant contact with her top advisers, talking to Oswald two or three times a week and Porchey nearly every day. Porchester made a strategic decision to send more of Elizabeth II's mares to the United States for breeding "to bring in new blood," said Michael Oswald. During the 1960s, she had sent some of her horses to France and several to the United States, but by 1970 it was clear that the best stallions were in Kentucky. Porchester advised the Queen to ship at least a half dozen mares across the Atlantic to several stud farms where they could be covered by such champions as Nijinsky. After weaning, the foals would then be transported back to England for training.

The Queen's prize horse in 1974 was a "long-striding filly" born to Highlight, a direct descendant of Feola — the great royal broodmare who had not only run well in the 1930s but had bred a string of winners in the following decades — and sired by Queen's Hussar, a stallion owned by Porchester's father, the 6th Earl of Carnarvon. The Queen named the filly Highclere, after the Carnarvon stud farm. Having captured the first classic title for the Queen in eighteen years by winning the 1,000 Guineas at Newmarket, Highclere was shipped to Chantilly in June to run in the prestigious Prix de Diane, also known as the French Oaks.

Accompanied by Henry Porchester, his wife, Jean, Michael Oswald, and Martin Charteris, the Queen flew from Windsor Castle to France on the 16th for lunch before the big race. France's newly elected president, Valéry Giscard d'Estaing, sent a big bowl of red roses, and Elizabeth II and her party drove down the racecourse in an open car against the backdrop of the Prince of Condé's château. The Queen knew from talking to the stable girl in the paddock that Highclere was in a "fiery mood," but as she watched the final furlongs from the royal box, she sat smiling, hands in prayerful position, while Porchester and Oswald jumped and shouted the filly home. "I'm very excitable on the race course," Porchester recalled, "too enthusiastic, not very British. I remember going mad and slapping the Queen on the back when Highclere won the Prix de Diane." It was the first victory for a British monarch in a French classic race.

The swarm of racegoers shouted "Vive la Reine,"

and when the Queen went to see Highclere, she was nearly mobbed by the crowds, protected only by Porchester, Oswald, and some gendarmes. That evening she invited the royal party, including her trainer Dick Hern and the winning jockey, Joe Mercer, to dinner at Windsor Castle with the Queen Mother, Prince Philip, Princess Anne, and Dickie Mountbatten. In the place of honor at the table's center was the Queen's new gold trophy. Highclere went on to win the King George VI and Queen Elizabeth Diamond Stakes at Ascot, and contributed to most of the Queen's £140,000 in winnings that year.

The Queen's triumph in France came on the eve of Royal Ascot, which in those days involved more elaborate entertainment than in later years. As many as sixty guests would be invited for the entire week at the castle. "I was assigned a valet, and every day we would be given a program with several options for activities," recalled a man who attended when he was in his early twenties. "I had to have morning dress for lunch and Ascot, and white tie for dinner every night. No one could ever be late, and the valets ensured that we were dressed correctly and showed up on time."

The Queen typically did her boxes in the morning while her friends opted for more vigorous pursuits such as riding, tennis, swimming, and swatting balls into nets from Philip's wooden polo pony (set up in a cage near the castle's indoor swimming pool). Others stayed indoors to read, do jigsaw puzzles, or play Scrabble. Sometimes she would invite several young male guests to ride with her for an hour before the luncheon, where she would appear looking thoroughly refreshed and pulled together after only a half hour in which to change. Every afternoon was devoted to the races. On Wednesday night there was a big formal dinner for 150 in the Waterloo Chamber, and on another night guests would be taken to a nearby theater followed by dinner. As with her dine-and-sleeps, the Queen devoted one evening to tours of the library and the royal art collection. Patrick Plunket organized everything to the minute.

Early in 1975, the Queen's great friend and consummate impresario was diagnosed with inoperable liver cancer. Plunket was admitted to King Edward VII hospital in mid-March, but after several days he insisted on leaving to attend an important reception at Buckingham Palace, saying, "I have to put on my white tie and medals." His pain dulled by morphine, he was driven to the Palace, where he retrieved his evening clothes from his room and announced all the guests. He finally returned to the hospital at 2 A.M. Hours later he found a letter on his breakfast tray from the Queen saying, "Patrick, I'm deeply grateful for what you did last night, Yours sincerely, Elizabeth R."

Patrick Plunket died ten days later on Easter Sunday at age fifty-one. The Queen honored him with a funeral in the Chapel Royal inside St. James's Palace, with plangent music sung by boy choristers. It was a small group — just members of the Plunket family along with the Queen and Philip. The royal couple also attended the standing-room-only memorial service in the Guards' Chapel across St. James's Park, where Philip read the lesson. At the funeral, Annabel Goldsmith glanced at the Queen and "caught a look of deep sadness."

According to Plunket's brother Shaun, the Queen had a hand in the *Times* obituary. "She certainly helped," he said. "It was quite light. There was a quotation that referred very much to his service." But she sent no condolence note, as is her custom. "I don't think we would have expected her to write," said Shaun Plunket. "We knew she missed him and that we missed him. She didn't have to put it on paper." His will designated that one of his favorite possessions, a seascape by the nineteenth-century English artist Richard Parkes Bonington, be given to the Queen. After his brothers presented it to her in her study at Buckingham Palace, she wrote them a gracious note of thanks.

She further expressed her gratitude by approving a distinctive memorial, a white pavilion atop a hill above the Valley Gardens in Windsor Great Park, with an engraved plaque saying, "In memory of Patrick Plunket for his service to the Royal Family." It was built with funds from his relatives and friends, including the Queen, Philip, and the Queen Mother. Elizabeth II took an interest in the design as well as the landscaping. "I'm sure I told the gardener I don't care for variegated hostas," she told Shaun Plunket on one inspection tour. "I can't think of why he put those there." Since the memorial is only minutes away from Smith's Lawn, where the Queen often comes to watch polo, she has walked over occasionally to sit on the bench and reflect.

With Plunket's death, the Queen lost not only a confidant but the sprightly tone he brought to court life. Her entertainments seemed more conventional, her guest lists less venturesome. Some even believe that if he had lived, he could have managed Diana, Princess of Wales, more effectively than anyone else in the royal household. A year after his death, someone asked the Queen, "Have you given some thought to who will replace Patrick Plunket?" Replied the Queen, "No one will ever replace him."

CHAPTER TWELVE
FEELING THE LOVE

Patrick Plunket's passing was the Queen's first major loss since the death of her father twenty-three years earlier, and she dealt with it by drawing on what one of her longtime friends calls her "profound religious existence," dating to her childhood, and reinforced by her consecration in 1953.

As the Supreme Governor of the Church of England, the monarch is the defender of the faith — the official religion of the country, established by law and respected by sentiment. Yet when the Queen travels to Scotland, she becomes a member of the Church of Scotland, which governs itself and tolerates no supervision by the state. She doesn't abandon the Anglican faith when she crosses the border, but rather doubles up, although no Anglican bishop ever comes to preach at Balmoral.

Elizabeth II has always embraced what former Archbishop of Canterbury George Carey called the "sacramental manner in which she views her own office." She regards her faith as a duty, "not in the sense of a burden, but of glad service" to her subjects. Her faith is also part of the rhythm of her daily life. "She has a comfortable relationship with God," said Carey. "She's got a capacity because of her faith to take anything the world throws at her.

She restated the pledge of lifelong service that she had made on her twenty-first birthday "in my salad days when I was green in judgment. I do not regret or retract a word of it."

The Queen wearing a hat trimmed with twenty-five small fabric bells, greeting the crowds celebrating her Silver Jubilee, June 1977. GETTY IMAGES

Her faith comes from a theology of life that everything is ordered."

She worships unfailingly each Sunday, whether in a tiny chapel in the Laurentian mountains of Quebec or a wooden hut on Essequibo in Guyana after a two-hour boat ride. But "she doesn't parade her faith," said Canon John Andrew, who saw her frequently during the 1960s when he worked for Archbishop of Canterbury Michael Ramsey. On holidays she attends services at the parish church in Sandringham, and at Crathie outside the Balmoral gates.

Her habit is to take Communion three or four times a year — at Christmas, Easter, Whitsunday, and the occasional special service — "an old-fashioned way of being an Anglican, something she was brought up to do," said John Andrew. She enjoys plain, traditional hymns and short, straightforward sermons. George Carey regards her as "middle of the road. She treasures Anglicanism. She loves the 1662 Book of Common Prayer, which is always used at Sandringham. She would disapprove of modern services, but wouldn't make that view known. The Bible she prefers is the old King James version. She has a great love of the English language and enjoys the beauty of words. The scriptures are soaked into her." The Queen has called the King James Bible "a masterpiece of English prose."

Because visiting clergymen preach at Sandringham and Balmoral, she often has them as houseguests. "The royal family treat clergy differently," said a minister in the Church of Scotland. "They tend to relax with us. It can get pretty perky. They say what they think in front of us." Once while visiting Sandringham, George Carey heard the Queen say to Princess Margaret, "Oh you silly woman." "It wasn't offensive," Carey recalled. "It was part of the family banter, but there was still deep affection." Occasionally the Queen's itinerant pastors have offered inadvertent comic relief. "For the delicious meal we are about to receive, and for the intercourse afterwards, may the Lord make us truly thankful," said a minister from Aberdeen before one dinner at Balmoral, which the Queen later recounted with perfect Scottish inflections for her friends.

In her role as head of state, Elizabeth II has known clergy high and low, from popes to parish priests. The American evangelist Billy Graham came several times to Windsor Castle to worship with her privately. She admired Graham, although when he asked her to sit in the royal box for his crusade at Wembley Stadium with a congregation of 100,000 people, she politely declined, drawing the line at such a public display.

She sees the Archbishop of Canterbury in regular audiences a half dozen times a year, and as needed when important spiritual matters come up. She is friendly with the other top Anglican prelates as well, but is probably closest to the Dean of Windsor, who "takes the place of a family confessor," said Margaret Rhodes. "He has contact with the Queen reasonably regularly because he is beside Windsor Castle. If she has things she would like to discuss, she can talk to him. She knows he can talk that kind of language."

Religion infuses Elizabeth II's public duties, not

only through her Christmas message, but her attendance at high-profile observances such as Remembrance Sunday (the only time she wears black during the year), the second weekend in November. Held at the Cenotaph in London, the commemoration honors the war dead of the nation and the Commonwealth.

Three days before Easter, she also marks Maundy Thursday, a modern ritual signifying humility that is based on Jesus washing the feet of his disciples at the Last Supper. In past centuries monarchs actually cleansed the feet of the poor, a practice that ended in 1685 with James II. Instead, they distributed alms, and in the Queen's reign, the recipients of "Maundy Money" have been elderly subjects chosen for their service to the community. At Philip's suggestion, she changed the location of the service in 1957 to a cathedral outside London for the first time, and since then she has traveled around the country. The pageantry is intricately orchestrated, with her white-ruffed and scarlet-coated Yeomen of the Guard carrying silver trays holding purses filled with specially minted silver coins. The Queen moves along a line of men and women in equal number based on the monarch's age, and hands each of them a purse, often adding a word of congratulations for their good work.

The Queen's primary role as Supreme Governor of the Church of England is appointing archbishops, bishops, and deans recommended by the prime minister. She can't reject his advice, but she can, as in her dealings on secular matters, raise questions and ask for more information. "It's a very clever subtle way of making the prime minister think again," said historian Kenneth Rose. "If the next week he comes back and says 'I still want that archbishop,' that is the end of it. The Queen will not imperil the constitution over something like that."

Harold Wilson took particular pleasure in making such appointments. "He found his ecclesiastical duties a peaceful oasis in the desert that most prime ministers inexorably make of their garden," wrote biographer Elizabeth Longford. The problems plaguing Britain weighed more heavily on Wilson than during his first government, and his stamina seemed diminished. Sensing his difficulties, the Queen was solicitous when she entertained the Wilsons at Balmoral. "They used to fetch us by car from Aberdeen, wrapping us tenderly in rugs," recalled Mary Wilson. "We went into the hall, and the Queen and Philip came to greet us. There were bowls on the floor, and corgis running around, and she put a vase of gentians in my room. The lady-in-waiting said the Queen thought I might like those. She gave a lot of thought to things like that."

During their September 1975 visit, Elizabeth II drove the Wilsons to a cabin, where she served them tea and cooked them dropped scones. Afterward, as she and Mary were washing the dishes, Wilson surprised the Queen by confiding that he intended to resign around his sixtieth birthday the following March. Since he later suffered from Alzheimer's disease, there has been speculation that he had recognized signs of his slipping cognitive powers and decided to leave before his ability to govern was affected. But Marcia Falkender said that as early as March 1974, "when he first got to Number 10, he said it would not be for long." In addition to his wife and Falkender, only Martin Charteris was informed, and he kept the prime minister's secret along with the Queen.

As the Wilsons were leaving Balmoral for the last time, Elizabeth II had some photographs taken. One shows her in a head scarf, smiling tentatively from under the hood of her macintosh, with Wilson at her side, dressed in a handsome tweed suit and holding a pipe in his hand, looking every inch the country gentleman. Wilson so treasured the image that he carried it in his wallet for years.

Gough Whitlam, the Labour prime minister of Australia, posed a different sort of challenge for the Queen that November. As Queen of Australia, Elizabeth II had an abiding affection for the distant realm she had visited five times since her coronation. When Whitlam was first elected in 1972, she was eager to win over the man who spoke frankly about wanting to eliminate the monarchy in his country. She invited him to stay at Windsor Castle in April 1973 on the night of her forty-seventh birthday, along with his wife, the "too-tall" and "ungainly" (in her own words) Margaret, nicknamed "Big Marge" by the Queen's courtiers. The royal household pulled out the stops to entertain the Whitlams, installing them in a suite overlooking the Long Walk that stretches two and a half miles through Windsor Great Park to the giant equestrian statue of George III on Snow Hill.

After dinner, Whitlam gave the Queen a birthday present: a "deep-piled cream sheepskin rug," which she and her sister flirtatiously sat upon after it had been spread on the floor of the drawing room. "That evening she was quite determined to catch her man," Martin Charteris told author Graham Turner. "A lot of her sexuality has been suppressed, but that night, she used it like a weapon. She wrapped Gough Whitlam round her little finger, knocked him sideways. She sat on that rug in front of him, stroked it and said how lovely it was. It was an arrant use of sexuality. I was absolutely flabbergasted." Whitlam later said to Charteris, "Well, if she's like that, it's all right by me!"

The royal couple built on that rapport during two subsequent trips to Australia. When the Whitlams bade them goodbye after their visit in October 1973, Margaret wrote that it was "almost too much and too moving for us all." But on November 11, 1975, good feelings counted for little when Whitlam was deadlocked with the Australian Senate over passage of his budget, raising the prospect of financial default by the government.

In each of her fifteen realms outside Britain, the Queen is represented by a governor-general whom she appoints on the advice of the country's prime minister and whose role and functions are comparable to those of the sovereign in the United Kingdom. Her governor-general in Australia at the time of the budget crisis was Sir John Kerr, a respected former judge. To break the legislative impasse, Kerr took the extraordinary step of exercising his "reserve power" to dismiss Whitlam and install Liberal Party leader Malcolm Fraser as caretaker prime minister pending the election that Whitlam had refused to call. The Queen had been briefed on events as they were unfolding, but Kerr purposely did not inform her before he took action because he wished to keep her out of the imbroglio — and above a political dispute. Kerr had consulted with Australia's chief justice, who confirmed that under the Australian constitution he had the right to use the reserve power to dismiss ministers.

An infuriated Whitlam and the Labour Party tried to get the Queen to fire her governor-general for overreaching, to no avail. She could terminate her representative only on the advice of the sitting Australian prime minister. Kerr's actions were legal. The new election swept in a coalition led by the Liberals; the government passed a budget and got down to business. Whitlam maintained a congenial relationship with the Queen, but he never forgave Kerr. The governor-general stepped down in 1977, when he was honored with the Knight Grand Cross of the Royal Victorian Order, a personal gift of the Queen. In 1986 the Australian parliament passed a law withdrawing the power of the governor-general to intervene as Kerr had done, although two thirds of the population still wanted to keep Elizabeth II as their Queen.

A crisis brewing within Elizabeth II's own family caused her great distress in the autumn of 1975 when the marriage of Princess Margaret and Tony Snowdon collapsed. For the first five years after their wedding, they had been the toast of London — beautiful, magnetic, and stylish, celebrated for their lively parties with scintillating guests drawn from the arts and society. They had two children, David in 1961 and Sarah in 1964, and Tony was achieving even greater success through his photographic commissions and his work as artistic adviser to the *Sunday Times* magazine as well as an unpaid consultant to the Council of Industrial Design.

But Margaret became bored, petulant, and increasingly possessive. Tony in turn buried himself more deeply in his work, escaping in the evenings to his studio at Kensington Palace and taking frequent assignments overseas. Despite their superficial compatibility — strong sexual attraction, quick wit, love of ballet and theater, and sybaritic enjoyment of parties in the evening and extended holidays in the sun at luxurious resorts — there were seeds of trouble from the outset. Margaret had married on the rebound from Peter Townsend. She had known Tony for only a year when they became secretly engaged late in 1959 shortly after Margaret heard that at age forty-seven Townsend was planning to marry a nineteen-year-old Belgian girl. "I received a letter from Peter in the morning," she recalled, "and that evening I decided to marry Tony." The princess was attracted to Tony at least in part because his creativity and uninhibited bohemian ways made him so different from her father's former equerry.

Margaret could not have known that Tony was a compulsive seducer. Both of them were solipsistic, craved constant entertainment, competed for center stage, and lacked the inclination or the ability to be introspective about their relationship. Tony wanted the freedom to come and go as he pleased. Margaret insisted on unrealistic standards of togetherness, even though he began his work early in the morning and she rarely appeared until close to noon, ready to socialize until the small hours.

As the tensions between them festered, his teasing took on a sadistic edge, and their amusing banter exploded into ugly alcohol-fueled fights in front of their friends. He took to leaving notes around listing "things I hate about you," while she loathed the cottage in the country that he had fastidiously restored. Each of them was repeatedly unfaithful. Among his dalliances was with the daughter of the Marquis and Marchioness of Reading, neighbors near his house in Sussex. Margaret's lovers included one of Tony's best friends, Anthony Barton.

Publicly Tony was diligent about his role accompanying her on royal engagements, walking two steps behind and always allowing her to speak first. They were at their best on royal tours abroad, smiling amiably during endless meet-and-greet receptions. In November 1965 they conducted a charm offensive during a three-week tour of five cities in the United States that included a formal dinner at the White House. President Lyndon Johnson called the princess "little lady" and offered a prescription for a happy marriage that couldn't have been more inappropriate for the royal pair: "First, let her think she's having her way. Second, let her have it."

The Snowdons lived increasingly separate lives, especially after Margaret began escaping to a villa on the Caribbean island of Mustique given to her by her friend Colin Tennant (later Lord Glenconner). Although Margaret talked to her sister and her mother nearly every day, she was circumspect about her marriage. As the Queen Mother said to one of Margaret's confidants, "I didn't bring up my daughter to discuss her husband with me!" Both the Queen and the Queen Mother were dazzled by Tony's artistry and ingenuity, not to mention his charm. In their company, he was always on his best behavior. "He pulled the wool over their eyes," said Anne Glenconner. "The Queen probably didn't realize what Tony was up to. It was not the sort of thing the Queen would talk about. She doesn't gossip."

The Queen did see Margaret behaving badly — when she took out her frustrations in rude remarks to the Queen Mother, or when she flouted protocol by refusing to turn when her sister did during meals, leaving the Queen to stare at the back of her dinner partner's head. She knew Margaret was drinking heavily; when her cousin Pamela Hicks had to cancel a party because of her husband's problems with alcohol, the Queen said, "I understand. I've been through it with Margaret." But as was her habit, the Queen avoided confronting the princess. "How's Margaret's mood?" she asked a friend of her sister before lunch at Royal Lodge. "Shall I venture out on the terrace?"

In 1973 Margaret fell for Roddy Llewellyn, an attractive and pliant dilettante nearly eighteen years her junior. The liaison infuriated Tony, and the Queen was upset by her sister's indiscretions, above all when Margaret began staying with Roddy at his bohemian upper-class commune in Wiltshire. By November 1975 the Snowdons had reached the breaking point. Tony sent a letter to the Queen telling her that "the atmosphere is appalling for all concerned," and they needed to separate. Several weeks later the Queen replied, saying that Tony's letter "had been devastating," wrote Snowdon biographer Anne de Courcy. "She intimated that she was aware of how bad their relationship had become before saying that she realized the situation was now intolerable for both of them." She asked only that they wait until after Christmas, and following discussions at the Palace, she advised that they make the separation announcement during the Easter holidays when their children could be with them. The Palace intended to say only that the Snowdons would "live apart" and that "there are no plans for divorce proceedings."

The Palace game plan blew up in late February 1976 when a tabloid photographer snapped a picture of Margaret and Roddy in their bathing suits, sitting together at a table in Mustique. Rupert Murdoch's *News of the World* splashed the suggestive image of the Princess and her toy boy, prompting Tony to move out. Although he had his own inamorata, Lucy Lindsay-Hogg, Tony managed to seize the moral high ground. He leaked the news of the separation to the *Daily Express,* which published it on March 17, two days before the planned announcement by the Palace. In the process, he eclipsed Harold Wilson's resignation announcement on the 19th — which, ironically, the prime minister had timed in part to deflect attention from the simmering Snowdon scandal.

Always deft with the media, Snowdon held his own press conference on the 17th in which he wished his wife well, asked for the understanding of their children, and professed his undying admiration and love for the royal family. His clever spin reinforced the view of Margaret as the guilty party, a self-indulgent and outré princess. "The Queen and the Queen Mother never took sides with Tony Snowdon over the separation," said one of the Queen's relatives, "but they never made an enemy of him. They realized their daughter and sister could be impossible to live with." Snowdon kept in the good graces of the Queen and her mother by never saying another unkind word about Margaret, and by remaining forever silent about the rest of the royal family.

Harold Wilson's retirement came as a surprise, not only to the public, but to members of his own party, which elected as its leader Foreign Secretary James Callaghan. The new prime minister, who kissed hands on April 5, 1976, had also served as chancellor of the exchequer and home secretary, so he was a known quantity in the corridors of Buckingham Palace. To honor the retiring premier, the Queen agreed to attend Wilson's farewell dinner at 10 Downing Street, the first time she had done so since Churchill left office twenty-one years earlier. The inspiration came from Charteris, and Wilson was flattered by the gesture. The sly wit of the Queen's private secretary was unmistakable as well, when she referred in her speech to herself and Wilson as the tenants of tied cottages at either end of the Mall.

The Queen hit her fiftieth birthday on April 21, 1976. She looked enviably youthful, a combination of good genes, healthy living, and an unfussy beauty regimen. "She doesn't sit in the sun and she doesn't hunt, which is very weathering," said one of her good friends. Her brown hair, which now showed some gray strands, was tended by her longtime hairdresser, Charles Martyn. Facing forward rather than the usual bending backward, she rested her chin inside a sink equipped with a large sprayer to have her hair washed with egg and lemon shampoo. Between setting and drying, Martyn would spend an hour and a half creating her unvarying hairstyle as she reviewed a stack of correspondence in her lap, scarcely glancing up to check her reflection in the mirror. For her skin she used an assortment of Cyclax products including milk of roses moisturizer, and she washed with milk and honey cleanser. She spent little time applying makeup, with just a dusting of powder, and she used bright red lipstick because it was more visible in public.

That June she hosted French president Valéry Giscard d'Estaing for a state visit and shrewdly orchestrated a public show of support for the supersonic Concorde airplane, an Anglo-French venture that French officials regarded as a useful collaboration, despite concerns about its high cost. Giscard was apprehensive about the Concorde because he had heard the British had lost enthusiasm for it. Before the state banquet at Buckingham Palace, the Queen instructed Martin Charteris to depart from protocol and applaud loudly when she mentioned the airplane in her speech. Charteris clapped on cue, and because of his senior position as the Queen's private secretary, he was joined resoundingly by the other British guests. At a press conference the next day, the French president said that after hearing the "spontaneous and loud applause," he was reassured of Britain's wholehearted support. Nicholas Henderson, a seasoned diplomat who watched the scheme unfold, considered it "a tribute to the Queen's understanding of the workings of guided democracy."

The following month, she returned to the United States for the first time in seventeen years. The idea of a state visit around the Bicentennial of American independence had been broached by President Nixon in early 1973, eighteen months before his resignation in the wake of the Watergate scandal. British officials thought the timing needed "careful consideration." As Robert Armstrong, Heath's principal private secretary, wrote to Martin Charteris at the time, "One would wish to consider whether it was right for The Queen to be associated in this way with the celebration of a rebellion from the British Crown." He added that the British Ambassador in Washington, Rowland Baring, the 3rd Earl of Cromer (husband of the Queen's lady-in-waiting Esme Cromer), "has some feeling that there may be a certain degree of uninhibited zest about the American celebrations of the Declaration of Independence with which it might not be entirely desirable that The Queen should be associated. . . . A certain amount of ballyhoo is inseparable from this sort of celebration in America, which would conspicuously lack dignity."

Despite those initial misgivings, a grand six-day state visit was arranged, beginning on July 6 with a stop in Philadephia. "July 4th was really pushing it," said David Walker of the British embassy. "Forgiveness can go so far." Among the Queen's entourage would be her good friend Virginia (Ginny) Airlie, the forty-three-year-old wife of the 13th Earl, who was her first American lady-in-waiting. Diminutive like the Queen, and described by Cecil Beaton as "a paragon of gaiety & dignity," Ginny Airlie had been appointed in 1973. She had initially demurred, saying she was an American subject with six children, the youngest only two years old, and suggested that the Queen "should get someone more steeped in it all." But the Queen had insisted. The unpretentious peer's wife fitted well with the royal household and adapted readily to the royal ways she had observed at parties and during shooting weekends at Sandringham and Balmoral. Even so, Woman of the Bedchamber Susan Hussey couldn't resist calling her "the American."

The royal party of twenty flew to Bermuda, where they embarked on *Britannia* for the three-day crossing to the United States. On the first night, they were hit with a force nine gale. Susan Crosland, the Baltimore-born wife of Foreign Secretary Anthony Crosland, noticed that during drinks before dinner amid the lurching seas, the Queen looked "philosophical, almost merry, twenty yards of chiffon scarf flung over one shoulder." Naval officer Philip, however, was "ashen and drawn," much as he had looked in 1951 when he had been seasick during their stormy voyage across the North Atlantic. Now, as then, the Queen was the only one to resist the nausea.

After coffee in the drawing room, the Queen grabbed the handle of a sliding door when a swell heaved the ship. As the door slid shut, the Queen exclaimed "Wheeeeee!" her chiffon scarf flying. The door slid open with another pitch of the waves, and again she cried, "Wheeeeee!" before turning to say "Good night." The next morning at breakfast she announced, "I have *never* seen so many grey and grim faces round a dinner table." Then a pause: "Philip was not well." Another pause, this time with a giggle: "I'm glad to say."

A crowd of five thousand greeted the Queen as *Britannia* docked at the same spot where William Penn had landed in 1681. It was a scorching day in Philadelphia as she walked from one historic spot to another among an estimated 75,000 well-wishers waving American flags and Union Jacks. Reporters were surprised by "her apparent eagerness to work a crowd."

At Independence National Park, she presented the six-and-one-half-ton commemorative Bicentennial Bell manufactured by London's Whitechapel Foundry, which had cast the original Liberty Bell in 1752. "I speak to you as the direct descendant of King George III," she said, noting that the Fourth of July "should be celebrated as much in Britain as in America . . . in sincere gratitude to the Founding Fathers . . . for having taught Britain a very valuable lesson. We lost the American colonies because we lacked that statesmanship 'to know the right time, and the manner of yielding what is impossible to keep.' . . . We learned to respect the right of others to govern themselves in their own ways. . . . Without that great act in the cause of liberty, performed in Independence Hall 200 years ago, we could never have transformed an empire into a commonwealth."

That evening she endured the casual protocol violations of Frank Rizzo, the beefy mayor of Philadelphia and former policeman who had campaigned on the slogan "I'm going to make Attila the Hun look like a faggot." During an elegant dinner for four hundred at the Philadelphia Museum of Art, Rizzo left her side to cruise the other tables and "press the flesh." "What a fascinating man he is," the Queen deadpanned. She escaped to the ladies' room — euphemistically known in royal circles as an "opportunity to tidy" or a "health break" — before a reception for yet another six hundred guests.

The temperature in Washington pushed one hundred degrees, but the Queen "never faltered in the day's walk-about under a remorseless sun," wrote Susan Crosland, who politely declined a revivifying pinch of snuff from Martin Charteris. After a welcoming ceremony on the White House South Lawn, President Gerald Ford and his wife, Betty, threw a white-tie dinner for 224 under a big tent in the Rose Garden hung with Japanese lanterns. Public television broadcast the banquet live, prohibited only from showing the Queen eating or dancing. In her yellow organza gown, diamond tiara, necklace, and earrings, Elizabeth II did not disappoint.

Henry Kissinger's wife, Nancy, smoked through the entire meal, and Vice President Nelson Rockefeller's wife, Happy, asked Philip about his German background. He retorted that he was Danish, prompting Happy to tell Tony Crosland, "Prince Philip is renouncing his German origins!" The East Room entertainment featured Bob Hope, followed by pop stars the Captain & Tennille, who sang their hit single "Muskrat Love" about a pair of rodents romancing by candlelight. Afterward, the Queen and Gerald Ford danced to "The Lady Is a Tramp," the iconic Rodgers and Hart tune popularized by Frank Sinatra. The Queen and Philip didn't leave for their quarters at Blair House until shortly before 1 A.M.

After another nonstop day of appearances, Elizabeth II reciprocated the next evening with her own white-tie, four-course dinner for eighty-four at the British embassy, preceded by a reception for 1,600 on the lawn, where she was trailed by television teams carrying high-powered lights. Suddenly the cameras and lights disappeared. Elizabeth Taylor had arrived "to make her grand entrance," recalled Michael Shea, then director of the British Information Services in New York. British ambassador Sir Peter Ramsbotham was fuming, but the Queen "was merely amused, seeing, for once, someone else at the center of media attention."

As she had in 1957, the Queen reached Manhattan by water, this time on the air-conditioned Royal Barge from *Britannia*. A hundred-yard walkabout in lower Manhattan turned chaotic as crowds pressed to get near her and the police "were overwhelmed by the enthusiasm," said Michael Shea. Not for the first time, she appeared cool amid the sweating multitude. "Luckily, I don't mind the heat," she said cheerfully.

She again met with the Pilgrims and the English-Speaking Union, this time over luncheon at the Waldorf-Astoria. As the Queen and Philip were driven uptown in an open car to visit the eighteenth-century Morris-Jumel mansion in Harlem — Manhattan's oldest house — she spotted a friend on the corner of Park Avenue and 61st Street. "Oh!" she exclaimed. "There's John Andrew!" The Anglican cleric waved and shouted back, "Hello, hello. I'll see you tonight." After she passed by, he thought to himself, "What a bloody fool. What a thing to say to the Queen."

The high point of her packed schedule that day was a visit to Bloomingdale's, which was highly orchestrated, unlike her stop at a supermarket nineteen years earlier. This time store officials swept her from one exhibition to another on three floors. She saw reproduction Chippendale chairs, noting that the seats were wider than in Britain, and she marveled at the Calvin Klein models wearing trendy tweed midi-skirts. "Gracious, do you really wear skirts *that* long here?" she asked. Philip had his own jovial tour that included a pet rock and talking calculator in a display of best-selling novelties.

The royal couple hosted a small dinner for three dozen guests on *Britannia,* which *The New York Times* likened to the "homey patched-elbow chic of an English country house, with flowered chintz slipcovers, family photographs, and rattan settees, interspersed with the occasional relic of Empire — shark's teeth from the Solomon Islands here, a golden urn commemorating Nelson's victory at Trafalgar there." An indiscreet crew member confessed to the *Times* reporter, "We have fabulous parties when the Queen's away and the Duke's on board." In fact, the evenings were often exuberant when Elizabeth II was there as well, with witty skits written by Martin Charteris and starring members of the family and household dressed in costume, singing and dancing to tunes played on the bolted-down piano.

Following the dinner, there was a reception for two hundred more guests, one of whom was Canon John Andrew. He was escorting Sharman Douglas, who had been a friend of the Queen since the late 1940s when Sharman's father, Lewis Douglas, served as U.S. ambassador to Britain. As soon as Elizabeth II saw Andrew, she threw back her head and laughed: "You looked so funny standing all alone on the corner of the street!" After she and Sharman Douglas had kissed hello, Philip came over, the lapel of his dinner jacket sporting one of the "Big Apple" cloth stickers featured in a popular promotional campaign for New York City. "What the hell is that?" asked John Andrew. The duke removed it and stuck it on the cleric's forehead. "There!" he said, which started the Queen laughing again.

Over the next two days, Elizabeth II traveled up and down the East Coast, first to visit Thomas Jefferson's Monticello and the University of Virginia, then to Newport, Rhode Island, where she entertained the Fords at a dinner on *Britannia*. She wrapped up her journey in Boston, "moving from one reminder of 1776 to another." In a speech at the old State House, she remarked that she was in the city where "it all began." Sailing out of Boston harbor on *Britannia,* for Halifax, Nova Scotia, the ship's band played "Auld Lang Syne." "I was reminded of the good that can flow from a friendship that is mended," Elizabeth II later reflected.

"Who would have thought 200 years ago that a descendant of King George III could have taken part in these celebrations?"

The Queen continued at the same pace for another two weeks in Canada, where she opened the Olympic Games in Montreal and watched her daughter compete as a member of the British equestrian team. During the cross-country event, Anne's horse hit a fence and threw her to the ground as the Queen stared intently, biting her nails and squinting with anxiety. Very much her mother's daughter, Anne climbed back on and continued the race, even after suffering bruises and a mild concussion that erased her memory of the competition.

The Queen's endurance, as always, was striking. Some years earlier, while she was touring Saskatchewan, Alvin Hamilton, then Canada's minister of northern affairs and national resources, had said to the Queen's private secretary, "I noticed, we've been going all day, and Her Majesty never requested even a health break." "You need not worry," the private secretary replied. "Her Majesty is trained for eight hours."

Whatever the setting, Elizabeth II appeared relaxed while carrying out her public duties. Onlookers were taken aback a few months later after a dinner during a royal tour in Luxembourg when the high-spirited Queen took to playing the drums, "keeping the rhythm and shaking her head." During a benefit for the Venice in Peril Fund featuring a screening of Luchino Visconti's *Death in Venice,* the evening's host, John Julius Norwich (the 2nd Viscount), was seated between the Queen and Princess Anne. He heard the monarch begin to sigh only a few minutes into the more than two-hour film. "I heard her sigh again," recalled Norwich. "It was a long sigh. I was in agony as the sighs continued throughout the film and I wondered what to say when the lights came up." But as the movie ended, she simply turned, flashed a bright smile, and said, "Well, that was a bit gloomy, wasn't it?" "She was trying to put me at ease," Norwich explained. "She could sense my discomfort."

In her 1976 Christmas message, the Queen spoke for the first time about her coming Silver Jubilee marking twenty-five years on the throne. "Next year is a rather special one for me," she said. "The gift I would most value . . . is that reconciliation should be found wherever it is needed." The Callaghan government initially opposed a Silver Jubilee celebration because of Britain's economic woes, but Charteris and his Palace colleagues successfully argued that it would provide a morale boost, and that the Queen should not only tour the country, but all her Commonwealth realms. She emphasized, however, her "express wish" that there should be "no undue expenditure." The press was predictably skeptical, with the pro-republican *Guardian* proclaiming on Sunday, February 6, that "apathy hits plans for Jubilee."

Although the Queen reached her landmark that Accession Day, she did not want to celebrate the moment her father died, so she spent the weekend quietly at Windsor Castle with her family. Four days later she embarked on the first of her two overseas jubilee tours, spending seven weeks traveling on *Britannia* to Western Samoa, Tonga, Fiji, Papua New Guinea, New Zealand, and Australia. Her reception gave the lie to *The Guardian*'s grim prediction. "Harbour entrances would be just packed with people everywhere," recalled Commodore Anthony Morrow. In Fiji a roof collapsed during a demonstration of native dances, although nobody was injured. One reporter noted that as the crowds headed to the scene, the Queen "seized the moment to whip out a lipstick and add another streak of red." On her return to England, Elizabeth II watched the three-year-old filly Dunfermline, her second great runner of the 1970s, win two of Britain's classic races, first the Oaks at Epsom and later in the summer the St. Leger at Doncaster.

The festivities began in earnest on May 4, 1977, with the Queen's appearance in Westminster Hall for "Loyal Addresses" from the Houses of Commons and Lords, followed by her reply. Like the Christmas broadcast, her message was personal and therefore noteworthy. As would be expected, she spoke glowingly of the Commonwealth, but she also said that Britain's entry into the European Economic Community was "one of the most significant decisions during my reign." Even more surprisingly, she frankly responded to the growing pressure to devolve power to Scotland and Wales. "I can readily understand these aspirations," she said, "but I cannot forget that I was crowned Queen of the United Kingdom of Great Britain and Northern Ireland. Perhaps this Jubilee is a time to remind ourselves of the benefits which union has conferred, at home and in our international dealings, on the inhabitants of all parts of this United Kingdom."

"That was significant, because it was the only political thing she has said, and all the more powerful because it was unique," said Simon Walker, who served as the Queen's communication and press secretary from 2000 to 2002. Nationalists in Scotland recognized the primacy of the union as her bedrock principle, and duly protested. But the Queen had been determined to speak her mind.

On Monday, June 6, Elizabeth II stood atop Snow Hill in Windsor Great Park, her hair shielded from the elements by her signature head scarf, poised to ignite a bonfire that would signal others around the country to light their own in celebration of their Queen. Unfortunately, a skittish soldier beat her to it, a glitch that amused rather than annoyed her. "Your Majesty, I'm afraid everything that could possibly go wrong is going wrong," said Major Sir Michael Parker, an impresario for royal events with an expertise in pyrotechnics. "Oh good, what fun!" she replied with a smile.

The apex of the festivities came the following day, when the Queen and Prince Philip rode in the Gold State Coach, accompanied by Household Cavalry, Yeomen of the Guard, and Prince Charles on horseback in a bearskin and the red uniform of Colonel-in-Chief of the Welsh Guards. It was the first time since the coronation that she had ridden in the freshly gilded and dizzyingly ornate carriage. "I had forgotten how uncomfortable that ride could be," the Queen later confided to a friend.

The carriage procession — which also featured the Irish State Coach, Queen Alexandra's State

Coach, and the Glass Coach carrying other members of the royal family — wended its way from Buckingham Palace to St. Paul's Cathedral, passing more than a million people, many of whom had camped out overnight in the rain. At the cathedral, a congregation of 2,700 guests included all of her five living prime ministers and an array of world leaders. Donald Coggan, the 101st Archbishop of Canterbury, praised the Queen as "an example of service untiringly done, of duty faithfully fulfilled, and of a home life stable and wonderfully happy," as the television camera panned across a row of her relatives. Princess Margaret, separated from Tony Snowdon for more than a year and still grabbing headlines for her escapades with Roddy Llewellyn, sat with her two children.

The Queen, wearing a bright pink shift dress, matching coat, and cloche hat trimmed with twenty-five small fabric bells, walked with her husband through the streets near the cathedral, shaking hands and exchanging pleasantries along the crowded barriers. At a luncheon in the Guildhall, she restated the pledge of lifelong service that she had made on her twenty-first birthday "in my salad days when I was green in judgment," adding, "I do not regret or retract a word of it."

As the Queen and Philip rode in an open carriage to Buckingham Palace, the roar of the vast crowd was so loud that her coachman couldn't even hear the horses' hooves hitting the pavement. The royal family fanned out on the famous Palace balcony, the men in uniform, the women like a pastel rainbow: the Queen in pink, the Queen Mother in daffodil, Margaret in slightly darker pink, and Anne visibly pregnant in aquamarine. Elizabeth II looked jubilant — laughing, talking, and waving, taking in a mass of humanity she had seen on numerous occasions stretching back to her father's coronation in 1937. But this time, more than any other, the crowds were genuinely cheering for *her,* for what she symbolized and what she had achieved. The Duchess of Kent, wife of the Queen's first cousin Edward the Duke of Kent, got so carried away she threw her arms around Elizabeth II and kissed her, exclaiming, "They *really* love you." Katharine Kent later explained that the Queen had been "totally bewildered and overwhelmed by this huge flood of affection directed towards her." An estimated 500 million television viewers around the world watched the spectacle.

Two days later the celebration topped itself with a barge procession down the Thames from Greenwich to Lambeth that was meant to evoke the majestic convoys of Tudor times. After dark, fireworks exploded across the sky, and another enormous crowd gathered in front of Buckingham Palace and along the Mall to catch the parade of illuminated carriages carrying the Queen and her family back to Buckingham Palace. Roy Strong, director of the Victoria and Albert Museum, was among the multitude — "basically middle class British. Educated voices could be heard," he recalled. "Men in suits passed by with Union Jacks tied to the end of their umbrellas." Clusters of onlookers spontaneously burst into "God Save the Queen" and "Rule Britannia." When the coaches clattered by, Strong felt a communal "surge of emotion." Elizabeth II and her family appeared on the Palace balcony, then reappeared after midnight, when Princess Margaret "more or less had to push them out as they failed to grasp the fervor of the crowd."

There were four thousand Silver Jubilee street parties in London alone, and an estimated twelve thousand in cities, towns, and villages around the country. The punk rock group Sex Pistols sounded one blatantly harsh note with their nihilistic take on "God Save the Queen," calling her the fascist leader of a country with no future. Although the BBC loyally refused to play the song, it nevertheless raced to number two in the charts.

Still, that dubious success didn't dim jubilee enthusiasm. Over the next several months, the Queen toured thirty-six counties in the United Kingdom. As the celebratory momentum grew, the crowds swelled to the point that over a million people came out on a single day in Lancashire. The Queen's last stop on her domestic itinerary was Northern Ireland, which she visited for the first time in eleven years.

Palace officials and government ministers had debated whether she should risk the trip. The conflict in Ulster since the beginning of the Troubles had been a continuing source of concern for the Queen. Following their deployment to Northern Ireland in the late 1960s, the British troops originally intended to protect the Catholic minority had become the targets of IRA bombs and snipers amid escalating tensions. In August 1971, the authorities began imprisoning Catholic militants without trial in an effort to control the violence.

"The Queen received me at one of my regular

audiences after she had been watching the coverage of riots in Belfast on the television, and was obviously shaken by the ferocity of the events in a part of her Kingdom," Edward Heath recalled. "In particular, she was horrified by the film of women's faces contorted with hate as they clung to the high wired fences protecting British troops. Whenever the Queen is accused of remoteness or indifference towards the tribulations of her subjects, I think back to that moment."

To protest the new internment policy, some ten thousand Catholic demonstrators had defied a ban on large gatherings to march through the streets of Londonderry on January 30, 1972. A British paratrooper regiment was dispatched to the scene, and after being assaulted by rocks and other objects, the forces opened fire in the panicky melee, killing thirteen and injuring fourteen, one of whom died later. There were armed IRA operatives in the crowd, but all those killed were unarmed Catholics, many of them cut down as they were fleeing.

The killings became known as Bloody Sunday, a turning point that rapidly escalated the IRA's battle to force a unification of Ulster and the Republic of Ireland. In the immediate aftermath, mobs burned down the British embassy in Dublin. The IRA boosted its membership with radicalized young recruits and intensified its campaign of terror against the British army and English civilians, along with Protestants in Northern Ireland, leading to thousands of casualties.

In several of her Christmas broadcasts after Bloody Sunday, the Queen had touched on what she called "our own particular sorrows in Northern Ireland," extending prayers and sympathy to those who were suffering, and encouraging Protestants and Catholics working together for peace "to keep humanity and common sense alive." She predictably bridled when officials had second thoughts in the summer of 1977 about her planned trip to Northern Ireland, just as she had resisted in 1961 when her trip to Ghana was nearly canceled. "Martin, we *said* we're going to Ulster," she told her private secretary. "It would be a great pity not to."

On August 10, she landed on the grounds of Hillsborough Castle outside Belfast by helicopter — judged by her security advisers to be "the safest way for the Queen to travel." It was her first trip on a helicopter, a means of transportation that had long made her nervous, despite her usual physical courage.

She was protected by extraordinary security during her two days in Ulster, with some 32,000 troops and police on alert. About seven thousand people were invited to her receptions, garden party, and investiture, all of which were broadcast on television. After visiting the New University of Ulster at Coleraine, she joined her family on *Britannia* for their annual Western Isles cruise and a two-month retreat at Balmoral. Her trip to Northern Ireland, she said in that year's Christmas broadcast, reminded her that "nowhere is reconciliation more desperately needed." Her ability to travel there allowed "people of goodwill" to be "greatly heartened by the chance they had to share the celebrations."

The second Commonwealth tour took her to

Canada and the Caribbean for nearly three weeks. She returned from Barbados on November 2 by Concorde, the distinctive beak-nosed supersonic jetliner that had gone into service in January 1976. Her three-hour-and-forty-five-minute trip gave a futuristic flourish to the end of her 56,000 miles of jubilee travels.

On November 15 at 10:46 A.M., she became a grandmother at age fifty-one with the arrival of Anne's first child, Peter Phillips. He was the first baby in the royal family to be born a commoner in five hundred years, since Mark Phillips had declined to take a title when he married Anne. They intended to raise their son — and his sister, Zara, born four years later — apart from the pressures of royal obligations, a decision that both children later welcomed.

That month Martin Charteris retired at age sixty-four after twenty-seven years of serving the Queen. Aside from Bobo MacDonald, no one in the royal household knew her better, had worked more intimately with her, or had seen her through so many stages of her life, from her formative years as a working princess through her grief over her father's early death to her evolution as a confident and capable sovereign. He had in every respect lightened her load, not only with his keen judgment but with the verve he brought to her speeches and his gentle prodding to open her mind to new approaches.

They said farewell at a brief audience in Buckingham Palace. To help keep her emotions in check, Elizabeth II brought along her flinty daughter, who wouldn't tolerate tears from her mother. "The

Queen knew Martin would cry, and he did," said Gay Charteris. "He was not inhibited by his emotions. She didn't cry, and in her view, the least said, the better." Some years later, Elizabeth II confided to her mother that when "my Martin" left, she missed him but she knew "he was still around if I needed to ask anything difficult." All she said that morning at the Palace was, "Martin, thank you for a lifetime," as she presented him with a silver tray inscribed with the same sentiment. When his tears abated, he mustered his customary levity. "The next time you see this," he said. "It will have a gin and tonic on it."

CHAPTER THIRTEEN
IRON LADY AND ENGLISH ROSE

The Queen's Silver Jubilee succeeded in lifting the nation's spirits during a troubled time, much as her wedding had done during the postwar gloom. Prime Minister James Callaghan had been struggling to jump-start Britain's stagnant economy from the moment of his election at age sixty-four in 1976. That year his government was forced to stave off bankruptcy with a loan of $3.9 billion from the International Monetary Fund. The money came with the sort of conditions — curbs on government spending and wage increases in the public sector — that were customarily imposed on developing countries.

The prime minister — nicknamed "Sunny Jim" — was an avuncular presence in his weekly meetings with the Queen, who was fourteen years his junior. The son of a chief petty officer in the Royal Navy and a schoolteacher, he had entered the civil service as a tax collector when he was unable to afford a university education. An unabashed monarchist, he enjoyed his meetings with the Queen, relieved to be in a setting where "conversation flowed easily and could roam anywhere over a wide range of social as well as political and international topics." After spending fifteen minutes or so on three

The Queen was always kind to Diana. But even after she had spent time in her mother-in-law's company, Diana remained "terrified of her."

Prince Charles and his future wife Lady Diana Spencer with the Queen shortly after the announcement of the couple's engagement, March 1981. PRESS ASSOCIATION IMAGES

prearranged agenda items, their talk over the next hour might touch on their families or perhaps the price of hay in Sussex, where he had a farm, compared to Norfolk or Scotland. Callaghan learned to respond adroitly to the Queen's fascination with political personalities, and he came to admire her oblique way of getting across her points: how she "weighs up" the problems of her prime minister, hinting at her thoughts in a "pretty detached" manner, and avoiding direct advice.

At six foot one, he was the tallest of the Queen's prime ministers, handsome, easygoing, ready with compliments and even mildly flirtatious. One week she memorably took him for a stroll in the Buckingham Palace gardens and coquettishly placed a sprig of lily of the valley in his buttonhole. Callaghan correctly summarized her evenhanded approach to all her prime ministers, with the exception of Winston Churchill, who was sui generis. "What one gets," Callaghan said, "is friendliness but not friendship."

For "poor old Jim Callaghan," as the Queen Mother referred to him, the Tuesday evening interludes offered a brief moment of tranquillity amid political strife. Despite the compelling need for austerity, the unions plunged ahead in 1978 with demands for fat wage increases, which meant higher government spending to placate public employees. Throughout what became known as the "Winter of Discontent" — one of the coldest on record — the country was crippled by a series of strikes by truck drivers, hospital orderlies, trash collectors, ambulance drivers, school janitors, and gravediggers. Piles of refuse filled the streets, a symbol of a nation that had lost its way.

On March 28, 1979, the Conservatives in the House of Commons introduced a vote of no confidence in the government, which is required under the constitution to have the support of a majority of the legislature. The Labour government lost the confidence motion by one vote (thanks mainly to the Liberal Party's backing of the Tory initiative), and a general election was called for May 3. The Conservative Party, led by fifty-three-year-old Margaret Thatcher, swept to power, winning 339 seats to 268 for Labour and 11 for Liberals. Thatcher's arrival at Buckingham Palace the next day to kiss hands as the first female prime minister was a historic moment for the ambitious young politician who had written twenty-seven years earlier that the accession of Elizabeth II could help remove "the last shreds of prejudice against women aspiring to the highest places." When thoroughbred trainer Ian Balding called the Queen shortly afterward, she said, "What do you think about Margaret Thatcher getting in?" "Ma'am," he replied, "I'm not sure I can get my head around a woman running the country." The Queen fell silent. "You know what I mean?" he said. This time she laughed, and said nothing in reply.

The two women were only six months apart in age. Impeccably dressed and meticulously coiffed, they were equally professional and hardworking, but they differed markedly in background and temperament. Margaret Roberts was the daughter of a successful grocer in Grantham, Lincolnshire, who lived above the store. She earned her Oxford degree in chemistry on a scholarship, married

Denis Thatcher, a prosperous divorced businessman, and worked as a lawyer before being elected
to Parliament in 1959.

She oversaw housing and education policy for
the various Conservative prime ministers, and in
1975 the party elected her as its leader, deposing
Edward Heath. She was determined to reverse the
country's economic decline by loosening the grip
of organized labor, dramatically cutting public
spending, reducing the dependence of citizens on
their government, deregulating business to promote growth, and, along the way, raising Britain's
stature on the world stage.

Thatcher was fearless and nimble in debate, and
passionate about her principles of bedrock con-
servatism shaped by such intellectuals as Milton
Friedman and Friedrich von Hayek. The conservative historian Paul Johnson admiringly called
her "the eternal scholarship girl. She loved learning, swotting things up, being tested, passing with
honours." Her zest for combat was antithetical to
the Queen's nonconfrontational nature. Nor could
the Queen share with her prime minister something like the irony of her conversation with Ian
Balding, because Thatcher's sense of humor was
barely discernible. For the next eleven years, there
would be none of the lively banter that Elizabeth II
enjoyed with James Callaghan, whatever she might
have thought of his policies. Conversations would
no longer be divided equally, since Thatcher had a
habit of lecturing. "The Queen found that irritating," said a top army general close to Elizabeth II.

Their audiences were formal and businesslike.
"The agenda included major topical events," said

Charles Powell, who was the prime minister's senior foreign policy adviser. "It was not a trivial agenda. Lady Thatcher wouldn't prepare. She would be fully up to speed anyway. She would want to know what the Queen would want to talk about, and what she might say to the Queen, who was working on the same information base. Lady Thatcher didn't need anything to impose discipline, because she was disciplined enough."

Afterward, the prime minister would join the Queen's private secretaries for a whisky. "She chatted with us," said a former courtier. "She was quite relaxed, which was rare for her. I think the audience was something like a tranquilizer." On returning to Downing Street, Thatcher might carry a request from the Queen, usually something to do with an army regiment. "She seemed to come back in a cheerful frame of mind," recalled Charles Powell. "She genuinely enjoyed the meetings. Her demeanor on returning did not say, 'Oh God, what a waste of time that was.' In fact it was the opposite."

After giving birth in 1953 to twins, Thatcher, like the Queen, had been an exception in her generation as a working mother, and had likewise relied on nannies for her children's upbringing. Both women had trouble discussing their feelings, which prevented them from venturing into personal topics that might have formed a bond — the push and pull of combining professional life and motherhood, and the challenges of having a husband in a subordinate position. One exception was the time the Queen ended an audience by offering wardrobe tips before the prime minister visited Saudi Arabia. Otherwise, the two women avoided any hint of "girl talk." "Mrs. Thatcher would have thought it impudent to have tried to establish a close relationship and would have expected the Queen to make the first move," said a former government adviser. Although no such move was forthcoming, the Queen treated her prime minister with courtesy and thoughtfulness. Whenever the Thatchers came to Windsor for a dine-and-sleep, Elizabeth II took care to choose items for the library exhibit with particular meaning: one year a selection of antique fans, another time a manuscript written by Mozart when he was ten years old.

Queen and prime minister thrived in a masculine world, but in different ways. Elizabeth II "was reserved but she could give you not quite a come-hither look, but one which was so friendly as to be encouraging," said her long-serving courtier Edward Ford. "She made us feel like men." Thatcher, who had just one woman in her cabinet, asserted her position with an intimidating firmness — earning the nickname "the Iron Lady" — that the Queen would have considered unnecessary if not unseemly for herself. *Spitting Image,* the satirical television show featuring large puppets that caricatured politicians, the royal family, and a slew of celebrities, famously presented a skit in 1984 showing the prime minister and her cabinet sharing a meal. "Would you like to order, sir?" the waitress asked Thatcher (dressed in a man's suit and tie, holding a cigar in her left hand). "Yes, I will have a steak," she replied. Waitress: "How'd you like it?" Thatcher: "Oh, raw please." Waitress: "And what about the vegetables?" Thatcher: "Oh, they'll have the same as me."

Princess Michael of Kent, the wife of one of the Queen's cousins, came up with a surprisingly apt description of the division of labor between Britain's two female leaders, each of whom had a powerful aura: "The Queen is the mother of the country," she explained to her children. "She sends you to school." Margaret Thatcher was "the headmistress who makes the rules you have to obey."

Yet the prime minister was scrupulously deferential to her sovereign. "No one could curtsy lower than Margaret Thatcher," said Charles Powell. "If I did it you would need a crane to pull me up. She came from a very patriotic lower middle class family who had huge respect for the royal family and the Queen, so as a result she would have been slightly formal." Thatcher once said that if she were a visitor from Mars required to create a constitutional system, "I would set up . . . a hereditary monarchy, wonderfully trained, in duty and in leadership, which understands example, which is always there, which is above politics, for which the whole nation has an affection and which is a symbol of patriotism."

One obligation the prime minister regarded as burdensome was the annual autumn pilgrimage to Balmoral, which she did "out of loyalty," said Charles Powell. She invariably arrived in a tweed suit and heels, utterly ill-equipped for country life. "Does the prime minister like to walk in the hills?" asked one frequent guest. "The hills?" replied the Queen. "The hills? She walks on the road!" Elizabeth II also knew that Thatcher never accepted the custom of withdrawing with the other women after dinner. "The Queen finessed it by always inviting the Thatchers to a barbeque, which was more informal than a dinner in the castle, so didn't follow the convention of having the ladies withdraw," explained a fellow guest. An equerry was assigned to play golf with Denis Thatcher, and the Queen routinely took the prime minister for tea at Birkhall, since the Queen Mother was an enthusiastic admirer of Thatcher. On the final day, the prime minister and her husband usually left at dawn.

Only three months after taking office, Margaret Thatcher encountered a surprisingly assertive Queen in her role as head of the Commonwealth. The cause was the outcast white minority government in Rhodesia led by Ian Smith that had been worn down by persistent attacks by black guerrillas. In late July and early August 1979, the Commonwealth leaders were set to meet in Lusaka, the capital of neighboring Zambia, to endorse a proposed conference in London between Smith and all factions including black guerrilla leaders Robert Mugabe (an avowed Marxist) and Joshua Nkomo to end the Rhodesian conflict and prepare for free and fair elections. The British prime minister regarded the guerrilla leaders as terrorists and favored a power-sharing agreement that Smith had already negotiated with a more moderate black party.

Because the guerrilla forces were operating out of bases in Zambia, Thatcher tried to prevent the Queen from attending the Commonwealth meeting on the grounds that she might be at risk. But Elizabeth II well remembered being banned by

Heath from the Singapore meeting eight years earlier, and she insisted on traveling to Africa. Before arriving in Lusaka, the Queen set aside nine days for state visits to Tanzania, Malawi, Botswana, and Zambia. What she heard made her increasingly concerned that a number of African countries could leave the Commonwealth unless the black majority took charge of governing Rhodesia. During the Malawi state banquet she was so engrossed by Dr. Hastings Banda, the country's "President for Life," that she let her manners slip and kept her elbows on the table as they talked at length. Little wonder, since Banda was one of Africa's most idiosyncratic leaders — a repressive dictator educated in the United States and Scotland who had practiced medicine in the United Kingdom, where he took to wearing Homburg hats and three-piece suits.

Elizabeth II arrived in Lusaka on July 27, 1979, two days before Thatcher, for meetings with Zambian president Kenneth Kaunda in which she urged him to subdue the anti-British rhetoric in the local press. During the four-day Commonwealth conference she followed her customary routine as the organization's symbolic head by hosting a reception and banquet for all forty-two leaders. That evening she uncharacteristically stayed until nearly midnight, "quartering the room and talking to the various heads of governments," recalled Chief Emeka Anyaoku of Nigeria. "I am convinced that the intervention spurred the organization — which was on the point of possibly splitting up — on to compromise."

Her informal role continued behind the scenes,

when she received each leader in a private audience for fifteen to twenty minutes in her bungalow. In those sessions, particularly with the Africans, she conveyed sympathy for their position without explicitly stating her own, and they came away impressed by her knowledge of their problems. By bringing down the temperature, the Queen made it easier for Thatcher to move toward the Commonwealth position, which others, notably her own foreign secretary, Peter Carrington, and Australian prime minister Malcolm Fraser, had openly urged her to do. The African leaders yielded as well, agreeing to consider a formula for some white representation in Rhodesia's new parliament.

No one could pinpoint what exactly the Queen had done beyond playing what Carrington called "an enormous role in calming everything down." By the end of the meetings, Thatcher signed the Lusaka Accord calling for a constitutional conference at London's Lancaster House in September. The Queen "talked to Mrs. Thatcher and to Kaunda," said Sonny Ramphal of Guyana, the Commonwealth's secretary-general at the time. "The fact that she was there made it happen."

Britain's prime minister enthusiastically embraced the peace process, which led to an agreement on December 21 calling for a cease-fire, free elections, and Rhodesia's independence in April 1980 as the Republic of Zimbabwe, the forty-third member of the Commonwealth, with Robert Mugabe as prime minister. Only in time did Thatcher's initial misgivings about Mugabe prove prescient, as he set himself up as an egregiously corrupt dictator, brutally crushed his political rivals, drove the white farmers from their land, and destroyed what had been Africa's most vibrant agricultural economy. In 2002 the Commonwealth suspended Zimbabwe's membership, and Mugabe permanently withdrew the following year.

Shortly after returning to England from Africa on August 4, 1979, the Queen headed to Balmoral for her annual holiday. Whenever she and Philip are having lunch together in the castle, courtiers are forbidden from disturbing them except in an emergency. So at midday on Thursday, August 27, when Robert Fellowes, her assistant private secretary, entered the dining room, Elizabeth II knew he bore bad news. That morning, during a holiday at the Mountbatten vacation home at Sligo in the Republic of Ireland, a twenty-seven-foot fishing boat carrying six members of their family and a local boy had been blown up by an IRA bomb. Philip's uncle and the Queen's cousin, seventy-nine-year-old Dickie Mountbatten; John Brabourne's eighty-three-year-old mother, Doreen; Nicholas Knatchbull, one of the Brabournes' fourteen-year-old twin sons; and Paul Maxwell, the fifteen-year-old Irish boy, had been killed. Patricia and John Brabourne and their surviving son, Timothy, were critically injured.

The Queen and her family were grief-stricken. Prince Charles considered Mountbatten "his closest confidant and the greatest single influence." Writing in his diary, Charles described his great-uncle as "someone who showed enormous affection, who told me unpleasant things I didn't particularly want to hear, who gave praise where it was due as well as criticism. . . . Life will *never* be the same now that he has gone."

The Queen called the hospital and had a long conversation with family members, but only Philip wrote a condolence letter. As a Red Cross doctor explained to Patricia Brabourne, "That kind of private person has strong feelings but doesn't want to convey them. She would feel what she might say would be totally inadequate, so why try." By contrast when her sister Pamela Hicks once wrote a note about the death of one of the royal corgis, the Queen replied with a six-page letter. "A dog isn't important," Hicks figured, "so she can express the really deep feelings she can't get out otherwise."

The royal family traveled to London for a full ceremonial funeral at Westminster Abbey on September 5, with massed military bands and 122 naval ratings pulling the gun carriage holding Mountbatten's coffin. The earl had planned every detail of his commemorative ceremony, and there had been numerous rehearsals in the previous week. When the family boarded the train to Romsey for the burial, the Queen said to her cousin Pamela, "Please sit with me and tell me everything that happened." "She hardly made any remark," Pamela Hicks recalled. "But she absolutely listened to every word." After the interment, the family gathered at Broadlands. In the absence of her parents, who were still hospitalized, Joanna Knatchbull, the eldest of the Brabournes' daughters, served as hostess, waiting at the front door. Elizabeth II stepped out of the car, her eyes reddened from crying. "Ma'am, would you like to go upstairs?" Joanna inquired. "Yes I think I would," replied the Queen.

A month later, Elizabeth II made her most meaningful gesture when she invited fourteen-year-old Timothy Knatchbull to stay at Balmoral after his release from the hospital. He arrived at the castle late at night with his older sister Amanda, when he spotted the Queen "striding down the corridor" like "a mother duck gathering in lost young." She greeted Timothy and his sister with kisses, served them soup and sandwiches, took them to their rooms, and started to unpack until Amanda persuaded her that she should go to bed. "She was in almost unstoppable mothering mode," Timothy recalled.

In the following days, the Queen monitored Timothy's bedtimes, suggested when he shouldn't attempt going out onto the grouse moor, and took care to ensure that her own doctor came to dress his wounds. "She was caring and sensitive and intuitive," he said. Seated next to him at lunch, she seemed to sense his need to talk about the terror attack. "She didn't probe. She has a brilliant way of using her ears as magnets and getting people to talk. I spoke to her in a way I hadn't spoken, articulating things other people hadn't drawn out of me."

When Prince Charles pondered the manner of his Uncle Dickie's death, he wrote, "I fear it will take me a very long time to forgive those people." Princess Margaret reacted even more harshly. During a visit to Chicago that autumn, when someone expressed sympathy over the attack, she said the Irish were pigs. Elizabeth II kept her own counsel.

"She had all the feelings of hurt and shock one could expect," said Timothy Knatchbull. "I would be surprised if she hadn't had flashes of anger and incredulity. But never has she departed from her high standards: a caring dignified stance, and a recognition that the peoples of both the United Kingdom and Ireland have sufferings and wounds of their own." In their many conversations, he saw "no evidence whatsoever" that she had hardened her views of Ireland.

One unlikely source of consolation for Prince Charles was his long-ago love, Camilla Parker Bowles, by then the mother of two children with a husband who was openly unfaithful. In 1979, after the birth of her second child, she and Charles had resumed their romance, a development noted by Andrew Parker Bowles's fellow officers in the Household Cavalry. One of them reported the affair to the Queen, who took it in but said nothing to her son.

At the same time, Charles had become acquainted with Lady Diana Spencer, the granddaughter of the Queen Mother's longtime friend and Woman of the Bedchamber, Ruth Fermoy (widow of the 4th Baron Fermoy), and the daughter of the Queen's former equerry Johnnie Spencer, the 8th Earl and scion of one of the great landed Whig families, with a fortune dating from the Middle Ages. The Spencers had been part of the group of English noblemen that had saved Britain from Catholic rule by bringing the Protestant Hanovers to England in 1714, a legacy that gave Diana a feeling of superiority over the royal family. Much later, after her marriage to Charles had fractured, she told her divorce lawyer, Anthony Julius, that she regretted marrying into a "German family."

Johnnie Spencer had been with the Queen and Prince Philip on their six-month Commonwealth tour after the coronation. Before they departed in November 1953, he had proposed to Frances Roche, the daughter of Ruth Fermoy, but he left the tour — highly unusual for a courtier — after only two months to return to England. "By the time we reached Australia, he was so love struck with Frances that the Queen said, 'Johnnie you have to go back,' " recalled Pamela Hicks, then a lady-in-waiting.

The Spencers lived at Park House in Norfolk, which they rented from the Queen, and had three daughters — Sarah, Jane, and Diana — and a son, Charles. But while they lived only a stone's throw from Sandringham, the family only had occasional contact with their royal neighbors after Johnnie resigned from the Queen's household to make his living as a gentleman farmer. In September 1967, when Diana was six, Frances left her husband for her lover, Peter Shand Kydd, which led to an acrimonious divorce followed by Frances's marriage to Shand Kydd. Sarah and Jane Spencer were away at boarding school, so Diana and her three-year-old brother felt the brunt of the bitterness — an experience that marked Diana deeply and contributed to her lifelong emotional instability. At age nine she went to the first of two boarding schools, both of which provided a nurturing environment, although she was a poor student, twice failing all of her O-level exams. After an unhappy six weeks at a

Swiss finishing school, Diana returned to England in 1978, and a year later took a job as an assistant at the Young England Kindergarten in London.

When Prince Charles finished his five years in the Royal Navy at the end of 1976, the tabloid press dedicated itself to chronicling his romantic pursuits, a campaign that intensified in November 1978 when he turned thirty, the benchmark he had set three years earlier as "a good age for a man to get married." One of his passing fancies was Sarah Spencer, but Diana caught his eye during a pheasant shoot at Althorp, the thirteen-thousand-acre estate in Northamptonshire that Johnnie Spencer inherited when his father died in 1975. Charles was twelve years older, but Diana at age sixteen shamelessly flirted with her sister's beau and developed a full-fledged crush on the heir to the throne. Over the next several years their paths crossed periodically, but it wasn't until July 1980, when they were guests at a house party in Sussex, that their romance began. Diana was alluringly pretty, with big and expressive blue eyes and a becoming blush to her cheeks, an "easy and open manner," and an apparent love of the country life Charles cherished. He was particularly moved by her compassion over his loss of Dickie Mountbatten the previous year.

A fast-paced courtship followed, with invitations to the Cowes races and Balmoral, where Diana had visited twice previously to stay with her sister Jane, who had married the Queen's adviser Robert Fellowes in 1978. But this time she was a guest of Elizabeth II, and when a tabloid reporter spotted the "perfect English rose," *The Sun* blared "LADY DI IS THE NEW GIRL." Over the following months, Charles vacillated about whether to propose, and two of his friends, Nicholas Soames and Penny Romsey, the wife of Mountbatten's grandson Norton Knatchbull, expressed doubts about Diana. Penny Romsey worried that she had seemingly "fallen in love with an idea rather than an individual." Soames bluntly dismissed her as "childish and very unformed" and said she and Charles were "too completely unalike."

Meanwhile the tabloids and paparazzi pursued Diana so relentlessly that in January 1981 Philip wrote his son a letter saying that he would damage her reputation unless he either proposed or quietly cut off the relationship. In his role as paterfamilias, Philip was presumably also expressing his wife's opinion, but she did not directly comment on Diana's fitness to be wife of the heir to the throne. After returning from a ski holiday, thirty-two-year-old Charles proposed to nineteen-year-old Diana at Windsor Castle on February 6, and the engagement was announced on February 24.

Charles would later say that his father's letter had wounded him and subjected him to undue pressure. "Prince Philip and the Queen felt responsible for Diana, particularly since Johnnie had been an equerry," said Pamela Hicks. "Prince Philip wrote a very helpful letter, but Prince Charles read it differently. He saw it as saying he must make a sacrifice now, and make up his mind. He kept the letter on him and would bring it out and read it."

In Charles's headlong rush into marriage to a young woman who satisfied the prevailing requirements of noble birth and virginal innocence, he and his parents focused on Diana's appealing traits — her charisma and humor, her warmth, her shy and winsome manner, her seemingly biddable nature. They knew that her parents had been divorced but they reckoned that she would welcome being part of the royal family. They also thought that since she had grown up in proximity to royal life, she would take to its demands effortlessly — a leap of faith, as it turned out. "There is a difference between being neighbors and being married and living in a palace, going to garden parties and banquets, knowing who the people are and what you say to them," said one of Diana's school friends in Norfolk.

If the royal family had taken the time to probe Diana's friends and relatives, they would have come across elements of Diana's character and background that would have given them pause: nagging insecurities that had been intensified by a troubled childhood, lack of discipline, shifting moods, signs of obsessive behavior, and difficulty telling the truth. Of these Ruth Fermoy was well aware, but as she later explained to Charles's biographer Jonathan Dimbleby, she felt unable to voice her misgivings. "If I'd said to him, 'You're making a very great mistake,' " she said, "he probably wouldn't have paid the slightest attention because he was being driven."

On June 13, only weeks before her eldest son's marriage, the Queen led her birthday parade up the Mall on Burmese, a nineteen-year-old black mare that the Royal Canadian Mounted Police had given her in 1969. Every day for the previous two weeks she had practiced her sidesaddle technique in the Royal Mews at Buckingham Palace, and early that June morning she had taken her favorite mount for a canter around the Palace gardens.

Riding on Burmese for the thirteenth time amid the cheering crowds on the Mall, she was dressed in the scarlet tunic of the Welsh Guards and her navy blue riding skirt. Her posture perfectly erect, she faced squarely ahead in the saddle, with both legs on the left side of Burmese as she held the reins lightly in her left hand and a crop in her right. She rode in front of Charles and Philip, in their red tunics and bearskins, as well as several members of the Household Cavalry.

Shortly before 11 A.M., as she turned right toward Horse Guards Parade for the start of Trooping the Colour, six shots rang out from the crowd. The Queen's startled horse cantered forward, and she instinctively pulled the reins with both hands, focusing completely on settling him. Her husband and son watched as guardsmen and onlookers immediately tackled the man with the gun, policemen streaked across the parade route to assist, and one of the cavalrymen spurred his horse and cantered to the Queen's side. She proceeded calmly at a walk, leaned down to pat Burmese with her left hand, smiled at the crowd, and continued with the ceremony. The shots were blanks, and the gunman, seventeen-year-old Marcus Sarjeant, was sentenced to five years in prison for "intent to alarm" the sovereign. The Queen later told friends and family that in a split-second glance she had seen Sarjeant in the crowd pointing the gun but couldn't believe her eyes.

The Queen's reaction was not only an impressive

display of expert horsemanship, but the first time the public had witnessed so vividly the unflinching physical courage and equilibrium that friends and courtiers had seen privately: standing quietly while surrounded by "dive bombing" colts, or sitting calmly when a ball crashed into an adjacent chair at a cricket match and everyone else jumped to their feet. "I never saw her scared in any way," recalled Sir Edward Ford, her assistant private secretary for fifteen years, even when a madman dropped a rock on her car during one of her early visits to Belfast and "she drove on as if nothing had happened."

Elizabeth II always understood the risks of appearing on horseback or in an open carriage, and she refused to accept protection that would intrude on her ability to be seen by the public. Her fatalistic attitude about the possibility of assassination was reinforced by the reassuring knowledge that an orderly succession was in place. Nevertheless, in 1982 the army instituted new procedures requiring two members of the household to flank the Queen in her birthday parade. "You know why you're there," she cheerily announced to Malcolm Ross as he took position beside her one year. "You're the one to get shot, not me." Periodically as they rode down the Mall, she would look over and say, in the manner of a strict riding instructor, "Left leg straight! Left leg straight!" The Queen continued to ride until 1986, when Burmese had to retire at age twenty-four. Rather than train a new mount, she switched to her horse-drawn Ivory Phaeton.

The press and public praised the Queen's handling of the shooting. "In every pub and club throughout the land the verdict is the same," wrote the *Daily Express.* "Her Majesty showed guts, courage, pluck, bravery and bottle." The admiration mingled with the growing excitement over Charles and Diana's wedding to create a surge of pro-royalist sentiment. A poll in July 1981 showed 86 percent support for the monarchy, compared to the consistent 80 percent since polling on the royal family began twelve years earlier.

One of the prominent guests at the wedding festivities was Nancy Reagan. The first lady had met Charles years earlier through Walter Annenberg, Nixon's envoy to Britain, and his wife, Lee, during a visit to California while the prince was serving in the Royal Navy. Nancy Reagan also endeared herself to the royal family by treating Charles to dinner in the private quarters of the White House the previous May, with a collection of guests that included Cary Grant, Audrey Hepburn, William F. Buckley, and Diana Vreeland. "I have fallen in love with Mrs. Reagan," Charles told Mary Henderson, wife of British ambassador Nicholas Henderson. "I wanted to kiss her!"

While the Queen couldn't entertain the new first lady herself, busy as she was with wedding preparations, she arranged for her cousin Jean Wills to host a luncheon in her honor on Tuesday, July 28, followed by coffee with the Queen Mother at Royal Lodge and a polo match at Smith's Lawn. Nancy Reagan and Josephine Louis, the wife of John Louis, the newly appointed ambassador to the Court of St. James's, dressed "in our best bib and tucker," as Josephine Louis recalled. "We were probably overdressed for polo." They were also surrounded by swarms of security that had been stepped up after an assassination attempt on President Ronald Reagan the previous March.

The match was already under way when a Land Rover appeared, and out popped the Queen from the driver's side, informally dressed in a tweed skirt and brogues, making her way through the crowd to the royal box, her protection officers virtually invisible. "She was wonderful that day," recalled Josephine Louis, "so warm and friendly." Nancy Reagan also clicked with the Queen Mother, who sent her a cordial note later that afternoon with a box of Bittermints as a reminder of the visit to the "little house in Windsor Great Park!"

The wedding the next day at St. Paul's Cathedral was yet another royal tonic at a time when Britain was plagued by urban race riots and rising unemployment. The atmosphere was exultant among the estimated 600,000 people who lined the London streets, and television viewership around the world exceeded 750 million. Diana looked dazzling in her voluminous silk taffeta wedding dress and twenty-five-foot train as Archbishop of Canterbury Robert Runcie memorably proclaimed to the congregation, "Here is the stuff of which fairy tales are made." Runcie later admitted he knew Charles and Diana were a misalliance, although he believed she would "grow into it."

Family, close friends, and royal guests went to the wedding breakfast for 180 at Buckingham Palace, while nonroyal heads of state attended a luncheon hosted by Margaret Thatcher at the Bank of England. That evening after Charles and Diana had left for their honeymoon, the Queen's cousin Lady Elizabeth Anson hosted a party at Claridge's for five hundred guests, including the Queen and Prince Philip. It was a high-spirited occasion, with television screens playing video loops of the wedding. The Queen perched on an ottoman, martini in hand, to watch what she had participated in hours earlier. "Oh Philip, do look!" she exclaimed. "I've got my Miss Piggy face on!"

The Queen invited Nancy Reagan, escorted by John Louis, and Princess Grace of Monaco to sit at her table for the buffet supper, while Philip presided nearby and fifty-year-old Princess Margaret sat on the floor eating scrambled eggs. The ballroom was decked out with a canopy of multicolored ribbons tied at the ends with apples, one of which hit Philip in the eye. The royal couple frequently took to the dance floor, although the Queen looked slightly uncomfortable dancing with the American ambassador, who at six foot four towered over her. Everybody danced to Lester Lanin's orchestra until nearly 1:30 in the morning, many of the revelers wearing Lanin's signature party beanies in every conceivable color, as well as boaters and bowlers with hatbands saying "Charles and Diana."

Finally the Queen regretfully prepared to leave, declaring, "I'd love to stay and dance all night!" John and Josephine Louis followed Elizabeth II and Prince Philip as they made for the exit, while Nancy Reagan ducked into a phone booth to call her husband at the White House and give him a full report on the evening. "The Queen was so mad at Philip because he wouldn't take off his beanie," Josephine Louis recalled. "She didn't think it was proper. She kept asking him, and he finally took it off. But as soon as they got in the car he slapped the beanie back on."

None of the guests at the party could have known that Charles and Diana's marriage was already beginning to unravel. The problems had begun when she was living in Buckingham Palace during their engagement and feeling isolated while Charles went about his royal duties. Secretly afflicted by bulimia, she rapidly lost weight, causing designer Elizabeth Emanuel to take in her wedding gown several times. Charles was thrown by his fiancée's mood swings, alarming dependence, and accusations about Camilla Parker Bowles, with whom he had broken off his affair. (She and her husband, Andrew, were among the 3,500 guests at the service but had been excluded from the reception by Diana.) By the time the newlyweds reached Balmoral for their honeymoon after a two-week cruise on *Britannia,* Diana was tearful and angry, down to a mere 110 pounds on her five foot, ten inch frame.

The princess made clear how much she hated Royal Deeside and all it represented — the rituals of life in the castle and on the grouse moors, especially the shooting. "It was just impossible," Philip recalled. "She didn't appear for breakfast. At lunch she sat with her headphones on, listening to music, and then she would disappear for a walk or a run." Nobody had ever flouted protocol as Diana did, or shown such disrespect to the Queen. Charles tried to cajole his wife, to no avail. He was ill equipped to deal with her demands so he either lost his temper or withdrew, dismayed by the "other side" of the "jolly girl" who had enchanted him with her sweetness. Finally, with his mother's agreement, Charles had Diana flown to London for psychiatric counseling, a gesture that she resented rather than welcomed.

The Queen couldn't avoid Diana's disquieting behavior, but she preferred to blame it on the stresses of her new life rather than more deep-seated problems. She didn't understand Diana — how for example she could be simultaneously empathetic and egocentric — in part because "the Queen is the least self-absorbed person you could ever meet," said one of her former top advisers. "She doesn't tend to talk about herself, and she is not interested in other people's efforts to dwell too much on themselves." Nor was she inclined to interfere in the lives of her family. "Regardless of how rude Princess Margaret is to her, she never says anything," said one of the Queen Mother's closest friends. "That is her policy. She never says anything to her children. She is a very decent person, but she won't intervene with anyone."

Underlying the Queen's aversion to confrontation is a high degree of tolerance. Back in London, Elizabeth II let her daughter-in-law know that she could call upon her any time. In the beginning, Diana, who called her "mama," visited her when she went to Buckingham Palace for a swim in the pool. "The Queen was always kind to Diana," said Lúcia Flecha de Lima, a confidante of the princess. "The Queen always received her." But even after she had spent time in her mother-in-law's company, Diana remained "terrified" of her, according to Robert Runcie.

The Queen also assigned forty-two-year-old

Lady Susan Hussey, her youngest lady-in-waiting, to guide Diana in royal ways. Hussey was somewhat formidable, and she was conscientious in carrying out the Queen's instructions. Known for her sharp sense of humor and for having "the briskest, deepest, most correct curtsy," she had helped Charles and Anne learn the ropes during their adolescence. But as a stickler for protocol, she may have been too exacting for Diana's haphazard temperament and insufficiently sympathetic to Diana's obvious frailties. Although Diana wrote letters of gratitude at the time, telling her she was like a wonderful older sister, the princess later said she mistrusted the lady-in-waiting's longtime friendship with Charles. One woman close to the royal family thought the Queen should have delegated her American Lady of the Bedchamber, Virginia Airlie, instead. Although six years older, she could have established better rapport. "She is pretty, soft and amusing," said the friend. "She would have given Diana honest advice and jollied her along." Perhaps inevitably, Diana had a major falling-out with Susan Hussey, telling friends she felt "betrayed" by her unquestioning loyalty to Charles.

Diana became pregnant during the honeymoon, but her condition put her even more on edge. Harassment by the tabloids so unnerved her that the Queen took the extraordinary step of meeting with twenty-one editors in Buckingham Palace in December 1981. Her press secretary, Michael Shea, told the group from Fleet Street that their intrusiveness was making Diana so "despondent" that she feared leaving home. When Barry Askew, editor of the sensational *News of the World,* wondered why the princess went out to buy candy at a shop rather than sending a servant, the Queen couldn't resist saying, "That's the most pompous thing I have ever heard."

CHAPTER FOURTEEN
A VERY SPECIAL RELATIONSHIP

When the new year began, the focus on Diana diminished as the public and the royal family faced the prospect of war in the South Atlantic between Britain and Argentina over the Falkland Islands. On Friday, April 2, 1982, Argentine forces invaded the islands, which had been a British colony since the eighteenth century, claiming that what they called the Malvinas really belonged to them. On the grounds that British sovereign territory had been violated, Margaret Thatcher immediately ordered a military expedition to retake the islands. The Queen wholeheartedly supported her prime minister's action, not only in her role as monarch of the invaded country, but as head of the Commonwealth.

She was also in the unusual position of considering whether her twenty-two-year-old son, Andrew, second in line to the throne, should be deployed into the war zone. In his brusque manner Andrew resembled his father, whose path he had followed to Gordonstoun. Unlike Charles, Andrew's more macho personality adapted easily to the rigors of the school. He spent six months in an exchange program at Lakefield College in Ontario, Canada, but on his graduation from Gordonstoun in 1979

The president described the Queen as "charming" and "down-to-earth," and observed that "she was in charge of that animal!"

The Queen and President Ronald Reagan taking a carefully orchestrated ride in the Windsor Home Park, June 1982. © Kent Gavin Associates

he skipped university and went directly into the Royal Navy after training at Dartmouth like his father. By the time of the Falklands War, Andrew was a fully accredited helicopter pilot.

The government expressed concern about the dangers of combat, but when Andrew insisted he go with his squadron on the HMS *Invincible* aircraft carrier, Elizabeth II backed him up. Her decision "brought into stark focus the responsibilities of being a mother and also being the sovereign," Andrew recalled. "The Queen and the Duke for that matter were entirely happy with me going. It was a straightforward decision." His participation "gave the country the feeling that actually the Queen was sharing in this whole dramatic expedition. [She] was going through the same thing that other parents were going through."

The war resulted in 255 British and 650 Argentine deaths before Argentina surrendered on June 14. Andrew was never involved in direct combat, although he flew a Sea King helicopter in a number of diversionary actions, transported troops, and conducted search and rescue operations — any of which could have put him in harm's way. He lost friends and colleagues, and once was on deck when Exocet missiles were fired at the ship. "I definitely went there a boy and came back a man," he said.

Margaret Thatcher's decisiveness in prosecuting the Falklands War greatly enhanced her image as "the Iron Lady" and Britain's reputation as a muscular and effective military power a quarter century after the Suez debacle. "We have ceased to be a nation in retreat," she said. Her staunch ally in the fight was Ronald Reagan, whose administration imposed economic sanctions on Argentina and supplied intelligence and key military equipment to the British forces, at the risk of alienating allies in South America. The bond between the two leaders, who had strong personal and ideological affinities, brought the British-American "special relationship" to its highest point since Churchill's time as prime minister. The Queen later rewarded Reagan and his secretary of defense, Caspar Weinberger, by investing them as honorary Knights Commander of the British Empire.

As it happened, President Reagan and his wife, Nancy, were scheduled to stay with the Queen and Prince Philip that June, an invitation that had come the previous July when the first lady was in London for the royal wedding. It was not a state visit arranged by the government. Rather, the Reagans were personal guests of the Queen for a "quiet two days between summit meetings" in France and Germany, and they were the first American presidential couple to stay overnight at Windsor Castle. The most anticipated element of the trip was a ride on horseback by the Queen and the president, the result of numerous meetings in Washington and London that began early in the year. British ambassador Nicholas Henderson noted that Reagan's key image maker, deputy chief of staff Michael Deaver, "invariably lit up at the prospect" of the ride. "Carter couldn't have done a thing like that," said Deaver. "Think of the photo opportunity."

Reagan's predecessor, Jimmy Carter, had met the Queen only twice, during her stop in Washington for the Bicentennial, and on his inaugural foreign trip as president to "the first country that I have visited outside my own" on May 5, 1977. He was in England for economic and foreign policy meetings, followed by a black-tie dinner for NATO leaders at Buckingham Palace. When Carter (wearing a bow tie three times the size of Philip's) greeted the Queen's seventy-six-year-old mother, he tried to flatter her by comparing her to his own beloved mother, "Miz Lillian," and in a burst of enthusiasm kissed her on the lips. "I took a sharp step backwards," the Queen Mother recalled, "not quite far enough." She commented afterward that she hadn't been kissed that way since the death of her husband twenty-five years earlier.

Ronald and Nancy Reagan arrived at Windsor Castle by helicopter on Monday, June 7, 1982. They were assigned the seven-room suite 240 in the Lancaster Tower — two bedrooms, two dressing rooms, two bathrooms, and a main sitting room with portraits of the Queen's ancestors by Hans Holbein — all with the sweeping view of the Long Walk. The Queen had arranged for a dedicated White House telephone line, as well as the installation of the first shower in Windsor Castle because her advisers were told "that was what he needed."

In the afternoon the royal couple took the Reagans on a tour of the gardens, and in the evening, the president and first lady, along with top officials and their spouses staying at the castle — Michael Deaver, Secretary of State Alexander Haig, Chief of Staff James Baker, and National Security Adviser William Clark — joined the royal family for a private black-tie dinner in the Crimson Room, the small dining room in the private apartments, preceded by drinks in the Green Drawing Room.

"We had the feeling we had come into a family dinner," said Carolyn Deaver. "They banter effortlessly in front of a stranger. They sort of make you feel a part, but you never are." Princess Anne and Mark Phillips were on hand, along with Charles and Diana, eight months pregnant and visibly miserable. "She was wearing a red dress and she had her head down," said Carolyn Deaver. "She was seated toward the end of the table and talked only a little to the people on either side."

The next morning Elizabeth II and Philip invited the Reagans to breakfast on a small terrace outside their bedroom. "It was surprisingly informal," Nancy Reagan recalled. "We had to walk through their bedroom, and lined up on a table were boxes of cereal. I said to Prince Charles, 'What do I do?' He said, 'Just help yourself.' It wasn't anything like what I had imagined."

At 9:30 it was time for the much heralded ride. The fifty-six-year-old Queen rode Burmese and wore tan jodhpurs, a checked woolen jacket, beige gloves, and a head scarf. The seventy-one-year-old president sported an open-collared shirt and light tweed jacket. He rode an eight-year-old stallion named Centennial and used an English saddle, "bobbing when he should have remained still." Neither of them wore a hard hat, which caused predictable criticism.

Before they headed into the mist of the 655-acre Home Park, Reagan joked with the swarm of 150 reporters shouting questions from behind a barrier. "Does it ride well?" yelled one. "Yes," replied Reagan with a grin. "If you stand still I'll take it over the top." The Queen, who never responds to such queries, glared, pulled at her reins, and trotted off, prompting Reagan to hastily catch up. They were followed by two of the Queen's equerries, two security men on horseback, and a Range Rover filled with Secret Service agents and British protection officers. Nancy Reagan rode in a four-in-hand carriage driven by Philip, who took her on her own tour around the park. Philip, who had given up polo in 1971 because of arthritis, had become a champion in competitive carriage driving marathons, and offered the first lady a running commentary on the finer points of the sport as well as the surrounding scenery.

For an hour, Elizabeth II and Reagan walked, trotted, and cantered on their eight-mile ride, stopping once to greet farmers in the middle of a field of cattle. As they followed a canal adjacent to the Thames, Reagan was waving so much to onlookers that the Queen worried he might ride straight into the water, and at one point took his reins and led his horse in the right direction. They finished at the top of Long Walk in Windsor Great Park, where protection agents lurked behind nearly every tree and bush, and reporters again shouted questions, prompting another flash of displeasure from the Queen when the president stopped to chat. He described her as "charming" and "down-to-earth," and observed that "she was in charge of that animal!"

Several hours later, Reagan praised Britain's Falklands campaign during a televised speech before both houses of Parliament, the first American president given that privilege. The Queen busied herself at Windsor with her boxes in her private sitting room. Carolyn Deaver spent the afternoon touring the castle, wandering along the Grand Corridor and marveling at the Canalettos. "Are you enjoying yourself?" piped a familiar voice from one of the doorways. "These paintings are just beautiful," the wide-eyed guest replied. "Take your time," said the Queen. "I'm glad you are enjoying it."

Carolyn Deaver was equally transfixed by the exacting day-long preparations in St. George's Hall for the evening's white-tie banquet. The 175-foot-long mahogany table was so wide (eight feet) that under-butlers strapped pillowlike dusters to their feet as they walked down the middle to set up the silver gilt candelabra and put flower arrangements in gold bowls.

At the banquet for 158 guests, the Queen told Reagan she was "much impressed by the way in which you coped so professionally with a strange horse and a saddle that must have seemed even stranger," adding in a more serious vein, "the conflict on the Falkland islands was thrust on us by naked aggression. . . . Throughout the crisis we have drawn comfort from the understanding of our position shown by the American people. We have admired the honesty, patience and skill with which you have performed your dual roles as ally and intermediary."

After dinner the Reagans and the royal couple walked down an aisle between the table and the chairs that footmen had pulled away, led by the sixty-six-year-old Lord Chamberlain, Lord Charles "Chips" Maclean, 27th chief of Clan Maclean, who walked backward. With growing alarm, Reagan glanced toward the Queen for reassurance about one of the monarchy's time-honored rituals. "I suddenly saw this tiny figure beside me walking along waving her hand," the president recalled. The Queen was steering Maclean, as she explained to Reagan, because "you know, we don't get those chairs even, and he could fall over one and hurt himself."

Diana had felt too ill to attend the banquet, but two weeks later she did her duty in providing a male heir, giving birth on June 21 to William Arthur Philip Louis. "It was a great relief because it was all peaceful again," she later recalled. "And I was well for a time." The Queen was among the first to visit St. Mary's Hospital and see the newborn prince, now second in line to the throne.

Scarcely a year after she had been targeted by Marcus Sarjeant, Elizabeth II had an even more unnerving jolt when she was awakened at 7:15 on the morning of Friday, July 9, by the slam of a door, something her staff never did. She knew Philip had left the Palace at 6 A.M. for an engagement outside the city. When she looked up, she saw a barefoot stranger in a T-shirt and jeans opening her curtains, then sitting at the foot of her bed with a shard of glass from a shattered ashtray, blood dripping from his right thumb onto her bedclothes.

In an egregious breach of security, thirty-one-year-old Michael Fagan had climbed over a fourteen-foot wall, entered the Palace through an open window, and walked freely along the corridors until he slipped undetected into the Queen's bedroom suite. It turned out he was an experienced Palace intruder, having broken in previously on June 7, when he amused himself by consuming a half bottle of wine.

"Get out of here at once!" the Queen said, but Fagan ignored her and started to pour out his personal troubles. Once she realized he meant no harm, she shifted gears quickly. For ten minutes, she listened patiently, finding common ground in talking about their children and interjecting sympathetic comments even as she tried several times to summon help by pushing her emergency button and twice calling the Palace switchboard. Fagan later commented that she had shown no sign of nerves. The situation uncannily recalled an incident at Windsor Castle in February 1941 when a mentally disturbed man emerged from behind the curtains of her mother's bedroom and grabbed her ankles. The Queen Mother refrained from screaming, saying instead, "Tell me about it," which he did as she eased across the room to sound the alarm bell.

Elizabeth II reacted similarly to Fagan, in part, she told friends, because "I am used to talking to people on street corners." But her preternaturally calm demeanor came into play as well, along with her physical courage and common sense. She seized an opening when he asked for a cigarette, and she directed him to a nearby pantry, which had a supply.

Out in the corridor they encountered chambermaid Elizabeth Andrew, who exclaimed, "Bloody 'ell, Ma'am, what's 'e doing 'ere?" (a reaction the Queen later recounted to friends with perfect mimicry of the girl's Yorkshire accent). Paul Whybrew, a six-foot-four-inch senior footman, arrived with the Queen's pack of corgis that he had been walking in the garden. As the dogs barked furiously, the footman gave Fagan a drink to steady him. Moments later, a contingent of police finally arrived. "Oh come on, get a bloody move on," said the Queen as one officer paused to straighten his tie.

"I wasn't scared," she later told her mother's equerry, Colin Burgess. "The whole thing was so surreal. He just came in, we chatted and then he went without incident, and that was that." Her response, according to one of her relatives, was "mostly shock and disbelief." The Queen appeared as scheduled at an 11 A.M. investiture and asked her advisers to keep the incident quiet while the government investigated the security failure. But the *Express* broke the story the following Monday with the headline "INTRUDER AT THE QUEEN'S BEDSIDE." That evening Margaret Thatcher came to her weekly audience a day early to apologize, and her home secretary, William Whitelaw, faced a barrage of questions in the House of Commons and offered to resign.

A week later, the IRA savagely bombed two groups of soldiers in Hyde Park and Regent's Park, killing eight members of the Household Cavalry and musicians of the Royal Green Jackets and injuring forty-seven others — a tragedy in the heart of London and a sobering reminder of the mayhem a terrorist could have caused inside the Palace. At public events the Queen's demeanor seemed subdued, and her doctors advised her to take some time off. Fagan was charged with stealing her wine but acquitted by a jury in September. Although he was confined to a mental hospital for five months, he effectively avoided any penalty and enjoyed a brief period of celebrity.

One happy interlude during these fraught times was the christening of Prince William on August 4, the Queen Mother's eighty-second birthday. The Queen yielded center stage to the youngest and oldest members of the royal family, allowing her mother to hold the baby in her stead. Diana put on a good show that day, but in fact she had sunk into postnatal depression that she later called her "dark ages." She had also resumed her secret bulimic bingeing and purging, and intensified her accusations about Camilla, refusing to believe that her husband had in fact broken off their affair. In September, while Diana and Charles were staying at Craigowan, a cottage on the Balmoral estate, she tried to cut herself with sharp objects, an alarming escalation of her erratic behavior that Charles did not share with his parents. Again he took Diana to London, where she underwent therapy with two different professionals before giving up after three months.

Her range of symptoms — depression, fear of rejection and abandonment, volatile moods, impulsive and self-destructive acts, and persistent feelings of loneliness and emptiness — suggested that she could have been suffering from borderline personality disorder, which is notoriously difficult to treat. But aside from the occasional glimpse

— Diana arriving late to the royal box at Albert Hall in November 1982 for the annual Festival of Remembrance, her demeanor tense and flustered after she and Charles had fought in front of their family — the public remained unaware of Diana's emotional turmoil and the misery of the Wales marriage.

That autumn Andrew returned from the Falklands on HMS *Invincible* after more than five months away. The Queen, Prince Philip, and Princess Anne flew to Portsmouth from Balmoral to be on hand for the homecoming. As cheering crowds along the shore held banners and waved flags, Elizabeth II appeared to wipe tears from her eyes. "It was actually very emotional," recalled Andrew, who lightened the atmosphere by greeting his mother with a red rose between his teeth.

In February 1983 the Queen realized her decades-long dream of visiting the West Coast of the United States, a trip that had been cut "for reasons of time and protocol" from her itinerary back in 1957. She had raised the matter with Nicholas Henderson before he took his post in Washington in 1979, so she was thrilled when Ronald and Nancy Reagan invited her during their visit to Windsor Castle. "What better time," she said, "than when the President is a Californian!" She expressly asked if she could see the Reagans' Rancho del Cielo on a mountaintop near Santa Barbara, where the president promised a Western-style ride on horseback.

The ten-day trip was planned to follow several weeks of state visits to Caribbean countries on

Britannia, and the royal couple looked forward to a mixture of official events and sightseeing in the fabled California sunshine. But they arrived on Saturday, February 26, in a downpour that followed them up the coast — the worst weather in two decades — and all the Queen's colorful silk day dresses went unseen as she donned her daily uniform of Burberry macintosh and black boots. At one point Princess Margaret called from England to suggest her sister buy a new coat.

The roads in San Diego, their first stop, were so flooded that the royal couple had to be transported in a big U.S. Navy bus — a development that astonished the pack of London reporters traveling with the royal entourage. "We said, 'But she's *never* been on a bus!' " recalled Peter McKay of the *Daily Mail.*

"They sat on the first two seats, and I thought they looked like two kids on an adventure," said Selwa "Lucky" Roosevelt, Reagan's chief of protocol. San Diego's acting mayor, William Cleaton, committed the ultimate faux pas during the Queen's harbor tour by guiding her with his palm on her back. "The Queen was visibly bothered and frowned her disapproval," according to the *Daily Express,* although she made no complaint to U.S. officials, and poor Cleaton was mortified. As they walked along a retaining wall, Philip suffered his own indignity when a seal jumped up and splashed him. The Queen burst out laughing, but the duke was not amused.

Philip played his consort role expertly, with occasional bursts of political incorrectness and pique over what he considered overzealous security.

"Are you expecting trouble?" he barked at Pete Metzger, Reagan's military attaché, who was assigned to shadow him during their tour of the USS *Ranger* aircraft carrier. "No, sir," replied Metzger. "Then back off!" said Philip. After shaking hands with five women from an official delegation in San Francisco, he asked, "Aren't there any male supervisors? This is a nanny city!" When he and Lucky Roosevelt were driving back to *Britannia,* he snapped at the Secret Service agents who asked him to turn off the light in the limousine, which they said made him a target. "Damned if I'll turn off the light," he said. "People came to see us." On arriving at the pier, he jumped out of the car and slammed the heavy armored door in the protocol chief's face. Halfway to the yacht, he realized what he had done, turned around, walked back, kissed Lucky Roosevelt's hand and said, "I am very sorry."

On Sunday after church, the Queen and Philip flew to Palm Springs for a luncheon at Sunnylands, the gated 208-acre estate of Walter and Lee Annenberg, where the table was set with a stunning array of Flora Danica china. "The Annenbergs have more than the Queen!" muttered one of the ladies-in-waiting. It was even raining in the desert, so after lunch Lee Annenberg took the group on a series of tours around the vast house (covering nearly an acre), which was filled with their collection of Impressionist and Post-Impressionist masterpieces — a private museum including van Goghs, Manets, Monets, Vuillards, and Corots. The Queen insisted on braving the elements to tour the grounds and the nine-hole golf course as well, so Mike Deaver rounded up five golf carts. They sped off under umbrellas, with the Queen and the ambassador in the maintenance cart filled with brooms and mops.

In the evening the Queen and Philip were honored at a dinner on Sound Stage 9 at 20th Century Fox for five hundred guests including such British and American film stars as Julie Andrews, Dudley Moore, Fred Astaire, and Bette Davis, with entertainment by George Burns, Frank Sinatra, and Perry Como and a menu that featured Ronald Reagan's favorite chicken pot pie from Chasen's restaurant in Hollywood.

The unrelenting downpour forced the royal party to travel to Santa Barbara on Tuesday by Air Force Two rather than *Britannia* for the long-promised trip to the Reagan ranch. They had to abandon their limousines at the base of the mountain and transfer to a caravan of four-wheel-drive vehicles. "There was a lot of talk at the time about whether we should try going up that road to the ranch," said Lucky Roosevelt, "but the Queen was game." "She said, 'If we can get there, let's go,' " recalled Charles Anson, the press attaché at the British embassy. Wearing black rubber boots, Elizabeth II clambered into a jeep, with Josephine Louis wedged beside her. "I don't know how happy she was being squeezed like that," said the ambassadress. "It was hard not to touch her and lean on her. I offered to put her purse aside. 'Oh no!' she said, and held it tightly."

Even on the clearest day, the 2,400-foot ascent on the intermittently paved seven miles of hairpin turns up Refugio Road is a terrifying prospect, intensified by sheer drops and a scarcity of guard-rails. For the Queen's journey, the road was cut in a half dozen places by torrents, and there was nearly zero visibility. She said little during the dangerous climb, but she appeared unfazed.

The ranch was shrouded in fog, causing the Reagans to apologize profusely that the weather had not only washed out the ride on horseback but obliterated the panoramic views. "Don't be silly," replied the Queen. "This is an adventure!" The foursome dined on Tex-Mex fare including tacos, enchiladas, and refried beans. "Mr. Deaver," the Queen said afterward. "That was so enjoyable, especially the used beans." As the royal couple and their entourage drove back down the mountain, the sun came out. "Damn it," said Reagan. "I told them it was going to clear."

Everyone flew back to Long Beach for dinner on *Britannia.* Mike Deaver played the piano for an after-dinner sing-along, and Nancy Reagan stayed overnight. "We talked at length," she recalled. "It was not the Queen and first lady but two mothers and wives talking about their lives, mostly our children. She was beginning to be concerned about Diana."

Rough seas prevented the royal couple from sailing to San Francisco, so with thirty staff and officials in tow, they flew instead on Air Force Two. As they made their approach, the pilot flew low over the Golden Gate Bridge, and the Queen excitedly joined the group on one side of the airplane to catch her first glimpse of the fabled span. The presidential and royal parties took over forty-six rooms on four floors at the St. Francis Hotel. The

Queen and Philip stayed in the $1,200 a night Presidential Suite, which Nancy Reagan's interior designer Ted Graber hurriedly dressed up with paintings and objects from local art museums.

On the spur of the moment, the Anglo-American group decided to have dinner in the Trafalgar Room at Trader Vic's. The Queen at first resisted, but her husband persuaded her. "I learned that night that she listened to him, and it wasn't completely 'my way or no way,' " said Carolyn Deaver. "I got the feeling he was a little more adventurous, and he wanted her to be too." Elizabeth II told the Deavers she hadn't dined in a restaurant in more than fifteen years, but when she got there, she laughed and tried the exotic rum punches. At the end of the meal, she cracked open her fortune cookie, read the fortune, showed it to Philip, and tucked it into her handbag.

On Thursday, March 3, the Queen and Philip were honored at a black-tie dinner at the de Young Memorial Museum. When Mike Deaver asked Philip Moore why the monarch took so long to prepare for the evening, the private secretary replied, "The Queen needs her tiara time!" Moore explained that she has a kit with tools that she uses to decorate certain diamond tiaras by hooking on pearl or gemstone drops, a pastime she much enjoys, according to former Crown Jeweler David Thomas.

For the banquet she chose pearls, but she detracted from the tiara, with its matching necklace and large drop earrings, by wearing an overdone evening gown of champagne-colored taffeta with "puff sleeves decorated with 'ruched' bands of lace edged with gold" and large bows on her shoulders. Peering through her reading glasses, she addressed the 260 guests in the vaulted Hearst Court: "I knew before we came that we have exported many of our traditions to the United States," she said, "but I had not realized before that weather was one of them." As she deadpanned, Reagan threw his head back with a mighty guffaw, inadvertently creating a hilarious juxtaposition with the sober and bespectacled queen in her ruffles and jewels.

The weather finally lived up to California's reputation on Friday when the royal couple flew to Sacramento for the day. The Queen's final dinner on *Britannia* honored the Reagans' thirty-first wedding anniversary. "I know I promised Nancy a lot when we were married," said the president, "but how can I ever top *this?*" Reagan expressed his fondness for the Queen by giving her a $24,000 Hewlett-Packard 250 business computer system. In no time she had it installed in Buckingham Palace to track her horse breeding, training, and racing activities.

The Queen and the Reagans had developed a genuine friendship that included other members of her family — Charles most prominently, but Princess Margaret as well. On October 1, 1983, the president and first lady entertained Margaret and a group of her friends at a dinner upstairs at the White House. She thanked the Reagans effusively for a "sparkling" evening and proclaimed her "abiding love for your country."

At age fifty-three, the Queen's sister was difficult to please: unattached, often unhappy, smoking heavily and drinking so much that she had to be hospitalized once for alcoholic hepatitis. She and Tony had divorced in July 1978, followed within months by his remarriage to Lucy Lindsay-Hogg. Roddy Llewellyn stayed in the picture for a while, although the Queen drew the line at inviting him to Margaret's fiftieth birthday party at the Ritz in August 1980.

The next year Llewellyn married fashion designer Tania Soskin, and Margaret wisely remained on good terms with her former lover and his new wife, who maintained a discreet silence about their royal friend. The princess continued to do the minimum of royal duties, but was more often photographed on her holidays in Mustique, or on the arm of a passing love interest. She was an attentive mother, however, ensuring that her son, David, and daughter, Sarah, grew up out of the limelight, and encouraging their artistic talents. "It is a curious irony that Margaret had such a messy life but produced two normal and nice children," said one of the Queen's former private secretaries.

Only weeks after Margaret's red-carpet treatment by the president, Reagan managed to profoundly offend the Queen when he ordered the invasion of the Caribbean island of Grenada by American forces. The island was a member of the Commonwealth and recognized the Queen as its head of state, but had been ruled by a Marxist dictator since 1979. In mid-October a more radical leftist group murdered the prime minister, Maurice Bishop, and a junta took power. Reagan believed the violent coup would destabilize the region and possibly endanger a group of American medical students on the island, so he responded sympathetically when other Caribbean nations asked for help from the United States. The president told Margaret Thatcher he was considering an invasion, and she warned him against such a measure. But without further consulting his most reliable ally, he ordered a military operation on October 25 and informed Thatcher only after the leaders of the coup had been captured and the safety of the American students secured.

Both the prime minister and the Queen were furious that Reagan had been so cavalier about intervening in the internal affairs of a Commonwealth nation, not to mention keeping them both in the dark. Elizabeth II was particularly indignant that her American friend had violated her role as the island's head of state. Yet the anger soon subsided, and at the Commonwealth leaders' conference in New Delhi that November, the emphasis was less on "debating about the past," as Thatcher put it, and more about doing "everything we can between us to help Grenada come to democracy." The following June, Reagan was in Europe to commemorate the fortieth anniversary of D-Day and attend a summit meeting in London. At a black-tie dinner at Buckingham Palace, he had the place of honor between the Queen and the Queen Mother.

Elizabeth II's 1984 foreign travel called for a state visit to Jordan in the spring, and two weeks in the western provinces of Canada in the autumn. As part of the second tour, she decided to have her first private holiday in the United States: five days in the legendary bluegrass horse country of

Kentucky, followed by three days in Wyoming at a ranch owned by Henry and Jean Porchester. On the final weekend of their West Coast trip the previous year, Elizabeth II and Philip had explored the majestic mountains and pine forests of Yosemite National Park, which whetted her appetite to see more of the American West. A visit to the Porchesters' Canyon Ranch below the rugged Big Horn Mountains offered the perfect opportunity. Philip had already stayed at the ranch for five days of hunting and fishing in 1969 and had little interest in visiting stud farms, so after accompanying his wife to Canada, he planned to fly to the Middle East.

The Queen's trip reflected her equine interests as well as her close relationship with the United States. Over six decades on the throne, she would visit America eleven times, five of those for private holidays — the most vacation time in any one place except Balmoral and Sandringham. By contrast, she would travel to Australia, one of her major realms, sixteen times.

While technically private, the visit to Kentucky was arranged with the same minute-by-minute precision as a state visit. The Queen wanted to take in the beauty of Kentucky, but her first priority was to visit the stud farms where her mares had boarded for nearly two decades, and to inspect more than sixty stallions for possible mating. To take advantage of the superior American breeding stock, she and Henry Porchester planned to send as many as five of her twenty-three broodmares to Kentucky in 1985.

At the suggestion of thoroughbred breeder

Paul Mellon, Elizabeth II arranged to stay with forty-five-year-old William Stamps Farish III and his wife, Sarah, at their 1,400-acre Lane's End Farm near Lexington. Mellon had been a trusted and generous friend of the Queen. He gave her a nomination every year to Mill Reef, the champion sire that he kept at the National Stud at Newmarket, waiving the usual stud fee of hundreds of thousands of dollars.

The Queen had met Will Farish only fleetingly in 1973 during a polo match at Smith's Lawn, but Mellon assured her that the Kentucky couple were low-key, unpretentious, and completely discreet. Their early-nineteenth-century brick home was beautifully appointed and architecturally distinctive — a long house only one room deep, with a row of arches and columns at the front entrance. Yet the interiors were becomingly modest, with a country kitchen under oak beams, an airy yellow sitting room lined with bookshelves, and a painting of jockeys by George Munnings on the dining room wall.

Will Farish was a multimillionaire from Houston who inherited family fortunes from Humble Oil (later Exxon) and Sears Roebuck, and Sarah was a du Pont heiress. For more than two decades, they had also been close friends of George H. W. and Barbara Bush, and Farish managed the vice president's blind trust during his time in office. Farish began breeding horses in Kentucky in 1963 and by 1984 had built Lane's End into one of the country's top thoroughbred operations.

When Elizabeth II landed in Lexington on Sunday, October 7, a woman from customs and immigration would not admit her without a passport. Catherine Murdock, a State Department protocol officer assigned to the Queen, explained that the sovereign doesn't carry one, but the official resisted until a call to Washington provided the necessary clearance. Arriving at Lane's End, the Queen immediately changed into her brogues, put on her raincoat and head scarf, and headed out for a walk in the wet grass. At teatime the Farishes brought out their new puppy, who promptly defecated in front of the Queen. "It put everyone totally at ease," said Catherine Murdock. "She has so many dogs she knows what to expect, but that was her introduction to the Farish household."

Each day the Queen moved in a caravan of cars from one storied farm to the next. At every stop, stable boys would lead out the stallions as trainers and breeders briefed the Queen and her advisers, who commented on the fine points of conformation and discussed bloodlines. The parade of champion horseflesh included Triple Crown winners Seattle Slew, Affirmed, and Secretariat, whose spirited antics delighted the Queen. At John Galbreath's Darby Dan Farm she visited Round Tower, her only broodmare then boarding in Kentucky. Having recently produced a foal, the mare was already expecting another.

Several owners entertained Elizabeth II at lunch and tea, but the pace allowed for little downtime. She attended the races at Keeneland, where she presented the winner of the Queen Elizabeth II Challenge cup for three-year-old fillies with a Georgian-style silver trophy that she had commissioned from a London jeweler. At Bloodstock Research Information Services, Henry Porchester's twenty-five-year-old son, Harry Herbert, showed her how to search for mating combinations within ten seconds on state-of-the-art computers, a program she intended to use on her recently installed computer system at Buckingham Palace. The directors of Keeneland also staged a mock auction in the large wood-paneled pavilion, re-creating the record-breaking sales of recent years as an equine quiz show in which the spectators had to guess the identity of the yearlings based on the description of their pedigrees.

Each night the Farishes had dinner parties for ten, where Elizabeth II unwound to an extent her advisers had not seen before. The guests were all from the horse world, many of whom the Queen already knew, and the conversation rarely strayed from thoroughbred topics. "She felt very much at home in Kentucky," said a courtier. "I saw an atmosphere of informality and gaiety that I never saw in England. No one was calling her Ma'am or Your Majesty. She was laughing and joking and having fun. She has a great soft spot for the United States."

Shortly before her departure on Friday, October 12, the Queen learned that a powerful IRA bomb had exploded during the Conservative Party conference at the Grand Hotel in Brighton. Margaret Thatcher, the prime target of the terror attack, had escaped injury, but five died and thirty-four were injured, including two of the prime minister's valued colleagues, Norman Tebbit and government chief whip John Wakeham. Thatcher had taken a hard line against prison hunger strikes in Northern Ireland four years earlier, and after the Conservatives increased their majority in the June 1983 general election, she had redoubled her resistance to the political demands of the IRA. The morning after the attack, she convened the conference at 9:30 A.M. as scheduled and gave a defiant speech announcing that "all attempts to destroy democracy by terrorism will fail."

Elizabeth II immediately sent a message of "sympathy and deep concern" to the prime minister, and Palace press secretary Michael Shea denounced the bombing as a "dreadful outrage." When she arrived in Wyoming, she called Thatcher, whose first words were, "Are you having a lovely time?" Elizabeth II's support "boosted one's morale," Thatcher recalled. The Queen then called Ronald Reagan, who shared his "deep regret," a sentiment underlined by the earlier attempt on his own life.

Despite the shadow of events in England, her weekend in Wyoming gave the Queen her first total relaxation in nearly a month as she settled into the Porchesters' two-story stone-and-clapboard house with dramatic views of the aspenglow, the golden foliage of autumn aspens on the slopes of the Big Horn Mountains. Her only annoyance was the proliferation of Secret Service agents, who scared off the elk and deer. But she took five-mile walks on the four-thousand-acre property, had several picnics along Little Goose Creek, and joined a morning shooting party, watching with the dogs as the guns brought down pheasants, partridges, and grouse. Meals were simple American fare such as rainbow trout, chicken pot pie, apple pie, ice cream, and cookies.

She made a couple of public forays to the Bradford Brinton Museum of Western and Indian Art in Big Horn, and Main Street in the town of Sheridan, where she did a walkabout against the advice of the Secret Service but to the delight of the one thousand local residents who had gathered to see her.

The Queen hosted a dinner on Saturday night for her staff and a dozen friends of the Porchesters at the Maverick Supper Club. It was the second time she was called upon to order from a restaurant menu in two years, and she seemed no more at ease with the process. She focused on the filet mignon, but puzzled over the king-sized and queen-sized cuts. "Queen sized-*fillette* cut, that's what I'll be having," she said, adding hash-brown potatoes with onions "because I have never tasted them." "What kind of salad dressing would you like?" asked the waitress. "Ya got French. Ya got Italian, ranch, honey mustard, or house." Genuinely perplexed, Elizabeth II diplomatically asked for a recommendation and chose the house dressing.

Before leaving on Monday, she handed out gifts to those who had helped her stateside — signed and dated photographs for all, and for the women, Halcyon Days enamel boxes monogrammed with her cypher. She also wrote a letter to Ronald Reagan to describe the time she had spent doing what she liked best — "looking at beautiful thoroughbreds" and "walking in the wide open spaces by the mountains."

■■■■

Back home she had a new grandchild to welcome her. Charles and Diana's second son, Henry Charles Albert David, had been born on September 15 while the Queen was at Balmoral. She had seen Prince Harry (as he would be known) only once, on a visit to Highgrove, her son's Gloucestershire estate, two days before her departure to Canada. Twenty-three-year-old Diana was in better spirits generally than she had been after the arrival of William, balancing motherhood, public engagements, and a fitness regimen. But by her own account, she had "closed off" from her husband and was disaffected with almost everything about him.

In addition to overseeing his charities, notably the Prince's Trust, which provided job training for youth in poor urban areas, Charles was attracting attention — and generating controversy — with his public stands on preserving the environment and resisting brutalist architecture. His speech in May 1984 denouncing a proposed new wing of the National Gallery as a "monstrous carbuncle on the face of a much loved and elegant friend" created an outcry in the architectural establishment but resulted in a far more congenial and traditional redesign.

Although he tried not to show it, Charles resented the adulation Diana received when they went out together. He had also become fed up with her moodiness and fixation on Camilla despite his repeated denials that he had even talked to his former lover much less seen her. Princess Michael of

Kent, the wife of Charles's cousin Prince Michael, told Roy Strong that Diana was a "catastrophe" and a "time bomb," and that Charles's unhappiness had deepened since his wife had become a "media queen."

To help boost Diana's confidence, Elizabeth II had earlier that year taken the extraordinary step of issuing an official statement of support through a Palace spokesman who said, "The Queen could not be more pleased with her daughter-in-law. She is very proud of the Princess's activities around the world and at home." By then Diana had become more conscientious about her royal duties and had signed on as a patron of seven new charities beyond the five she had previously adopted, organizations dedicated to the arts as well as education and medicine. In her public engagements, Diana could be exceptionally effective, connecting with people, particularly the ill and downtrodden, with a warmth and empathy that other members of the royal family did not project. Combined with her celebrated beauty and high style, her egalitarian manner gave her an aura that was powerful — and potentially dangerous when she turned it against her husband.

When Charles and Diana visited Washington in the autumn of 1985, they showed no sign of their private discord. Diana was jealous of anyone close to her husband, including Nancy Reagan, whom he unabashedly adored. Only a year earlier, Diana had confided to Andrew Neil, the editor of *The Sunday Times,* that the president was a "Horlicks" — a boring old man — and that the first lady cared only about being photographed with members of the royal family. Neil found the comments surprisingly "bitter." But the princess was all smiles at the White House dinner in their honor, where she memorably danced with John Travolta, as well as Neil Diamond and Clint Eastwood.

Three days after Elizabeth II turned sixty the following spring, the Duchess of Windsor died at age eighty-nine. Led by the Queen, the royal family attended her funeral at St. George's Chapel and burial at Frogmore next to her husband. Diana Mosley, a friend and fellow expatriate in France, wrote to her sister Debo Devonshire that the Queen "in her clever way gave the best seats to Georges and Ofelia" — the duchess's French butler and his wife. Surprisingly, Elizabeth II was in tears at the graveside, "touched perhaps by the sadness of those wretched lives," noted diarist James Lees-Milne.

She was back in the United States less than a month later on her second "working holiday," this time four days in Kentucky. Once again Will and Sarah Farish offered the Queen their hospitality as she appraised the results of the mating decisions she and Henry Porchester had made eighteen months earlier and inspected a new group of potential sires. Most of the bluegrass breeders who serviced her mares did so without charge, saving the Queen an estimated $800,000 in exchange for claiming a royal pedigree for the offspring of their stallions. By the mid-1980s her horses had won nearly three hundred races and some $2 million in prize money. But Britain's most prestigious racing event, the Epsom Derby, continued to elude her.

The Derby in early June marked the start of the annual "season" of sporting events, parties, and royal pageantry that on July 23, 1986, culminated with the wedding of the Queen's second son at age twenty-six. Prince Andrew had chosen a fetching twenty-six-year-old named Sarah Ferguson (popularly known as "Fergie"), a redhead who compensated for her limited education — a second-rate boarding school and secretarial courses — with an open-hearted enthusiasm. Like Diana, she came from a troubled background, although she masked her insecurities more effectively behind her gregarious demeanor.

Fergie's parents were commoners, but they were respectable country gentry who boasted aristocratic forebears and relatives including the 6th Duke of Buccleuch and Princess Alice, the Duchess of Gloucester. Her father, Major Ronald Ferguson, had given up a career as a cavalry officer in the Life Guards to run his family's farm in Hampshire, and her mother, the former Susan Wright, had been presented at court during the 1954 debutante season. Both parents were accomplished equestrians who moved easily in the upper echelons of English society.

When Sarah was thirteen years old, her mother bolted to marry Argentine polo player Hector Barrantes and moved to South America, leaving her former husband to raise Sarah and her older sister. Ronald Ferguson played polo with Prince Philip, served as Prince Charles's polo manager, and ran the Guards Polo Club at Windsor, connections that inevitably brought his daughter together with Andrew.

By the summer of 1985, when their romance began, the tabloids had already named the prince "Randy Andy" for his flamboyant exploits with an assortment of women, including Koo Stark, an American actress who had appeared in a soft-core pornography movie in 1976. Rather than trying to control her second son, the Queen indulged him. One of her ladies-in-waiting recalled a time when she and the Queen were writing letters together under an awning at Sandringham. "Suddenly from the bushes to the left there were screams and giggles," said the lady-in-waiting. "Around the corner came Andrew dragging the gardener's daughter, her dress in disarray. The Queen took no notice and kept on dictating the letters."

Andrew and Sarah delighted in crude jokes and boisterous behavior. Still, Elizabeth II was charmed by Sarah, who loved to stalk, shoot, and fish at Balmoral — all of which gave her an automatic edge over Diana. Fergie regularly rode with the Queen, and "felt favored and blessed. . . . I was robust and jolly and not too highly strung." It also helped that Fergie's cousin was Robert Fellowes, recently promoted to deputy private secretary. "She's very sharp and clever," said Princess Michael of Kent, "and she has made very great friends with the Queen."

On their wedding day, the Queen conferred on Andrew and his wife the titles Duke and Duchess of York. As they stood together on the Buckingham Palace balcony after their service in Westminster Abbey, they thrilled the crowds with a distinctly un-royal and lusty kiss. Three of the Queen's four children were now married, and she already had four grandchildren, with the expectation of more to come. To all appearances, she was the matriarch of a happy and burgeoning family.

CHAPTER FIFTEEN
FAMILY FRACTURES

Amid the wedding celebrations, the Queen had to confront news reports that raised serious questions about her professional conduct. On Sunday, July 20, 1986, Rupert Murdoch's *Sunday Times* splashed a sensational page-one story claiming that Elizabeth II was dismayed by the policies of Margaret Thatcher. The Queen purportedly took issue with her prime minister's opposition to the Commonwealth's advocacy of economic sanctions against South Africa to bring an end to apartheid, her tough tactics to break the miners' union during a long and violent strike in 1984 and 1985, her granting the United States permission to refuel at British airbases before launching a bombing mission against Libya the previous April, and her assaults on entitlement programs that had been supported by a "consensus" of Tories and Labour since the end of World War II. According to the *Sunday Times* report, the Queen not only regarded Thatcher's approach to governing as "uncaring, confrontational and divisive," she had become an "astute political infighter who is quite prepared to take on Downing Street when provoked."

Elizabeth II's senior advisers were dining at Boodle's, the men's club on St. James's Street, with the

"No one could curtsy lower than Margaret Thatcher."

Prime Minister Margaret Thatcher curtsying to the Queen at 10 Downing Street, December 1985. TIM GRAHAM/GETTY IMAGES

private secretaries to sovereigns of eight countries on Saturday night when a call came through that the story was breaking. The courtiers dispatched an assistant press secretary to Victoria Station to grab copies of the newspaper as the truck delivered them at eleven o'clock. "It was like a scene out of Trollope," said one of the courtiers. "This serene dinner with dignitaries was going on, and at the other end of the room one private secretary was on the phone with Buckingham Palace, another with *The Sunday Times,* and another with Downing Street trying to defuse the story."

"Margaret Thatcher was very upset," said Charles Powell. "She was furious that someone put that in the papers, but she didn't think it was the Queen." More than anything, the prime minister worried that "ordinary people" would be offended that she could be "upsetting the Queen." Elizabeth II was angry as well. She called Thatcher on Sunday from Windsor Castle to say that the allegations were completely untrue, and the two women "commiserated with each other," according to a senior courtier.

Palace press secretary Michael Shea issued a swift denial. He was more distraught than his colleagues, and they began to suspect that he had been indiscreet. A graduate of Gordonstoun with a doctorate in economics from the University of Edinburgh, he had served for fifteen years as a diplomat before joining the Palace in 1978 to run the press office — an appointment that raised eyebrows at the time because he was said to have a skeptical view of the monarchy.

There had been press reports in previous weeks

speculating that Elizabeth II was concerned that some members could leave the Commonwealth over Thatcher's South Africa policy. At the October 1985 meeting of Commonwealth leaders in Nassau, Thatcher had vigorously opposed a package of harshly punitive economic sanctions, arguing that they would lead to black unemployment in South Africa, harm the exports of British businesses, and push the white minority government headed by P. W. Botha even further to the right. The Queen had encouraged Canadian prime minister Brian Mulroney, who was serving as chairman of the Commonwealth, to work with the other leaders to find a unified position in their efforts to end apartheid.

Elizabeth II offered no opinion about sanctions. But as in Lusaka six years earlier, she dispelled tensions in her individual meetings with the leaders, this time in her stateroom on *Britannia,* emphasizing the "moral obligation" to keep talking. Thatcher eventually compromised by signing the group's communiqué denouncing apartheid, calling for curbs on bank loans and trade missions, and establishing a group of seven leaders to meet in London the following August to consider further actions. The *Sunday Times* article landed only days before the so-called mini-summit was scheduled to begin.

The newspaper's sweeping claims about domestic as well as foreign policy ran counter to the Queen's ironclad rule, which she had followed for the thirty-four years of her reign, to be utterly discreet about political matters. "She never expressed her views on sensitive topics," said one of her senior advisers. Nor did she have any fore-knowledge of the *Sunday Times* article, which her private secretary, William Heseltine, emphatically denounced as false. The question became not only who would leak such an account, but why.

To shield its informant, *The Sunday Times* had misleadingly said it had multiple sources, but by the end of the week the culprit was unmasked as Shea. He admitted that he had spoken to reporter Simon Freeman on a background basis several times by telephone, thinking he was briefing him for a speculative story on the monarchy in the twenty-first century. Shea said he talked in general terms and that Freeman and the newspaper's political editor, Michael Jones, had "misinterpreted" his words. Freeman insisted that Shea had specifically attributed left-of-center opinions on a range of issues to the Queen, and that the story had been cleared by the press secretary before publication. Shea countered that Freeman had withheld "crucial parts" when he read back the story.

The press secretary's colleagues, none of whom had known about Shea's dealings with the *Sunday Times* reporter, concluded that Andrew Neil, the newspaper's editor, had cooked up a provocative story line, that Freeman had used a combination of cajolery and flattery, and that Shea had gone overboard in a burst of ego and vanity. Even Rupert Murdoch told *Times* and *News of the World* columnist Woodrow Wyatt, "I think he has megalomania." Shea was also venting his own liberal views that friends had heard him express at dinner parties. "He personally didn't go for Margaret

Thatcher," said Elizabeth II's friend Angela Oswald. "He put words in the Queen's mouth that she never said. She was brought up never to get involved in party politics. She would never imply that she favored one politician over another."

A week after the story was published, the Queen and her prime minister were at Holyroodhouse in Edinburgh, where Shea was seated between them at a luncheon. He apologized to Thatcher, who simply said, "Don't worry, dear." Later that day in a phone conversation, Woodrow Wyatt told Thatcher that the Queen should fire Shea or force him to resign. "Well, I can't do anything about that," she said. "It's up to her. But we will have to see whether new arrangements are made to prevent such a thing happening again. I think they will be." In a matter of months Shea left his job at the Palace to work in private industry.

On August 4, 1986, Elizabeth II hosted the first "working dinner" of her reign when she gathered the seven Commonwealth leaders at Buckingham Palace after their first round of mini-summit meetings at 10 Downing Street. Foreign Secretary Sir Geoffrey Howe called it a "deliberate act by the Queen . . . to remind us all of our commitment to get on with each other." Earlier that day, Zambian president Kenneth Kaunda had strenuously attacked Thatcher, unfairly accusing her of sympathizing with apartheid. Deploying remarkable sangfroid, Thatcher calmed him by taking his arm and saying, "Now Kenneth, we must get ourselves lunch before we have another vigorous discussion this afternoon." That night at dinner, the Queen glanced at Kaunda and said with a twinkle to Indian prime minister Rajiv Gandhi, "How is the emotional one?"

"There was no doubt that Her Majesty sided with the Commonwealth," said Brian Mulroney. "But she couldn't speak out. You had to understand the nuances and body language. She did it by allusion and by indirection. At the dinner she was a great moderating influence on everyone. She led us through an elevated discussion of human rights. I don't know how much opinion she expressed, but she would nudge everyone in a certain direction." By the end of the conference, Thatcher joined the other six leaders on a set of recommendations to be presented later to all forty-nine Commonwealth members. "What saved the day," recalled Brian Mulroney, "was that Margaret was aware Her Majesty certainly wanted some kind of resolution. So we were able to put in three or four financial things that Margaret accepted, which allowed us to move on to the next meeting without rupture."

After their annual Balmoral holiday, the Queen and Prince Philip traveled to the People's Republic of China in mid-October, the first time a British monarch had visited the Chinese mainland. The planning had begun several years earlier. The Queen read extensive briefs on history and culture, as well as on the habits of Deng Xiaoping, the country's eighty-two-year-old leader, including his bridge playing and incessant smoking. The royal couple's itinerary took them from Beijing to Shanghai, Kunming, and the ancient city of X'ian, where they walked among the vast army of life-size terra-cotta warriors that had recently been unearthed by archaeologists.

Elizabeth II charmed Deng when they were having lunch and she detected that he was becoming restless. Turning to Geoffrey Howe, she said, "I think Mr. Deng would be rather happier if he was told he was allowed to smoke." Recalled Howe, "I've never seen a man light up more cheerfully. It was a very human touch and he appreciated it." When the Chinese leader let fly into a spittoon several feet away, the Queen "didn't move a muscle," said Michael Shea.

The trip was going smoothly until Philip encountered a group of British students in X'ian and cautioned them that they would get "slitty eyes" if they stayed in China much longer. The tabloid pack howled with glee and filed stories about the duke's insult to the entire Chinese nation, sweeping aside all the positive coverage of the Queen's diplomatic bridge building.

"The British press went nuts," said one of the Queen's advisers, "but we couldn't figure out why after the slitty-eyed remark there was no comment in China." The courtiers assumed their hosts didn't want to spoil the visit, but senior officials in the Chinese government said later that they had scarcely noticed because they used the term privately among themselves.

For Philip, it was the latest in a long line of gaffes attributed to him by the press when he was trying, in the view of his friend Sir David Attenborough, to "puncture the balloon" during earnest royal rounds. "I don't know why he has the gift of trying to think of something funny that ends up offending," said one of the Queen's former private secretaries. "There is a degree of insensitivity, and once the press gets hold, it looks for further examples and ignores everything else."

Philip's wisecracks masked the considerable intellect and surprising dimensions behind his brusque personality, as well as the substantive role he played at the Palace. As chancellor of both Cambridge and Edinburgh universities, he encouraged innovation, especially in technology. "My only claim to fame is that I'm the most experienced visitor of technological facilities," he once said. "I've been doing it professionally for forty years. I can claim to have petted the first microchip on the head." The thousands of books in his library included substantial collections devoted to religion, wildlife (with a particular passion for ornithology), conservation, sports, and horses as well as poetry and art. His little recognized artistic talent ranged from his oil painting to a flair for designing jewelry, including a gold bracelet entwined with E and P and set with diamonds, rubies, and sapphires that he had given to his wife on their fifth wedding anniversary.

By 1984 he had written nine books — anthologies of speeches, essays on religion, philosophy, science, and conservation, as well as the complete rules for competition carriage driving. He had also appeared on the documentary series *Nature* to plead for the preservation of rain forests in Brazil — a cause his son Charles would take up decades later. In 1982 he began driving a Bedford Smith electric van around the Sandringham estate, and the solar panels he installed there were among the first to be used in Britain — an "energy saving," he conceded, rather than a replacement for other sources.

"Sometimes I would take an idea to the Queen — not a constitutional issue, because she would ask her private secretary for that," recalled one of her former courtiers. "She would say, 'What does Philip think?' She would make it clear that she wanted you to take the idea to him first, rather than clutter her time with him talking about routine business."

In his discussions with his wife's advisers, "Prince Philip would ask for lots of lines of inquiries," the courtier said. "She might say, 'Have you thought of x or y?' It would not be the same way you would engage with Prince Philip. It is not that the Queen does not have the mind for it, but there is a lot that comes across her desk, and she is not the sort to zero in and peel the skin of the onion away every time until you get to the heart of it. He has a sort of Defence Staff rigor, the ability to pull an idea to bits, find the good parts and the parts that need work. You take it back to the Queen once you know that Prince Philip's view is there, and then you go over it. You know if he is happy with the idea, she will probably be too."

A crucial issue facing the Queen in the mid-1980s was an unprecedented top-to-bottom review of the administration and expenses at Buckingham Palace conducted by David Airlie, who became her Lord Chamberlain on December 1, 1984, at age fifty-nine after retiring as chairman of Schroders, the venerable merchant banking firm. As a lifelong friend, he was a known quantity. One of his favorite photographs shows Airlie with five-year-old Princess Elizabeth on his fifth birthday after his parents had given him a shiny pedal car. When his father suggested he let the princess ride in it, David resisted mightily until he finally yielded. In the picture, she is happily steering the car while the future 13th Earl of Airlie is pushing it with a furious scowl on his face.

The Queen knew that Airlie was due to retire from banking at the end of November, the same time that Chips Maclean was retiring from the Lord Chamberlain post after thirteen years running the household at Buckingham Palace. Maclean, who had served in the Scots Guards with Airlie, asked if he would consider taking on the job. Soon afterward Airlie was at Sandringham on a shoot when the Queen said, "Do you really want to be Lord Chamberlain?" That was the extent of his job interview with his future boss, but in fact a good deal of thought had been given to his recruitment.

Airlie was known as a tough and highly successful businessman as well as a debonair aristocrat — just the sort who had the credibility and expertise to bring a fresh eye to Palace operations. He was struck immediately that Elizabeth II was "enormously practical" and "extremely businesslike." If he wrote her a memorandum requiring an answer, she would invariably return it within twenty-four hours. If not, he would know that she hadn't made up her mind and wanted "to sit on it and think about it." Although he had been in her company socially for years, Airlie discerned for the first time her powers of observation during public engagements. "The reason why she moves slowly is that she wants to absorb what's going on in the room and the people in the room," he said. "You can see her looking around the room as she walks in and taking it all in and my goodness me what she takes in never ceases to amaze me."

After he had spent six months looking and listening, he advised her to hire an outside consultant for an internal review, to ensure that the result would be evenhanded and unassailably professional. With the Queen's backing, he brought in thirty-five-year-old Michael Peat, a fellow Old Etonian who had graduated from Oxford and received an MBA from the prestigious INSEAD business school in France. Peat had worked for more than a decade at his family's accounting firm, KPMG, the auditor of the Palace books, and Airlie had gotten to know him while he was at Schroders.

Under Airlie's supervision, Peat spent more than a year preparing a 1,393-page report with 188 recommendations for streamlining the household and instituting the "best practices" that were being adopted by many businesses. These included setting up a more professional personnel department and creating the Royal Collection Department to oversee the monarchy's artistic holdings as well as the retail shops and other commercial enterprises. Among the suggestions were personnel cutbacks, but at the Lord Chamberlain's insistence to be achieved only by natural attrition rather than by actually firing people.

Airlie kept both Elizabeth II and Philip informed as the review was under way, although not in detail. The Lord Chamberlain understood that the Queen distrusted change for change's sake, but was open to well-reasoned argument. By the time the report was issued in December 1986, the Queen

473

accepted everything, and within three years, 162 of the reforms were put into effect.

While the modernizers at the Palace were making progress, they were incapable of controlling the antics of the Queen's children, three of whom made fools of themselves when they participated in a television game show. The idea came from twenty-three-year-old Prince Edward, who was trying to make his mark in the entertainment business. After graduating from Gordonstoun and earning a degree at Cambridge, he had obediently followed his family's military tradition by enlisting with the Royal Marines. He was a keen athlete who competed vigorously at court tennis, but temperamentally was shy and sensitive.

Shortly before finishing the Marines' six-month training course in January 1987, he unexpectedly announced that he was resigning his commission. His reservations about a military career were more mental than physical, and the press reported that his father had reacted angrily to Edward's decision. But a letter to the Marine commandant — later leaked to *The Sun* — showed that Philip had in fact been understanding and sympathetic. "They always try to make him out as a brute," the Queen Mother told Woodrow Wyatt. "In fact he's extremely kind to his children and always has been."

Edward instead decided to pursue his interest in theater and television. For his first project he proposed a variation on a popular show called *It's a Knockout* that pitted contestants dressed in silly costumes against each other in equally ludicrous games. His idea, titled *It's a Royal Knockout,* was to raise money for royal charities by featuring his siblings vying with celebrities. Charles declined to participate, and vetoed his wife's appearance as well, but Anne, Andrew, and Fergie signed on.

Because of the proposed involvement of family members, Edward needed the approval of his mother. She was dubious. William Heseltine expressed concern that the show could cast the royal family in a poor light, and he and her other top advisers urged her to veto the project. But she succumbed to her impulse to indulge her children and gave Edward her permission. The only caveat was that her children appear as "team captains" rather than participants in the games.

Televised live on June 19, 1987, the program featured Edward, Anne, Andrew, and Fergie dressed in faux royal costumes. They hopped around shouting on the sidelines while an assortment of British and American actors including John Travolta, Michael Palin, Rowan Atkinson, Jane Seymour, and Margot Kidder engaged in mortifying stunts such as pelting each other with fake hams. During interviews with the royal participants, the show's hosts lampooned deference with exaggerated bows that made the group look even sillier. The spectacle was more undignified than the courtiers feared, eclipsing the £1 million raised for the World Wildlife Fund, Save the Children Fund, Shelter for the Homeless, and the Duke of Edinburgh International Award for Young People.

Princess Anne in particular should have known better, having spent the better part of a decade rehabilitating her public image. When she began taking on more royal duties in the early 1970s she had appeared supercilious and short-tempered, particularly with journalists, whom she couldn't abide. While she was riding in the Badminton Horse Trials, she famously told reporters to "Naff off!" They responded with the nickname "Her Royal Rudeness." She couldn't shed her prickly temperament, but she eventually earned widespread respect if not affection for her tireless efforts on behalf of her charities, particularly Save the Children. Just six days before the *Knockout* program, the Queen had rewarded her daughter's hard work and professionalism by designating her "The Princess Royal," a title reserved only for the eldest daughter of the monarch.

Edward compounded the embarrassment at a press conference after the show. "Well, what did you think?" he asked, prompting laughter among the more than fifty reporters. He was so annoyed by their reaction that he stalked out, and the press called him arrogant as well as foolish. The show not only managed to trivialize the participants, but the institution of the monarchy itself. The consensus at the Palace and among the Queen's friends was, in the words of Michael Oswald, "It was a disaster and should never have been allowed."

Given the family tensions that summer, it was probably a blessing that *Britannia* was out for a complete refit and unavailable for the annual Western Isles cruise. Instead, the Queen traveled north to spend two nights at the Castle of Mey — the only time she ever stayed overnight — for some quiet time with her eighty-seven-year-old mother.

The Queen Mother relinquished her own bedroom, with its views of her prize Aberdeen Angus cattle and North Country Cheviot sheep out in the pastures, and moved into "Princess Margaret's Bedroom," which had never actually been slept in by her younger daughter, who dismissed Mey as "cold, drafty, and expensive."

The two queens took walks through the nearby woods and down to the sea, and attended the village of Mey's version of the Highland games on a muddy football field. In the evenings, the Queen Mother hosted jolly dinner parties with friends from the area, including the local minister, who brought his guitar. After dinner he played Scottish songs and everyone, including the Queen, sang along with gusto.

Several months later, Martin Charteris told Roy Strong that the younger generation of the royal family had been "stripped naked" and needed to "put the mystery back." The faithful former courtier couldn't have anticipated how much worse the Queen's problems with her children would get.

By the late 1980s, all three marriages were showing signs of strain. In 1985 Diana had taken up with one of her bodyguards, Barry Mannakee, who had a wife and two children, and in November of the following year, over dinner at Kensington Palace, she began an intense romance with Captain James Hewitt of the Life Guards, who had been her riding instructor. Charles, meantime, had resumed his affair with Camilla in 1986 for her "warmth . . . understanding and steadiness."

The tabloids didn't yet know about these infidelities, but they periodically reported rumors about troubles in the Wales marriage after they stayed in separate bedrooms during a state visit to Portugal and then took a number of holidays apart, even on their sixth anniversary. While the Queen was unaware of the extent of their estrangement, the tension was obvious enough in the autumn of 1987 that she invited them to meet with her one evening in Buckingham Palace shortly before they were due to leave for an official tour of West Germany. She urged them to pull themselves together, and for a time thereafter they seemed to heed her advice.

They had not in fact reconciled. Rather, they were giving each other "civilized space," with Charles operating mainly out of Highgrove in Gloucestershire, and Diana out of their London home at Kensington Palace, an arrangement that allowed them to maintain a more harmonious public facade in the following months. The press proclaimed a "new Diana" who was more attentive to her charities and royal duties, with 250 engagements in 1988 compared to 153 for Fergie and 665 for the indefatigable Anne.

By early 1988 Fergie was pregnant with the first of two daughters, Princess Beatrice, yet she was increasingly dissatisfied with her marriage to Andrew. His naval career meant he was home only forty-two days a year, leaving her behind in their unstylish and surprisingly modest three-bedroom apartment at Buckingham Palace. Beyond the availability of servants and other perquisites, Sarah was expected to live on Andrew's £35,000 ($55,000) annual salary, but her extravagant tastes plunged her into debt that began an inexorable climb into six figures.

Her spending sprees were fueled in part by her competition with Diana, who had access to her husband's Duchy of Cornwall annual income of around £1 million ($1.5 million). The sisters-in-law vacillated between rivalrous sniping and juvenile behavior — capering like schoolgirls on the ski slopes and poking rolled umbrellas into the backside of a friend at Ascot. Tabloid reporters who had previously hailed Fergie for being refreshingly approachable declared her to be the "bad royal . . . crass, rude, raucous, and bereft of all dignity." Even her father fit the new stereotype when he was discovered frequenting a London massage and sex parlor.

For a number of years there had been rumblings around dinner tables in London and at house parties in the country that Anne and her husband, Mark Phillips, had both been having affairs and were leading separate lives. She was linked to Peter Cross, one of her security officers, as well as Camilla's husband, Andrew Parker Bowles, whom Anne had dated before meeting Phillips. The definitive story emerged in April 1989 when the tabloids revealed four purloined love letters to the thirty-eight-year-old princess from Commander Timothy Laurence, the Queen's thirty-four-year-old equerry.

In an echo of Princess Margaret's romance with Peter Townsend, Anne had grown close to Laurence after he joined the royal household in 1986. The letters, written over eighteen months, called her "darling" and were written in "affectionate terms" without specifically suggesting intimacy. The Palace confirmed the authenticity of the letters, which *The Sun* turned over to Scotland Yard. Soon afterward, Anne and her husband announced their separation, while in a tacit show of support for her popular equerry the Queen kept Laurence on her staff. The public responded sympathetically but witnessing her daughter's marital unhappiness was a blow to the Queen.

Elizabeth II found escape from her family travails in her equine pursuits. At the end of 1988 she had been reading in two American magazines, *Blood Horse* and *Florida Horse,* about a new technique for "starting" horses developed by a fifty-three-year-old California cowboy named Monty Roberts. Rather than "breaking" yearlings to accept human riders by tying their legs and heads with ropes, Roberts had devised a method based on "advance-and-retreat" body language, eye contact, and subtle signals that appeal to a horse's herd instinct. He had grown up observing wild mustangs discipline their difficult colts, and after receiving a degree in psychology and animal science from California Polytechnic State University in 1955, he began his career training thoroughbreds, determined to avoid the violent tactics that his father had used.

The Queen sent Lieutenant Colonel Sir John Miller, who had recently retired after twenty-six years as her Crown Equerry — the man in charge of all her horses except racehorses — to Roberts's ranch north of Santa Barbara for a demonstration. After Miller reported that he found the new approach compelling, the Queen invited Roberts to Windsor Castle so she could judge for herself. He agreed to conduct demonstrations over five days starting on April 10, 1989. She invited some two hundred guests to watch him start sixteen horses, although she said she would be present only for an hour on the first day. If she found his technique useful, she promised to send him on a twenty-one-city tour throughout the United Kingdom to educate others in the horse world.

On the Saturday before the trials, Roberts went with Miller to the indoor riding school at the castle to inspect the newly installed fifty-foot round pen where he would work with the horses. Into the riding hall strode the Queen, dressed in jodhpurs and a handsome hacking jacket, moving quickly to speak to Miller. She was "confident, in a hurry, with things to do," recalled Roberts. Her presence was at odds with the "indelibly engraved image" he had from sightings at Ascot, Epsom, and Newmarket — "always in a dress, a strolling lady, purse over her arm, a smile for everyone, a tranquil lady, never in a hurry in public, everything lined up for her."

A suddenly attentive Miller made the introduction as Elizabeth II extended her hand to the stocky horseman with a deep tan and alert blue eyes. "Come show me this lions' cage of yours," she said. "Do I need a whip and a chair?" "She said it not only with a twinkle, but her method of addressing me — clearly her talent — was to put me at ease," Roberts recalled.

The following Monday morning at nine, he faced not only the Queen, but Prince Philip and the

Queen Mother, whose filly was first into the pen. The royal group, along with Miller, Michael Clayton, the editor of *Horse and Hound* magazine — the only journalist Elizabeth II ever befriended — and Lieutenant Colonel Seymour Gilbart-Denham, the new Crown Equerry, sat in a glass-enclosed viewing platform at one end of the high-ceilinged hall with arched Gothic-style windows. The grooms stood along the walls, gazing suspiciously.

Roberts went through his paces, tossing a light cotton line toward the horse, who responded by trotting around the perimeter of the pen. Over the next fifteen minutes the filly shifted from fear to trust, encouraged by Roberts's glances and gestures, including turning his back on the horse, until she began following him. After ten more minutes, she first accepted his touch — "joining up" in his nomenclature — then a bridle and saddle. Moments later Roberts's assistant was riding the filly around the pen. "That was beautiful," the Queen said to Roberts, impressed by his gentle but effective approach. Philip gave him a hard handshake and asked if Roberts could work with his carriage ponies. With tears in her eyes, the Queen Mother said, "That was one of the most wonderful things I've ever seen in my life."

Roberts watched in amazement as the Queen began issuing orders. "That surprised me," he said. "You don't see the Queen doing that in real life." Several of the girl grooms had told her they suspected Roberts of tranquilizing the filly by throwing powder into her nose. In response, Elizabeth II asked for a more rigorous test in the afternoon with two raw three-year-old stallions to be transported from the stables at Hampton Court. She had changed her plans and would be returning after lunch.

That afternoon, nearly a hundred guests were on hand. The Queen stood directly by the pen, arms folded, watching intently with her girl grooms nearby. Both of the stallions were "riled up, big, moving and sweating," but Roberts started each of them after a half hour of training. To his surprise, the Queen's schedule miraculously cleared and she came to the morning and afternoon demonstrations every day that week to watch him work with twenty-two horses. She called the top trainers around the country to encourage them to attend the demonstrations she had set up, and she arranged for Michael Clayton to chronicle the tour for his magazine. She even supplied a bulletproof Ford Scorpio for Roberts to drive.

The sovereign and the cowboy struck up a fast friendship, connected by their compatible view of equine psychology and their prodigious memories for racehorse pedigrees. Speaking precisely and slowly, his voice gentle but strong, Roberts answered her numerous questions over lunch in the castle gardens. "I saw a mind open up that through decades of training and interest had been encapsulated in the traditional approach," recalled Roberts. "She saw it was a better way."

He was struck that she "knew every move, knew why it was there and why it was executed." When he told her something she didn't know, she sat on the edge of her chair "with a humility like a first grader." He was equally surprised that she offered him ideas on how to present his concepts to an

English audience. "You need to ease up," she said, "so you don't appear to be too competitive." Her advice showed "an incredible ability to read intention, just like a horse does."

His friendship with the Queen changed Monty Roberts's life. Not only did she adopt his approach for many of her own horses, she encouraged him to write an autobiography that would incorporate his training techniques. She critiqued his drafts, urged him to make major revisions, and introduced him to publishers. When *The Man Who Listens to Horses: The Story of a Real-Life Horse Whisperer* was published in 1997, it sold more than two million copies. The Queen praised him not only for producing the book but for "getting it right." He has gone on to establish training centers around the world, teaching his methods to some 1,500 students a year. All along the way, the Queen has tracked his progress and received updates during his visits to Windsor twice a year. In 2011 she rewarded Roberts by making him an honorary Member of the Royal Victorian Order.

Horse racing had always been a source of unalloyed joy for the Queen, but in 1989 the pleasure of making a new friendship with Monty Roberts and discovering the possibilities of his teachings was marred by controversy and disappointment, both on and off the track. A central character was a long-striding colt called Nashwan, the offspring of Height of Fashion, a prize mare the Queen had bred a decade earlier.

As a filly, Height of Fashion had won five of her seven races in 1981 and 1982, catching the eye of

Sheikh Hamdan al Maktoum of the Dubai royal family. He offered to buy the horse for more than £1 million — at the time an extravagant amount for an untested "maiden" broodmare. Acting on Henry Porchester's advice, Elizabeth II decided to sell, using the proceeds to buy the West Ilsley stables in Berkshire. Her highly regarded trainer, Major Dick Hern, who was living in a nearby rectory, also purchased by the Queen, then signed a seven-year lease on the stable.

Hern had worked for Elizabeth II since 1966 and also trained for other prominent owners, including the Maktoum family. He had trained two of the Queen's most successful horses, Highclere and Dunfermline, and had been part of the group that celebrated the Prix de Diane victory at Windsor Castle.

In 1984, Hern broke his neck in a hunting accident. He was paralyzed below the waist but valiantly continued training from a wheelchair and turning out winners. Four years later he had another setback when he underwent major heart surgery. As Hern was recuperating in the hospital in August 1988, the Queen's veteran racing manager — now known as the 7th Earl of Carnarvon after inheriting the title on his father's death the previous year — informed the sixty-seven-year-old trainer that he would have to leave West Ilsley at the end of his lease the following year. Porchey's insensitivity provoked an outcry in the racing world.

Hern briefly resumed training for Elizabeth II, but she announced in March 1989 that he would be replaced by William Hastings-Bass, the future

Earl of Huntington. The anger at Henry Carnarvon turned toward the Queen, not only for firing her trainer, but for evicting him from the rectory where he had lived since 1962. Ian Balding, a good friend of Hern, told Robert Fellowes, "If you don't make some sort of arrangement for Dick Hern, it will be the most unpopular thing the Queen has ever done, and she risks having her horses booed in the winners' enclosure."

That never happened, but something close occurred when Nashwan won at Newmarket in May, and the crowd greeted Hern, who had trained the horse for Maktoum, with "loud and sustained applause" as he "swept off his Panama" to welcome the horse into the winners' enclosure. "The Queen has done something I thought was impossible," Woodrow Wyatt told the 18th Earl of Derby's wife, Isabel. "She is turning the Jockey Club and the racing world into republicans."

The worst, at least for a competitive owner like the Queen, was yet to come. On June 7, Elizabeth II attended the Epsom Derby, the race she most wanted to win. None other than Nashwan, the horse who could have been hers, galloped to a dramatic, five-length victory.

By then, she had countermanded Carnarvon's advice and arranged to let Hern remain at the West Ilsley stables through 1990, sharing the training with Hastings-Bass for a year. Even more significant, she allowed Hern to stay in his home for as long as he wanted. The Maktoum family bought and renovated a new stable for the veteran trainer, and he worked successfully for them until he retired in 1997. Elizabeth II was forgiven the biggest blunder of her career as a thoroughbred breeder, in large measure due to the magnanimity of Hern, who greeted her cordially after his Derby win and never spoke ill of her.

The new year brought a welcome resolution of one of the most troubling problems of the Queen's reign. South Africa's newly elected white president, Frederik Willem de Klerk, made the stunning announcement on February 2, 1990, that he would free Nelson Mandela, the leader of the African National Congress, who had been imprisoned for twenty-seven years for resisting apartheid policies. Nine days later Mandela walked through the prison gates as a free man. De Klerk legalized the ANC and set in motion the dismantling of apartheid and establishment of universal democratic elections.

Both leaders yielded to internal and external pressures, and their successful reconciliation earned them the Nobel Peace Prize in 1993. Mandela believed that the Commonwealth's anti-apartheid stance had been vital, as was the Queen's role in keeping the organization unified. "Sonny Ramphal [secretary-general of the Commonwealth] was sitting in London with [Thabo] Mbeki and [Oliver] Tambo from the ANC," recalled Canada's Brian Mulroney. "He would pass on everything that went on in the Commonwealth, and they would pass it on to Mandela. In the area of moral leadership, Mandela would say that the Commonwealth saved South Africa."

The South African denouement came as a relief to Margaret Thatcher as she began her eleventh year as prime minister after leading the Tory party to victory three times — in 1979, 1983, and 1987. Britain's difficult years of stringent monetary policy, high unemployment, and union busting had been eclipsed by an economic boom in the late 1980s. Thatcher had broken the back of inflation, encouraged entrepreneurs, expanded the number of homeowners, privatized state industries, reduced the size of government, and opened London's financial markets to foreign investment. Internationally, she had bolstered the country's image with her strong anticommunist stance (in concert with Ronald Reagan), and her economic policies offered a model to the rising Eastern European countries that had elected noncommunist governments after the breakup of the Soviet Union that began in 1989.

In July 1990, David Airlie presented the prime minister with a new proposal to fund the Civil List. Having instituted most of the Peat Report reforms, he was able to show the government that Palace officials could be "in charge of our own destiny." His presentation called for returning to the ten-year funding set by the Civil List Act of 1972, a formula that the Labour government had superseded in 1975 with a law reverting to annual requests for increases. Thatcher agreed to raise the annual Civil List payment from £5.1 million to £7.9 million through 2000.

Persuaded by the professionalism and efficiency of the Queen's advisers, the prime minister also shifted the job of managing the finances of the occupied royal palaces — Buckingham, St. James's, Kensington, Marlborough House, Clarence House, Windsor Castle, and assorted properties in Windsor Great Park and the Home Park — from the Department of the Environment to the royal household, with Michael Peat serving in the new position of director of finance and property services. Thatcher defended the Civil List plan by emphasizing that it would "give much more dignity and continuity to the Crown," adding that "an overwhelming number of people in the nation regard the royal family as the greatest asset that the United Kingdom has and greatly admire everything that it does."

Despite Thatcher's numerous successes, she faced growing opposition in the electorate as well as within the Conservative Party. To raise revenue for local services such as education and trash collection, she had abolished property taxes and created instead a poll tax. Every adult was required to pay the same amount, but local authorities used the new system to impose rates that caused many low-income people to pay considerably more than they had previously. The widespread unpopularity of the poll tax threatened the prospects for a Tory victory in the 1991 general election.

Inside Tory ranks, liberal members objected to Thatcher's increasingly "Euro-skeptic" position as the European Economic Community moved toward greater integration in the post–Cold War period. She emphatically opposed abandoning the pound sterling to join a single European currency, a policy advocated by several of her senior ministers. One of them, Foreign Secretary Geoffrey Howe, resigned in protest on November 1, 1990. Two weeks later, Michael Heseltine, who had left

Thatcher's cabinet in 1986, challenged her leadership.

Although she won a majority in the first ballot on Tuesday, November 20, she needed a wider margin under party rules to win decisively. She was in Paris at the time and returned to London Wednesday morning, determined to prevail in the second ballot. But after meeting with her principal supporters, she decided to consult each of her cabinet ministers individually. One by one, her erstwhile liege men told her she would lose the vote. By that evening, Thatcher decided to withdraw her name from the second ballot rather than face defeat. On Thursday morning she went to Buckingham Palace to inform the Queen she would be resigning. "She's a very understanding person," Thatcher said later. "She understood . . . the rightness of the decision I was taking. . . . It was very sad to know that was the last time I'd go to the Palace as prime minister after eleven-and-a-half years."

When the second ballot took place on the 27th, Thatcher's nemesis, Michael Heseltine, was defeated by John Major, the chancellor of the exchequer and her preferred candidate. The next morning Margaret Thatcher submitted her resignation to the Queen, and forty-five minutes later Major arrived at the Palace to accept the sovereign's invitation to form a government. At age forty-seven, he was the youngest prime minister in more than a century.

The Queen showed her esteem for Thatcher by quickly awarding her the sovereign's two most prestigious personal honors, the Order of the Garter and the Order of Merit. Founded in 1902 by

King Edward VII for distinction in the military, arts, and sciences, the Order of Merit, like the Garter, only has twenty-four members at a time and has included just three previous prime ministers: Winston Churchill, Clement Attlee, and Harold Macmillan. "The Garter tends to go to all ex–prime ministers in time, but the Order of Merit is mostly scientists and academics. That really mattered to her," said her longtime adviser Charles Powell.

The Queen Mother was deeply upset by Thatcher's departure, calling her "very patriotic" and expressing the hope that she would come to stay at Balmoral after she left office. "She said they [meaning the royal family] think it is desperately unfair and an appalling way to do things," her friend Woodrow Wyatt recorded in his diary two days after Thatcher stepped down. "They admire her, they think she was wonderful, and she did so much for Britain, not only at home but in the world at large." According to Wyatt, any stories about the Queen disliking Thatcher were "pure invention."

CHAPTER SIXTEEN
ANNUS HORRIBILIS

Of all Elizabeth II's prime ministers, John Major had the most unusual background, as exotic as it was humble. His father had sought his fortune in the United States, working in the steel mills of Pittsburgh before making a career as a circus trapeze artist and performer on the vaudeville circuit in America and Britain. After the death of his first wife, he married a young dancer and built a business selling novelty garden ornaments. John was their fourth child, born when his father was sixty-four and had suffered financial reversals.

The family moved to the Brixton slums, and John had to leave school at sixteen to help support his parents. He worked in a variety of odd jobs until he took up banking, where he found success. Attracted to politics, he rose from his local council to Parliament and entered the Thatcher cabinet in 1987. He was known for his steady hand, mastery of policy detail, quiet determination, and shrewd judgment.

When he became prime minister, Major focused on conciliating the bitterly divided factions of the Tory party. After five months in office, he scrapped the hated poll tax and replaced it with a newly crafted property tax based on the value of a resi-

"Scrutiny...can be just as effective if it is made with a touch of gentleness, good humor and understanding."

Queen Elizabeth II making her "Annus Horribilis" *speech about her family's troubles, November 1992.* TIM GRAHAM/GETTY IMAGES

dence as well as the number of its occupants. He built on the economic gains of the Thatcher years and successfully negotiated advantageous terms in the 1991 Maastricht Treaty that kept Britain in the strengthened European Union (formerly the European Economic Community) without ceding independence on issues such as workers' wages, health and safety, or abolishing the pound for the continent's proposed single currency.

In the presence of her courtiers, the Queen treated the amiable Major just as she did his brisk predecessor. "I couldn't pin down a difference between the two," said one of her senior advisers. Major was "totally relaxed and cheerful" before his audiences. "Afterward when he was with the private secretaries, the conversation was almost always about cricket."

Shortly after assuming power, the new prime minister led Britain into a coalition with the United States and thirty other nations to free Kuwait from Iraqi forces that had invaded the previous August. Britain was a key player in the successful air bombardment of Iraq that began on January 17, 1991, followed by a ground campaign that swept to victory on February 28. Major gave the Queen regular briefings, and as the ground assault began on Sunday the 24th, she made the first wartime broadcast of her reign, reassuring the nation that she was praying for victory.

A cease-fire ended the occupation of Kuwait, although it did not remove Iraqi dictator Saddam Hussein from power. Still, the war was hailed as a significant success for Major as well as for Reagan's successor, George H. W. Bush. The two leaders bonded tightly as allies and "had a lot in common," wrote Ray Seitz, Bush's ambassador to the Court of St. James's.

Three months later, Bush welcomed the Queen to Washington for her third state visit. The patrician Bushes and royal Windsors established an easy camaraderie from the start. As near contemporaries, the forty-first president and the Duke of Edinburgh had both seen action in the Pacific during World War II. The two families shared similar Anglo-Saxon traditions and values, and they counted the Queen's hosts in Kentucky, Will and Sarah Farish, as good friends. "The Queen is rather formal," Bush recalled. "But I never found her reserve stand-offish. It's hard to explain really, but she is very, very easy to be with. Conversation comes easily."

Elizabeth II's arrival in Washington on Tuesday, May 14, came when gratitude for Britain's assistance in the Gulf War was running high. Bush rolled out an imposing welcome on the South Lawn with military bands, fife and drum corps, and twenty-one-gun salute fired by howitzers on the Ellipse. But after his effusive remarks welcoming her as "freedom's friend," neither he nor his aides remembered to pull out a step for the five-foot-four-inch Queen to use behind the podium intended for the six-foot-two-inch president. As she made her reply, the cluster of microphones covered most of her face, and television viewers could glimpse only her eyeglasses beneath a broad-brimmed purple and white striped hat.

At a small luncheon in the private quarters of the White House with Bush family members, the British and American ambassadors, and the Farishes, "we had a good laugh" about the hat incident, recalled Bush. "Her humor made it all seem fine." It was also the first time the sixty-five-year-old Queen met the president's eldest son, forty-four-year-old George W. Bush, the future forty-third president, who was then running the Texas Rangers baseball team. "The first thing I noticed was the twinkle in her eye, which I took as a sign of an easy spirit," he recalled. "Much to my delight, she certainly didn't give off the vibe that 'I'm better than you.' "

He told Elizabeth II that his cowboy boots were custom-made and usually were printed with "Texas Rangers." "Is that on those boots?" she inquired. "No, Ma'am," young Bush joked. "God Save the Queen." She was most amused and impishly asked, "Are you the black sheep in the family?" "I guess so," he said. "All families have them," the Queen replied helpfully. "Who's yours?" asked Bush. "Don't answer that!" interjected his mother. The Queen took the first lady's cue and escaped the conversation gracefully.

After lunch the president escorted the Queen onto the Truman Balcony to show her the view of the Tidal Basin and Jefferson Memorial. The White House was being repainted, and twenty layers had been stripped off the facade, laying bare pale stone and raw wood. Visible on a nearby pilaster were scorch marks dating from 1814 when British troops had set fire to the presidential mansion. "I teased her that it was her folks who had done this," the president recalled. "We talked about the fact that the burn marks were 'enshrined.' "

That night at a state dinner for 130 the president kept up the jocular tone by complimenting the Queen on her intrepid walking, which "left even the Secret Service panting. . . . I'm glad my fibrillating heart was not taxed by a competitive walk." The essence of their toasts reaffirmed the Anglo-American friendship recently strengthened by a wartime alliance. "No wonder I cannot feel a stranger here," said the Queen. "The British have never felt America to be a foreign land." She praised Bush for his conduct of the Gulf War "not with bombast and rhetoric but thoroughness and courage."

The Queen jammed eighteen engagements into her three days in the nation's capital, including the first address by a British monarch to a joint session of Congress. She opened her remarks by saying, "I do hope you can see me today from where you are," prompting a burst of laughter and standing ovation. She also watched her first Major League Baseball game between the Baltimore Orioles and Oakland Athletics. As with her other events, she had studied briefing papers on America's national pastime. After greeting gum-chewing players lined up in the dugout, she received a full tutorial from Bush, a former varsity first baseman at Yale, as they sat together in the owner's box.

The most diverting moment of her visit occurred in one of the city's downtrodden neighborhoods, where Elizabeth II visited a 210-pound African American great-grandmother, sixty-seven-year-old Alice Frazier. The purpose was to see Frazier's newly built home, which she had purchased under a private-public program for low-income first-time owners. As the Queen entered the house, Frazier vigorously shook her hand, said, "How are you doin'?," then wrapped her arms around her guest and gave her an exuberant bear hug. Elizabeth II smiled gamely over Frazier's shoulder as she stiffly leaned forward, arms held tightly at her waist until she was released. "It's the American way," Frazier said afterward. "I couldn't stop myself."

For their brief moments of respite, Elizabeth II and Philip retired to their five-room, two-bath suite in Blair House. They took their breakfast in the upstairs library, served by their page, but otherwise the Queen remained in her quarters while Philip busied himself by turning off lights, muttering, "What a waste, what a waste." One morning Benedicte Valentiner, the Blair House general manager, was standing in the front hallway when the Queen came downstairs before her first engagement. "She was standing stock still," Valentiner recalled. "It was as if she were looking inward, getting set. I admired that enormously. This was how she wound up her batteries. There was no chit chat, but standing absolutely still and waiting, resting in herself. It was a remarkable coping mechanism."

On Friday the Queen and her nearly fifty-strong entourage plus four and a half tons of luggage — hers always marked with yellow labels imprinted "The Queen" — left on a chartered British Airways Concorde for official visits to six U.S. cities and another three-day vacation in Kentucky. They landed in Miami and spent ten hours touring the city before boarding *Britannia* to host a black-tie dinner for fifty dignitaries including the Reagans and the Fords.

It was a particularly welcome reunion with the Reagans, who remained affectionate friends of Elizabeth II and Philip. Just a year earlier, Ronald Reagan had heard about the death of Burmese and had written the Queen a letter of condolence. Her grateful two-page reply reported that while walking her dogs she had last seen the twenty-eight-year-old mare "grazing happily" in her field at Windsor. The next morning, Burmese had died of a heart attack after "a long life for a horse."

Elizabeth II was in high spirits on *Britannia* as she caught up with the fortieth American president, who was complaining about the onerous costs of big government. "If you've got two-thirds of the fund paying for the bureaucrats," Reagan said, "and you give only one-third to the needy people, something's wrong there." "Well you see all the democracies are bankrupt now," the Queen replied emphatically, "because of the way that the services are being planned for people to grab." As he decried the incentives for bureaucrats to spend rather than cut costs, she agreed: "Obviously, yes . . . I think the next generation are going to have a very difficult time." Her spontaneous — and prescient — remarks not only reflected an affinity with the Reagan-Thatcher political philosophy, but she made them while a BBC crew was capturing their private conversation for a documentary about her.

After a quiet weekend on *Britannia* sailing through the Dry Tortugas in the Gulf of Mexico, the royal party disembarked for a three-hour visit to Tampa where the Queen conferred an honorary knighthood on General Norman Schwarzkopf, the commander of coalition forces in the Gulf War. They flew by Concorde to Austin for a sweep through the Lone Star State — an overnight stop in Austin, two hours in San Antonio, seven hours in Dallas, and two nights and a day in Houston. "I am an amazing woman!" she exclaimed during a black-tie dinner in her honor at Houston's Museum of Fine Arts. "Yesterday I made four major Texas cities! I woke up in one, went to bed in another, and visited two cities in between!" One of the highlights of her time in Houston was a guided tour of Mission Control at the Johnson Space Center. Once again she could indulge her fascination with astronauts, asking how they could see through the gold visors of their space suits and why food adhered to the plate rather than drifting away during space travel.

For the fourth time, Philip declined the offer to see the legendary Kentucky bluegrass and instead flew home at the end of their nine-day working marathon. When Elizabeth II landed in Lexington for the weekend, Sarah Farish greeted her with a kiss on the cheek — a display of affection seen frequently in private among friends but rarely in public.

Her hectic days in the United States were halcyon compared to what awaited her in London. The tabloids were working themselves into a speculative frenzy over the state of the Wales marriage as Charles and Diana approached their tenth wedding anniversary. Tabloid reporters knew that Charles had gone back to Camilla, and they were on the scent of Diana's affair with James Hewitt as well. Andrew Morton of *The Sun* was the most brazen, writing that Diana felt "humiliated that her husband prefers to spend so much time with Camilla rather than with her." Several weeks before the July 29 anniversary, the princess began secretly collaborating with Morton on a tell-all book through a series of interviews conducted by Dr. James Colthurst, a mutual friend who acted as an intermediary to give author and subject deniability.

Andrew and Fergie were misbehaving in their own way, living lavishly in a new fifty-room home called Sunninghill Park that the Queen had financed at an estimated cost of more than £3.5 million. Their second daughter, Princess Eugenie, was born in 1990. But motherhood couldn't match the allure of nightclub hopping in London and expensive vacations in Morocco, the Swiss Alps, and the south of France while Andrew was at sea. The tabloids took particular note of her getaways with thirty-five-year-old Texas millionaire Steve Wyatt.

The atmosphere of decadence and frivolity created by the Queen's children led the editor of *The Sunday Times,* Andrew Neil, to write a sharply critical editorial that resonated throughout the media. The perception took hold that not only were public funds being wasted on unproductive members of the royal family, but that it was time for the Queen to pay taxes on her substantial private income.

In fact, the wheels were already turning quietly, albeit slowly, inside Buckingham Palace for the monarch to contribute her fair share. A prime mover was Robert Fellowes, who succeeded William Heseltine as private secretary in 1990 at age forty-nine. An Old Etonian and former officer in the Scots Guards, Fellowes was the most uniquely connected of all the Queen's private secretaries. Not only was he a cousin of Fergie and brother-in-law of Diana, his father, Major Sir William "Billy" Fellowes, had been the Queen's Land Agent at Sandringham for twenty-eight years. "This is the first time I have got a private secretary I held in my arms as a baby," Elizabeth II said on making the appointment.

Fellowes was an eminently reliable counselor, having served the Queen in the private secretary's office since 1977. He was scrupulously honest, abstemious in his habits (he rode a bicycle to work and carried his father's battered leather briefcase), and completely loyal to the Queen. Yet behind his bespectacled reserve, he held surprisingly progressive views — to the extent that his friends in the men's clubs in St. James's regarded him as "a frightful pinko." Even before the press began kicking up dust about taxes, Fellowes and his deputy, Robin Janvrin, had begun a discussion on the subject.

The Queen balked at first. She was worried about "exposing too much of the inner workings of the monarchy to the public gaze," said one courtier. Of equal concern was her father's insistence that immunity from taxation was a principle worth defending. But both Queen Victoria and King Edward VII had paid taxes on their incomes, and only under the reign of George V had that obligation been reduced and eventually eliminated.

After some study, Elizabeth II's senior advisers concluded that an income tax would not be overly burdensome for the monarchy. When Fellowes presented their findings on her return to London from Sandringham early in 1992, he was prepared for stiff resistance, but she readily agreed to set up a working group of officials from the Palace and the government to prepare a detailed plan for her consideration. "She was not worried about how much she would pay," recalled a courtier. The most persuasive argument was its symbolic importance — that "doing it could do the monarchy a lot of good."

The Queen was set to mark her fortieth year on the throne in 1992, an occasion that normally would call for celebration. But she chose to commemorate the anniversary in a subdued way, at least in part because the lives of her children were so unsettled. Andrew and Fergie had told the Queen at Christmas that they were considering a separation, and she asked them to postpone their decision for six months. Less than a month later the *Daily Mail* published photographs of Fergie and Steve Wyatt on vacation in Morocco. An infuriated Andrew called in the lawyers, and the Queen braced herself for the inevitable separation.

In an effort to blunt the negative publicity and refocus attention on the purpose of the monarchy, Elizabeth II had allowed the BBC to follow her around in 1991 for a documentary intended to show how she went about her work. The resulting film, *E II R,* aired on her Accession Day, February 6, 1992. It turned out to be the high point of her worst year on the throne in the most tumultuous decade of her life.

The admiring portrait included a voice-over of her own reflections that she had recorded at the conclusion of the filming — not an interview per se, but an unusual personal statement similar to little noticed remarks she had made in previous films about racing and the Commonwealth. "Most people have a job and then they go home, and in this existence the job and the life go on together, because you can't really divide it up," she mused. "You have to sort of work out in your own mind the hard work, and then what you enjoy in retrospect from it." She said she was accustomed to living "very much by tradition and by continuity," adding rather forlornly, "I think this is what the younger members find difficult, the regimented side of it." Most pointedly, she observed that hers was a "job for life," putting to rest rumors floated by friends of the Prince of Wales that she would abdicate on her Accession Day.

The press greeted the film respectfully, praising its depiction of the Queen as a model of duty, sensibility, understatement, and wisdom. But even a well-crafted reminder of her worthy conduct couldn't compete with the multiplying distractions of her family's troubles, not to mention what one tabloid called "the dynamic sexiness of Princess Diana or the glorious naffness of Fergie."

Diana had reached a new and perilous stage in her relationship with the media — from realizing that she was a magnet for attention, to craving the attention, to seeking the attention, and now to using it as a weapon against Charles. In February, during their tour of India, she took aim with deadly accuracy by posing for photographers in "wistful solitude," as the *Daily Mail* put it, in front of the romantic Taj Mahal. Her unspoken message was that "the marriage was indeed on the rocks," wrote Charles's biographer Jonathan Dimbleby.

Andrew and Fergie officially announced their separation in March, the divorce of Anne and Mark Phillips became final on April 23, and Fergie moved out of Sunninghill Park in May. But no one was prepared for the seismic events in June — a festive season that would ordinarily have been filled with tributes to the Queen's milestone year.

On the 7th, *The Sunday Times* published the first of two excerpts from Andrew Morton's explosive book, *Diana: Her True Story.* It was filled with vivid details about Diana's severe emotional problems, but far more dangerous was its indictment of Charles as a cold and unfaithful husband (with chapter and verse about his affair with Camilla) and an uncaring father, and its depiction of the royal family as remote and strange. When asked several times by her brother-in-law Robert Fellowes if she had cooperated with the book, Diana lied and denied any role. Despite persistent rumors that she had been involved, Fellowes chose to take Diana at her word and sanctioned a condemnation by the Press Complaints Commission.

He was with the Queen on a state visit to Paris later that week when it became clear that Diana had deceived him. He immediately offered his resignation for embarrassing the press commission, but the Queen insisted that he remain in his job. Known for his integrity and lack of guile, Fellowes was astonished and angered by Diana's dishonest behavior, which severely damaged their relationship and distanced the princess from her sister

Jane Fellowes as well.

The Queen proceeded with her program in Paris even as she was fielding media queries behind closed doors from her forty-eight-year-old press secretary, Charles Anson. "Not once was there the slightest hint of annoyance," recalled Anson, an unflappable and urbane veteran of two decades in the diplomatic service. "The doors would open and the Queen would walk out into the public gaze as if she didn't have a care in the world." She was, in fact, distressed. In consultations with Fellowes and her other advisers, she emphasized that despite Diana's betrayal, she wanted to try to keep the marriage together, if only for the sake of William and Harry and to avoid any constitutional repercussions that might result for a divorced heir to the throne.

The second *Sunday Times* excerpt landed on June 14 when the Queen was back at Windsor, and the book came out two days later, on the first day of Royal Ascot. That Tuesday afternoon Charles and Diana met with his parents at the castle. It was an emotional encounter, according to Diana, who spoke about it with her butler, Paul Burrell, as well as Morton's collaborator, James Colthurst. The possibility of separation and divorce was discussed, but according to Burrell's account, the Queen and Philip told the couple that they should stay together and "learn to compromise, be less selfish, and try to work through their difficulties for the sake of the monarchy, their children, the country and its people."

Charles and his mother said little during the meeting, while Diana tearfully unloaded on her husband and Camilla, and Philip vented the family's distress about the Morton book. For the first time since the Morton crisis began, Diana lied directly to her in-laws and her husband, reiterating that she had not helped the author. "Mama despaired as she listened to me," Diana told Burrell. "All I seemed to be doing was relaying to her my anguish."

With the lines of communication now open, the Queen asked Diana and Charles to return for a second meeting the following day. Not only did Diana refuse to come, she packed up and left Windsor Castle, prompting Philip to write her a two-page letter expressing his disappointment while offering some suggestions for dealing with her troubled marriage. It was the first of five thoughtful letters he wrote from June through September "in a friendly attempt to resolve a number of family issues," each followed by a lengthy reply from Diana.

Acting in his role as head of the family, Philip tried to persuade his daughter-in-law to recognize her own faults as well as those of her husband, even as he praised her for the good work she had done. To promote compromise, he emphasized what she and Charles had in common, and he cited his own experience in giving up his independent career when his wife became Queen. In an effort to provide perspective, he wrote that being the wife of the heir to the throne "involved much more than simply being a hero with the British people."

Although Diana described her father-in-law's words as "stinging," "wounding," and "irate," Philip's private secretary, Brigadier Sir Miles Hunt-Davis, said later in sworn testimony that there was "not a single derogatory term within the correspondence." Diana's replies began "dearest Pa" and ended with "fondest love." She told him she was "particularly touched" by his guidance, thanked him for being "heartfelt and honest," and expressed admiration "for the marvelous way in which you have tried to come to terms with this intensely difficult family problem." When Philip wrote that he was eager to "do my utmost to help you and Charles to the best of my ability" while conceding "I have no talents as a marriage counselor!!!" she responded, "You are very modest about your marriage guidance skills and I disagree with you! This last letter of yours showed great understanding and tact." Implicit in Philip's entreaties was the Queen's support, which Diana acknowledged at one point by sending "much love to you both."

In the end, Philip's advice failed to move her, according to a friend who saw the letters, because "he never touched Diana's heart. He couldn't, because he argued in terms of duty and not love."

The entire royal family had swung over to Charles's side now that they understood the full scale of Diana's treachery. Before the Morton book, Charles had been unable to talk to his parents about his troubles. "I think it took a long time to accept that the faults were not more his than hers," said Patricia Brabourne. "The Queen could see through Diana's manipulation, but in personal situations it was difficult to really know the truth. There were two sides to the story and you had to work out how to put them together." Charles welcomed his parents' newfound sympathy; Philip even sent his son a long letter referring to his "saint-like fortitude."

Andrew, who among the siblings had been closest to Diana, moved into his older brother's corner, along with Anne, whose relationship with Diana had always been cool, and Edward, who had kept his sister-in-law at arm's length. The one family member with whom Diana had enjoyed the greatest kinship was Princess Margaret, who shared her love of ballet and quick sense of humor. Margaret had shown compassion for Diana's vulnerability, and Diana could relate to the sadness of Margaret's star-crossed love life. But Margaret viewed the Morton book as an attack on her sister, and never had another kind word for Diana.

The Queen confided her unhappiness to members of her close circle while trying "to keep a calm view," said one of her relatives. Over dinner with John and Patricia Brabourne, she said, "Can you imagine having two daughters-in-law like this?" "It was nonplussing," Patricia Brabourne recalled. "You don't know how to behave when someone is making such a mess. You want to help them mend, but how to do it?"

George Carey, who by then had been Archbishop of Canterbury for over a year, gathered intelligence from two ladies-in-waiting, Susan Hussey and Richenda Elton, the wife of the 2nd Baron Elton. "If I wanted help in understanding I would talk to them," he said. "I would never worry about the Queen's mood, which was constant. I would say to them, 'What is on her mind?' and they would tell me directly."

The archbishop conveyed to Elizabeth II his

sense that the estrangement between Charles and Diana was too deep for anyone to make a difference. "The personalities were so different," said Carey. "The Queen understood that. She could offer support and put them into her prayers." She was also concerned about the possibility of Charles marrying Camilla. "There was a moment when we were talking very candidly about divorce," said Carey. "I remember her sighing and saying, 'History is repeating itself.' I saw despair. What she was talking about was the Duke and Duchess of Windsor. She thought Charles was in danger of throwing everything out the window by rejecting Diana and forging another relationship. It was a very worrying moment, and my role was to reassure her."

The Queen was fortunate to have a prime minister with a placid temperament in those tense times. John Major relied on her as a dispassionate and confidential sounding board, and she leaned on him equally to work through complicated family matters. Their Tuesday audiences "became almost mutual support sessions," wrote royal biographer William Shawcross. "Major knew that the scandals were devastating for her." Years later Major said, "People don't realize quite how strong she is. I think the way she behaved in those years has saved the monarchy from far worse problems that otherwise they might have faced."

In July, the prime minister contacted George Carey to say that the couple would likely separate in the autumn and divorce was now a distinct possibility. The prime minister asked the archbishop to participate in "some preparatory work on constitutional matters" along with Lord Mackay of Clashfern, the Lord Chancellor; cabinet secretary Robin Butler; and Foreign Secretary Douglas Hurd. Carey also met separately with Diana and Charles. "It was my pastoral duty to assist them to conclude their marriage with grace and understanding," he wrote. In the process, he came to see "with some sorrow that Charles was more sinned against than sinning. There was a streak in Diana's psychological make-up that would not allow her to give in."

The annual Balmoral holiday brought no escape from the family turmoil, this time created by Fergie, who was there at Andrew's invitation. On Thursday, August 20, the *Daily Mirror* ran a page-one exposé headlined "FERGIE'S STOLEN KISSES." It featured ten pages of photographs showing the thirty-two-year-old Duchess of York lounging bare-breasted on the French Riviera with her two daughters and her "financial advisor," a thirty-seven-year-old American named John Bryan. In one shot, Bryan was shown kissing Fergie's toes, and in another they were embracing in front of two-year-old Eugenie.

At breakfast that morning, the royal family, their houseguests, and courtiers were confronted with the humiliating display. "It would be accurate to report that the porridge was getting cold," Fergie wrote in her memoir. "Eyes wide and mouths ajar, the adults were flipping through the *Daily Mirror* and the rest of the tabloids. . . . I had been exposed for what I truly was. Worthless. Unfit. A national disgrace." She immediately apologized to the Queen, who was "furious" over her daughter-in-law's stunningly poor judgment. "Her anger wounded me to the core, the more because I knew she was justified," Fergie recalled. After three more days of chilly stares from her estranged in-laws, the disgraced duchess returned to London. She did not see Balmoral again for sixteen years.

Philip never forgave Fergie for dishonoring the family. "I don't see her because I don't see much point," he told author Gyles Brandreth. But the Queen, in her typically tolerant fashion, remained on good terms. During the Christmas holidays at Sandringham, she even arranged for Fergie to stay at nearby Wood Farm so her daughters could join her after celebrating with the rest of the family. "The Queen had an affection for her daughter-in-law, who often got things wrong," said one of her senior advisers. "In a sense, though, Fergie was disarmingly guileless and you could see what she was doing up to a mile away." Diana was another matter — secretive and scheming — and so was more difficult to forgive.

Four days after the *Mirror* scoop, the rival *Sun* dropped its own bombshell headlined "MY LIFE IS TORTURE." The article quoted extensively from a surreptitiously recorded telephone conversation between Diana and thirty-three-year-old James Gilbey, an intimate friend who had also cooperated with the Morton book. The recording had been made at the end of December 1989 while Diana was staying at Sandringham. Their conversation was sprinkled with endearments (he repeatedly called her "Squidgy" and she referred to him as "darling") and sexual innuendo. She revealed her duplicity when she proposed various cover stories for their assignations. Most damning were her bitter comments about Charles and his relatives. "Bloody hell," she said, "after all I've done for this fucking family."

The Palace declined to comment, while Elizabeth II strove to maintain her equilibrium. After Margaret left Scotland for a holiday in Italy, she wrote to the Queen that she "personally found great comfort in being with you" at such a difficult time and said she hoped her sister could find some solace in the beauty of the Highlands.

Diana didn't flee Balmoral as Fergie had done. Instead, she turned, in the words of her private secretary Patrick Jephson, "alternately despairing, defiant, or lost in self-pity" and announced she would not accompany Charles on an official visit to Korea in November. Once again, the Queen intervened, this time with the help of Philip, and persuaded her to make the trip. It was a fig leaf at best. Back in London that autumn, both Charles and Diana consulted lawyers, but neither was able to take the difficult first step toward official separation.

The rush of sensational stories whipped up further attacks on the Queen for her exemption from taxes. Early in September, government officials began suggesting she might be ready to reverse the policy. That autumn the working group had nearly completed its review, with further details to be ironed out in the final proposal. David Airlie intended to present the plan to the Queen when he and his wife came to stay at Sandringham for a shooting weekend in early January — an approach he often used for difficult issues. That way, he could meet with Elizabeth II in a relaxed setting, "take time and talk round it and have Philip there," said a senior adviser. Once she gave the go-ahead, officials reasoned, the announcement could be made in the spring of 1993.

Fate intervened on Friday, November 20, the forty-fifth wedding anniversary of the Queen and Philip. She was going into an audience in the late morning when Andrew rang from Windsor to tell her that part of the castle was ablaze. A number of rooms were being rewired when a spotlight ignited a curtain in the Private Chapel, causing a fast-moving fire that spread from the Chester Tower to Brunswick Tower, destroying or damaging nine state rooms — including St. George's Hall, the State Dining Room, Crimson Drawing Room, Green Drawing Room, Grand Reception Room, and Octagon Dining Room — and more than one hundred others. Because of the ongoing restoration work, much of the artwork had been removed from the rooms hit hardest. Andrew joined scores of volunteers including members of the Household Cavalry and the Dean of Windsor to rescue nearly all the remaining paintings, furniture, and other valuables threatened by the fire.

The Queen arrived at around 3 P.M. "It was the most shaken I ever saw her," said one of her senior advisers. Windsor was the home that meant the most to Elizabeth II, and the conflagration seemed like cruel retribution for the misbehavior of her wayward family. Bundled in her macintosh, a rain hat, and wellies, her hands thrust into her pockets, she stood in the middle of the courtyard looking bereft as the fire roared, and the roof above the state apartments began to collapse. The image captured her ultimate solitude more tellingly than either of her Annigoni portraits.

She spent about an hour in the gray drizzle before going to the private apartments to help her staff move out precious possessions in case the fire spread further. After the firefighters brought the blaze under control, she and Andrew inspected the damage.

Though Philip was away at a conference in Argentina, he spoke with his wife at length on the phone. The Queen Mother invited her daughter to spend the weekend with her at Royal Lodge, an occasion for extended conversation and some soul searching. "It made all the difference to my sanity after that terrible day," the Queen wrote to her mother the following week.

Heritage Secretary Peter Brooke announced that the estimated £20 million to £40 million cost for restoration would be borne by the government. It was entirely appropriate because royal residences cannot be commercially insured. Moreover, the expenses of running and restoring Windsor Castle — including those under way when the fire broke out — were customarily paid by the government. But to the astonishment of both the Queen and John Major, the *Daily Mail* led an angry populist crusade against this plan, fueled by cumulative resentment of the royal family's younger generation. At a time of economic recession the cry went up for the Queen to pay for the restoration, and to start paying taxes as well.

In a matter of days, Palace officials scuttled their timetable and gained the Queen's approval of their tax plan. She and Prince Charles would voluntarily pay tax on their private income from the Duchy of Lancaster and the Duchy of Cornwall, respectively, starting in 1993. The Queen would also reimburse the government from her private funds for the £900,000 a year in Civil List payments to Andrew, Anne, Edward, and Margaret to cover their official expenses. To help finance the Windsor Castle restoration, she agreed to open the state rooms at Buckingham Palace to members of the public for an admission fee.

The impetus for the new Buckingham Palace policy came from Michael Peat, strongly supported by David Airlie, and had been debated for many months. At first the Queen felt it would be "lifting too much veil on the mystery of monarchy," said a courtier. "Being invited to the Palace was a special privilege and being inside was a special privilege. Would tours cheapen it?" On the other hand, "She could see that it was a good thing for a more open monarchy, providing access to the royal collection, which after all belongs to the nation," said another senior adviser. "Everyone could see the point of it, but the Queen was concerned about how to make it work without impinging on the working of the Palace and on security." The Prince of Wales advocated the idea, but the Queen Mother, who took a dim view of change, was strongly opposed, as she had been in 1977 when the Queen first began offering public tours of Sandringham House.

Elizabeth II ultimately embraced a compromise to admit the public to the Palace during the months when she was in residence at Balmoral. The Queen Mother accepted the new policies, although she insisted to Woodrow Wyatt that her daughter "let Major persuade her" to pay taxes, adding that Margaret Thatcher "never would have suggested that or allowed it." Major had actually been reluctant at first, and he was indignant about the uproar in the press over financing Windsor Castle, which he called a "very miserable and mealy-mouthed response. It just seemed so mean spirited and out of character for the British nation."

Yet opening the Palace became "one of the central features of innovation of the Queen's reign," said one of her senior advisers. It also proved a revenue bonanza, not only financing three quarters of the £37 million tab for the castle restoration (with the rest from cost savings measures at all the palaces) but helping to cover the ongoing costs of upkeep.

Four days after the fire, the Queen appeared at the Guildhall in the City of London for a luncheon hosted by the Lord Mayor to honor her forty years on the throne. She was suffering from a severe cold, with a temperature of 101 and a raw throat from the smoke she had inhaled. Wearing a dark green dress and matching hat with an upturned brim, she looked drawn, and her voice was raspy and thin as she began her remarks. Robert Fellowes had drafted the speech, but it bore the Queen's touchingly personal imprint. "Nineteen ninety-two is not a year on which I shall look back with undiluted pleasure," she said. "In the words of one of my more sympathetic correspondents, it has turned out to be an *'Annus Horribilis.'* "

She went on to mildly rebuke "some contemporary commentators" by saying that the judgment of history offered an opportunity for "moderation and compassion — even of wisdom — that is sometimes lacking in the reactions of those whose task it is in life to offer instant opinions on all things great and small." She acknowledged the value of criticism, noting that "no institution . . . should expect to be free from the scrutiny of those who give it their loyalty and support, not to mention those who don't" — an oblique but unmistakable reference to her republican critics. "Scrutiny . . . can be just as effective if it is made with a touch of gentleness, good humor and understanding," she added. "This sort of questioning can also act, and it should do so, as an effective engine for change."

The audience of dignitaries gave her a standing ovation. Even the *Daily Mail* praised her "intense and complex" remarks as an indication that she was open to some necessary reforms in the monarchy's conduct. *"Annus horribilis"* became one of the memorable catchphrases of the Queen's long reign, although its author, former assistant private secretary Sir Edward Ford, admitted that as a classical scholar he should have more precisely said *"annus horrendus,"* meaning a horrid year. *"Horribilis,"* he later explained, meant "a year capable of scaring you." In many respects that description was equally apt.

At the time of her Guildhall speech, the Queen knew that more bad news would soon be emerging about Charles and Diana. During their trip to Korea in early November, Diana had privately been "in a state of desperation, overcome by nausea and tears." She seemed to be sleepwalking through her public appearances, her expression either bored or anguished, and Charles looked intensely uncomfortable. The tabloids pounced on the visible signs of strain, calling the royal couple "The Glums."

Shortly after their return to England, Diana pushed Charles to the breaking point when she informed him at the last minute that she and their sons would not be attending his annual shooting party at Sandringham. At that moment, Charles decided that "he had no choice but to ask his wife for a legal separation." The day after his mother's *"annus horribilis"* speech, he met with Diana at Kensington Palace and told her of his decision.

On Wednesday, December 9, John Major stood before the House of Commons to announce that the heir to the throne and his wife would be separating. He hastened to add that they had "no plans to divorce and their constitutional positions are unaffected. . . . The succession to the Throne is unaffected by it . . . there is no reason why the Princess of Wales should not be crowned Queen in due course." Major's case was less than persuasive, since the notion of a bitterly estranged but still married royal couple going through a coronation together took the monarchy into hazardous territory. "With hindsight it was a mistake to have said that," said cabinet secretary Robin Butler. "It was seen as softening the blow, showing that she was not being thrown into outer darkness."

Some relief from the turmoil came the following Saturday when Princess Anne married Commander Timothy Laurence in Crathie Church at Balmoral on an overcast and frigid day. Anne wanted a religious wedding, but as a divorcée she could not be married in the Church of England, so she chose the more forgiving Church of Scotland. The arrangements were so hastily made that the Queen Mother had to leave her weekend house party at Royal Lodge in the morning and fly back to London to rejoin her guests for dinner.

The forty-two-year-old bride and her thirty-seven-year-old groom exchanged vows in a private half hour ceremony before a congregation of thirty guests that included her two children, three brothers, and her aunt as well as her parents and grandmother. Laurence wore his Royal Navy uniform, and Anne was dressed in a knee-length white suit. Instead of wearing a veil, she tucked a small bunch of white flowers in her hair. Her only attendant was her eleven-year-old daughter, Zara. Since Balmoral Castle was shuttered for the winter, the group repaired to Craigowan Lodge for a short reception after the ceremony. It was a far cry from the pageantry of Anne's first wedding two decades earlier.

In her Christmas message, the Queen revisited her time of troubles, mainly to express her gratitude for the "prayers, understanding and sympathy" that had given her and her family "great support and encouragement." Never one for self-pity, she sought to give her "sombre year" context by emphasizing those who put service to others above their difficult circumstances. She singled out Group Captain Leonard Cheshire, a former RAF pilot who had become an advocate for the disabled. His heroism and "supreme contempt for danger" during World War II had earned him the Victoria Cross, and the Queen had further honored him in 1981 with the Order of Merit.

She had seen him earlier in the year at an Order of Merit gathering not long before he died from a "long drawn-out terminal illness." The encounter "did as much as anything in 1992 to help me put my own worries into perspective," she said. "He made no reference to his own illness, but only to his hopes and plans to make life better for others." He had "put Christ's teaching to practical effect," and his "shining example" could "inspire in the rest of us a belief in our own capacity to help others." Drawing from Cheshire's inspiration, she pledged — yet again — her "commitment to your service in the coming years." With her characteristic resilience, she put the year behind her, turning to meet the "new challenges" of 1993 "with fresh hope" in her heart.

CHAPTER SEVENTEEN
TRAGEDY AND TRADITION

Another wave of tabloid headlines in mid-January abruptly dashed the Queen's hopes for a dignified new year. Both the *Daily Mirror* and *The Sun* published compromising transcripts of a telephone conversation between Charles and Camilla that had been secretly recorded in mysterious circumstances during December 1989, the same month as Diana's now infamous "Squidgy" tape. In much of the conversation, Camilla tried to boost Charles's spirits ("You're a clever old thing, an awfully good brain lurking there, isn't there?"). But attention focused on their inane sexual banter, especially Charles's juvenile wish to be reincarnated as a tampon so he could "live inside your trousers." The Palace declined comment, but the tapes were undeniably authentic and confirmed Diana's allegations about her husband's affair. In a poll published by the tabloid *Today,* 68 percent of the respondents thought Charles had tarnished his reputation, and 42 percent thought ten-year-old Prince William should be the next king.

The Queen briefly managed to shift attention from the scandal when David Airlie held a press conference in February "to explain to the media exactly why the Queen had decided to pay tax

Uncertain how the people would react, the Queen betrayed a trace of anxiety in her expression. As she and Philip walked toward the floral display, the crowd began clapping.

The Queen and Prince Philip surprise the crowds outside Buckingham Palace by walking among the thousands of floral tributes to Diana, Princess of Wales, September 1997. CAMERA PRESS LONDON

and the way in which it was going to be done." The Queen's senior advisers did not speak for the record, on the principle that "courtiers should be neither seen nor heard." But the Queen wanted her Lord Chamberlain to show her willingness not only to move with the times, but to answer all questions openly on her behalf.

Airlie intentionally held the briefing in the historic Queen Anne Room at St. James's Palace under the huge portraits of kings — a not so subtle reminder that he was representing centuries of tradition. He spelled out the details of taxes to be paid on Elizabeth II's private income as well as capital gains, after various deductions, including stipends paid to Prince Philip and the Queen Mother for their official expenses. The press pounced on the most important exclusion, asking why inheritance tax would not be paid on assets such as Sandringham, Balmoral, and the Duchy of Lancaster that were passed on to her successor.

"Is she not like us?" asked one reporter. "She isn't like you!" Airlie bantered, explaining that the sovereign must have private resources that shouldn't be dissipated through inheritance. Airlie's presentation helped mollify complaints about royal finances, although questions remained about the magnitude of the Queen's wealth and the level of expenses for luxuries such as *Britannia.*

Later that year, while the Queen was at Balmoral, Bobo MacDonald, her beloved former nursemaid and longtime dresser, died in her suite at Buckingham Palace at age eighty-nine. She had been semiretired from her duties for a number of years, but remained close to Elizabeth II, who had hired two nurses to provide round-the-clock care after Bobo's health began to fail. The Queen came down to London from Scotland to attend the funeral, which she arranged at the Chapel Royal in St. James's Palace. Joining her were other family members and staff, including Bobo's sister Ruby, also a longtime employee in the royal household. Bobo had served her "little lady" for sixty-seven years, and the Queen marked her passing with typical restraint.

None of the Queen's children stirred up further problems in 1993, although Diana proved to be a continuing distraction. On the one hand, she devoted herself to a range of charitable causes such as drug and alcohol abuse, hospice care, debilitating illnesses such as AIDS, and services for mentally handicapped children. But behind the scenes she was feeding information on her whereabouts to Richard Kay, the royal reporter at the *Daily Mail,* in an effort to upstage Charles as well as other members of the royal family. She was also cooperating with Morton on yet another book.

She had ended her affair with James Hewitt, her former riding instructor, in 1991 when he became the focus of press surveillance. "She simply stopped ringing and taking my calls," he said years later. She then became involved with a married art dealer named Oliver Hoare. It was a tempestuous relationship, something of an obsession for the princess, who pestered the Hoare household with anonymous telephone calls that prompted a police inquiry. The press got wind of the romance and began reporting sightings toward the end of 1993. Around the same time, Diana tearfully announced that she was retiring from public life and needed "time and space" to get her bearings and focus on her sons, blaming the intolerable pressure of "overwhelming" media attention. Both the Queen and Prince Philip had urged her to proceed quietly if she wished to disengage from her royal obligations and her charities. Even though she opted for public melodrama, they still invited her to join the family at Sandringham for Christmas. In an atmosphere thick with tension, the Queen got particularly cross when a pack of tabloid "snappers" showed up to take pictures of the princess as she arrived.

Elizabeth II was riding at Sandringham several weeks later when she suffered a rare accident as her horse tripped and fell. She had her hand on the horse's neck, which allowed her to give him a push when he was rolling over on his side. But he landed on her nevertheless, severely injuring a ligament in her left wrist. Her mount was Centennial, the stallion famously ridden twelve years earlier by Ronald Reagan, who sent her a solicitous letter. "I wasn't paying enough attention!" she wrote in her reply to the former president. She went on to describe the accident in detail and share her frustration at having her arm encased in plaster.

Still in a cast, she embarked on a three-week tour of six Caribbean countries and Bermuda in February and March. Visiting that part of the world gave her special satisfaction. "She has no regard for color," said longtime BBC correspondent Wesley Kerr, a native Jamaican raised by white foster parents in Britain. "Jamaica is her fourth-biggest realm. When she refers to herself as the Queen of

Jamaica she says it with utter conviction. In the Caribbean there is a closeness."

The Queen knew Kerr had a large extended family in Jamaica that numbered nineteen half siblings on his father's side. "Did you see your father, Mr. Kerr, and did he see me?" she asked during one gathering. On another day, Kerr marveled at her composure during a walkabout in Kingston. "A group of women were grabbing her and saying 'Nice! Nice!'" said Kerr. "She didn't flinch but her bodyguards almost grabbed her. She didn't mind the contact. She didn't want to be like a piece of china."

Three months later, Elizabeth II observed a meaningful event in her own life and that of her country when she marked the fiftieth anniversary of D-Day on June 6, 1994. She also had her first extended time with the forty-second American president, Bill Clinton, and his wife, Hillary. On the eve of the celebrations at the Normandy beaches, Elizabeth II and Philip hosted a banquet in Portsmouth and invited the Clintons to spend the night on *Britannia.*

Seated next to the sixty-eight-year-old Queen at dinner, the forty-seven-year-old president was taken with "the clever manner in which she discussed public issues, probing me for information and insights without venturing too far into expressing her own political views. . . . Her Majesty impressed me as someone who but for the circumstance of her birth, might have become a successful politician or diplomat. As it was, she had to be both, without quite seeming to be either." From her place between Prince Philip and John Major, Hillary watched as the Queen "nodded and laughed at Bill's stories." The next day on the beach at Arromanches, the Queen "was clearly happy as the veterans — her generation — marched past," wrote William Shawcross. "There was a rare catch in her voice as she and the old men reveled in their pride in each other. Her heir, Prince Charles, also there, was equally moved."

The evident harmony between mother and son was dispelled later that month when Charles shocked his parents by appearing in a television interview with journalist Jonathan Dimbleby. The prince had been cooperating with Dimbleby for two years on the TV program and a companion biography, ostensibly to highlight his charitable ventures on the twenty-fifth anniversary of his investiture as Prince of Wales. Of equal importance to Charles was the chance to counteract the negative portrait of his character that Diana had given to Morton and others in the press.

After the project was well under way, Charles briefed his parents on its general contours, and they advised him to avoid any frank discussion of private matters. He had other ideas. The two-and-a-half-hour documentary on June 29, 1994, covered a wide range of anodyne topics, but all were eclipsed by a brief exchange addressing the "damaging charge" that Charles had been "persistently unfaithful" to Diana "from the beginning" of the marriage. Charles said he had been "faithful and honorable" to his wife until their marriage "became irretrievably broken down, us both having tried." He didn't mention Camilla as other than "a friend for a very long time," but it was clear she was his mistress, and that their affair had resumed five years after Charles and Diana were married.

Charles genuinely believed his straightforward response would put to rest "the myth that he had never intended to make his marriage work." He gained public sympathy largely because of his demeanor, which was tormented and remorseful rather than callous. Still, his public admission of adultery embarrassed his mother and violated her code of discretion. It also raised the ante with Diana, provoking her to consider her own retaliatory television appearance.

Two months later the Queen had even greater cause for dismay when she learned that Charles had provided Dimbleby with diaries, letters, and official papers. John Major was concerned as well, telling Woodrow Wyatt that he might use the Official Secrets Act (a British law that shields state secrets) to prevent publication of anything from ministerial documents. Charles complied when the Queen asked for the return of the confidential papers, but their relationship was so strained that he didn't visit his parents at Balmoral, staying instead with the Queen Mother at Birkhall.

Elizabeth II was beginning a historic four-day trip to Russia in mid-October — the first visit by a British monarch since her great-grandfather King Edward VII met with Tsar Nicholas II in 1908 aboard a yacht in Russian waters — when an excerpt of the Dimbleby book appeared in *The Sunday Times*. The contents of the 620-page book drove a deeper wedge between Charles and his parents. He portrayed his mother as a remote figure during his unhappy childhood, and described his father as overbearing and insensitive. Elizabeth II and Philip were stung by these characterizations, according to their friends. She refrained from comment, although all three of Charles's siblings were indignant and rebuked him to his face. When asked about the controversy, the Queen Mother signaled her disdain with a wave of her hands and exclaimed, "That Jonathan Dimbleby!"

While the press focused on the Dimbleby revelations at home, the Queen carried on in Moscow and St. Petersburg. Her visit tapped dark historical currents. The Romanov rulers of the Russian empire and the British royal family had been close relatives. When the Bolsheviks murdered Tsar Nicholas II and his family in 1918, it was the Queen's grandfather King George V who sealed their fate by refusing to give political asylum in Britain to his Romanov first cousin. Paradoxically, the Soviet Communist Party had always shown the British royal family considerable respect. Still, the Queen could not in good conscience visit Russia until the Soviet Union collapsed in 1991.

The Russians were eager to receive her in 1994. "The monarchy is unshakeable," said the Russian newspaper *Izvestia*. "No matter what happens in the country, the British know that there is an institution that will survive any difficulty." Boris Yeltsin, the first democratically elected president of Russia, was as enraptured by the Queen as Khrushchev had been, confiding to her how difficult it was to promote democracy after so many years of totalitarian rule. When he tried to draw out her opinions, she referred him to her foreign secretary, Douglas Hurd.

At a performance of *Giselle* by the Bolshoi ballet, Elizabeth II wore her spectacular diamond and sapphire tiara, necklace, and bracelet and received a ten-minute standing ovation. "I thought the jewels were too much," she fretted afterward to David Thomas, the Crown Jeweler. "No, Ma'am, everyone loved it," said Thomas, who felt it was important to "fly the flag." Douglas Hurd said that "the Queen evoked a sort of nostalgia" among the Russians, who "were groping for their own past."

Back home, the new year got off to a rocky start when Martin Charteris offered an unintentionally candid glimpse of the Queen's scandal-plagued family when he gave an interview to *The Spectator* magazine. He later confessed he had been lulled by the "attractive" reporter and thought he was speaking on background — "very conceited of me, I know." He said out loud what many in royal circles had been saying sotto voce: that Sarah Ferguson, the Duchess of York, was "vulgar, vulgar, vulgar" and that Charles and Diana would "likely divorce," an outcome that would "clear the air" and would not prevent Charles from someday becoming king.

The retired courtier also put the Queen in perspective, describing her as a realist "far more than you would imagine." He said she was determined to "sit it out," knowing that the monarchy goes through "phases." When asked about the comments several months later, the Queen Mother assured her friend Woodrow Wyatt that she and the rest of the family weren't cross with Charteris in the least. "He's got such a lot of wisdom," she said.

Elizabeth II had "one of the outstanding experiences of my life" in March 1995 when she stepped foot on South African soil for the first time in nearly five decades. She was greeted as "Elizabeth" by Nelson Mandela, her host for a state visit. (He and Kenneth Kaunda of Zambia were the only world leaders to call her by her Christian name, without causing offense.) She had initially met him in 1991 during a conference of Commonwealth heads of government in Zimbabwe. As leader of the ANC, Mandela had been invited only as an observer, and South Africa still remained outside the Commonwealth. Lacking head of government status, he technically couldn't be included in the Queen's traditional banquet. But Robert Fellowes urged the Queen to make an exception. "Let's have him," she responded instantly. At the time, her decision was potentially controversial; just four years earlier Margaret Thatcher had branded Mandela a terrorist.

In April 1994, he was elected president of South Africa in the country's first democratic election open to all races. The Commonwealth welcomed the former rogue nation as a member soon afterward, and the Queen attended a special service in Westminster Abbey to mark the occasion that July. Her South Africa visit eight months later attracted large and enthusiastic crowds, notably in the black townships where people held up signs saying, "THANK YOU FOR COMING BACK." It was "a huge emotional charge for everybody," said Douglas Hurd.

Elizabeth II was less reassured about her standing in her own country, where she continued to be overshadowed by Diana's exploits — news reports about the princess's telephone stalking of Oliver Hoare, a book detailing her affair with James Hewitt, derided by the tabloid press as the "love rat," the Andrew Morton sequel that included gruesome specifics of Diana's self-mutilation, and headline-grabbing accounts of what she characterized as her "re-launched" life as a global charity worker — less than a year after her vow to retire.

With the approach of the fiftieth anniversary of the end of the Second World War in Europe on May 8, 1995, the Queen was uncharacteristically hesitant about what to do. "She was nervous about the fact that the monarchy was not doing well in the public's esteem," recalled Robert Salisbury, the Tory leader in the House of Lords who was in charge of organizing the celebration. "I wanted to reproduce the crowds at Buckingham Palace. She was afraid they would not turn out, so she wanted to have it in the Horse Guards Parade, where crowds would be smaller. I said, 'No, I can fill it.' I was extremely nervous. If I had called it wrong I would have felt an awful idiot."

The crowds ended up even larger than they had been in 1945. Looking across the sea of people from the balcony with her sister and ninety-four-year-old mother — the very trio who had stood in the same spot with King George VI fifty years earlier — she wore the stony-faced expression she used to suppress strong feelings. "The Queen's eyes were brimming," said one of her ladies-in-waiting. "But she was absolutely determined that nobody should see when they got back inside. She quickly took a large gin and tonic and knocked it back."

As was so often the case in those years, the benefits of the touching royal tableau were only temporary. On November 14 — quite intentionally, the forty-seventh birthday of Prince Charles — Diana informed officials at Buckingham Palace that she would be appearing shortly on the BBC's respected public affairs program *Panorama.* Unbeknownst even to her private secretary or press secretary, she had already taped the fifty-five-minute interview in her apartment at Kensington Palace with Martin Bashir, a little known reporter and producer for the network.

The program aired on November 20, the forty-eighth wedding anniversary of Elizabeth II and Philip. It was Diana's ultimate revenge against her estranged husband. No longer shielded by an intermediary, she had been furnished the questions in advance and had rehearsed the answers. Barbara Walters, who later talked to Diana about the interview, called it a "superb performance." The princess spoke unflinchingly about her emotional torment, her romance with Hewitt, and her shattered marriage, and she portrayed the royal family as insensitive to her problems, preferring to dismiss her as "unstable."

She reserved her most withering fire for Charles, whose fitness for the throne she undermined by saying he would find the role of king "suffocating." The "top job," she said, "would bring enormous limitations to him, and I don't know whether he could adapt to that." As for his affair with Camilla,

534

Diana memorably said, "There were three of us in this marriage, so it was a bit crowded." She conveniently ignored the fact that during the time referred to — from 1986 onward — there were in fact four in the marriage, including James Hewitt. The other line that resonated with the fifteen million TV viewers in Britain and millions more overseas was her wish to be "a queen of people's hearts."

Her close friend Rosa Monckton later wrote that the performance was "Diana at her worst." Charles's friend Nicholas Soames said the interview showed "advanced stages of paranoia." The damage, both self-inflicted and to the royal family, was far greater than that caused by the Morton book, although a Gallup survey registered an initial positive response for the princess, with 77 percent saying she had a right to present her side of the story. More worrying for the Queen, 46 percent of respondents believed Charles was unfit to be king, an increase of 13 percent in two years. Over lunch in Mayfair, Martin Charteris told Woodrow Wyatt that Diana was "very dangerous" as well as "unbalanced," and that a divorce was now "inescapable."

The Queen did not watch Diana's interview. Charles Anson, her press secretary, made it clear to the media on her authority that she "never watched *Panorama,*" an unusual expression of her personal preference that "took the BBC aback," said one courtier. Her advisers did tune in and briefed her on the salient points. After consulting further with John Major and George Carey, she informed the prime minister on December 12 that she would write to Charles and Diana individually asking them to agree to an "early divorce . . . in the best interests of the country." Since they had been officially separated for more than two years, Charles could file for an uncontested divorce if Diana concurred. The Queen signed her precisely phrased instructions — in effect, a royal command — to her daughter-in-law, "with love from Mama."

The biggest controversy over the divorce had nothing to do with money or child custody or perquisites, but with Diana's title. In a meeting with the Queen at Buckingham Palace on February 15, 1996, attended by deputy private secretary Robin Janvrin, who took notes, Diana volunteered to give up "Her Royal Highness." Elizabeth II remained predictably noncommittal, but she urged Diana to sit down with Charles for a detailed discussion of all the issues. Afterward, Diana told Paul Burrell that her mother-in-law had shown her "sensitivity and kindness."

When Charles and Diana finally met at St. James's Palace on February 28, Diana agreed to a divorce. They would share the upbringing of their two sons, and she would be known simply as Diana, Princess of Wales, relinquishing "Her Royal Highness." But Diana again overreached by immediately revealing the confidential details of the discussion to the press, along with her own particularly damaging spin (transmitted to her ally at the *Daily Mail,* Richard Kay) that the Queen and Charles had pressured her to drop her royal title. That assertion was false, and Elizabeth II had the notes from her meeting with the princess to prove it. She authorized Charles Anson to make an unusually direct statement: "The decision to drop the title is the Princess's and the Princess's alone. It is wrong that the Queen or the Prince asked her. I am saying categorically that is not true. The Palace does not say something specific on a point like this unless we are absolutely sure of the facts."

As Charles and Diana's complicated negotiations proceeded, Andrew and Fergie's divorce became final on May 30, a decade after their wedding. Along the lines of Diana's agreement, Fergie gave up "Her Royal Highness" and was called Sarah, Duchess of York. But unlike the Waleses, the Yorks parted amicably despite Fergie's frequent misbehavior. In bringing up their daughters, they described themselves as "co-parents," and Fergie said they were in fact the "happiest unmarried couple."

Charles's generous divorce settlement for Diana was disclosed that summer: a £17 million lump sum along with more than £385,000 annually for Diana's office expenses. She would live and work out of Kensington Palace, and Charles would do the same at St. James's Palace. She would conduct her charity activities separately from the royal family, but she would need to secure permission from the Queen as well as the Foreign Office for any overseas travel in the line of work. The state apartments at St. James's Palace would be available to her for entertaining, and she could use royal transport for her official engagements. Diana tried at the last minute to hang on to her "HRH," but she finally yielded when fourteen-year-old William told her it didn't matter to him. To bolster her status as a semiroyal, the Palace took pains to say that she would still be "regarded as a member of the royal family." Whenever she attended state or national occasions she would rank as an "HRH."

The Queen found blessed relief from her family travails when Nelson Mandela arrived for a triumphant four-day state visit on Tuesday, July 9. Tens of thousands of spectators — the biggest crowd for a foreign visitor in decades — turned out to cheer the African leader as he and Elizabeth II were driven by carriage to Buckingham Palace after the ceremonial welcome on Horse Guards Parade. At the state banquet that evening, the seventy-year-old monarch paid tribute to the seventy-seven-year-old South African leader as the savior of a country that "has a special place in my heart and in the hearts of the British people." Her praise for his wisdom and understanding after suffering twenty-seven years in prison was borne out three days later when he met for twenty minutes with his former adversary, Margaret Thatcher — in the spirit, he said, of "let bygones be bygones."

Instead of the traditional "return" dinner at South Africa House on Thursday night, Mandela chose to bend protocol by hosting a "Two Nations" concert at Royal Albert Hall. Prince Charles helped organize the event starring Phil Collins, Tony Bennett, and Quincy Jones along with Hugh Masekela and other prominent South African musicians. Mandela, who was well known for dancing to the toe-tapping rhythms of South African music, sat with the Queen, Philip, Charles, and other members of the royal family in the royal box. At intermission he took aside Robin Renwick (Baron Renwick of

Clifton), who had served as British ambassador to South Africa. "Should I dance?" Mandela asked. "By all means," said Renwick. "What about the Queen?" said Mandela. "You should do it," replied Renwick. "Don't worry."

When the all-male a cappella singing group Ladysmith Black Mambazo began performing, Mandela, dressed in a black silk shirt, stood up in the royal box and started to dance. Philip tentatively rose to join him, followed by Charles, swaying and clapping along with the music. "To everyone's surprise," said Robin Renwick, "the Queen stood up and did a little side by side movement too." As the *Daily Telegraph* noted the next day, Elizabeth II "has seldom been known to boogie in public."

On August 28, the Wales divorce became final, to the enormous relief of the royal family. But they had not anticipated that Diana had every intention of staying in the limelight. She forged a strategic new alliance with Tony Blair, leader of the Labour Party and candidate for the general election to be held in 1997. Early in the new year they met quietly at several private dinner parties where the dynamic young politician took Diana's measure. He was mesmerized by her beauty and charisma, and she offered him advice on photo opportunities for his political campaign, speaking in "fairly calculating terms of how she had 'gone for the caring angle.' "

Blair welcomed her "radical combination of royalty and normality . . . a royal who seemed at ease, human, and most of all, willing to engage with people on an equal basis." At the same time he could see that she was "an unpredictable meteor" who had entered the royal family's "predictable and highly regulated ecosystem." Although she didn't specify her political inclinations, he sensed her "perfect fit" with his plans for the Labour Party "in temperament and time, in the mood she engendered."

Just as Diana created a less formal royal style, Blair flouted political convention by seeking a "Third Way" that defied Labour orthodoxy. Fundamentally, they were both accomplished actors. "We were both in our ways manipulative people," he later wrote, "perceiving quickly the emotions of others and able instinctively to play with them." That chameleon quality served Blair well as he fashioned a campaign to defeat John Major's steady but dull leadership. Blair's "New Labour" agenda promised youthful vigor and modernization that incorporated market-based Conservative ideas rather than diehard socialism. On May 1, 1997, Labour won in a landslide, and Blair, who took office four days before his forty-fourth birthday, became the first prime minister to be born after the Queen's accession.

Blair was the product of an upwardly mobile Scottish family. His father, Leo's, adoptive parents came from the Glasgow shipyards, and his maternal grandfather had been a butcher. Leo worked his way through law school and became a barrister and law lecturer at Durham University in England before turning to Conservative politics — a career cut short by a crippling stroke.

He insisted on the best private education for Tony, sending him to Fettes College, a boarding school in Edinburgh known as the Eton of Scotland. Blair studied law at Oxford and did a stint as a barrister in London where he met Cherie Booth, an ambitious and skilled lawyer from Liverpool who became his wife. He took up Labour politics and won a seat in Parliament in 1983, casting himself as a reformer. Boyishly handsome with a gleaming smile — the Queen Mother slyly observed that he was "all teeth and no bite" — Blair attracted attention with his glib and earnest rhetoric, and he gathered support with his engaging personality. "He had the nicest manners of any prime minister I have come across, in Britain or anywhere else," wrote conservative historian Paul Johnson.

In 1994, after the death of Labour leader John Smith, Blair revealed his toughness when he won election as leader of the opposition, cutting off his friend and colleague Gordon Brown, who had been lining up support for his own run. Brown accused Blair of "betrayal," and Blair mollified him with an "understanding" that he would eventually make way for Brown to succeed him. The residue of that deal was a bitter animosity between the two politicians that lasted throughout the years they worked together.

Blair made a memorable appearance at Buckingham Palace for "kissing hands" on May 2, 1997. After receiving his instructions from the Queen's equerry, he tripped on the edge of the carpet and fell upon the Queen's outstretched hand he was supposed to brush with his lips. Scarcely missing a beat, Elizabeth II told him that he was her tenth prime minister. "The first was Winston," she said. "That was before you were born." Their conversation turned up with some dramatic embellishment in the film *The Queen,* which also accurately conveyed Blair's extreme nervousness. "I got a sense of my relative seniority, or lack of it, in the broad sweep of history," Blair recalled in a 2002 interview. "But it was immediately apparent, even at that meeting . . . she was someone who took every care to try to make sure that you were put at ease."

After some twenty minutes of "general guff" about Labour's legislative plans, a Palace aide brought in Cherie, a militant republican often derided for her failure to give the monarch adequate respect. "I can't remember not curtsying," Cherie vaguely recalled, "so I probably did." The two women discussed the practical logistics of moving a family — the Blairs had three children at the time — into 10 Downing Street, the Queen "generally clucking sympathetically." Elizabeth II "kept the conversation going for just the right length of time," the prime minister recalled, until "by an ever so slight gesture, she ended it and saw us out."

Elizabeth II had quietly celebrated her seventy-first birthday eleven days earlier at Windsor Castle. She went riding, entertained her ninety-six-year-old "mama" at lunch, and contemplated the beauty of the garden at Frogmore in the "hot spring sunshine," as she described the day to Nancy Reagan.

At an age when most in her generation had settled into comfortable retirement and narrowing views, the Queen's unique position required her to broaden her perspective to keep abreast of changes in the culture. On March 6, she had switched on the first royal website, containing 150 pages of information on the monarchy. She remarked that the Internet "opens the door to a huge range of knowledge which has no national boundaries." Still, in other respects, as Blair observed, "there's a bit of her that is very strongly unchanging" — mainly regarding traditions that preserve "the mystery and the majesty of the monarchy."

One of the new prime minister's ticklish early decisions had to do with the forty-three-year-old yacht *Britannia*. In a cost-cutting measure, the Major government had decided three years earlier to end the royal yacht's service in 1997. The Tories had been reluctant to finance the necessary £11 million upgrading as well as escalating yearly maintenance costs. "A lot of people thought *Britannia* should be kept," said a former senior Palace official. "A lot of people in the street thought it was important. It was a wonderful symbol of the monarchy." Some argued that the yacht helped promote British trade around the world with its "Sea Days" for businessmen that brought some £3 billion to the Treasury from 1991 to 1995. But in the end, *Britannia* had come to symbolize politically incorrect extravagance and privilege at public expense, and the Queen told the government she was prepared to give it up.

Despite the political sensitivity, the Major government had nevertheless considered building a new state-of-the-art royal yacht that would be less expensive to operate, and the Ministry of Defence developed plans with an estimated cost of £80 million. When Blair attended the ceremonial handover of Hong Kong's sovereignty to the People's Republic of China on June 30, 1997, he was impressed with the value of having a floating embodiment of Britain. After the Union Jack was lowered at midnight, Blair watched the floodlit yacht dramatically sail out of Hong Kong harbor. "What an asset," he said. But his government soon scuttled any successor to *Britannia* — a decision that seemed small-minded compared to Blair's own misguided construction project, the £750 million Millennium Dome, which came to symbolize pointless big-government excess.

That August the royal family took *Britannia* on its final Western Isles cruise on their way to Balmoral, a sentimental journey with the usual stop at the Castle of Mey. "Lilibet" and "Philip" put their signatures in the Queen Mother's guest book commemorating *Britannia* Day for the last time, followed by Andrew and his two daughters; Anne and her second husband, Tim Laurence, with her son and daughter; Edward and his girlfriend Sophie Rhys-Jones; Margaret's daughter, Sarah, and Sarah's husband, Daniel Chatto; as well as Margaret's son, David Linley, and his wife, Serena. The traditional luncheon was "somewhat melancholy," but they all rose to the occasion with their usual ship-to-shore exchange of doggerel as *Britannia,* accompanied by two destroyers, steamed past the coast twice before disappearing over the horizon.

The Queen Mother's verse was written by her friend Ted Hughes, Britain's poet laureate, and said, in part:

With all our memories of you, so happy and dear
Whichever course your captain takes,
You steer into this haven of all our hearts, and here
You shall be anchored forever.

The Queen's sixteen-line reply from *Britannia* to the Queen Mother's "castellated pad" marveled:

Oh what a heavenly day, happy glorious and gay
Delicious food from the land
Peas shelled by majestic hand
Fruit, ice cream from foreign lands
Was it India or Pakistan?

As the Queen, her family, and friends fell into the leisurely pace of Balmoral life, they were confronted each morning with a display of newspapers on the drawing room table carrying stories of Diana's escapades. Since the divorce, the princess had presented a brave face to the world, taking on important new causes such as banning the use of land mines. But her emotional life was more turbulent than ever as she attached herself to men who were increasingly unsuitable. She doted on William and Harry and tried to expose them to everyday life as much as possible, giving them, as she said in her *Panorama* interview, "an understanding of people's emotions, people's insecurities, people's distress, and people's hopes and dreams." Yet she also began to burden her sons — William in particular — with too much information about her boyfriends and her problems.

She hit a new low in mid-July when she took up with Dodi Fayed, the son of Egyptian tycoon Mohamed Fayed, who had been repeatedly denied British citizenship by the U.K. government. Mohamed Fayed had befriended Diana as a generous benefactor of several of her charities. He appealed to her, according to Andrew Neil, a sometime consultant for Fayed, "by cultivating the idea that both were outsiders and had the same enemies."

Diana met Dodi while she and her sons were staying at the ten-acre Fayed estate in Saint-Tropez. At age forty-two, Dodi was a classic case of arrested development: spoiled, ill-educated, unemployed, rootless, and irresponsible, with a taste for cocaine and fast cars. He showered Diana with extravagant gifts, including an $11,000 gold Cartier Panther watch, and sybaritic trips on his father's plane and yachts. From the moment the story of their romance broke on August 7, the tabloids covered the couple's every move with suggestive photographs and lurid prose. William and Harry, who were at Balmoral with their father, mistrusted Dodi, and they were embarrassed by their mother's exhibitionistic behavior.

At around 1 A.M. on Sunday, August 31, a call came through to Robin Janvrin at Craigowan Lodge from the British embassy in Paris with a chilling message: Diana and Dodi had been in a horrific car crash in the tunnel underneath the Place d'Alma. Janvrin immediately hustled to Balmoral Castle for urgent conferences with the Queen, Philip, and Charles. Shortly after 4 A.M. they received word that Diana was dead at age thirty-six, along with her lover and the driver of the car.

They decided to let William and Harry sleep, and the Queen wrote a note to be shown to her mother when she awakened. At 7:15 A.M. Charles told his sons, then aged fifteen and twelve, about the tragedy. From that moment on, Elizabeth II alternated between consoling her two grandsons and working with her senior advisers to make arrangements for honoring their mother.

Robin Janvrin stayed with the Queen at Balmoral while her other courtiers set up a makeshift command center at Buckingham Palace in the Chinese Dining Room overlooking the Victoria Memorial. David Airlie called off his trip to Italy, Lieutenant Colonel Malcolm Ross, the comptroller of the Lord Chamberlain's office, flew in from Scotland, and Robert Fellowes came down from Norfolk. At the same time, Tony Blair and his top aides began managing what they perceived as a "global event like no other" and a fast-moving crisis for the monarchy.

By the time Blair spoke with Elizabeth II that morning, the Palace had issued a terse statement: "The Queen and Prince of Wales are deeply shocked and distressed by this terrible news." She told the prime minister she had no plans to say anything further about the deaths. Blair found her to be "philosophical, anxious for the boys, but also professional and practical. She grasped the enormity of the event, but in her own way, she was not going to be pushed around by it." When Blair told her he planned to make a comment before church, she raised no objection. Reading from some scribbles on the back of an envelope, he indelibly called Diana "the People's Princess," described how he felt the public's pain, alluded to "how difficult things were for her from time to time," and applauded those who "kept faith" with the deceased princess.

His words were meant to be placatory, and in some respects they were, simply by filling a vacuum and crystallizing inchoate feelings of affection and loss. But the royal family thought that Blair's choice of "People's Princess" helped stir up rather than pacify public feeling. George Carey worried that the description might "encourage the temptation of some to make her an icon to set against the royal family. Those fears were to be realized that week."

The Queen and her family attended the regular Sunday service at Crathie. No mention of Diana was made in the prayers, which is customary in the Church of Scotland, where the ministers "don't pray for the souls of the departed, because God has discharged them," said a former senior official in the church who has often preached at Balmoral. But the press chose to portray the omission as an insult to Diana's memory, and criticized the Queen for taking William and Harry to church only hours after their mother's death. "They handled it like ostriches," said Jennie Bond of the BBC. In fact, the princes wanted the comfort of religion at that moment. By one account, William said he wished to "talk to Mummy." Everyone including the boys behaved as the royal family always does, with stiff stoicism in the face of emotional pain, which prompted still more criticism for their seeming insensitivity.

At that point, the family withdrew from the public gaze. The Queen's intentions were pure from the outset — the kind of "unstoppable mothering" she had shown Timothy Knatchbull after the Mountbatten bombing in 1979. She believed William and Harry should be kept in the Highlands for as long as possible, surrounded by those who loved them. Like their father, the boys had been imbued with an enjoyment of the countryside. The Queen made certain the princes could stalk and fish with their cousin Peter Phillips, and gather with the family on the hills for barbecues. "To take them away to have nothing to do in Buckingham Palace would have been horrible," said Margaret Rhodes.

The Queen secured a Royal Air Force plane to fly Prince Charles, along with Diana's sisters, Sarah and Jane, to Paris to bring back the princess's body. Elizabeth II also asked that Blair meet the plane at RAF Northolt airport on Sunday afternoon. In recognition of the Queen's wish that the late princess be treated like a member of the royal family, Diana's coffin was draped with her own Royal Standard, an adaptation of the sovereign's heraldic banner in red, gold, and blue.

Elizabeth II initially yielded to the wish of the Spencer family that Diana's funeral be private, but after conferences with her advisers, she recognized the need to do something akin to a royal ceremonial funeral at Westminster Abbey — although not a full-blown state funeral. She was helped by Robert Fellowes, who brought his wife, Jane, and the rest of the Spencers around. The funeral plans for members of the royal family are not only exhaustively planned in advance, they have code names: London Bridge for the Queen, Tay Bridge for the Queen Mother, Forth Bridge for Prince Philip. But there were no plans in place for Diana's funeral because she was no longer technically a member of the royal family. "We can't look at the files," David Airlie told his colleagues. "We have to do it *de novo*."

Working throughout Sunday and long into the night, the courtiers at Buckingham Palace planned a funeral for the following Saturday that combined elements of the traditional and the modern: Diana's coffin on a horse-drawn gun carriage (primarily so it could be seen better than in a hearse) with twelve pallbearers from the Welsh Guards, followed by five hundred workers from Diana's charities instead of the standard military procession, which she would have disliked. "We wanted the people who had benefited from her charities, not the chairmen and trustees," said David Airlie. "It was also important to bring a cross-section of the public not normally invited to the Abbey — the people Diana associated with." Rather than a lying-in-state at Westminster Hall, the courtiers came up with condolence books for the public to sign at Kensington Palace and St. James's Palace, where Diana's body would rest privately on a catafalque in the Chapel Royal until the funeral.

Airlie phoned Janvrin at Balmoral early Monday morning to relay the outlined plan. By 9 A.M. the Queen had given her approval. "She was very happy with the charity workers," recalled Ross. It would be "a unique funeral for a unique person," the Palace announced.

The Lord Chamberlain supervised a series of meetings with all interested parties including the police and military as well as several of Blair's key operatives specifically invited by Airlie. They hammered out the details for what the press was now calling the "people's funeral," including such unconventional touches as a solo by Elton John and a reading by the prime minister, while excluding such traditional fanfare as trumpeters and drums. By Tuesday afternoon they had written everything down and transmitted it to Balmoral so the Queen could "see the totality." Again she approved their proposals readily and without discussion. "She is much better with paper, especially for something long and complicated," said Ross. "She speed reads. She is very quick with paper."

Contrary to popular mythology about hidebound courtiers, the Queen's men showed flexibility and ingenuity that week. Airlie had been at the vanguard of modernizing Buckingham Palace operations for more than a decade. Robert Fellowes proved surprisingly "shrewd and savvy," in Tony Blair's view. Robin Janvrin was "completely au fait with where it was all heading," Blair recalled. Even Alastair Campbell, the prime minister's antimonarchist press spokesman, remarked that the courtiers "encouraged creative thinking and even risk-taking." The Queen trusted them and responded decisively to such suggestions as doubling the route of the funeral procession to give greater access to the crowds and putting giant video screens in Hyde Park to televise the funeral.

But she dug in her heels over what she considered unreasonable demands from the press and public that violated deeply embedded traditions as well as her family's wish to deal with the tragedy privately. By Tuesday it was clear that Diana's death had triggered an unprecedented display of mass grieving by mourners who poured into London, by one estimate "at a rate of 6,000 per hour." They heaped flowers, stuffed animals, signs, balloons, condolence notes, and other tributes along the railings of Buckingham Palace and Kensington Palace, and they camped out in the parks, hugging and weeping as if for a close relative or intimate friend. By Wednesday night some three quarters of a million people had stood in line, some for more than ten hours, to sign the condolence books that multiplied rapidly from four to thirty-four in two days. It seemed as if Diana's own displays of raw emotion — leading "from the heart not the head," as she said in her *Panorama* interview — had prompted the citizenry to abandon the dignified restraint they had shown after the deaths of King George VI and Winston Churchill.

The crowds at first had vented against the tabloids, inflamed by Diana's brother, Charles, Earl Spencer, who said hours after his sister's death, "I always believed the press would kill her in the end." Outside Kensington Palace on Sunday, mourners had shouted at a group of reporters, "Happy now?" But by midweek, the anger turned against the Queen for remaining sequestered in the Highlands and failing to acknowledge the pain felt by her subjects in London. "If only the royals dared weep with the people," said *The Independent* in a critical editorial on Wednesday. "The media were circling, looking to blame someone other than themselves," said one of Elizabeth II's top advisers. "They needed to direct it at the other target," Blair observed. "And to be fair, they were releasing genuine public feeling." As a symbol of the Queen's apparent indifference, the press focused on the empty flagpole above Buckingham Palace and demanded that a flag be flown at half-staff to honor Diana.

By centuries of custom, the only flag to fly at the Palace was the Queen's Royal Standard, and only while she was in residence. It could never be flown at half-staff because once a monarch dies, the heir immediately takes the throne in an unbroken chain of sovereignty. But the crowds had no patience for such distinctions, and their mood verged close to mutinous. "I think the thing that impressed me most was the silence, which I found worrying," said David Airlie, who took several walks outside the Palace.

On Wednesday the Queen's London advisers suggested that she put aside tradition and fly the Union Jack at half-staff, but she was unyielding, as was Philip. "Robin had to describe the feeling in London," said Malcolm Ross. "It was a torturous process because she felt so strongly. Robin said he metaphorically had blood pouring down his face because she had scratched his face metaphorically. He had to come back to her again and again."

Later that day a Palace spokesman tried to defuse the growing pressure by saying that "all the royal family . . . are taking strength from the overwhelming support of the public who are sharing their tremendous sense of loss and grief." Tony Blair publicly defended the Queen as well, although he knew, he later said, that "the fact that I was speaking only served to emphasize the fact that she wasn't." Reluctant to confront Elizabeth II himself and be "as blunt as I needed to be" with "very direct advice," Blair called Charles, who said he would speak to his mother. Charles told Blair that he agreed the Queen could no longer "hide away" and needed to "come to London to respond to the public outpouring."

There is a Brigadoon quality at Balmoral that makes it difficult to appreciate the emotional temperature 550 miles away. But the Queen had been willing on a number of occasions to fly south when duty called — to accept Macmillan's resignation when he was hospitalized, to have lunch with Richard Nixon at Chequers, to greet her son Andrew at Portsmouth after the Falklands campaign, and to attend Bobo MacDonald's funeral. Her unwillingness this time was impelled by a desire to shield her grandsons from further upset. For the Queen it was an ironic turnabout. After being criticized so often for putting duty over family, she found herself being pilloried for doing the reverse. "If she had come down, there would have been adverse press about the heartless grandmother leaving her grandchildren in a time of grief," said Dickie Arbiter, a former press spokesman for the Queen.

The tabloids on Thursday morning turned up the heat with headlines screaming "SHOW US YOU CARE" (*The Daily Express*); "WHERE IS OUR QUEEN? WHERE IS HER FLAG?" (*The Sun*); and "YOUR PEOPLE ARE SUFFERING: SPEAK TO US, MA'AM" (*The Daily Mirror*). A survey by MORI (Market & Opinion Research International) found that 25 percent of the public felt the monarchy should be replaced, a significant rise from the 19 percent average dating back to 1969. Alastair Campbell called Fellowes and Janvrin to report that the mood on the street had become "dangerous and unpleasant." "Robin Janvrin told me the Queen was composed but distressed by the way the nation assumed she did not care," said George Carey. In a conference call that morning with the London team, the Queen grasped the gravity of the situation — not only that her absence was endangering the monarchy itself, but that she needed to fulfill her role as the nation's leader in a time of crisis.

The vehemence of the press played a part in her decision, but more important was the persuasiveness of her advisers. Rather than traveling to London overnight by train for arrival shortly before the 11 A.M. funeral on Saturday, she and the family would fly down on Friday. That evening, she would make a televised speech, and she would pay her respects at Diana's coffin in the Chapel Royal. Once she left Buckingham Palace on Saturday for the funeral, the Royal Standard would be lowered, and for the first time a Union Jack would rise on the flagpole, to remain at half-staff in tribute to Diana.

The Queen also asked Andrew and Edward to visit Diana's coffin on Thursday afternoon and then walk among the crowds on the Mall back to Buckingham Palace — the family's first overt gesture of public sympathy. The princes chatted with the mourners, who greeted them warmly. "It was an extraordinary experience feeling the atmosphere outside the Palace," Andrew recalled. "It was unreal . . . completely unreal, beyond anybody's expectation or understanding."

At midday Blair called the Queen at her request so they could discuss the new plans. "It was the first time I'd heard him one on one with the Queen, and he really did the ma'am stuff pretty well," recalled his press spokesman, Alastair Campbell, who was listening in. "He said he felt she had to show that she was vulnerable and they really were feeling it. He said, 'I really do feel for you. There can be nothing more miserable than feeling as you do and having your motives questioned.' " Blair remembered that the Queen "was now very focused and totally persuaded. It wasn't easy, but it was certain."

That afternoon, Palace press secretary Geoffrey Crawford stood in front of St. James's Palace to read an unusual statement that not only explained what would happen the next day, but displayed a new softness in describing the Queen's feelings. "The royal family have been hurt by suggestions that they are indifferent to the country's sorrow," he said, adding that Diana's sons "miss her deeply." Crawford reiterated the wish of William and Harry to be in the "quiet haven" of Balmoral and the Queen's efforts to help them "come to terms with their loss" as they prepared themselves "for the public ordeal of mourning their mother with the nation."

Though she was willing to show some emotion in order to comfort her people, above all, Elizabeth II had to be a strong leader for her family as well as the nation. Her sister, Margaret, later thanked her for "how you kindly arranged *everybody's* lives after the accident and made life tolerable for the two poor boys . . . there, always in command, was you, listening to everyone and deciding on all the issues. . . . I just felt you were wonderful."

Philip suggested that on the eve of their return

to London the family attend a service at Crathie. Unlike the previous Sunday, Diana's name was mentioned by the minister, Bob Sloan, this time in a prayer of comfort for the grieving royal family. Afterward, they stopped in front of a horde of photographers at the Balmoral gates — the boys in dark suits and the men in their customary tweed jackets and tartan kilts — to inspect the flowers left by mourners. At 2:40 P.M. on Friday — five days after Diana's death — Elizabeth II and Philip arrived at the Buckingham Palace gates, with the unannounced intention of making the same gesture.

When they emerged from their Rolls-Royce, the royal couple faced crowds extending twenty deep to the Victoria Memorial, and thousands of bouquets wrapped in cellophane heaped six feet high along the Palace railings. "There was a very ugly atmosphere in the crowd that was lining the Mall," said assistant private secretary Mary Francis. Uncertain how the people would react, the Queen betrayed a trace of anxiety in her expression. As she and Philip walked toward the floral display, the crowd began clapping.

"It wasn't completely over with, but you could feel the atmosphere change," said Francis. One young girl held out a bouquet. "Would you like me to place them for you?" asked the Queen. "No, Your Majesty, they're for you," the girl replied. The Queen spoke to a few more women in the line of mourners, asking them questions ("Have you been queuing a long time?"), and leaning in to listen to their comments. "I just said how sorry I was," recalled Laura Trani, a student from Hampshire. "I said that William and Harry were now her main concern. She must take great care of them. She said she would. She said it was so hard for them because they were so young and loved their mother very much."

Inside the Palace, the Queen and Philip "spent a long time talking about what the mood was, and what was on people's minds," said Mary Francis, "wanting to understand but not quite being able to be just out there and mingle and hear as private individuals."

Elizabeth II was preparing for her much awaited speech — only the second such special televised address of her reign (the first was on the eve of the Gulf War in 1991). She was meant to tape her remarks in the late afternoon for airing later that evening. "She knew it was something she should do," said one of her senior advisers. "She was clear about what she wanted to say."

Robert Fellowes had written the first draft, assisted by David Airlie and Geoffrey Crawford, and transmitted it to Robin Janvrin at Balmoral. In a collaboration similar to the Christmas broadcasts, the Queen and Philip discussed and amended the remarks with her senior staff. Like her annual telecast, her words would reflect her own views, not those of the government.

As she did with her Christmas message, the Queen sent the speech to 10 Downing Street as a courtesy. Both Blair and Campbell read the text, and Campbell suggested that the Queen say she was speaking not only as the Queen, but "as a grandmother" — one of the most affecting phrases, as it turned out. "There were some last-minute discussions about her precise words," recalled Blair. "But it was plain from the language and tone that once she had decided to move, she moved with considerable skill."

Late on Friday afternoon, the Queen's advisers decided she would be more effective if she read the speech live. They also agreed — with encouragement from Alastair Campbell — to seat her in the Chinese Dining Room in front of an open window with the crowds outside the Palace as a backdrop. A technician placed an additional microphone adjacent to the window to capture the ambient murmur outdoors.

The Queen wasn't a fan of live broadcasts — decades earlier she had switched to tape for her Christmas message — but always rose to the occasion when asked. Wesley Kerr of the BBC could hear her rehearsing from the TelePrompTer on an open line. "One run-through," she said.

At 6 P.M. she appeared, bespectacled and perfectly coiffed, wearing a simple black dress adorned with a triangular diamond brooch, a triple strand of pearls, and pearl earrings. She spoke for three minutes and nine seconds, and the thousands of people behind her — walking about, sitting on the Victoria Memorial — lent a dramatic, almost eerie, touch.

Her speech was pitched perfectly: her mien sober, with just a hint of emotion. She said what she meant, straightforwardly and with no gush. She knew all too well Diana's failings, and the damage she had done to her eldest son. But she also recognized that her difficult daughter-in-law had struck a chord with the public, and that elements of her approach — her informality and her empathy — had been a force for good.

Diana's death had caused "an overwhelming expression of sadness," she said. "We have all been trying in our different ways to cope." Speaking "from my heart," she praised the late princess as "an exceptional and gifted human being." In an oblique reference to Diana's emotional troubles, she said, "In good times and bad, she never lost her capacity to smile and laugh, nor to inspire others with her warmth and kindness."

Elizabeth II said — no more or less than she felt — "I admired and respected her, for her energy and commitment to others and especially for her devotion to her two boys." She emphasized that "we have all been trying to help William and Harry come to terms with the devastating loss that they and the rest of us have suffered." Signaling her understanding of the need to adapt to changing times, the Queen said, "I for one believe there are lessons to be drawn from her life and from the extraordinary and moving reaction to her death. I share in your determination to cherish her memory."

After thanking everyone for their outpouring of support and "acts of kindness," she exhorted her viewers to think of Diana's family and the families of the others who died in the accident, and to unite "in grief and respect" at her funeral. She closed in typically understated fashion, by thanking God "for someone who made many, many people happy," a tacit acknowledgment that others may have been less than happy.

Reaction to the speech was overwhelmingly

positive. The Queen's long-ago arch-critic John Grigg, the former Lord Altrincham, pronounced it "one of the very best speeches" and said she had "stabilized the situation." George Carey thought it "showed her compassion and understanding. It went a very long way towards silencing her critics and removing the misunderstanding that had developed." Tony Blair considered the broadcast "near perfect. She managed to be a Queen and a grandmother at one and the same time."

A dissenting view came from playwright and novelist Alan Bennett, who had cleverly portrayed the Queen in his play *A Question of Attribution*. Bennett found the broadcast "unconvincing" because Elizabeth II "is not a good actress, indeed not an actress at all." He regretted that the Queen had not been directed "to throw in a few pauses and seem to be searching for words," and expressed disappointment that "she reels her message off, as she always does." The "difference between Princess Diana and the Queen," he wrote, was "one could act, the other can't."

Yet the Queen's inability to pretend, much less to prevaricate, has always been one of her greatest assets. After forty-five years on the throne, her character was clear as she sat in front of the television camera. Her uncomplicated authenticity made her words that much more powerful. "There's no putting on of a face in order to be more popular," said Simon Walker, who would serve as her communications secretary from 2000 to 2002, "because it just wouldn't work."

That night at dinner in Buckingham Palace, Prince Philip helped resolve one of the lingering questions about the funeral: would William and Harry follow the tradition of royal males and walk with their father and uncle Charles Spencer behind their mother's coffin? Both boys, especially William, had been reluctant all week to commit to something so public. William had resisted mainly because he was "consumed by a total hatred of the media" after their hounding of his mother, according to Alastair Campbell. Palace officials feared that if the Prince of Wales walked without his sons, he risked "being publicly attacked," Campbell recorded in his diary.

On Friday evening, Philip — who as a seventy-six-year-old former father-in-law had not been scheduled to walk — said to William: "If you don't walk, you may regret it later. I think you should do it. If I walk, will you walk with me?" William and his brother unhesitatingly agreed. They would join the procession as it passed St. James's Palace — a solemn row of four royal princes and an earl behind Diana's coffin.

The atmosphere on the sunny morning of Saturday, September 6, 1997, was uncannily calm. Central London was closed to all traffic except security vehicles and cars transporting mourners to the Abbey, and airplane routes had been redirected. Over a million people lined the four-mile funeral route and filled the city's parks. The crowds stood still and silent, making the clip-clop of the horses drawing the gun carriage all the more pronounced.

The funeral cortege headed down Constitutional Hill from Kensington Palace toward Buckingham Palace. In yet another surprise, the Queen led her sister and the rest of the family through the gates to stand near the crowd. As the gun carriage passed, Elizabeth II spontaneously bowed to Diana's coffin. "It was completely unexpected," said Mary Francis, who was standing nearby. "I don't think there had been any discussion of it, certainly not with her advisers beforehand. But instinctively she had done it, and it was the right thing to do." It was also a vivid demonstration "that there was already a readiness to be more flexible," said Ronald Allison, the Queen's former press secretary.

The royal family joined the congregation of two thousand inside the Abbey. Loudspeakers enabled the nearby crowds outside to hear the entire proceedings, which were also visible on the giant video screens. The television audience in Britain was an estimated 31 million, with 2.5 billion tuning in around the world. The service, presided over by the Very Reverend Dr. Wesley Carr, Dean of Westminster, and George Carey, Archbishop of Canterbury, was "unashamedly populist and raw with emotion," Carey recalled. Diana's sisters each read inspirational poems, and Tony Blair offered a somewhat overheated reading from First Corinthians. The musical selections were eclectic, from traditional hymns and an excerpt from Verdi's *Requiem* to Elton John's reworking of "Candle in the Wind" for "England's Rose" and the haunting strains of a contemporary composition by John Tavener.

An unexpected flash point came toward the end of Charles Spencer's eloquent and emotional tribute to Diana when he turned to the sorrow of William and Harry, pledging that the Spencers, "your blood family, will do all we can to continue the imaginative and loving way" their mother was raising them. The Spencers had no more claim as a "blood family" than the Windsors, and "those unnecessary words," as Carey later called them, insulted the Queen, Prince Philip, and their family seated in a row of scarlet and gilt chairs next to Diana's coffin on the catafalque. Even worse, as Spencer's remarks echoed outside the Abbey, the crowd began applauding. "It sounded like a rustle of leaves," recalled Charles Moore, the editor of the *Daily Telegraph,* who was in the Abbey. Members of the congregation picked up the clapping — itself a breach of Church of England practice — even William and Harry, although the Queen and Philip refrained from joining in. "It was a Shakespearean moment," said Moore, "one family's blood against the other. It was an incredibly powerful speech."

After the funeral, the royal family returned to its Highlands redoubt. Tony and Cherie Blair arrived the next day. It was supposed to have been their first prime minister's weekend at Balmoral, but under the circumstances they came only for luncheon with Elizabeth II and some of her friends. The Queen and Philip "were very kind," Cherie Blair recalled, but not a word was spoken about Diana or the previous week's earth-shaking events. Listening to the conversation about deer stalking, agriculture, and fishing, Cherie thought, "This is really weird. Yesterday at the lunch in Number 10 following the funeral, there I was sitting next to Hillary Clinton and Queen Noor of Jordan, talking about current affairs, and here I am today with our head of state talking about the price of sheep."

The prime minister had his audience with the Queen in the drawing room. As he made the rookie's mistake of trying to sit in Queen Victoria's chair, he heard a "strangled cry" from a footman and saw "a set of queenly eyebrows raised in horror." Blair was admittedly tense, and he later felt he had been presumptuous and somewhat insensitive in their conversation. When he spoke about possible lessons to be learned, he thought that she "assumed a certain hauteur." But she acknowledged his points generally and he "could see her own wisdom at work, reflecting, considering and adjusting."

Blair scarcely knew the Queen at that stage, so during the week after Diana's death there had been fewer direct interactions between prime minister and monarch than was generally believed. Blair and his aides did not overtly stage-manage Elizabeth II and Philip, as depicted in the film *The Queen.* But they did help guide the family's thinking through close coordination with receptive Buckingham Palace courtiers.

In part because Blair had come to know Diana personally, he understood her character and had more quickly grasped the impact of her death than either the Queen or her advisers. Sensing that the outpouring of grief was turning into a "mass movement for change," Blair decided his job was to "protect the monarchy." It's impossible to gauge the degree to which his "People's Princess" comment, however well-meaning, contributed to the volatile atmosphere. But had he been standoffish or negative, the monarchy would doubtless have sustained greater damage. Instead he tried to channel popular anger and recast the Queen's image in a more positive way. The Queen's courtiers were pivotal, but it also took Blair's behind-the-scenes prodding, including his use of Prince Charles as an intermediary, to push the Queen into acting in a way that went against her grain. In her eighth decade, Elizabeth II had come to understand that she needed to loosen the grip of tradition to keep the monarchy strong.

CHAPTER EIGHTEEN
LOVE AND GRIEF

In the autumn, when the Queen returned to London, she could look forward to celebrating a happy occasion for a change: the opening of the magnificently restored state rooms at Windsor Castle in time for her golden wedding anniversary on November 20, 1997, five years to the day from the devastating fire. The prime movers behind the restoration were Philip and Charles, who worked together on a project that reflected their common interests in art, architecture, and design. They shared a passion for painting, and both favored landscapes. Charles worked in watercolors on a small scale in a soft palette with delicate brushstrokes, while Philip painted in oils, using vivid colors and bold strokes with a more contemporary feel.

Both men appreciated the sort of traditional approach to architecture and exacting standards of craftsmanship required for the ornate rooms at Windsor. Philip chaired the overall advisory committee for the massive project, which included restoring five state rooms to their previous splendor. Charles was in charge of a design subcommittee that focused on reimagining rooms in areas that had been destroyed. The Queen offered ideas to

"Time is not my dictator," said the Queen Mother. *"I dictate to time. I want to meet people."*

The Queen with her sister, Margaret, and her mother on the Buckingham Palace balcony during the celebration of the Queen Mother's hundredth birthday, August 2000. PRESS ASSOCIATION IMAGES

her husband and her son, and she made all the final decisions.

To replace the gutted private chapel, Charles supervised the neo-Gothic design of an octagonal Lantern Lobby and adjacent private chapel in medieval style. Philip's sketches inspired the creation of the chapel's new stained glass windows with images of a salvage worker, a firefighter, and St. George stabbing an evil flame-breathing dragon. When Philip disagreed with the proposal for a decorative floor in the Lantern Lobby that he thought would be too noisy and slippery, Charles came up with a compromise calling for a carpet woven with the Garter Star to be used when necessary. Charles also oversaw a "modern reinterpretation" of a medieval hammer beam roof in the majestic St. George's Hall.

Originally scheduled to be completed by the spring of 1998, the restoration was finished six months ahead of time and came in £3 million under the estimated £40 million budget. The Queen marked the completion with a party in the restored rooms on November 14 for 1,500 contractors who worked on the project. During the reception, a Pakistani carpenter approached her and said, "Your Majesty, Your Majesty, please come with me. I want you to meet someone." He took her over to his brother for an introduction. As she was chatting with someone else, the carpenter returned and again said, "Your Majesty, please come with me." He then introduced her to a second brother who had helped carve the castle's woodwork. Rather than being offended, she was amused by his enthusiastic audacity. Recounting the story to a senior Indian diplomat several years later in a flawless South Asian accent, she laughed and said, "I began to worry that he might have 12 brothers!"

The wedding anniversary commemoration reflected a reverence for tradition as well as a new openness adopted by the royal family after Diana's death. On Wednesday, November 19, Philip paid tribute to his wife and family in a speech at a luncheon for the couple hosted by the Lord Mayor of London at the Guildhall. With the Queen seated next to him, Philip observed that "tolerance is the one essential ingredient of any happy marriage. . . . It is absolutely vital when the going gets difficult." His wife, he said, "has the quality of tolerance in abundance." Mindful of the family's recent "tribulations," he also singled out his children for praise, saying they "have all done rather well under very difficult and demanding circumstances."

On the 20th, Elizabeth II and Philip attended a service of thanksgiving at Westminster Abbey, where they had walked down the aisle fifty years earlier. In addition to their four children and six grandchildren, the royal couple was honored by seven kings, ten queens, a grand duke, twenty-six princes, and twenty-seven princesses, as well as fifty other couples, all ordinary citizens, who were also married in 1947. With memories still fresh from Diana's funeral eleven weeks earlier, there was an added undercurrent of solemnity, especially when William and Harry arrived with their father. In a "throat-catching moment," George Carey blessed the Queen and Philip as they knelt before him. "I found myself wondering if our nation was actually worthy of their devotion and unflagging sense of duty," the archbishop recalled.

The nod to modernity came afterward at a "people's banquet," a luncheon orchestrated in New Labour style and hosted by Tony Blair. Rather than having the royal couple at a head table on a dais surrounded by luminaries, the prime minister invited 350 guests from all walks of life and placed them at round tables without regard for rank or privilege. Dining with the Queen were an autoworker, a policeman, a jockey, and a maintenance worker, and she was seated next to a twenty-four-year-old leader of the Girl Guides.

In a speech at the luncheon, Blair thanked Elizabeth II anew for her conduct during "the terrible test" of Diana's death when "hurtful things" were said. He understood "how moved you were by the outpouring of grief. . . . You sought, at all times . . . to help and do the best by the boys, and that is the way it should have been and was." He affirmed his support for "a strong and flourishing monarchy" led by a Queen representing "those values of duty and service that are timeless." It was on this occasion that Blair memorably hailed Elizabeth II as "a symbol of unity in a world of insecurity where nothing stays the same. You are our Queen. We respect and cherish you. You are, simply, the Best of British."

In her speech, the Queen not only praised her husband but expanded on the notion of "lessons to be drawn" that she had first broached in her remarks about Diana. Surveying her five decades of married life, she remarked on such innovations as television, mobile telephones, and the Internet, which "to be honest" meant in her case that she had "listened to other people talking about surfing the Net."

She reflected on the "huge constitutional difference between a hereditary monarchy and an elected government," both of which depend on the consent of the people. "That consent, or lack of it," she said, "is expressed for you, Prime Minister, through the ballot box. It is a tough, even brutal, system but at least the message is a clear one for all to read."

For the royal family, "the message is often harder to read, obscured as it can be by deference, rhetoric or the conflicting currents of public opinion. But read it we must." She said she had done her best "with Prince Philip's constant love and help to interpret it correctly" and assured her audience that they would "try together to do so in the future." She expressed gratitude for the support she received after Diana's death. "It is you, if I may now speak to all of you directly, who have seen us through," she said, "and helped us to make our duty fun."

She closed with a frank but tender homage to Philip, who "all too often, I fear . . . has had to listen to me speaking." She acknowledged his help in crafting her speeches — expressing his views "in a forthright manner." Admitting his unwillingness to "take easily to compliments," she said he had, "quite simply, been my strength and stay all these years, and I, and his whole family, and this and many other countries, owe him a debt greater than he would ever claim, or we shall ever know."

The Queen's marital milestone inevitably

prompted speculation in the press about how much her celebrated tolerance had been tested. For years there had been rumors that Philip had a roving eye, and in 1996 author Sarah Bradford had stated flatly in her biography of the Queen that "Philip's obvious flirtations and his affairs" had made "no difference to a marriage as firm and indeed fond as theirs."

Philip had been linked to women in high aristocratic circles — usually close friends of the couple such as Jane, the Countess of Westmorland, who had been a great beauty; Penny Romsey, who often rode with the duke in carriage driving competitions; his (and the Queen's) cousin Princess Alexandra; and Sacha Abercorn, wife of the 5th Duke of Abercorn, a contemporary of the Prince of Wales. In none of those cases was there any evidence of an affair.

Martin Charteris sought to put the gossip to rest shortly before the golden wedding anniversary in an interview with the *Daily Mail*'s Anne de Courcy. "I simply don't know of anyone who has claimed to be his mistress or to have had a particularly close relationship," he said in early November 1997. "If anybody had enjoyed such a relationship, do you think for one minute we wouldn't have heard about it? He's a man, he likes pretty girls, he loves fun. But I am absolutely certain there was nothing that would in any way have shaken that marriage."

Patricia Brabourne, the royal couple's Mountbatten cousin, subsequently explained Philip's relationship with her daughter-in-law, Penny Romsey, by saying that she is "Philip's great friend. The friendship there is largely based on their carriage driving. She goes and is visible." Brabourne was also "absolutely certain" that he had been faithful to the Queen. "He would never behave badly," she said. "He has always loved the Queen. . . . He wouldn't want to do anything to hurt her."

Sacha Abercorn spoke out as well, with the same objective of shooting down the rumors. She told author Gyles Brandreth that she and Philip had become friendly in the 1970s through their mutual interest in the writings of Swiss psychiatrist Carl Jung, about whom they had "riveting conversations." When Brandreth asked why she was seen holding hands with the duke on the island of Eleuthera, she explained, "It was a passionate friendship, but the passion was in the ideas. . . . I did not go to bed with him. It probably looked like that to the world . . . but it didn't happen. . . . He isn't like that. . . . He needs a playmate and someone to share his intellectual pursuits."

The Queen, according to her cousin Pamela Hicks, "doesn't mind when he flirts. He flirts with everyone, and she knows it means absolutely nothing." She recalled the time Philip "bitterly said to my sister that he has never had an affair since he has been married." He vehemently added, "The way the press related it, I had affairs with all these women. I might as well have and bloody enjoyed it." Even biographer Sarah Bradford eventually backed off, telling *The Times,* "quite honestly, what real evidence is there? . . . The Queen relies on him tremendously. Through all those troubles they certainly did get closer. They are very close. They understand each other."

The royal couple said goodbye to one of the most visible emblems of their partnership when *Britannia* was decommissioned on December 11, 1997, in Portsmouth. (The yacht would later be made into a museum in Edinburgh.) Before the service, the royal family and courtiers went aboard for a last luncheon in the State Dining Room, with its long mahogany table, Hepplewhite chairs, and travel mementos, among them a narwhal tusk, a Sioux peace pipe, and a whalebone Philip had retrieved from a beach on Deception Island in Antarctica. The Queen and her entourage walked around her "country house at sea" and bid farewell to the ship's company. "It was awful and she cried," said one of her courtiers.

The quayside service, conducted by naval chaplains and attended by 2,200 former *Britannia* officers and yachtsmen, was seen by a television audience of millions. As the band of the Royal Marines marched away, they played "Auld Lang Syne" and saluted the yacht one final time. The Queen, dressed in red, raised a black-gloved hand to her eye and wiped away a tear. Some commentators in the press criticized her for weeping over a mere ship. But to the Queen and her family, *Britannia* held decades of memories. "It had not just been for work," said a lady-in-waiting. "It had been their floating home." More than anything, the royal yacht "represented freedom to her," said one of the Queen's relatives.

By early 1998 the royal household had begun to take concrete steps toward applying some of the lessons from the era of Diana. After support for a republic peaked in the days following her death, it dropped to 12 percent after the Queen's televised speech, and in the following month it returned to around 19 percent, where it had been for three decades. But the volatility of opinion during that period sent deputy private secretary Robin Janvrin to visit Robert Worcester, the American expatriate professor who had founded the MORI poll.

Since Michael Shea's appointment as press secretary to the Queen in 1978, her advisers had been periodically meeting with Worcester over lunch in London to pick his brain about trends in public opinion toward the monarchy. Now Janvrin told Worcester that he had a budget for private polling and wanted to hire MORI. In briefings at the Palace, the pollsters assessed support for the monarchy versus a republic by region, gender, age, social class, and other demographic characteristics. Through focus groups they also developed a list of ten attributes (promoting Britain abroad, importance to Britain, highly respected, supporting and promoting charitable institutions, hardworking, in touch with lives of ordinary people, well advised, good value for money, up to date, relevant) and assessed their relative importance to the public.

The two main concerns among the Queen's senior counselors at the outset were that the monarchy was losing support among the young, and that the royal family was perceived to be "too myopic and inward looking." In general, the research, which included some focus groups as well as traditional surveys, established that support for the monarchy is a stable and enduring value for the British people, transcending the headline of the moment — knowledge that gave the Palace greater confidence and enabled it to take a long view. The results of the private polling over the first several years also confirmed that while support for a republic among people in their twenties ranged from 28 percent to 35 percent, by the time they reached their mid-thirties, they would "revert to the mean" of 19 percent. "People start thinking about the future, about raising kids, living in a decent country," said Robert Worcester. "That is why the monarchy is such a deep value and so consistent." The most conspicuous area of weakness for the royal family was the perception that they were out of touch, which was held by more than a third of the British people when polling began in the late 1990s.

While Palace officials found much of the research reassuring, they began to develop strategies to respond to public opinion and show that the royal family was "in touch." Surveys helped the Palace choose places the Queen should visit and themes for events she sponsored. They upgraded the press secretary's job to "communications secretary" and recruited a public relations professional from British Gas, thirty-nine-year-old Simon Lewis, on a two-year secondment, with half his salary paid by his corporate employer. He first met the Queen and Prince Philip on a Friday afternoon at the end of May 1998.

"My abiding impression was how remarkably open they were," Lewis recalled. "We had a discussion of what I would do and what the challenges were. It was more discursive than I had anticipated." Lewis was struck "by the interaction between the two of them, how comfortable and easy they were, and how they had both thought about this role together. It was a very balanced discussion." Philip in particular "had thought carefully about the communications area. The probing discussion was led by him. He was very interested in the nascent website, and he was pushing the idea of direct contact with the public. He had given up on the traditional media, which he thought was unwinnable. In his view, the only way was direct communication. I was impressed by how farsighted he was."

The royal family began to manage its public duties more closely as well. In late 1994 David Airlie had started the Way Ahead Group to bring together the Queen, Prince Philip, their four children, and senior advisers twice a year to coordinate their plans. Now they focused on shaping the family's activities to incorporate some of the best of what Diana had done, lessening the formality (instructing people before meeting members of the royal family that the bow and curtsy were optional), and consistently taking a more unassuming approach to public engagements — sitting down for tea in public housing projects, or walking around a classroom rather than peering in the door. "It is not heart on the sleeve or contrived," explained one courtier. "But showing more empathy."

The watchword became "imperceptible evolution," based on an analogy that Robin Janvrin called "the Marmite theory of monarchy." The salty food spread found in British cupboards for over a century has a distinctive red, yellow, and green label that is comforting in its familiarity. But only by comparing a fifty-year-old Marmite jar with one on contemporary shelves is it possible to see pronounced differences. The jar evolved so gradually and slowly that the changes were imperceptible. By Janvrin's theory, the monarchy needed to change the same way — incrementally over time, small steps rather than large steps, so people were reassured that the institution was staying the same while adapting.

But Janvrin and his colleagues did make the occasional misstep, such as when they arranged for the Queen to greet people outside a McDonald's restaurant in a display of populism. Determined to cast the visit in a poor light, the press ran photographs of her Rolls-Royce under the fast-food sign, making the appearance look contrived. Elizabeth II had a word with Robin Janvrin afterward, but she didn't belabor the matter. "She has incredibly good instincts about how something will be perceived," said Simon Lewis. "I was struck by her pragmatism and her sense of what would work. She has a finely tuned sense of the moment. On occasion ideas would be put to her and she would say, 'We can't do that. It's far too grand.' "

The final years of the twentieth century brought the Queen a new round of worries, this time about her mother and her sister. The Queen Mother was inevitably growing more fragile as she neared her hundredth birthday, although she still had her doughty spirit, refusing offers of a wheelchair and even balking at using a cane. "Time is not my dictator," said the Queen Mother. "I dictate to time. I want to meet people."

She continued her royal rounds even after she had

her right hip replaced in November 1995. While visiting the Sandringham Stud in January 1998, she fell and broke her left hip, which required a second replacement surgery. At age ninety-seven, she made another remarkable comeback and appeared at the end of March at St. James's Palace for her annual Clothing Guild meeting — the first of forty-six public engagements that year.

Margaret's problems were psychological as well as physical. She had suffered from a range of ailments over the years — migraines, depression, bronchitis, gastroenteritis, and alcoholic hepatitis — resulting mainly from her excessive drinking and smoking. She had surgery in 1985 to remove a small portion of her lung. Although it wasn't malignant, she had tried — unsuccessfully — to stop smoking, and she had cut back on her Famous Grouse whisky.

The two sisters kept up their daily phone calls, and when Margaret traveled overseas, she would call the Queen first thing on arrival. At Balmoral, Margaret "was almost like a poor relation," said one courtier. "The Queen felt sorry for her." "Sometimes Margaret was a very lonely person," said her longtime friend Jane Rayne. "After Tony, then Roddy, no one else made her happy," observed a man who was friendly with Margaret. "At dinner parties she would often indicate that I should drive her home. She would ask me in, and offer me a drink, then she would talk about all her personal problems."

In late February 1998 Margaret suffered a mild stroke at age sixty-seven. She recovered well, although she showed signs of fatigue as well as forgetfulness. Almost exactly a year later, she badly scalded her feet while taking a bath in her house on Mustique. The Queen arranged for her to be flown by Concorde back to England, where she was treated at King Edward VII Hospital. Afterward she had difficulty walking and often relied on a wheelchair. There were other signs of decline as well. Since the early 1980s, Margaret had faithfully corresponded with Nancy Reagan, but in 1999 her lady-in-waiting Annabel Whitehead had to begin writing on her behalf.

As late as May 1999 the Queen was unsure whether her ailing sister could attend the wedding the following month of Prince Edward to thirty-four-year-old Sophie Rhys-Jones, a middle-class career woman who bore a passing resemblance to Diana. The daughter of an auto parts salesman and a homemaker, Sophie had grown up in the Kentish countryside and attended Kent College Pembury, a well-regarded girls school. After working in a variety of public relations jobs, she started her own firm in 1996. She met Edward while promoting a charity tennis tournament in 1993, and after dating for five years, they announced their engagement in January 1999.

Following the debacle of *It's a Royal Knockout,* Edward had made a modestly successful career as a producer of films including documentaries on haunted castles in Wales, his great-uncle the Duke of Windsor, and the restoration of Windsor Castle. But as the last of the Queen's children to marry, thirty-five-year-old Edward had also been subjected to such a persistent whispering campaign about his sexuality that Sophie herself denied publicly that he was gay. "How I'd love to be able to go out and sing from the rooftops: IT IS NOT TRUE," she said. "I want to prove it to people, but it's impossible to do that."

Unlike the other royal siblings, Edward and Sophie had a relatively low-key wedding in St. George's Chapel at Windsor Castle on June 19 that they organized as much as possible on their own. The Queen gave them the titles of Earl and Countess of Wessex and set them up in a fifty-six-room Victorian house in Surrey called Bagshot Park that was criticized as excessive for their position in the royal family. They both continued in their jobs and were known professionally as Edward and Sophie Wessex, determined to combine royal life with everyday work.

Elizabeth II lost one of the stalwart figures in her life that December with the death of Martin Charteris at eighty-six. He had been diagnosed early in the month with advanced liver cancer and was immediately admitted to King Edward VII Hospital. While he was there, the Queen came for an hour-long visit. "They picked up right away on topics that were current," recalled Gay Charteris. "They talked about all sorts of issues. I had never seen them talk that way together." At no point did the Queen commiserate with her long-serving adviser about his terminal condition. "She knew that was pointless," said his widow, "and that Martin wanted to talk about the kinds of things they had talked about when he worked for her."

After three weeks, he left the hospital and died at his home in Gloucestershire on December 23.

A year later the Queen invited the Charteris family to Windsor Castle for the installation of a cast-iron fireback that he had been sculpting in the last year of his life. He had died before finishing it, so a young sculptor at Eton completed the job. The design had all the royal emblems, and in a fanciful touch, three corgis as well. "I know if Martin had lived, one of the corgis would have lifted its leg," said his widow. The Queen placed the fireback in St. George's Hall, a reminder of the man who was her friend as well as her courtier.

To celebrate Millennium Eve on December 31, 1999, the Blairs invited the Queen and Prince Philip, along with Anne and her husband, to the vast Millennium Dome in Greenwich. Originally intended as an exhibition center that would symbolize New Labour's "Cool Britannia" image, the dome had been plagued by cost overruns and poor planning. Tony Blair promised that the opening night extravaganza would be nothing less than "the greatest show on earth." It featured acrobats in the nether reaches of the structure, a concert, and, shortly before midnight, a prayer read by the Archbishop of Canterbury.

Alastair Campbell observed that Elizabeth II "at least managed the odd smile," while the others "looked very pissed off to be there." Anne, in particular, "was like granite." One reason may have been the absence of heat, which caused the Queen, among thousands of other guests, to keep her coat buttoned. "It was pretty clear they would rather be sitting under their traveling rugs at Balmoral," recalled Campbell. As the clock struck twelve everyone was expected to link arms and sing "Auld Lang Syne." The Queen merely stared ahead and lightly clasped the fingers of Blair and Philip, who gave her a rare public kiss on the cheek. Even Blair called the touchy-feely moment "ghastly."

Despite her obvious discomfort on New Year's Eve, the Queen had established a fond relationship with Blair. She had presided over the opening of the Scottish Parliament and witnessed the establishment of the National Assembly for Wales — two essential pieces of New Labour's program to devolve some legislative powers away from the British Parliament in Westminster after decades of nationalist pressure. "The Queen had a central role in the devolution process," said Simon Lewis. "So it was important for her to be there and visible. As the country was changing, she needed to be seen to be involved." In accepting devolution, she was careful to point out that politicians should be mindful that "the kingdom can still enjoy all the benefits of remaining united. . . . The parts are only fragments of a whole," and with unity "we can be much more than the sum of those fragments."

In the early going, Blair was not as assiduous about his weekly audiences at the Palace as he later became, and he was known to do an irreverent impersonation of Her Majesty: "Now Blair, no more of this people's princess nonsense, because I am the people's Queen." In time, he developed a "high regard for her street smarts," said Jonathan Powell, Blair's chief of staff, and her skill "at assessing people and situations." Blair recognized that she kept her finger "steadily on the national pulse — more, probably, than people would perhaps perceive." "Her quality is the ability to get underneath what is happening," Blair said. "It's not just a question of knowing the facts on this and this and this. . . . It's also being able to sense . . . the small p politics of something."

Like his predecessors, Blair came to regard the Queen's audience room as a sanctuary. "He was always working flat-out, one meeting after another," said another of his advisers. "When he climbed into the car with his private secretary it was a moment for decompression. It was a time of tranquillity for him, to walk in and sit down and talk about what the Queen wanted to discuss." He appreciated that she was "very to the point" and "very direct." He learned, he later wrote, that "you don't get matey with the Queen. Occasionally she can be matey with you, but don't try to reciprocate or you get The Look."

Cherie Blair mellowed in her view of the royal family after a rocky beginning in which she had frosty exchanges with both Princess Margaret and Princess Anne, who declined to call her Cherie because, said Anne, "it's not the way I've been brought up." "I have a soft spot for Prince Philip," Cherie said. "He and I share a great interest in the Internet." The prime minister's wife enjoyed the barbecues at Balmoral that initially flummoxed her husband when "the person who you have grown up with as the Queen" was "fussing around you and looking after you." Mostly Cherie was impressed by the way Elizabeth II played with the Blairs' two-year-old son, Leo, during a visit to the Highlands, patiently teaching him how to toss biscuits to the corgis and reacting with benign tolerance when he threw a handful around the room.

Elizabeth II, as always, was circumspect about her own views of her tenth prime minister, although once when asked by a friend she said, "I think he's in the wrong party." "It was a throw-away observation," explained her friend, "matter of fact, reflecting a common perception that he was not a traditional Labour Party figure." Philip was predictably more outspoken, telling Gyles Brandreth that he was a modernizer but "not for the sake of buggering about with things in some sort of Blairite way."

In March 2000 the Queen traveled to Australia for her thirteenth visit at a time of uncertainty in the country's relationship with Britain. The previous November there had been a landmark referendum on the future of the monarchy. By 54 percent to 45 percent, Australians had voted to keep the Queen as their head of state despite opinion polls indicating strong republican sentiment. In the view of many observers, the people had rejected the republican proposal only because it advocated electing a president by both houses of parliament rather than directly by the country's twelve million voters — reflecting more of a distrust of politicians than an endorsement of the sovereign.

When the Queen had greeted Martin Charteris in his hospital room a month after the vote, "the first thing they talked about was whether Australia would become a republic," said Gay Charteris. Elizabeth II took the philosophical view that someday the British sovereign would no longer serve as the monarch of Australia. In a speech on March 20, 2000, at the Sydney Opera House, she struck a balance — on the one hand reminding her listeners that she had "felt part of this rugged, honest creative land" since she "first stepped ashore" in February 1954, while frankly acknowledging that "the future of the monarchy in Australia is an issue for you, the Australian people, and you alone to decide by democratic and constitutional means." She pledged that "whatever the future may bring," her "lasting respect and deep affection" would "remain as strong as ever."

The well-being of her mother and her sister remained a major preoccupation for the Queen, especially when she was away for two weeks in distant Australia. "The Queen was always wondering if her mother would be all right, would she fall again, and that poor old leg was never healing," said her cousin Pamela Hicks.

With the Queen Mother pointing toward her one hundredth birthday in August, Elizabeth II organized a series of unforgettable occasions. The first, a grand ball in the state apartments at Windsor Castle on Wednesday, June 21, also celebrated the seventieth birthday of Princess Margaret, the fiftieth of Princess Anne, and the fortieth of Prince Andrew. The list of more than eight hundred guests included European kings and queens, princes and princesses, leading figures from the British aristocracy, flamboyant international celebrities, and royal estate managers and horse trainers. Longtime royal nanny Mabel Anderson was there, along with Roddy Llewellyn and his wife, Captain Mark Phillips and his new wife, Sarah, Duchess of York, and Camilla Parker Bowles and her husband. Bars were set up in four different rooms, and three dance bands alternated in the Waterloo Chamber while a disco boomed in the Queen's Presence Chamber.

There had been grumbling four years earlier when the press revealed that the Queen Mother was running an overdraft at Coutts bank of £4 million. Critics questioned the Queen's acceptance of her mother's extravagance, and the £643,000 allocated for her annual Civil List allowance. But few begrudged the ninety minutes of pageantry at Horse Guards Parade on July 19 in tribute to the Queen Mother's century: a cast of thousands in a gaily costumed procession, the Royal Philharmonic Orchestra, servicemen, choirs, bands, bulls, sheep, chickens, horses, one hundred doves, and an aerial display by vintage RAF airplanes. Earlier that week there had been a service at St. Paul's Cathedral and congratulatory messages from the House of Lords and the House of Commons.

Two weeks later on August 4, 2000, the day she turned one hundred, the Queen Mother rode with the Prince of Wales in a flower-bedecked carriage up the Mall to Buckingham Palace, where a crowd of forty thousand waited to cheer her arrival. "It was three years after the death of the Princess of Wales and I was struck by how far the monarchy had come," said Simon Lewis. "I was standing in the forecourt at Buckingham Palace thinking, 'If there was any question how people feel about the monarchy, there was a sense of joy that day.' It was a tiny reminder that the institution had come through tough times and was in great shape."

■■■■

Planning began that summer for the Queen's own celebration two years later of her Golden Jubilee, marking fifty years on the throne. The task fell to Robin Janvrin, who had taken over as private secretary when Robert Fellowes retired in 1999. The son of a vice admiral, Janvrin had graduated with honors from Oxford and served as an officer in the Royal Navy and as a diplomat before joining the royal household in 1987. Having witnessed some of the worst years of the Queen's reign, he had become the leading modernizer among her top advisers.

His first recruit was Simon Walker, head of communications for British Airways, to replace Simon Lewis, who was returning to British Gas following his two years at the Palace. A South African by birth, Walker was outside the classic courtier mold, having worked not only in the Labour Party but for John Major in his last two years at 10 Downing Street. The Queen's advisers wanted another press manager with an outside perspective and a more realistic idea of how stories would play. After a half dozen meetings with various officials in the household — mainly to determine if Walker harbored republican ideas — Janvrin said, "Only one person can decide if you are right for the job, and that is the Queen."

Walker's interview with Elizabeth II was late on a Wednesday afternoon in June 2000. She asked if he minded standing since she had been sitting for a portrait for three hours. As they talked, one of the Queen's corgis insistently tugged at Walker's trouser leg, which made standing still a challenge. The Queen didn't try to stop the dog, nor for that matter did she seem to take notice at all, and Walker began to think that his ability to endure the distraction was meant to test his unflappability.

Their conversation was friendly and informal, and the Queen was well briefed. Her purpose was not to conduct the sort of forensic interview common in private industry, but rather to get a sense of how Walker might fit in and work with her. "There was definitely a subtlety to it," he recalled.

Walker joined the household in September, when preparations for the Golden Jubilee got under way. He and his colleagues were mindful of "Millennium fatigue" created by Blair's overhyped approach to the dome. "Under-promise and over-delivery were seen to be critical to the Jubilee's media prospects," recalled Walker. The festivities would avoid simply copying the Silver Jubilee and its multitude of street parties, emphasizing instead inclusiveness to capture the multicultural changes that had occurred during the Queen's reign. The focus would be on the Queen herself rather than on the institution of the monarchy, and communities of all stripes would be encouraged to celebrate in their own way, along with the major events forming the centerpiece of the official celebrations in London.

One striking emblem of the modern mood at the Palace was the portrait in progress on the day Simon Walker met the Queen. Of all the depictions of the Queen throughout her reign, it was one of the most controversial. The artist was Lucian Freud, widely regarded as Britain's greatest living realist painter, and the grandson of psychoanalyst Sigmund Freud. The idea for the painting had come from Robert Fellowes, whose portrait Freud had painted in 1999. It was a risky commission, since Freud's portraits (including the one of Fellowes) were often brutal, even grotesque images, rendered in thick brushstrokes. Freud said his goal was to produce "the interior life of 'inner likeness' behind such an instantly recognizable face." For that reason, he remarked that his task was as challenging as "a polar expedition."

Rather than working in the ornate Yellow Drawing Room at Buckingham Palace looking out across the Mall, where artists over the decades had painted the Queen, Freud insisted they meet in the Friary Court Studio at St. James's Palace, a room used for painting restoration. He sat the Queen in front of a stark beige wall and had her pose in the diamond and pearl diadem shown on postage stamps and bank notes, which made an odd juxtaposition with her tailored blue suit and usual triple strand of pearls. From May 2000 through December 2001 he painted her in fifteen sittings, a source of frustration for the artist, who was accustomed to many more. At age seventy-seven, Freud worked with a vigor matching that of his seventy-four-year-old sitter.

Because of the diadem's value, several protection officers stood guard in the studio with them, but Freud found their presence distracting, so the Queen asked them to go outside. She told the artist that she had met one of them while on a shoot at a friend's estate. She was picking up as she always did when a wounded cock pheasant flew out of a hedge straight at her, flapping and clawing, and knocked her down. There was blood on her clothing from the bird's scratches, and the detective standing nearby feared she had been shot. He threw himself on top of her and began giving her mouth-to-mouth resuscitation. "I consider we got to know each other rather well," she told Freud. Afterward, she hired the man for her protection force.

The Queen not only proved equal to Freud's notoriously penetrating gaze, the artist shared with his sitter an enthusiasm for horses. He had been fascinated by the equine personality since his childhood, when he slept in the stables to be near the animals, and he had painted a number of arresting portraits of horses. "Lucian had a whale of a time with the Queen," said his longtime friend Clarissa Eden. "They talked about racing and horses. She kept on saying, 'We must stop talking. We must get on with this portrait.' "

Memories of the unfortunate escapades of Elizabeth II's children resurfaced in April 2001 when Prince Edward's wife, Sophie Wessex, was entrapped in a sting by Mazher Mahmood, a reporter for *News of the World* impersonating an Arab sheikh interested in signing on as a client of her public relations firm. Mahmood secretly taped their conversation, and his newspaper ran the transcript in a sensational "World Exclusive." The other tabloids reported incorrectly that Sophie called the Queen "an old dear," the Queen Mother "the old lady," Conservative leader William Hague "deformed," and Cherie Blair "horrid." She said none of those things, but she was indiscreet, telling the fake sheikh that the royal family referred to the prime minister as "President Blair because he thinks he is," that Hague has "got this awful kind of way he talks. . . . He sounds like a puppet unfortunately," and that John Major was "completely wooden." She called the Labour budget "a load of pap," and said its "increase in everybody's taxes is something frightening."

In an effort to prevent the publication of the transcripts, Sophie gave an interview to the newspaper, with the approval of the Buckingham Palace press office. That was when she denied Edward was gay, and she spoke as well of the pressures created by comparisons to Diana, usually unfavorable. "I have been reduced to tears," she said. "I don't deny that we do look alike, and it's a huge compliment for me when people say that. But I couldn't ever compete with Diana's public image. I'm not Diana." It was an excruciating experience for the novice member of the royal family, and she sent apologies to those she had insulted. But she not only remained in royal favor, she and her husband grew even closer to the Queen. "Sophie first of all respects her as the Queen, then as a mother-in-law, but she also understands that she is a human being and treats her that way," said the Queen's cousin Elizabeth Anson.

A few months later, the Queen entertained her tenth American president on July 19 when recently elected George W. Bush arrived at Buckingham Palace with his wife, Laura, for lunch before traveling to Genoa for the G-8 conference. Accompanying them was the Queen's good friend Will

Farish, the new U.S. ambassador to the Court of St. James's. They alighted under the portico of the Grand Entrance, where they stood at attention for "The Star-Spangled Banner" expertly played by the band of the Coldstream Guards. As the forty-third president and the Duke of Edinburgh walked out into the quadrangle to inspect the guard of honor, it began to pour, soaking Bush's trousers and shoes. Philip got a good laugh, but Elizabeth II tactfully refrained from comment. Ten years after their first meeting in his father's White House, Bush felt a "natural connection" with the Queen, who created a relaxed and welcoming atmosphere.

The Anglo-American alliance deepened less than two months later when al Qaeda Islamist terrorists carried out the 9/11 attacks. The Queen was at Balmoral, and unlike the reaction to Diana's death four years earlier, her reflexes were sure and swift. She issued a statement of condolence to President Bush expressing her "growing disbelief and total shock," and she prepared to return to London for a special service at St. Paul's Cathedral to honor the nearly three thousand victims, sixty-seven British citizens among them.

Malcolm Ross called Balmoral from London to ask that the Union Jack at Buckingham Palace be lowered to half-staff for the second time since Diana's death (the Queen had authorized the same gesture of respect the previous October after the death of Donald Dewar, the first minister of Scotland). Ross also made the novel suggestion that at the next Changing of the Guard the American as well as British national anthem be played, with a two-minute silence between. The Queen instantly approved both proposals, and Robin Janvrin asked the American embassy to participate. That Thursday, two days after the attack, Will Farish and Prince Andrew stood at attention in the Palace forecourt as the Coldstream Guards band played "The Star-Spangled Banner," and a large crowd of spectators wept outside the railings.

The Queen suffered yet another loss on September 11 when her friend of many years, Henry Carnarvon, was stricken with a fatal heart attack at age seventy-seven. Like Elizabeth II and millions around the world, Carnarvon and his wife, Jean, had been watching television as the horrors unfolded in the United States. Just after the second hijacked airplane hit the World Trade Center, he collapsed. In the ambulance on the way to the hospital, he turned to his wife and said, "Would you call the Queen?" He died shortly afterward in the operating room, and his daughter, Lady Carolyn Warren, phoned Balmoral with the news. "The Queen was devastated," said Jean Carnarvon. "It was so unexpected. It caught us all."

On Friday, September 14, the Queen joined a congregation of 2,700, most of them Americans, at St. Paul's Cathedral for a memorial service honoring the September 11 victims. Prince Philip read the lesson, and everyone sang "The Battle Hymn of the Republic," which hadn't been heard there since the 1960s when it was played for John F. Kennedy and Winston Churchill. "When our National Anthem was played, I watched the Queen as she sang all the words," recalled Jackie Davis, the wife of an official at the American embassy. "I thought to myself, 'If she can do that, then I can learn the words to "God Save the Queen." ' "

On September 20, Tony and Cherie Blair traveled to New York to participate in another memorial for the victims at St. Thomas's Church on Fifth Avenue. The prime minister did a reading from Thornton Wilder's *The Bridge at San Luis Rey,* but "A Message from Her Majesty the Queen," read by British ambassador Sir Christopher Meyer, most eloquently caught the intense sadness of the moment. Written by Robin Janvrin, it ended with what Bill Clinton called a "stunning sentence": "Grief is the price we pay for love." Those words were so evocative, and so true, that they were carved in stone not only at St. Thomas's, but at a memorial in Grosvenor Square near the American embassy in London.

Tony Blair kept the Queen up to date on developments over the following weeks that led to the October invasion of Afghanistan by the United States, Britain, and other NATO forces. Their mission was to unseat the fundamentalist Muslim Taliban forces and root out the al Qaeda terrorists who had trained there for the devastating attacks. It was the first step in the global war on terrorism that escalated two years later with the invasion of Iraq and ouster of dictator Saddam Hussein, who was suspected of illegally making weapons of mass destruction intended for use against the United States and its allies.

From time to time during this period, Blair relied on the Queen for guidance. "Obviously there was a huge focus on the Arab world," he recalled, "and that is something she has immense experience of.

She has dealt with many of the royal families, with many of the ruling families, over a long, long period of time, and she has a lot of real insight into how they work, how they operate, how they think, the best way of trying to make sure that we reach out to them."

Lucian Freud unveiled *Her Majesty the Queen* at Buckingham Palace on December 20 and donated it to the Royal Collection in honor of the Golden Jubilee. Much of the reaction from the press was negative: "extremely unflattering," said the *Daily Telegraph;* "a travesty," pronounced *The Sun.*

The painting is shocking in several respects, starting with its size: only nine inches by six inches. Because it is so small, it is peculiarly concentrated, showing only the Queen's head and a small part of her shoulders. Without the diadem, she would be barely recognizable. "You gaze at it for half a minute," said Clarissa Eden, who was also painted by Freud. "Suddenly you realize it is the Queen." Her face is harsh, the expression a scowl, the eyes hooded, the skin a rough patchwork of white and orange streaks, the heavy chin with a masculine five-o'clock shadow.

Yet despite Freud's failure to show such attributes as her expressive eyes and luminous skin, he does capture in a mesmerizing way the essence of her dutiful and determined nature, as well as her strength and stoicism. "This is a painting of experience," said Adrian Searle, art critic for *The Guardian.* So too is it an artwork of its time. "It could not have been painted ten years earlier," said Sandy Nairne, director of the National Portrait

Gallery since 2002.

Freud said the Queen looked at the portrait while she was being painted but she did not tell him what she thought. Sir Hugh Roberts, director of the Royal Collection, reflected the official Palace view when he called the portrait a "remarkable work." Even more telling was a commentary by Jennifer Scott, the assistant curator of paintings for the collection, who wrote that it "feels real and earthy, almost as if Freud peeled away the layers of deportment that come so naturally to a monarch and painted the person underneath."

Christmas at Sandringham was unsettled that year. Margaret, now seventy-one, had suffered two more strokes in the beginning of 2001, leaving her partially paralyzed and bedridden as well as blind. When she made a brief appearance at the one hundredth birthday party for her aunt Princess Alice, the Dowager Duchess of Gloucester, on December 12 at Kensington Palace, Margaret wore sunglasses, and her face was swollen from steroid medications. Anne Glenconner, Margaret's longtime friend and Norfolk neighbor, came to Sandringham and arranged to have a television installed in the princess's room, along with a hot plate so her nurse could make scrambled eggs. "What a good idea!" the Queen said. Prince Charles was especially solicitous, sharing with Anne Glenconner the task of reading aloud to his aunt, who by then could barely speak. "Her quality of life was not good," said Glenconner.

Four months past her 101st birthday, the indomitable Queen Mother was fading as well. She came down with a respiratory infection that kept her confined mainly to her room at Sandringham. In early February, Margaret was driven back to Kensington Palace, while her mother remained in Norfolk to recuperate. As the princess was wheeled to the car, the Queen Mother "carried out the family tradition of waving a white handkerchief in farewell."

Accession Day, on February 6, was usually observed privately by the Queen. But to mark the fiftieth anniversary of taking the throne, she not only appeared publicly, she sent out a message of thanks with a modern twist — on the Internet through her official jubilee website. She started the day at Sandringham with an early morning ride, then traveled by car to nearby King's Lynn to open a new cancer unit at the Queen Elizabeth Hospital, where she talked to patients and toured the facility. Her visit was intended in part as a tribute to her late father's struggle with lung cancer.

Two days later, Margaret had another stroke. After she showed signs of heart problems, she was rushed to King Edward VII Hospital late that night. With her son and daughter at her bedside, the princess died at 6:30 A.M. on Saturday, February 9. The Queen was at Windsor Castle, while Philip had stayed on at Sandringham for a shooting weekend. Charles immediately drove to Norfolk to console his grandmother. Resolutely positive as always, she told her grandson that her daughter's death "had probably been a merciful release."

Margaret's funeral took place at 3 P.M. in St. George's Chapel on Friday the 15th — fifty years to the day since her father, King George VI, was laid to rest. She had been eligible for a "royal ceremonial funeral," but her wish was to "depart without a fuss," so she requested a "royal private funeral," by definition a less public ceremony. Unusually for a member of the royal family, she also requested cremation, with instructions that her ashes be placed with her father's remains in his vault at the chapel.

The princess had selected the readings and the music for the service, which showed not only what her good friend George Carey called her "rooted and firm" adherence to the Church of England, but her love of ballet. As the 450 mourners entered the chapel, the organist played Tchaikovsky's *Swan Lake.* The congregation included thirty-seven members of the royal family, and friends from show business such as actresses Judi Dench and Felicity Kendal. Roddy Llewellyn and Tony Snowdon were there as well.

The Queen Mother had fallen at Sandringham and cut her arm two days earlier. But she had insisted on attending the funeral, and the previous day had been flown to Windsor by helicopter. She arrived at the chapel by wheelchair after the Queen and was seated near her daughter's coffin, which was covered with Margaret's personal Royal Standard and arrangements of white roses and pink tulips.

Following the service, eight Royal Highland Fusiliers in tartan trousers and dark jackets carried out the coffin as trumpeters sounded "The Last Post" and "Reveille." A bagpiper played "The Desperate Struggle of the Bird," which seemed a suitably melancholy lament for a princess who had seen so much unhappiness. The Queen Mother managed to stand briefly as Margaret's coffin passed, and she kept her emotions in check, but as the Queen stood outside the chapel watching the coffin being placed in the hearse, she lowered her head to wipe away tears. "It was the saddest I have ever seen the Queen," said Reinaldo Herrera, Margaret's good friend.

By the time family members joined Elizabeth II at the castle for tea afterward, she had regained her composure. She was already turning her attention to her departure in three days for Jamaica, the first stop on a two-week Golden Jubilee Commonwealth tour that would also take her to New Zealand and Australia.

"She went as scheduled," said a member of the royal household. "You never would have known. She was doing her duty, smiling, laughing, engaged in everything. Maybe privately she showed her grief, but we didn't see it." The Jamaicans gave a flag-waving welcome to the woman known in the local patois as "Missis Queen" and "The Queen Lady."

The crowds in New Zealand and Australia surpassed expectations as well. Sir Edmund Hillary, whose conquest of Mount Everest had coincided with Elizabeth II's coronation, attended a garden party for her in Auckland and said, "Most people much prefer to have a Queen as head of state rather than a broken-down old prime minister." In Queensland thirty thousand people stood in the rain to hear her remarks at the "people's day" fair. When Queenslander Ted Smout told her he was 104 years old, she said, "Oh, my mother is only

601

101!" In private she talked "constantly" of Margaret, and she called every day to check in with her mother. On her return to England on Sunday, March 3, she went immediately to Royal Lodge for a visit.

Nearly a month later, she was back at Windsor for Easter weekend. The Queen Mother had become noticeably weaker, but she had been lucid enough in the previous week to call friends and relatives with various instructions that were meant to be final wishes. On the morning of March 30, 2002 — Easter Saturday — the Queen was out for her customary ride when she received a message from the doctors attending her mother that the end was approaching. When Elizabeth II arrived in her riding clothes, the Queen Mother was in a chair by the fireside in her dressing gown. The two women exchanged a few private words, and the Queen Mother did not speak again. Shortly afterward she closed her eyes and fell unconscious as Canon John Ovendon, chaplain of the Royal Chapel of All Saints in Windsor Great Park, held her hand and prayed.

Elizabeth II went back to the castle to change and returned to Royal Lodge with Margaret's children, David Linley and Sarah Chatto. The Queen Mother's niece and close friend Margaret Rhodes was there as well. She lived nearby in the Great Park and had been faithfully visiting her aunt every day. At 3:15 in the afternoon the Queen Mother died peacefully at age 101, surrounded by her surviving daughter, her two grandchildren, and her niece, all of whom were crying. Tony Blair spoke to the Queen that evening and found her "very sad but dignified." Prince Charles, who was in Klosters, Switzerland, on a skiing holiday with his sons, rushed to Windsor the next day to pay his respects to the grandmother he called "the original life enhancer."

The Queen Mother's "Tay Bridge" funeral plan unfolded as she had meticulously planned. By custom, it was not called a state funeral — reserved for reigning monarchs, with rare exceptions such as Winston Churchill — but a royal ceremonial funeral that was identical in its trappings. The Queen and her advisers were concerned at first whether there would be sufficient public interest to justify the nine days of official mourning, including three days of lying in state. These misgivings were prompted in part by modest-sized crowds outside Buckingham Palace and lines for the condolence books at St. James's Palace, and by coverage in admittedly pro-republican newspapers such as *The Guardian,* which ran a headline on the day after the Queen Mother's death: "UNCERTAIN FAREWELL REVEALS A NATION DIVIDED."

By Friday, April 5, when the Queen Mother's coffin was taken on a gun carriage in an elaborate procession from St. James's Palace to Westminster Hall for the lying in state, the naysayers were proved wrong, as an estimated 250,000 people lined the route, in some places twenty deep. Draped over the coffin was her red, gold, white, and blue personal standard emblazoned with the familiar heraldic designs as well as bows and rampant lions from her family coat of arms. Resting on top was a wreath of white camellias bearing a card saying "In loving memory — Lilibet." In front of the flowers was a purple velvet cushion holding the Queen Mother's glittering coronation crown set with the legendary 105-carat Koh-i-Noor diamond.

The horses of the King's Troop pulled the gun carriage, and 1,600 members of the armed forces representing regiments from Britain and the Commonwealth marched to the somber music of military bands accompanied by muffled drumbeats. Immediately following the coffin were all the male members of the royal family plus, for the first time, Princess Anne. Like her brothers Charles and Andrew, she wore a naval uniform with trousers, a privilege of her rank as an honorary rear admiral.

They met the Queen and Margaret's daughter, Sarah Chatto, at the door of Westminster Hall, and the pallbearers carried the coffin to the seven-foot-high catafalque where George VI had lain in state five decades earlier. After the Archbishop of Canterbury conducted a brief prayer service for the family, the Queen and Prince Philip were driven back to Buckingham Palace. As she waved to the crowds, Elizabeth II's expression was ineffably sad. As their car left Parliament Square and turned into Whitehall, the crowds of silent mourners unexpectedly burst into applause that continued along the Mall. "It was very emotional for her," said one of her relatives. "It made her realize people really cared." The Queen said that the moment was "one of the most touching things" that had ever happened to her.

When the soaring medieval hall was opened to members of the public, they stood in lines that

First Lady Laura Bush, and United Nations Secretary General Kofi Annan among numerous dignitaries. There were ordinary people as well who had known the Queen Mother through the more than three hundred charities of which she was patron or president. In the spirit of the Queen's address, the midday funeral service combined solemn pageantry with reminders of how, "like the sun," the Queen Mother "bathed us in her warm glow," in the words of George Carey, the Archbishop of Canterbury. She embodied, he said, "one of the most fundamental of all roles and relationships — that of simply being a mother, a mum, the Queen Mum."

A significant shift had taken place that week. For fifty years, Elizabeth II had deferred to her mother, and the object of that deference was gone. The Queen now took on the mantle of her mother's role as well as her own. She moved up a generation and became the nation's grandmother, or as Margaret Rhodes put it, "the senior royal lady." Much as the Queen adored her mother, she had been slightly overshadowed by the Queen Mother's merry and approachable presence, so beloved by the people. Elizabeth II had always been admired, but now the depth of affection for the Queen Mother began to merge with the equally deep respect for the Queen.

Still, the deaths of her sister and her mother within the space of seven weeks gave seventy-five-year-old Elizabeth II "a terrible wallop of grief," said Margaret Rhodes. "It was a huge thing," said Elizabeth Anson. "The two people she talked to every day on the phone — neither of them was there." The full impact of those losses — and of her altered relationship with the public — would become more evident later. In the meantime, Elizabeth II found solace in her duty.

CHAPTER NINETEEN
MOVING PICTURES

"The British have lost the habit of proper partying," said historian David Starkey at the end of January 2002, explaining that changes in the nature of British society meant the celebratory atmosphere of the Silver Jubilee could not possibly be duplicated twenty-five years later. Starkey was part of a chorus of skeptics predicting the Golden Jubilee would be a flop. As it had in 1977, *The Guardian* led the charge, joined by *The Independent* — the same newspapers that had predicted a tepid response to the death of the Queen Mother.

Even after the outpouring of enthusiasm for the monarchy shown by the crowds for her funeral, much of the press had remained dubious. In keeping with its "softly, softly" strategy of holding down expectations, Buckingham Palace advisers concentrated on refining their ambitious plans. The celebration was privately financed, and had taken eighteen months to map out. Shipping magnate Jeffrey Sterling, Lord Sterling of Plaistow, who had successfully run the Silver Jubilee, was appointed chairman of the Golden Jubilee committee. Within a matter of months, he raised nearly £6 million from corporations and individuals who wanted to honor their Queen.

"Suddenly they got the point of the Queen, who had been doing her job for fifty years."

Queen Elizabeth II and Prince Philip riding in the Gold State Coach from Buckingham Palace to St. Paul's Cathedral for the Golden Jubilee service of thanksgiving, June 2002. REBECCA NADIN/PRESS ASSOCIATION IMAGES

A crucial part of the Palace strategy involved an advisory group of outsiders that met fifteen times in 2001 over lunches hosted by Robin Janvrin in the Chinese Dining Room. Its members were drawn from the senior ranks of public relations, broadcasting, magazines, and newspapers, including Libby Purves, a columnist for *The Times* who articulated the views of "middle Britain." In the spirit of their more open approach, Janvrin and Simon Walker also invited such critics of the monarchy as Waheed Alli, a Labour peer who was a highly successful television producer and gay rights activist. The committee members made their own suggestions and commented on plans presented by Palace officials. Neither the committee's membership nor details of its deliberations ever leaked.

Private polling and focus groups measured the Queen's popularity by region. This research helped the Queen's advisers plan her three-month-long progress starting on May 1 with sixteen regional tours throughout the United Kingdom. The Palace intentionally launched the tours in Cornwall and Devon, counties that showed some of the highest support for the monarchy. To ensure maximum coverage, the press office briefed three thousand community organizations even before conducting off-the-record briefings for national and regional media, followed by meetings with the international press.

On April 25, 2002, the Queen had a reception at Windsor Castle for more than 750 journalists representing the smallest regional newspapers as well as the major dailies in London. Alastair Campbell acidly observed that "there was something truly pathetic about these so-called hardened hacks, many of them self-proclaimed republicans, bowing and scraping." The Queen "moved effortlessly between them and left grown men in little puddles of excitement." Afterward, Simon Walker suggested to the Queen that they should have a similar party in five years' time. She said she preferred ten.

Four nights later, Tony and Cherie Blair hosted a dinner at 10 Downing Street for Elizabeth II and Philip and her surviving prime ministers — Heath, Callaghan, Thatcher, and Major — and the families of the others. "What a relief!" the Queen said as she greeted the Blairs. "No need for any introductions!" Campbell detected a marked difference in the Queen's manner from her evening at Windsor "when she had been doing her professional small-talk thing," and at No. 10, "where she seemed genuinely happy."

The following day, Elizabeth II addressed the Joint Houses of Parliament in Westminster Hall, where her mother's body had lain in state only three weeks earlier. As was the case in the same setting in 1977, her words were personal, and they reflected the essential message of her jubilee year. "Change has become a constant," she said. "Managing it has become an expanding discipline. The way we embrace it defines our future." She emphasized the importance of Britain's enduring values of moderation and pragmatism, inventiveness and creativity, and fairness and tolerance, as well as its tradition of service.

In keeping with her theme of inclusiveness, she cited "the consolidation of our richly multicultural and multi-faith society" as a "major development" since 1952, achieved "remarkably peacefully and with much goodwill." (Only days earlier, the Palace had announced that during her travels over the summer, she would visit a Hindu temple, a Jewish museum, a Sikh temple, and an Islamic center — her first time inside a mosque.) At seventy-six years of age, she made clear — yet again — "my resolve to continue, with the support of my family, to serve the people of this great nation of ours to the best of my ability through the changing times ahead." One thousand peers and members of Parliament rose to their feet and gave her a loud and prolonged round of applause — the magnitude of which seemed to both move and embarrass her.

After her first three regional swings through England, she traveled to Northern Ireland on May 13 for a three-day tour in an atmosphere far different from her tense visit during the Silver Jubilee. On April 10, 1998, the Good Friday Agreement had brought peace to Ulster with a compromise to share power between the Protestant majority and Catholic minority in a newly created legislative assembly (ending direct London rule). The accord also put aside the idea of a united Ireland unless approved by the voters in both Ulster and the Republic of Ireland.

Four years later, Elizabeth II addressed legislators from the new Northern Ireland Assembly for the first time as their Queen at a reception in the parliament buildings at Stormont. She told them they had "an historic opportunity to bring the administration of Northern Ireland closer to the people whom you serve" and to "meet the aspirations both of those who are proud to be

British and of those who feel a strong sense of Irish identity."

The centerpiece of the Golden Jubilee festivities was a four-day "people's party" at the beginning of June, with two unprecedented concerts in the gardens at Buckingham Palace. Each concert was attended by twelve thousand fans randomly selected from nearly two million applicants, and both were televised live by the BBC. The music was classical on Saturday the 1st and pop on Monday the 3rd.

Initiating the pop concert required some delicate maneuvering. "It was important to have young support for the jubilee," said Simon Walker. Robin Janvrin ultimately won over the Queen, who made it clear she had no interest in spending three hours listening to pop singers. As a compromise, the courtiers arranged for her to arrive about thirty-five minutes before the end.

The concert began dramatically with Brian May, the guitarist from Queen, standing on the roof of Buckingham Palace playing his idiosyncratic version of the national anthem. When Elizabeth II appeared, Eric Clapton was singing "Layla," and the comedian Dame Edna Everage introduced her as the "Golden Jubilee girl." The Queen, who wore yellow earplugs, sat with Philip, the Blairs, and twenty-four members of the royal family in the VIP box for the remaining acts, which ended with Paul McCartney singing "Hey Jude." Accompanied by her husband, Charles, William, and Harry, she joined the performers on the stage as Charles greeted his "mummy" and saluted her "50 extraordinary years," adding, "You have embodied something vital in our lives — continuity. You have been a beacon of tradition and stability in the midst of profound, sometimes perilous, change." The audience cheered, and the heir to the throne gave his mother a kiss.

Afterward, Elizabeth II ignited a beacon in front of the Victoria Memorial, one of more than two thousand bonfires blazing in the United Kingdom and Commonwealth countries. In Kenya, a fire was lit near Treetops, where she became Queen. The evening ended with a spectacular fireworks display and light show on the Palace facade, before a crowd of a million people who had gathered in the Mall and nearby parks. The Queen and Philip watched from a reviewing stand, beaming as an illuminated version of the Union Jack rippled across the front of the Palace.

The final day of celebration, on Tuesday the 4th, featured the ceremonial drive in the ornate Gold State Coach from the Palace to St. Paul's for a jubilee service, followed by a Guildhall luncheon in which Tony Blair told the Queen, "Deference may be inherited but affection is earned, and the affection this country feels for you is real." In the afternoon the Queen and Philip attended a festival along the Mall with twenty thousand participants, including a gospel choir of five thousand singers and representatives of the fifty-four Commonwealth countries in native costumes. By teatime the vast crowd had completely filled the Mall, waving flags, cheering, and singing, as they had twenty-five years before, "Land of Hope and Glory" and "God Save the Queen," while Elizabeth II and her family waved back from the Buckingham Palace balcony. Above them at only 1,500 feet flew a Concorde followed by the RAF's Red Arrows in synchronized formation.

The festivities continued throughout the summer as the Queen covered some 3,500 miles by Royal Train and visited seventy cities and towns. She had garden parties at Sandringham and Balmoral as well as Buckingham Palace and Holyroodhouse. She did some private celebrating as well. Fifty men who had been pages at royal events in their boyhood treated her to a black-tie dinner at White's club, where women were permitted only on rare occasions. According to a story told by members afterward, a buffer spotted her arriving and grumbled: "The Queen coming to White's — the thin edge of the wedge!" (A photograph taken that night of the Queen and her former pages hangs proudly in the loo at the club.)

The Golden Jubilee was an enormous success. "People woke up and realized that Her Majesty was about stability, serenity, continuity, calm through adversity, and humor when things are going wrong," said her former press secretary Charles Anson. "Suddenly they got the point of the Queen, who had been doing her job for fifty years." Press coverage turned effusive with the popular tide. The jubilee events "have proved conclusively," noted the BBC, "that the Queen and the monarchy are still held in high esteem by millions of British people." The results emerging from the private polls also augured well. "The public felt the Queen was paying attention to them and was having a good time," said Robert Worcester of MORI. When the polling for the Palace began, those who felt the monarchy was out of touch registered nearly 40 percent, but that number dropped to the mid-20s in the years after the jubilee.

In the autumn of 2002 the Queen became embroiled in a controversy over an encounter she had had five years earlier with Paul Burrell, the butler to the late Princess of Wales. He was known as Diana's "rock" for his total devotion if not, as it turned out, discretion. Before working for Diana, Burrell had been a footman at Buckingham Palace, and the Queen had rewarded his service by investing him with the Royal Victorian Order, one of her personal honors. She was told that he was torn up with grief over Diana's death, so when he asked for an audience at the Palace, she was open-hearted enough to oblige.

On Thursday afternoon, December 18, 1997, Burrell had a lot on his mind when he arrived at her private sitting room on the first floor overlooking the gardens. During their ninety minutes together, he spoke "at length" about Diana's troubles and her feelings toward Charles. He said that Diana's mother, Frances Shand Kydd, had been shredding her daughter's letters and memos during visits to Kensington Palace, and he told the Queen "he had taken some of the princess's papers for safekeeping" — just one topic among many before he and the Queen parted company.

Three years later, in January 2001, acting on a tip from another former royal servant, police raided Burrell's home. They turned up more than three hundred items from Diana's estate, including designer clothing, jewelry, handbags, and furniture, as well as a lesser number of belongings allegedly taken from Charles and William. The former butler was charged with theft. As the investigation progressed, the Queen was briefed several times by Robin Janvrin, but she didn't mention her talk with Burrell because, as she later said, she didn't think his passing reference to safeguarding Diana's papers was relevant in the context of the charges Burrell faced. Nor, for his part, did Burrell disclose the nature of their meeting to his own lawyers because, he said, it was "private."

Burrell's trial began on Ocrtober 14, 2002, the day before the Queen returned to England from her ten-day Golden Jubilee tour of Canada. On Friday the 25th, while being driven to a memorial service, Philip and Charles were discussing the much-publicized case. Philip mentioned to Charles that the Queen had met with Burrell after Diana's death and that the butler had talked about keeping some documents. This was apparently the first Charles had heard of the meeting. He immediately relayed the information to his private secretary, who alerted the authorities. On November 1, the prosecution dropped the case because it was based "on a false premise that Mr. Burrell had never told anyone that he was holding anything for safekeeping." Even though what Burrell told the Queen pertained only to an unspecified number of papers out of the substantial hoard of valuable belongings, it was enough to stop the trial.

The press pounced on the dramatic turn of events and suggested that the Queen and her son had somehow tried to halt the trial to prevent embarrassing public testimony about the late princess and the royal family. Equally damaging was the alternative explanation — that she was an "old woman being forgetful."

In fact, the Queen had not forgotten the incident at all. Earlier in the autumn at Balmoral, when the upcoming trial was in the news, Elizabeth II had been entertaining her guests over drinks before setting off for a barbecue. "She was playing patience, very content and very relaxed," said a friend sitting with her that day. "Almost in passing, she talked about the conversation she had had with Burrell. Her recollection was very clear, that Burrell had told her he had taken a few documents as opposed to hundreds of things." The impression she gave was that Burrell's disclosure was minor. "She told me she thought no more about it," said her friend. "It only became a topical matter because the trial was going to be taking place and it was on people's minds. What she said was so matter-of-fact that she must have discussed it on other occasions."

Michael Peat, who by then had moved from Buckingham Palace to be Charles's private secretary, conducted an exhaustive examination of whether there was "anything improper or remiss" in the termination of the Burrell trial. Peat found "no evidence" that the revelation was meant to derail the trial. He pointed out that if the Palace had wanted such an outcome, there had been "numerous prior opportunities to intervene to prevent or stifle the prosecution." It was only after the trial unfolded that press accounts reported the crux of the prosecution's case, which was to prove that Burrell had spirited away hundreds of items without telling anyone.

A week after the trial collapsed, the Queen took on a task her mother had carried out faithfully every year, visiting the Field of Remembrance outside Westminster Abbey, where nineteen thousand tiny crosses had been planted in tribute to members of the British armed forces who had died in combat, a tradition that began in 1928 to honor those killed in World War I. The Queen Mother had invariably stayed longer than expected, stopping to speak to as many former servicemen and members of deceased veterans' families as she could. The previous November she had braved freezing temperatures to plant her cross, and now the Queen planted her own during a brief prayer ceremony attended by several thousand people. As the service concluded with a minute of silence, Elizabeth II had tears streaming down her cheeks.

If the Queen showed traces of emotional fragility after the ups and downs of 2002, her physical health was as robust as ever. At the Windsor Horse Show the previous May, spectators had marveled at her vigor while following Philip on one of his competitive carriage driving marathons in Windsor Great Park. "She drove her own Range Rover to each of the obstacles every half mile," recalled Nini Ferguson, one of the American competitors. "Philip was driving four horses. She would watch him do the obstacles, then run back and jump in her car. She was in her wellies, with her scarf flying, followed by four or five corgis. She had such spirit and energy, and she seemed so young."

In early January 2003, Elizabeth II slipped while walking on uneven ground at Sandringham after visiting Desert Star, one of her most promising colts. She tore cartilage in her right knee, which required arthroscopic surgery. In a letter to Monty Roberts, she expressed her frustration over being stuck "languishing indoors," unable to ride or walk her dogs. She recovered well and had an identical operation on her left knee less than a year later to repair minor cartilage damage that her doctors had discovered. She walked for several weeks with a cane, but was soon back into her weekly riding routine. Her one concession to age was using Fell ponies as her mounts rather than the larger horses she had been riding for decades. "They are about 14 hands high, solid squat things," said Michael Oswald. "Not many her age ride at all, so they are safe conveyances."

With her mother and sister gone, Elizabeth II came to rely more on her extended family for companionship. Her long-standing ritual on Sundays at Windsor had been to have a midday drink at Royal Lodge after attending the service at the Royal Chapel of All Saints. Now she would go instead to visit her cousin Margaret Rhodes, a small and sprightly countrywoman. Her cottage in Windsor Great Park is simple and cozy, with modest furnishings and rubber toys for Gilda, her West Highland terrier, strewn on the floor. The tables in her sitting room are filled with photographs of the Queen Mother, King George VI, and Elizabeth II in her Balmoral garb.

When Margaret's husband was stricken with terminal cancer in 1981, the Queen gave them the house so they could be closer to London hospitals than their farm in Devon. "How would you like to live in suburbia?" the Queen asked. "It was the answer to a prayer," Margaret Rhodes recalled.

Each Sunday the Queen takes the wheel of her Jaguar for the short drive from the church. Her cousin greets her with a curtsy, and the Queen perches on the faded sofa in the sitting room, her hat firmly in place, ready for the return trip to the castle. As Elizabeth II sips her gin and Dubonnet, the two women talk about the events of the previous week, and swap news about family matters and various people they know — the health of an elderly stalker at Balmoral, for example.

The events of 2002 — her personal losses as well as the acclaim for her jubilee — had turned a page, and the difficulties of the 1990s had now been relegated to history. The Queen was smiling more in public. She seemed warmer, more approachable, and more relaxed, in some ways more like her mother. "This may sound impertinent," said Robert Salisbury, "but I would guess the Queen has rather blossomed since her mother died." Monty Roberts felt that she was showing "more understanding of the wonders of life than she had before."

During a small dinner in 2003 with a group of Grenadier Guards in the Officers Mess at St. James's Palace — a handsome high-ceilinged room decorated with antiques, regimental silver, a wooden officers' latrine door from the trenches of World War I, and a portrait of the young Queen Victoria — laughter and loud conversation could be heard through the open windows. A call came through from the Queen's comptroller, Malcolm Ross, who had an apartment in the Palace. He was complaining about the noise, not knowing the identity of the guest that evening. The officer of the guard conveyed the message to the Queen, who replied, "Oh tell Malcolm not to be so silly."

Robert Salisbury detected a shift in Elizabeth II's manner when he was seated next to her at the seventieth birthday party for Ginny Airlie at Annabel's in February 2003. The Queen told friends how much she had been looking forward to the party because it was the first time she had been in a nightclub since the early days of her marriage. "Never have I seen anyone have such a good time," said Annabel Goldsmith (after whom the club had been named), who was also seated with the Queen. "Here was this austere woman laughing and joking. She was amusing the whole table."

The next day, Elizabeth II had an engagement at St. Alban's Abbey, north of London. As she was being introduced to dignitaries, the dean of the abbey spotted Robert Salisbury, and asked the Queen whether she had met him before. "Oh yes," said the Queen in ringing tones. "Robert and I were in a nightclub last night till half past one."

She also acquired a new confidante in Angela Kelly, who had taken Bobo MacDonald's place. Twenty-five years the Queen's junior, Kelly had been a soldier who joined the royal household as a maid and worked her way up through the ranks to dresser, a title Kelly herself upgraded to "personal assistant." Like Bobo, who was the daughter of a railwayman, Kelly had modest origins in Liverpool, where her father worked in the dockyards. But unlike Bobo, who kept a low profile, Kelly, a plump blonde with an effervescent personality, became a visible presence in the Queen's entourage.

When Kelly is with the Queen "there is lots of jolly laughter," said Anne Glenconner. "She has moved into the vacuum created by the death of the Queen's sister and her mother," according to one of the Queen's relatives.

Kelly tends to the royal wardrobe in a rigorously professional way, adapting the traditions of Hartnell and Amies with an eye to the theatrical requirements of the Queen's public appearances. Kelly often accompanies household officials on reconnaissance trips ("recces") for foreign tours, checking the backgrounds where the Queen will be appearing and researching national colors as well as hues that might have positive and negative significance. "Angela understands the Queen needs to wear something that sets her apart from the crowd when she is at a distance, and that inside she can wear beige and grey, things that are more neutral," said a senior royal adviser. Kelly uses new couturiers such as Stewart Parvin, but she also designs many of the Queen's dresses, coats, and hats herself and has them made in-house at lower cost.

The Queen has long taken a keen interest in her jewelry and knows the history of the pieces in her extensive private collection. She enjoys displaying her beautiful jewelry whether in public or private, sometimes at dinner parties wearing multiple rings, even on her index fingers. Once, when she was introduced to Joel Arthur Rosenthal, the American creator of JAR jewelers, at a Winfield House dinner, she said, "I have heard that Damien Hirst has been using diamonds to make a jeweled skull, but I prefer the diamonds around my neck."

Angela Kelly has built on her boss's expertise by developing computerized inventories so she can have the most up-to-date facts at her fingertips when she sets out a tray with pieces for the Queen's selection. "Angela will come up with something she has found God knows where," said a lady-in-waiting. "If the brooch is from Mexico, she will say where the stones are from. She is interested in it, and she makes it fun."

On Wednesday, November 19, 2003, the Queen and her courtiers awoke to a "World Exclusive" in the *Daily Mirror:* a page-one photograph of a footman on the famous Buckingham Palace balcony with INTRUDER emblazoned above his head. Another headline explained: "As Bush arrives, we reveal Mirrorman has been a Palace footman for TWO MONTHS in the biggest royal security scandal ever." Inside the paper were fourteen pages of surreptitiously snapped photographs and descriptions of royal family routines and private quarters, punctuated by equally sensational headlines ("I COULD HAVE POISONED THE QUEEN"). It was all the handiwork of twenty-six-year-old *Mirror* reporter Ryan Parry, who lied his way into a job as a footman and bolted with his story, violating the confidentiality agreement he signed when he was hired.

The newspaper tried to frame the stunt as a public service, but it was mainly a peek into the private lives of the Queen and her family. The most talked-about photograph was of the breakfast table laid for the Queen and Prince Philip with white linen, a floral centerpiece, silver cutlery, and bone china, along with an inexpensive transistor radio and three perfectly aligned Tupperware boxes containing cornflakes and porridge oats. Parry wrote that the Queen preferred her toast "with light marmalade," but she ended up feeding most of it to the corgis under the table.

He reported that each royal tea tray had its own map, that Prince Andrew was a teetotaler who sometimes swore at his footman, and that Princess Anne required her breakfast bowl to "contain a very black banana and ripe kiwi fruit," and went about her business "without a fuss." Parry described Sophie Wessex as "kind and grateful," and the Queen came across as chatty and congenial — "not nearly haughty enough for the job," observed *The Sunday Times.*

Photographs and descriptions of the private apartments highlighted Andrew's penchant for stuffed toys and pillows embroidered with messages such as "Eat, Sleep, and Remarry," Anne's sitting room where "every surface is covered with books, ornaments, piles of paper and magazines," and Edward and Sophie Wessex's modern decor and tidy housekeeping. Parry even snapped a picture of the carpeted Wessex bathroom adorned with a cartoon showing the Queen speaking to a group of penguins in "royal garments."

The next day the *Mirror* struck again, with "our man's exposé of Windsor," showing Parry on page one petting two of the Queen's corgis in front of the castle, followed by eleven pages of photographs and descriptions of his weekend working for the Queen. His picture of her breakfast table included her lineup of morning newspapers: as always, the

Racing Post was on top, followed by the *Daily Mail, Express,* and *Mirror* (with its revelation of the day, an excerpt from Paul Burrell's tell-all book about the royal family), then the *Daily Telegraph* and *The Times.*

Parry recounted that the Queen dined alone while watching her surprisingly lowbrow choice of television programs: *The Bill,* a popular police drama ("I don't like 'The Bill,' " she told Parry as he poured her coffee, "but I just can't help watching it"), the long-running soap opera *EastEnders,* and, somewhat improbably, *Kirsty's Home Videos,* a comedy show featuring footage of ordinary people that included "a fair share of bare bottoms." There was also a photo spread of the castle's luxurious Victorian summerhouse, with its potted plants, sculptures, swimming pool, indoor badminton court, table tennis, and netted cage surrounding Philip's wooden polo practice horse.

The Queen was furious, and her lawyers took immediate legal action against the newspaper, citing "a highly objectionable invasion of privacy, devoid of any legitimate interest." She obtained a permanent injunction that prevented the *Mirror* from publishing anything further and restrained the newspaper's ability to reprint many of the photographs. The newspaper paid £25,000 toward the Queen's legal costs, gave the Palace all unused photographs, and destroyed its unpublished stories.

But the *Mirror*'s editor, Piers Morgan, who went on to become a television personality in the United States, had succeeded in his mission. Not only did he embarrass the royal family, he timed publication

— with its predictable cascade of coverage in the other newspapers — to coincide with the arrival of George and Laura Bush for the second state visit by a United States president. The only other American leader to be entertained on the same scale at Buckingham Palace over several days was Woodrow Wilson in December 1918.

The Bushes' historic trip was already clouded by security concerns and the prospect of thousands of protesters marching against the war in Iraq. As a result, the Queen was forced to shelve the traditional welcoming ceremony in Horse Guards Parade followed by a procession of carriages along the Mall to Buckingham Palace. Instead, there was a truncated version in the forecourt behind the railings where the Changing of the Guard usually took place. The Bushes were driven from the rear of the Palace (where they had spent the night) around to the front. They walked up the red-carpeted stairs into a specially built pavilion to greet the Queen and a line of dignitaries. The Household Cavalry trotted past, the president and the Duke of Edinburgh inspected the guard of honor, and everyone then walked inside for lunch — all of which had an improvised feel that the press roundly mocked.

The Bushes, however, were delighted, and the Queen, who already had an easygoing relationship with the first couple, made them feel welcome. "She was unruffled by the protests," George Bush recalled. "She had seen a lot during her life, and it didn't seem to faze her. Nor did it faze me."

That evening the Queen hosted a white-tie state banquet for 160 guests. The following night George and Laura Bush returned the hospitality with a smaller and less formal dinner hosted by Will and Sarah Farish at Winfield House. Among the sixty guests were prominent Americans in Britain such as U.S. senator George Mitchell and Rose Marie Bravo, the CEO of Burberry. "It was like old friends week," said Catherine Fenton, the White House social secretary. "The Queen and the Duke of Edinburgh greeted the Farishes affectionately, and there was lots of laughter."

There were protesters in the streets that week heckling Blair as well as Bush, but in the prime minister's case, they were objecting to the protracted campaign by the Labour Party to ban fox hunting. When Blair tried to explain the issue, Bush said, "Whatever did you do that for, man?" The president, Blair observed, was "as ever getting right to the point."

The proposed ban united animal rights activists concerned about the well-being of the foxes (typically killed by a pack of hounds at the end of each hunt) with a populist assault on the aristocracy. Blair embraced the measure as a purely political ploy to assuage the left wing of his party. Debate over the ban consumed more than seven hundred hours in Parliament — the largest amount for any piece of legislation during the Blair era. It also galvanized a series of protests by a "countryside alliance" in London that attracted vast peaceful crowds ranging from landed peers to humble countrymen dependent on the sport for their livelihood. Although the Prince of Wales didn't join the protest, he and his sons were avid hunters, and he openly defended the sport, telling Tony Blair the ban was "absurd." Blair, in turn, warned Charles against trying to "play politics with him." Sophie Wessex reflected the prevailing view in the royal family when she said, "Fox hunting is just vermin control but people think it's the aristocracy running round doing what the hell they like." She added that Blair was "ignorant of the countryside," which he later acknowledged was correct.

Elizabeth II necessarily had to remain neutral. But as her cousin Margaret Rhodes observed, "She is a countrywoman at heart. She would defend hunting as one of the glues to keep the countryside together." In her own quiet way, the Queen lobbied Blair during a weekend at Balmoral several years before the ban came to a vote. She patiently explained to him over dinner that hunting was an activity not only for the upper class but for regular people as well. Some of the riders, she said, were far from well-off and rented their horses from livery stables. She naturally assumed that Blair knew about these facilities, which were a staple of rural areas, but he had never heard of them.

Her briefing helped him understand the economic as well as social significance of hunting for rural communities, and he later admitted that the ban was "one of the domestic legislative measures I most regret." He claimed he could do nothing to stop the momentum toward eventual passage of the Hunting Act of 2004. In fact, he "allowed a compromise proposal to be overruled by his own party," wrote Charles Moore in *The Spectator,* permitting a bill "to be invoked . . . to force through a total ban." As a practical matter, fox hunting with hounds continued as clever huntsmen found various loopholes, and the anticipated widespread arrests never happened. Still, all members of the royal family had to stop fox hunting since it had become technically illegal.

On Saturday, April 9, 2005, the Prince of Wales finally married the love of his life, Camilla Parker Bowles, thirty-four years after they first met, and nearly two decades after they resumed their romance in the mid-1980s. He was fifty-six and she fifty-seven.

Camilla and her first husband had divorced in 1995, and she had been gradually brought into the fold in the years since Diana's death. Her appearance at the two Golden Jubilee concerts in the Buckingham Palace gardens was the first time she had been seen in public with the Queen and the rest of the royal family. Although Camilla's love affair with Charles had aggravated his problems with Diana, the Queen recognized her good qualities — salty humor, resilience, warmth, common sense, and above all devotion to Charles. Camilla enjoyed the field sports so important to the royal family, and she embraced all their traditions. Through years of vilification, Camilla maintained a discreet silence, which also impressed the Queen. "Camilla never whines," said one of her longtime friends. "She takes things as they come and tries to turn them into something humorous." When the tabloids were stirring up trouble in the weeks before the wedding, Camilla joked, "It's just two old people getting hitched."

Under liberalized Church of England guidelines, the two divorcés could have been married in a religious ceremony, but church leaders agreed that given the couple's well-known adultery, such a service would have offended too many priests and parishioners. Instead, they exchanged their vows at the Windsor Guildhall.

As Supreme Governor of the Church of England, the Queen decided it would be inappropriate to attend the civil service at the Guildhall, which was witnessed by twenty-eight family members. "Her decision assuredly had nothing to do with her private feelings but everything to do with her public role," wrote Jonathan Dimbleby at the time. "Much as they might have wished otherwise, her advisers knew that they had no chance of persuading her otherwise — however un-motherly or even out of date it may have made her appear." The Queen and Philip did attend the "Service of Prayer and Dedication" afterward at St. George's Chapel.

The congregation of 720 guests that filled St. George's Chapel included the Blairs and other political leaders as well as representatives from royal houses in Europe and the Middle East, numerous titled aristocrats, and television and film stars such as Kenneth Branagh and Prunella Scales. The traditional service conducted by Rowan Williams, the 104th Archbishop of Canterbury, used the 1662 Book of Common Prayer, which Charles preferred to the more modern version. In contrast to the elaborate naval commander's uniform he wore in Westminster Abbey a quarter century earlier, Charles was dressed in a morning suit, and Camilla chose an elegant floor-length pale blue silk coat dress with gold embroidery. When they emerged from the West Door of the chapel, they declined to kiss before two thousand well-wishers who had been admitted by ticket to the castle grounds, although Charles and Camilla, now known as the Duchess of Cornwall, did a five-minute walkabout, shaking hands and accepting congratulations.

Everyone was in high spirits at the reception hosted by the prince's mother in the state apartments at the castle. "I have two very important announcements to make," said the Queen. "I know you will want to know who was the winner of the Grand National. It was Hedgehunter." After the applause died down, she turned to Charles and Camilla, and said, "Having cleared Becher's Brook and the Chair [the most dangerous and highest fences on the steeplechase course] the happy couple are now in the winners' enclosure." "There was a huge roar of approval, very un-monarchical," wrote veteran broadcaster Melvyn Bragg, who was thrilled to be among "the great gangs of England" celebrating the marriage. Charles paid tribute to "my darling Camilla," thanking her for "taking on the task of being married to me." When Joan Rivers, a friend of the couple, was introduced to the Queen, the comedian said, "I'm going on Larry King tonight, and I'm going to tell him how beautiful your pin is." "Thank you," replied the slightly puzzled Queen.

As the newlyweds left the castle for their honeymoon at Birkhall, they paused at the sovereign's entrance where Camilla and the Queen kissed goodbye, the first time they had done so publicly. Princes William and Harry kissed their new stepmother as well before she climbed into the waiting car with "Prince" and "Duchess" scrawled across its windshield.

■■■■

William graduated from St. Andrews University in Scotland the following June. His younger brother, Harry, had already embarked on a career in the military, and William wanted to do the same. But first he worked on his father's farm in Gloucestershire and at Chatsworth, home of the Duke and Duchess of Devonshire, to gain experience in estate management. He spent three weeks visiting financial institutions including the Bank of England, the London Stock Exchange, and Lloyd's of London, which gave him "a better understanding of how all the different financial institutions work and how they fit together." By January 2006 he was enrolled at the Royal Military Academy at Sandhurst, where Harry was completing his training.

At twenty-two, William was already showing he knew how to meet royal expectations with a determination, not unlike his mother's, to do things in his own way. When he sensed he was being "pushed," he could be "quite stubborn," yet he said he remained "open for people saying I'm wrong because most of the time I am." He had learned to live in the glare of publicity, though he found being in the spotlight "kind of awkward." At the same time, he emphasized that he valued "the normality I can get, doing simple things, doing normal things, more than anything, rather than getting things done for me." He even liked to do his own shopping, paying with his credit card because "I'm not organized enough to have cash."

The Queen and Prince Philip were a visible and

important force in the lives of their grandchildren, who now numbered seven with the addition of Edward and Sophie's first child, Louise, in November 2003. Elizabeth II paid particular attention to William as second in line to the throne. During his student days at Eton, he had often come to tea with his grandmother at Windsor Castle, and he had observed her from the time he was a little boy.

In a November 2004 interview he said he was "very close" to both his grandparents. The Queen had been "brilliant. She's a real role model," he said. "She's just very helpful on any sort of difficulties or problems I might be having. But I'm quite a private person as well, so I don't really talk that much about what I sort of feel or think." His grandfather "makes me laugh. He's very funny. He's also someone who will tell me something that maybe I don't want to hear, but still tell me anyway and he won't care if I get upset about it. He knows it's the right thing to say, and I'm glad he tells me because the last thing I want is lots of people telling me what I want to hear." William flashed his own self-deprecating wit when asked if he ever had to wear a disguise like a wig. "That's a different issue actually," said the prematurely balding prince. "But no, I haven't."

On Thursday, July 7, 2005, Islamist terrorists detonated bombs on London's subways and buses, killing fifty-two people and injuring seven hundred others. That day the Queen ordered the Union Jack over Buckingham Palace lowered to half-staff. The next day she made the rounds of hospitals to console the injured, and she visited the wreckage of one of the bombings. Epitomizing the "Keep Calm and Carry On" attitude of Londoners during the Blitz and years of terror attacks by the IRA, she said, "I want to express my admiration for the people of our capital city, who in the aftermath of yesterday's bombings are calmly determined to resume their normal lives." Looking up for emphasis, she added, with a trace of steel in her voice "*That* is the answer to this outrage."

A week after the bombings, a moment of silence was observed throughout Europe to honor the dead. The Queen assembled the royal family in the Palace forecourt as Big Ben chimed to 12 and everything came to a standstill. "There in one of the archways stood the Queen," said a courtier, "with her handbag, for two minutes, all alone, symbolizing unity and stability."

That October, Margaret Thatcher celebrated her eightieth birthday with a reception at the Mandarin Oriental Hotel on Hyde Park. Unlike her royal contemporary, the erstwhile Iron Lady had slowed considerably, her mind impaired by several strokes. But she was visibly excited that the Queen was coming to the party. "Is it all right if I touch her?" asked Thatcher as Elizabeth II was approaching. She extended her hand, which the Queen held steady as her former prime minister curtseyed, although not as low as before. The Queen then tenderly guided Thatcher through the crowd of 650 guests. "That was unusual for the British, who know you are not supposed to touch the Queen," said Charles Powell. "But they were hand in hand, and the Queen led her around the room."

By the time Elizabeth II reached her own eightieth birthday six months later, she and her children had reached a welcome state of equipoise. Charles did a televised tribute to his "darling mama" and hosted a formal dinner for twenty-five family members at Kew Palace with the Queen seated between himself and William. The heir to the throne was happily settled with Camilla, dedicating himself to his hundreds of charities and causes, Andrew had been working for five years as Britain's special representative for international trade and investment, Anne and her husband assiduously went about their duties, and Edward and Sophie had left the private sector to work full-time for the "Firm." On Edward's marriage in 1999, the Queen had announced that he would become Duke of Edinburgh when his father died. Although Philip at age eighty-five continued to keep a heavy schedule of engagements, his youngest son was now sharing a number of commitments including the Duke of Edinburgh's Award Scheme for young people who had met high standards for physical stamina and community service.

On serious issues, Elizabeth II remained vigilant about avoiding public comment unless advised by government officials, and her advisers were continually on guard to shield her political views. But on duty in private settings, she occasionally let her commonsense opinions slip out. Her friend Will Farish had been unhappy as ambassador to the Court of St. James's and had resigned in the summer of 2004. When his successor, Robert H. Tuttle, was presenting his credentials to the Queen the following year, the American embassy was embroiled in a controversy with Ken Livingstone, the left-wing mayor of London, who had imposed a "congestion charge" on vehicles entering the city, ostensibly to reduce traffic. Officials at the embassy had decided not to pay the charge, contending that it was a form of taxation from which Americans were exempt.

After the credentials ceremony at Buckingham Palace, the Queen said to Tuttle, "I understand you think the congestion charge is a tax." "Yes, ma'am," replied Tuttle. "Well, it *is* a tax," she said. "I looked at Michael Jay, who was the head of the diplomatic corps," recalled Tuttle, "and he sort of blanched."

The Queen seemed to take pleasure in being less formal, and less inclined to stand on ceremony. On her fifteenth visit to Australia, in March 2006, she attended the Commonwealth Games, which she liked to call the "Friendly Games." In that spirit, she joined the competitors in their canteen for lunch, and happily posed with one woman athlete who put her arm around the Queen's back. Nor did Elizabeth II flinch when Eddie Daniel, a twenty-year-old boxer from the Cook Islands, slid into a seat next to her and enthusiastically kissed her on the cheek. She "just smiled back" at what he called his mark of respect. "She is so cool, man," he added.

On the first day of Royal Ascot that June, the Queen opened a completely rebuilt racecourse and grandstand. The complex had been demolished two years earlier (with Royal Ascot in the intervening year held at York Racecourse), and both Elizabeth II and Philip had been intensely involved in the plans and £200 million redevelopment of the site, which is leased from the Crown Estate. Peregrine Cavendish, the 12th Duke of Devonshire (known as Stoker to his friends), whom the Queen appointed as her representative at Ascot, oversaw the project and consulted with the royal couple from the inception of the plans in 1996. "Prince Philip has experience with all sorts of building projects," explained Devonshire, "so he looked at it from a practical use angle, while she looked from a racing angle."

The Queen's interest was far-reaching and at times surprisingly detailed — from the particulars of the turf to the construction of the smaller but no less well-appointed royal box: two curved rows of four comfortable armchairs, television monitors below showing four different angles of the course, an area in the rear of the box where the other guests could stand to watch the race, and a tearoom with round tables behind. "She was most interested in the actual racing surface," said Stoker Devonshire, "and in how it would affect the horses." They grew special grass on seventy acres in Lincolnshire, harvested it at the right time, and returfed the track.

The new stand was a soaring structure with a light-filled galleria behind the boxes and general admission seats. Numerous old-timers complained about its sleek modernity and said its escalators reminded them of an airline terminal. They also objected to diminished sight lines for some racegoers, a less picturesque paddock, the quality of the food, and the general difficulty getting around.

The Ascot management spent an additional £10 million to improve the viewing at the lower levels, and the Queen brought in her cousin Lady Elizabeth Anson, a veteran party planner, to enhance the look and feel of the hospitality tents in the Royal Enclosure, and to improve the menus.

To mark her eightieth year, the Queen permitted two anodyne documentaries devoted to her life and work, neither of which presented the personal glimpses she had allowed nearly four decades earlier in *Royal Family.* She also participated in a somewhat contrived film about a new portrait of her being painted by seventy-five-year-old Rolf Harris, an Australian-born television entertainer and artist. When the BBC proposed the project, the Palace took only two days to say yes — further evidence of the Queen's willingness to be seen by the public in less traditional ways.

All efforts by her advisers to shape the Queen's image paled beside the impact of *The Queen* when it appeared in theaters in the autumn of 2006 to popular and critical acclaim. The director, Stephen Frears, said, "We made the Queen a Hollywood star" — not a notion she would savor. But the film did serve to define her anew and, odd as it seems, merged the real Queen in the public imagination with Helen Mirren, a lifelong republican whose newfound admiration for Elizabeth II made her into a "Queenist." Although much of the dialogue and many of the scenes were pure invention by screenwriter Peter Morgan (Prince Philip may have called his wife "Sausage," but never "Cabbage"), the film was thoroughly researched and grounded in reality.

Its appeal lay in imagining moments that contrasted the Queen's exalted status with her appearance in curlers as her worst nightmare unfolded after Diana's death, in balancing her shortcomings with an essential goodness, and in satisfying the public's need for her to reflect their own anxieties, doubts, and sadness. "What is brilliant is that the film has a mythical quality," said Frances Campbell-Preston, lady-in-waiting to the Queen Mother for thirty-seven years. Although the words were "not necessarily the Queen's words," she said, "there is a truth."

"I gather there's a film," Elizabeth II said to Tony Blair in an audience just after the movie opened. "I'd just like you to know that I'm not going to watch it. Are you?" "No, of course not," said Blair. One of her relatives gave her a full rundown on the telephone as the Queen listened silently. When told the film was good for the monarchy, she asked why. "Because it showed why you didn't come down to London, that you were being a grandmother as opposed to temporarily not being queen," said her relative, who added that she shouldn't see it because it would be "a reminder of a really ghastly week" and that "to see herself portrayed by someone would be irritating."

One of Elizabeth II's friends gently ribbed her by sending a cartoon titled "The Queen" from *The Spectator* magazine. It showed the interior of a movie theater with someone's view of the screen being obstructed by a person wearing a crown. The Queen was tickled by the cartoon, but she told her friend she was holding to the agreement she had with Blair — stubbornness perhaps, but also a sign of her lack of self-absorption. When the film came up in a conversation with Monty

Roberts, she asked him not to see it, even when he told her he heard it was flattering. "I suppose it depends on your point of view," the Queen said. "I think she preferred me to know her the way I know her," he recalled.

Nearly everyone else who knew the Queen did go, and they almost unanimously felt that the portrayal "rang true," as Nancy Reagan said — from the way it captured aspects of her character and personality to her sturdy walk and the way she put on her spectacles. But they also observed that because of the tragic circumstances of the film, Mirren's Elizabeth II was more like her restrained public image than her relaxed and jolly private self. Most agreed that the depiction of Philip was unduly harsh, and that both the Queen Mother and Robin Janvrin had been mischaracterized. But even Elizabeth II understood the phenomenon created by the film, according to her friends. Palace officials were delighted when the movie spawned articles in fashion magazines about "Balmoral chic" as sales of Barbour waxed jackets surged.

"You know, for fifty years and more Elizabeth Windsor has maintained her dignity, her sense of duty and her hairstyle," said Helen Mirren to appreciative laughter after winning the Oscar for best actress in February 2007. "She's had her feet planted firmly on the ground, her hat on her head, her handbag on her arm, and she's weathered many many storms, and I salute her courage and her consistency." Holding the Oscar aloft, she concluded, "Ladies and gentlemen, I give you 'The Queen!' "

CHAPTER TWENTY
A SOLDIER AT HEART

In April 2007, the Queen sat for her first portrait by an American, the celebrity photographer Annie Leibovitz. Not only was the sitting limited by her schedule to just twenty-five minutes, it was to be filmed for yet another television documentary about the Queen carrying out her duties. She agreed to wear the stunning Queen Mary tiara, the Nizam of Hyderabad diamond necklace, a white satin gown embroidered with gold, and her flowing dark blue Garter robe. Leibovitz was surprised to learn that Elizabeth II did her own makeup and got her hair done just once a week.

In a brief conversation the evening before the photo shoot, the Queen spoke fondly to Leibovitz about British photographer Jane Bown, an octogenarian who had done her portrait the previous year. "She came all the way by herself!" the Queen said. "I helped her move the furniture." Leibovitz replied, "Well, tomorrow is going to be the opposite of that."

Unusually for a woman who prided herself on punctuality, the Queen arrived twenty minutes late for her sitting. "I don't have much time," the Queen said to the photographer, who noticed that the dressers "were staying about 20 feet away from her."

"She's a real role model. She's just very helpful on any sort of difficulties or problems I might be having."

Prince William escorting his grandmother during a visit to his base in Wales, where he worked as a search-and-rescue helicopter pilot, April 2011. Ian Jones Photography

Elizabeth II was clearly vexed to be surrounded by the photographer's large entourage. When Leibovitz asked her to remove her "crown" to make the image less dressy, the Queen said, "Less dressy! What do you think this is?" But she calmed down and yielded to the photographer's requests to vary her costume and her pose. Leibovitz later said she loved the Queen's "feisty" personality and respected her willingness to fulfill her commitment, however tiring and stressful.

The resulting images were stunning. The most striking showed the Queen without the tiara and wearing a simple navy boat cloak with gleaming brass buttons, her arms and hands unseen, standing in front of a digitally superimposed background of a wintry sky and the bare trees of the Palace gardens. It was a frank attempt by Leibovitz to evoke earlier iconic images by Beaton and Annigoni symbolizing the Queen's solitude, as well as "an appropriate mood for this moment in the Queen's life."

The photos were unveiled on the eve of the Queen's tenth trip to the United States, and her third state visit, this time hosted by George and Laura Bush. Before her departure, she gave a reception at Buckingham Palace for 350 prominent Americans in London. *Washington Post* correspondent Kevin Sullivan joined one of the small semicircles of people to be introduced to the Queen, which also included Don Johnson, who was starring in *Guys and Dolls* in the West End, Terence Kooyker and Andrew Wright, who were rowers at Oxford, and Brian McBride, one of the top players for the Fulham professional football team.

The Queen showed no sign of knowing that Johnson had starred in the hit television series *Miami Vice,* but when she was introduced to the rowers, she asked to see their big hands, which were covered with calluses and blisters. "The Queen examined them closely, and sympathized as if the young men were her grandchildren," recalled Sullivan, who also noticed that she had "a disarming habit of smiling only when she finds something funny" and lacked "the political perma-smile." As she was talking to McBride, another man ignored protocol and barged into the group. "Do you play football too?" the Queen asked. "No," he replied. "I sell pancake and waffle mix, mostly in the Middle East." "How interesting what people will eat," said the Queen, as she turned to approach another group.

Elizabeth II and Philip arrived in Richmond, Virginia, on Thursday, May 3. In a speech to the Virginia legislature she expressed her condolences for the massacre at Virginia Tech the previous week in which a lone gunman killed thirty students and teachers before committing suicide. She also adjusted her schedule to meet a group of survivors of the shooting. Then she traveled to Jamestown, where she commemorated the four hundredth anniversary of the first British settlement — fifty years after her first visit during the Eisenhower presidency. Surveying the archaeological relics, she spotted exhibit 15, an iron spatula labeled "for severe constipation." She beckoned her traveling physician, Commander David Swain, who was always only a few steps away with his large black case containing vital medications and blood plasma. Pointing at the crude implement, she exclaimed, "You should have some things like that!"

Over the weekend she fulfilled her lifelong dream of attending the Kentucky Derby, and for the fifth time she was a guest at the Farish farm. The former ambassador and his wife remained close to the Queen, and once again Sarah Farish greeted her by publicly kissing her on both cheeks.

Elizabeth II was no longer sending as many mares to Kentucky. The center of gravity among breeders had shifted to the powerhouse stud farms of Ireland, which offered high-caliber stallions for her to choose from without subjecting her mares to transatlantic travel. It had been politically impossible for her to send her mares across the Irish Sea until the 1998 Northern Ireland peace settlement took effect. Now her new bloodstock adviser, Henry Carnarvon's son-in-law John Warren, was trying to invigorate the royal thoroughbred line and make it more competitive, in the hopes that the Queen could finally win the elusive Derby at Epsom.

But the Queen still enjoyed relaxing in bluegrass country with like-minded friends she had known for decades, and for the first time Philip was along to share the experience. In the garden at Lane's End Farm, she sipped a late afternoon martini and fretted about the performance of Princess Anne's daughter, Zara Phillips, at the Badminton Horse trials. "Nobody pays any attention to what Granny thinks!" she said.

At the Kentucky Derby on Saturday, the Queen was intrigued by the winning jockey, Calvin Borel, a Cajun who could barely read and write but was known for his uncanny affinity for horses. Anticipating the Queen's interest, Laura Bush had set aside two places at the state dinner two days later and extended an invitation to Borel. Amy Zantzinger, her social secretary, arranged for him to be outfitted in white tie, and for a Louisville dress shop to be opened on Sunday so his fiancée could buy a gown.

George Bush managed to inject a note of unintended levity in his opening remarks on the White House South Lawn before seven thousand guests on Monday, the 7th. "You helped our nation celebrate its bicentennial in 177— uh 1976," he said. After a beat, he winked at the Queen and said, "She gave me a look only a mother could give a child." Elizabeth II and Philip had a quiet lunch upstairs in the Yellow Oval Room with members of the Bush family, including the forty-first president and Barbara Bush, who accompanied the royal couple to the World War II memorial on the Mall, the last stop in a fast-paced two-day visit that included stops at NASA and the Children's National Medical Center.

Other than a short walk with the president and first lady from the White House to Blair House across the street on the first day, the Queen was barely seen by the general public. The crowd of one thousand in the cordoned area included numerous children, and the Queen stopped to talk to them along the way. One member of her entourage commented that "it was sad that security was so tight. Even the walk was stage-managed."

That afternoon at the British embassy garden party, the Queen spotted her friend Frolic Weymouth and went straight over to him. "So glad to see you," she said with a smile. "How are you? I heard you were sick." The artist knew she collected pepper grinders, so earlier in the year he had sent her one made of plastic that he found in an Italian restaurant. It was in the shape of a waiter, and with a turn of the head, a recording inside said in an Italian accent, "You're breaking my neck!" Weymouth had received a prompt thank-you note from the Queen saying how much she had laughed. At the garden party as they finished their conversation, he said, "Oh Ma'am, do you need another pepper shaker?" At that point, Weymouth recalled, "she lost it. She started laughing and hitting her pocketbook. Then she became dignified again and moved on."

Calvin Borel met Elizabeth II in the receiving line at the state dinner that night. Posing for an official photograph between the monarch and the first lady, Borel did what Laura Bush called "the sweetest thing" as he wrapped his arms around both women. By now infringements of protocol such as touching the Queen were becoming almost routine. In her toast, the Queen spoke fondly of the "vital wartime alliance" forged by Winston Churchill that had carried forward across the decades as a "partnership always to be reckoned with."

The following night she hosted a dinner in honor of the Bushes at the British embassy. All day her advisers had been urging her to include in her toast a lighthearted reference to the president's verbal stumble the previous day until she finally relented. "I wondered whether I should start this toast by saying, 'When I was here in 1776 but I don't think I will,' " she said as the guests laughed knowingly. "It was the perfect retort," recalled Bush. When the Sovereign's Standard was lowered from the embassy flagpole at the conclusion of the evening, the Queen and Philip were whisked to Andrews Air Force Base for their flight home, he in black tie and she in her gown and tiara.

On June 27, 2007, Tony Blair resigned as prime minister under pressure from his fifty-six-year-old chancellor of the exchequer, Gordon Brown. It was a quiet coup by the Scotsman after a decade of playing second fiddle to the charismatic prime minister. Largely because of widespread opposition to the Iraq War, Blair had become deeply unpopular, which strengthened the Labour bloc led by Brown. Blair finally yielded two months after passing the Labour Party record of ten years as prime minister.

The son of a minister in the Church of Scotland, Brown had been a scholastic prodigy, entering the University of Edinburgh at age sixteen and eventually earning a doctorate. He had a brooding manner matched by a burly and sometimes disheveled appearance, and he advanced in politics despite what Blair called "a lacuna — not the wrong instinct, but no instinct at the human, gut level. Political calculation, yes. Political feelings, no. Analytical intelligence, absolutely. Emotional intelligence, zero." Brown's success was fueled by his prodigious energy, formidable intellect, and intense focus. But he was an odd duck: capable of quick wit, but more often socially maladroit and programmed in his casual social interactions.

Brown was touched by tragedy as well. An accident while playing rugby as a teenager left him blind in one eye, and his vision was also impaired in the other eye. He didn't marry until age forty-nine, and he and his wife, Sarah, lost their first child ten days after her birth in 2002. They later had two sons, one of whom was afflicted with cystic fibrosis.

Elizabeth II knew Brown from a decade of his briefings before presenting the annual budget. In his audience the previous year he had assured her that he had "some good information about how we're trying to support the troops." "They're very pushed now, in so many places," the Queen commented. When she told him that Prince Andrew had recently visited Iraq, Brown assured her the government was "doing some investment in helicopters." "It would be good if the helicopters we bought actually could work," she pointedly replied.

The Queen treated Brown correctly, and the prime minister was "tremendously respectful of the royal family," said Simon Lewis, who served as Brown's press secretary for his last year in office. "If any Palace-related issues came up, he would say, 'Simon, make sure we're on top of that.' He was sensitive to the nature of the relationship and getting on smoothly." Compared to the thoroughly urban Tony Blair, it helped that Brown came from a country background, with a home overlooking the Firth of Forth.

Brown said he relied on the Queen's knowing "what works and what doesn't. Sometimes you go back and change a bit of your speech." But he especially valued her sense of humor and how "she'll be talking about things that make both her and me laugh." When the Queen was with friends, he sometimes was the target of that humor; her talent for mimicry and years of listening to Scottish brogue enabled her to render a spot-on imitation of her new prime minister. Brown's visits to Balmoral, said Margaret Rhodes, "brought a certain amount of heavy weather."

Elizabeth and Philip hit another milestone on November 20, 2007, as the first Queen and consort to celebrate sixty years of marriage. "With the absence of her mother and sister, the Duke of Edinburgh has been her emotional touchstone," said one of the Queen's senior advisers. When he was away, staying at Wood Farm on a shooting weekend at Sandringham, for example, he would ring her up every day. "They are not physically demonstrative, but they have a strong connection," said another courtier. "She still lights up when he walks into the room. She becomes softer, lighter, and happier."

Their religious bond deepened as well. Her unwavering faith was ingrained from childhood, while Philip's meandered from the Greek Orthodox beliefs of his parents through his confirmation as an Anglican to his probing of theological and interfaith issues. "His approach is much more restless than the Queen, more focused on the intellectual side," said George Carey. "He is searching, and he has been a bridge builder, putting faiths together. He has more time to do that, and the Queen stands back and lets him."

Yet Elizabeth II and Philip, according to their cousin Pamela Hicks, are "not a sweet old Darby and Joan by any means. They're both *very* strong characters." One point of disagreement concerned the press. "I don't read the tabloids," Philip sputtered to Jeremy Paxman, the BBC's grand inquisitor, in 2006. "I glance at one [broadsheet]. I reckon one's enough. I can't cope with them. But the Queen reads every bloody paper she can lay her hands on!"

After Philip took one too many spills in his competitive carriage driving, Elizabeth II put her foot down and insisted that he stop, although he continued to drive for pleasure. On other matters, she simply avoided confrontation. When her husband's dressing room at Sandringham needed to be repainted, "on Her Majesty's instruction we had to match the dirty paintwork so he wouldn't know," said Tony Parnell, for more than three decades the foreman responsible for looking after the house. "I don't think he ever knew."

Elizabeth II gave Philip the latitude to experiment in his supervision of her estates. At Sandringham he created a truffière, an orchard designed to produce organic truffles, in addition to breeding French partridges ("incredibly stupid birds," he said) and growing fruits for the production of apple juice and black currant cordial. He was responsible for their private art collection, buying at shows in Edinburgh, where he had an eye for up-and-coming artists, and hanging the paintings himself in their private apartments. The Queen, however, continued to supervise the decor in their private homes. "Her taste was very modest in terms of decoration and fabrics," recalled Tony Parnell. "It was almost replacing like for like."

Philip frequently rode through London inconspicuously in his own Metrocab, sometimes taking the wheel himself. Once he drove his taxi to a dinner with friends at a modest flat on the edge of Belgravia belonging to Jane Westmorland, widow of the 15th Earl. "He wore a cap like a taxi driver and the detective sat in the back seat," recalled Frolic Weymouth. "He drove around and around in the circle out front to show us how easily the cab could turn."

When they were together in public, Philip could still cause his wife anxiety with his unpredictable comments within earshot of the press. Labour MP Chris Mullin recalled a time in 2003 when the Queen was attending the Commonwealth conference in Nigeria. After an official read a statement at the opening of the new British Council offices in Abuja, Philip huffed, "That speech contained more jargon per square inch than any I've heard for a long time." He then turned to a group of women and asked if they were teachers. They replied that their job was to "empower" people. *"Empower?"* he boomed. "Doesn't sound like English to me!" As Mullin recorded in his diary, "By now the Queen, noticing that trouble is brewing, has turned and is pointing vaguely over the balcony. 'Look . . .' The Duke, stopping mid-sentence, retreats instantly to her side, somewhat bemused. '. . . at the pottery.' When they have gone, I go and look. I see no pottery."

At the Queen's request, the celebrations of their diamond wedding anniversary were muted and family-oriented. The couple visited Broadlands on Sunday, November 18, and spent time searching for a tree where they were photographed during their honeymoon. The Queen appeared in the same double strand of pearls and sapphire brooch ringed with diamonds that she had worn six decades earlier. For their official anniversary photograph on the grounds of the Mountbatten estate, Elizabeth II and Philip re-created a nearly identical pose — her right hand tucked into his left elbow as they smiled at each other. He looked less jaunty, but the warmth of her gaze was remarkably similar. That evening, Charles and Camilla hosted a black-tie family dinner party at Clarence House.

The next day the Queen and Philip attended a commemoration at Westminster Abbey, where Prince William's reading from the Book of John included the line "Let us love one another because love is from God." Judi Dench recited verse composed by poet laureate Andrew Motion that commended "a life where duty spoke in languages their tenderness could share, a life remote from ours because it asked each day, each action to be kept in view."

The royal couple flew to Malta on the 20th for a sentimental journey to the island where they had enjoyed unencumbered happiness and a brief spell of normality as a young married couple. A month later they received a belated anniversary gift with the birth of their eighth grandchild, James Alexander Philip Theo Wessex. As they had with his older sister, Edward and Sophie decided their son would not be known as a Royal Highness, enabling both of the children to pursue a life outside the royal orbit.

Throughout the celebrations, Elizabeth II and Philip were keeping a secret: their twenty-three-year-old grandson, Prince Harry, a second lieutenant in the Household Cavalry regiment of the Blues and Royals, was about to be sent to Helmand Province in Afghanistan for a seven-month deployment. Since the invasions of Afghanistan in 2001 and Iraq in 2003, Elizabeth II had received regular updates from top officials in the military and Foreign Office, so she was well aware of the treacherous combat conditions facing the British military in both places.

Her role as the head of armed forces is one of her most sacrosanct duties. With her hierarchies, rituals, traditions, and clothing created with a military-style sense of occasion, she is a soldier at heart. Members of the military are acutely aware that they are fighting for Queen and Country. "The royal family has pride and joy in the military," said General Charles Guthrie, Baron Guthrie of Craigiebank, who was the chief of the Defence staff from 1997 to 2001. "Come hell or high water, the military is loyal to the Queen, who is their commander in chief."

Since her days with the garrison at Windsor Castle during World War II and her brief service in uniform with the Auxiliary Territorial Service, she has taken a keen personal interest in military matters, meeting informally with the top brass over lunch and dinner as well as in audiences. She visibly relaxes in the company of soldiers, not thinking twice about walking into a battalion of a thousand men. Once she helpfully sent a commander a photograph from a magazine showing a piebald shire stallion she considered suitable for service as a drum horse for the Household Cavalry.

Her knowledge of military traditions and practices is encyclopedic, as officers serving her quickly learn. When Johnny Martin-Smith, a lieutenant on guard duty at Windsor Castle, was invited to dinner with the Queen, she turned to him and said, "Do the Welsh Guards have new uniform requirements? Are red socks allowed?" She had been looking out the window that day at a Welsh Guards soldier setting up a bandstand who had worn red instead of regulation green socks.

"The Queen has an eagle eye, possibly better than 15 eagles," said a Palace courtier. After her annual birthday parade, she gives her critique to senior officers, sometimes asking why a soldier was standing several feet out of position or moving his fingers on his rifle. "I hope that man who cut his hand is going to be all right," she said one year to the officer in charge. A soldier in the front row had cut himself on his bayonet and nobody else had noticed except the Queen, who had been standing at some distance. "Cut himself, ma'am?" replied the officer. "Yes," said the Queen, "the one in the middle, the 3rd or 4th man."

The Queen "wouldn't read a three-volume history of Afghanistan," said Charles Guthrie, who met with her frequently. But through her briefings by officers and meetings with soldiers returning from the front lines, along with reading her boxes and newspapers and watching reports on television, her knowledge is impressively up to date. "You could tell her what you thought," said Guthrie. "You could be critical of government, and she would listen. She would not comment. She would not get into gossip. She would question on certain things that were topical, but it wasn't an interrogation. It was a conversation. She absolutely understands her constitutional prerogatives and does not stray into areas that could be unconstitutional. She doesn't try to run the army."

When the Labour government consolidated many of the army's historic regiments in 2006 to cut costs, she made inquiries but stayed out of the debate. "She knew we had too many regiments," said senior Blair adviser Jonathan Powell. "She was concerned, but she was not a lobbyist pushing an agenda." Speaking to one of the army chiefs, however, she couldn't conceal her sadness when the venerable Black Watch was merged with five other regiments to become a battalion within the new Royal Regiment of Scotland. The Queen Mother had been colonel-in-chief of the Black Watch for sixty-five years, and three of her brothers, including one who died in battle during World War I, had served in the regiment.

The Queen fully supported the decisions by William and Harry to enter the military. "It is a traditional thing to do, a good thing to do," explained Charles Guthrie, who discussed it with her. "It teaches a lot about leadership. It mixes up royals with different examples of society, people from poor backgrounds, which is helpful and certainly very good." Choosing the army rather than the navy, where the princes' father, uncle, and grandfather had served, reflected the practical reality of modern warfare and the decline of Britain's importance as a naval power. The military gave William and Harry jobs that kept them away from the limelight — and the press. ⱴ

The imposition of discipline in the context of regimental camaraderie was particularly good for Harry, whose high spirits threatened to turn him into a scapegrace. He got caught using marijuana when he was seventeen, prompting his father to march him off to visit a drug rehabilitation center and listen to recovering addicts. There were other unfortunate incidents involving the third in line to the throne — sightings of drunkenness at London clubs and at a costume party where Harry wore a swastika armband. Because of his red hair and freckles, it had long been rumored that his father was James Hewitt ⱴ despite the well-documented fact that Diana didn't meet the cavalry officer until after Harry was born. While Diana strongly resembled her maternal grandmother, Ruth Fermoy, she scarcely looked like her father's side of the family. Harry, however, inherited the ginger looks of the Spencers.

It was first proposed early in 2007 that Harry be posted to Iraq. He was determined to serve with his regiment, but when publicity about the prospect led to terrorist threats against him, Army Chief of Staff Sir Richard Dannatt vetoed his participation. The Queen had favored his deployment, and she helped talk Harry through his frustration. She supported his resolution to "turn to the right and carry on," he recalled.

When the Blues and Royals regiment was called

to Afghanistan later in the year, Dannatt consulted with Gordon Brown, the Prince of Wales, and the Queen. They decided to deploy Harry under an embargo reached with selected news organizations that agreed to publicize the details of his experience once he had returned safely to Britain. As with her decision to back Andrew twenty-five years earlier, the Queen didn't hesitate. She broke the news to her grandson in December on a weekend at Windsor Castle. "I think she's relieved that I get the chance to do what I want to do," he said at the time. "She's a very good person to talk to about it."

From his arrival only days before Christmas, Harry served on the front lines at a forward operating base under regular fire from machine guns, snipers, rockets, and mortars. He called in air strikes and routinely went out on foot patrol through dangerous Taliban-held terrain. As a troop leader responsible for eleven soldiers doing reconnaissance work, he was undeniably in danger. At the same time, he was " 'mucking in' with every other soldier, cooking his own rations, taking his turn making brews for himself and his mates, cleaning his rifle and equipment," wrote Colonel Richard Kemp, former commander of British forces in Afghanistan.

The secret of his deployment held for ten weeks, until an Australian magazine and a German newspaper broke the blackout, and an American website, the Drudge Report, picked up the news. The Ministry of Defence withdrew Harry from Helmand, at least in part to ensure the safety of his battle group. Before leaving, the prince said, "All my wishes have come true. I managed to get the job done." He was also grateful, he said, because "it's very nice to be sort of a normal person for once. I think it's about as normal as I'm going to get."

The final months of 2007 marked the appearance of another work of fiction that captured the public imagination about the Queen. In *The Uncommon Reader,* Alan Bennett's fictionalized Elizabeth II discovers a passion for reading — an opsimath, she calls herself, delighted to find a word describing a late-blooming learner. She neglects her official chores as she breezes through an eclectic canon including Mitford, Austen, Balzac, Pepys, Byatt, McEwan, Roth, and even the memoirs of Lauren Bacall, whose life she envies for having "had a much better bite at the carrot." The Queen confuses those she meets by asking about their reading habits, throws her courtiers and her family into a state of high alarm, and eventually decides to take up writing and redeem her life "by analysis and reflection."

It is a thoroughly fanciful plot, given the Queen's deep-seated sense of duty and practical turn of mind. But as in *A Question of Attribution* twenty years earlier, Bennett zeroes in on the Queen's underestimated qualities and depicts a shrewd, observant, and inquisitive character whose sly wit ("Oh do get *on!*" she mutters while reading Henry James at teatime) is a believable facsimile of Elizabeth II's tart asides.

The book was a runaway bestseller in Britain and the United States, propelled by word of mouth and rave reviews. After *The Queen,* wrote Jeremy McCarter in *The New York Times Book Review,* the book "offered yet another reason to think warmly of Her Majesty, another reminder that marble has veins." Like the film, Bennett's book tapped into a yearning for Elizabeth II to break out of the royal cocoon, and to show some of her repressed mischief. The most touching aspect of Bennett's depiction is his character's discovery of egalitarian anonymity when immersed in a book: "It was shared, it was common. . . . Between these covers she could go unrecognized."

The real Queen keeps her views of literature well guarded, but she does take a special interest in the annual Commonwealth Writers' Prize, a competition for authors around the world. She reads the winning novels for pleasure intermingled with obligation. Most of them are historical fiction, and in recent years she has enjoyed *The Secret River* by Kate Grenville, on the early colonization of Australia; *Mister Pip* by Lloyd Jones, about Papua New Guinea; and *The Book of Negroes* by Lawrence Hill, on the slave trade with Canada. Each summer she invites the winner to Buckingham Palace for an audience. "It's very informal," said Mark Collins, director of the Commonwealth Foundation, who accompanies the authors. "It's upstairs in her private apartments, and we're knee-deep in corgis running around." For twenty minutes she conducts an earnest discussion touching on the writer's roots, the source of inspiration, and how the book developed. "She asks how the locations came to be selected, and the characters, and any reflections on the country that the author might have," recalled Collins. "The discussion rattles along tidily."

Elizabeth II is not the sort to brood about mortality, but in the early years of her ninth decade she almost seemed to be making her way down a sort of royal bucket list, checking off things she hadn't done before, and places she hadn't seen. In June 2008, she attended her first luncheon at Pratt's, an exclusive men's club in St. James's owned by the Duke of Devonshire. At the invitation of a conservation group called the Shikar Club, she joined her husband and ten other members for drinks in front of a large fireplace, followed by a robust meal of smoked salmon, lamb cutlet, and treacle tart. The following July she watched the annual Swan Upping, a ritual dating to the twelfth century when the swans on the Thames (which belong to the sovereign) are officially counted. She even started taking a regular commuter train to and from King's Lynn in Norfolk for her annual winter break at Sandringham. She didn't sit with the regular passengers, however; for security reasons, she and her small party took over a first-class compartment.

For shooting, stalking, and fishing weekends at Sandringham and Balmoral she began including more guests a generation younger. "We have seen less of them," said a woman who had been a regular guest of Elizabeth II and Philip since the 1950s. "They don't just see the old fogies."

The children of her longtime friends found that she responded readily when they invited her to informal dinners, where she took time to chat with their own teenage children, asking them questions and listening intently. When one of her brides-maids, Lady Elizabeth Longman (known to her friends as "Smith"), turned eighty, Elizabeth II went to a cocktail party in her honor in a small flat. While a female protection officer waited in the car, a guest escorted the Queen up in a rickety eleva-tor. She stayed for more than an hour and spent a full fifteen minutes talking to Smith's grandson, Freddy Van Zevenbergen, a designer who built scale models of grand houses.

For the first time in nine years, the Queen had a winner on the final day of Royal Ascot in June 2008. Her two-year-old colt Free Agent was run-ning behind what John Warren called "a wall" of ten other horses with only three furlongs to go in the Chesham Stakes. But Free Agent, ridden by Richard Hughes, broke through and won by two and a quarter lengths. "I've done it!" the Queen shouted. Seated between Warren and her hus-band, she jumped up and punched the air with her fist — an unusual public display captured by BBC cameras for the evening newscasts. "It was a moment of real joy," said John Warren. Afterward, "she raced to the paddock like she was 20," said her fifty-two-year-old bloodstock adviser. "We were struggling to keep up with her. The jockey was trying to explain what had happened but all the Queen wanted to do was touch her horse."

Earlier in the week at Ascot, Helen Mirren was in attendance to present a trophy, and the Queen asked her cinematic alter ego to the royal box for tea. "I wouldn't have been invited to tea if she had hated the film," said Mirren. "I was very touched to be invited." The Queen said, "Hello, it's lovely to meet you," followed by some "horsey chat." It was only the second time Elizabeth II had met an actress who played her. Some years earlier she had encountered Prunella Scales, who portrayed the Queen in *A Question of Attribution*. When Scales bowed to Elizabeth II in a receiving line, the Queen said, "I expect you think I should be doing that to you."

Elizabeth II's eldest son celebrated his sixtieth birthday in November 2008, making him the oldest Prince of Wales in history, passing King Edward VII, who was fifty-nine when he succeeded Queen Victoria on her death in 1901. Elizabeth II hosted a black-tie reception, orchestral concert, and dinner in Charles's honor at Buckingham Palace on the eve of his birthday on the 14th. More noteworthy was the visit she and Philip made a day earlier to the headquarters of his signature charity, the Prince's Trust, which since its founding in 1976 had helped more than a half million disadvantaged youths learn skills and find jobs.

Throughout his life Charles has craved the approval of his parents, and the Queen's remarks that day represented a rare public expression of support for his philanthropic work with his twenty charities and as patron or president of 350 other organizations. "For Prince Philip and me there can be no greater pleasure or comfort than to know that into his care are safely entrusted the guiding principles of public service and duty to others," the Queen said.

Charles overtook his sister, Anne's, record as

"hardest working royal," with 560 official engagements in 2008. (She came close with 534.) His mother logged 417 visits in the U.K. and overseas that year — down only slightly from 440 in 2007. At age eighty-two — seventeen years past Britain's mandatory retirement age at the time — she had no intention of slowing down. The previous December she had become the oldest-ever monarch when she passed Queen Victoria, who lived eighty-one years and 243 days.

She continued to carry out her duties as she had since her accession, serving as head of state — representing her government officially at home and abroad — as well as head of nation, connecting with people to reward their achievements and remain in touch. But while in the early years of her reign she presided over twenty-six investitures a year, that number was gradually pared to fifteen, with Prince Charles and Princess Anne splitting the rest.

"All her programs are done with great cleverness," said Malcolm Ross, her former comptroller. "They have reduced the pace for her without it showing." But whenever her advisers try to sneak something too obvious into her schedule to give her a rest, "she instantly spots it and asks why she is not doing more," said a source close to the Palace household. "She doesn't miss anything."

Robin Janvrin, the Queen's private secretary and leading advocate of modernizing, retired in 2007. Janvrin was replaced by forty-six-year-old Christopher Geidt, a like-minded veteran of the Foreign Office with degrees from King's College London and Cambridge University. He made a smooth transition, setting the tone with brisk efficiency and easy humor.

The all-important Palace communications apparatus was now run by two women in their late thirties, both mothers of small children. Samantha Cohen, communications and press secretary to the Queen, had written for regional newspapers in her native Australia, and before joining the royal household had been head of communications for National Grid, the international electricity and gas company. Deputy press secretary Ailsa Anderson came out of regional newspapers in Essex to work in the civil service. She served as press officer for Conservative Nicholas Soames at the Ministry of Defence and for Labour politician Margaret Beckett when she served in Tony Blair's cabinet. Bright, skillful, straightforward, and tough, Cohen and Anderson managed to protect the Queen's private life while boldly projecting her image as a symbol of modernity.

Elizabeth II began responding more quickly to crises, and showing more emotion in public. She had her portrait done as a hologram. She chatted comfortably with pop singer Lady Gaga without flinching at the performer's shiny red latex outfit, and cheerfully welcomed to Buckingham Palace fashion designer Zandra Rhodes, who sported a pink wig, and photographer David Bailey, who wore ratty jeans. When the world financial meltdown hit in the fall of 2008, the Queen made a trip to the London School of Economics. After listening to a presentation on the origin of the credit crisis, she asked the one essential question: "Why did no one see it coming?" "The general feeling is she is more approachable, human, empathetic, and in touch," said a Palace official.

Although the Queen had received her first computer twenty-five years earlier from Ronald Reagan, she had lagged behind her husband in adapting to technology. Philip began writing letters on a computer in the 1980s and became an avid user of email and the Internet, especially while researching his speeches. Elizabeth II eventually took up cell phones to send text messages to her grandchildren, and computers to keep track of her horses. At the suggestion of Prince Andrew, she acquired an iPod in 2005. While firmly committed to paper and pen, she began exchanging emails with family members. Ten years after launching the royal website in 1997, the Queen got her own channel on YouTube in December 2007, with a million hits in the first week.

There was no better indicator of her embrace of the new than her visit to the London headquarters of Google in the fall of 2008. The dynamic young company honored Elizabeth II by incorporating her image and a crown into the "Google doodle" logo on its U.K. home page on the day of her visit. The Queen and Philip ("a great googler," said one of the Queen's senior advisers. "He is always googling, and sharing it with the Queen") spent more than an hour in the company's offices, meeting a predominantly youthful and casually dressed group of employees. "Just come back from jogging?" Philip inquired when he met marketing executive Matthew Trewhella, who was wearing a hooded top, chinos, and sneakers.

During her visit, Elizabeth II uploaded onto her

Royal Channel a video of a reception at Buckingham Palace in 1968 for Olympic athletes, delicately guiding the mouse with her black-gloved right hand. When she and Philip were shown the famous "laughing baby" on YouTube, they caught the contagion and started to giggle. "Lovely little thing isn't it?" she said to her husband. "Amazing a child would laugh like that."

Even as she kept her focus on the here and now, in various ways, publicly and privately, the Queen honored her late mother, whose memory she kept close. During a shooting weekend at Sandringham in January 2009, she lost an important link with the death of Emma, the last of the Queen Mother's corgis. A visibly saddened Queen went around the room before dinner and gave the news to each of the guests as Philip tried to console her.

The following month the family and a throng of friends were out in force on the terrace below Carlton House to unveil a bronze statue more than nine feet tall of a faintly smiling Queen Mother in her Garter robes. She was portrayed at age fifty-one because the memorial stood below a bronze statue of George VI, also in Garter attire, at age fifty-six, the year of his death. "At long last my grandparents are reunited," said Prince Charles after his mother had pulled a cord to remove the blue satin cover. The £2 million memorial, paid for by the sale of coins commemorating Elizabeth II's eightieth birthday, also featured two eleven-foot-long bronze friezes that captured the Queen Mother's spirit by depicting her comforting homeless families in London's East End during World War II, being applauded with one of her winning race-horses, and sitting with two of her corgis in the garden at the Castle of Mey.

Several months later the Queen turned up as a surprise guest at a fund-raising reception for the Castle of Mey Foundation. The Queen Mother's favorite residence had been opened to the public in August 2002, and private funds helped maintain both castle and gardens. Elizabeth II was only scheduled to make a brief appearance at the Goring Hotel near Buckingham Palace. Instead, she spent ninety minutes circulating through the room and conversing with patrons and potential donors. One British businessman was so taken by his encounter that he later wrote a £20,000 check to the foundation.

An advantage Elizabeth II has had over all her prime ministers is her vast knowledge of the United Kingdom that she gathers in visits called "awaydays" to cities as well as tiny hamlets. "She knows every inch of this country in a way that no one else does," said Charles Powell, who came to appreciate the Queen's expertise when he worked as private secretary to Margaret Thatcher and John Major. "She spends so much time meeting people that she has an understanding of what other people's lives are like in Britain. I think she understands what the normal human condition is."

In March 2009 she visited Kingston upon Hull in East Yorkshire — described by *The Times* as one of the country's "few dogged bastions of republicanism" — for the first time in ten years. Before her maiden visit in 1957, one of her advisers wrote a speech that began "I am very pleased to be in Kingston today." The Queen decisively crossed out the "very" and said, "I will be *pleased* to be in Kingston, but I will not be *very* pleased." Whether the adverb applied fifty-two years later she did not say, but she was eager to assess the impact of the economic downturn on the once thriving shipping center, which had also suffered extensive flood damage from torrential rains two years earlier.

Palace advisers worked with Susan Cunliffe-Lister, the lord lieutenant of East Yorkshire, and other local officials to organize the itinerary for the four-hour awayday. When the Queen was younger, she would pack in as many as eight different stops, but now she did a maximum of four, ending with lunch. To help prepare the Queen, Cunliffe-Lister sent seventy pages of briefings: rundowns on the people she would meet, descriptions of the places she would see, and menus and seating plans for a luncheon in the Guildhall. Palace officials produced a seventeen-page single-spaced schedule that included every step the Queen would take.

To minimize disruption to the rail system and ensure an on-time arrival, Elizabeth II and Philip spent the night before their visit on the Royal Train near Hull. The shiny maroon train, a staple of royal travel since Queen Victoria ordered the first version in 1842, is endearingly old-fashioned, its functional decor dating from the 1970s. The Queen and Philip each have a separate carriage — "saloon" in royal parlance — divided into a bedroom, bathroom and sitting room with a desk and small dining table. The furniture is blond wood, the floors are covered in plain wall-to-wall carpet, and the plastic walls are adorned with Scottish landscapes and Victorian prints of rail journeys.

When the train pulled into the Hull station at 10:20 A.M. on March 3, the Queen and Philip were greeted on the platform by the predictable lineup of dignitaries that the Palace calls the "chain gang," so named for the ceremonial chains and other regalia worn by the lord mayor, the high sheriff, and beadles in their robes, knee breeches, buckled shoes, and plumed hats. The royal retinue was small — a lady-in-waiting, an assistant private secretary, an equerry, and several personal protection officers — but there was a large local security contingent.

At the Queen's request, she met more ordinary people than luminaries. Waiting nearby was the royal Bentley (transported the previous day in a truck) with the hood ornament of St. George slaying the dragon and the distinctive shield bearing the Queen's arms attached to the roof. After a five-minute walkabout of approximately twenty paces along the barriers outside the station, Elizabeth II was driven to the Queen's Center for Oncology and Haematology, where she spent nearly an hour talking to patients, doctors, and nurses.

Phil Brown, the forty-nine-year-old manager of the Hull City football team, sat next to the Queen at the Guildhall luncheon. "She has an amazing ability to scan right across the classes, to come to my level and to go back to being regal," he said. She talked across the table to a "lollipop lady" (a school crossing guard), an ambulance driver, and an "environmental community volunteer." Maria Raper, the crossing guard, was transfixed not only by the sight of the Queen applying lipstick after polishing off her Tian of Triple Chocolate Mousse, but by the way she "was picking at her bread roll the whole time. She opened it and picked little bits off, and at the end of the meal there was her bread plate with a collection of small bits of bread." Throughout the day, Elizabeth II smiled frequently and moved unhurriedly, mindful of Martin Charteris's edict to "spread a carpet of happiness." The next morning's *Hull Daily Mail* rewarded her efforts with the banner headline "SHE'S A ROYAL TONIC."

Several weeks later she shifted her focus to the international sphere for a state visit by Felipe Calderón, the president of Mexico. After hosting ninety-six state visits, the Queen was no less attentive to the minutiae of ceremony and protocol. Every place setting for the state banquet in the ballroom was precisely measured, and all the fruit on the table was polished to a high gloss.

In the middle of the Mexican visit, the Queen and Prince Philip hosted a reception at Buckingham Palace for twenty world leaders attending the G-20 summit. Before the reception began they had their first meeting with the new American president, forty-seven-year-old Barack Obama, and his forty-five-year-old wife, Michelle.

Although Gordon Brown had spent many summers vacationing in Provincetown on Cape Cod, his relationship with the United States was not as close as that of Blair, who had forged personal ties with both Bill Clinton and George W. Bush. Obama had also shown a coolness toward the "special relationship." Shortly after taking office, he returned the bronze bust of Winston Churchill that George W. Bush had proudly displayed for seven years. The British government had lent the bust after 9/11 "as a signal of the strong transatlantic relationship," and Obama decided to discontinue the loan.

But the forty-fourth American president and his wife had an air of expectancy when they arrived at the private Garden Entrance of the Palace. The first lady even confided to a courtier that she was nervous about meeting the sovereign. The Queen arranged to have her American lady-in-waiting, Ginny Airlie, greet the couple before Master of the Household David Walker escorted them upstairs to the private apartments, where they had twenty minutes of congenial small talk with Elizabeth II and Philip. The royal couple presented their standard gift — a signed framed photograph — and the Obamas gave the Queen a video iPod loaded with forty classic show tunes, photographs, and footage of her 2007 and 1957 visits to the United States, as well as the audio of the president's speech to the 2004 Democratic National Convention and his inaugural address, along with a selection of inaugural pictures.

Elizabeth II and Prince Philip greeted the rest of the heads of state visiting for the G-20 summit in a receiving line before they made their way into the Picture Gallery, with its extraordinary array of paintings, including works by Canaletto, Rubens, Rembrandt, Vermeer, and Holbein. "The Queen knows when she enters the room she is the most compelling head of state in the room," former Canadian prime minister Brian Mulroney once observed. "She is number one even though her country is not number one."

The atmosphere was electric with concentrated power as the Queen informally circulated among the world leaders, with no need for introductions by her equerries and ladies-in-waiting, who lingered nearby mainly to engage guests as they waited for a chance to speak. Secretary of State Hillary Clinton was working the room like a political candidate, stopping at one point to talk to French president Nicolas Sarkozy over the Queen — a maneuver that Elizabeth II doubtless thought "frightfully funny," said one of her ladies-in-waiting.

With the American president standing six foot one and his wife nearly as tall, the Obamas towered over nearly everyone. As Michelle Obama and the Queen were talking, they turned toward lady-in-waiting Susan Hussey to remark on their disparity in size. The first lady wrapped her arm around the Queen's back, and Elizabeth II responded in kind, lightly placing her arm around Michelle's waist. After ten seconds, the Queen dropped her arm to her side, but the first lady kept her hand in place and even gave the sovereign's shoulder a reassuring rub.

"It happened spontaneously," said Peter Wilkinson, the Queen's videographer, who recorded the moment. "The Queen and Michelle were lifting up their heels to compare the size. The Queen came up to Michelle's shoulder, and when they put their arms around each other, the Queen jokingly looked skyward. Sue Hussey was laughing. They sort of did it together as they compared their heights."

The newspapers grabbed Wilkinson's footage off the television screens and made a fuss about an "unthinkable" breach of protocol by the first lady. But after the Queen's encounters in the United States and Australia in recent years, not to mention her hugs and kisses with close friends, she was more relaxed about gestures of familiarity. Palace officials hastened to say there was neither an offense nor a faux pas in what a spokeswoman described as a "mutual and spontaneous display of affection and appreciation." "You can't analyze it," said a courtier. "It just happened. We'd never seen it before, but the Queen was happy, the event was going so well, which is why there was a spontaneous happy expression."

The following November Elizabeth II was off on her big foreign tour of the year — two days in Bermuda, followed by a three-day state visit in Trinidad and Tobago combined with the biennial meeting of Commonwealth leaders. They were sent on their way, according to custom, at Heathrow Airport by the Queen's Lord Chamberlain, William Peel, the 3rd Earl, a ritual that invariably prompted Philip to exclaim, "Mind the shop!"

At age eighty-three, the Queen studied her briefs as conscientiously as ever — biographical summaries of all the people she would meet (with difficult pronunciations phonetically spelled out) along with Foreign Office guidance on questions that the foreign leaders might raise. Her itineraries, prepared by the host countries and Palace officials, had been approved in detail by the Queen, with time splits down to the half minute. Every conceivable scrap of information was included in a four-by-six-inch spiral-bound blue book called the "Mini" — names, logistics, security details, dress requirements, and the number of paces from point to point (13+7 signifying 13 steps, a pause, then 7 steps), rehearsed repeatedly by her staff during a series of reconnaissance trips.

The visit to Bermuda was to mark the four hundredth anniversary of the island's settlement by English voyagers marooned after a shipwreck. It was fifty-six years to the day since she had first set foot on her distant territory in the Atlantic as she began her coronation tour.

After her eight-hour flight with no time to nap, she arrived in mid-afternoon to a ceremonial welcome led by Bermuda's governor, Sir Richard Gozney (resplendent in a white uniform and white cocked hat decorated with swan feathers) and Premier Ewart Brown, followed by a walkabout and a ninety-minute cocktail party with 150 prominent Bermudians at Government House, the governor's Italianate home on the island's north shore.

The Queen was a smiling icon moving through the crowd at the reception, careful not to engage too much. For all her expansiveness in private, her remarks in these settings seemed to escape like wisps of vapor. After decades in the public eye, she had become like a Rorschach test, saying little and allowing others to superimpose their impressions. At a small dinner afterward, Richard Gozney noted that she showed "no visible signs of flagging. She is clearly a master of pacing herself. You don't see it, but she organizes her own energies and output accordingly." She had a four-hour stretch of downtime in the next day's twelve-hour schedule, which she used to do her boxes in her three-room suite.

As she crisscrossed the island, she walked whenever she could, was driven through the streets of Hamilton in an open landau, and slowed her motorcade whenever possible — knowing, as she had said decades earlier, that "I have to be seen to be believed." An estimated twenty thousand people lined the roads, in some places four deep, far exceeding the turnout on her previous visit in 1994. The enthusiastic support for the monarch was seen as a rebuke to Ewart Brown's advocacy of independence for the island, which had been rejected repeatedly in public opinion polls.

For her four-hour flight to Trinidad the next day, more than sixty people were on board the British Airways 777, including two private secretaries, her equerry, two ladies-in-waiting, a physician, her personal assistant, a hairdresser, footmen, maids, administrative support personnel, and security officers, along with fifteen members of the broadcast and print media, all spread out in an aircraft that usually accommodates 230.

The royal couple had First Class to themselves, members of the household occupied Business Class, and press and security men occupied Economy. The premium Economy section, with all the center seats removed, held a pile of securely strapped royal luggage overseen by Matthew King, the Traveling Yeoman. The Queen brought thirteen outfits, along with four spare dresses, two diamond tiaras, and an array of brooches, necklaces, earrings, and bracelets. In years past, when the royal party traveled on *Britannia,* the entourage was much larger, with several chefs and a large military contingent, and the household brought abundant quantities of food, wine, and spirits, as well as linen, china, flatware, and such equipment as the Queen's monogrammed electric kettle for tea. Since the decommissioning of the royal yacht, the Queen relied on the host country to meet most of those needs. In Port of Spain, Trinidad, the Queen and her household took over the entire twelve-story Carlton Savannah hotel.

Elizabeth II was back in her element in the Caribbean. Trinidad and Tobago had obtained independence in 1962 and had voted to become a republic in 1976, but the country remained in the Commonwealth and kept strong financial and cultural ties with Britain, along with an enduring affection for the Queen. She showed her respect during the state dinner on the first night by wearing an Angela Kelly–designed "emblem dress" embroidered with images of the country's national birds, the scarlet ibis and the cocrico, and the national flower, the wild poinsettia.

She opened the Commonwealth conference the next day by attending an elaborate ceremony in the country's performing arts center, where she gave a five-minute speech reminding the group that they should work together on environmental problems, especially by helping smaller and more vulnerable countries. "Every word she says is listened to carefully," said Kamalesh Sharma, an Indian diplomat who was serving as the Commonwealth's secretary-general.

"The Commonwealth is very much her legacy," said Brian Mulroney. "For her it is a major achievement and platform." Without the Queen's leadership and example, "many of us would have left," said Kenneth Kaunda, the former president of Zambia. Lacking executive power, she had nevertheless learned to use her role to exert influence and to work quietly behind the scenes to defuse crises. Through her own sources of information, she came to know more about the issues and concerns of Commonwealth countries, particularly in Africa, than her government's top officials. She developed better relationships with Commonwealth leaders, even the Marxists, than her prime ministers. She could discuss grazing rights in Somalia, or a particular leader's fishing habits and favorite hymns. Prince Philip said she became the "Commonwealth psychotherapist."

While in the past she would have twenty-minute audiences with every head of government, in Trinidad she limited herself to a private reception with the fifteen leaders who had taken office since the previous Commonwealth conference two years earlier. At her dinner that evening for all the leaders at the Hyatt Hotel — where each place was set with silver gilt Commonwealth goblets sent over from London the previous week and stored in a vault at the Central Bank in Port of Spain — Gordon Brown was just one among many, a diffident presence at the end of the receiving line.

All the events on the Queen's tour were stage-managed by press secretary Samantha Cohen. She helped set up photographers' shots, mindful of vantage points and background colors, and worked with reporters on human interest angles that would appeal to their editors. Unlike the Queen Mother, Elizabeth II "doesn't look at photographers," said Robin Nunn, a longtime photographer of the royal family. "Over time you know that she'll look in a certain direction, so you can catch her."

Elizabeth II was interested in seeing as much Caribbean culture as possible, so Eric Jenkinson, the British high commissioner in Port of Spain, organized a series of musical performances, followed by a walkabout among masses of children costumed for Carnival. The Queen seemed unperturbed by the frenzy, the noise, and the heat as a scrum of still and video photographers rushed close, little girls dressed as butterflies and hummingbirds twirled and swayed to the rhythms of drums and steel pans, and adults scrambled to catch the scene on their camera phones. Nearly a dozen protection officers formed a cordon by placing themselves nearby, while Samantha Cohen kept her arms on photographer Tim Rooke's waist as she guided him along. Videographer Peter Wilkinson worked intently but never closer than five feet away, filming for the monarchy's website as well as a private DVD so the Queen could recall events and see people she missed.

Her final engagement — her fifth evening out — was a garden party for sixty-five worthies at the peach stucco residence of the British high commissioner on a hilltop overlooking Port of Spain. Although she had been going nearly nonstop since mid-morning, she seemed remarkably fresh and no less disciplined as she talked to seven groups arranged by themes such as sport, environment, and culture. The schedule called for 4.5 minutes per group, but Elizabeth II and Philip spent more than the allotted time, somehow managing to cross paths exactly in the middle of the terrace.

With each encounter, the Queen leaned forward, offering a smile and pertinent comment. One young man from Kenya cheekily asked for her favorite song on the iPod given to her by Barack Obama the previous March. "I don't have time to use it much!" she replied, escaping the query without giving offense. It was a hot night, and the faces of several Palace officials were dripping sweat, but as usual the Queen's maquillage showed no hint of moisture.

Pausing briefly inside with Jenkinson and his wife, Maire, the Queen had a soft drink and prepared for her long flight home. The royal couple walked into the night and climbed into their car, which remained illuminated as they were driven away while waving to the guests lining the driveway. "That was a seamless beautiful moment," said one of the security men.

Elizabeth II and her entourage landed on Sunday morning at Heathrow, where they were greeted by Willie Peel, the Lord Chamberlain. After only two days off, she was back on a full work schedule, with an investiture, visits to Wellington College and the Ashmolean Museum, and a dinner party for twenty-five at Windsor Castle. "I sometimes think her advisers don't realize she is 83 years old," said her cousin Margaret Rhodes. "But maybe she doesn't want them to slow her down."

CHAPTER TWENTY-ONE
LONG LIVE THE QUEEN

The only other sovereign in the history of the British monarchy to spend sixty years on the throne was Queen Victoria. In 1897, during the six-mile carriage procession that was the high point of her Diamond Jubilee celebration, Victoria, then seventy-eight, was so overcome by the tumultuous reception that she wept openly. "How kind they are to me!" she said repeatedly. Too infirm to walk into St. Paul's Cathedral, she sat outside in her carriage for a brief service of thanksgiving, surrounded by clergy and dignitaries as the choir sang a *Te Deum,* followed by an unconventional exhortation from the Archbishop of Canterbury: "Three cheers for the Queen!" Victoria died at age eighty-one on January 22, 1901, after sixty-three years and 216 days on the throne — a record that Queen Elizabeth II would surpass in September 2015.

Elizabeth II's Diamond Jubilee was arranged with some concessions to her eighty-six years. She won't cover the forty thousand miles overseas that she logged during her Golden Jubilee travels, but her tours throughout England, Scotland, Wales, and Northern Ireland will cover ten regions. Members of the royal family will visit all fifteen of the

"There was sunshine and laughter and happiness that everyone could join in."

Queen Elizabeth II and Prince Philip, her husband of sixty-three years, during the wedding of their grandson Prince William to Catherine Middleton at Westminster Abbey, April 2011. IAN JONES PHOTOGRAPHY

Queen's other realms as her representatives. The plan has many of the same elements — parades, concerts, luncheons, dinners, garden parties, religious services, themed events, and fireworks — to capture the affection and admiration that have grown stronger since the last jubilee. "Her reputation now is as high as at any time since the golden early years when everyone was intensely loyal to the new Queen, and Churchill was flat on his back with admiration," said Margaret Thatcher's senior adviser Charles Powell.

Her regional tours will begin in May of 2012 following Accession Day on February 6, always a time of quiet commemoration for the Queen. The apex of the public celebration spans four days of events on the first weekend in June that includes national holidays on Monday and Tuesday. The timing of the Summer Olympic Games six weeks later promises to extend the festive atmosphere, and to give Britain's athletes added incentive to win for their Queen as well as their country.

With the exception of security and a special grant from the Treasury of £1 million to cover costs such as additional staffing, funding for the jubilee has come from nongovernment sources, with broadcasters and private organizations underwriting concerts and other events. The Thames Diamond Jubilee Foundation organized and funded "the largest flotilla to be assembled on the river in modern times," scheduled for Sunday, June 3. Featuring at least one thousand boats and covering seven and a half miles, the river pageant was designed to surpass the Silver Jubilee barge procession, which had only 140 vessels. At the head of the waterborne progress will be a special barge for the Queen and Prince Philip, modeled on an eighteenth-century royal galley and powered by oarsmen that London mayor Boris Johnson joked could be "oiled and manacled MPs."

On Saturday she will celebrate by watching the Derby at Epsom, and Monday will feature a concert produced and financed by the BBC and attended by twelve thousand people chosen by lottery as they were a decade earlier. They will attend a garden party at Buckingham Palace, followed by the musical program, which will include selections from classical to popular. The Queen will again light a national beacon as others are lit around the United Kingdom and Commonwealth. The stage will have the Palace as its dramatic backdrop, stands will be built around the Victoria Memorial, and large video screens will be placed down the Mall.

On Tuesday the Queen will be honored at a service of thanksgiving at St. Paul's Cathedral, and her carriage procession afterward will trace part of Queen Victoria's route. None of the celebrations could be considered modest, nor will they be extravagant, in keeping with the Queen's wishes to minimize the expenditure of public funds.

Planning for the jubilee began in 2009, which the Palace called its "ideas" year. The elements of the celebration were rolled out in a low-key fashion to tamp down expectations, as had been done for the 2002 festivities. The Queen's advisers were mindful that opposition to the monarchy had dwindled considerably, and they were determined to keep it that way. "Republicanism isn't even an esoteric political position in Britain these days," wrote *Times* columnist Hugo Rifkind in 2009. "It's barely even a political position at all." Forty years after surveys about the monarchy's popularity began in 1969, the Queen continues to enjoy an approval rating of around 80 percent.

Evidence of the monarchy's strong emotional hold, not only over the British people but around the world, could be seen in the popularity of the Oscar-winning film *The King's Speech,* the inspiring tale of how Elizabeth II's father, George VI, overcame his stutter through perseverance and discipline. The film touched people's hearts but also tapped into a yearning for the monarchy's enduring values of duty, integrity, and courage. In one movie theater after another, audiences applauded after the final scene.

Intrigued by the response to the film, the Queen saw it in a private screening. "On the whole she quite liked it," said Margaret Rhodes. "I'm glad she saw it. It's always difficult to see your own parents depicted, but she wasn't violently either pro or con. Obviously there were a few bits that were not characteristic, but she thought it was okay."

A powerful source of the Queen's success as sovereign has been her inscrutability and avoidance of controversy. With the exception of a few relatively inconsequential remarks over the years, her political views remained a matter of conjecture long after *The Sunday Times* tried to portray her as a soft Tory against Margaret Thatcher's hard line. Sometimes she has hinted at progressive thinking: applauding the Commonwealth's multilateralism and initiatives to combat climate change, and speaking of "redressing the economic balance between nations" in her Christmas speech in 1983 by urging prosperous countries to share modern technology with poorer countries. But even then, her public statements have been well within constitutional bounds, and congruent with her government's policies. Above all, the arguments against the monarchy as antidemocratic and backward-looking have been overwhelmed by the Queen's dependable and consistent presence — what David Airlie, her former Lord Chamberlain, calls "the sheet anchor in the middle for people to hang on to in times of turbulence."

On Tuesday, May 11, 2010, Elizabeth II greeted her twelfth prime minister, Conservative leader David Cameron. At age forty-three, he was the youngest politician to take that office since Lord Liverpool was appointed in 1812. Born in the fifteenth year of her reign, Cameron was also junior by three years to Prince Edward, the Queen's youngest child. She had first glimpsed the future PM when he appeared at age eight with Edward in a school production of *Toad of Toad Hall.* It was a remarkable trajectory from her first prime minister, who was born in the nineteenth century and served in her great-great-grandmother's army.

Cameron made the time-honored trip to the Palace five days after the general election on Thursday, May 6, resulted in the first hung Parliament since 1974. The Tory party had won 306 seats, but it was twenty shy of the majority needed to govern. Labour tallied 258 seats, and the minority Liberal Democrats (the party created in 1988 when the Liberals merged with the Social Democratic Party) captured fifty-seven seats, placing their forty-three-year-old leader, Nick Clegg, in the role of power broker as he considered overtures from the two other parties. The Liberal Democrats were in many respects more in line with Labour, but Cameron moved more nimbly than Gordon Brown, offering terms for a deal that Labour couldn't match.

At one point Brown's chief negotiator, Peter Mandelson, sought advice from Private Secretary Christopher Geidt at the Palace, who said Brown had a "constitutional obligation, a duty, to remain in his post" until a new government could be formed. As the period of limbo extended through the weekend, Geidt made regular trips to 10 Downing Street to get briefings. "It was important for Geidt to be visible, and to show that he was very much there on behalf of the Queen," recalled Brown's press spokesman and Palace veteran Simon Lewis.

During his final encounter with Clegg on Tuesday, Brown said, "I can't keep the Queen waiting. Make up your mind, Nick." In the end, Clegg accepted what Cameron later described as "a big generous offer to have a coalition government" that included making the Liberal Democrat leader deputy prime minister. Still, the deal for the first two-party government since World War II was subject to ratification by Clegg's party. When Cameron met with the Queen after Brown's resignation, "I said I couldn't be totally sure about what sort of government I was going to form," he recalled. "I said that I hoped to form a coalition government but I might have to come back in the morning and tell her it was something rather different."

Cameron was the first Old Etonian to become prime minister since Alec Douglas-Home left office in 1964. The new prime minister came from a wealthy family of bankers interlaced with aristocrats including the 7th Earl of Denbigh. His father, Ian, was a stockbroker who taught his son about coping with adversity. Born with severely deformed legs, Ian managed to play tennis and cricket, endured repeated surgery, and finally suffered through amputation, always steadfast and devoid of self-pity. After attending Heatherdown with Prince Edward, David went to Eton and graduated from Oxford with honors. He spent much of his early career as a backroom strategist for the Conservative Party and honed his ability to get his message across during seven years as a public relations executive at Carlton Communications, one of Britain's leading media companies.

Once he was elected to Parliament in 2001, Cameron rose to the top in just four years, working to modernize the Tory party by emphasizing individual initiative as well as social justice while tackling government excesses. Handsome, easygoing, and quick on his feet, he struck the right notes in the way Tony Blair had done with the Labour Party. His wife, Samantha, the daughter of a baronet, cut a stylish figure, and they had three young children. The eldest, Ivan, born with cerebral palsy and severe epilepsy, was unable to eat on his own, speak, or walk. Although he required round-the-clock care (including twenty-six doses of medicine a day), the Camerons tried to include him in as many family activities as possible and expose him to the outside world.

In 2009, Ivan died at age six from the complications of his illness. Gordon Brown, who knew the pain of losing a child as well as caring for one with a serious chronic illness, spoke of his rival's tragedy with unusual feeling on the floor of the House of Commons. Three months after her husband became prime minister, Samantha Cameron gave birth to their third daughter, although their happiness dimmed just two weeks later when Ian Cameron died of a stroke at age seventy-seven while on vacation in France.

David Cameron's combination of matter-of-fact strength and ingenuous openness about his hardships simultaneously aligned him with the Queen's instinctive stoicism and the post-Diana emotional accessibility she had come to accept as part of modern life. Aside from Cameron's school days in the shadow of Windsor Castle, he and the eighty-four-year-old Queen found other common ground. He had grown up in the countryside, in a small village in Berkshire, where he enjoyed hunting and shooting. His father had a passion for horse racing, taking shares in several thoroughbreds. Like the Queen, the prime minister had a practical turn of mind, and spoke in an unusually forthright way for a politician. There was, in short, an ample comfort zone for the weekly audiences at Buckingham Palace, which Cameron could readily fill with self-deprecating humor and a companionable personality.

The coalition led by Cameron immediately had

to come to grips with a brutal recession compounded by Labour's legacy of government spending that had expanded from 40 percent of gross domestic product in 1997 to nearly half of GDP by 2010. The new government imposed cuts of nearly 20 percent across the board to slash a swollen budget deficit, and also raised taxes and tuition fees at universities. Students protested in the streets, but otherwise the British public endured the stern medicine after watching the economies of Greece, Ireland, and Portugal nearly collapse under the weight of unaffordable entitlements.

The royal budget was not immune from either scrutiny or action when the ten-year funding for the Civil List expired in 2010. During the twenty years since Margaret Thatcher fixed an annual stipend of £7.9 million to cover the Queen's duties as head of state, there had been no increases. The original formula had been set higher than the Palace had budgeted because at the time inflation was running above 9 percent. With yearly inflation at a far more modest average of 3 percent through the 1990s, the Queen's treasurer took the surplus cash and invested it in a rainy day fund that grew to £35.6 million by the end of the decade.

When the Thatcher agreement ended in 2000, Tony Blair froze the Civil List for the following ten years, assuming that the reserve fund would top off the rising costs of running the royal household. By 2009, yearly Civil List expenses had climbed to more than £14 million, largely due to inflation, requiring a £6.5 million annual supplement from the Queen.

When George Osborne, the chancellor of the

exchequer, presented his report on royal finances in June 2010, he praised the "careful housekeeping" at the Palace over the previous decade and said that the freeze on the Civil List amount would need to continue for two more years, which would exhaust the Queen's remaining £15.2 millon reserve fund. In addition, Elizabeth II planned to spend nearly £1.3 million of her more than £13 million personal income from her Duchy of Lancaster portfolio to support the official expenses of three of her four children and other royal relatives working for the "Firm." (Charles spent £9 million on his "official duties and charitable activities" out of his Duchy of Cornwall income of £17.1 million in 2009.) The costs of security provided by the police and the military for the entire family and the palaces remained a closely kept secret; estimates put it at more than £50 million annually.

In October 2010 the chancellor announced that the Queen's household had further agreed to cut spending for 2012 by 14 percent, in line with the government's austerity budget. At the same time, Osborne unveiled a historic change in financing the monarch's official activities that he had devised in collaboration with Palace officials. Starting in 2013 the Civil List and various government grants will be scrapped. The new arrangement will give the royal household a single Sovereign Support Grant based on 15 percent of net income from the vast Crown Estate portfolio of property and investments that has belonged to the monarchy since the eleventh century. The Queen's income will be pegged to the profit from two years previously.

Osborne's solution is elegant in its simplicity and

pragmatic in its consequences. It restores to the monarch a portion of the Crown Estate profits that King George III had relinquished in 1760 in exchange for the Civil List stipend. It also removes the need to periodically negotiate a payment plan with Parliament "so that my successors do not have to return to the issue so often," said Osborne. With its capital value of £7.3 billion, the Crown Estate's projected net income in 2011–12 of some £230 million is expected to yield about £34 million in 2013 for the Queen's official business and provide the government treasury with £196 million.

The new arrangement is meant to keep pace with inflation, and will place safeguards on the downside and limits on the upside so the income will not be "adversely high." Critics have argued that the monarch would no longer be accountable to Parliament, but in fact the Palace agreed for the first time to yearly scrutiny by the National Audit Office, which will report its findings to Parliament. The new system will also permit the royal household to decide how to allocate resources rather than rely on separate dedicated funds for maintenance and travel. Shoring up aging infrastructure will be an urgent priority. Buckingham Palace has been losing pieces of masonry from its facade, and the roof over the ballroom has sprung leaks.

Aside from landmark events and regular entertainments like the annual garden parties, diplomatic receptions, and state dinners, the Queen had already begun paring expenses in various ways. The era of periodic grand balls for friends and family was long over. To recognize two of her ladies-in-waiting, Susan Hussey and Mary Morrison, for serving fifty years apiece, the Queen hosted a low-key private reception at Buckingham Palace in June 2010 called "A Century of Waiting." She recycled her outfits regularly, and for a state visit to Slovenia in October 2008 she asked Angela Kelly to create a gown for the state banquet out of silver and gold brocade fabric that had been given to her during a visit to the Middle East two decades earlier — a gesture the Palace called "credit crunch couture." In the autumn of 2010, Elizabeth II announced that she was canceling the annual Christmas party at Buckingham Palace, cutting an estimated £50,000 from her £1.3 million catering and hospitality budget. A headline in the *Evening Standard* captured the mood: "EVERYONE LOSES . . . EVEN THE QUEEN."

The royal family's relations with the press became less troublesome in the first decade of the twenty-first century. The main reason was the disappearance of a parallel court presided over by Diana that fed morsels of information to tabloid favorites. At the same time, the Palace had developed a more sophisticated view of the media. "We have no experts in royal history, but we understand the way the media works," said one senior official.

Although Philip complained that the Queen read too many "bloody" newspapers, her daily habit has given her a good feel for the press. She had long since learned to sort out what was important and what was irrelevant, and how to distinguish between media opinion and public opinion. The Palace press office reached out to a greater cross section of "opinion formers" as well as local papers, and offered more frequent background briefings. "We are not about demystifying the royal family," said one official. "It is about telling people what they do."

As the circulation of newspapers dropped with the rise of the Internet, the Queen's advisers realized they could get their message directly to the public — and particularly what Palace officials call "the space of young people" — through the monarchy's website and its YouTube channel. Keeping pace with emerging technologies, the Palace launched its British monarchy Twitter account in 2009, although its use was confined to bulletins about the comings and goings of the royal family. By early 2011 there were more than 100,000 followers of the royal family on Twitter. Four months after its launch on November 7, 2010, more than 300,000 "likes" were registered on the Queen's Facebook page.

But the social media only softened the lash of Britain's national newspapers, which remained more influential than the press in the United States. In 2010 and 2011 their prime target was Prince Andrew, Britain's special representative for trade and investment since 2001. His global peregrinations earned him the nickname "Air Miles Andy," and he was severely criticized for his contacts with unsavory dictators in places like Kazakhstan and Azerbaijan, not to mention the American billionaire Jeffrey Epstein, who had served time in prison for pedophilia. Reporters routinely questioned the value of Andrew's unsalaried role, which cost the British government nearly £600,000 annually for overseas travel, hotels, and entertaining — plus his £249,000 annual allowance from the Queen to run his private office.

Government officials credited Andrew with helping British firms win multibillion-pound contracts for such projects as the Dubai metro and jet engines for Air Asia. His lobbying for British industry was most effective in Asia and the Middle East, where he was friendly with leaders such as Jordan's King Abdullah II, with whom he hunted in Morocco and Tanzania. "It's not about the power of royalty, it's about personal relationships," said Andrew. "If you know the right people you can have a positive outcome. . . . If you are competing with other countries, you have to deploy as many assets as you can. I am one of those assets." Nevertheless, Andrew's questionable associates and poor judgment disturbed the Queen and her advisers, and in July 2011 he stepped down from his job after serving for ten years. He still intended to promote British business, but on an unofficial basis, while focusing on helping develop apprenticeships for young people.

Andrew's image had also been badly dented when his ex-wife got caught a year earlier exploiting her husband's position in a mortifying episode that recalled the royal family's misadventures of the late twentieth century. After their divorce in 1996, Fergie had been more than £3 million in debt, but she had returned to financial solvency by pursuing an array of lucrative business ventures. She even won the approval of her former mother-in-law, who included her in a weekend at Balmoral in August 2008 with Andrew and their daughters, Beatrice and Eugenie, the first time the outcast duchess had been to the royal Highland retreat since her hasty exit in 1992.

Fergie continued to maintain a profligate lifestyle, however, employing eleven full- and part-time staff, compared to Andrew's five. Her finances began to implode again in 2009 as her income declined and her debts grew to more than £2 million. In the spring of 2010 the fifty-year-old duchess was in a desperate mood when Mazher Mahmood, the *News of the World* reporter who had entrapped Sophie Wessex nine years earlier, enticed Sarah into a sting by posing as an Indian businessman. With hidden cameras recording the meeting in a Mayfair apartment, Fergie sold access to her former husband in exchange for £500,000, including a $40,000 cash down payment that she carried off in a computer bag. She repeatedly emphasized that Andrew "never does accept a penny for anything" and said she only wanted "a lick of the spoon."

In an effort to defuse the potential damage from the incriminating footage, which was an instant sensation on YouTube, Fergie quickly issued a statement saying she was "sincerely sorry." She explained that her finances were "under stress," but said this was "no excuse for a serious lapse of judgment." Both she and Andrew said that he had been unaware of her contacts with the phony businessman. After consulting with the Queen, Andrew covered a portion of his ex-wife's debts and helped her restructure the rest. That July Fergie fired all her employees and agreed to operate under the supervision of Andrew's office.

The following month, the Queen and Philip gathered their children and most of their grandchildren (William and Harry were off on military duty) for a nostalgic ten-day Western Isles cruise aboard the *Hebridean Princess* to celebrate the sixtieth and fiftieth birthdays of Anne and Andrew. The guest of honor was eighty-three-year-old retired nanny Mabel Anderson, who lived rent-free in one of the Queen's grace-and-favor houses in Windsor Great Park and remained close to her former charges, particularly Charles.

For the first time since the royal yacht was decommissioned in 1997, the family re-created *Britannia* Day by stopping at the Castle of Mey, where Charles customarily stayed in his grandmother's faithfully preserved pale blue bedroom for a week at the beginning of August. On August 2, 2010, Charles assumed the role of his late grandmother and hosted the family for a tour of the castle, proudly showing off various improvements he had overseen — the new visitor center as well as the recently built turret in the southeast corner of the walled garden. The Queen queried the staff about visitor numbers, inquired about the new radiant heating on the ground floor of the castle, and climbed up the turret to look out at the Orkney Islands through a monocular. After their tour, the royal party sat down to the traditional lunch, which featured *oeufs Drumkilbo*, just the way the Queen Mother had served them.

In his seventh decade, Prince Charles had not only found contentment in his new life with Camilla, but fulfillment in the job he had invented to give meaning to his role as heir to the throne. The Prince of Wales doggedly promoted a wide-ranging agenda embracing architecture, historic preservation, the environment, sustainable farming, rain forest conservation, health, education, and job training. A number of his views, such as the value of organic produce and the need for human-scale architecture to build new communities, were initially derided but later moved into the mainstream. He raised more than £110 million each year for his personal charities, which have extended his reach to projects in China, Afghanistan, Guyana, and Jamaica.

He had grown more comfortable in his own skin and committed himself to establishing his legacy through the job that, as he frequently said, "I made up as I went along." "He has made a full life for himself," said Nancy Reagan. "He does so much more than any previous Prince of Wales." Yet his approach to his role is diametrically opposed to his mother's more deliberate operation at Buckingham Palace. Much of what the Queen does she is advised to do, while her firstborn son tends to do mainly what he wants to. Charles "is high octane because he is so driven," said one of his aides. "He is always at full tilt."

The differences in temperament between mother and son are striking. "He is probably an instinctively glass half empty person, while she is more a half full one," said her cousin Margaret Rhodes. The Queen "has no illusions about what can and can't be changed," said her former press secretary Charles Anson. "She has an acceptance of the way life deals its cards that is rare in the Western world, and stems partly from her religious conviction and partly from her life experience." Prince Charles is more emotional than the Queen, easily offended and short-tempered, with an inclination to brood and to need reassurance. "Camilla soothes things and anticipates what could go wrong," said Anne Glenconner.

He is more impressionable than his mother, and over the years was influenced by gurus such as Laurens van der Post and the mystical poet Kathleen Raine. But while the Queen can be persuaded by a well-crafted proposal, Charles dislikes advice contrary to his beliefs. There are few, even among his close friends, who feel comfortable challenging him for fear of being judged insensitive or disloyal. His father, by contrast, welcomes robust argument. While Philip can squash an opponent on occasion, he is more than happy to accommodate the views of someone he feels has mastered his brief.

Charles is also less direct than either of his parents, who can be counted on for a straight answer. "You sense he maneuvers," said a longtime friend of Camilla. "People have to maneuver with him." Charles enjoys gossip more than the Queen (although she likes political scuttlebutt) and wonders whether "that person is for or against me, in this or that camp," said one of Elizabeth II's former advisers. "The Queen doesn't think that way. It is more, 'What is the problem? What do we do?' She only wants to know who is in what camp if it is obstructing a decision that needs to be taken."

No one would deny that the Queen sets high standards for her household, but Charles is more extravagant. Elizabeth II knows what everything costs and economizes when necessary. Guests at routine Buckingham Palace receptions are served wine, potato chips, and nuts, while at Clarence House they get gourmet hors d'oeuvres, and the dinner parties have elaborate floral displays and theatrical lighting. "It is fair to say when he feels something should be done well, he doesn't stint," said Patricia Brabourne. When he goes to stay at Sandringham for a week on his own, Charles brings along vans filled with vegetables and meats from Highgrove, even though there is a farm on the Norfolk estate. At dinner parties, he is known to eat a different meal from his guests, sometimes with his personal cutlery.

Such behavior may seem persnickety and spoiled, but Charles has a capacity for empathy that was underestimated in the Diana era. His ability to engage with people is "as good if not better than the Queen," said a former courtier. "He has natural warmth with the Queen's sense of duty and Philip's ability to make a guy laugh." He is more imaginative and intuitive as well, and his thoughtfulness is legendary. When Anne Glenconner's sister got cancer, Charles wrote her a seventeen-page letter with ideas about alternative treatments.

While the Queen has four private secretaries, Charles has eleven — nine full-time and two part-time — plus separate directors for each of the twenty charities he founded and a commercial enterprise that produces his Duchy Originals line of organic products ranging from Sicilian Lemon All Butter Shortbread to Mandarin Zest and Rose Geranium shampoo. All the profits, totaling more than £6 million in two decades, have been donated to charitable causes.

Along with Charles's independence has come a

boldness to proselytize for his causes in speeches, publications, and regular letters to government ministers in his distinctive scrawl. "There is nobody I admire more for his energy, ambition and enthusiasm," said Sir Malcolm Ross, who served for two years as Charles's Master of the Household after eighteen years in the senior ranks at Buckingham Palace. "He wants to save the world. The problem is he wants to save the world this afternoon and every other day." In recent years Charles has urged that the global economic system be overhauled and questioned the values of a materialistic consumer society, denounced climate change skeptics, called for a "revolution" in the Western world's "mechanistic approach to science," and praised Islam for its belief that there is "no separation between man and nature." He has twice taken on one of Britain's most prestigious architects, Sir Richard Rogers, and derailed his multimillion-dollar projects for being incompatible with their neighborhoods, much to the relief of nearby residents.

His outspokenness has periodically put him at odds with his family, especially his father. After Charles first condemned genetically modified crops in 1998 for jeopardizing the delicate balance of nature, Philip vehemently disagreed on the grounds that such crops are necessary to feed the world. In 2000, when Charles intensified his attack on bioengineered agriculture, both his father and Princess Anne publicly took issue with his position, which his sister witheringly called a "huge oversimplification." Philip pointed out in an interview with *The Times* that "we have been genetically modifying animals and plants ever since people started selective breeding."

Tony Blair, whose government supported genetically modified farming, had already complained a year earlier to the Queen about Charles's public pronouncements and had fumed to Alastair Campbell that the prince was using "the same argument that says if God intended us to fly, he would have given us wings." The prime minister expressed his concern privately to Charles through cabinet minister Peter Mandelson that his remarks "were becoming unhelpful" because they were "anti-scientific and irresponsible in the light of food shortages in the developing world."

The Queen has typically remained above the fray and avoided confrontation with the heir apparent. "She has allowed Prince Charles to work at his interests, his aims and his ambitions," said Malcolm Ross. At the same time, she has found many of his ideas baffling, and has expressed concern to her advisers when he has become embroiled in public controversies. "It is not a cozy relationship, and never has been," said Margaret Rhodes. "They love each other, but the family is not set up to be cozy." In recent years tensions between the Queen and her heir have eased, and they regularly meet for a private dinner.

She has gradually called on Charles to share more of her duties, presiding over investitures, receiving dignitaries in audiences, and reading sensitive documents in his own dark green boxes. Palace courtiers anticipate that if Philip dies before the Queen, additional responsibility will shift to Charles, who will become more of a chief executive officer to his mother's chairman of the board. "That will be a defining moment," said one of her former advisers. "Prince Philip is such a part of her life and her role."

Advisers who work with mother and son see contrasts in their approach to the duties a sovereign is expected to carry out. The Queen has investitures down to a science, allocating forty seconds to each of the nearly one hundred encounters during the hour-long ceremony in the Buckingham Palace ballroom. After a quick prompt from her equerry, she leans forward to present the insignia, smoothing the sash or ribbon, as Cecil Beaton once said, like a "hospital nurse or nanny." Keeping eye contact, she smiles brightly, steps back, asks a question, and listens intently until her inner alarm sounds and she extends her hand to say goodbye. When Charles does the honors, he tends to linger and chat more, which lengthens the proceedings by as much as fifteen minutes.

Elizabeth II is more efficient, systematic, and disciplined than her son in other ways as well. She never falls behind on her official boxes, while he often does when he gets caught up in what one of his aides described as "furiously writing letters, rewriting speeches, and reading documents" — behavior the Queen would consider self-indulgent. (In 2009–10 he personally wrote 1,869 letters.) He avoids reading newspapers, a hangover from the Diana era, preferring to get daily reports from his aides and a digest of current events from *The Week* magazine, which the Queen worries will limit his knowledge, not to mention the perspective on the media she has developed through long experience.

At various times Charles has ruminated to friends and colleagues about the possibility of his mother's abdication, once drawing a sharp rebuke from her in November 1998 when his press secretary, Mark Bolland, leaked to the media that the Prince of Wales would be "privately delighted" if his mother were to step down from the throne. When confronted by the Queen, Charles apologized and said the story was untrue. The idea of abdicating is anathema to Elizabeth II, who takes seriously her oath and anointment with holy oil during her coronation. When George Carey went to her in 2003 to say he was ready to retire as Archbishop of Canterbury, she sighed and said, "Oh, that's something I can't do. I am going to carry on to the end."

The only caveat, as the Queen said to her cousin Margaret Rhodes, would be "unless I get Alzheimer's or have a stroke." "But even then she wouldn't retire," said Rhodes. If the Queen were incapacitated, Prince Charles would become Regent, acting on her behalf under the terms of the Regency Act of 1937.

In the royal tradition, the Queen, her husband, and her eldest son have state funeral plans with scripts they have approved. The name of Philip's "Forth Bridge" plan derives from the bridge over the Firth of Forth in Scotland, Charles's "Menai Bridge" is named after the span that connects the mainland of Wales and the island of Anglesey, and the Queen's "London Bridge" is self-explanatory. All three plans are overseen by the Lord Chamberlain's office and have similar elements stretching over nine days from death to burial, with processions, lying in state, and services mapped out.

"The principals don't tweak the plans," said Malcolm Ross, who was involved in the preparations. "We report back to reassure them. The last thing they want to do is crawl all over their own funerals. They are more involved with the basics." At least once a year, senior Palace aides talk through the arrangements and do tabletop exercises.

Although Edward VII, George V, and George VI had funerals at St. George's Chapel, Windsor, after lying in state at Westminster Hall, the Queen has planned her service for Westminster Abbey, where George II was the last monarch to have a funeral, in 1760. Both St. George's Chapel and the Abbey are "Royal Peculiars," which means they belong to the sovereign rather than a diocese. But according to a former senior Palace official, the Queen regards the Abbey "as the central church to her and to the Church of England." Burial will be at Windsor, where her parents and her sister are interred at St. George's Chapel.

When asked by NBC's Brian Williams in a television interview in November 2010 what would happen when his mother died, Charles gave a tortured reply. "It is better not to have to think too much about it," he said. "Except, you know, obviously, if it comes, then you have to deal with it. I think about it a bit, but it's much better not. This is something that, you know, if it comes to it, and regrettably it comes as the result of the death of your parent which is, you know, not so nice, to say the least."

In the same conversation, the Prince of Wales addressed for the first time the tricky matter of his wife's status on his accession. When he married

Camilla Parker Bowles, in 2005, Palace advisers finessed the question of her eventually becoming queen by saying she wished only to be "Princess Consort" — a title devised to placate those who still sympathized with Diana. As Camilla has conscientiously carried out her duties by his side, formerly hostile public sentiment about her years as Charles's mistress has softened. Privately, he has indicated that he wants her to be his Queen Consort, just as his grandmother was for George VI. Anything less would constitute an unacceptable "morganatic" marriage of two unequal partners. "The settled rule and strong custom says the wife shall take the style and precedence of the husband," said royal historian Kenneth Rose. "In settled law there is nothing to prevent Queen Camilla." When NBC's Williams queried Charles directly if Camilla would be queen, he replied, "We'll see, won't we? That could be."

Unless he predeceases his mother, Charles will be the next head of state. The prospect of a King Charles III (or, if he were to choose one of his other names with happier associations, King George VII) raises several issues that could open the door to republican reformers. In the early years of the twenty-first century, both Labour and Conservative governments have raised the possibility of changing the 1701 Act of Settlement as well as the law of primogeniture, two vital underpinnings of the hereditary monarchy.

The eighteenth-century act was devised to guarantee a Protestant monarch by barring anyone in the line of succession from either being Roman Catholic or marrying a Roman Catholic. Advocates of altering the law contend that it is discriminatory, arguing that there is nothing to bar someone in the succession from marrying a Jew or Hindu or Muslim. As a practical matter, the act has worked smoothly for centuries and hasn't prevented Catholics from marrying members of the royal family. In recent times, the Queen's cousin, Prince Michael of Kent, removed himself from his distant position in the succession to marry a Catholic, while Peter Phillips's wife converted to the Anglican faith so he could keep his eleventh place.

Overturning the Act of Settlement outright could challenge the legitimacy of the Queen and all other descendants of the House of Hanover, whose right to the throne was created by the law. (Several Stuart descendants live in Germany and could conceivably lay claim to the throne.) Even altering the Catholic exclusion would call into question the requirement that the sovereign be Anglican, since a central tenet of Catholicism is a pledge to raise children as Roman Catholics. A further complication is the prerequisite under the 1931 Statute of Westminster that any change in the act must have the consent not only of the British Parliament but of the other fifteen realms for which the Queen is head of state.

Primogeniture, which is based on common law dating to the Middle Ages, requires the firstborn son to inherit a family's hereditary title and estate. In the monarchy, it means that males take precedence over females in the succession regardless of their position in the birth order. Among the Queen's children, Charles became heir to the throne, followed by Andrew and Edward, with second-born Anne in fourth position. All three siblings were superseded by Charles's two sons.

The marriage of Prince William gave new impetus to proposals that the crown go to the eldest child of the sovereign, whether a boy or a girl. Despite concerns that pulling out one strand from the laws of the monarchy could provoke additional constitutional questions, in October 2011 at the biennial conference of Commonwealth leaders in Perth, Australia, David Cameron secured the agreement of the Queen's fifteen other realms to join Britain and introduce legislation to change the law of primogeniture to one of "gender equality." Cameron also proposed amending the Act of Settlement to permit members of the royal family to marry Roman Catholics.

The Queen subtly signaled her approval in her speech opening the Commonwealth summit, urging the fifty-four nations to "find ways to allow girls and women to play their full part." However, she has taken no official position on changing the laws, largely because the hurdles are high and the constitutional questions complex. "This is a matter for the government," said a senior Palace official. "The monarchy is an institution which is great and solid and long-lasting. The framework has endured for centuries. It is not personal to her. She is a female monarch ironically as have been other great monarchs."

Charles has said little publicly about his vision of kingship in the twenty-first century, but he has dropped some tantalizing hints. In 1994 he declared that rather than being the Defender of the Faith, he wished to be the "defender of faith," in itself a difficult notion for a king pledged to uphold the Church of England as the legally established religion. Sixteen years later, he went further and said he was "absolutely determined to be the defender of nature. . . . That's what the rest of my life is going to be concerned with."

He has avoided discussing what if anything he would do to change the trappings of the monarchy, although he has indicated he would like to see the number of working members of the royal family decreased. There have been suggestions as well that he could keep Clarence House as his residence and use Buckingham Palace as his office, setting a more low-key tone. Courtiers have said he could cut back some of the ceremonial parts of the coronation while keeping its historical and religious elements intact, and that he might have a second service that would embrace other cultures and faiths. As for his closely tended charities, "obviously it would be nice if some things were taken on by my sons," he said in 2008, "but I don't know. It all depends on their interests."

When Charles turned sixty in 2008, his biographer Jonathan Dimbleby wrote that he wanted to be an "active" king, ready "to speak out on matters of national and international importance in ways that at the moment would be unthinkable." It would be a "waste of his experience and accumulated wisdom," Dimbleby added, "for it to be straitjacketed within the confines of an annual Christmas message or his weekly audience with the prime minister." When commentators in the press raised alarms, Clarence House officials hastened to say that Charles "fully accepts that as king, his power to discuss issues close to his heart would be severely curtailed."

Yet Charles has signaled that he intends to do things "in a different way than my predecessors . . . because the situation has changed." He has said he would use his "convening power" — the allure of a royal invitation to gather important people to discuss big issues and mobilize to solve problems. In an interview with *Vanity Fair*'s Bob Colacello in the autumn of 2010, he cited his education at Gordonstoun and Cambridge, saying, "Of course they really shouldn't — should they — have sent me to a school which was precepted on taking the initiative. Or to a university where you inevitably look into a lot of issues. So it's their bad luck, but that's the way I intend to continue."

Charles is difficult to pigeonhole politically. Tony Blair wrote that he considered him a "curious mixture of the traditional and the radical (at one level he was quite New Labour, at another definitely not) and of the princely and insecure." He is certainly conservative in his old-fashioned dress and manners, his advocacy of traditional education in the arts and humanities, his reverence for classical architecture and the seventeenth-century Book of Common Prayer. But his forays into mysticism and his jeremiads against scientific progress, industrial development, and globalization give him an eccentric air.

"One of the main purposes of the monarchy is to unite the country and not divide it," said Kenneth Rose. When the Queen took the throne at age twenty-five, she was a blank slate, which gave her a great advantage in maintaining the neutrality necessary to preserve that unity. It was a gentler time, and she could develop her leadership style quietly. But it has also taken vigilance and discipline for her to keep her views private over so many decades.

Charles has the disadvantage of a substantial public record of strong and sometimes contentious opinions, not to mention the private correspondence with government ministers protected by exemptions in the Freedom of Information Act that could come back to haunt him if any of it is made public. One letter that did leak was written in 1997 to a group of friends after a visit to Hong Kong and described the country's leaders as "appalling old waxworks."

Even if as sovereign he continues to advocate his views in what he considers a less provocative way, he still runs the risk of alienating some portion of the population. If that number approaches half or more, he could chip away at the consent necessary for the survival of the monarchy. He could come into conflict with government policy as well, politicizing his position and creating a constitutional crisis.

Many of his supporters hope that by the time he takes the throne — likely in his seventies if not late sixties, which would make him the oldest new monarch, superseding King William IV, who was sixty-four when he succeeded his older brother George IV in 1830 — he will have had his fill of controversies and made his points, and will be ready to embrace his constitutional obligations. "With a bit of luck, he will be old enough not to be tempted down less wise paths," said Robert Salisbury.

Veteran courtiers expect that the very act of becoming king will be transformative for Charles, instilling the solemn recognition that he can no longer act as an individual but as an institution representing the nation. "Life changes overnight when you inherit the throne," said David Airlie. A diplomat who once worked with Charles on a government speech found that he was "not spoiled or stubborn" when it came to taking official advice. "When you tell him what he can't do, he doesn't like it but he will listen," said the diplomat. "If you take out sections saying you can't say this, it is not government policy, he gets cross but he goes along with it." As Prince of Wales he has had the luxury of declining to shake the hand of a Chinese leader because of his poor human rights record, as he did when he refused to attend the banquet President Jiang Zemin had for the Queen during his state visit in October 1999. But as king "he will have to shake the bloody hand of murderous leaders if it is in Britain's national interest," said historian Andrew Roberts.

That task would include some heads of Commonwealth governments. Charles will not automatically inherit the job of head of the Commonwealth when the Queen dies. He must be voted in by the fifty-four-nation membership, which is by no means certain. A survey published in March 2010 by the Royal Commonwealth Society reported that fewer than 20 percent of those polled thought Charles should be the next head, and that many favored rotating the position among member states. "Whilst the vast majority of people greatly admire the role Queen Elizabeth II has played in uniting and guiding the Commonwealth," wrote the authors of the study, "there is a significant debate about whether this role should be passed on to the next British monarch when the time comes. Many people are vehemently opposed to the idea."

Charles considers heading the Commonwealth an important part of the monarch's job, and he has cultivated his own relationships with member countries, visiting thirty-three of them since he became Prince of Wales. But he has attended the biennial heads of government meeting only twice, most recently in 2007 in Uganda when he joined his mother at the opening session. The Commonwealth's director of political affairs, Amitav Banerji, indicated in a memo leaked in November 2010 that Charles did not "command the same respect" as his mother, but that the organization was "trying quietly to get him more involved."

Three of the biggest countries in the Commonwealth could replace the British sovereign with their own head of state whenever the crown changes hands. Australia, where polls have long shown substantial numbers favoring a republic, would likely go first, possibly followed by New Zealand. Unlike the two Antipodes with their own historical traditions separate from Britain, Canada has a greater natural affinity for the monarchy, which helps create an identity distinct from its powerful neighbor to the south. But there is a strong republican strain in Canada as well. The Queen is a realist and has said that each nation should decide its own destiny. Her main concern is that if they become republics they remain in the Commonwealth.

■■■■

An undercurrent to the speculation about Charles as king is that he is destined to be a transitional figure with a short reign before the succession of his more popular son, Prince William. There is a saying that a strong sovereign must either be young and beautiful, or old and venerable; the Queen through her long reign has managed to be both. If Charles gets the venerable part right, he will be judged a success. But it is William that monarchists count on to keep the dynasty strong in the new millennium. The Palace is fully aware that the monarchy's future depends not only on reaching young people but emphasizing its own next generation.

Public opinion polls in recent years have shown that a majority would like to see William as the next king rather than Charles. An ICM research poll in Britain at the end of 2010 found 64 percent in favor of William and only 19 percent for Charles. When William visited Australia and New Zealand in January 2010 on his first official overseas tour, he attracted larger than anticipated crowds and boosted the popularity of the monarchy. He dressed in open-neck shirts and sneakers, and he endeared himself at a children's hospital by getting down on his knees with toddlers. Before his visit, polls consistently showed 60 percent favoring a republic in Australia; afterward one survey showed that number had dropped to 44 percent.

Just over a year later, William was back Down Under, this time to console victims of natural disasters in both countries, where his empathy and genuine manner struck a chord. "My grandmother once said grief is the price you pay for love," he told the residents of Christchurch, New Zealand, who had endured a calamitous earthquake. "You are an inspiration to all people." "He came, he saw, he charmed their bloody socks off," wrote the *Herald Sun* in Queensland, Australia.

But succession to the next in line is preordained, with no provision for skipping a generation. Even if Charles were to take the throne and abdicate immediately in favor of King William V, there would be numerous complications. A law would have to be passed by the British Parliament, and the legislatures in the other fifteen realms would need to agree. The resulting debate could have the unintended consequence of tipping some of those countries toward republics, and of igniting republican forces in Britain to push for a presidency to replace the monarchy. If William became king while his father was still alive, Charles could not return to being Prince of Wales and Duke of Cornwall, titles that are reserved for the eldest son of the sovereign. He would likely lose the resources of the Duchy of Cornwall, which would revert to the crown until William's first child reaches the age of eighteen. Deciding on a title for an erstwhile king would be equally problematic.

"There is no question in Prince William's mind that the Prince of Wales will be the next monarch," said a senior royal adviser. "He has no desire to climb the ladder of kingship before his time." The courtier added that William is "very close to his father and incredibly supportive of him and his work as the Prince of Wales. Both of them will let nature take its course."

Yet the juxtaposition of an aging heir to the throne with his vibrant young successor inevitably sets up the possibility of upstaging, however unintentional. Simply by being himself, William has become a "people's prince," and a magnet for publicity. An important part of his appeal is that he is half Spencer, the pure English bloodline. He represents a powerful combination of good looks and tragedy, but without a trace of self-pity.

Handsome and tall like his mother (at six foot three, he towers over the rest of the Windsors), he embodies her magic in his informal and accessible personality, irreverent humor, and high-wattage smile. Like his father, he engages people with a steady gaze and speaks with poise, conviction, and sensitivity. He lacks the deep-seated insecurities and attention-craving impulses of Diana and the old-fashioned formality and awkward mannerisms of Charles. He has his mother's soulful eyes, and his father's thinning hair. He projects confidence without arrogance, although he shows a streak of willfulness that can be traced to both parents. "The future could not be more optimistic," said Malcolm Ross. "William is stunning, very sensible, incredibly polite, and very, very good with people."

In the years following their mother's death, both sons have grown closer to their "Pop," who has been an engaged and affectionate parent. "We get along really well, Harry and I and my father," William said at age twenty-two. "We're a very close family. There are disagreements, obviously, as all families have and when they are, they are big disagreements. But when they're happy times we have a really good time."

William has been schooled in the British institutions that he needs to understand as an heir to the throne. As was the case with Elizabeth II and Charles, much of William's royal education has come from observing and developing an instinctive feel for what is proper for a monarch to do. "He learns a lot by osmosis," said one of his father's senior advisers. "It is an unusual situation to have three generations. There is an inevitable tension, but they are all quite close. Communication among the offices is much better coordinated than it used to be."

William seemed ready to leave the Household Cavalry at the end of 2008 to join the "Firm" full-time. But with his father's concurrence, he unexpectedly decided to sign on for five years with the Royal Air Force and train as a search-and-rescue helicopter pilot. Both William and Harry, who gained great confidence by qualifying as an Apache helicopter pilot, take pride in their professional expertise. "They don't want to be *Hello* magazine princes," said a senior Palace adviser.

Working on Anglesey island in a remote part of northwest Wales offered William the added benefit of preserving a quasi-normal life for as long as possible — something that was denied his father. After Charles was named Prince of Wales at age ten, he had to become a little adult as a young teenager, when he was pushed out to do royal duties. Even at Cambridge he was called "Sir." "With William and Harry we are easing into that," said a Clarence House adviser in 2010. "Now they are

Prince William and Prince Harry, but not yet 'Sir' or 'Your Royal Highness.' They don't want that yet. Maybe when they leave the military they will have to be that, but not until."

Although their jobs in the armed forces mean their royal duties are only part-time, the princes are nevertheless assuming a higher profile. In 2009 they used a six-figure bequest from their late mother to endow their own charitable foundation. Robin Janvrin, their grandmother's trusted former courtier, was appointed as chairman of the trustees. At twenty-seven and twenty-five, William's and Harry's collaboration signaled not only their closeness but also their long-term commitment to public service. They set up their own private office in St. James's Palace with a private secretary and press secretary.

Even more significant was the Queen's assertiveness in personally recruiting a seasoned diplomat, David Manning, to serve as a mentor to the princes, William in particular. Known for his keen intelligence and sound judgment, as well as his experience as Britain's ambassador to the United States and Israel, Manning is widely regarded as a "safe pair of hands." "He is not only wise," said Charles Anson, "but he doesn't act in self-interest, a quality that is highly valued in the household." When William visited Australia and New Zealand in 2010 and 2011, Manning came along, and his guidance contributed to the young prince's success.

Several days before Christmas in 2009, William spent a freezing night "sleeping rough," as he put it, with homeless teenagers in an alley near London's Blackfriars Bridge. The overnight was organized by the Centrepoint charity, where he followed his mother's footsteps to become a patron. William went incognito in a hooded sweatshirt and knit cap, and his easy rapport with far less fortunate contemporaries was apparent. His purpose, he said afterward, was to show how poverty, substance abuse, and mental illness contribute to the homeless problem. "These kinds of events are much more fulfilling to me than dressing up in a suit," he said.

The challenge for William will be to find the sort of balance that his grandparents mastered early: to project a freshness and glamour without succumbing to the allure of celebrity. He will need to embrace serious and often boring routines even as he experiences the satisfactions of inspiring people, doing good works, and exploring the world. As the first heir to the throne brought up to blend in with his contemporaries rather than believe he was different from everyone else, he will need to learn how to be "ordinary" in a way that preserves regal dignity. During his first trip to Australia he crossed into undignified ordinary territory when he was bantering with a group of rap musicians and blurted out, "I had the piss taken out of me for my taste in music."

The yearning for William has been heightened by the addition of Kate Middleton, whose natural beauty and sophisticated style evoke Diana, but in a more demure manner reminiscent of Jacqueline Kennedy. The romance began when they were undergraduates at the University of St. Andrews in Scotland. Away from the prying eyes of the paparazzi they fell in love and lived together, sharing such mundane chores as shopping at the supermarket and doing the dishes. Her advantages were modest, but important: a good education at the prestigious Marlborough College boarding school and an upbringing in a tightly knit and nurturing family with a sister and a brother and happily married parents. Michael and Carole Middleton achieved the ultimate middle-class dream by leaving their jobs as an airplane dispatcher and flight attendant to build a prosperous mail order business creating party products for busy mothers. William grew close to Kate's parents, who were "loving and caring."

After eight years of tabloid speculation, their engagement announcement on November 16, 2010, came first on Twitter, followed by the Queen's Facebook page. When the two twenty-eight-year-olds appeared together in the splendor of the Entrée Room at St. James's Palace, they were as warm as they were dazzling, a marked contrast to Charles and Diana's uneasy debut nearly three decades earlier.

Elizabeth II and Philip were "absolutely delighted" by William's choice. The Queen had approved of the match from afar, but had actually spent little time with Catherine, as the Palace instantly began referring to her. They had met several times, but always in groups. Their first encounter was at the wedding of Princess Anne's son, Peter Phillips, at St. George's Chapel at Windsor in May 2008, when the Queen came over and "had a little chat." Prince Charles said he was "thrilled" on hearing of the engagement and joked, "They have been practicing long enough!" David Cameron heard the news in a cabinet meeting and announced that it was met with "a great cheer" and a "banging of the table" by everyone in the room.

Both inside and outside the royal family, the consensus was that a well-grounded, middle-class British girl, the first future queen to be a university graduate, would be good news for the Windsors. After all the Queen's heartaches over her children in the 1980s and 1990s, she accepted with equanimity the less conventional choices made by the next generation, including marriage to middle-class commoners, which had become the rule for the royal family.

While Princess Anne's daughter, Zara Phillips, was a student at Gordonstoun, she turned up at age seventeen with a metal stud in her tongue, and later fell in love with Yorkshire native Mike Tindall, a professional rugby player described as a "big, beer-loving lug" whose misshapen nose had been broken eight times. The Queen didn't look askance when the couple lived together for five years before announcing their engagement, nor did she object when Zara's brother, Peter, lived with his future wife, Autumn Kelly, for two years before they were married. Kelly was a Canadian management consultant who had studied Mandarin and Japanese history at McGill University and worked as a barmaid to pay her tuition. When the Phillipses' daughter, Savannah, was born in December 2010, the Queen's first great-grandchild was hailed by Canadians as one of their own.

Catherine Middleton's enthusiastic welcome by the royal family was even more consequential, because she was marrying a man destined to be king. The Queen's embrace of an "ordinary" young woman undercut a core republican argument that the monarchy is hidebound and remote from its subjects. Even Carole Middleton's working-class roots in the coal mines of Durham were seen as an example of the monarchy's more inclusive spirit. "From the pit to the Palace in three generations!" said longtime courtier Malcolm Ross.

In their first television interviews, William and his future queen presented an image that augured well for the monarchy's future — self-possessed, contented, and clearly in love. Like William, Catherine came off as intelligent and reflective. "We're both down-to-earth," he said, "and take the mickey out of each other a lot." Catherine paid homage to Diana, calling her an "inspirational woman to look up to." But unlike the late princess, she seemed instinctively to understand that her "daunting" role would require her to keep her husband in the forefront. "Over the years, William's really looked after me," she said, calling him "a great, loving boyfriend." William patted his fiancée's hand protectively, emphasized that "there's no pressure" to fill his mother's shoes, and said that Kate would make her "own future and . . . destiny."

William and Catherine timed their wedding to avoid any conflict with the Queen's full schedule of engagements in the spring and summer. The wedding date, April 29, 2011, was also comfortably distant from two fraught milestones — Diana's fiftieth birthday on July 1, and the thirtieth anniversary of Charles and Diana's wedding on July 29.

After attending the weddings of twenty of their friends, William and Catherine had firm ideas about what they wanted for their own. The Queen was deeply involved in the planning as well. She tasted the food for the reception and approved the menu as well as the flowers. The celebration was intended to blend old and new, starting with the ceremony in Westminster Abbey, where Elizabeth II and Prince Philip were married, rather than St. Paul's Cathedral, the choice of Charles and Diana. The 1,900 invitations to the Abbey came from the Queen, not Charles, using traditional royal wording specifying the marriage of William "with" Catherine rather than the more conventional "to." Elizabeth II also invited 650 guests to a midday reception at Buckingham Palace. Instead of the customary seated "wedding breakfast," guests were to be served Pol Roger vintage champagne and hot and cold canapés prepared by twenty-two Palace chefs. In another departure from past practice, William and Catherine designated twenty-six charities to receive donations in lieu of gifts.

The young couple controlled the guest list, which was heavily weighted toward their contemporaries and representatives of William's charities. To accommodate the couple's preferences, ambassadors were invited, but their spouses were not. Even the Queen and Prince Philip had an allocation of only forty places, not unlike most twenty-something weddings, where the grandparents' circle is rarely in evidence. Elizabeth II was able to invite such members of her extended family as Margaret Rhodes (who had been one of her own bridesmaids), and she arranged for Angela Kelly's staff of in-house seamstresses to make her cousin a pale blue dress, coat, and hat.

A month before the nuptials, the Queen attended a private party at St. James's Palace given by her cousin Lady Elizabeth Anson to celebrate the fiftieth year of her party planning business. For more than ninety minutes, Elizabeth II mingled with the crowd of six hundred that included aristocrats as well as caterers and florists. "Usually when members of the royal family come into a room, there is a vacuum around them," said one partygoer. "But tonight everyone is crowded in around her." The Queen was in a merry mood, smiling and chatting informally with old friends and strangers alike, without the benefit of Palace aides to smooth her path. "Come on, you two, get together!" she said with an emphatic gesture as she made one spontaneous introduction. Later she remarked on how much she enjoyed spending time with such a diverse group of people. "And everyone was so friendly to me!" she exclaimed.

With eight days to go before her grandson's big event, she celebrated her eighty-fifth birthday, which coincided with her annual Maundy Service, held at Westminster Abbey for the first time in a decade. She spent nearly a half hour presenting red and white purses of Maundy money to eighty-five men and eighty-five women, walking with a sure stride and showing no sign of the pain in one of her knees that had been bothering her for several months. (She had even given up riding for a while, but had resumed her daily outing on horseback when she and her court moved to Windsor for their annual stay during April.) Philip, looking trim in his morning suit, watched her intently as she carried out her solemn act of humility, and the elderly recipients greeted her with bows and curtsys. Midway through the service, he walked to the pulpit to read the second lesson, from the Book of Matthew, in a clear and strong voice. At the end, the congregation of nearly two thousand sang a thunderous "God Save the Queen" accompanied by military trumpeters and the organ at full volume.

By the following Friday, the Abbey had been transformed into a leafy bower, with the strategic placement along the nave of twenty-foot-tall maple and hornbeam trees in large planters brimming with lilies of the valley. Under the majestic Gothic arches, Catherine wanted to create the illusion of the countryside as she walked down the red-carpeted aisle with her father. It was a bold and successful move, one of numerous examples of the distinctly modern stamp she and William put on their day. The Order of Service not only featured a stunning photograph of the couple by Mario Testino, it included an informal message of thanks to the public for its "kindness" and "incredibly moving . . . affection" that "touched us both deeply."

That morning the Queen had given them the titles of Duke and Duchess of Cambridge. But even more significantly, they overrode protocol by announcing that they could be known by their own names as well. "It is absolutely natural that the public might want to call them Prince William and Princess Catherine," said Paddy Harverson, press secretary to Prince Charles (technically, "princess" is used only for someone born a princess), "and no one is going to have any argument with that."

At the heart of the celebration was the infectious joy of a young man and woman who both loved and understood each other. They showed a sense of restraint and respect for the monarchy's one-thousand-year-old traditions, along with what Rowan Williams, the Archbishop of Canterbury, called a "deeply unpretentious" style. Standing at the altar in the dashing scarlet and gold-braided uniform of the Irish Guards, his regiment as an honorary colonel, William turned to Catherine when she reached his side. "You are beautiful," he said, taking in her simple yet exquisitely detailed dress with bodice and sleeves of handmade lace, her gossamer veil, and the delicate diamond "Halo" tiara lent to her by the Queen. As they left the Abbey in the horse-drawn 1902 State Landau, Catherine said, "Well, are you happy?" "Yes," replied William. "It was amazing. I'm so proud you're my wife."

The Queen also pronounced the service "amazing." A vibrant figure in a buttercup yellow coat and matching hat, she had watched approvingly while keeping her emotions in check, seated in the front row below the high altar with Prince Philip in their wooden and gilded chairs with crimson silk cushions. The bride and groom radiated strength and stability under the scrutiny of forty television cameras transmitting their every expression and word to an estimated two to three billion viewers in 180 countries around the world. They were also being followed by 400 million people on the Internet, with 237 tweets per second.

The wedding service was unabashedly British and Anglican, and it dramatically displayed the royal family's role as a repository of unself-conscious patriotic pride, providing a chance "for the nation to come together without partisan disagreement, without excuse for political discord," wrote *The Times.* At a time of economic distress and low morale, "there was sunshine and laughter and happiness that everyone could join in."

The year 2002 had been a turning point for the Queen, but 2011 was a turning point for the monarchy — the arrival of what David Cameron called "the team of the future" for an institution "that's helped bind the country together" and "has produced incredible people." Nobody made a direct reference to Diana in the Abbey, but her presence was inescapable, not only through the inclusion of a hymn from her funeral in the same setting, but the memory of William's stoical sadness that day. Fourteen years later, he had found happiness as well as redemption, closing the book on a painful past.

The Queen was beaming during the six-minute appearance on the Buckingham Palace balcony when the newlyweds kissed not once but twice for the jubilant multitude around the Victoria Memorial. Elizabeth II modestly kept to one side, but when it was time to go, she took charge and led the Windsors and the Middletons back inside. As in the Abbey, the atmosphere was surprisingly intimate in the vast state rooms, where the springtime floral decorations included cow parsley and daffodils from Scotland. "The venue was palatial," said the author Simon Sebag Montefiore, "but really it felt as cozy, informal and effervescent as a traditional British family wedding."

Few would have noticed that the Queen was recovering from a cold that had been bothering her earlier in the week. One who knew was John Key, prime minister of New Zealand. During a visit with her at Windsor Castle two days earlier, he had given her a jar of his country's manuka honey, which is known for its infection-fighting properties — a thoughtful gesture that she mentioned to a number of guests at the reception. In New Zealand the popularity of William and Catherine had sparked an impressive surge of support for the monarchy. More than half of the country's adults watched the royal wedding, and a new poll indicated that only 33 percent expected New Zealand to vote out the monarchy, compared to 58 percent in 2005.

The Queen made no public remarks at the reception, but both future kings spoke from a dais in the Picture Gallery. Charles said he was "thrilled to have a daughter" who was his son's "soulmate," teased the groom about his hereditary bald spot, and said he hoped William would care for him in his old age, although he worried his eldest son might "push his wheelchair off a cliff." William introduced "Mrs. Wales" as "a wonderful girl" with whom he was "in love." He thanked his grandparents not only for "allowing us to invade your house," but the Queen in particular "for putting up with numerous telephone calls and silly questions" in the weeks before the wedding.

At 3:30 on the dot, after all the guests had assembled in the garden, Catherine, still in her bridal gown, and William, now in a dark blue Irish Guards frock coat, climbed into Charles's 1970 Aston Martin convertible, decorated with shiny balloons, ribbons, and a license plate saying "JU5T WED." They drove through the Palace gates onto the Mall for the short ride to Clarence House, as one of William's Sea King helicopters hovered above, trailing a Union flag. The crowds exuberantly cheered as they passed. "William and Catherine were coming down to earth," said Margaret Rhodes. "They were like an ordinary couple driving out in their little open car."

By every measure, the wedding was the biggest media sensation of the twenty-first century, with nonstop coverage by six thousand accredited journalists and as many as four thousand unaccredited — numbers that astonished Palace officials, and the Queen as well. A million spectators hailed the royal couple on the streets of London and another 24 million in Britain watched on television, nearly 40 percent of the population of 62 million. In a YouGov poll taken for *The Sunday Times,* 73 percent of respondents said Catherine would help revivify the royal family.

Following the newlyweds' ten-day honeymoon in the Seychelles, Catherine readied herself for a gradual adoption of royal duties with a limited number of charity patronages and official engagements. The couple agreed to make their first overseas tour together to Canada, the Queen's largest realm, for nine days in July 2011, followed by three days in the United States, choosing California rather than Washington, D.C., or New York for their stay — another sign of their fresh approach.

William and Catherine made clear their intention to live their own way as well as the royal way, in a Welsh farmhouse near his RAF base for at least two years without the customary domestic staff of valets and maids, and emerging periodically on the public stage. They deliberately chose a path that would allow them to enjoy the normal rhythms of married life while preserving the mystery necessary for the monarchy's image.

Two weeks after the wedding, the Queen made a historic state visit to the Republic of Ireland — the first since her grandfather, King George V, toured Dublin a century earlier when the country was still part of the United Kingdom. Thirteen years after the Good Friday Agreement was signed, Elizabeth II's four days in Ireland were laden with symbolism. In her most resonant gesture, she silently bowed her head at Dublin's Garden of Remembrance after laying a wreath, honoring those who had fought against Britain for Irish independence. She also paid homage to the nearly fifty thousand Irishmen who had died while serving with their British comrades in World War I and some seventy thousand who had volunteered in World War II despite Ireland's official position of neutrality.

Elizabeth II moved with quiet dignity from one carefully chosen location to another amid massive security provided by ten thousand police and soldiers. She unflinchingly confronted her nation's bloody past by visiting Croke Park, the stadium where British troops had fired into the crowd of five thousand at a football game in 1920, killing fourteen spectators in reprisal for the assassination of fourteen British undercover agents by an IRA hit squad. She toured historical sites, business enterprises, education and research institutions, and even three legendary stud farms in County Kildare. The Queen wore emerald green, the British flag flew, and Irish bands played "God Save the Queen" for the first time as leaders of both countries emphasized the value of reconciliation and the potential from strengthening Anglo-Irish ties.

Speaking at a state banquet in Dublin Castle, for centuries the headquarters for British colonial rule, the Queen began with an unscripted greeting in perfect Gaelic — the language once banned by the British — prompting Irish president Mary McAleese to mouth, "Wow, wow, wow," and for the assembled luminaries to applaud. The relationship between the two neighboring countries had "not always been straightforward," said the Queen, "nor has the record over the centuries been entirely benign." She stressed "the importance of forbearance and conciliation," and, in an echo of her earlier gesture, "of being able to bow to the past, but not be bound by it."

She directly addressed the "painful legacy" of "heartache, turbulence and loss," including events that touched "many of us personally" — a clear allusion to the assassination of her Mountbatten cousin. "To all those who have suffered as a consequence of our troubled past I extend my sincere thoughts and deep sympathy," she said. "With the benefit of historical hindsight we all see things which we would wish had been done differently or not at all."

Her restrained and subtle language was inherently powerful, and her manner was heartfelt. But the impact came mainly from the moral authority that the Queen has earned over her long reign. She didn't need to issue an abject apology; with her words and her actions, Elizabeth II offered the Irish — and the British — a gentle catharsis. She "helped to release . . . sorrow for the sufferings of the past, relief that they are over, hope for a decent future," wrote *The Irish Times*. Even Gerry Adams, president of Sinn Fein, the IRA's political arm, praised the Queen's "sincere expression of sympathy."

Her trip to Ireland was hailed as one of the most significant of her reign. "I don't think anybody could have achieved what she has," said Elaine Byrne, a lecturer in politics at Trinity College Dublin. "It just seemed more personal and real." The Irish people enveloped her with warmth and enthusiasm, marveling at her stamina for an octogenarian — her prolonged standing and her walking across distances and up steps with surprising agility — and pleased that she seemed to be having such a good time. At a concert in her honor, the audience gave her a five-minute standing ovation as she stood on the stage and smiled appreciatively. During her final rounds in the city of Cork, known for its history as a bastion of republican rebels, she took an unscheduled walkabout and greeted cheering onlookers, some even waving union flags. The Queen's visit, said Byrne, "left us feeling a bit better about ourselves for the first time in a long time."

Scarcely pausing to catch her breath, Elizabeth II

entertained Barack and Michelle Obama at Buckingham Palace during a state visit the following week — the 101st of her reign. Obama had forged a warmer relationship with David Cameron than with his predecessor, and the British prime minister was eager to honor the American president as a sign of what the two leaders were now calling the "essential" rather than the "special" relationship. It was, as Obama himself acknowledged, a singular moment "for the grandson of a Kenyan who served as a cook in the British army."

Security concerns caused the Queen to move the official arrival ceremony from the public setting of Horse Guards Parade to the privacy of the Buckingham Palace gardens. There was no white pavilion bedecked with flags and national insignia, nor even the usual entourage of dignitaries in ceremonial uniforms. Only the Queen, Prince Philip, Charles, and Camilla stood with the Obamas on the West Terrace overlooking the lawn. The band of the Scots Guards played "The Star-Spangled Banner" as a forty-one-gun salute boomed out in nearby Green Park, and the president inspected the guard of honor with Prince Philip.

In every other respect, the Obamas — with whom the royal couple had evident rapport — were treated to all the pomp of the traditional state visit: luncheon with the royal family, a display of historical documents in the Picture Gallery, an exchange of gifts, a state banquet in the ballroom, and two nights in the Belgian Suite among paintings by Canaletto and Gainsborough. (The Queen herself gave them a tour of their quarters.) The one unusual twist came just before the ceremonial welcome when the Obamas were escorted to the 1844 Drawing Room for a private twenty-minute meeting with William and Catherine, their first official appearance since the wedding. The encounter made headlines and reinforced the special status of the newlyweds — although they did not stay for either the luncheon or the banquet, where their presence could have overshadowed the guests of honor.

In June Elizabeth II celebrated the ninetieth birthday of Prince Philip — still largely defined in the press by his acerbic humor and outspokenness, although increasingly admired for the breadth of his interests and the extent of his contributions to a range of British institutions as well as to causes around the world. William and Catherine reappeared to attend the Queen's private party for her husband at Windsor Castle. They also took center stage at Trooping the Colour, where William participated in the ceremonial parade on horseback for the first time.

While the Diamond Jubilee was not set to get under way for another year, the royal wedding of 2011 was a fitting prelude. It brightened the outlook for the House of Windsor, seventy-five years after destiny touched a ten-year-old princess and placed the burden of leadership on her small shoulders. Elizabeth II fulfilled her duty with steadfast determination and clarity of purpose, exerting influence without grasping for power, retaining her personal humility despite her public celebrity — and above all, in good times and bad, spreading a carpet of happiness.

ACKNOWLEDGMENTS

In the spring of 2008, Gina Centrello, president and publisher of Random House, suggested that I write a book about Queen Elizabeth II, to be published in conjunction with her Diamond Jubilee marking sixty years on the throne. I instantly said yes.

Elizabeth II is at once the most public and most private woman in the world, and my challenge was to show her private side while explaining how she has handled her public role — to portray her in the round, in many different settings, surrounded by a great cast of characters. As an American, I thought I could bring a fresh perspective, enhanced by more than a quarter century of frequent visits to Britain, which have led to numerous friendships and family ties as well.

This is not an authorized account of her reign; the royal family will not choose an official biographer until after she dies. But the staff at Buckingham Palace gave me invaluable assistance. They opened doors, offered guidance and information, and arranged for me to watch the Queen and Prince Philip in action — on overseas and domestic tours as well as at key events on the yearly royal calendar, including an investiture, a state visit, a

Buckingham Palace garden party, and the Maundy Service. I also met the Queen at a garden party at the British ambassador's residence in Washington and at two private parties at St. James's Palace.

The Queen has a firm policy against granting interviews, but I was gratified that people who have known her from many angles — family, close friends, senior advisers, religious leaders, politicians, diplomats, world leaders, generals, artists, horse trainers, dog handlers, and estate managers among them — were willing to share their insights and knowledge. I also visited all the Queen's homes in England and Scotland as well as the royal yacht *Britannia,* took a private tour of the Royal Stud at Sandringham, and spent the night at the Queen Mother's Castle of Mey.

To conduct my research I spent six months in the United Kingdom, and I was blessed by the hospitality of my dear friends Joan and Bernie Carl, whose apartment on the top floor of their London home became the "writer's roost" I had first enjoyed while researching my book on Diana, Princess of Wales. During my long stays, Pauline Taplin and Tony Stephens looked after me with care and thoughtfulness. For Joan and Bernie's exceptional generosity, I am eternally grateful.

Of the more than two hundred people I interviewed, about forty asked to remain anonymous. I am indebted to everyone for taking the time out of their busy lives to assist me. Many thanks to those who spoke on the record:

Lord Airlie, Canon John Andrew, Charles Anson, Lady Elizabeth Anson, Lady Avon, Pamela Bailey, Ian Balding, Bruce Bent, Barbara Taylor Bradford,

Peter Brown, Ruth Buchanan, George H. W. Bush, George W. Bush, Lady Frances Campbell-Preston, Lord Carey, Lady Carnarvon, Lady Charteris, Lady Mary Clayton, Mark Collins, Mina Jones Cox, the late Lady Cromer, Susan Cunliffe-Lister, Lady Dartmouth, Jackie Davis, Carolyn Deaver, the Dowager Duchess of Devonshire, the 12th Duke of Devonshire, Lord and Lady Dudley, the Honourable Dominic Elliot, Isabel Ernst, Oliver Everett and Diana Jervis-Reed, Lady Falkender, Michael Fawcett, Catherine Fenton, Nini Ferguson, Stephen Frears, the late Lucian Freud, Lady Anne Glenconner, Lady Annabel Goldsmith, Didy Grahame, Lord Guthrie, Nicholas Haslam, Reinaldo Herrera, Lady Pamela Hicks, Min Hogg, Wesley Kerr, James Ketchum, Timothy Knatchbull, Simon Lewis, Lady Elizabeth Longman, Josephine Louis, Johnny Martin-Smith, Anita McBride, Sir Paul McCartney, David Metcalfe, Pete and Ande Metzger, Dame Helen Mirren, Paul Moorhouse, Howard Morgan, Peter Morgan, Lady Mountbatten, the Right Honourable Brian Mulroney, Catherine Murdock, Sandy Nairne, John Julius Norwich (2nd Viscount), Robin Nunn, Columbus O'Donnell, Lady Angela Oswald, Sir Michael Oswald (including his tour of the Sandringham Stud), Debbie Palmer, the Honourable Shaun Plunket, Jonathan Powell, Lord and Lady Powell, Lady Rayne, Nancy Reagan, Lord Renwick, the Honourable Margaret Rhodes, John Richardson, Andrew Roberts, Monty Roberts, Tim Rooke, Selwa "Lucky" Roosevelt, Kenneth Rose, Lieutenant Colonel Sir Malcolm Ross, Lady Salisbury, Lord Salisbury, Richard Salmon, Jean Seaton, Kamalesh and Babli Sharma, Lady Soames, Sir Roy Strong, Kevin Sullivan, Marjorie Susman, Monica Tandy, David Thomas, Robert Tuttle, Benedicte Valentiner, Freddy Van Zevenbergen, Simon Walker, George "Frolic" Weymouth, Lady Wilson, Ashe Windham, Robert Worcester, Anne Wyndham, David Wynne-Morgan, and Amy Zantzinger.

On the Queen's visit to Bermuda: Sir Richard Gozney (the governor), Kenneth Bascombe, Graham Foster, Ed Harris, Fiona and Marty Hatfield, and Dr. David Saul.

On the Queen's visit to Trinidad and Tobago: Eric Jenkinson (the British high comissioner), Matthew Albert, Ulric Cross, James Dolan, Thora Dunbell, Rosalind Gabriel, Brian Lara, David Miliband, Lyle Pauls, Commander Andrew Stacey, Air Vice Marshal David Walker (master of the household), and Dwight Yorke.

On the Queen's visit to Hull: Susan Cunliffe-Lister (the lord lieutenant of East Yorkshire), Elaine Garland (lord mayor), Bryan Bradley, Phil Brown, Alan Cook, Doris Gagen, and Maria Raper.

At Balmoral: Martin Leslie (retired factor).

At Sandringham: Tony Parnell (retired foreman).

At the Castle of Mey: James Murray (managing director of the Castle and Gardens of Mey), Christina Murray, Shirley Farquahar, Helen Markham, Nancy McCarthy, Grant Napier, and June Webster.

I would also like to thank Her Majesty the Queen for permission to quote excerpts from personal papers at the Castle of Mey.

Special thanks to the team at the Buckingham Palace Press Office for patiently responding to numerous queries and for kindly making so many arrangements on my behalf: Ailsa Anderson, Samantha Cohen, Zaki Cooper, Meryl Keeling, Nick Loughran, Ed Perkins, David Pogson, Colette Saunders, Jen Stebbing, and Peter Wilkinson, the Queen's videographer.

I am grateful as well for the assistance of Paddy Harverson, communications secretary to the Prince of Wales and the Duchess of Cornwall.

I also offer heartfelt thanks for the support, hospitality, and ideas of friends and acquaintances alike: Piers Allen, Suzy Allen, Philip Astor, Geoffrey and Kathryn Baker, Bob Balaban and Lynn Grossman, Oliver Baring, Darcie Baylis, Peter and Amy Bernstein, Linda Boothby, Chris and Wendy Born, John Bowes Lyon, Graydon and Anna Carter, Victor and Isabel Cazalet, Robert Chartener, Jane Churchill, Caroline Clegg, Colin and Amanda Clive, Bob Colacello, Pat and Bill Compton, Mary Copeland, Jean Cox, Jim and Susan Dunning, John and Jodie Eastman, Jane Elliot, Michael Estorick, Barbara Evans-Butler, Pamela Fiori, Brian and Jane FitzGerald, April Foley, Tom Foley, Christopher "Kip" Forbes, Joanna Francisco, Mary Mel French, Alexander Gaudieri, Douglas and Sue Gordon, Sarah Gordon, Anne Greenstock, Debbie Haddrell, Rupert and Robin Hambro, Catherine Hamill, David and Kathleen Harvey, Rod and Kay Heller, Robert Higdon and David Deckelbaum, Patrick and Annie Holcroft, Lord and Lady Howard, Brit and Kim Hume, Brenda Johnson, Stanley and Jenny Johnson, Annie Jones, David Ker, Michael-John Knatchbull, Henry Koehler, Anne Kreamer, Tony Lake,

Wayne Lawson, Mark Lloyd, Sharon Lorenzo, Jeff and Elizabeth Louis, Grant Manheim, Roz Markstein, Alyne Massey, Betty Mattie, Mike Meehan, Sir Christopher and Lady Meyer, Anne-Elisabeth Moutet, Liz Newman, Peggy Noonan, the Honourable James and Lady Caroline Ogilvy, Giulia Orth, Maureen Orth, Christopher and Ginny Palmer-Tomkinson, Christopher and Brina Penn, Helen Phelps, Justine Picardie, Olga Polizzi, Pat Roberts, Michele Rollins, Margot Roosevelt and George Girton, Bertie Ross, Charlotte Rothschild, Hannah Rothschild, Jim and Cindy Rowbotham, Martha Smilgis, Jeremy Soames, Bobby Spencer, Nadia Stanfield, Francesca Stanfill, Claire Stapleton, Will Swift, Miner Warner, Sandy and Patsy Warner, Margaret Westwood, and Jacqueline Williams.

My friend David Harvey deserves particular thanks for giving me a wonderfully vivid account written by his father, Major Thomas Harvey, private secretary to Queen Elizabeth the Queen Mother, "Notes on the Birth of Prince Charles," dated November 14, 1948. Carolyn Deaver, another friend, shared her sharp-eyed journal of the Queen's trip to California in 1983. I am grateful as well to those who showed me personal letters from the Queen.

I owe a great debt to numerous biographers and historians, memoirists and diarists who have helped me appreciate how Elizabeth II has confronted challenges at various stages of her reign. Among the works that were particularly helpful were *Queen and Country,* an illuminating book and accompanying BBC documentary by William

Shawcross, who also wrote the masterly *Queen Elizabeth the Queen Mother: The Official Biography;* Sarah Bradford's *Elizabeth;* Gyles Brandreth's *Philip and Elizabeth;* Jonathan Dimbleby's *The Prince of Wales;* Robert Lacey's *Majesty* and *Monarch;* Elizabeth Longford's *Elizabeth R;* Ann Morrow's *The Queen;* Ben Pimlott's *The Queen: A Biography of Elizabeth II;* Graham Turner's *Elizabeth: The Woman and the Queen;* and Hugo Vickers's *Elizabeth the Queen Mother.*

William Shawcross was also a source of wisdom and encouragement, and Sarah Bradford, Robert Lacey, and Hugo Vickers kindly shared information and offered helpful advice, as did a number of other journalists and fellow authors: Sarah Baxter, Anne de Courcy, Roland Flamini, Flora Fraser, Robert Hardman, Rachel Johnson, Alan Jones, Valentine Low, Anne McElvoy and Martin Ivins, Peter McKay, Jon Meacham, Simon Sebag Montefiore, Charles Moore, and Justin Webb.

From my research in the late 1990s for *Diana in Search of Herself,* I drew on interviews with Jane Atkinson, the late Elsa Bowker, the late Lord Deedes, Roberto Devorick, Jonathan Dimbleby, Lucia Flecha de Lima, Andrew Knight, Andrew Neil, and Barbara Walters.

I am deeply grateful to Nancy Reagan, who not only shared her reminiscences with me over two enjoyable lunches in Los Angeles but granted me exclusive access to the personal correspondence she and President Reagan had with members of the royal family. Fred Ryan, chairman of the board of trustees for the Ronald Reagan Presidential Foundation, gave me good guidance, and Wren

Powell, Nancy Reagan's executive assistant, efficiently arranged my visit to the Reagan Presidential Library, where Joanne Drake and Mike Duggan assisted my study of the correspondence files.

This is the third time I have relied on the intrepid Mike Hill for essential research. Once again he rounded up books and periodicals and found valuable nuggets of information in presidential libraries. At the Virginia Historical Society, he combed through the diaries of longtime American ambassador to the Court of St. James's David Bruce, with the assistance of Nelson Lankford. I was also fortunate to rely on the research skills of Jack Bales, the reference and humanities librarian at Mary Washington University.

My archival and periodical research in England was capably handled by Annabel Davidson, and Edda Tasiemka unearthed obscure clippings from her extensive collection.

I am fortunate indeed to have Kate Medina as my editor. She is patient, wise, and imaginative, with great instincts honed by experience, and I deeply appreciate her enthusiasm for this project from day one. Editor Lindsey Schwoeri asked perceptive questions about the manuscript and expertly steered the book through the publication process. Anna Pitoniak, Kate's assistant, was invariably efficient and cheerful. Production editor Steve Messina supervised the meticulous work of copy editor Fred Chase and fielded numerous emails.

Gina Centrello's publishing team at Random House is the best in the business — creative and smart about every aspect of *Elizabeth the Queen*. My thanks to Tom Perry, executive vice president and deputy publisher, and Sally Marvin, vice president and director of publicity, for their excellent ideas on promotion, along with publicists Bridget Fitzgerald and Alex Chernin. I am also grateful for the attentiveness of Avideh Bashirrad, Kelly Gildea, Erika Greber, Denise Cronin, Toby Ernst, Joelle Dieu, and Ken Wohlrob. Thanks as well to Laura Goldin and Deborah Foley, and to art director Paolo Pepe, jacket designer Belina Huey, and interior designer Susan Turner for making my book look beautiful inside and out. Carol Poticny once again threw herself into the task of photo research, resourceful and persistent as always. Thanks as well to my website designer, Shannon Swenson, and to Tony Hudz and Rosalyn Landor for their impeccable audio recording of the book.

I was delighted to have Max Hirshfeld, as congenial as he is gifted, back to take my author photograph, along with his lovely wife, Nina, stylist, Kim Steele, and assistant, Mike Jones — all of whom turned the photo session into a queen-for-a-day experience.

Amanda Urban, my longtime agent and treasured friend for even longer, has been my stalwart advocate as well as a fount of valuable advice.

In the middle of my research, my daughter, Lisa, was married in London at the Guards' Chapel — only a stone's throw from Buckingham Palace — to a charming and brave English army officer, Dominic Clive. Their wedding on the Fourth of July brought together an exuberant Anglo-American crowd, which somehow gave this project an extra dimension of kismet. Lisa and Dom, along with my sons, Kirk and David, were a constant source of love and support, especially when I was immersed in the solitude of writing for more than a year.

After living through my six biographies for nearly three decades, my loving husband, Stephen, might be expected to show some impatience with the all-consuming nature of these projects. To the contrary, he was endlessly understanding, even when I left for long stretches of interviewing in London. He introduced me to English friends who helped me with ideas and further introductions. He buoyed me when I was feeling discouraged, making me laugh at least once every day. He happily shared my thrill of discovery. He offered astute suggestions about structure and writing. He edited my manuscript not once but twice on weekends and evenings when he was exhausted after long days of running a newspaper. As I was wrestling with options for a title, he came up with a brilliantly concise winner in about five seconds — the fourth time he has done so. Somewhat against his nature, he even agreed to provide comic relief when I wrote in my preface about his protocol infractions with the Queen. As an expression of my love and my everlasting gratefulness, *Elizabeth the Queen* is dedicated to him.

SALLY BEDELL SMITH
Washington, D.C.
July 2011

SOURCE NOTES

Preface

Elizabeth fell in love: John W. Wheeler-Bennett, *King George VI: His Life and Reign,* p. 749.

"She never looked at anyone else": Margaret Rhodes interview.

"People will not realize": Nigel Nicolson, *Vita and Harold: Letters of Vita Sackville-West and Harold Nicolson,* p. 414.

"Her private side took me": Howard Morgan interview.

"She stacked the plates!": George "Frolic" Weymouth interview.

"You can hear her laughter": Tony Parnell interview.

"intentionally measured and deliberate pace": William Shawcross, *Queen Elizabeth the Queen Mother: The Official Biography* [QEQM], p. 347.

"She can uphold the identity": Margaret Rhodes interview.

"to watch her sidle into a room": Graham Turner, *Elizabeth: The Woman and the Queen,* pp. 58–59.

When her cousin Lady Mary Clayton: Author's observation.

"the only thing that comes between": Monica

Tandy interview.

"like a bat out of hell": Margaret Rhodes interview.

"interest and character to the face": Elizabeth Longford, *Elizabeth R: A Biography,* p. 9.

"To be that consistent": Dame Helen Mirren interview.

"It's just like scrubbing your teeth": Jean Seaton interview, recounting conversation between her late husband, Ben Pimlott, and Queen Elizabeth II.

"It's not really a diary": *E II R* documentary, BBC, Feb. 6, 1992.

"I had no idea what to say": Gwen, the Countess of Dartmouth, interview.

"A great battle is lost": Martin Gilbert, *Winston S. Churchill,* Vol. 8, *"Never Despair," 1945–1964,* p. 835.

"She makes a dictatorship more difficult": Robert Gascoyne-Cecil, the 7th Marquess of Salisbury, interview.

"the right to be consulted": Walter Bagehot, *The English Constitution,* p. 75.

"a symbol of unity in a world": William Shawcross, *Queen and Country* [*Q and C*], p. 216.

"When she says something": Gay Charteris interview.

"There is a weed in Scotland": Lady Elizabeth Anson interview.

"supporting the Queen": Gyles Brandreth, *Philip and Elizabeth: Portrait of a Royal Marriage,* p. 228.

"Prince Philip is the only man": Ibid., p. 347.

"never having to look": John Julius Cooper, the 2nd Viscount Norwich, interview.

"She has two great assets": Sarah Bradford, *Elizabeth: A Biography of Britain's Queen,* pp. 358–59; Turner, p. 195, quotes Martin Charteris saying the Queen is "as strong as a yak."

"present[s] the house to her": Tony Parnell interview.

I first met Queen Elizabeth II: Author's observation.

generating considerably more searches: Google Trends: www.google.com/trends.

It was probably fitting: Author's observation.

One: A Royal Education

"Does that mean": Longford, *Elizabeth R,* p. 81.

"catching the days": Margaret Rhodes interview.

"an air of authority": Shawcross, *Q and C,* pp. 21–22.

"neat and methodical": Marion Crawford, *The Little Princesses: The Story of the Queen's Childhood by Her Nanny, Marion Crawford,* p. 171.

"She liked to imagine herself": Mary Clayton interview.

"I never wanted this to happen": Wheeler-Bennett, p. 294.

"It was when the Queen was eleven": Helen Mirren interview.

"I have a feeling that in the end": *E II R* documentary.

"It was unheard of for girls": Patricia Knatchbull, 2nd Countess Mountbatten of Burma, interview (her husband was John Knatchbull, 7th Baron Brabourne, and she has been known either as Patricia Mountbatten or Patricia Brabourne).

"hopeless at math": Mary Clayton interview.

"to write a decent hand": Crawford, p. 19.

"as fast as I can pour it": Shawcross, *QEQM*, p. 535.

"a first-rate knowledge": Ben Pimlott, *The Queen: A Biography of Elizabeth II,* p. 69.

"the corners of the Commonwealth": Mark Collins interview.

"stood me in good stead": Robert Lacey, *Monarch: The Life and Reign of Elizabeth II,* pp. 406–7.

"a dramatic, racy, enthusiastic": Longford, *Elizabeth R,* p. 304.

"entirely at home with him": Crawford, p. 85.

"Hide nothing": Sir Alan "Tommy" Lascelles, *King's Counsellor: Abdication and War: The Diaries of Sir Alan Lascelles,* edited by Duff Hart-Davis, p. 208.

"somewhat rambling structure": Lacey, *Monarch,* p. 116.

"a consultative and tentative absolutism": Ibid., p. 117.

"it was as if she were studying": Ibid., p. 118.

"cool clear precision": David Horbury, "A Princess in Paris," *Royalty Digest: A Journal of Record* 6, no. 3 (September 1996): 88.

"to appraise both sides": Longford, *Elizabeth R,* p. 116.

"fresh, buxom altogether 'jolly' ": *Time,* April 29, 1929.

"The way that Dame Pearl": Shawcross, *QEQM,* p. 555.

"The arches and beams": Jane Roberts, *Queen Elizabeth: A Birthday Souvenir Album,* facsimile reproduction of "The Coronation 12th May, 1937, To Mummy and Papa In Memory of Their coronation, From Lilibet, By *Herself.*"

"No, none": *The Queen, by Rolf,* BBC documentary, Jan. 1, 2006.

"intelligent and full of character": Gerald Isaaman, "A Forgotten Artist Who Had a Brush with Grandeur," *Camden New Journal,* Jan. 15, 2004.

"horrid . . . He was one of those": *The Queen, by Rolf,* BBC documentary.

The second artist to capture: Pimlott, p. 33.

"It's quite nice": *The Queen, by Rolf* documentary.

"horses are the greatest levelers": Frolic Weymouth interview.

"moving carpet": Sally Bedell Smith, *Diana in Search of Herself: Portrait of a Troubled Princess,* p. 149.

"They're heelers": *The Queen, by Rolf* documentary.

"It was a very inhibiting experience": Turner, p. 11.

"Never do that to royalty": James Ogilvy interview.

"a glass curtain": Crawford, p. 81.

"real people": Ibid., p. 31.

"quite fierce": Lady Pamela Mountbatten (Hicks after her marriage to interior designer David Hicks) interview.

"was brought up knowing": Patricia Brabourne interview.

"if you find something or somebody": Ann Morrow, *The Queen,* p. 16.

"You must *not* be in too much of a hurry": Crawford, p. 89.

"particularly easy and pleasant": Shawcross,

QEQM, p. 465.

"sometimes I have tears": Ibid., p. 468.

"almost continually 'on show' ": Ibid., p. 478.

"The Queen knows the prayer book": George Carey, the 103rd Archbishop of Canterbury and later Lord Carey of Clifton, interview.

"She comes from a generation": Ibid.

"sit up at a slight distance": Clarissa Eden, the Countess of Avon, interview.

"a lady's back should never touch": Shawcross, QEQM, p. 780.

"brought up her children": Mary Clayton interview.

"never shout or frighten": Shawcross, QEQM, p. 336.

"remember to keep your temper": Ibid., p. 583.

"She was brought up by strict": Confidential interview.

"small, very smart, and rather peremptory": John Dean, H.R.H. Prince Philip Duke of Edinburgh: A Portrait by His Valet, p. 60.

"The Queen just enjoyed": Mary Clayton interview.

"clothes tidy": Crawford, p. 172.

"internal fast beat": Helen Mirren interview.

who wore a tiara every night at dinner: Deborah Devonshire, the Dowager Duchess of Devonshire, Home to Roost and Other Peckings, p. 62.

"look anyone straight in the face": Cecil Beaton, Self Portrait with Friends: The Selected Diaries of Cecil Beaton, edited by Richard Buckle, p. 264.

"Queen Mary wore tiaras like she wore her toques": Devonshire, Home to Roost and Other Peckings, p. 62.

Queen Mary touchingly said: Longford, *Elizabeth R,* p. 196.

"all the people who'll be waiting": Ibid., pp 73–74.

"new ideas held no terrors": Gilbert, p. 809.

"a happy childhood": Crawford, p. 18.

"wonderful memory training": Ibid., p. 43.

"steadfastness": Robert Lacey, *Majesty: Elizabeth II and the House of Windsor,* p. 92.

Six weeks later: Crawford, p. 106.

Crawfie directed the princesses: Ibid., p. 108.

"purdah": Lacey, *Majesty,* p. 105.

"I was brought up amongst men": Longford, *Elizabeth R,* p. 122.

"the first requisite of a really good officer": Crawford, p. 150.

"a rather shy little girl": Ibid., p. 134.

"never forgot there was a war on": Longford, *Elizabeth R,* p. 122.

"the whistle & scream": Shawcross, *QEQM,* p. 527.

"looking different": Ibid., p. 531.

"Though they are so good": Ibid., p. 586.

"pink cheeks and good appetites": Ibid., p. 542.

"All seemed to breathe": Christopher Hibbert, *Queen Victoria: A Personal History,* p. 177.

shot her first stag: Margaret Rhodes interview.

caught her first salmon: Lascelles, p. 257.

Tommy Lascelles imitating a St. Bernard: Ibid., p. 54.

"young men and maidens": Ibid., p. 184.

"the best waltzer in the world": Frances Campbell-Preston, *The Rich Spoils of Time,* edited by Hugo Vickers, p. 221.

"confidence and vigour": Horace Smith, *A Horseman Through Six Reigns: Reminiscences of a Royal Riding Master,* p. 150.

"What a beastly time": Shawcross, *QEQM,* p. 576.

"and give her a little picture": Crawford, p. 142.

"all the happiest memories": Bradford, p. 86.

The girls earned their cooking badges: Crawford, p. 148.

With their Cockney accents: Ibid., pp. 117–18.

"I think I've broken the prop-shaft": Peter Morgan, *The Queen* screenplay, p. 65.

She told Labour politician: Barbara Castle, *The Castle Diaries, 1964–1976,* p. 213.

"I've never worked so hard": Bradford, p. 108.

That night, she and Margaret Rose: Margaret Rhodes, *The Final Curtsey,* pp. 66–67; Longford, *Elizabeth R,* p. 124, recounting Toni de Bellaigue's memories.

"provided us with sandwiches": Longford, *Elizabeth R,* p. 124.

"Out in crowd again": Rhodes, p. 69.

"It was a unique burst of personal freedom": Ibid., p. 68.

"walked miles . . . Ran through Ritz": Ibid., p. 69.

"the princesses wished to be treated": *The Times,* Aug. 8, 1945.

Two: Love Match

"There was a whole battalion": Lady Anne Glenconner interview.

"boulevardier": Hugo Vickers, *Alice Princess Andrew of Greece,* p. 210.

"The family broke up": Brandreth, pp. 33–34.

"He was one of those boys": Sir Trevor McDonald, *The Duke: A Portrait of Prince Philip,* Indigo Television for ITV, May 13, 2008.

"born leader": Wheeler-Bennett, p. 748.

"intelligence and spirit": Brandreth, p. 39.

"Prince Philip is a more sensitive": Patricia Brabourne interview.

"never took her eyes off him": Crawford, p. 101.

"been in love for the past eighteen": Bradford, p. 105.

"intelligent, has a good sense of humour": Shawcross, *QEQM,* p. 579.

"the simple enjoyment": Ibid., p. 578.

All he left: Vickers, *Alice,* p. 321.

"descants and ditties": Shawcross, *QEQM,* p. 598.

"pink and fawn": Longford, *Elizabeth R,* p. 126.

She invited Mrs. Vicary Gibbs: Mabel, Countess of Airlie, *Thatched with Gold: The Memoir of Mabel, Countess of Airlie,* edited by Jennifer Ellis, pp. 223–24.

"absolutely natural": Campbell-Preston, p. 217.

"danced every dance": Ibid., p. 219.

He was a frequent visitor: Crawford, pp. 175–77.

"all the good things which have happened": Shawcross, *QEQM,* p. 625.

"Philip had a capacity for love": Turner, p. 34.

"would not have been a difficult person": Patricia Brabourne interview.

"pin-up": Michael Dewar, editor, *All the Queen's Horses: A Golden Jubilee Tribute to Her Majesty the Queen,* p. 11.

"sugar pink": Cecil Beaton, *The Strenuous Years: Diaries, 1948–1955,* p. 143.

"She sort of expands": Margaret Rhodes interview.

"was always trying to catch up": Anne Glenconner interview.

"one of the most becoming frocks": Crawford, p. 165.

"I think people thought 'Aha!' ": Patricia Brabourne interview.

"Royal Firm": Longford, *Elizabeth R,* pp. 15, 140.

"a practical little man": Shawcross, *QEQM,* p. 602.

The first several days: Gaumont British Newsreel (Reuters), "Royal Family on Board the HMS *Vanguard.*"

Elizabeth carried a photograph: Crawford, p. 185.

The princesses were enchanted: Gaumont British Newsreel (Reuters), "Royal Welcome to Capetown"; "Royal Family Visits Ostrich Farm"; "Royal Visit to Durban and Zululand"; "Royal Family Tour the Kruger National Park."

"guilty that we had got away": Shawcross, *QEQM,* p. 612.

"quite sucked dry sometimes": Ibid., p. 619.

her mother's ability to still his "gnashes": Ibid., pp. 618–19.

"terrible and glorious years": "21st birthday speech," April 21, 1947, Official Website of the British Monarchy.

The address was written: Brandreth, p. 153.

"the trumpet-ring": Ibid.

Reading the text for the first time: Helen Cathcart, *Her Majesty the Queen: The Story of Elizabeth II,* p. 80.

"200 million other people cry": Ibid.

"a lump into millions": S. Evelyn Thomas, *Princess Elizabeth: Wife and Mother: A Souvenir of the Birth of Prince Charles of Edinburgh,* p. 47.

"Of course I wept": Shawcross, *QEQM,* p. 621.

"solid and endearing": May 13, 1947, LASL 4/4/17, Sir Alan Lascelles Papers, Churchill College, Cambridge University.

"an astonishing solicitude": Sir Alan Lascelles to Lady Lascelles, April 30, 1947, LASL 4/4/17, Lascelles Papers.

They had made a great effort: Gaumont British Newsreel (Reuters), "Royal Tour Reaches Pretoria and Johannesburg"; "Tribesmen Gather for Royal Visit."

the princesses sometimes in their dressing gowns: Shawcross, *QEQM,* p. 615.

After boarding the *Vanguard:* Gaumont British Newsreel (Reuters), "Capetown Bids Farewell to Royal Family."

"real": Pimlott, p. 110.

"There was luxury, sunshine and gaiety": Pimlott, p. 124, citing Jock Colville unpublished diary, end of Aug. 1947, Sept. 21 and 29, 1947.

In 1947 the Crown Estate provided: Zaki Cooper, assistant press secretary to the Queen, email, June 17, 2010.

"sensational evening": Noel Coward, *The Noel Coward Diaries,* p. 96.

"he dealt them out like playing cards": Lady Elizabeth Longman interview.

"busy refilling the cigarette boxes": Dean, p. 46.

"suddenly and apparently without difficulty": Ibid.

"very brave or very foolish": Patricia Brabourne interview.

"Nothing was going to change for her": Ibid.

"a flash of colour": Gilbert, p. 359.

"patience, a ready sympathy": British Pathé Newsreel, "The Princess Weds," Nov. 20, 1947.

"tumultuous expression of good will": Ibid.

"the bride snugly ensconced": Cathcart, p. 92.

As they alighted: Ibid.

"like a female Russian commando": Rhodes, p. 35.

"I only hope that I can bring up": Shawcross, *QEQM,* p. 630.

"Cherish Lilibet?": Ibid., p 631.

Three: Destiny Calls

"serious questions": Eleanor Roosevelt, *This I Remember,* p. 209.

"social problems": Eleanor Roosevelt, *The Autobiography of Eleanor Roosevelt,* p. 230.

"brimming with tears": Horbury, "A Princess in Paris," *Royalty Digest,* Sept. 1996, p. 88.

"published good photographs": Ibid.

"in black lace, with a large comb": Henry Channon, *Chips: The Diaries of Sir Henry Channon,* edited by Robert Rhodes James, p. 425.

"I never realized": Patricia Brabourne interview.

a hospital suite had been prepared: Alfred Wright, Jr., "A Royal Birth," *Life,* Nov. 8, 1948.

Around 9 P.M. senior members: Major Thomas Harvey, private secretary to Queen Elizabeth the Queen Mother, "Notes on the birth of Prince Charles," Nov. 14, 1948.

"I knew she'd do it!": Ibid.

"any spare pages": Ibid.

"Glad it's all over": Ibid.

"never been so pleased": Ibid.

"just a plasticene head": Ibid.

"I had no idea that one": *Daily Telegraph,* March 31, 2011.

"fine, long fingers": Anthony Holden, *Charles Prince of Wales,* p. 67.

"when someone complained": Bradford, p. 145.

"Philip is terribly independent": Shawcross, *QEQM,* pp. 630–31.

"suspended from a crown": Dean, p. 113.

"In England the upper class": Pamela Hicks interview.

"some of the darkest evils in our society today": Pimlott, p. 160.

"were advised that conditions": Dean, p. 121.

At the outset she fulfilled: Gaumont British Newsreel (Reuters), "Princess Elizabeth Leaving for Malta"; "Princess Joins Duke in Malta"; "Princess Elizabeth Visits Mdina Cathedral in Malta"; "Princess Elizabeth Unveils War Memorial and Visits Maternity Hospital."

"I think her happiest time": Margaret Rhodes interview.

"noticed that she was slow": Longford, *Elizabeth R,* p. 160.

The royal couple lived: Pamela Hicks interview.

Elizabeth dispensed: Dean, pp. 121–22.

They cheered: Pamela Hicks interview; Gaumont British Newsreel (Reuters), "Lady Pamela Mountbatten Wins Ladies Race"; "Princess Goes Dancing and Views U.S. Warship."

"loathed": Pamela Hicks interview.

"a very fast, very dangerous": Ibid.

"Don't say anything": McDonald, *The Duke* documentary.

who was enraptured: Gay Charteris interview.

"vulgar": Pimlott, p. 138.

"giving himself an ecstatic hug": Shawcross, *QEQM*, pp. 644–45.

he helped his wife: *Time,* Feb. 18, 1952.

for the first time she took the salute: Gaumont British Newsreel (Reuters), June 1951, "The Royal Family Watches Trooping the Colour Parade."

"the happiest of my sailor life": Dean, p. 130.

"I thought I was going to have a career": Brandreth, p. 178.

The double-decker plane: Gaumont British Newsreel (Reuters), Oct. 1951, "The Royal Stratocruiser and Crew."

"one of the largest military parades": Ibid., "Royal Tour Reaches Quebec," October 1951.

In Toronto: Ibid., "Royal Tour Continues to Toronto and Niagara Falls."

"comfort, softness, and discretion": Confidential interview.

"My face is aching": Pimlott, p. 171.

When the royal couple watched: Gaumont British Newsreel (Reuters), "Royal Tourists in the Cowboy Country."

"a good investment": Longford, *Elizabeth R,* p. 165.

"much refreshed and strengthened": Shawcross, *QEQM,* p. 650.

"He was impatient": Brandreth, p. 208.

"This will ruin my hair!": Gaumont British Newsreel (Reuters), "Royal Tour Continues to Toronto and Niagara Falls."

when she saw the skyline: Ibid., "Royal Tour Continues in Windsor and Winnipeg."

"recovered so promptly": Ibid., "Washington Hails the Princess."

"tells me when everyone": Ibid.

"fairy princess": Pimlott, p. 172.

"free men everywhere": Gaumont British Newsreel (Reuters), "Washington Hails the Princess."

She later told Martin: Betty Beale, *Power at Play: A Memoir of Parties, Politicians and the Presidents in My Bedroom,* p. 34.

a reception at the Statler Hotel: Gaumont British Newsreel (Reuters), "Washington Hails the Princess."

"welcome ornament": Ibid., "Busy Days in Washington."

Only Elizabeth managed: Dean, p. 140.

"Where is your sword?": Gaumont British Newsreel (Reuters), "The Royal Couple Return to Buckingham Palace After Their Trip to Canada."

"Britain's heiress presumptive puts her duty first": Ibid.

When the City of London: Ibid., "City Welcomes Princess and Duke."

The red-brick facade: *Country Life,* May 28, 2008.

"sturdily philistine": Elizabeth Longford, *The Queen Mother: A Biography,* p. 157.

"HEAD & FACE ONLY": Deborah Devonshire and Patrick Leigh Fermor, *In Tearing Haste: Letters Between Deborah Devonshire and Patrick Leigh Fermor,* edited by Charlotte Mosley, p. 212.

The King felt well enough: Shawcross, *QEQM,* p. 651.

Dressed in khaki trousers: Dean, p. 147.

"Look, Philip, they're pink!": *Time,* Feb. 18, 1952.

After a pleasant day shooting hares: Shawcross, *QEQM,* pp. 652–53.

"the most appalling shock": Shawcross, *Q and C,* p. 16.

"pale and worried": Dean, p. 148.

"Oh, thank you": Pamela Hicks interview.

"seized her destiny with both hands": Shawcross, *Q and C,* p. 17.

Four: "Ready, Girls?"

"What are you going to call yourself?": Longford, *Elizabeth R,* p. 176.

"It was all very sudden": *E II R* documentary.

"she looked as if she might": Dean, p. 149.

"was like the Rock of Gibraltar": Turner, p. 41.

"Lilibet, your skirts are much too short": Dean, p. 149.

"by the sudden death": BBC, "On This Day," Feb. 8, 1952, news.bbc.co.uk/onthisday.

by several accounts she was in tears: Morrow, p. 73; Bradford, p. 168.

"protection and love": Longford, *Elizabeth R,* p. 180.

"I cannot bear to think of Lilibet": Shawcross, *QEQM,* pp. 654–55.

"I tried to cheer him up": Gilbert, p. 697.

"my father realized very quickly": Mary Soames interview.

"He was impressed by her": Brandreth, p. 217.

"Extraordinary thing": Longford, *Elizabeth R,* p. 196.

"a fair and youthful figure": Gilbert, p. 700.

"if, as many earnestly pray": Shawcross, *Q and C*, p. 121.

"People need pats on the back": *E II R* documentary.

"gallantry and utter contempt": "Investiture at Buckingham Palace" on Wednesday, 27th February 1952, at 11 o'clock a.m.: To be Decorated: Private William Speakman, The King's Own Scottish Borderers. Buckingham Palace Press Office.

"my little lady": Dean, p. 60.

"I like my rooms to look really lived in": Morrow, p. 65.

"a bureaucrat's dream": Turner, p. 46.

"rather personal to oneself": *E II R* documentary.

"a piece of 300 to 900 words": Government chief whip to Mr. R. T. Armstrong, Feb. 22, 1975, National Archives, Kew.

"low wattage": Mr. Bernard Weatherill, His Humble Duty [to HMTQ], Parliamentary Proceedings from Monday 14th February to Friday 18th February, 1972, National Archives, Kew.

"as well informed": Morrow, p. 158.

Michael Adeane estimated: Pimlott, p. 401.

"If I missed one once": Confidential interview.

"my way of meeting people": *E II R* documentary.

she reverted to her nursery ways: Morrow, p. 92.

"She is not particular": Confidential interview.

In her first gesture of modernity: Jonathan Dimbleby, *The Prince of Wales: A Biography*, p. 22.

"a final romp": Dean, p. 172.

"Why isn't Mummy": Ibid., p. 173.

"For a real action man": McDonald, *The Duke* documentary.

"wielded over the Sovereign": G. Lytton Strachey, *Queen Victoria,* p. 93.

"The Monarchy changed": Brandreth, p. 215.

"Refugee husband": Ibid., p. 147.

"Philip was constantly being squashed": Ibid., p. 218.

"My father was considered pink": Patricia Brabourne interview.

"the House of Mountbatten now reigned": Hugo Vickers, *Elizabeth the Queen Mother,* p. 311.

"She was very young": Patricia Brabourne interview.

"I am the only man": Pimlott, p. 185.

"I'm nothing but a bloody amoeba": Hugh Massingberd, *Daydream Believer: Confessions of a Hero-Worshipper,* p. 148.

"that old drunk Churchill": Ibid.

"Churchill never forgave my father": Patricia Brabourne interview.

"save her a lot of time": McDonald, *The Duke* documentary.

"would submit entirely": Dimbleby, p. 59.

"she was not indifferent so much as detached": Ibid.

"her struggle to be a worthy head of state": William Deedes interview (Jan. 20, 1998).

"In the first five years she was more formal": Confidential interview.

she once attended a ball: *New York Times,* Feb. 8, 1996.

"How *much* nicer": Nancy Mitford, *Love from Nancy: The Letters of Nancy Mitford,* edited by Charlotte Mosley, p. 291.

"must seem very blank": Bradford, p. 169.

"engulfed by great black clouds": Victoria Glendinning, *Edith Sitwell: A Unicorn Among Lions,* p. 299.

a small run-down castle: Author's observations and tour by Nancy McCarthy.

"How sad it looks": *Aberdeen Press and Journal,* Jan. 9, 2009.

"escape there occasionally": Shawcross, *QEQM,* p. 670.

"The point of human life": Ibid., p. 769.

"the great mother figure": Beaton, *The Strenuous Years,* p. 147.

"like a great musical comedy actress": Roy Strong interview.

"pink cushiony cloud": Cecil Beaton, *The Unexpurgated Beaton: The Cecil Beaton Diaries as He Wrote Them,* introduction by Hugo Vickers, p. 52.

"They were great confidantes": Dame Frances Campbell-Preston interview.

"an Edwardian lady": Ibid.

"A lot of the importance": Confidential interview.

"The Queen Mother was always": Confidential interview.

The two women deferred to each other: Margaret Rhodes interview.

"very much the Sovereign": Nicolson, *Vita and Harold,* p. 405.

"millions outside Westminster Abbey": The Queen's First Christmas Broadcast, Dec. 25, 1952, Official Website of the British Monarchy.

"henceforth have, hold and enjoy": Longford, *Elizabeth R,* p. 194.

"not those of a busy": Beaton, *The Strenuous*

Years, p. 120.

"We took it for granted": Gay Charteris interview.

"quite inappropriate for a King": Bradford, p. 184, citing 98th and 99th Conclusions, 18 and 20 Nov. 1952, National Archives, Kew.

"What a smug stinking lot": Michael Bloch, *The Secret File of the Duke of Windsor,* p. 279.

"like a phoenix-time": Pimlott, p. 193.

"the emblem of the state": *Washington Post,* June 3, 1953.

She met several times: Canon John Andrew interview.

"I'll be all right": Longford, *Elizabeth R,* p. 199.

"All the deposed monarchs are staying": Mini Rhea, with Frances Spatz Leighton, *I Was Jacqueline Kennedy's Dressmaker,* p. 162.

"and that takes a bit of arranging": Deane Heller and David Heller, *Jacqueline Kennedy,* p. 81.

"a great big, warm personality": Beaton, *The Strenuous Years,* p. 143.

"swathed in purple silk": *Baltimore Sun,* June 3, 1953.

"She was relaxed": Anne Glenconner interview.

"You must be feeling nervous": Shawcross, *Q and C,* p. 182.

"Ready, girls?": Anne Glenconner interview.

"plucked indiscriminately": *Baltimore Sun,* June 3, 1953.

"backwards and forwards": Beaton, *The Strenuous Years,* p. 144.

she gave a slight neck bow: British Pathé Coronation newsreel, Part 1, June 3, 1953.

"Lord Cholmondeley had to do": Anne Glenconner interview.

"It was the most poignant moment": Ibid.

"Some small interest was generated": *Baltimore Sun,* June 3, 1953.

"The real significance": John Andrew interview.

"gentleness in levying taxes": British Pathé Coronation newsreel, Part 2, June 3, 1953.

"intense expectancy": Beaton, *The Strenuous Years,* p. 144.

"Look, it's Mummy!": Associated Press, June 2, 1953.

"sadness combined with pride": Beaton, *The Strenuous Years,* p. 143.

"She used to say": Frances Campbell-Preston interview.

"never once did she lower": Associated Press, June 2, 1953.

"Oh ma'am you look so sad": Anne Glenconner interview.

"as a simple communicant": Beaton, *The Strenuous Years,* p. 145.

Before leaving the chapel: Anne Glenconner interview.

"We were all running": Ibid.

"anchored them in her arms": Beaton, *The Strenuous Years,* p. 147.

"Elizabethan explorers": William Manchester, *Baltimore Sun,* June 3, 1952.

"the Coronation has unified": Earl Warren, governor of California, to Dwight D. Eisenhower, report on coronation, June 30, 1953, Dwight D. Eisenhower Presidential Library and Museum.

Future prime minister John Major: William Shawcross, *Queen and Country,* BBC Four-Part

Documentary Series, 2002.

"It was a thrilling time": Sir Paul McCartney interview.

"he was never anointed": Jeremy Paxman, *On Royalty: A Very Polite Inquiry into Some Strangely Related Families,* p. 125.

"television lunch": *Baltimore Sun,* June 3, 1953; Paul Johnson, *Brief Lives: An Intimate and Very Personal Portrait of the Twentieth Century,* p. 111.

Five: Affairs of State

"She would pull on all sorts": Jean, the Countess of Carnarvon, interview.

The Queen was driven down: Universal International Newsreel, June 6, 1953.

"marvelous sport": Longford, *Elizabeth R,* p. 239.

"seemed to be just as delighted": BBC Sport, June 2, 2003.

"Winston of course": Longford, *Elizabeth R,* p. 214.

"Oh, racing": Shawcross, *Q and C,* p. 70.

"they spent a lot of the audience": Mary Soames interview.

"I could not hear": Lascelles, p. 430.

"mingled, with perfect facility": Lytton Strachey, p. 33.

"Not a bit of it": Nicolson, *Vita and Harold,* p. 405.

"What did you think": Longford, *Elizabeth R,* p. 213.

"in a frightful fury": Ibid.

"If it was a case of teaching": Mary Soames interview.

"rather rough on the Poles": Gilbert, p. 810.

"the strain": Winston and Clementine Churchill, *Winston and Clementine: The Personal Letters of the Churchills,* edited by Mary Soames, p. 569.

"fatigue": Ibid., p. 570.

writing a lighthearted letter: Gilbert, p. 852.

"They want you": Ibid., p. 884.

"prevaricated continuously": Clarissa Eden, *Clarissa Eden: A Memoir from Churchill to Eden,* p. 142.

"a devilish bad equerry": Lascelles, p. 211.

"It is not necessary for you": Longford, *Elizabeth R,* p. 119.

"She would not listen ever": Mary Clayton interview.

"Margaret was an awful tease": Ibid.

"The Queen never shows off": Kenneth Rose interview.

"unusual, intense beauty": Kenneth Rose, *Intimate Portraits of Kings, Queens and Courtiers,* p. 273.

"in a black hole": Pimlott, p. 199.

"deeply in love": Lascelles, p. 398.

"formidable obstacles": Ibid.

"fluff": BBC, "On This Day," October 31, 1955, news.bbc.co.uk/onthisday.

"This is most important!": Lascelles, p. 399.

"employment abroad as soon as possible": Ibid.

"stood on the sidelines": Obituary of Peter Townsend, *The Independent,* June 21, 1995.

"the Queen, after consulting": Lascelles, p. 400.

He was scheduled to retire: Ibid., p. 405.

"She strongly believed": Elizabeth Anson interview.

By one accounting: Longford, *Elizabeth R,* p. 206.

"She sees herself fused": Brian Mulroney interview.

Sir Philip Moore, her private secretary: Oliver Everett interview.

"The transformation of the Crown": The Queen's Speech at the Luncheon in the Guildhall to mark her Silver Jubilee, Tuesday 7th June 1977, Buckingham Palace Press Office.

the Queen supervised the creation: *Daily Telegraph,* June 23, 2009.

"looked so young and vulnerable": Coward, p. 222.

"the good of the world": Gilbert, p. 942.

Otherwise, Elizabeth II watched: Gaumont British Newsreel (Reuters), "Fiji Hails the Queen."

"Didn't you LOVE this?": Pamela Hicks interview.

"The Queen suffered through that": Ibid.

"the Crown is not merely": Queen Elizabeth II Christmas Broadcast, Dec. 25, 1953, Official Website of the British Monarchy.

Two keen listeners: Vickers, *Elizabeth the Queen Mother,* p. 329.

"He is intensely affectionate": Shawcross, *QEQM,* p. 692.

by one count, three quarters: Shawcross, *Q and C,* p. 59.

"world's sweetheart": Pimlott, p. 222.

"The level of adulation": Brandreth, p. 181.

"How moving & humble making": Shawcross, *QEQM,* p. 691.

"I remember her complaining": Pamela Hicks interview.

"never . . . a superfluous gesture": Beaton, *The*

Strenuous Years, p. 144.

"she has no intermediate": Pimlott, p. 250.

"The trouble is that unlike": *Daily Mail,* Sept. 16, 2008, excerpt from *Killing My Own Snakes,* by Ann Leslie.

"Don't look so sad, sausage": Longford, *Elizabeth R,* p. 209–10.

"What meaneth then": Morrow, p. 44.

"One plants one's feet": Susan Crosland, *Tony Crosland,* p. 346.

"It was almost like a lady's prop": Phil Brown interview.

"is a very practical down-to-earth lady": Confidential interview.

"I watched the Queen open her handbag": Confidential interview.

"I'm always fascinated by their toes": Morrow, p. 92.

"a way of relieving the boredom": Turner, p. 63.

"Do come in, you have nothing to do": Pamela Hicks interview.

To a gathering of scientists: HRH the Prince Philip Duke of Edinburgh, *Selected Speeches, 1948–1955,* p. 82.

Her attendants noticed: Pamela Hicks interview.

"We were all pouring sweat": Debbie Palmer interview.

"There are certain people whose skin runs water": Pamela Hicks interview.

the new 412-foot royal yacht: Author's observation; *The Royal Yacht Britannia Official Guidebook.*

"country house at sea": *The Royal Yacht Britannia Official Guidebook,* p. 17.

"truly relax": Ibid., p. 14.

"You may find Charles much older": Shawcross, *QEQM,* p. 692.

"No, not you dear": Holden, *Charles Prince of Wales,* p. 88.

The private reunion was warm: Pamela Hicks interview.

"enchanting": Shawcross, *QEQM,* p. 692.

"No, Not You Dear": Anthony Holden, *Charles: A Biography,* p. 15.

"One saw this dirty commercial river": Gilbert, p. 976, citing Queen Elizabeth II reflections in *Queen and Commonwealth,* television documentary produced by Peter Tiffin, April 22, 1986.

"seemed less truculent": Eden, p. 168.

"dragged out longer and longer": Gilbert, p. 1124.

The Queen remained patient: Ibid., p. 1115.

"felt the greatest personal regrets": Ibid., p. 1117.

"young, gleaming champion": Ibid., p. 1121.

"never be separated": Ibid., p. 1123.

"wished to die in the House of Commons": Ibid., p. 1124.

"will ever, for me, be able to hold": Ibid., p. 1127.

"to keep Your Majesty squarely confronted": Ibid.

"the case was not a difficult one": Ibid., p. 1125.

"Well, Ma'am?": Eden, p. 190.

"the best looking politician": Ibid., p. 122.

"odd and violent temper": Cynthia Gladwyn, *The Diaries of Cynthia Gladwyn,* edited by Miles Jebb, p. 198.

"Anthony was telling her": Eden, p. 215.

"They were chatting away and laughing": Clarissa Eden interview.

"It is only by seeing him": *Daily Telegraph,* Nov. 7, 2009.

"COME ON MARGARET!": Christopher Warwick, *Princess Margaret: A Life of Contrasts,* p. 197.

In early October the Edens visited: Eden, p. 219.

"high place": *The Times,* Oct. 24, 1955.

Although her sorrowful statement: BBC, "On This Day," Oct. 31, 1955, news.bbc.co.uk/onthisday.

"in a cottage": Rose, p. 189.

"selfish and hard and wild": Bradford, p. 287.

captured her in seven sessions: "1954 Sir William Dargie: Her Majesty Queen Elizabeth II," artistsfootsteps.com.

"straight back . . . never slumped once": Ibid.

"a nice friendly portrait": Laura Breen, "Dargie's Wattle Queen," *reCollections: A Journal of Museums and Collections,* Nma.gov.au.

The only other portrait: *The Queen, by Rolf* documentary.

"kind, natural and never aloof": Pietro Annigoni, *An Artist's Life: An Autobiography,* p. 84.

"watching the people and the cars": Ibid., p. 82.

"alone and far off": Ibid., p. 83.

Margaret praised the artist's success: Ibid., p. 86.

The following year Margaret sat thirty-three times: Ibid., p. 96.

"Mine was better than hers": Frolic Weymouth interview.

she visited the Oji River Leper Settlement: Gaumont British Newsreels (Reuters), "Royal Tour of Nigeria 1956."

"qualities of grace and compassion": Barbara Ward, "The Woman Who Must Be a Symbol,"

New York Times Magazine, Oct. 13, 1957.

On May 11, 1956: Andrew Duncan, *The Queen's Year: The Reality of Monarchy: An Intimate Report on Twelve Months with the Royal Family,* p. 152.

which some participants liken: Morrow, p. 91.

Once one of her corgis had an accident: Oliver Everett interview.

"looking very smart": Eden, p. 230.

"She was dressed": Nikita Khrushchev, *Khrushchev Remembers,* translated and edited by Strobe Talbott, p. 406.

"The Queen said to me": Eden, p. 231.

"Nothing was kept from her": Pimlott, p. 253.

"she understood what we were doing": Lacey, *Majesty,* p. 212.

He began taking Benzedrine: Gladwyn, p. 198.

"edgy": Pimlott, p. 255.

"I think the Queen believed Eden was mad": Ibid.

"Are you sure you are being wise?": Ibid.

"nor would I claim that she was pro-Suez": Lacey, *Majesty,* p. 212.

"I don't think she was really for it": Gay Charteris interview.

"in such a bad way": Gladwyn, p. 198.

Churchill, who criticized: Gilbert, p. 1222.

"the real enemy": Ibid.

"it is most interesting": Ibid., p. 1223.

"highly valued": Shawcross, *Q and C,* p. 74.

"wise and impartial reaction": Pimlott, p. 273.

"choose the older man": Lacey, *Majesty,* p. 215.

Six: Made for Television

"it would have been much simpler": HRH Prince

Philip Duke of Edinburgh, *Prince Philip Speaks: Selected Speeches by His Royal Highness the Prince Philip, Duke of Edinburgh, K.G., 1956–1959,* edited by Richard Ollard, p. 38.

"remote communities": McDonald, *The Duke* documentary.

"by profession a sailor": Prince Philip, *Selected Speeches, 1948–1955,* p. 105.

"allegiance to another": Ibid., p. 148.

He pursued his fascination: Prince Philip, *Selected Speeches, 1956–1959,* p. 137.

"full set": British Pathé newsreel, "The Duke Visits the Outposts."

In a nostalgic touch: Pamela Hicks interview; McDonald, *The Duke* documentary.

"Philip's Folly": Longford, *Elizabeth R,* p. 225.

although he did send the Queen white roses: Ibid.

"willing to serve others": Prince Philip, *Selected Speeches, 1956–1959,* p. 38.

"He has one of those minds": Confidential interview.

"whole man": Prince Philip, *Selected Speeches, 1956–1959,* p. 131.

"sub-health": Ibid., p. 95.

The story of the "party girl": Brandreth, p. 254.

"very hurt, terribly hurt, very angry": Pimlott, p. 271, citing Brook Productions, *The Windsors,* interview transcript.

"It is quite untrue": *Irish Times,* Feb. 12, 1957.

"nothing at all": Prince Philip, *Selected Speeches, 1956–1959,* p. 43.

The idea had come: Pimlott, p. 272.

"Most of our people have never had": Alistair

Horne, *Harold Macmillan,* Vol. 2, *1957–1986,* p. 64.

although she sometimes became irritated: Charles Williams, *Harold Macmillan,* pp. 293, 319.

"instinctive reverence": Horne, p. 169.

"We all knew about it": Woodrow Wyatt, *The Journals of Woodrow Wyatt, Vol. 2,* p. 546.

"a mask of impenetrable calm": Williams, p. 474.

"Victorian languor": Horne, p. 308.

astonished him from the outset: Ibid., p. 14.

"a great support": Ibid., p. 168.

"She never reacted excessively": Lacey, *Majesty,* p. 217.

"be made to smile more": Ibid., p. 218.

"had always assumed people wanted": Ibid.

Dickie Mountbatten blamed the delay: Massingberd, p. 148.

"just as calm and composed": Eleanor Roosevelt, *My Day: The Best of Eleanor Roosevelt's Acclaimed Newspaper Columns, 1936–1962,* p. 247.

"haven of security": Dimbleby, p. 40.

"She let things go": Gay Charteris interview.

Six-year-old Charles flopped onto: Eden, p. 201.

Clarissa Eden was mildly amused: Clarissa Eden interview.

"the natural state of things": McDonald, *The Duke* documentary, quoting Pamela Hicks.

that Charles make his bed: Lacey, *Majesty,* p. 235.

"a very gentle boy": Bradford, p. 329.

"not a vessel to be filled": Hill House International Junior School Website.

being in a classroom with other boys: Dimbleby, pp. 32–33.

educating the "whole" child: Cheam School Website.

"Children may be indulged at home": Dimbleby, p. 43.

"I always preferred my own company": Ibid., p. 44.

He had no idea what was coming: Ibid., p. 49.

"dread": Queen Elizabeth II to Anthony Eden, Jan. 16, 1958, Lord Avon Papers.

"not necessarily fitted to serve": *Time,* April 8, 1957.

"tight little enclave": "The Monarch Today," *National and English Review,* Aug. 1957, pp. 61–67.

"efficient public relations set-up": *New Statesman,* Oct. 22, 1955.

"to pit his infinitely tiny": Pimlott, p. 281.

"a very silly man": *Time,* Aug. 19, 1957.

"95 per cent of the population": Ibid. In 1963 after Parliament passed a law allowing peers to renounce their titles, Altrincham would disclaim his and become known as John Grigg.

"real watershed": Roy Strong, *The Roy Strong Diaries, 1967–1987,* p. 430.

By some accounts, Prince Philip: *Sunday Graphic,* Nov. 17, 1957.

With help from her husband: *Sunday Times,* Dec. 22, 1957.

The following year marked the last: Fiona MacCarthy, *Last Curtsey: The End of the Debutantes,* pp. 1, 17–18.

"those who mix socially": Malcolm Muggeridge, "Does England Really Need a Queen?," *Saturday Evening Post,* Oct. 19, 1957.

He was harassed: Longford, *Elizabeth R,* p. 229.

She used a TelePrompTer for the first time: *Washington Post,* Oct. 14, 1957.

"shy, a bit bashful": *New York Times,* Oct. 14, 1957.

"I want to talk to you": *Washington Post,* Oct. 14, 1957.

"taking part in a piece": *New York Times,* Oct. 15, 1957.

"there does seem to be a much closer": Queen Elizabeth II to Anthony Eden, Oct. 11, 1957, Lord Avon Papers, Birmingham University.

"devoted friendship": *The Papers of Dwight David Eisenhower: NATO and the Campaign of 1952,* Vol. 13, letter to Queen Elizabeth the Queen Mother, Feb. 7, 1952, p. 947.

he liked to recount: "Suggested Remarks: Welcome for Prince Charles and Princess Anne," July 15, 1970, Richard Nixon Presidential Library and Museum.

"We all dived under the table": *Daily Mail,* Jan. 15, 2011, citing unused footage from the 1969 documentary *Royal Family.*

"If [Eisenhower] and his party": Rhodes, p. 57.

"was so staggered": *Daily Mail,* Jan. 15, 2011.

A crowd of ten thousand greeted: *Illustrated London News,* Oct. 26, 1957.

"enlightened and skilled statesmen": *Washington Post,* Oct. 17, 1957.

As they waited to take off: Wiley T. Buchanan, Jr., with Arthur Gordon, *Red Carpet at the White House: Four Years as Chief of Protocol in the Eisenhower Administration,* p. 130.

"He was flustered": Ruth Buchanan interview.

"the little British sovereign": *Washington Post,*

Oct. 18, 1957.

"very certain, and very comfortable": Ruth Buchanan interview.

"staggering amount": *New York Times,* Oct. 19, 1957.

"rather startling ideas": Richard Nixon to Queen Elizabeth II, Oct. 19, 1957, Nixon Library.

"match": *Washington Post,* Oct. 19, 1957.

"could see how American housewives": *New York Times,* Oct. 20, 1957.

Dressed in a $15,000 mink coat: Buchanan, p. 132.

"perturbed": *Washington Post,* Oct. 20, 1957.

"parade of industries": *New York Times,* Oct. 20, 1957.

"How nice that you can bring your children": *Washington Post,* Oct. 20, 1957.

"Good for mice!": Ibid.

"amazed and scared": Ibid.

On their final day: Ibid., Oct. 21, 1957.

"as it should be approached": *New York Times,* Oct. 22, 1957.

"Wheeeee!": *New York Daily News,* Oct. 21, 1957.

"a row of great jewels": Alistair Cooke, *Manchester Guardian,* Oct. 22, 1957.

"Hi Liz": *Washington Post,* Oct. 22, 1957.

"I never realized": *New York Daily News,* Oct. 21, 1957.

"a teaser": *New York Times,* Oct. 22, 1957.

"a thunderous standing ovation": *Washington Post,* Oct. 22, 1957.

"kept standing up": Ibid.

"tremendous": *New York Times,* Oct. 22, 1957.

"the evening sky was purple": *Manchester Guard-*

ian, Oct. 22, 1957.

eating striped bass with champagne sauce: Anne Pimlott Baker, *The Pilgrims of the United States: A Centennial History,* pp. 128–29.

Guests could watch: *New York Times,* Oct. 22, 1957.

"one time during the program": Ibid.

"straight as a ruler": Buchanan, p. 149.

"Philip . . . look at all those people": Ibid., pp. 149–50.

"You both have captivated": Dwight D. Eisenhower to Queen Elizabeth II, Oct. 20, 1957, Eisenhower Library.

"extraordinarily successful": *New York Times,* Oct. 22, 1957.

"has buried George III for good and all": Horne, p. 55.

"Why did she have to cross": *Washington Post,* Oct. 27, 1957.

"gone beyond the stage": Prince Philip, *Selected Speeches, 1948–1955,* p. 55.

"Television is the worst of all": Queen Elizabeth II to Anthony Eden, Oct. 11, 1957, Lord Avon Papers.

Philip, who had urged her: *Sunday Dispatch,* Oct. 6, 1957.

"more vivacious": *Daily Mirror,* Oct. 11, 1957.

Philip took a particularly active role: *Sunday Times,* Dec. 22, 1957.

In addition to getting the knack: *Sunday Graphic,* Dec. 22, 1957.

"My husband seems to have found": *Daily Express,* Dec. 27, 1957.

A few days before the broadcast: *News Chronicle,*

Dec. 27, 1957.

The Queen spoke: Queen Elizabeth II Christmas Broadcast, Dec. 25, 1957, Official Website of the British Monarchy.

her husband standing behind: *News Chronicle,* Dec. 27, 1957.

"post-Altrincham royal speech": *Daily Express,* Dec. 27, 1957.

"unstrained and natural": *News Chronicle,* Dec. 27, 1957.

"All her charm": *Daily Express,* Dec. 27, 1957.

"lovely statement": *News Chronicle,* Dec. 27, 1957.

"The final draft was, in fact": Pimlott, p. 291.

one year her butler noted: Paul Burrell, *A Royal Duty,* p. 19.

"the working pieces of kit": David Thomas interview.

"There is one thing to remember": Ibid.

"looking like culprits": Diaries of David Bruce, Nov. 3, 1964, Richmond Historical Society.

"I think I have made the dullest": Annigoni, p. 181.

"my neck is still feeling": Ibid.

"many millions of my subjects": "The Queen's Speech," Oct. 28, 1958.

"were scarcely separated": Lacey, *Monarch,* p. 214.

"I am going to have a baby": Pimlott, p. 305.

Mayor Richard Daley rolled the red carpet: *Chicago Tribune,* July 17, 2005.

"Chicago is yours!": Longford, *Elizabeth R,* p. 311.

"he had never witnessed": Dwight D. Eisenhower to Queen Elizabeth II, July 7, 1959, Eisenhower Library.

"this will be an insult": Horne, p. 147.

friends including the Earl of Westmorland: Eisenhower Archives, guest list, Aug. 21, 1959, Eisenhower Library.

"The Queen and Eisenhower got on": Dominic Elliot interview.

"When there are fewer I generally put": Queen Elizabeth II to Dwight D. Eisenhower, Jan. 24, 1960, Eisenhower Library.

"perfect in every respect": Dwight Eisenhower to Queen Elizabeth II, Aug. 30, 1959, Eisenhower Library.

Philip gave eight speeches: Prince Philip, *Selected Speeches, 1956–1959*, pp. 32–34.

"great national awakening": Ibid., p. 33.

"The Queen only wishes": Williams, p. 357.

"absolutely set her heart": Anthony Howard, *Rab: The Life of R. A. Butler*, p. 276.

"in tears": Bradford, p. 286.

"de-royalised": Harold Macmillan, *Pointing the Way, 1959–1961*, p. 161.

at the urging of Dickie and Prince Charles: Dimbleby, p. 234; Massingberd, p. 148.

"a great load off her mind": Bradford, p. 286.

"The Queen has had this in mind": Longford, *Elizabeth R*, p. 251.

Seven: New Beginnings

"Nothing, but *nothing*": Turner, pp. 46–47.

"Pigmy-Peep-a-toes": *The Mitfords: Letters Between Six Sisters*, edited by Charlotte Mosley, p. 287.

"slightly explosive drawl": Strong, p. 158.

"If you missed the 'royal' ": Confidential interview.

"I don't measure the depth": Peter Morgan, *The Queen,* p. 5.

"You mustn't worry": Shawcross, *QEQM,* p. 847.

"I felt the Queen was not served well": Patricia Brabourne interview.

"whole atmosphere": Coward, p. 437.

"endless, vivid herbaceous borders": Ibid., p. 438.

"pale . . . a bit tremulous": Ibid.

"scowl a good deal": Ibid.

"When she is deeply moved": Richard Crossman, *The Diaries of a Cabinet Minister,* Vol. 2, *Lord President of the Council and Leader of the House of Commons, 1966–1968,* Sept. 20, 1966, p. 44.

The £26,000 cost: Bradford, p. 292.

the Macmillan government picked up: Lacey, *Monarch,* p. 216.

refurbished at a cost: Bradford, p. 402.

£50,000 of which was allocated: Anne de Courcy, *Snowdon: The Biography,* p. 105.

"an opportunity to consider": Horne, p. 169.

"assiduity with which she absorbed": Ibid.

"the wind of change is blowing": Macmillan, *Pointing the Way,* p. 156.

"The official text is weak": Horne, p. 205.

"to appeal to de Gaulle's sense of grandeur": Ibid., p. 223.

"well informed about everything": Charles de Gaulle, *Memoirs of Hope: Renewal and Endeavor,* p. 235.

"Only Rose Kennedy came into the room": Brian

Mulroney, *Memoirs,* p. 326.

"eaten into [JFK's] soul": Isaiah Berlin Oral History, John F. Kennedy Presidential Library and Museum.

"the greatest man he ever met": Ibid.

"young cocky Irishman": Horne, p. 288.

"strange character . . . obstinate, sensitive, ruthless": Ibid., pp. 281–82.

"We seemed to be able (when alone)": Harold Macmillan to Jacqueline Bouvier Kennedy, Feb. 18, 1964, Harold Macmillan Archive, Bodleian Library, Oxford University.

"surrounded himself with a large retinue": Macmillan, *Pointing the Way,* p. 352.

"special relationship within": Henry Brandon Oral History, Kennedy Library.

"professional statesman": Raymond Seitz, *Over Here,* p. 41.

"completely overwhelmed": Horne, p. 303.

"put on a good show": Diaries of David Bruce, June 2, 1961.

"pretty heavy going": Gore Vidal, *Palimpsest: A Memoir,* p. 372.

"they were all tremendously kind": Cecil Beaton, *Self Portrait with Friends,* p. 341.

"the Queen was human only once": Vidal, p. 372.

He had an Egyptian wife: David E. Lilienthal, *The Journals of David E. Lilienthal,* Vol. 4, *The Road to Change, 1955–1959,* p. 338.

"corrupt and tyrannical regime": Gilbert, p. 1331.

"widespread uneasiness": Ibid., p. 1330.

"her wish is to go": Ibid., p. 1331.

"fainthearts in Parliament and the press": Horne, p. 399.

"How silly I should look": Longford, *Elizabeth R,* p. 320.

"the greatest Socialist monarch": Horne, p. 399.

"fell for her": Longford, *Elizabeth R,* p. 321.

"how muddled his views on the world": Pimlott, p. 308, summarizing letter from Queen Elizabeth II to Henry Porchester, Nov. 24, 1961.

"I have risked my Queen": Horne, p. 399.

"brave contribution": Ibid.

This time Elizabeth II gave the American sisters: Diaries of David Bruce, March 28, 1962.

"It was a great pleasure": Queen Elizabeth II to John F. Kennedy, May 20, 1962, Kennedy Library.

"the stuff he is made of": Prince Philip, *Selected Speeches, 1956–1959,* pp. 134–35.

"prison sentence": Dimbleby, p. 69.

"hell . . . especially at night": Ibid., p. 78.

"an awful cloud came down": David Ogilvy, the 13th Earl of Airlie, interview.

"She loves her duty": Macmillan, *Pointing the Way,* p. 472.

"fashionable London call girl": John F. Kennedy and Arthur Schlesinger, telephone recording transcript, March 22, 1963, Presidential Papers, Office Files, Presidential Recordings, Kennedy Library.

"political squalor": Schlesinger to John F. Kennedy, "The British Political Situation," March 25, 1963, W. Averell Harriman Papers, Library of Congress.

"grossly deceived": Diaries of David Bruce, June 17, 1963.

"pitiable and extremely damaging": Horne, p.

483, quoting Bruce cable to Dean Rusk, June 18, 1963.

"greatly undermined": Diaries of David Bruce, June 15, 1963.

"deep regret at the development": Harold Macmillan, *At the End of the Day, 1961–1963,* p. 445; Horne, p. 485.

"charmingly consoling letter": Horne, p. 486.

The Palace approved: Charles Powell, Baron Powell of Bayswater, interview.

"in animated conversation": Ibid.

"firm step, and those brightly shining eyes": Macmillan, *At the End of the Day,* p. 515.

"there were in fact tears": Horne, p. 565.

"seemed moved": Macmillan, *At the End of the Day,* p. 515.

"the Queen asked for my advice": Ibid.

"take his soundings": Ibid., p. 516.

"magic circle": Pimlott, p. 334.

"too remote": Ibid., p. 332.

"excruciatingly amusing": Diaries of David Bruce, July 20, 1961.

"taking women into a parliamentary embrace": "The Life Peerages Act 1958: The passage of the Act," lifepeeragesact.parliament.uk.

"friendly headmaster": Lacey, *Majesty,* p. 260.

"guide and supporter": Macmillan, *At the End of the Day,* p. 519.

"continue to take part in public life": Ibid.

"It is almost incredible": Diaries of David Bruce, Nov. 12, 1963.

"The unprecedented intensity": Queen Elizabeth II speech at Runnymede, May 14, 1965, itnsource.com (Reuters TV).

She insisted on having: Diaries of David Bruce, Nov. 26, 1963, Nov. 28, 1963.

"generosity, sympathy and understanding": Ibid., May 14, 1965.

"doom laden period": Queen Elizabeth II speech at Runnymede, May 14, 1965, itnsource.com (Reuters TV).

"wit and style": Diaries of David Bruce, May 14, 1965.

"you share with me thoughts that lie too deep": Ibid.

"immensely valuable": Woodrow Wyatt, *The Journals of Woodrow Wyatt,* Vol. 1, edited by Sarah Curtis, p. 249.

"The Queen knew for years": Ibid.

"I find that I can often put things out": Turner, p. 57.

"She has a compartmentalized brain": Margaret Rhodes interview.

"She talked of all sorts of things": Diaries of David Bruce, April 28, 1964.

"She regards Windsor as her home": Longford, *Elizabeth R,* p. 303.

"better than any dry cleaner in London": Confidential interview.

"unnerving to be descended upon": Strong, p. 220.

"It is always amusing to see": Confidential interview.

the "Windsor Uniform": John Martin Robinson, *Windsor Castle: The Official Illustrated History,* p. 81.

"I need to explain about the napkins": Paxman, p. 121.

"The Queen told me it was all right": Isabel

Ernst interview.

"She never batted an eye": Jean, Countess of Carnarvon, interview.

"The selections are to entertain": Oliver Everett interview.

"It gives people something to talk about": Jean Seaton interview.

"I suppose landscape is quite nice": *The Queen, by Rolf* documentary.

"he experimented terribly": Ibid.

"she was steered away from the unmade bed": *The Mitfords: Letters Between Six Sisters,* p. 798.

"Her assessment of a picture": Bradford, p. 500.

"She is neither an art historian": Oliver Everett interview.

"beauty in nature": Pimlott, p. 544.

"refrain from offering presents": Diaries of David Bruce, April 29, 1964.

"What surprised me": Strong, p. 219.

"the Lord Chamberlain is commanded": Author's invitation for July 7, 2009.

When the Palace doors open: Author's observations.

"drank her tea": Confidential interview.

"standing talking quietly": Beaton, *The Unexpurgated Beaton,* p. 259.

"I suppose": Harold Wilson, Wikipedia.

"I got a bleak look": Sir Michael Oswald interview.

"read all his telegrams": Lacey, *Majesty,* p. 260.

"We have to work very hard": Confidential interview.

"a bit touchy . . . uncomfortable": Woodrow Wyatt, *The Journals of Woodrow Wyatt,* Vol. 3, edited by Sarah Curtis, p. 505.

"tamed him": Vickers, *Elizabeth the Queen Mother,* p. 409.

"Harold was never a republican": Marcia Williams, Baroness Falkender, interview.

"real ceremonies of the monarchy": Shawcross, *Q and C,* p. 99.

"She started with Winston Churchill": Mary Wilson, Lady Wilson of Rievaulx, interview.

"He was surprised that she used to sit": Marcia Falkender interview.

Eight: Refuge in Routines

"Operation Hope Not": John Pearson, *The Private Lives of Winston Churchill,* p. 400.

"It was entirely owing": Mary Soames interview.

President Lyndon Johnson was supposed: Diaries of David Bruce, Jan. 25, 1965.

"living entity to be fostered": Independent Television from London, "The State Funeral of Sir Winston Churchill," narrated by Sir Laurence Olivier, Paul Scofield, and Joseph C. Harsch.

Johnson desperately pressed: Diaries of David Bruce, Jan. 27, 1965.

The president's designated replacement: Ibid.

"a great maker of history": Dwight D. Eisenhower remarks, Jan. 30, 1965, Winstonchurchill.org.

"acknowledge our debt of gratitude": Gilbert, p. 1361.

who equipped it with rugs: Longford, *Elizabeth R,* p. 282.

"Waiving all custom and precedence": Gilbert, p. 1362.

"we were not to curtsy": Mary Soames interview.

"most enthusiastically rendered": Diaries of David Bruce, Jan. 30, 1965.

"the clouds of cold": Cecil Beaton, *Beaton in the Sixties: More Unexpurgated Diaries,* introduction by Hugo Vickers, p. 17.

"It hit between wind and water": Diaries of David Bruce, Jan. 30, 1965.

"only the Queen decides": Gilbert, p. 823.

"mark of Royal favour": Official Website of the British Monarchy.

who had regularly hosted: Ian Balding, *Making the Running: A Racing Life,* pp. 99, 103–4.

"Well, here it is": Mary Soames interview.

"Whoever invented these robes": "The Queen Off Duty," YouTube video.

"she is highly practical": *The Mitfords: Letters Between Six Sisters,* p. 765.

"no hanging about": Deborah Devonshire, *Wait for Me!: Memoirs of the Youngest Mitford Sister,* p. 314.

Following the luncheon: Author's observations, June 15, 2009.

"The Queen is always very concerned": Lt. Col. Sir Malcolm Ross interview.

"It's always very lucky": "The Queen Off Duty," YouTube video.

"hats off, hair down": *The Mitfords: Letters Between Six Sisters,* p. 766.

"had very good views on everything": Marcia Falkender interview.

"justify any proposals to her": Shawcross, *Q and C,* p. 99.

"restraining influence": Horne, p. 171.

"The fact that she was Queen": Marcia Falkender interview.

When he was worried: Kenneth Rose interview.

"large, shambolic bisexual": A. N. Wilson, *Our Times: The Age of Elizabeth II*, p. 150.

"terribly degrading": Tony Benn, *Out of the Wilderness: Diaries, 1963–1967,* p. 168.

"the most miniature bow": Ibid., p. 169.

"lovely laugh . . . really very spontaneous": Crossman, *The Diaries of a Cabinet Minister,* Vol. 2, p. 44.

"Oh that woman": *Daily Telegraph,* Dec. 29, 2007.

"natural charm": Shawcross, *Q and C,* p. 100.

"You and I would never have got": Castle, p. 25.

"which kept the conversation going": Bradford, p. 321.

She patiently listened: Benn, pp. 230–32.

"She took him for a mug": Kenneth Rose interview.

"I'm sure you'll miss your stamps": Benn, p. 446.

"except in knowledge of horse flesh": Diaries of David Bruce, April 23, 1968.

"walking wounded": Michael Oswald interview.

The Royal Stud at Sandringham: Author's observations.

"a horse had a good shoulder": Longford, *Elizabeth R,* p. 249.

"She reads a lot, and she knows a lot": Michael Oswald interview.

"rests always with the Queen": Arthur FitzGerald, *Thoroughbreds of the Crown: The History and Worldwide Influence of the Royal Studs,* p. 136.

"Maternity Help and Marriage Guidance Center": Michael Oswald interview.

"She is very matter-of-fact": Ibid.

"dive bombing": Ian Balding interview.

"Oh, that was scary": Ibid.

"She has the ability to get calmer": Monty Roberts interview.

"talking to her is almost like talking": Turner, p. 75.

"If she had been a normal person": Ian Balding interview.

"Some trainers suit a particular horse": Turner, p. 75.

"She would watch": Balding, p. 115.

She revisits her horses: Ian Balding interview.

"I had a feeling that it was incredibly dusty": Ibid.

"used to be bananas about it": Jean Carnarvon interview.

"I really think it is ridiculous": Ian Balding interview.

"I never have": Ibid.

"keen to win at all costs": Dewar, ed., p. 62.

"He drives it": Monty Roberts interview.

"She has an ability to get horses": Pimlott, p. 107.

"She gets into it and investigates": Monty Roberts interview.

"the Ascot Vigil": Vickers, *Elizabeth the Queen Mother,* p. 409.

"formal day wear": Diaries of David Bruce, June 20, 1962.

"The great thing about racing": Michael Oswald interview.

"Look, it's on the wrong leg": *E II R* documentary.

"I don't think that horse stayed": Longford, *Elizabeth R,* p. 249.

"As a human being one always has hope": *E II R* documentary.

The 1950s brought her a string: Dewar, ed., pp. 29–30.

"Racing is incredible": Shawcross, *QEQM,* p. 691.

"The Queen Mother accepted gratefully": Ibid., p. 790.

"great gastronome": Diaries of David Bruce, March 4, 1969.

She had one serious health scare: Shawcross, *QEQM,* pp. 816–17.

"Oh, the Cake!": *The Mitfords: Letters Between Six Sisters,* p. 308.

"She really is superb": Ibid., p. 433.

the Queen Mother even joined: Diaries of David Bruce, June 4, 1962.

"the Japs": Beaton, *The Unexpurgated Beaton,* p. 52.

"so nice & so nasty": Shawcross, *QEQM,* p. 348.

"They were naked": Confidential interview.

"Darling, you must have them close": Jane FitzGerald interview.

"Look at us. We are just ordinary people": Wyatt, Vol. 2, p. 311.

In 1967 even seventeen-year-old Princess Anne: Shawcross, *Q and C,* p. 102.

"major blunder": Coward, pp. 601–2.

"Tomorrow night, Ma'am": Paul McCartney interview.

"lovely . . . She was like a mum": Ibid.

"platoon of bagpipers": Seitz, p. 316.

"little creep": Ibid.

"the Queen talked at some length about violence": Diaries of David Bruce, Aug. 2, 1968.

"I think she thought this was a bit too much": Longford, *Elizabeth R,* p. 328.

"Queen Anne's dying": Ibid.

Driven by an impulse: de Courcy, p. 148.

"People will be looking after me": Lacey, *Monarch,* p. 223.

"As a mother, I'm trying to understand": *Sunday Times,* Oct. 30, 1966.

"It's nice to hibernate": *E II R* documentary.

The long drive from the gates: Author's observations.

trucks filled with clothing: Martin Leslie interview.

"There is a certain fascination": *E II R* documentary.

"The furniture has barely been moved": Margaret Rhodes interview.

"Every new person goes for it": Jean Carnarvon interview.

"Her Majesty is aware": Martin Leslie interview.

"Hooray!": Confidential interview.

"steep frowning glories": Dimbleby, p. 35.

"At Balmoral, she knows every inch": Malcolm Ross interview.

"It was always fun to see a new stalker": Margaret Rhodes interview.

She shot her last stag: Confidential interview.

a practice she was forced to stop: Confidential interview.

"the hoovers": Turner, p. 73.

"If I'd known you were all watching": Ibid.

"She shows you to your room": Confidential interview.

"as if a switch has flipped": Malcolm Ross interview.

"She is conversing as she is playing": Confidential interview.

"she has to have it absolutely right": Anne Glenconner interview.

"Our lunch was over": Confidential interview.

"Woe betide if you put": Confidential interview.

"At Balmoral, she never forgets": Confidential interview.

"engrossed in the sufferings of Swann": Alan Bennett, *The Uncommon Reader,* p. 62.

For many years she would choose: Oliver Everett interview.

"You can go out for miles": *E II R* documentary.

Nine: Daylight on the Magic

"Goodness what fun": Bradford, p. 325.

"was very impressed": Mary Wilson interview.

Displeased by her harsh treatment: Dimbleby, p. 39.

The Queen was not intimidated: Ibid., p. 40.

"work and responsibilities and duties": *The Queen at 80,* Sky News, 2006.

"he could hear the younger children": Min Hogg interview.

"dodge-ems": *The Queen at 80,* Sky News, 2006.

"pick us up and say": Ibid.

"caustic lot": Longford, *Elizabeth R,* p. 273.

"exert her authority": Bradford, p. 338.

"an utterly detached sensation": Longford, *Elizabeth R,* p. 273.

Having ridden since the age: Princess Anne the

Princess Royal, with Ivor Herbert, *Riding Through My Life,* p. 2.

"crème de la crème": Dimbleby, p. 135.

"on level grown-up terms": *Daily Mirror,* Feb. 28, 1968.

"I remember the patience": Mary Wilson interview.

"charming . . . with his desire to please": Gladwyn, p. 343.

"Right from the beginning": Turner, p. 118.

"it just beggars belief": Brandreth, p. 301.

"great difference": Ibid., p. 296.

"was too proud to admit it": Dimbleby, p. 189.

"an escape place": *E II R* documentary.

"pure luxury . . . miles of stubble fields": Princess Anne, p. 2.

"the autumn colours": Ibid., p. 16.

It was one of the few times: Margaret Rhodes interview.

the Queen Mother had been preparing: Helen Markham interview.

"There is a grave shortage": Display at Castle of Mey; copyright HM the Queen.

"A meal of such splendour": Castle of Mey Visitors Book, Aug. 15, 1991; copyright HM the Queen.

In the distance through binoculars: Nancy McCarthy interview.

"She did not have to worry": Vickers, *Alice Princess Andrew of Greece,* p. 335.

"Bubby-kins": Ibid., p. 382.

"Yaya": Ibid., p. 360.

"Oh, I thought you were saying": Ibid., pp. 351–52.

"cuddly granny": Ibid., p. 361.

"compartmentalize": Ibid.

Andrew and Edward often came: Lacey, *Monarch,* p. 232.

even joining the elderly princess: Annigoni, p. 173.

"not arguments, but let's say": Vickers, *Alice Princess Andrew of Greece,* p. 391.

Her worldly goods: Ibid., p. 394. At a later date, according to her instructions, the remains of Princess Alice were transferred to Jerusalem for burial. In April 1993 she was recognized by the Holocaust Memorial in Jerusalem for her heroism in hiding a family of Jews from the Nazis in Greece during World War II.

"We are not publicity agents": *Time,* April 11, 1949.

he had hosted a second program: McDonald, *The Duke* documentary.

"I was quite a different kind": Shawcross, *Q and C,* p. 151.

"I think it is quite wrong": *The Times,* Nov. 10, 1969.

"You can do it": Pimlott, p. 379.

"the Queen goes with what she has to do": Gay Charteris interview.

"She suddenly discovered": Pimlott, p. 381.

"Can't we avoid a shadow here?": Morrow, p. 89.

"She never underplays the importance of ceremony": Confidential interview.

implying she meant the hapless Annenberg: Diaries of David Bruce, Nov. 27, 1968.

"infinitely rewarding and impressive": Walter Annenberg to Richard Nixon, May 1, 1969, Nixon

Library.

"flustered envoy . . . verbal felicity": Christopher Ogden, *Legacy: A Biography of Moses and Walter Annenberg,* p. 429.

Through speech therapy, he had learned: Ibid., p. 430.

"When we reviewed the film": Ibid., p. 432.

"came through as a great character": Beaton, *Beaton in the Sixties,* p. 342.

"we must not let in daylight upon magic": Bagehot, p. 59.

"like a middle-class family in Surbiton or Croydon": *Evening Standard,* June 26, 1969.

"depends on mystique": Bradford, p. 353.

"rotten idea": William Shawcross, *Queen and Country* documentary.

"language and culture": Dimbleby, p. 149.

"grand and simple": BBC News interview with Lord Snowdon, June 29, 2009.

"I didn't want red carpets": BBC Colour TV coverage, July 1, 1969, YouTube.

"that it was her show not his": Gladwyn, p. 346.

"By far the most moving": Dimbleby, p. 163.

"She gaily shattered": Coward, p. 678.

Ten: Ring of Silence

"Everything about her seemed smaller": Annigoni, p. 172.

"At every sitting": Ibid., p. 174.

"I see Your Majesty": Ibid., pp. 176–77.

The Queen had become fascinated: Diaries of David Bruce, April 22, 1969.

"and to the American people": Queen Elizabeth II message to Richard Nixon, Department of State telegram, July 1969, Nixon Library.

"it filled us with wonder": Annigoni, p. 184.

"he was so drunk": Ibid., p. 185.

"You must have emptied": Shaun Plunket interview.

"people who never in the past": Confidential interview.

"He knew everybody": Margaret Rhodes interview.

"She realized quickly that Patrick": Shaun Plunket interview.

"often with a smile": Ibid.

"a great protector": Annabel Goldsmith, *No Invitation Required: The Pelham Cottage Years,* p. 87.

"Ma'am, do you feel I ought to close": Shaun Plunket interview.

Afterward, he would regale: Annabel Goldsmith interview.

Philip was relieved: Shaun Plunket interview.

Plunket found a kindred spirit: Gay Charteris interview.

"Martin was someone he could relate to": Ibid.

"would have been too late": Ibid.

"One of the pleasant things": Diaries of David Bruce, Feb. 4, 1969.

"There are no set plays": Confidential interview.

"She will say, 'Can you cope?' ": Confidential interview.

"a glare": Anne Glenconner interview.

"fierce whisper": Johnson, p. 105.

"It would be ghastly": Esme, the Dowager Countess of Cromer, interview.

"easy to relax": Campbell-Preston, p. 270.

"We never talked": Esme Cromer interview.

They had shared a bedroom: Crawford, p. 121.

"Bobo could say anything": Margaret Rhodes interview.

"The sketches were put all over": Valerie Rouse interview, Hardyaimes.com.

"Bobo will give me hell": *Daily Mail,* Nov. 11, 1997.

"She knew everything": Confidential interview.

"quite friendly when thawed": Dean, p. 60.

Bobo wandered away: Jean Carnarvon interview.

"sound, very human, very wise": Patricia Brabourne interview.

"ring of silence": Turner, p. 188, quoting an anonymous former cabinet secretary.

"Those who see the private side": Confidential interview.

"She is not someone who is enormously intimate": Confidential interview.

"One of her greatest strengths": Robert Salisbury interview.

"the Colonel": Shawcross, *QEQM,* p. 626.

"There is absolutely no such thing as snobbism": Patricia Brabourne interview.

"I nearly died of fright": Jean Carnarvon interview.

The hostess sends her the guest list: Esme Cromer interview.

"easy and gay and ready to giggle": Coward, p. 634.

Two years later: Columbus O'Donnell interview.

She even showed up: Duncan, p. 188.

"You have mosquitoes": *Daily Mail,* Sept. 16, 2008.

"I get kicked in the teeth": Prince Philip speech

at Edinburgh University, May 23, 1969.

"the monarchy functions": Prince Philip interview on Grampian Television, Feb. 21, 1969.

"The answer to this question": Duncan, p. 65.

he even jumped into a swimming pool: Lacey, *Majesty,* p. 257.

Three years later, President Nixon organized: Dinner at the White House, guest list for Tuesday, Nov. 4, 1969, at 8:00 P.M., Nixon Library.

"I had never thought of the President": Barbara Walters, *Audition: A Memoir,* pp. 177–78.

"Might Queen Elizabeth ever abdicate?": Ibid.

"means of unlocking": Ibid.

"particularly charming and intelligent": Prince Philip to Richard Nixon, Nov. 7, 1969, Nixon Library.

"Duke of Edinburgh jousts": *Time,* Nov. 7, 1969.

"We go into the red": *Meet the Press,* Nov. 9, 1969.

Consumer prices had risen by 74 percent: Lacey, *Majesty,* p. 275.

Eleven: "Not Bloody Likely!"

The ball was a Patrick Plunket production: Beaton, *The Unexpurgated Beaton,* pp. 71–73.

"We had been expecting to put up with Wilson": Ibid., p. 75.

"I was told that he blushed": Ibid.

"celibate": Philip Ziegler, *Edward Heath: The Authorised Biography,* p. 230.

"cold and uncompassionate": Ibid., p. 231.

He described her as a patient listener: Andrew Marr, *An Intimate Portrait of the Queen at 80,* BBC, 2006.

"a good deal": Longford, *Elizabeth R,* p. 346.

"The fact that she has all these years": Ibid.

"very useful . . . particularly on overseas stuff": Ziegler, p. 319.

"deeply unhappy": John Campbell, *Edward Heath: A Biography,* p. 494.

"It's like Nanny being there": Lacey, *Monarch,* pp. 260–61.

"actively sought to downgrade": Ziegler, p. 374.

their first trip: Suggested Remarks: Welcome for Prince Charles and Princess Anne, July 15, 1970, Nixon Library.

"I learnt the way a monkey learns": Longford, *Elizabeth R,* p. 279.

"At nineteen years old suddenly being dropped": Shawcross, *Queen and Country* documentary.

Nixon laid on an ambitious program: Department of State, Office of the Chief of Protocol, "Administrative Arrangements for the Visit to Washington, D.C.: His Royal Highness the Prince of Wales, K.G. and Her Royal Highness the Princess Anne," Nixon Library.

More than three decades later: Confidential interview.

"hopes and aspirations": Henry Kissinger to Richard Nixon, July 17, 1970, Nixon Library.

"pointed out one must not": Dimbleby, p. 180.

The Queen, who was on vacation: Ziegler, p. 375.

"suitable for entertaining": Michael Adeane to Charles Morris, M.P., Nov. 18, 1970, National Archives, Kew.

"during his four-hour stay": Robert T. Armstrong to Michael Adeane, Nov. 18, 1970, National Archives, Kew.

"signal kindness": Richard Nixon to Queen Elizabeth II, Oct. 7, 1970, Nixon Library.

"Taking a lively interest": Appendices to the Minutes of Evidence Taken Before the Select Committee on the Civil List, 1971, p. 111.

"expensive kept woman": Pimlott, p. 404.

"Martin was given his chance": Gay Charteris interview.

"Your job is to spread a carpet of happiness": Ibid.

"ridiculous disease": Queen Elizabeth II to Edward Heath, Nov. 28, 1971, National Archives, Kew.

"to commiserate with you": Edward Heath to Queen Elizabeth II, Nov. 23, 1971, National Archives, Kew.

"from *them* — one can't win from a virus!": Queen Elizabeth II to Edward Heath, Nov. 28, 1971, National Archives, Kew.

During her thirties and forties: *Evening Standard,* April 28, 1971.

"She has a theory that you carry on": Confidential interview.

"how unnerving it was to get under the bed-clothes": Min Hogg interview.

"can do no harm": Wyatt, Vol. 3, p. 423.

Among Blackie's more exotic treatments: Morrow, p. 55.

"for whatever was wrong with them": Min Hogg interview.

the Queen had extended an olive branch: Diaries of David Bruce, March 28, 1965.

But in 1968 the Queen complied graciously: Bradford, pp. 347–48.

"If the Duke of Windsor were to die": Christopher Soames confidential telegram, May 10, 1972, National Archives, Kew.

Accompanied by an entourage of thirty-six: State Visit of the Queen and the Duke of Edinburgh to France, Monday 15th–Friday 19th May, 1972, List of Party, National Archives, Kew.

"We may drive on different sides": *Time,* May 29, 1972.

driving to Rouen at the mouth of the Seine: *The Times,* May 23, 1972.

"She went on board *Britannia*": Mary Soames interview.

"a conspicuous demonstration": *The Observer,* May 21, 1972.

"had seduced and conquered": Ibid.

"With the Queen's visit": *Time,* May 29, 1972.

"prattled away": Dimbleby, p. 217.

"He gave up so much for so little": Ibid., p. 218.

"showed a motherly and nanny-like tenderness": Beaton, *The Unexpurgated Beaton,* p. 256.

"The new links with Europe": Queen Elizabeth II Christmas Broadcast, Dec. 25, 1972, Official Website of the British Monarchy.

"scratch our heads": Prince Philip on *Meet the Press,* Nov. 9, 1969.

"pyramid of snobbery": Andrew Knight interview (May 7, 1998).

"Action Man": Dimbleby, p. 221.

"slightly sexy, ginny voice": Confidential interview.

"feeling of emptiness": Dimbleby, p. 232.

"shock and amazement": Ibid.

"We had to be told": "Princess Anne and Her

Fiancé, Captain Mark Phillips, Talk About Marriage," BBC, Nov. 10, 1973.

"interest, fascination": Dimbleby, p. 233.

"few sentences": *The Times,* Jan. 1, 2004.

Undaunted by his censorship: Ibid.

"The Queen could only await": *The Guardian,* Feb. 14, 2010.

"our relaxed intimacy": Pimlott, p. 419.

"the Queen . . . let it be known": Beaton, *The Unexpurgated Beaton,* p. 370.

"Not bloody likely!": "The Princess Royal at 60," BBC *Inside Sport* special, Aug. 12, 2010.

"as if it were a perfectly normal": Dimbleby, p. 254.

"It wouldn't have been much good": "Heavy Security as Princess Anne Visits Her Husband's Home Village: Princess Describes Her Reaction to Attempt to Kidnap Her," ITV Reuters, March 22, 1974.

whose grave she marked with a copper beech: FitzGerald, p. 146.

"Henry was the Queen's closest personal friend": Ian Balding interview.

They would cover not only her own: FitzGerald, pp. 135–36.

"to bring in new blood": Michael Oswald interview.

Porchester advised the Queen: FitzGerald, p. 136.

"long-striding filly": Dewar, ed., p. 30.

Valéry Giscard d'Estaing, sent a big bowl: FitzGerald, p. 137.

"fiery mood": Ibid., p. 138.

"I'm very excitable on the race course": *New York*

Times, Oct. 5, 1984.

"Vive la Reine": FitzGerald, p. 138.

"I was assigned a valet": Confidential interview.

"I have to put on my white tie and medals": Shaun Plunket interview.

"Patrick, I'm deeply grateful": Ibid.

"caught a look of deep sadness": Annabel Goldsmith, *Annabel: An Unconventional Life: The Memoirs of Lady Annabel Goldsmith,* p. 125.

"She certainly helped": Shaun Plunket interview.

After his brothers presented it: Ibid.

"I'm sure I told the gardener": Ibid.

Some even believe: Annabel Goldsmith interview.

"Have you given some thought": Shaun Plunket interview.

Twelve: Feeling the Love

"profound religious existence": Confidential interview.

"sacramental manner in which she views": George Carey interview.

"not in the sense of a burden": George Carey, *Know the Truth: A Memoir,* p. 401.

"She has a comfortable relationship with God": George Carey interview.

"she doesn't parade her faith": John Andrew interview.

"an old-fashioned way of being": Ibid.

"middle of the road": George Carey interview.

"a masterpiece of English prose": Queen Elizabeth II Christmas Broadcast, Dec. 25, 2010, Official Website of the British Monarchy.

"The royal family treat": Confidential interview.

"Oh you silly woman": George Carey interview.

"For the delicious meal": *Daily Mail,* Nov. 11, 1997.

She admired Graham, although when he asked: Diaries of David Bruce, June 17, 1966.

"takes the place of a family confessor": Margaret Rhodes interview.

The pageantry is intricately orchestrated: Author's observations, Maundy Service and Office for the Royal Maundy, Westminster Abbey, April 21, 2011.

"It's a very clever subtle way": Kenneth Rose interview.

"He found his ecclesiastical duties": Longford, *Elizabeth R,* p. 347.

"They used to fetch us by car": Mary Wilson interview.

During their September 1975 visit: Ibid.

"when he first got to Number 10": Marcia Falkender interview.

Wilson so treasured the image: Mary Wilson interview.

"too-tall . . . ungainly": Susan Mitchell, *Margaret Whitlam: A Biography,* p. 213.

"Big Marge": Turner, p. 13.

installing them in a suite: Margaret Whitlam, *My Day,* p. 41.

"deep-piled cream sheepskin rug": Mitchell, p. 213.

"That evening she was quite determined": Turner, p. 13.

"almost too much and too moving": Whitlam, p. 130.

Tony was achieving even greater success: de

Courcy, pp. 102, 112.

"I received a letter from Peter": "Margaret: Unlucky in Love," BBC News, Feb. 9, 2002.

Tony wanted the freedom: de Courcy, p. 130.

"things I hate about you": Ibid., p. 177.

Among his dalliances: Ibid., p. 194.

Margaret's lovers included: Ibid., p. 142.

"little lady": James Ketchum interview.

"First, let her think": "Princess Goes to Washington: Princess Margaret and Lord Snowdon Visit Washington," Nov. 21, 1965, British Pathé, WPA Film Library.

"I didn't bring up my daughter": Confidential interview.

"He pulled the wool": Anne Glenconner interview.

when she flouted protocol: Confidential interview.

"I understand": Pamela Hicks interview.

"How's Margaret's mood?": Confidential interview.

"the atmosphere is appalling": de Courcy, pp. 234–35.

"had been devastating": Ibid.

"live apart": Ibid., p. 243.

"The Queen and the Queen Mother never took sides": Confidential interview.

"She doesn't sit in the sun": Confidential interview.

was tended by her longtime hairdresser: Morrow, pp. 60–61.

For her skin she used an assortment: Ibid.

shrewdly orchestrated a public show: Nicholas Henderson, *Mandarin: The Diaries of an Ambassa-*

dor, 1969–1982, pp. 120–21.

"a tribute to the Queen's understanding": Ibid.

"careful consideration": Robert T. Armstrong to Martin Charteris, Feb. 6, 1973, National Archives, Kew.

"One would wish to consider": Ibid.

"July 4th was really pushing it": *New York Times,* June 13, 1976.

"a paragon of gaiety & dignity": Beaton, *The Unexpurgated Beaton,* p. 334.

"should get someone more steeped": Confidential interview.

couldn't resist calling her "the American": Confidential interview.

they were hit with a force nine gale: Crosland, p. 344.

"philosophical, almost merry": Ibid., p. 345.

"Wheeeeee!": Ibid., pp. 345–46.

"her apparent eagerness to work a crowd": *New York Times,* July 8, 1976.

"I speak to you as the direct descendant": Ibid., July 7, 1976.

"I'm going to make Attila the Hun": *Time,* Oct. 24, 1977.

"press the flesh": Crosland, p. 347.

"What a fascinating man": Bradford, p. 374.

"never faltered in the day's walk-about": Crosland, p. 348.

Henry Kissinger's wife, Nancy: Ibid.

"Prince Philip is renouncing": Ibid.

"to make her grand entrance": *Edinburgh Evening News,* June 19, 2003.

"were overwhelmed": Shawcross, *Q and C,* p. 173.

"Luckily, I don't mind the heat": *New York Times,* July 10, 1976.

"There's John Andrew!": John Andrew interview.

"Gracious, do you really wear skirts": *New York Times,* July 10, 1976.

"homey patched-elbow chic": Ibid., July 9, 1976.

In fact, the evenings were often exuberant: Gay Charteris interview.

"You looked so funny standing all alone": John Andrew interview.

"moving from one reminder": *New York Times,* July 12, 1976.

"I was reminded of the good that can flow": Queen Elizabeth II Christmas Broadcast, December 25, 1976, Official Website of the British Monarchy.

Very much her mother's daughter: "The Princess Royal at 60," BBC *Inside Sport* special, Aug. 12, 2010.

"I noticed, we've been going all day": Confidential interview.

"keeping the rhythm and shaking her head": Morrow, p. 41.

"I heard her sigh again": John Julius Norwich interview.

"Next year is a rather special one for me": Queen Elizabeth II Christmas Broadcast, December 25, 1976, Official Website of the British Monarchy.

"express wish": *Daily Telegraph,* Dec. 29, 2007.

"apathy hits plans": *The Guardian,* Feb. 6, 1977.

"Harbour entrances would be just packed": Shawcross, *Q and C,* p. 114.

"seized the moment to whip out a lipstick": Morrow, p. 59.

"one of the most significant decisions": The Queen's Reply, Westminster Hall, May 4, 1977.

"That was significant": Simon Walker interview.

"Your Majesty, I'm afraid": *The Times,* Sept. 13, 2008. Major Sir Michael Parker was an Englishman who worked on numerous royal events, not to be confused with Lieutenant Michael Parker, the Australian naval officer who had worked for Prince Philip.

"I had forgotten how uncomfortable": Burrell, p. 30.

"an example of service untiringly done": BBC, "On This Day," June 7, 1977, news.bbc.co.uk/onthisday.

"in my salad days when I was green": Ibid.

the roar of the vast crowd was so loud: Shawcross, *Q and C,* p. 115.

"They *really* love you": Strong, p. 194.

"basically middle class British": Ibid, p. 193.

"more or less had to push": Ibid., p. 194.

"The Queen received me": Shawcross, *Q and C,* pp. 108–9.

"our own particular sorrows": Queen Elizabeth II Christmas Broadcast, Dec. 25, 1972, Official Website of the British Monarchy.

"Martin, we *said* we're going": Bradford, p. 377.

"the safest way for the Queen": BBC, "On This Day," Aug. 10, 1977, news.bbc.co.uk/onthisday.

"nowhere is reconciliation more desperately": Queen Elizabeth II Christmas Broadcast, Dec. 25, 1977, Official Website of the British Monarchy.

He was the first baby in the royal family: *The Guardian,* Nov. 16, 1977.

"The Queen knew Martin would cry": Gay Charteris interview.

"he was still around": Shawcross, *QEQM,* p. 895.

"Martin, thank you for a lifetime": Gay Charteris interview.

Thirteen: Iron Lady and English Rose

"conversation flowed easily": *Sunday Times,* Feb. 7, 1982.

their talk over the next hour might touch: Longford, *Elizabeth R,* p. 350.

"weighs up": Ibid., p. 349.

One week she memorably took him for a stroll: Shawcross, *Q and C,* p. 112.

"What one gets . . . is friendliness": Longford, *Elizabeth R,* p. 348.

"poor old Jim Callaghan": Wyatt, Vol. 2, p. 36.

"the last shreds of prejudice": Shawcross, *Q and C,* p. 121.

"What do you think about Margaret Thatcher": Ian Balding interview.

"the eternal scholarship girl": Johnson, p. 263.

"The Queen found that irritating": Confidential source.

"The agenda included major topical": Charles Powell interview.

"She chatted with us": Confidential interview.

"She seemed to come back in a cheerful": Charles Powell interview.

One exception was the time: Morrow, p. 167.

"Mrs. Thatcher would have thought it impudent": Pimlott, pp. 460–61.

Whenever the Thatchers came: Monica Tandy tour of Windsor Castle; Longford, *Elizabeth R,* p. 376.

"was reserved but she could give you": Turner, pp. 48–49.

"Would you like to order, sir?": *Spitting Image,* YouTube.

"The Queen is the mother of the country": James Lees-Milne, *Diaries: 1984–1997,* abridged and introduced by Michael Bloch, p. 141.

"No one could curtsy lower": Charles Powell interview.

"I would set up . . . a hereditary monarchy": Longford, *Elizabeth R,* p. 358.

"out of loyalty": Charles Powell interview.

"The hills? . . . The hills? She walks on the road!": Confidential interview.

"The Queen finessed it": Ibid.

she let her manners slip and kept her elbows: Morrow, pp. 147–48.

"quartering the room": Paxman, p. 315.

"an enormous role in calming everything": Shawcross, *Q and C,* p. 123.

"talked to Mrs. Thatcher and to Kaunda": Pimlott, p. 468.

Whenever she and Philip are having lunch: Confidential interview.

"his closest confidant": Dimbleby, p. 213.

"someone who showed enormous affection": Ibid., p. 324.

The Queen called the hospital: Timothy Knatchbull, *From a Clear Blue Sky: Surviving the Mountbatten Bomb,* p. 115.

"That kind of private person": Pamela Hicks interview.

"A dog isn't important": Ibid.

"Please sit with me": Ibid.

"Ma'am, would you like to go upstairs?": Timothy Knatchbull interview.

"striding down the corridor": Knatchbull, p. 176.

"She was in almost unstoppable mothering mode": Ibid.

"She was caring and sensitive and intuitive": Timothy Knatchbull interview.

"I fear it will take me": Dimbleby, p. 324.

she said the Irish were pigs: Wilson, p. 259.

"She had all the feelings": Timothy Knatchbull interview.

One unlikely source of consolation: Smith, p. 87.

"German family": *Sunday Times,* Jan. 31, 2010.

"By the time we reached Australia": Pamela Hicks interview.

"a good age for a man": *Woman's Own,* Feb. 1975.

"easy and open manner": Dimbleby, p. 338.

"LADY DI IS THE NEW GIRL": *The Sun,* Sept. 8, 1980.

"fallen in love with an idea": Dimbleby, p. 341.

"Prince Philip and the Queen felt responsible": Pamela Hicks interview.

"There is a difference": Confidential interview.

"If I'd said to him": Dimbleby, p. 340.

"intent to alarm": Morrow, p. 131.

sitting calmly when a ball crashed: Jean Carnarvon interview.

"I never saw her scared": Turner, p. 46.

"You know why you're there": Malcolm Ross interview.

"Left leg straight!": Ibid.

"In every pub and club": Dewar, ed., p. 17.

A poll in July 1981: Longford, *Elizabeth R,* p. 357.

The first lady had met Charles: Prince Charles

to Nancy Reagan, June 6, 2004, The Ronald Reagan Presidential Foundation & Library.

Nancy Reagan also endeared: Henderson, pp. 395–97.

"I have fallen in love": Mary Henderson to Nancy Reagan, May 3, 1981, Reagan Library.

"in our best bib and tucker": Josephine Louis interview.

"She was wonderful that day": Ibid.

"little house in Windsor Great Park!": Queen Elizabeth the Queen Mother to Nancy Reagan, July 28, 1981, Reagan Library.

The atmosphere was exultant: BBC, "On This Day," July 29, 1981, news.bbc.co.uk/onthisday.

"grow into it": *Daily Mail,* Sept. 10, 1996.

It was a high-spirited occasion: Josephine Louis interview; Nicholas Haslam interview; confidential interview.

"Oh Philip, do look!": Morrow, p. 7.

"I'd love to stay and dance": Ibid.

"The Queen was so mad": Josephine Louis interview.

she rapidly lost weight: Andrew Morton, *Diana: Her True Story — In Her Own Words,* p. 56.

down to a mere 110 pounds: Smith, p. 145.

"It was just impossible": Paxman, p. 274.

"other side . . . jolly girl": Dimbleby, p. 345.

Charles had Diana flown: Smith, p. 151.

"the Queen is the least self-absorbed": Confidential interview.

"Regardless of how rude Princess Margaret": Confidential interview.

"The Queen was always kind": Lucia Flecha de Lima interview (Nov. 10, 1997).

"terrified": *Daily Mail,* Sept. 10, 1996.

"the briskest, deepest, most correct curtsy": Morrow, p. 40.

Although Diana wrote letters of gratitude: Jonathan Dimbleby interview (Dec. 10, 1997).

"She is pretty, soft and amusing": Confidential interview.

"betrayed": Confidential interview.

"despondent": Smith, p. 155.

"That's the most pompous thing": Longford, *Elizabeth R,* p. 409.

Fourteen: A Very Special Relationship

"brought into stark focus": *The Queen at 80,* Sky News, 2006.

"I definitely went there a boy": *Daily Telegraph,* Feb. 13, 2010.

"We have ceased to be a nation in retreat": Margaret Thatcher, speech to Conservative rally at Cheltenham, July 3, 1982, Margaret Thatcher Foundation Website.

"quiet two days": *New York Times,* June 7, 1982.

"invariably lit up at the prospect": Henderson, p. 434.

"the first country that I have visited": Jimmy Carter, London, England, remarks on arrival at Heathrow Airport, May 5, 1977.

"I took a sharp step backwards": Shawcross, *QEQM,* p. 900.

The Queen had arranged: *New York Times,* June 8, 1982.

"that was what he needed": Michael Fawcett interview.

"We had the feeling we had come": Carolyn

Deaver interview.

"It was surprisingly informal": Nancy Reagan interview.

"bobbing when he should have remained": *Daily Mirror,* June 9, 1982.

"Does it ride well?" Associated Press, June 8, 1982.

offered the first lady a running commentary: Nancy Reagan interview.

"charming . . . down-to-earth . . . she was in charge": *Daily Telegraph,* Aug. 17, 1982.

the first American president: Ronald Reagan, *The Reagan Diaries,* p. 88.

"Are you enjoying yourself?": Carolyn Deaver interview.

"much impressed by the way": United Press International, June 8, 1982.

"the conflict on the Falkland islands": *Daily Mirror,* June 9, 1982.

"I suddenly saw this tiny figure": *Daily Telegraph,* Aug. 17, 1982.

"It was a great relief": Martin Bashir interview with Diana, Princess of Wales, *Panorama,* BBC, Nov. 20, 1995.

The Queen was among the first to visit: Morrow, p. 238.

"Get out of here at once!": Ibid., p. 232.

"Tell me about it": Shawcross, *QEQM,* p. 533.

"I am used to talking to people": Confidential interview.

"Bloody 'ell, Ma'am": Morrow, p. 232.

"Oh come on, get a bloody move": Ibid., p. 233.

"The whole thing was so surreal": Colin Burgess, *Behind Palace Doors: My Service as the Queen*

Mother's Equerry, p. 156.

"mostly shock and disbelief": Confidential interview.

"dark ages": Morton, p. 61.

she underwent therapy with two different professionals: Ibid., pp. 140–41.

"It was actually very emotional": *The Queen at 80,* Sky News, 2006.

"for reasons of time and protocol": *Newsweek,* Oct. 21, 1957.

She had raised the matter: Henderson, p. 273.

"What better time": *Time,* March 14, 1983.

She expressly asked: Henderson, p. 485.

At one point Princess Margaret called: Selwa "Lucky" Roosevelt interview.

"We said, 'But she's *never* been' ": Peter McKay interview.

"They sat on the first two seats": Lucky Roosevelt interview.

"The Queen was visibly bothered": *Time,* March 14, 1983.

Philip suffered his own indignity: Josephine Louis interview.

"Are you expecting trouble?": Pete Metzger interview.

"Aren't there any male supervisors?": *Time,* March 14, 1983.

"Damned if I'll turn off the light": Lucky Roosevelt interview.

"The Annenbergs have more than the Queen!": Carolyn Deaver journal, Feb. 27, 1983.

They sped off under umbrellas: Ibid.

"There was a lot of talk at the time": Lucky Roosevelt interview.

"She said, 'If we can get there, let's go' ": Shaw-cross, *Queen and Country* documentary.

"I don't know how happy she was": Josephine Louis interview.

Even on the clearest day: Author's observations.

She said little: Josephine Louis interview.

"Don't be silly": Nancy Reagan interview.

"That was so enjoyable": Pamela Bailey interview.

"Damn it . . . I told them": *Time,* March 14, 1983.

"We talked at length": Nancy Reagan interview.

As they made their approach: Pete Metzger interview; Carolyn Deaver interview.

Ted Graber hurriedly dressed up: Nancy Reagan interview.

"I learned that night that she listened": Carolyn Deaver interview.

At the end of the meal, she cracked open: Ibid.

"The Queen needs her tiara time!": Ibid.

she has a kit with tools: Ibid.; David Thomas interview.

"puff sleeves decorated": Hardy Amies, *Still Here: An Autobiography,* p. 119.

"I knew before we came": *Time,* March 14, 1983.

"I know I promised Nancy": Nancy Reagan interview.

Reagan expressed his fondness: *Time,* March 14, 1983.

In no time she had it installed: Michael Oswald interview; Associated Press, Oct. 11, 1984.

"sparkling": Princess Margaret to Ronald and Nancy Reagan, Oct. 6, 1983, Reagan Library.

"It is a curious irony": Confidential interview.

"debating about the past": Margaret Thatcher radio interview with David Spanier of IRN (New Delhi Commonwealth Conference), Nov. 29, 1983, Margaret Thatcher Foundation Website.

At a black-tie dinner: Reagan, *The Reagan Diaries,* p. 246.

On the final weekend: *Time,* March 14, 1983.

Philip had already stayed: Jean Carnarvon interview.

To take advantage: *New York Times,* Oct. 9, 1984.

He gave her a nomination: FitzGerald, p. 140.

When Elizabeth II landed: Catherine Murdock interview.

the Queen immediately changed: Lady Angela Oswald interview.

"It put everyone totally at ease": Catherine Murdock interview.

The directors of Keeneland also staged: Ibid.

Each night the Farishes had dinner parties: Ibid.

"She felt very much at home": Confidential interview.

"all attempts to destroy democracy": Margaret Thatcher speech to Conservative Party conference, Oct. 12, 1984, Margaret Thatcher Foundation Website.

"sympathy and deep concern": Associated Press, Oct. 12, 1984.

"Are you having a lovely time?": Jean Carnarvon interview.

"boosted one's morale": Shawcross, *Q and C,* p. 128.

"deep regret": United Press International, Oct. 15, 1984.

Her only annoyance: Jean Carnarvon interview.

But she took five-mile walks: Ibid.; Tad Bartimus, "Queen Elizabeth Visits Wyoming," *American West,* March/April 1985.

Meals were simple American fare: *Time,* Oct. 22, 1984.

"Queen-sized *fillette* cut": Catherine Murdock interview.

"because I have never tasted them": Bartimus, "Queen Elizabeth Visits Wyoming," *American West,* March/April 1985.

"What kind of salad dressing": Catherine Murdock interview.

she handed out gifts: Ibid.

"looking at beautiful thoroughbreds": Queen Elizabeth II to Ronald Reagan, Oct. 14, 1984, Reagan Library.

"closed off": Morton, p. 51.

"monstrous carbuncle": Dimbleby, p. 384.

"catastrophe . . . time bomb": Strong, p. 361.

"The Queen could not be more pleased": *The Sun,* April 12, 1984.

"Horlicks . . . bitter": Andrew Neil interview (May 6, 1998).

she memorably danced: Prince Charles to Ronald Reagan, Nov. 11, 1985, Reagan Library.

"in her clever way": *The Mitfords: Letters Between Six Sisters,* p. 712.

"touched perhaps by the sadness": Lees-Milne, *Diaries, 1984–1997,* p. 93.

Most of the bluegrass breeders: *Washington Post,* May 29, 1989.

"Suddenly from the bushes to the left": Anne Glenconner interview.

"felt favored and blessed": Sarah, the Duchess of

York, with Jeff Coplon, *My Story,* p. 108.

"I was robust and jolly": Ibid., p. 107.

"She's very sharp and clever": Wyatt, Vol. 3, p. 410.

Fifteen: Family Fractures

The Queen purportedly took issue: *Sunday Times,* July 20, 1986.

"astute political infighter": Ibid.

"It was like a scene out of Trollope": Confidential interview.

"Margaret Thatcher was very upset": Charles Powell interview.

"ordinary people": Shawcross, *Q and C,* p. 133.

"commiserated with each other": Turner, p. 181.

He was more distraught: Confidential interview.

an appointment that raised eyebrows: *The Times,* Oct. 20, 2009.

There had been press reports: Wyatt, Vol. 1, p. 167.

The Queen had encouraged Canadian: Brian Mulroney interview.

"moral obligation": Ibid.

Thatcher eventually compromised: Mulroney, p. 404.

"She never expressed her views": Confidential interview.

To shield its informant: *The Times,* Oct. 20, 2009.

"misinterpreted": *Daily Telegraph,* Oct. 19, 2009.

"crucial parts": *The Times,* Oct. 20, 2009.

The press secretary's colleagues: Confidential interviews.

"I think he has megalomania": Wyatt, Vol. 1, p. 173.

"He personally didn't go for Margaret Thatcher": Angela Oswald interview.

"Don't worry, dear": Pimlott, p. 514, citing interview with Sir John Riddell.

"Well, I can't do anything": Wyatt, Vol, 1, p. 178.

"deliberate act by the Queen" Shawcross, *Q and C,* pp. 133–34.

"Now Kenneth": Brian Mulroney interview.

"How is the emotional one?": Mulroney, p. 466.

"There was no doubt": Brian Mulroney interview.

"I think Mr. Deng would be rather happier": Shawcross, *Q and C,* p. 176.

"didn't move a muscle": Shawcross, *Queen and Country* documentary.

"The British press went nuts": Confidential interview.

"puncture the balloon": McDonald, *The Duke* documentary.

"I don't know why he has the gift": Confidential interview.

"My only claim to fame": *Austin American-Statesman,* May 21, 1991.

including a gold bracelet: *Daily Telegraph,* Jan. 12, 2011.

In 1982 he began driving: McDonald, *The Duke* documentary.

"energy saving": Ibid.

"Sometimes I would take an idea": Confidential interview.

One of his favorite photographs: David Airlie interview.

"Do you really want to be": Confidential interview.

"enormously practical . . . extremely business-like": BBC interview with David Airlie: transcript, Feb. 21, 1994.

"to sit on it and think": Ibid.

"The reason why she moves": Ibid.

After he had spent six months: David Airlie interview.

the press reported that his father: *The Guardian,* Jan. 8, 2010.

"They always try to make him out": Wyatt, Vol. 1, p. 309.

"It was a disaster": Ibid., p. 492.

"cold, drafty, and expensive": James Murray interview.

The two queens took walks: June Webster interview; Helen Markham interview.

After dinner he played: Confidential interview.

"stripped naked": Strong, p. 430.

In 1985 Diana had taken up: Smith, p. 197.

in November of the following year: Ibid., p. 212.

"warmth . . . understanding and steadiness": Dimbleby, p. 481.

the tension was obvious enough: *Sunday Times,* Sept. 24, 1988.

"civilized space": Penny Thornton, *With Love from Diana,* p. 52.

"new Diana": Smith, p. 234.

Sarah was expected to live: Ibid., p. 239.

"bad royal": Sarah, the Duchess of York, p. 148.

"crass, rude, raucous, and bereft": Ibid., p. 155.

For a number of years": *People,* April 24, 1989.

She was linked: Ibid.

as well as Camilla's husband: *Daily Mail,* June 22, 2007.

"darling . . . affectionate terms": *People,* April 24, 1989.

At the end of 1988 she had been reading: Monty Roberts interview.

"advance-and-retreat": Monty Roberts, *The Man Who Listens to Horses: The Story of a Real-Life Horse Whisperer,* p. xxxi.

The Queen sent: Monty Roberts interview.

She invited some two hundred guests: The description of Roberts's demonstration at Windsor Castle and the reactions from the royal family are drawn from author's interview with Roberts and from his autobiography.

"I saw a mind open up": Monty Roberts interview.

"knew every move": Ibid.

"getting it right": Ibid.

In 2011 she rewarded Roberts: *The Mirror,* June 11, 2011.

He offered to buy the horse: FitzGerald, p. 149.

The anger at Henry Carnarvon: *Daily Telegraph,* May 23, 2002.

"If you don't make some sort": Phil Dampier and Ashley Walton, *What's in the Queen's Handbag and Other Royal Secrets,* p. 107; Ian Balding interview.

"loud and sustained applause . . . swept off his Panama": *Daily Telegraph,* May 23, 2002.

"The Queen has done something": Wyatt, Vol. 2, p. 81.

By then, she had countermanded: *Daily Telegraph,* May 23, 2002.

"Sonny Ramphal . . . was sitting in London": Brian Mulroney interview.

"in charge of our own destiny": David Airlie interview.

"give much more dignity and continuity": Margaret Thatcher statement to the House of Commons on the Civil List, July 24, 1990.

She was in Paris at the time: Charles Powell interview.

"She's a very understanding person": Shawcross, *Q and C,* p. 138.

"The Garter tends to go": Charles Powell interview.

"very patriotic": Wyatt, Vol. 2, p. 403.

Sixteen: *Annus Horribilis*

"I couldn't pin down a difference": Confidential interview.

"had a lot in common": Seitz, p. 320.

"The Queen is rather formal": George H. W. Bush interview by email, Aug. 25, 2009.

"freedom's friend": *Boston Globe,* May 15, 1991.

"we had a good laugh": George H. W. Bush interview.

"The first thing I noticed": George W. Bush interview by email, Jan. 18, 2011.

"No, Ma'am . . . God Save the Queen": Ibid., Jan. 19, 2011.

"I teased her that it was her folks": George H. W. Bush interview.

"left even the Secret Service": *New York Times,* May 15, 1991.

"No wonder I cannot feel a stranger": *Washington Post,* May 15, 1991.

"I do hope you can see me today": *Dallas Morning News,* May 17, 1991.

"How are you doin?": *Washington Post,* May 16, 1991.

"It's the American way": United Press International, May 15, 1991.

"What a waste": Benedicte Valentiner interview.

"She was standing stock still": Ibid.

"grazing happily": Queen Elizabeth II to Ronald Reagan, July 15, 1990, Reagan Library.

"If you've got two-thirds": *E II R* documentary.

"I am an amazing woman!": *Houston Chronicle,* May 23, 1991.

Once again she could indulge: Ibid.

Sarah Farish greeted her with a kiss: *Daily Express,* May 24, 1991.

"humiliated that her husband": *The Sun,* May 20, 1991.

Andrew and Fergie were misbehaving: *People,* March 11, 1991.

a sharply critical editorial: *Sunday Times,* Feb. 10, 1991.

"This is the first time": Gay Charteris interview.

he rode a bicycle: Smith, p. 276.

"a frightful pinko": *Daily Telegraph,* Nov. 14, 2008.

"exposing too much of the inner workings": Confidential interview.

she readily agreed to set up a working group: David Airlie interview.

"She was not worried about how much she would pay": Confidential interview.

An infuriated Andrew called in: Wyatt, Vol. 2, p. 651.

an unusual personal statement: Confidential interview.

"Most people have a job": *E II R* documentary.

"the dynamic sexiness": *Today,* May 18, 1991.

"the marriage was indeed on the rocks": Dimbleby, p. 592.

On the 7th: *Sunday Times,* June 7, 1992.

Despite persistent rumors: Smith, p. 276.

Known for his integrity: Ibid., p. 277.

"Not once was there the slightest hint": Charles Anson interview.

In consultations with Fellowes: Smith, p. 278.

It was an emotional encounter: Burrell, p. 159.

"learn to compromise": Ibid.

"Mama despaired": Ibid., p. 158.

"in a friendly attempt to resolve": Transcript of hearing into the death of Diana, Princess of Wales, Dec. 13, 2007, quoting statement from Prince Philip on Nov. 23, 2002.

"involved much more than simply": Burrell, p. 161.

"stinging . . . wounding . . . irate": Smith, p. 280.

"not a single derogatory term": Brigadier Sir Miles Hunt-Davis testimony, transcript of hearing, Dec. 13, 2007.

"dearest Pa" and subsequent quotes from letters: Ibid.

"he never touched Diana's heart": Smith, p. 280.

Before the Morton book: Dimbleby, p. 588.

"I think it took a long time": Patricia Brabourne interview.

"saint-like fortitude": Bradford, p. 475.

"to keep a calm view": Confidential interview.

"Can you imagine having two": Patricia Brabourne interview.

"If I wanted help in understanding": George

Carey interview.

"The personalities were so different": Ibid.

"became almost mutual support sessions": Shawcross, *Q and C,* p. 201.

"People don't realize quite how strong": Shawcross, *Queen and Country* documentary.

"some preparatory work": Carey, p. 402.

"It was my pastoral duty": Ibid., p. 405.

On Thursday, August 20: *Daily Mirror,* Aug. 20, 1992.

"It would be accurate to report": Sarah, the Duchess of York, p. 21.

"I had been exposed for what I truly was": Ibid., p. 19.

"furious": Ibid., p. 23.

"I don't see her because": Brandreth, p. 329.

"The Queen had an affection": Confidential interview.

Four days after the *Mirror* scoop: *The Sun,* Aug. 24, 1992.

"personally found great comfort": Shawcross, *QEQM,* p. 892.

"alternately despairing, defiant": P. D. Jephson, *Shadows of a Princess: An Intimate Account by Her Private Secretary,* p. 307.

Once again, the Queen intervened: Burrell, p. 165.

Early in September: Wyatt, Vol. 3, p. 94.

"take time and talk round it": Confidential interview.

She was going into an audience: *The Queen at 80,* Sky News.

"It was the most shaken I ever saw her": Confidential interview.

"It made all the difference to my sanity": Shawcross, *QEQM,* p. 892.

"lifting too much veil": Confidential interview.

"She could see that it was a good thing": Confidential interview.

as she had been in 1977: James Lees-Milne, *Diaries, 1971–1983,* p. 234.

"let Major persuade her": Wyatt, Vol. 3, p. 133.

"very miserable and mealy-mouthed": Shawcross, *Queen and Country* documentary.

"one of the central features": Confidential interview.

She was suffering: Shawcross, *QEQM,* p. 893.

"Nineteen ninety-two is not a year": *Annus Horribilis* speech, Nov. 24, 1992, Official Website of the British Monarchy.

"intense and complex": *Daily Mail,* Nov. 25, 1992.

"a year capable of scaring you": Shawcross, *Queen and Country* documentary.

"in a state of desperation": Dimbleby, p. 593.

"The Glums": Smith, p. 284.

"he had no choice": Dimbleby, p. 595.

"no plans to divorce": Ibid.

"With hindsight it was a mistake": Shawcross, *Q and C,* p. 204.

The arrangements were so hastily made: Shawcross, *QEQM,* p. 894.

"prayers, understanding and sympathy": Christmas Broadcast, Dec. 25, 1992, Official Website of the British Monarchy.

"with fresh hope": Ibid.

Seventeen: Tragedy and Tradition

"You're a clever old thing": *Sunday Mirror,* Jan.

17, 1993.

In a poll published: Smith, p. 284.

"to explain to the media": BBC interview with David Airlie: transcript, Feb. 21, 1994.

"courtiers should be neither seen": Ibid.

"She isn't like you!": David Airlie interview.

died in her suite: *Los Angeles Times,* Sept. 25, 1993.

who had hired two nurses: *The Scotsman,* Nov. 12, 2002.

The Queen came down: Margaret Rhodes interview.

"She simply stopped": *Daily Express,* Sept. 3, 1998.

It was a tempestuous relationship: Smith, p. 317.

"time and space": *Today,* Dec. 4, 1993.

Both the Queen and Prince Philip had urged: Smith, p. 310.

In an atmosphere thick with tension: Bradford, p. 487.

"I wasn't paying enough attention!": Elizabeth II to Ronald Reagan, Feb. 13, 1994, Reagan Library.

"She has no regard for color": Wesley Kerr interview.

"Did you see your father": Ibid.

"the clever manner in which she discussed": Bill Clinton, *My Life,* p. 599.

"nodded and laughed": Hillary Rodham Clinton, *Living History,* p. 238.

"was clearly happy": Shawcross, *Q and C,* p. 229.

but all were eclipsed by: Jonathan Dimbleby, *Prince Charles: The Private Man, the Public Role,* ITV, June 29, 1994.

"the myth that he had never intended": *Sunday*

Telegraph, July 3, 1994.

John Major was concerned: Wyatt, Vol, 3, p. 403.

"That Jonathan Dimbleby!": Ibid., p. 453.

Paradoxically, the Soviet Communist Party: *The Independent,* Oct. 16, 1994.

"The monarchy is unshakeable": Ibid.

When he tried to draw out: Shawcross, *Q and C,* p. 177.

"I thought the jewels were too much": David Thomas interview.

"the Queen evoked a sort of nostalgia": Shawcross, *Q and C,* p. 207.

"attractive . . . very conceited": Wyatt, Vol. 3, p. 466.

"vulgar, vulgar, vulgar": *Daily Mail,* Jan. 6, 1995.

"He's got such a lot of wisdom": Wyatt, Vol. 3, p. 504.

"one of the outstanding experiences": Shawcross, *Queen and Country* documentary.

He and Kenneth Kaunda: Robin Renwick, Baron Renwick of Clifton, interview.

"Let's have him": Turner, p. 193.

"huge emotional charge": Shawcross, *Queen and Country* documentary.

"re-launched": Smith, p. 339.

"She was nervous about the fact": Robert Salisbury interview.

"The Queen's eyes were brimming": Pimlott, p. 575.

"superb performance": Barbara Walters interview.

The princess spoke unflinchingly: Bashir interview, *Panorama.*

"Diana at her worst": *Sunday Telegraph,* Sept. 7, 1997.

"advanced stages of paranoia": *The Guardian,* Nov. 21, 1995.

a Gallup survey registered: *Daily Telegraph,* Nov. 27, 1995.

"very dangerous": Wyatt, Vol. 3, p. 577.

"took the BBC aback": Confidential interview.

"early divorce . . . in the best interests": *Daily Telegraph,* Dec. 21, 1995.

"with love from Mama": Burrell, p. 222.

Elizabeth II remained predictably noncommittal: Jane Atkinson interview (Dec. 3, 1998).

"sensitivity and kindness": Burrell, p. 229.

But Diana again overreached: Jane Atkinson interview.

"The decision to drop the title": *Daily Mail,* March 1, 1996.

"co-parents": Meredith Vieira interview with Prince Andrew, *Today,* Jan. 29, 2008.

"happiest unmarried couple": Sarah Ferguson interview with Sky News, Feb. 24, 2010.

"regarded as a member of the royal family": "Status and Role of the Princess of Wales," statement from Buckingham Palace, July 12, 1996.

"has a special place in my heart": ITN Reuters Television, July 10, 1996.

"let bygones be bygones": *New York Times,* July 13, 1996.

"Should I dance?" Robin Renwick interview.

"To everyone's surprise": Ibid.

"has seldom been known": *New York Times,* July 13, 1996.

Early in the new year they met: Tony Blair, *A Journey: My Political Life,* p. 135.

"fairly calculating terms": Alastair Campbell,

The Blair Years: Extracts from the Alastair Campbell Diaries, p. 152.

"radical combination": Tony Blair, p. 135.

"an unpredictable meteor": Ibid., p. 136.

"perfect fit": Ibid., p. 134.

"We were both in our ways": Ibid., p. 140.

"all teeth and no bite": Burgess, p. 76.

"He had the nicest manners": Johnson, p. 37.

"betrayal . . . understanding": *The Mirror,* Sept. 4, 2010.

he tripped on the edge: Cherie Blair, *Speaking for Myself: My Life from Liverpool to Downing Street,* p. 186.

"The first was Winston": Tony Blair, p. 16.

"I got a sense of my relative seniority": *The Times,* May 22, 2002.

"general guff": Tony Blair, p. 16.

"I can't remember not curtsying": Cherie Blair, p. 180.

"generally clucking sympathetically": Tony Blair, p. 16.

"hot spring sunshine": Queen Elizabeth II to Nancy Reagan, April 24, 1997, Ronald Reagan Library.

"opens the door": *Royalty Digest,* No. 70, April 1997, p. 316.

"there's a bit of her that is very": Marr, *The Queen at 80,* BBC.

"A lot of people thought *Britannia*": Confidential interview.

"Sea Days" for businessmen: *The Royal Yacht Britannia Official Guidebook,* p. 56.

"What an asset": Alastair Campbell, p. 218.

"Lilibet" and "Philip": Castle of Mey Visitors

Book, Aug. 16, 1997.

"somewhat melancholy": Shawcross, *QEQM,* p. 909.

steamed past the coast twice: June Webster interview.

"With all our memories of you": Castle of Mey Visitors Book, Aug. 16, 1997, Copyright HM the Queen.

"Oh what a heavenly day": Ibid.

"an understanding of people's emotions": Bashir interview, *Panorama.*

Yet she also began to burden: Roberto Devorick interview (March 10, 1998); Elsa Bowker interview (Dec. 12, 1997).

"by cultivating the idea": Andrew Neil interview (May 6, 1998).

they were embarrassed: Lacey, *Monarch,* p. 358.

the Queen wrote a note: Shawcross, *QEQM,* p. 910.

"global event like no other": Tony Blair, p. 138.

"The Queen and Prince of Wales are deeply shocked": *Daily Mail,* Sept. 4, 1997.

"philosophical, anxious for the boys": Tony Blair, p. 140.

"the People's Princess": Ibid., p. 141.

"how difficult things were": Lacey, *Monarch,* p. 360.

But the royal family thought: Alastair Campbell, p. 246.

"encourage the temptation": Carey, p. 407.

"don't pray for the souls": Confidential interview.

"They handled it like ostriches": *Diana: The Week She Died,* ITV documentary, 2006.

the princes wanted the comfort: *Daily Telegraph,*

Sept. 27, 2009.

"talk to Mummy": Lacey, *Monarch,* p. 358.

"To take them away to have nothing to do": Margaret Rhodes interview.

"We can't look at the files": David Airlie interview.

"We wanted the people who had benefited": Ibid.

"She was very happy with the charity workers": Malcolm Ross interview.

"unique funeral for a unique person": *New York Times,* Sept. 2, 1997.

"people's funeral": Alastair Campbell, p. 236.

"She is much better with paper": Malcolm Ross interview.

"shrewd and savvy": Tony Blair, p. 144.

"completely au fait": Ibid.

"encouraged creative thinking": Lacey, *Monarch,* p. 367.

"at a rate of 6,000 per hour": Wilson, p. 326.

They heaped flowers: Author's observations.

By Wednesday night: *Daily Mail,* Sept. 4, 1997.

"from the heart not the head": Bashir interview, *Panorama.*

"I always believed the press would kill": *New York Times,* Sept. 1, 1997.

"Happy now?": Ibid.

"If only the royals dared weep": *New York Times,* Sept. 4, 1997.

"The media were circling": Confidential interview.

"They needed to direct it": Tony Blair, p. 144.

"I think the thing that impressed": Shawcross, *Queen and Country* documentary.

"Robin had to describe": Malcolm Ross interview.

"all the royal family": *New York Times,* Sept. 4, 1997.

"the fact that I was speaking": Tony Blair, p. 148.

"as blunt as I needed to be": Ibid., p. 149.

"very direct advice": Ibid., p. 148.

"hide away": Ibid., p. 149.

"If she had come down": *Diana: The Week She Died* documentary.

The tabloids on Thursday morning: *Washington Post,* Sept. 5, 1997.

A survey by MORI: Robert Worcester interview.

"dangerous and unpleasant": Alastair Campbell, p. 240.

"Robin Janvrin told me": George Carey interview.

more important was the persuasiveness: Malcolm Ross interview.

"It was an extraordinary experience": *The Guardian,* Feb. 13, 2010.

"It was the first time I'd heard": *The Guardian,* Jan. 16, 2011, excerpt from Alastair Campbell Diaries, Vol. 2, *Power and the People.*

"was now very focused": Tony Blair, p. 149.

"The royal family have been hurt": *Washington Post,* Sept. 7, 1997.

"how you kindly arranged": Shawcross, *QEQM,* p. 911.

Philip suggested that on the eve: Alastair Campbell, p. 241.

"There was a very ugly atmosphere": Marr, *The Queen at 80* documentary.

"It wasn't completely over with": Ibid.

"Would you like me to place them": Lacey, *Monarch,* pp. 378–79.

"Have you been queuing": Marr, *The Queen at 80* documentary.

"I just said how sorry I was": Shawcross, *Queen and Country* documentary.

"spent a long time talking": Marr, *The Queen at 80* documentary.

"She knew it was something she should do": Confidential interview.

"as a grandmother": Alastair Campbell, p. 243.

"There were some last-minute discussions": Tony Blair, p. 149.

"One run-through": Wesley Kerr interview.

"an overwhelming expression of sadness": Queen Elizabeth II speech following the death of Diana, Princess of Wales, Sept. 5, 1997, Official Website of the British Monarchy.

"one of the very best speeches": Shawcross, *Queen and Country* documentary.

"showed her compassion": Carey, p. 409.

"near perfect": Tony Blair, p. 149.

"unconvincing": Alan Bennett, *Untold Stories,* pp. 214–15, Sept. 5, 1997, diary entry.

"There's no putting on of a face": Simon Walker interview.

"consumed by a total hatred": *The Guardian,* Jan. 16, 2011, excerpt from Campbell Diaries, Vol. 2.

"If you don't walk": *Daily Mail,* Oct. 17, 2009, quoting Gyles Brandreth diary, Sept. 6, 1997.

The atmosphere on the sunny morning: Author's observations.

"It was completely unexpected": Marr, *The Queen at 80* documentary.

"that there was already a readiness": Shawcross, *Queen and Country* documentary.

"unashamedly populist and raw": Carey, p. 410.

"your blood family": "Diana, Princess of Wales," BBC recording of the funeral service, BBC Worldwide Music, Sept. 6, 1997.

"those unnecessary words": Carey, p. 411.

"It sounded like a rustle of leaves": Charles Moore interview.

"were very kind": Cherie Blair, p. 207.

"This is really weird": Ibid.

"strangled cry": Tony Blair, p. 151.

"assumed a certain hauteur": Ibid., p. 152.

"mass movement for change": Ibid., p. 143.

"protect the monarchy": Ibid., p. 145.

Eighteen: Love and Grief

Philip chaired the overall: Adam Nicolson, *Restoration: The Rebuilding of Windsor Castle,* pp. 74–75.

To replace the gutted private chapel: Ibid., pp. 231–40.

Philip's sketches inspired: Ibid, pp. 264–65.

When Philip disagreed: Ibid., p. 240.

"modern reinterpretation": BBC News, Nov. 17, 1997.

"Your Majesty, Your Majesty": Confidential interview.

"tolerance is the one essential": BBC News, Nov. 19, 1997.

"throat-catching moment": Carey, p. 412.

"people's banquet": Associated Press, Nov. 20, 1997.

Dining with the Queen: BBC News, Nov. 19, 1997.

"the terrible test": Shawcross, *Q and C,* p. 216.

In her speech: Golden Wedding Speech, Nov. 20, 1997, Official Website of the British Monarchy.

"Philip's obvious flirtations and his affairs": Bradford, p. 401.

"I simply don't know of anyone": *Daily Mail,* Nov. 11, 1997.

"Philip's great friend": Patricia Brabourne interview.

"absolutely certain": Ibid.

"He would never behave badly": Ibid.

"riveting conversations": Brandreth, p. 281.

"doesn't mind when he flirts": Pamela Hicks interview.

"quite honestly, what real evidence": *The Times,* April 18, 2009.

"It was awful and she cried": Confidential interview.

"It had not just been for work": Confidential interview.

"represented freedom to her": Confidential interview.

After support for a republic peaked: Robert Worcester interview.

Now Janvrin told Worcester: Ibid.

"too myopic and inward looking": Confidential interview.

In general, the research: Robert Worcester interview.

"People start thinking about the future": Ibid.

"My abiding impression": Simon Lewis interview.

"It is not heart on the sleeve": Confidential interview.

"imperceptible evolution . . . the Marmite theory": Simon Walker interview.

"She has incredibly good instincts": Simon Lewis interview.

"Time is not my dictator": Shawcross, *QEQM,* p. 903.

At age ninety-seven, she made another: Ibid., p. 912.

She had suffered: BBC News, Feb. 9, 2002.

she would call the Queen first thing: Josephine Louis interview.

"was almost like a poor relation": Confidential interview.

"Sometimes Margaret was a very lonely": Jane Rayne interview.

"After Tony, then Roddy, no one else": Confidential interview.

Since the early 1980s: Annabel Whitehead to Nancy Reagan, Aug. 24, 1999, Reagan Library.

As late as May 1999: Queen Elizabeth II to Nancy Reagan, May 6, 1999, Reagan Library.

"How I'd love to be able to go out": *News of the World,* April 1, 2001.

they organized as much as possible: Ibid.

"They picked up right away": Gay Charteris interview.

"I know if Martin had lived": Ibid.

"the greatest show on earth": *New York Times,* Dec. 31, 1999.

"looked very pissed off": Alastair Campbell, p. 513.

"It was pretty clear": Ibid.

"ghastly": Tony Blair, p. 261.

"The Queen had a central role": Simon Lewis interview.

"the kingdom can still enjoy": Queen Elizabeth II Christmas Broadcast, Dec. 25, 1997, Official Website of the British Monarchy.

"Now Blair, no more of this": *The Guardian,* Jan. 16, 2011, excerpt from Campbell Diaries, Vol. 2.

"high regard for her street smarts": Jonathan Powell interview.

"steadily on the national pulse": *The Times,* May 22, 2002.

"It's not just a question of knowing": Marr, *The Queen at 80* documentary.

"He was always working flat-out": Confidential interview.

"very to the point . . . very direct": *The Times,* May 22, 2002.

Cherie was impressed by: Cherie Blair, p. 304.

"I think he's in the wrong party": Confidential interview.

"not for the sake of buggering about": Brandreth, p. 225.

"the first thing they talked about": Gay Charteris interview.

"felt part of this rugged": Queen Elizabeth II Sydney Opera House speech, March 30, 2000, Official Website of the British Monarchy.

"The Queen was always wondering": Pamela Hicks interview.

The list of more than eight hundred guests: Program: Reception and Dance to Mark the Decade of Birthdays of Queen Elizabeth the Queen Mother, the Princess Margaret, Countess of Snowdon, the Princess Royal, the Duke of York, State Apartments, Windsor Castle, Wednesday, 21st June 2000.

There had been grumbling: Shawcross, *QEQM,* pp. 907–8.

the £643,000 allocated: Civil List Annual Report 2009, p. 60.

a cast of thousands: Shawcross, *QEQM,* pp. 1–2, 922.

"It was three years after": Simon Lewis interview.

"Only one person can decide": Confidential interview.

As they talked, one of the Queen's corgis: Simon Walker interview.

"There was definitely a subtlety": Ibid.

"Under-promise and over delivery": Simon Walker, speech to PR Week Conference, March 2002.

emphasizing instead inclusiveness: Simon Walker interview.

The idea for the painting had come: BBC News, Dec. 20, 2001.

"the interior life or 'inner likeness'": Jane Roberts, *Royal Treasures: A Golden Jubilee Celebration,* catalogue entry 36, p. 110.

"a polar expedition": Ibid.

he painted her in fifteen sittings: Oliver Everett interview.

a source of frustration for the artist: Richard Salmon interview; Jan. 25, 2011, email from Sarah Howgate, curator of Lucian Freud exhibit at the National Portrait Gallery.

She told the artist: Lucian Freud and Nicholas Haslam interview.

"I consider we got to know each other": Ibid.

He had been fascinated: *Daily Telegraph,* March

13, 2004.

"Lucian had a whale of a time": Clarissa Eden interview.

She said none of those things: *News of the World,* April 8, 2001.

"President Blair because": Ibid.

"I have been reduced to tears": Ibid., April 1, 2001.

"Sophie first of all respects her as the Queen": Elizabeth Anson interview.

As the forty-third president and the Duke: *The Times,* July 20, 2001.

"natural connection": George W. Bush interview.

"growing disbelief and total shock": *The Guardian,* Aug. 18, 2002.

Malcolm Ross called Balmoral: Malcolm Ross interview.

the Queen had authorized the same gesture: Simon Walker interview.

Ross also made the novel suggestion: Malcolm Ross interview.

"Would you call the Queen?": Jean Carnarvon interview.

"The Queen was devastated": Ibid.

"When our National Anthem was played": Jackie Davis interview.

"stunning sentence": Shawcross, *Q and C,* p. 233.

"Grief is the price we pay for love": Christopher Meyer, *DC Confidential: The Controversial Memoirs of Britain's Ambassador to the U.S. at the Time of 9/11 and the Iraq War,* p. 199.

they were carved in stone: Ibid., p. 201.

"Obviously there was a huge focus": *The Times,* May 22, 2002.

"extremely unflattering . . . a travesty": BBC News, Dec. 21, 2001.

"You gaze at it for half a minute": Clarissa Eden interview.

"This is a painting of experience": BBC News, Dec. 21, 2001.

"It could not have been painted ten years earlier": Sandy Nairne interview.

Freud said the Queen looked: Lucian Freud interview.

"remarkable work": *The Scotsman,* Dec. 21, 2001.

"feels real and earthy": Jennifer Scott, *The Royal Portrait: Image and Impact,* p. 185.

"What a good idea!": Anne Glenconner interview.

"Her quality of life was not good": BBC News, Feb. 9, 2002.

"carried out the family tradition": Shawcross, *QEQM,* p. 929.

But to mark the fiftieth anniversary: BBC News, Feb. 6, 2002.

"had probably been a merciful release": Shawcross, *QEQM,* p. 930.

"depart without a fuss": Carey, p. 415.

"rooted and firm": Ibid., p. 413.

"It was the saddest I have ever seen": Reinaldo Herrera interview.

she had regained her composure: Confidential interview.

"She went as scheduled": Confidential interview.

"Missis Queen . . . The Queen Lady": BBC News, Feb. 19, 2002.

"Most people much prefer to have a Queen":

Reuters, Feb. 26, 2002.

"Oh, my mother is only 101!": *Daily Telegraph,* March 4, 2002.

"constantly": Ibid.

but she had been lucid enough: Shawcross, *QEQM,* p. 931.

On the morning of March 30, 2002: Ibid., p. 932.

The two women exchanged a few private words: Margaret Rhodes interview.

At 3:15 in the afternoon: Ibid.

"very sad but dignified": Alastair Campbell, p. 611.

"the original life enhancer": Shawcross, *QEQM,* p. 935.

The Queen and her advisers were concerned: Alastair Campbell, p. 610.

"UNCERTAIN FAREWELL REVEALS": BBC News, April 9, 2002.

"It was very emotional for her": Confidential interview.

"one of the most touching things": Shawcross, *QEQM,* p. 935.

"beloved mother": BBC News, April 9, 2002.

"the most magical grandmother": *The Guardian,* April 2, 2002.

Sophie Wessex, Princess Anne: Ibid., April 9, 2002.

Just before the Queen's broadcast: BBC News, April 9, 2002.

They described how they had taught: *The Observer,* April 7, 2002.

"Darling, lunch was marvelous": Ibid.

Crown Jeweler David Thomas was up: David

Thomas interview.

"like the sun": Carey, p. 417.

"the senior royal lady": Margaret Rhodes interview.

"a terrible wallop of grief": Ibid.

"It was a huge thing": Elizabeth Anson interview.

Nineteen: Moving Pictures

"The British have lost the habit": *The Independent,* Jan. 27, 2002.

In keeping with its "softly, softly": Simon Walker interview.

Shipping magnate Jeffrey Sterling: *The Times,* March 14, 2002; Aug. 5, 2002.

A crucial part of the Palace strategy: Simon Walker interview.

Private polling and focus groups: Robert Worcester interview.

The Palace intentionally launched: Simon Walker interview.

"there was something truly pathetic": Alastair Campbell, p. 618.

Afterward, Simon Walker suggested: Simon Walker interview.

"What a relief!": Cherie Blair, p. 270.

"when she had been doing her professional": Alastair Campbell, p. 619.

"Change has become a constant": *Daily Telegraph,* May 1, 2002.

Only days earlier: *The Guardian,* April 24, 2002.

"an historic opportunity to bring": Queen Elizabeth II speech during visit to Parliament buildings on Tuesday, May 14, 2002, Northern Ireland Assembly Website.

"It was important to have young support": Simon Walker interview.

When Elizabeth II appeared: *The Guardian,* June 4, 2002.

who wore yellow earplugs: Ibid.

"50 extraordinary years": *The Independent,* June 4, 2002.

"Deference may be inherited": Ibid., June 5, 2002.

Fifty men who had been pages: Confidential interviews.

"The Queen coming to White's": Confidential interviews.

"People woke up and realized": Charles Anson interview.

"have proved conclusively": BBC News, June 5, 2002.

"The public felt the Queen was paying attention": Robert Worcester interview.

"at length": Burrell, p. 321.

He said that Diana's mother: Ibid.

"he had taken some of the princess's papers": Buckingham Palace chronology of the Queen's involvement in the Paul Burrell Case, Nov. 12, 2002, Official Website of the British Monarchy.

just one topic among many: Burrell, pp. 318–22; Report to His Royal Highness the Prince of Wales by Sir Michael Peat and Edmund Lawson QC, March 13, 2002 (Peat Report), p. 75.

Three years later: Burrell, pp 340, 342–43.

the Queen was briefed several times: Buckingham Palace chronology; Peat Report, p. 76.

she didn't think his passing reference: Peat Report, p. 74.

"private": Ibid., p. 76.

Philip and Charles were discussing: Buckingham Palace chronology, Peat Report, p. 74.

"on a false premise": *New York Times,* Nov. 1, 2002.

"old woman being forgetful": *The Independent,* Nov. 3, 2002.

"She was playing patience": Confidential interview.

"anything improper or remiss": Peat Report, p. 77.

The previous November: *The Times,* Nov. 8, 2002.

"She drove her own Range Rover": Nini Ferguson interview.

which required arthroscopic surgery: Buckingham Palace announcements, Jan. 13, 2003, Jan. 14, 2003, Official Website of the British Monarchy.

"languishing indoors": Queen Elizabeth II to Monty Roberts, Jan. 19, 2003.

had an identical operation: Buckingham Palace announcements, Dec. 9, 2003, Dec. 12, 2003, Official Website of the British Monarchy.

"They are about 14 hands high": Michael Oswald interview.

Now she would go instead: Margaret Rhodes interview.

Her cottage in Windsor Great Park: Author's observations.

"How would you like to live in suburbia?": Margaret Rhodes interview.

Each Sunday the Queen takes the wheel: Ibid.

"This may sound impertinent": Robert Salisbury interview.

"more understanding of the wonders": Monty Roberts interview.

a handsome high-ceilinged room: Author's observations.

"Oh tell Malcolm not to be so silly": Malcolm Ross interview.

"Never have I seen anyone": Annabel Goldsmith interview.

"Oh yes . . . Robert and I were in a nightclub": Robert Salisbury interview.

Twenty-five years the Queen's junior: *Daily Mail,* April 11, 2006.

"there is lots of jolly laughter": Anne Glenconner interview.

"She has moved into the vacuum": Confidential interview.

"Angela understands the Queen needs": Confidential interview.

"I have heard that Damien Hirst": Piers Allen interview.

"Angela will come up with something": Confidential interview.

"As Bush arrives, we reveal Mirrorman": *The Mirror,* Nov. 19, 2003.

Inside the paper were fourteen pages: Ibid.

"not nearly haughty enough": *Sunday Times,* Nov. 23, 2003.

"our man's exposé of Windsor": *The Mirror,* Nov. 20, 2003.

"a highly objectionable invasion": *Daily Express,* Nov. 25, 2003.

he timed publication: *The Guardian,* Nov. 21, 2003.

all of which had an improvised feel: Ibid., Nov. 29, 2003.

"She was unruffled": George W. Bush interview.

"It was like old friends week": Catherine Fenton interview.

"Whatever did you do that for, man?": Tony Blair, p. 305.

Debate over the ban consumed: *The Spectator,* Sept. 11, 2010.

"absurd": Tony Blair, p. 306.

"play politics with him": *The Guardian,* July 2, 2011, excerpting *Power and Responsibility: The Alastair Campbell Diaries,* Vol. 3, *1999–2001,* by Alastair Campbell.

"Fox hunting is just vermin control": *News of the World,* April 8, 2001.

he later acknowledged: Tony Blair, p. 305.

"She is a countrywoman": Margaret Rhodes interview.

In her own quiet way, the Queen lobbied: Confidential interview.

"one of the domestic legislative measures": Tony Blair, p. 304.

"allowed a compromise proposal": *The Spectator,* Sept. 11, 2010.

Her appearance at the two Golden Jubilee concerts: *People,* June 17, 2002.

"Camilla never whines": Confidential interview.

"It's just two old people": *The Times,* April 9, 2005, April 10, 2005.

"Her decision assuredly had nothing": Ibid., April 8, 2005.

"I have two very important announcements": *Sunday Times,* April 10, 2005.

"There was a huge roar of approval": Ibid.

"my darling Camilla": *The Times,* April 11, 2005.

"I'm going on Larry King": Confidential interview.

Princes William and Harry kissed: *Daily Telegraph,* April 11, 2005.

"a better understanding": Clarence House press release, Nov. 26, 2005.

"pushed . . . quite stubborn": BBC interview with Prince William, Nov. 19, 2004.

"I want to express my admiration": Marr, *The Queen at 80* documentary.

"There in one of the archways": Confidential interview.

"Is it all right if I touch her?" Confidential interview.

"That was unusual for the British": Charles Powell interview.

"darling mama": *The Times,* April 21, 2006.

"I understand you think": Robert Tuttle interview.

In that spirit, she joined: *Daily Express,* March 17, 2006.

"just smiled back": *Daily Telegraph,* March 31, 2006.

"Prince Philip has experience": Peregrine Cavendish, 12th Duke of Devonshire, interview.

"She was most interested": Ibid.

When the BBC proposed: Interview with Rolf Harris, January 2006, Royal Insight, Official Website of the British Monarchy.

"We made the Queen a Hollywood star": Stephen Frears interview.

a lifelong republican whose newfound admiration: Helen Mirren interview.

"What is brilliant": Frances Campbell-Preston interview.

"I gather there's a film": Graydon Carter interview with Tony Blair, June 24, 2009, VF.com.

"Because it showed why": Confidential interview.

One of Elizabeth II's friends gently ribbed: Confidential interview.

"I suppose it depends on your point of view": Monty Roberts interview.

"rang true": Nancy Reagan interview.

Palace officials were delighted: Confidential interview.

"You know, for fifty years and more": Helen Mirren Oscar acceptance speech, Feb. 25, 2007.

Twenty: A Soldier at Heart

Leibovitz was surprised to learn: Annie Leibovitz, *At Work,* p. 189.

"She came all the way by herself!": Ibid., pp. 186–87.

"I don't have much time": Ibid., p. 189.

"Less dressy!" Ibid.

"feisty": Ibid.

"an appropriate mood": Ibid., p. 184.

"The Queen examined them closely": *Washington Post,* April 5, 2007.

"Do you play football too?": Kevin Sullivan interview.

"You should have some things like that!": *Daily Telegraph,* May 5, 2007.

Now her new bloodstock adviser: Michael Oswald interview.

"Nobody pays any attention": Confidential interview.

Anticipating the Queen's interest: Amy Zantzinger interview.

"She gave me a look": CBS News, March 31, 2009.

"it was sad that security was so tight": Confidential interview.

"So glad to see you": Frolic Weymouth interview.

"the sweetest thing": Laura Bush, *Spoken from the Heart,* p. 390.

"vital wartime alliance": White House Press Office transcript of remarks by President Bush and Queen Elizabeth II at a White House state dinner, May 7, 2007.

"It was the perfect retort": George W. Bush interview.

"a lacuna": Tony Blair, p. 608.

"some good information": Robert Hardman, *Monarchy: The Royal Family at Work,* p. 170.

"tremendously respectful of the royal family": Simon Lewis interview.

"what works and what doesn't": Hardman, p. 170.

"she'll be talking about things": Ibid.

When the Queen was with friends: Anne Glenconner interview.

"brought a certain amount of heavy weather": Margaret Rhodes interview.

"With the absence of her mother and sister": Confidential interview.

When he was away: Margaret Rhodes interview.

"They are not physically demonstrative": Confidential interview.

"His approach is much more restless": George Carey interview.

"not a sweet old Darby and Joan": McDonald, *The Duke* documentary.

"I don't read the tabloids": Paxman, p. 237.

After Philip took one too many: *Daily Express,* May 2, 2010.

"on Her Majesty's instruction": Tony Parnell interview.

"incredibly stupid birds": McDonald, *The Duke* documentary.

"Her taste was very modest": Tony Parnell interview.

"He wore a cap like a taxi driver": Frolic Weymouth interview.

"That speech contained more jargon": Chris Mullin, *A View from the Foothills: The Diaries of Chris Mullin,* p. 429.

The Queen appeared in the same double strand: *Daily Mail,* Nov. 19, 2007.

"Let us love one another": BBC News, Nov. 19, 2007.

"a life where duty spoke": *Daily Telegraph,* Nov. 20, 2007.

As they had with his older sister: *Daily Mail,* April 21, 2008.

Since the invasions: Gen. Charles Guthrie interview.

"The royal family has pride and joy": Ibid.

Once she helpfully sent: Ibid.

"Do the Welsh Guards have new uniform": Johnny Martin-Smith interview.

"The Queen has an eagle eye": Confidential interview.

"wouldn't read a three-volume history": Charles Guthrie interview.

"You could tell her what you thought": Ibid.

"She knew we had too many regiments": Jonathan Powell interview.

Speaking to one of the army chiefs: Confidential interview.

"It is a traditional thing to do": Charles Guthrie interview.

despite the well-documented fact: Smith, p. 212.

He was determined: *Daily Telegraph*, Feb. 28, 2008.

Army Chief of Staff Sir Richard Dannatt vetoed: Prince Harry deployment update, PrinceofWales. gov.uk, May 15, 2007.

"turn to the right and carry on": BBC News interview with Prince Harry, Feb. 28, 2008.

They decided to deploy Harry: Sky News, Feb. 28, 2008.

"I think she's relieved": BBC interview with Prince Harry, Feb. 28, 2008.

" 'mucking in' with every other soldier": *Daily Telegraph,* Feb. 29, 2008.

"All my wishes have come true": Ibid.

"it's very nice to be sort of a normal person": BBC News interview with Prince Harry, Feb. 28, 2008.

an opsimath, she calls herself: Bennett, p. 48.

"had a much better bite at the carrot": Ibid.

"by analysis and reflection": Ibid., p. 113.

"Oh do get *on!*": Ibid., p. 49.

"offered yet another reason to think warmly": *New York Times Book Review,* Sept. 30, 2007.

"It was shared, it was common": Bennett, p. 31.

"It's very informal": Mark Collins interview.

At the invitation of a conservation group: Confidential interviews.

The following July she watched: BBC News, July 20, 2009.

She even started taking: *Daily Mail,* Dec. 17, 2009; *Daily Telegraph,* Feb. 8, 2010.

"We have seen less of them": Confidential interview.

The children of her longtime friends: Confidential interview.

When one of her bridesmaids: Elizabeth Longman interview; Freddy Van Zevenbergen interview.

"a wall": *Daily Telegraph,* June 21, 2008.

"I've done it!": Ibid., June 19, 2008; Ian Balding interview.

"I wouldn't have been invited": Helen Mirren interview.

"I expect you think": *The Guardian,* Nov. 24, 2006.

"For Prince Philip and me": BBC News, Nov. 12, 2008.

"All her programs are done with great cleverness": Malcolm Ross interview.

"she instantly spots it": Confidential interview.

"Why did no one see it coming?": *The Guardian,* Nov. 18, 2008.

"The general feeling is she is more approachable": Confidential interview.

Philip began writing letters: *Daily Mail,* April 17, 2009.

Elizabeth II eventually took up cell phones: *The Times,* Oct. 17, 2008.

At the suggestion of Prince Andrew: *Daily Telegraph,* April 1, 2009.

"a great googler": Confidential interview.

"Just come back from jogging?": *Daily Mail,* Oct. 17, 2008.

"Lovely little thing isn't it?": *The Times,* Oct. 17, 2008.

During a shooting weekend: Confidential interview.

"At long last my grandparents are reunited": Ashe Windham, "A Fitting Memorial to Queen Elizabeth," *Friends of the Castle of Mey Newsletter,* April 2009. p. 5.

Elizabeth II was only scheduled: Elizabeth Anson interview.

"She knows every inch": Charles Powell interview.

"few dogged bastions of republicanism": *The Times,* April 29, 2011.

"I am very pleased to be in Kingston": David Pogson, senior press officer, Buckingham Palace Press Office.

When the Queen was younger: Confidential interview.

To help prepare the Queen: Susan Cunliffe-Lister interview.

When the train pulled into the Hull station: Author's observations.

"She has an amazing ability to scan": Phil Brown interview.

She talked across the table: Author's observations.

"was picking at her bread roll": Maria Raper interview.

"SHE'S A ROYAL TONIC": *Hull Daily Mail,* March 6, 2009.

"as a signal of the strong": *Daily Telegraph,* Feb. 16, 2009.

The first lady even confided: Confidential interview.

"The Queen knows when she enters": Brian Mulroney interview.

"frightfully funny": Confidential interview.

After ten seconds, the Queen dropped: *Daily Mail* timed sequence of photos, April 3, 2009.

"It happened spontaneously": Peter Wilkinson interview.

"unthinkable": *The Guardian,* April 2, 2009.

"mutual and spontaneous display": Confidential interview.

a ritual that invariably prompted: Confidential interview.

The Queen was a smiling icon: Author's observations.

"no visible signs of flagging": Sir Richard Gozney interview.

She had a four-hour stretch: Confidential interview.

"I have to be seen to be believed": Longford, *Elizabeth R,* p. 5.

For her four-hour flight: Author's observations.

In years past: Duncan, p. 19; Morrow, pp. 111, 118.

"Every word she says": Kamalesh Sharma interview.

"The Commonwealth is very much her legacy": Brian Mulroney interview.

"many of us would have left": Shawcross, *Q and*

C, p. 48.

She could discuss grazing rights: Bradford, p. 229.

or a particular leader's fishing habits: Shawcross, Q and C, p. 201.

favorite hymns: Margaret Rhodes interview.

"Commonwealth psychotherapist": The Times, April 16, 1986.

"doesn't look at photographers": Robin Nunn interview.

Elizabeth II was interested in seeing: Eric Jenkinson interview.

The Queen seemed unperturbed: Author's observations.

filming for the monarchy's website: Peter Wilkinson interview.

The schedule called for 4.5 minutes: Eric Jenkinson interview.

"I don't have time to use it much!": Author's observations.

Pausing briefly: Eric Jenkinson interview.

"That was a seamless": Confidential interview.

"I sometimes think": Margaret Rhodes interview.

Twenty-One: Long Live the Queen

"How kind they are to me!": Lytton Strachey, p. 156.

"Three cheers for the Queen!": Lacey, Monarch, p. 40.

"Her reputation now is as high": Charles Powell interview.

"the largest flotilla": Diamond Jubilee Foundation statement, April 5, 2011.

"oiled and manacled MPs": *The Guardian,* April 5, 2011.

"ideas" year: Confidential interview.

"Republicanism isn't even an esoteric": *The Times,* Nov. 13, 2009.

In one movie theater after another: *The Guardian,* Nov. 12, 2011.

"On the whole she quite liked it": Margaret Rhodes interview.

"redressing the economic balance": Queen Elizabeth II Christmas Broadcast, Dec. 25, 1983, Official Website of the British Monarchy.

"the sheet anchor in the middle": David Airlie interview.

She had first glimpsed: *Daily Mail,* May 10, 2010.

"constitutional obligation": Ibid., July 29, 2010.

"It was important for Geidt": Simon Lewis interview.

"I can't keep the Queen waiting": Ibid.

"a big generous offer": *Daily Mail,* July 29, 2010.

"I said I couldn't be totally sure": Ibid.

the Queen's treasurer took: Civil List Act of 1972, Report of the Royal Trustees, June 22, 2010 (Treasury Report), "Background Information and Review of Performance," p. 6.

By 2009, yearly Civil List: Treasury Report, p. 33.

"careful housekeeping" HM Treasury, Budget Announcement on the Civil List for 2011, June 22, 2010.

In addition, Elizabeth II planned: Treasury Report, p. 61.

Charles spent £9 million: The Prince of Wales and the Duchess of Cornwall Annual Review 2010

(PoW Annual Review), p. 40.

"so that my successors do not": *The Independent,* Oct. 21, 2010.

"adversely high": *The Mail,* Oct. 24, 2010.

Buckingham Palace has been losing: *The Mail,* July 5, 2010.

To recognize two of her ladies-in-waiting: Confidential interview.

"credit crunch couture": *The Times,* Oct. 22, 2009.

her £1.3 million catering: Treasury Report, p. 33.

"We have no experts in royal history": Confidential interview.

"We are not about demystifying": Ibid.

"the space of young people": Ibid.

which costs the British government: *Daily Telegraph,* May 30, 2010.

plus his £249,000: *Daily Mail,* July 12, 2010.

Government officials credited: *Financial Times,* May 23, 2010.

His lobbying for British industry: *The Guardian,* Nov. 29, 2010.

"It's not about the power": *Daily Telegraph,* Oct. 24, 2009.

Nevertheless, Andrew's questionable associates: Buckingham Palace statement, July 21, 2011; BBC News, July 21, 2011.

She even won the approval: *Daily Telegraph,* Aug. 9, 2010.

employing eleven: *Daily Mail,* May 29, 2010; *Financial Times,* May 23, 2010.

"never does accept a penny . . . lick of the spoon": *Sunday Times,* May 23, 2010.

"sincerely sorry": *The Independent,* May 24, 2010.

The guest of honor was: *Daily Telegraph,* Aug. 1, 2010.

On August 2, 2010, Charles assumed: Ashe Windham interview.

He raised more than £110 million: PoW Annual Review, p. 24.

"He has made a full life": Nancy Reagan interview.

"is high octane": Confidential interview.

"He is probably an instinctively": Margaret Rhodes interview.

"has no illusions": Charles Anson interview.

"Camilla soothes things": Anne Glenconner interview.

"You sense he maneuvers": Confidential interview.

"that person is for or against": Confidential interview.

"It is fair to say when he feels": Patricia Brabourne interview.

When he goes to stay at Sandringham: Confidential interview.

he is known to eat a different meal: Roy Strong interview and confidential interview.

"as good if not better": Confidential interview.

When Anne Glenconner's sister got cancer: Anne Glenconner interview.

Charles has eleven: PoW Annual Review, pp. 54–56.

"There is nobody I admire more": Malcolm Ross interview.

"revolution . . . mechanistic approach": *Daily Mail,* Dec. 18, 2010.

"no separation between man and nature": *Wall Street Journal,* June 15, 2010.

"huge oversimplification": BBC News, June 6, 2000.

"we have been genetically modifying": Ibid.

"the same argument that says": *The Guardian,* July 2, 2011, excerpt from Vol. 3, *The Alastair Campbell Diaries.*

"were becoming unhelpful": *Daily Mail,* July 18, 2010.

"She has allowed Prince Charles to work": Malcolm Ross interview.

"It is not a cozy relationship": Margaret Rhodes interview.

"That will be a defining moment": Confidential interview.

allocating forty seconds to each: Malcolm Ross interview.

"hospital nurse or nanny": Beaton, *The Unexpurgated Beaton,* p. 231.

Keeping eye contact: Author's observations; Strong, pp. 313, 317.

"furiously writing letters": Confidential interview.

In 2009–10 he personally wrote: PoW Annual Review, p. 45.

"privately delighted": Lacey, *Monarch,* p. 391.

"Oh, that's something I can't do": George Carey interview.

"unless I get Alzheimer's": Margaret Rhodes interview.

"But even then she wouldn't retire": Ibid.

"The principals don't tweak": Malcolm Ross interview.

"as the central church to her": Confidential interview.

"It is better not to have to think": Bloomberg News, Nov. 19, 2010.

"The settled rule and strong custom": Kenneth Rose interview.

"We'll see, won't we?": *Daily Mail,* Nov. 19, 2010.

"find ways to allow girls and women": Speech opening the Commonwealth Heads of Government meeting, Oct. 28, 2011, Official Website of the British Monarchy.

"This is a matter for the government": Confidential interview.

"defender of faith": *Sunday Times,* Nov. 16, 2008. Jonathan Dimbleby wrote, "Prince Charles told me in 1994 that when he inherits the crown he wants to become 'defender of faith.' . . . This does not mean that he foresees any difficulty in swearing to become "defender of the faith." . . . He sees no constitutional or spiritual contradiction in being both that and a 'defender of faith.' "

"absolutely determined to be the defender of nature": *Vanity Fair,* Nov. 2010.

"obviously it would be nice": *Daily Telegraph,* Nov. 13, 2008.

"active . . . to speak out on matters": *Sunday Times,* Nov. 16, 2008.

"fully accepts that as king": *Daily Mail,* Nov. 17, 2008.

"in a different way than my predecessors": *Vanity Fair,* Nov. 2010.

"Of course they really shouldn't": Ibid.

"curious mixture of the traditional and the radical": Tony Blair, p. 146.

"One of the main purposes of the monarchy": Kenneth Rose interview.

"appalling old waxworks": Paxman, p. 181.

"With a bit of luck, he will be old enough": Robert Salisbury interview.

"Life changes overnight when you inherit the throne": David Airlie interview.

"not spoiled or stubborn": Confidential interview.

"he will have to shake the bloody hand": Andrew Roberts interview.

"Whilst the vast majority": *Daily Telegraph,* March 8, 2010.

"command the same respect": *Daily Mail,* Nov. 30, 2010.

An ICM research poll: *Time,* Nov. 22, 2010.

Before his visit, polls consistently showed: *The Mail on Sunday,* Jan. 24, 2010.

"My grandmother once said": *New Zealand Herald,* March 19, 2011.

"He came, he saw, he charmed": *Herald Sun,* March 20, 2011.

"He would likely lose the resources": As part of the Sovereign Grant bill passed by Parliament in October 2011 to change the funding of the royal family, Duchy of Cornwall revenues will be given to an heir to the throne who is not the Duke of Cornwall, enabling a firstborn daughter to receive that significant inheritance for the first time.

"There is no question in Prince William's mind": *Sunday Telegraph,* Nov. 27, 2010.

"The future could not be more optimistic": Malcolm Ross interview.

"We get along really well": BBC interview, Nov.

19, 2004.

"He learns a lot by osmosis": Confidential interview.

"They don't want to be *Hello* magazine princes": Confidential interview.

"With William and Harry we are easing into that": Confidential interview.

Even more significant was the Queen's assertiveness: Confidential interview.

"He is not only wise": Charles Anson interview.

"sleeping rough": Associated Press, Dec. 22, 2009.

"These kinds of events are much more fulfilling": *Sunday Times,* Dec. 27, 2009.

"I had the piss taken out of me": *Sunday Telegraph,* Jan. 24, 2010.

"loving and caring": Tom Bradby interview with Prince William and Catherine Middleton, ITV, Nov. 16, 2010.

"absolutely delighted": Confidential interview.

"had a little chat": Bradby interview, ITV, Nov. 16, 2010.

"They have been practicing long enough!": BBC News, Nov. 16, 2010.

"a great cheer . . . banging of the table": *Daily Telegraph,* Nov. 16, 2010.

"big, beer-loving lug": Ibid., Dec. 26, 2010.

Kelly was a Canadian management consultant: CTV, Dec. 30, 2010.

"From the pit to the Palace": Malcolm Ross interview.

"We're both down-to-earth": Prince William and Catherine Middleton photocall interview, St. James's Palace, Nov. 16, 2010.

"great, loving boyfriend": Bradby interview, ITV, Nov. 15, 2010.

The Queen was deeply involved: Confidential interview.

Even the Queen and Prince Philip had an allocation: Ibid.

she arranged for Angela Kelly's staff: Margaret Rhodes interview.

For more than ninety minutes, Elizabeth II mingled: Author's observations.

"Usually when members of the royal family": Confidential interview.

"Come on, you two": Author's observations.

"And everyone was so friendly": Confidential interview.

She spent nearly a half hour: Author's observations.

but had resumed her daily outing: Confidential interview.

"It is absolutely natural": *Daily Telegraph,* May 1, 2011.

"deeply unpretentious": BBC News, April 21, 2011.

"You are beautiful": *Daily Mail,* April 30, 2011.

"Well, are you happy?" *The Mail on Sunday,* May 1, 2011.

"amazing": *Daily Mail,* April 30, 2011.

They were also being followed by 400 million: *The Times,* April 30, 2011.

237 tweets per second: *The Independent,* May 1, 2011.

"for the nation to come together": *The Times,* April 30, 2011.

"the team of the future": *Daily Mail,* April 29, 2011.

where the springtime floral decorations included: Confidential interview.

"The venue was palatial": *Sunday Telegraph,* May 1, 2011.

During a visit with her: *New Zealand Herald,* April 27, 2011.

a thoughtful gesture that she mentioned: Confidential interview.

More than half of the country's adults: *Daily Telegraph,* May 4, 2011.

"thrilled to have a daughter": *The Times,* April 30, 2011.

"push his wheelchair": *Sunday Times,* May 1, 2011.

"allowing us to invade": Confidential interview.

"for putting up with numerous": *Sunday Times,* May 1, 2011.

"William and Catherine were coming down to earth": Margaret Rhodes interview.

numbers that astonished Palace officials: Confidential interview.

In a YouGov poll: *Sunday Times,* May 1, 2011.

"Wow, wow, wow": BBC News, May 20, 2011.

"not always been straightforward": Reuters, May 18, 2011.

"helped to release . . . sorrow": *Irish Times,* May 21, 2011.

"sincere expression of sympathy": *Daily Telegraph,* May 20, 2011.

"I don't think anybody could have achieved": *Financial Times,* May 20, 2011.

"left us feeling a bit better": Ibid.

"essential": *The Economist,* May 26, 2011.

"for the grandson of a Kenyan": *The Guardian,*

May 25, 2011.

The Queen herself gave them a tour: *New York Times,* May 24, 2011.

a private twenty-minute meeting: *Daily Mail,* May 26, 2011.

BIBLIOGRAPHY

BOOKS

Airlie, Mabel, Countess of. *Thatched with Gold: The Memoir of Mabel, Countess of Airlie.* Edited by Jennifer Ellis. London: Hutchinson, 1962.

Amies, Hardy. *Still Here: An Autobiography.* London: Weidenfeld & Nicolson, 1984.

Princess Anne the Princess Royal, with Ivor Herbert. *Riding Through My Life.* London: Pelham, 1991.

Annigoni, Pietro. *An Artist's Life: An Autobiography.* London: W. H. Allen, 1977.

Bagehot, Walter. *The English Constitution.* New York: Cosimo Classics, 2007.

Baker, Anne Pimlott. *The Pilgrims of the United States: A Centennial History.* London: Profile, 2003.

Balding, Ian. *Making the Running: A Racing Life.* London: Headline, 2005.

Beale, Betty. *Power at Play: A Memoir of Parties, Politicians and the Presidents in My Bedroom.* Washington, D.C.: Regnery Gateway, 1993.

Beaton, Cecil. *Beaton in the Sixties: More Unexpurgated Diaries.* Introduction by Hugo Vickers. London: Weidenfeld & Nicolson, 2003.

————. *Self Portrait with Friends: The Selected Diaries of Cecil Beaton.* Edited by Richard Buckle. London: Pimlico, 1991.

————. *The Strenuous Years: Diaries, 1948–1955.* London: Weidenfeld & Nicolson, 1973.

————. *The Unexpurgated Beaton: The Cecil Beaton Diaries as He Wrote Them.* Introduction by Hugo Vickers. London: Weidenfeld & Nicolson, 2002.

Benn, Tony. *Out of the Wilderness: Diaries, 1963–1967.* London: Arrow, 1988.

Bennett, Alan. *Plays Two.* London: Faber & Faber, 1998.

————. *The Uncommon Reader.* New York: Farrar, Straus and Giroux, 2007.

————. *Untold Stories.* New York: Farrar, Straus and Giroux, 2006.

Blair, Cherie. *Speaking for Myself: My Life from Liverpool to Downing Street.* New York: Little, Brown, 2008.

Blair, Tony. *A Journey: My Political Life.* New York: Alfred A. Knopf, 2010.

Bloch, Michael. *The Secret File of the Duke of Windsor.* New York: Bantam, 1988.

Boothroyd, Basil. *Prince Philip: An Informal Biography.* New York: McCall, 1971.

Bradford, Sarah. *Elizabeth: A Biography of Britain's Queen.* New York: Riverhead, 1997.

Brandreth, Gyles. *Philip and Elizabeth: Portrait of a Royal Marriage.* New York: W. W. Norton, 2005.

Buchanan Jr., Wiley T., with Arthur Gordon. *Red Carpet at the White House: Four Years as Chief of Protocol in the Eisenhower Administration.* New York: E. P. Dutton, 1964.

Burgess, Colin. *Behind Palace Doors: My Service as*

the Queen Mother's Equerry. London: John Blake, 2007.

Burrell, Paul. *A Royal Duty.* New York: G. P. Putnam's Sons, 2003.

Bush, Laura. *Spoken from the Heart.* New York: Scribner, 2010.

Campbell, Alastair. *The Blair Years: Extracts from the Alastair Campbell Diaries.* New York: Alfred A. Knopf, 2007.

Campbell, John. *Edward Heath: A Biography.* London: Jonathan Cape, 1993.

Campbell-Preston, Frances. *The Rich Spoils of Time.* Edited by Hugo Vickers. London: Dovecote, 2006.

Carey, George. *Know the Truth: A Memoir.* London: Harper Perennial, 2005.

Castle, Barbara. *The Castle Diaries, 1964–1976.* London: Papermac/Macmillan, 1990.

Cathcart, Helen. *Her Majesty the Queen: The Story of Elizabeth II.* New York: Dodd, Mead, 1965.

Channon, Henry. *Chips: The Diaries of Sir Henry Channon.* Edited by Robert Rhodes James. London: Weidenfeld & Nicolson, 1967.

Churchill, Winston and Clementine. *Winston and Clementine: The Personal Letters of the Churchills.* Edited by their daughter Mary Soames. Boston: Houghton Mifflin, 1999.

Clinton, Bill. *My Life.* New York: Alfred A. Knopf, 2004.

Clinton, Hillary Rodham. *Living History.* New York: Simon & Schuster, 2003.

Coward, Noel. *The Noel Coward Diaries.* Edited by Graham Payn and Sheridan Morley. London: Papermac/Macmillan, 1983.

Crawford, Marion. *The Little Princesses: The Story of the Queen's Childhood by Her Nanny, Marion Crawford.* New York: St. Martin's, 2003.

Crosland, Susan. *Tony Crosland.* London: Coronet/Hodder & Stoughton, 1983.

Crossman, Richard. *The Diaries of a Cabinet Minister,* Vol. 1, *1964–1966.* New York: Holt, Rinehart & Winston, 1976.

————. *The Diaries of a Cabinet Minister,* Vol. 2, *Lord President of the Council and Leader of the House of Commons, 1966–1968.* London: Hamish Hamilton and Jonathan Cape, 1976.

————. *The Diaries of a Cabinet Minister,* Vol. 3, *Secretary of State for Social Services, 1968–1970.* London: Hamish Hamilton and Jonathan Cape, 1977.

Dampier, Phil, and Ashley Walton. *What's in the Queen's Handbag and Other Royal Secrets.* Sussex, England: Book Guild Publishing, 2007.

Dean, John. *H.R.H. Prince Philip Duke of Edinburgh: A Portrait by His Valet.* London: Robert Hale, 1954.

de Courcy, Anne. *Snowdon: The Biography.* London: Weidenfeld & Nicolson, 2008.

de Gaulle, Charles. *Memoirs of Hope: Renewal and Endeavor.* New York: Simon and Schuster, 1971.

Devonshire, Deborah. *Wait for Me!: Memoirs of the Youngest Mitford Sister.* London: John Murray, 2010.

Devonshire, Deborah the Dowager Duchess of Devonshire. *Home to Roost and Other Peckings.* London: John Murray, 2009.

Devonshire, Deborah, and Patrick Leigh Fermor. *In Tearing Haste: Letters Between Deborah Devon-*

shire and Patrick Leigh Fermor. Edited by Charlotte Mosley. London: John Murray, 2008.

Dewar, Michael, editor. *All the Queen's Horses: A Golden Jubilee Tribute to Her Majesty the Queen.* London: MDA, 2002.

Dimbleby, Jonathan. *The Prince of Wales: A Biography.* New York: Warner, 1995.

Duncan, Andrew. *The Queen's Year: The Reality of Monarchy: An Intimate Report on Twelve Months with the Royal Family.* Garden City, N.Y.: Doubleday, 1970.

Eden, Clarissa. *Clarissa Eden: A Memoir from Churchill to Eden.* London: Phoenix, 2008.

Eisenhower, Dwight David. *The Papers of Dwight David Eisenhower: NATO and the Campaign of 1952,* Vol. 13. Edited by Louis Galambos. Baltimore: The Johns Hopkins University Press, 1970.

FitzGerald, Arthur. *Thoroughbreds of the Crown: The History and Worldwide Influence of the Royal Studs.* Guildford, U.K.: Genesis Publications, 1999.

Gilbert, Martin. *Winston S. Churchill,* Vol. 8, *"Never Despair," 1945–1964.* Boston: Houghton Mifflin, 1988.

Gladwyn, Cynthia. *The Diaries of Cynthia Gladwyn.* Edited by Miles Jebb. London: Constable, 1995.

Glendinning, Victoria. *Edith Sitwell: A Unicorn Among Lions.* New York: Alfred A. Knopf, 1981.

Goldsmith, Annabel. *Annabel: An Unconventional Life: The Memoirs of Lady Annabel Goldsmith.* London: Weidenfeld & Nicolson, 2004.

———. *No Invitation Required: The Pelham Cottage Years.* London: Weidenfeld & Nicolson, 2009.

Hardman, Robert. *Monarchy: The Royal Family at Work.* London: Ebury, 2007.

Heller, Deane, and David Heller. *Jacqueline Kennedy.* Derby, Conn.: Monarch, 1963.

Henderson, Nicholas. *Mandarin: The Diaries of an Ambassador, 1969–1982.* London: Weidenfeld & Nicolson, 1994.

Hibbert, Christopher. *Queen Victoria: A Personal History.* Cambridge, Mass.: Da Capo, 2001.

Holden, Anthony. *Charles: A Biography.* London: Bantam, 1998.

———. *Charles Prince of Wales.* London: Pan, 1980.

Horne, Alistair. *Harold Macmillan,* Vol. 2, *1957–1986.* New York: Viking Penguin, 1989.

Howard, Anthony. *Rab: The Life of R. A. Butler.* London: Jonathan Cape, 1987.

Jay, Antony. *Elizabeth R: The Role of the Monarchy Today.* London: BBC Books, 1992.

Jephson, P. D. *Shadows of a Princess: An Intimate Account by Her Private Secretary.* New York: HarperCollins, 2000.

Johnson, Paul. *Brief Lives: An Intimate and Very Personal Portrait of the Twentieth Century.* London: Hutchinson, 2010.

Junor, Penny. *The Firm: The Troubled Life of the House of Windsor.* New York: Thomas Dunne Books/St. Martin's Griffin, 2008.

Khrushchev, Nikita. *Khrushchev Remembers.* Translated and edited by Strobe Talbott. Boston: Little, Brown, 1970.

Knatchbull, Timothy. *From a Clear Blue Sky: Surviving the Mountbatten Bomb.* London: Hutchinson, 2009.

Lacey, Robert. *Majesty: Elizabeth II and the House of Windsor.* New York: Harcourt Brace Jovanovich, 1977.

———. *Monarch: The Life and Reign of Elizabeth II.* New York: Free Press, 2002.

Lascelles, Sir Alan "Tommy." *King's Counsellor: Abdication and War: The Diaries of Sir Alan Lascelles.* Edited by Duff Hart-Davis. London: Weidenfeld & Nicolson, 2006.

Lees-Milne, James. *Diaries, 1971–1983.* Abridged and introduced by Michael Bloch. London: John Murray, 2007.

———. *Diaries, 1984–1997.* Abridged and introduced by Michael Bloch. London: John Murray, 2008.

Leibovitz, Annie. *At Work.* New York: Random House, 2008.

Lilienthal, David E. *The Journals of David E. Lilienthal,* Vol. 4, *The Road to Change, 1955–1959.* New York: Harper & Row, 1969.

Longford, Elizabeth. *Elizabeth R: A Biography.* London: Coronet/Hodder & Stoughton, 1984.

———. *The Queen Mother: A Biography.* London: Granada, 1981.

Lytton Strachey, G. *Queen Victoria.* Teddington, Middlesex: Echo Library, 2006.

MacCarthy, Fiona. *Last Curtsey: The End of the Debutantes.* London: Faber & Faber, 2007.

Macmillan, Harold. *At the End of the Day, 1961–1963.* London: Macmillan, 1973.

———. *Pointing the Way, 1959–1961.* London: Macmillan, 1972.

Major, John. *The Autobiography.* London: HarperCollins, 1999.

Massingberd, Hugh. *Daydream Believer: Confessions of a Hero-Worshipper.* London: Pan, 2002.

Mellon, Paul, with John Baskett. *Reflections in a Silver Spoon: A Memoir.* New York: William Morrow, 1992.

Meyer, Christopher. *DC Confidential: The Controversial Memoirs of Britain's Ambassador to the U.S. at the Time of 9/11 and the Iraq War.* London: Weidenfeld & Nicolson, 2005.

Mitchell, Susan. *Margaret Whitlam: A Biography.* Sydney: Random House Australia, 2006.

Mitford, Nancy. *Love from Nancy: The Letters of Nancy Mitford.* Edited by Charlotte Mosley. Boston: Houghton Mifflin, 1993.

The Mitfords: Letters Between Six Sisters. Edited by Charlotte Mosley. London: Harper Perennial, 2008.

Morrow, Ann. *The Queen.* London: Granada, 1983.

Morton, Andrew. *Diana: Her True Story — in Her Own Words.* New York: Simon & Schuster, 1997.

Mullin, Chris. *A View from the Foothills: The Diaries of Chris Mullin.* London: Profile, 2010.

Mulroney, Brian. *Memoirs.* Toronto: A Douglas Gibson Book/McClelland & Stewart, 2007.

Nicolson, Adam. *Restoration: The Rebuilding of Windsor Castle.* London: Michael Joseph in association with the Royal Collection, 1997.

Nicolson, Nigel. *Vita and Harold: Letters of Vita Sackville-West and Harold Nicolson.* New York: G. P. Putnam's Sons, 1992.

Ogden, Christopher. *Legacy: A Biography of Moses and Walter Annenberg.* Boston: Little, Brown, 1999.

Paxman, Jeremy. *On Royalty: A Very Polite Inquiry into Some Strangely Related Families.* New York: PublicAffairs, 2007.

Pearson, John. *The Private Lives of Winston Churchill.* New York: Simon & Schuster, 1991.

HRH the Prince Philip, Duke of Edinburgh. *Selected Speeches, 1948–1955, by His Royal Highness the Prince Philip Duke of Edinburgh.* London: Oxford University Press, 1957.

―――. *Prince Philip Speaks: Selected Speeches by His Royal Highness the Prince Philip Duke of Edinburgh, K.G., 1956–1959.* Edited by Richard Ollard. London: Collins, 1960.

Pimlott, Ben. *The Queen: A Biography of Elizabeth II.* New York: John Wiley & Sons, 1997.

Powell, Anthony. *Journals, 1987–1989.* London: Heinemann, 1996.

Prochaska, Frank. *The Eagle and the Crown: Americans and the British Monarchy.* New Haven: Yale University Press, 2008.

―――. *Royal Bounty: The Making of a Welfare Monarchy.* New Haven: Yale University Press, 1995.

Reagan, Ronald. *The Reagan Diaries.* New York: HarperCollins, 2007.

―――. *Ronald Reagan: An American Life.* New York: Simon & Schuster, 1990.

Rhea, Mini, with Frances Spatz Leighton. *I Was Jacqueline Kennedy's Dressmaker.* New York: Fleet Publishing, 1962.

Rhodes, Margaret. *The Final Curtsey.* London: Umbria, 2011.

Roberts, Jane. *Queen Elizabeth: A Birthday Souvenir Album.* London: Royal Collection Enterprises, 2006.

————. *Royal Treasures: A Golden Jubilee Celebration.* London: Royal Collection Enterprises, 2002.

Roberts, Monty. *The Man Who Listens to Horses: The Story of a Real-Life Horse Whisperer.* New York: Random House, 1997.

Robinson, John Martin. *Windsor Castle: The Official Illustrated History.* London: Royal Collection Publications, 2004.

Roosevelt, Eleanor. *The Autobiography of Eleanor Roosevelt.* London: Hutchinson, 1962.

————. *My Day: The Best of Eleanor Roosevelt's Acclaimed Newspaper Columns, 1936–1962.* Cambridge, Mass.: Da Capo, 2001.

————. *This I Remember.* London: Hutchinson, 1950.

Rose, Kenneth. *Intimate Portraits of Kings, Queens and Courtiers.* London: Spring, 1989.

Sarah, the Duchess of York, with Jeff Coplon. *My Story.* New York: Simon & Schuster, 1996.

Scott, Jennifer. *The Royal Portrait: Image and Impact.* London: Royal Collection Publications, 2010.

Seitz, Raymond. *Over Here.* London: Weidenfeld & Nicolson, 1998.

Shawcross, William. *Queen and Country.* Toronto: McClelland & Stewart, 2002.

————. *Queen Elizabeth the Queen Mother: The Official Biography.* London: Macmillan, 2009.

Smith, Horace. *A Horseman Through Six Reigns: Reminiscences of a Royal Riding Master.* London: Odhams, 1955.

Smith, Sally Bedell. *Diana in Search of Herself: Portrait of a Troubled Princess.* New York: Signet: New American Library, 2000.

Strong, Roy. *The Roy Strong Diaries, 1967–1987.* London: Phoenix, 1998.

Thomas, S. Evelyn. *Princess Elizabeth: Wife and Mother: A Souvenir of the Birth of Prince Charles of Edinburgh.* London: S. Evelyn Thomas Publication, 1949.

Thornton, Penny. *With Love from Diana.* New York: Pocket Books, 1995.

Turner, Graham. *Elizabeth: The Woman and the Queen.* London: Macmillan/*The Daily Telegraph,* 2002.

Vickers, Hugo. *Alice Princess Andrew of Greece.* New York: St. Martin's, 2002.

———. *Elizabeth the Queen Mother.* London: Arrow, 2006.

Vidal, Gore. *Palimpsest: A Memoir.* New York: Penguin, 1995.

Walters, Barbara. *Audition: A Memoir.* New York: Alfred A. Knopf, 2008.

Warwick, Christopher. *Princess Margaret: A Life of Contrasts.* London: André Deutsch, 2000.

Wheeler-Bennett, John W. *King George VI: His Life and Reign.* New York: St. Martin's, 1958.

Whitlam, Margaret. *My Day.* Sydney: William Collins, 1974.

Williams, Charles. *Harold Macmillan.* London: Weidenfeld & Nicolson, 2009.

Wilson, A. N. *Our Times: The Age of Elizabeth II.* London: Hutchinson, 2008.

Wilson, Mary. *New Poems.* London: Hutchinson, 1979.

Wyatt, Woodrow. *The Journals of Woodrow Wyatt,* Vol. 1. Edited by Sarah Curtis. London: Pan, 1992.

———. *The Journals of Woodrow Wyatt,* Vol. 2. Edited by Sarah Curtis. London: Macmillan, 2000.

———. *The Journals of Woodrow Wyatt,* Vol. 3. Edited by Sarah Curtis. London: Macmillan, 2000.

Ziegler, Philip. *Edward Heath: The Authorised Biography.* London: HarperPress, 2010.

Guidebooks

Balmoral: Highland Retreat of the Royal Family Since 1852: Guide to the Castle and Estate. Heritage House Group, 2007.

Buckingham Palace: Official Souvenir Guide. Royal Collection Publications, 2008.

The Castle and Gardens of Mey. The Queen Elizabeth Castle of Mey Trust.

The Crown Jewels: Official Guidebook. Historic Royal Palaces, 2002.

The Royal Yacht Britannia Official Guidebook. Someone Publishing Ltd.

Sandringham, by His Royal Highness the Duke of Edinburgh. Jarrold Publishing.

Television Programs

Diana: The Week She Died. ITV, 2006.

The Duke: A Portrait of Prince Philip. Sir Trevor McDonald. Indigo Television for ITV, May 13, 2009.

E II R. BBC, Feb. 6, 1992.

An Intimate Portrait of the Queen at 80. Andrew Marr. BBC, 2006.

Panorama. Martin Bashir interview with Diana, Princess of Wales. BBC, Nov. 20, 1995.

Prince Charles: The Private Man, the Public Role. Jonathan Dimbleby. ITV, June 29, 1994.

Queen and Country. William Shawcross. BBC four-part documentary series, 2002.
The Queen at 80. Sky News, 2006.
The Queen, by Rolf. BBC, Jan. 1, 2006.

Unpublished Papers

Lord Avon Papers, Birmingham University.

The Diaries of David Bruce, Richmond Historical Society.

Dwight D. Eisenhower Presidential Library and Museum.

W. Averell Harriman Papers, Library of Congress.

John F. Kennedy Presidential Library and Museum.

Sir Alan Lascelles Papers, Churchill College, Cambridge University.

Harold Macmillan Archive, Bodleian Library, Oxford University.

Paul Mellon Collection, Yale Center for British Art.

Morgan, Peter. *The Queen* screenplay. Courtesy of Peter Morgan.

The National Archives, Kew.

Richard Nixon Presidential Library and Museum.

The Ronald Reagan Presidential Foundation & Library.

ABOUT THE AUTHOR

Sally Bedell Smith is the author of bestselling biographies of William S. Paley; Pamela Harriman; Diana, Princess of Wales; John and Jacqueline Kennedy; and Bill and Hillary Clinton. A contributing editor at *Vanity Fair* since 1996, she previously worked at *Time* and *The New York Times,* where she was a cultural news reporter. She is the mother of three children and lives in Washington, D.C., with her husband, Stephen G. Smith.

www.sallybedellsmith.com